Shakespeare's Verse

Iambic Pentameter and the Poet's Idiosyncrasies

American University Studies

Series IV
English Language and Literature

Vol. 41

PETER LANG
New York · Bern · Frankfurt am Main · Paris

Marina Tarlinskaja

Shakespeare's Verse

Iambic Pentameter and the Poet's Idiosyncrasies

PETER LANG
New York · Bern · Frankfurt am Main · Paris

Library of Congress Cataloging-in-Publication Data

Tarlinskai͡a, Marina.
  Shakespeare's verse.

  (American university studies. Series IV, English language and literature; vol. 41)
    Bibliography: p.
    Includes index.
    1. Shakespeare, William, 1564–1616—Versification.
2. English language—Early modern, 1500–1700—Versification.   3. Iambic pentameter.   I. Title.
II. Series.
  PR3085.T37   1987   821'.3   86-27560
  ISBN 0-8204-0344-X
  ISSN 0741-0700

CIP-Kurztitelaufnahme der Deutschen Bibliothek

Tarlinskaja, Marina:
Shakespeare's verse: iambic Pentameter and the poet's idiosyncrasies / Marina Tarlinskaja. –
New York; Bern; Frankfurt am Main; Paris: Lang, 1987.
  (American University Studies: Ser. 4, English Language and Literature; Vol. 41)
    ISBN 0-8204-0344-X

NE: American University Studies / 04

Cover design: ©Sofya Liberman

© Peter Lang Publishing, Inc., New York 1987

All rights reserved.
Reprint or reproduction, even partially, in all forms such as microfilm, xerography, microfiche, microcard, offset strictly prohibited.

Printed by Weihert-Druck GmbH, Darmstadt, West Germany

Contents

	Page
Tables	ix
Figures	xi
Acknowledgements	xiii
Preface	xv
Foreword	xix

Chapter 1

Meter: In General and In Its Particulars

1.1	General concepts. "Vertical" and "horizontal" analyses of meter	1
1.1.1	Main structural feature of syllabo-tonic verse	1
1.1.2	The two basic problems	4
1.1.3	Most general form of iambic meter: "vertical" analysis	5
1.1.4	English iambic pentameter defined	7
1.1.5	"Horizontal" analysis for comparing metrical subsystems	15
1.2	Problems of attribution	18
1.3	Links between verse form and meaning	25
	Notes	28

Chapter 2

Evolution of Stress Profiles. Periodization

2.1	Principles of stressing	31
2.1.1	Stress vs. non-stress	31
2.1.2	Word and phrase stress in prose and in verse	32
2.1.3	Stressing monosyllabic words	36
2.2	Background: stress profiles of loose and rigid verse	39
2.3	Chambers' and Wentersdorf's chronologies	47
2.4	Evolution of ictic stresses in Shakespeare	53
2.5	Evolution of non-ictic stresses in Shakespeare	67
2.6	Evolution of ictic stresses in Marlowe's and Byron's poetic cycles	79

2.7	Shakespeare's non-dramatic verse	85
2.8	Evolution of syllabic structure of Shakespeare's verse	87
	Note	93

Chapter 3

Homogeneous and Heterogeneous Plays: Authorship and Style

3.0	Preliminary notes	95
3.1	Rhythm variation by acts	96
	3.1.1 Evolution tendencies in Shakespeare	96
	3.1.2 Homogeneous and heterogeneous plays: typology	105
3.2	Contrast between groupings of acts or scenes in three questionable or stylistically heterogeneous plays	121
3.3	Play-in-Play	131
	Note	133

Chapter 4

How Personages Speak: Rhythmical Differentiation of Characters

4.0	Preliminary remarks	135
4.1	Formal analysis of utterances	136
	4.1.1 Lines split between speakers	136
	4.1.2 Utterances of different lengths	148
4.2	Character study	152
	4.2.1 Differentiation of characters through rhythm	152
	4.2.2 Evolution of characters	174
	Note	176

Chapter 5

Line Endings: Accentual and Syllabic Structure

5.1	Problems; principles of analysis	177
5.2	General evolution of line endings in Shakespeare	181
5.3	Some particulars of the evolution of line endings	190
5.4	Line endings of acts and scenes in four controversial plays	192
	Note	201

Chapter 6

Phrase Endings: Aspects of Rhythm; Author's Idiosyncrasy

6.1	The problem	203
	6.1.1 Linguistic aspect	204

6.1.2	Verse theory aspect	206
6.1.3	The aspect of epochs and individual styles	207
6.2	Material	207
6.3	Grammatical types of proclitic and enclitic phrases. General information	208
6.4	General analysis of proclitic and enclitic phrases: rhythm and the authors' idiosyncrasy	214
6.5	Particular grammatical patterns of proclitic and enclitic phrases: grammatical and semantic aspects of rhythm	219
6.6	Resum: grammar and word semantics as aspects of rhythm	225
6.7	Postscript: Word Boundary Rhythm and the Epoch	226
	Notes	228

Chapter 7

Rhythmical Figures: Structural Types, Grammatical Features and Compositional Functions

7.1	Preliminary remarks. Aim and material	231
7.2	Types of "rhythmical figures" in English iambic verse: general characteristics	233
7.3	Incidence of different rhythmical figures in Shakespeare's verse and in the texts of later poets	239
7.4	Grammatical features of rhythmical figures	241
7.4.1	Morphology	241
7.4.2	Syntax	253
7.5	Rhythmical-grammatical patterns	265
7.6	Compositional function of rhythmical figures in rhymed verse	266
7.6.1	Correlation with stress profiles	267
7.6.2	Distribution in verse lines of a stanza and poem	278
7.7	Summing up	280
	Notes	288

Chapter 8

Rhythm and Meaning

8.0	Preliminary remarks	287
8.1	A more general stylistic analysis of monosyllabic figure W	288
8.2	Analysis of the disyllabic figure SW	292
8.2.1	Adjectives in SW-1	292
8.2.2	Method of componental analysis for rhythmical figures	293
8.2.3	Semantic characteristics of SW-1 containing a verb	295
8.2.4	Semantic characteristics of nouns in SW-1	299
8.2.5	Adjectives forming SW-1	301

8.2.6	Preliminary conclusions	302
8.3	The disyllabic figure WS-1	303
8.3.1	General stylistic (expressive) characteristics of the verbs	303
8.3.2	Semantic characteristics of verbs in WS-1	305
8.4	The trisyllabic figure WSW-1	312
8.5	The disyllabic figure WS-2	315
8.6	The trisyllabic figure WSW-2	321
8.7	General resum of semantic functions of rhythmical figures	321
8.7.1	Semantic categories coupled with all rhythmical figures	322
8.7.2	Semantic differences among the rhythmical figures	323
8.7.3	Connections between parts-of-speech and syntactic properties of rhythmical figures and semantic information	323
8.7.4	Rhythmical-grammatical-semantic-lexical patterns	324
8.7.5	Genre and period characteristics in use of semantic and stylistic potential of rhythmical figures	328
Notes		329

Chapter 9

Conclusion: Iambic Pentameter and Shakespeare's Idiosyncrasy

9.0	Preliminary remarks	331
9.1	English iambic meter and Shakespeare's verse	331
9.1.0	Basic accentual-syllabic features of phrase structure in English	331
9.1.1	Most general definition of English iambic pentameter	332
9.1.2	Stress profiles as an element of meter	333
9.1.3	Meter and rhythmical figures	336
9.2	Problems of genre and style: rhythmical markers	339
9.2.1	Shakespeare's genres; dramatic and non-dramatic verse	339
9.2.2	Stylistic differentiation within texts, compositional laws and structural isomorphism	341
9.2.3	Rhythmical-grammatical-semantic-lexical patterns	344
9.3	Verse form and meaning	345
9.3.1	Variations of iambic pentameter and meaning	345
9.3.2	Rhythmical figures and meaning	346
9.4	Verse form and the poet's idiosyncrasy	347
9.4.1	General summary	347
9.4.2	Four questionable plays	348
9.5	Final remarks	350
Bibliography		353
Sources analysed and quoted		370
Index		373

Tables

1.1	Stress profile data for Russian, English and Italian verse and verse models	10-11
2.1	Shakespeare: stress profiles of ictic positions by periods	46
2.2	Stress profiles (ictic positions) of Shakespeare's works	49-51
2.3	Stress profiles of Shakespeare's older and younger contemporaries	52
2.4	Synchronic comparison of plays by different authors	66
2.5	Shakespeare: non-ictic stress profiles by periods	68
2.6	Stress profiles (non-ictic) of Shakespeare's works	69-71
2.7	Differentiated stress profiles, non-ictic	74-75
2.8	Stress profiles (ictic) of Marlowe's dramas	81
2.9	Stress profiles (non-ictic) of Marlowe's dramas	82
2.10	Stress profiles (ictic) of Byron's dramas	84
2.11	Stress profiles (non-ictic) of Byron's dramas	85
2.12	Syllabic structure of dramatic verse	93
3.1	Stress profiles of separate acts in Shakespeare's dramas, arranged chronologically	97-102
3.2	Range of rhythm variation by acts, Shakespeare's plays	107
3.3	Comparison of range of dispersion of Shakespearean with other plays	109
3.4	Stress profiles of separate acts, 13 non-Shakespearean plays	110-112
3.5	Range of dispersion by acts of 13 non-Shakespearean plays	113
3.6	Mean deviation of ictic stressing by acts	118-119
4.1	Places of utterance junctures in Shakespeare's dramas	137-138
4.2	Places of utterance junctures generalized by periods	139
4.3	Places of utterance junctures in Byron's dramas	140
4.4	Stress profiles of whole texts compared with split lines	141
4.5	Stress profiles of long, medium and short utterances in 24 role texts	153-155
4.6	Rhythmical characteristics of 26 personages	158-159
5.1	Structure of line endings by periods	182
5.2	Structure of line endings in Shakespeare's dramas	183-184
5.3	Structure of line endings in Marlowe's dramas	186
5.4	Structure of line endings in Byron's dramas	189
5.5	Feminine endings in "Titus Andronicus"	193
6.1	Proclitic and enclitic phrases	215
6.2	Proportion of proclitic vs enclitic attributive phrases	219
6.3	Proportion of proclitic vs enclitic verb + adverb phrases	220
7.1	Incidence of types of polysyllabic rhythmical figures	240
7.2	Part-of-speech correlation of monosyllables on W and S	242

Tables—continued

7.3	Part-of-speech correlation of monosyllables in SW-1	243
7.4	Part-of-speech correlation of monosyllables in WS-1	244
7.5	Part-of-speech correlation of disyllabic words in WS-2	249
7.6	Part-of-speech correlation of monosyllabic words in verse outside of multi-syllabic figures	250
7.7	Part-of-speech correlation of monosyllabic words in prose	250
7.8	Part-of-speech correlations in the (⊥__) form in verse outside rhythmical figures	251
7.9	Part-of-speech correlations in (⊥__) forms in prose	251
7.10	Syntactic functions of monosyllabic verbs in WS-1	259
7.11	Syntactic functions of disyllabic verbs in WS-2	263
7.12	Stress profiles for each line of "The Rape of Lucrece"	268
7.13	Stress profiles for each line of Shakespeare's sonnets	269-270
7.14	Stress profiles for each line of iambic tetrameter stanzas rhymed abab	271
7.15	Stress profiles for each line of iambic tetrameter stanzas rhymed aabb	271

Figures

1.1	Stress profiles and iambic indices of Russian, Italian and English verse	12
2.1	Stress profiles of speech model and canonized and decanonized iambic pentameter	42
2.2	Stress profiles comparing early and late Shakespeare with earlier, contemporaneous and later plays	45
2.3	Stress profiles for four periods of Shakespeare's canon	55
2.4	Rigidity indices for Shakespeare's plays plotted by theater season	64
3.1	Stress profiles of acts I, III, V of four plays	103
3.2	Mean percent stress variation by acts	120
3.3	Stress profiles of four plays divided into two groups	123
4.1	Split lines: percentage and mean position plotted chronologically	142
4.2	Stress profiles of long vs short utterances	149
4.3	Stress profiles of 16 major character roles	161
5.1	Evolution of features of line endings in Shakespeare's dramas	185
6.1	Proportion of proclitic vs enclitic micro-phrases	216
7.1	Morphological characteristics of three main rhythmical figures	245
7.2	Stress profiles of the first and last lines of Shakespeare's sonnets contrasted with the mean	273
7.3	Stress profiles for each line of iambic tetrameter stanzas rhymed abab	277
8.1	Emotive connotations of adjectives in SW-1 in texts of Shakespeare, Shelley and Arnold	291
8.2	Percent of WSW-1 figures with semantic loading in texts of Shakespeare, Pope, Shelley and Arnold	313

Acknowledgements

This book is, in a way, a continuation of my first, *English Verse: Theory and History*. Shakespeare was, originally, merely one personage in the long row of English poets; but because he was so great, and wrote so much, he began to dominate my study more and more until he finally became the hero.

To turn specifically to English dramatic verse was, years ago, one of the valuable pieces of advice I got from V.M. Žirmunskij, whom I always remember with gratitude.

R.O. Jakobson has been encouraging my efforts for years; his support and praise have been a continuous source of stimulation. Whatever I do is, in a way, in memory of Roman Jakobson.

I am especially grateful to M.L. Gasparov, whose invaluable advice and friendly assistance have been of enormous significance during all my life as a scholar. Working alongside each other is a memory to cherish. Even now that we are so far apart I keep consulting him – in my mind and in letters.

My warmest gratitude goes to James Bailey, also a friend of many years, for his untiring readings of my writings, his comments and suggestions. His help in final editing of this book is hard to overestimate.

All my life I have been blessed with friends; I had wonderful friends in my old home, and now I am getting new friends. One of them is George T. Wright; I cannot overrate his interest in my work and his advice as an "insider" of American English departments.

Another is Terry V. Brogan, a warm and encouraging friend, whose editorial and bibliographical advice has always been ready to me.

And finally, my boundless indebtedness to my husband, L.K. "Coach" Coachman, who helped smuggle out the first variant of the book (I was not supposed to take out of the Soviet Union one single page of manuscript), who has encouraged me through the hard years of getting used to a new country; who has tirelessly read and edited the book, formatted the manuscript for printing, and provided the kind of inspiration a loving – and loved – friend can. This book is for him.

Marina Tarlinskaja
Seattle, WA.
April, 1986

Preface

Although the Russian linguistic-statistical method for studying poetic rhythm has existed for over seventy years, the approach still has not become familiar to metrists who do not have access to basic works written in several Slavic languages by Tomaševskij, Jakobson Taranovsky, and Gasparov. From what is available in English, the apparent emphasis on description over theory, preoccupation with statistics, and attention to linguistic details may seem to offer little which might help to explain the mysteries of English meters. Such impressions probably arise because of a different attitude toward language and poetry. Rather than imposing external metrical rules derived from a small selection of material, indulging in an endless quest for classical feet, or taking delight in "lilting iambs" and "tripping trochees", the "Tomaševskij school" tries to discover how poets utilize the prosodic features of their language to create meters, analyzes large amounts of material, generalizes the results statistically, and only then deduces theory. The difference in emphasis may be subtle, but it leads to objective conclusions which can be checked by other scholars.

For English metrists one of the chief stumbling blocks in understanding the Russian method concerns the opposition between meter and rhythm. Meter is the abstract idea, scheme, or model, while rhythm is concretely realized in the language of a poem. Without implying any equivalence between poetic and musical rhythm, one may refer to the analogous distinction which musicians make between meter and rhythm; meter is what a conductor indicates with a baton and rhythm is what an orchestra actually plays. The Russian method assumes that an interaction takes place between meter and rhythm; meter may coincide with the rhythm but may also diverge so that metrical expectation is frustrated. The meter/rhythm dichotomy develops clearly in Russian because a word has essentially one stress, full stressed vowels are opposed to reduced unstressed vowels, and stress is free, that is, it can fall on any syllable of a word. In iambic verse, the ictuses, or positions for the metrical stress on the even syllables, frequently but not always receive a stress in the rhythm; in addition, non-metrical stresses may occasionally occur on the odd syllables, a phenomenon which may be expressed in analogous musical terms as syncopation. Complete observance of a metrical scheme produces rhythmical monotony, but too large a divergence disrupts the meter. The Russian approach seeks to determine the frequency and the limits in poetic practice between the poles of rhythmical monotony and rhythmical diversity.

Analysis of the rhythm in English meters is much more difficult. Degrees of stress tend to depend on the grammatical function of a word (usually form words are more strongly stressed than function words), function words may acquire a strong stress when the meaning requires it, and English meters evidently are based on a combination of word and phrase stress. Furthermore, the stress of many English words may shift according to the immediate rhythmical context; such shifts are not shown by citation forms in dictionaries but can be perceived in speech. Yet another stubborn problem of English metrics involves the differences between the spelling of many words and their phonetic forms in speech. Do poets in English have the right to exercise their artistic choice and include colloquial syllabic variants long existing in the English language? Or, according to the "antiphilologism" implied in Saintsbury's trisyllabic substitution, do the poets have to observe contemporary spelling norms and ignore what they hear?

Through her background and training in both Russian and English, and through her numerous studies published over the past twenty years, Dr. Marina Tarlinskaja is uniquely qualified to introduce the Russian approach to English readers. In the present volume she has made the methods developed by Russian scholars accessible to English metrists through analysis of English verse itself. In her detailed investigation of what is undoubtably one of the most demanding and complex meters in the European languages, the English iambic pentameter, she describes how poets adapt the English language to a meter, summarizes the results in statistics, and on that basis derives metrical norms established by the poets themselves. Her analysis shows that poets develop their own distinctive rhythms and that some poets resort to departures from the metrical scheme more than do other poets. Dr. Tarlinskaja demonstrates that many rhythmical patterns are determined by syntactic patterns typical for English and that certain ones are favored by English poets. By comparing the frequency of syntactic combinations in prose with those in poetry, she shows how the poets select those most suitable for a meter while rejecting others which do not fit the meter. Most important, Dr. Tarlinskaja describes in precise detail how the English iambic pentameter alternates between periods of comparatively regular observance of the metrical scheme and periods of free treatment which leads virtually to a disintegration of the meter. In some poetic epochs the amount of rhythmical diversity which the poets regard as being acceptable is relatively narrow, but in other epochs the amount of acceptability is strained to the limit. In reality, the English iambic pentameter has several possible rhythmical realizations.

Following some recent leads by Russian metrists, Dr. Tarlinskaja turns her attention toward elucidating the "semantic aureole" associated with each metrical form, a fascinating subject which requires much supporting data if deductions are to be substantiated. On the most immediate level, she delineates rhythmical differences among lyric, narrative, and dramatic works in iambic pentameter. But beyond this, she connects specific rhythmical patterns with certain broad themes, and demonstrates how different types of rhythm may distinguish high and low characters, or positive and negative personnages in plays. Shakespeare could be called the "silent hero" of Dr. Tarlinskaja's book because rhythmical analysis of his plays is central to her study. She takes up the problem of attribution and proposes a revised chronology of Shakespeare's plays which no serious student of his work can afford to neglect.

Dr. Tarlinskaja's book is not especially easy reading, particularly for those who feel that close analysis kills poetry, shy away from statistics, or do not care for linguistic detail. But for those who wish to pass beyond the outer beauties of English poetry into the poet's linguistic workshop and are willing to try to discover how poets wield their craft, her work will provide new insights into the way poets create their rhythms within their language. The result may be a more conscious appreciation of poetry and a deeper admiration for the abilities of the finest poets who are as original in their rhythms as they are in other aspects of poetry. Through her comparative analysis of the English, Italian, and Russian forms of the iambic pentameter Dr. Tarlinskaja has emphasized once more the value of comparative metrics which is capable of bringing the rhythmical characteristics of a meter in different languages into sharper focus than would otherwise be possible.

Dr. Tarlinskaja's book on English versification is a path-breaker because she has at long last performed the spadework necessary to turn the study of English metrics into a solid and professional academic field.

James Bailey
The University of Wisconsin, Madison.

Forward

Literary critics and linguistic scholars have often relied on each other's studies while pursuing their own interests, and they have regularly disagreed about the nature of the material before them. Poems and novels, after all, are both language and literature and can be inspected from a variety of points of view. The literary study of language is not at all identical with the linguistic study of literature, and the gap between them divides more than two branches of humanistic study. Linguistics aspires to the status of a science, criticism to the condition of an art. The linguist finds in poetic meter a special case of linguistic activity, which operates there under special conditions and perhaps under local rules. These rules and conditions the linguistic scientist is eager to formulate. The critic's attention is on the artistry with which the poet handles the meter, the linguist's on the material handled, and though either kind of study can shed light on the other, the difference in these approaches is so sharp as to generate suspicion and disdain. Critics are likely to find linguists insensitive and abstract; linguists find critics unmethodical and imprecise.

A more genial relation between these two branches of scholarship used to obtain, even in English. Early study of Old and Middle English literature had to be both philological and literary, and the editing of Renaissance texts has always involved complex problems which only a detailed knowledge of phonology and morphology could help resolve. More recently, formalist critics have taken advantage of the insights of structural linguists. But generative metrics, now the most fashionable approach among American linguists, has put off most literary critics by its increasingly cumbersome terminology and its shaky theoretical foundations. If critics and linguists have always been faintly wary of each other, the gap between them now seems wider than ever.

In this situation it is more than refreshing to welcome to the American linguistic scene a metrist of a different and more intelligible persuasion, who yet represents a well-established European tradition of linguistic inquiry. Until Marina Tarlinskaja appeared, no representative of the Russian Formalist approach to meter had concentrated on the development of English poetry, so it is hard to know whether the methods of that school could help us understand English meters better. In 1976 her formidable work *English Verse: Theory and History* showed us how much can be learned about the history of English verse from statistical studies, guided by well-formulated questions. Ten years later, the present book offers us an equally thorough exploration of some extremely important aspects of Shakespeare's poetry. It is easy to predict that future literary scholars who want to say anything accurate about Shakespeare's metrical verse will be gratefully citing her tables and figures and her lucid explanatory chapters.

Contemporary linguists usually write as if (and sometimes state explicitly that) the whole problem of meter is to describe the fit between the stress system of English ("prose rhythm") and the stress system of particular meters. Literary critics know that there is much more to rhythm than that, including analysis of how metrical verse is sounded and performed, and inquiry into the dramatic or aesthetic purposes of different meters and of variations from metrical norms, two huge subjects which linguists avoid as subjective and unresponsive to their own classifying and abstracting skills. Nevertheless, what linguists have to say about the fit between the two stress systems is bound to be of great interest to literary students of meter, for it is usually through the divergences between phrasal rhythmic patterns and metrical norms that poets achieve their most expressive rhetorical effects. Unfortunately, the methods of many modern linguists (especially generative metrists) lead them to fix as their central preoccupation the distinction between metrical and "unmetrical" lines of verse, a distinction not useful to literary metrists except as a means of differentiating generally the practice of one poet from another: Shakespeare writes certain kinds of lines that Milton avoids, Donne some that Shakespeare avoids. For such linguists, the chief task is to formulate the "rules" which, never formulated by the poets, have induced them to accept some kinds of lines and reject others.

These highly rational abstract studies retain little connection with any reader's actual experience of verse, whether read in private or heard in the theater. The empirical studies of Marina Tarlinskaja are very different in spirit. Her chief concern is not the border between metrical and "unmetrical" lines— that dubious terrain way off on the fringes of the subject—but the patterns that the poets do use. What makes her research far more pleasing to literary scholars than most other linguists' is one crucial difference of focus: she studies norms, not rules; variations, not violations. Her basic subject remains essentially simple: the extent to which speech stress falls on ictic and non-ictic positions in iambic pentameter verse. This, for her, is the key to the poets' use of meter and to any study of the differences we find in the metrical styles of poets, of periods, and of national poetries. Specifically, it opens up for her the means of formulating accurately the relationships that hold between meter and other linguistic levels, grammar and semantics; and of comparing typologically the iambic form of English verse with the stricter Russian and the looser Italian forms. These are important matters, and her approach succeeds impressively in illuminating them.

The discriminations she makes are sometimes very small—i.e., the disparities she finds between two poets' stressing of syllables in any one position in the line may be only a few lines out of a hundred—but her method is statistical and involves the observation of hundreds of thousands of lines. For her data to be reliable, it is absolutely essential that her definitions of stress and her decisions about particular lines be made with great sensitivity to the poetic line and with great logical exactitude. Tarlinskaja's great care about these matters makes a non-linguist reader feel confident that her results can be relied on, that what she is saying about the poetry's meter is valid and is important to any serious study of English metrics. Her work is amazingly methodical and systematic, her procedures always logical. The questions she asks are pertinent, and her research designs precisely fitted to her questions. Her basic tools—statistical data compiled and displayed with an enviable resourcefulness and skill, tables and figures expertly constructed—have never, to my knowledge, been used with such purposefulness and good sense by anyone before her in this field. She brings to the world of English prosody a maturity of judgement as well as a sensitivity to poetry that makes most American linguists who study meter look like mischievous children in comparison. Furthermore, though the terminology she uses is often difficult, her style of presentation is lucid and tactful. She really wants not to impress or befuddle her readers, but to share her knowledge with them.

How useful is her work to literary scholars and critics? Her findings can be extremely helpful to literary historians, who are still trying, after more than a century of attribution studies, to fix the authors and dates of doubtful plays or scenes and who may find here the best available stylistic data for this purpose. Her studies also help us understand more precisely the relations between meter and language—meter and phrasing, meter and grammar, meter and meaning—and to account more intelligibly for our intuitions about poetic and metrical styles. We can learn much from this book about how Shakespeare developed new ways of patterning his verse and fitting the rhythms of English to it, and about how his practice altered from play to play, from genre to genre, from period to period, and even from character to character, perhaps even from one character-type to another. As she illuminates these matters, her assumptions need not alienate the literary scholar. Her methods are tough, precise, and consistent, and her claims reasonable and clearly formulated. She also, I think, implicitly recognizes where the domain of linguistic analysis ends and futher work must be left to literary criticism. However technical her arguments become, she does not wish us to forget that the material of her study is poetry and that it is justly valued primarily for its literary merits, not because it is grist for the linguist's mill.

George T. Wright
University of Minnesota

Chapter 1

Meter: In General and in its Particulars

1.1 General concepts. "Vertical" and "horizontal" analyses of meter

1.1.1. Shakespeare's verse has been subjected to detailed study for over one hundred years, but its metrical form has never been analyzed in any systematic and well-rounded fashion. It is the correlation of actual stresses with the metrical scheme that constitutes the main structural feature of a syllabo-tonic verse text, i.e., the type of verse in which both the total number of syllables per line and the number and distribution of stressed and unstressed syllables in the line are structurally-relevant features.

Every reader of poetry knows that the actual distribution of stresses in individual lines can take on a seemingly infinite variety. The first impression of an unsophisticated reader is that no two lines in a poem have precisely the same rhythm. More reading experience, however, makes him realize that there is a certain general law of stressing in, say, an iambic poem. An even more sophisticated reader knows this general law before he reads a poem; the reader instantly recognizes the law after scanning the first few lines. In keeping with this general law the poet stresses some syllabic positions in the lines more often and more strongly than others; in an iambic poem the even-numbered positions (2,4,6. . .) are on the whole stressed more often than odd ones (1,3,5. . .); among the even positions, the last (10 in an iambic pentameter poem) is stressed more often than the penultimate even position (8), and 4 more often than 2. The reader comes to expect this regularity and notices if it is broken (for example, he will certainly notice a missing stress on the final even position). So there is a general law, the reader finds, that guided the poet into some specific stress-patterning of his verse lines. Now the reader, growing more sophisticated, begins to wonder whether the poet was continually conscious of the law that guided his distribution of stresses, or was it an unconscious, inspiration-guided process? The reader comes across poems written in the same general stress-pattern law but belonging to different authors and discovers that they do not sound alike. Our inquisitive reader speculates further: since the poems are on the whole alike, there obviously is a general law; on the other hand, some poems are so rhythmically dissimilar it seems almost as if each poet construed the law to suit himself. Therefore, there must be a law to provide general guidelines for the poet but which also allows him to exercise considerable individuality in style. How general is the law? Phrased another way, how far can poets deviate in stressing their lines from the general law of stress distribution (the meter), yet still remain within it?

This most general law of stress distribution, the meter, can be formulated in several ways, more superficially, or deeper, with more attention to various details. Examples are: (a) only as a general line scheme of stressing alternation; (b) as a list of "rules" permitting without any limitation certain rhythmical combination of words in the verse line, restricting other combinations, while forbidding all other combinations of words; or (c) as a finite list of permissible ("metrical") accentual and word boundary types of verse lines within a given literary tradition (Tomaševskij 1929:94-137). The frequency of each type in actual verse texts may vary considerably.

One poet may differ from another not so much by the types of lines he uses, but by a different proportion of the same line type. For example, a line like *Chloe stepp'd in and kill'd him with a frown* (Pope, "The Rape of the Lock" V:68), metrical for all English poets, is more typical of Shakespeare or Shelley than of Pope, and it is the different proportions of the same line types that are largely responsible for the dissimilar rhythm of Shakespeare's, Pope's, and Shelley's verse.

The idiosyncratic features of a poet's verse system (e.g., Shakespeare's iambic pentameter) can be abstracted from all, or a large part, of his works and presented in the form of a model. In relation to one work of the poet (e.g., "Richard II") such a model plays the same "background" role as does the model of a national form of meter (e.g., English iambic pentameter) in relation to an individual author's style (e.g., Shakespeare's rhythmical system of iambic pentameter).

Here it is necessary to clarify my use of the terms meter and rhythm. In the so-called Russian school of verse study, to which I belong, it is customary to apply the term "meter" to the most general features of a particular verse system which characterize the whole tradition as it developed within a national literature, for example, German, Russian, or English. Thus we can speak of the English, or Russian, iambic meter. The realization, and variation, of the meter in a particular epoch, or in the works of a particular poet, is usually called "rhythm",[1] for example, the rhythm of Puškin's iambic pentameter. Some scholars, however, have begun to apply the term "meter" also in relation to its more specific, individual features, discovered in the verse of a certain epoch or poet (cf. Proxorov 1984:89), and even in one long poem (cf. Gindin 1981). If a poem is viewed, as it were, in isolation from all other works in the same meter, then its structural features, abstracted from the text, may be said to form a "microsystem" of their own, a particular version of "meter". To avoid misunderstanding, I shall use the term "meter" when discussing the most general features of English iambic pentameter. The variant a meter assumes during a certain epoch will be referred to as a "metrical subsystem", while individual variations of meter in the works of one poet will be generally termed "rhythm", even though it can also be viewed as a "metrical microsystem", a poet's "metrical idiolect".

Special methods of verse analyses devised in the past decades make it possible to discover both the most general laws of a syllabo-tonic verse (meter) and their idiosyncratic realizations in individual verse styles (rhythm). This study attempts to do both for a large body of English verse written in the most commonly used syllabo-tonic binary meter—iambic pentameter, the verse form in which Shakespeare wrote almost exclusively.

Only very recently have scholars begun to devise ways of studying the correlation between actual stresses and the metrical law in English verse. Chambers (1930), who felt that "variations within the blank verse cadre itself . . . become part of the unconscious or subconsious instinct of a writer and are more likely to be significant of a chronological development than those which involve deliberation," had to admit that "variations of stress have not so far received much study" (Chambers 1930:I,258-259,267). The situation did not change for many years, if naive works like Feuillerat (1953) are disregarded (cf. Schoenbaum 1966:140). "Surprisingly enough, the metrical structure of English poems has seldom been studied from the statistical point of view . . . Statistical studies of line and stanza patterns are common in Europe . . . But the statistical measurement of English poetry . . . has not been often undertaken," wrote Richard Bailey in 1969 (R.W. Bailey 1969:231). The most recent studies on English verse in which the underlying meter is statistically "extracted" from long portions of text are Tarlinskaja and Teterina 1974, James Bailey 1975, and Tarlinskaja 1976.

Among the most recent works on Shakespeare's verse are those of Kiparsky 1975, 1977, Hayes 1983, Tarlinskaja 1983, and Suhamy 1984. Kiparsky and Hayes formulated certain "metrical rules" for Shakespeare's Sonnets in contrast to the rules for other poets, mainly Milton; the metrical rules are concerned with "deviating" ("mislabeled") syllables on adjacent metrical positions and their correlation with the phonological and grammatical characteristics of words causing these "deviations". This approach makes it possible to discover some minute particulars of a poet's style. Neither Kiparsky nor Hayes, however, studied the types of whole lines, for example, the places of "deviating" groups of syllables and their correlation with other "deviations" in the same line; nor did they study the correlation of various line types in the poems of different authors.

Suhamy's (1984) detailed study of Shakespeare's verse concentrates on the proportion of verse and prose in the dramas, the syllabic volume of lines (and certain types of polysyllabic words), on different places of "splits" in the lines, and various types of line endings. The study of line accentuation in its interaction with the meter occupies only 63 pages (Chaper II) of the book almost eight hundred pages long. Suhamy not only does not generalize, or trace any evolution in Shakespeares' rhythmical style; also his approach is in several ways faulty. For example, he confuses the notions of "ictus" and "stress". This confusion results, on the one hand, in his attempt to consider even articles stressed if they fall on an ictus (e.g., Suhamy 1984:154,159,178). On the other hand, confusing ictus and stress brings him back to the old concept of "feet substitution" (e.g., Suhamy 1984:201), much critizised (e.g., Bailey 1973b) for the theoretical consequences to which it leads. For example, any line of free verse, or even any segment from a newspaper, may be interpreted as an "iambic verse line" where such-and-such "feet" substitute for "iambic feet". Suhamy's otherwise very thorough study does not shed any new light on the problem of Shakespeare's iambic pentameter.

Tarlinskaja (1983) did a statistical evaluation of stress on each metrical position of the whole text of every drama by Shakespeare (their "stress profiles"); this type of analysis provides a general insight into a poet's rhythmical idiosyncrasy and its evolution but ignores minute details. In the present study both "vertical" (stress profile) and "horizontal" (line type) analyses are combined to achieve a detailed picture of Shakespeare's rhythmical idiosyncrasy and to pinpoint the place of his idiolect in the English tradition of iambic pentameter.

1.1.2. Thus, the two basic problems addressed in this study are: what, in general, constitutes iambic pentameter? and what particular forms did it assume in Shakespeare's poetry? Key corollary questions are: what is meter? What forms does the same meter assume in different literary traditions? What constitutes an author's rhythmical idiosyncrasy? These problems were in part stated in 1.1.1; here are some additional considerations.

Any meter, defined most generally, is an accepted principle of organizing the language material in a verse line in a way that generates a perceptible alternation of phonologically marked (e.g., long, or stressed) and unmarked (e.g., short, or unstressed) syllables.[2] The same general metrical principle, e.g., iambic, historically assumes different forms in different languages and in different literatures, e.g., English vs. German vs. Russian iambic meter. The forms which a meter assumes in different languages and literatures will be called, for lack of a better term, "national forms of meter". (No implication of a "national spirit"!) Rhythmical idiosyncrasy, i.e., an author's particular rhythmical style, can only be identified if we describe the background against which the poet's verse can be matched. A poet's individual rhythmical style must be viewed, first of all, within the framework of the national variant of the meter taken as a whole, e.g., Shakespeare's iambic pentameter must be compared to English iambic pentameter in general (in contrast with, for example, Russian or German). Secondly, the poet's individual metrical style must be compared to those of his contemporaries, predecessors, and followers, matching not only epoch to epoch but also genre to genre.

These conditions require that the notions of "meter" and "rhythm" be defined on several different levels of abstraction from the verse texts. The definition on the highest level disregards the national peculiarities of meter, stating only the most general principles of, say, the iamb or trochee. On the next level of abstraction the definition takes into account the most general national characteristics, e.g., English iamb as opposed to German and Russian, or even more specifically, English iambic pentameter as opposed to its German and Russian counterparts. On a still lower level of abstraction, when the definition begins to distinguish period variations of a metrical form, for example, the English iambic pentameter of eighteenth-century Classicism as opposed to nineteenth-century Romanticism, "meter" begins to slip into the realm of "rhythm". An even more specific definition will take into account genre features within a period, for example, Elizabethan lyrical poetry as opposed to drama. Next come definitions of poets' individual subsystems, for example, Shakespeare's iambic pentameter as opposed to Fletcher's; next follow definitions of period and genre particulars within every poet's canon viewed as a whole, for example, Shakespeare's early and late dramas; and, finally, we define peculiarities of an individual text, for example, Shakespeare's "Othello". The differentiation can cut even deeper into the text and become more text-style oriented, for example, different rhythmical subsystems used by a poet to oppose his dramatis personae, for example the role text of the villain Iago vs. the text spoken by the noble hero Othello in acts I-II, or passages of pathos vs. comic scenes (see Chapter 4).

The definitions of meter and rhythm, moving from more general (e.g., the meter of English iambic pentameter) to the most specific (e.g., the rhythm of the part of Iago) pass from more abstract rules that exist "outside" and "before" a particular text, to their more concrete materialization in a particular text or its part. Such rhythmical particulars are, naturally, derived from the text, "after" it has been written.

The closer the formulation defines specific verse texts, the more particulars it is based on. The higher the level of abstraction, the lower is the language level invoked for the definition. The most general formulations of meter are based on the phonological level of the language, the more specific definitions of meter and rhythm must take into account also grammatical and even lexical peculiarities of text elements (see Chapters 6 and 7). The determination of the tendencies in the distribution of the grammatical and lexical categories in verse specifies the notion of meter and differentiates rhythmical styles; it can also be a first step toward statistical modeling of the semantic structure of verse (cf. Levy 1969:108, Tarlinskaja 1985).

1.1.3. In its most general form iambic meter can be defined as an alternation of weak and strong syllabic positions in the model of a verse line. The weak positions are generally associated with phonologically unmarked syllables (unstressed, or short) and the strong positions with phonologically marked syllables (stressed, or long). Just how rigid is this general requirement of meter? How strong is this link between weak positions—and unmarked syllables, or strong positions—and marked syllables? The degree of rigidity varies in different national literary traditions. The correlation between a certain position and a certain phonological type of syllable can be rigidly constant (absolutely obligatory), everywhere in the line, or at least in certain parts of the line; the correlation may be less rigid: the link is still there, but it is not realized 100%; or the link can be even weaker and exist only in the form of a tendency. If there is no link, there is, naturally, no meter. Specifying the degree of rigidity, the strength of the link between a certain metrical position and a certain phonological type of syllable, helps to define the national form of meter in a most general way.

The most general definition of any national form of iambic meter must specify the permissible "minimum": how often can weak positions be filled with the theoretically untypical, phonologically marked syllables (e.g., stressed) and strong positions with the theoretically untypical, phonologically unmarked syllables (e.g., unstressed)? The "minimum" varies from language to language, from literature to literature. Russian iambic meter, for example, is more demanding than English, particularly with respect to weak syllabic positions: they cannot normally be filled by phonologically marked syllables, i.e., stressed syllables of polysyllabic words (cf. Bailey 1973a:134-135), while in English iambic verse they can, though with certain constraints (cf. Gasparov 1973, Tarlinskaja and Teterina 1974, Tarlinskaja 1976, Kiparsky 1977, Hayes 1983).

The different degrees of metrical acceptability which identify the different national forms of meter are usually explained by the specific features of each particular language, and by the verse tradition as it developed in each particular national literature. Among language characteristics that are metrically relevant are the following features: the typical length of words; strength of word stress and its correlation with phrasal accent; and freedom in word stress. In a language, the longer the words, the stronger the word stress and the less its subordination to phrasal accent, and the less fixed the place of stress in a word, the more suitable for the language seem to be the tonic and syllabo-tonic systems of versification; vice versa, the shorter the words, the weaker the word stress and the stronger its domination by phrasal accent, and the more fixed the place of stress in a word, the more suitable for the language seems to be the syllabic system of versification. Russian is an example of a language better suited for tonic and syllabo-tonic systems of versification and French is a language more suitable for a syllabic system of versification, while English occupies an intermediate position (see Jakobson 1979a, Žirmunskij 1977:375, Xolševnikov 1984a; cf. Bjorklund 1978:404-441).

Gasparov, however, gives a higher priority to the processes within a national literature and its needs at every particular epoch than to the "language givens". In eighteenth-century Russia, for example, syllabo-tonic verse replaced syllabic not because the former suited the Russian language any better than the latter. On the contrary, the syllabic system of verse is much closer to the Russian prose characteristics than any syllabo-tonic meter. That is precisely why metrical systems of versification, being more artificial and constraining, and more clearly opposing verse to prose, were more acceptable to the developing Classicism (Gasparov 1984a:22,31).

The role of literary tradition in the national forms of meter is hard to overestimate. For example, one of the reasons why English iambic meter is less rigid than Russian is the fact that the English syllabo-tonic verse system developed gradually in the course of a lengthy process several centuries long and was influenced not only by a foreign, Romance system of versification but also by its own folk verse, which was moving in the syllabo-tonic direction anyhow (cf. Lehmann 1956, Smirnickaja 1970). In contrast, Russian iambic verse developed during a short period of time and underwent a drastic qualitative change as a result of the Trediakovskij-Lomonosov reform; it developed as a literary form of verse within seventeen years (1735-1752), was little connected with the Russian folk traditions, and assumed, consequently, a more rigid form of meter (Gasparov 1984a:21).

These factors affect both the most general and more specific characteristics of national variants of the same meter, e.g., iambic pentameter.

The most general features of iambic meter can be best disclosed by a "vertical" analysis utilizing the text as a whole or large portions of text, because the general features are obscured when only individual lines are examined (the inherent variations in stressing). The proper approach in "vertical" analysis is statistical: the number of stressed syllables in each syllabic position are counted and expressed as a percentage of the total of all the lines of the text. The correlation between the indices expressed statistically is called the "stress profile" of the text.[3] Thus the degree of rigidity will have a numerical expression, and such notions as "constantly" stressed or unstressed, "predominantly" stressed or unstressed, and "optionally" stressed (cf. Trubetzkoy 1963, Kolmogorov and Proxorov 1968, Gasparov 1973, 1980, 1984b, Xolševnikov 1984b) can be assigned numerical indices.

1.1.4. To define what constitutes English iambic pentameter, I compared three national systems of verse: Russian and English iambic pentameter, and Italian hendecasyllabic verse. Most common definitions of Italian verse treat it as syllabic—the type of verse structure which is based on the number of syllables per line and exhibits a great variety in distribution of stresses. However, some authors (e.g., Giammati 1972, Elwert 1968: 23) admit that there is a certain degree of regularity in Italian syllabic verse which results in an optional iambic cadence at least in certain parts of the line. Analyzing the existing definitions, Gasparov (1980) assumed that there are possible four accentual variants of the Italian hendecasyllabic verse: a purely syllabic type, **A**, a syllabo-tonic type, **D**, not unlike the English iambic pentameter, and two transitory types, **B** and **C**, that move from a purely syllabic form to syllabo-tonic. Types **B** and **C** are the most common in the Italian verse tradition. Gasparov analyzed hendecasyllabic verse of twelve Italian poets, from Dante to D'Annunzio, and compared actual verse to its language probability models of the four types (**A-D**).[4] He introduced the notion of "iambic index"[5]: the difference between the mean stress on even ("ictic", or "strong") and odd ("non-ictic", or "weak") positions (the constantly stressed final ictus was disregarded); in actual Italian verse it is never less than 33% (the **B** type), while in Gasparov's model of purely syllabic verse (type **A**) it is only 4%. This means that Italian hendecasyllabic verse has an iambic tendency. It therefore can be compared with other national variants of iambic pentameter as an example of a syllabic extreme.

To differentiate between degrees of rigidity of links between syllabic positions and particular accentual types of syllables that fill the positions, I first started with the system introduced by Trubetzkoy in 1937 (Trubetzkoy 1963:56-57). He distinguished three types of metrical positions: obligatorily stressed (−), obligatorily unstressed (∪), and arbitrarily stressed (x). A similar system was adopted by Jakobson (1935) (cf. Kolmogorov and Proxorov 1968, Xolševnikov 1984b, Gasparov 1984b).

Trubetzkoy defined Russian iambic tetrameter verse in the following way:

$$\cup \ x \ \cup \ x \ \cup \ x \ \cup \ -$$

Similarly, Russian pentameter can be defined:

$$\cup \ x \ \cup \ x \ \cup \ x \ \cup \ x \ \cup \ -$$

This means that (a) non-ictic positions in Russian iambic verse are obligatorily unstressed, (b) the final ictic position is obligatorily stressed (in fact 100%), while (c) stressing on non-final ictic positions is optional: they can be filled by either stressed or unstressed syllables.

Gasparov (1973:414), using my stress profile data for English verse (later published in Tarlinskaja and Teterina 1974, Tarlinskaja 1976), suggested that English iambic meter might be defined in the following way:

$$x \ - \ x \ - \ x \ - \ x \ - \ x \ -$$

In this definition ictic positions are assumed to be obligatorily stressed, while non-ictic positions are optionally stressed. Gasparov noticed, however, that ictic positions in English pentameter are not rigidly filled by stressed syllables and came to a conclusion he himself called a paradox: in English pentameter both ictic and non-ictic positions are optionally stressed. This turns English pentameter into purely syllabic verse, which is absurd.

Stress profile data for Russian iambic pentameter show that non-terminal ictic positions are also not quite "optionally" stressed; actually, only ictus IV has truly optional stressing, while others are predominantly stressed, not less than in English verse (cf. Xolševnikov 1984b criticizing Trubetzkoy). Therefore, a re-examination of the definition of Russian and English verse based on a re-examination of the notions "obligatory stress", "obligatory nonstress", and "optional stress", seemed in order. Trubetzkoy's definition, "optional stress", is much too wide a range: it is everything between 0 and 100%. I decided to narrow the range of "optional stress" and also to add the notions "predominantly stressed" and "predominantly unstressed" (cf. Xolševnikov 1984b:170). I assigned ranges of numerical values to the following types of positions: (1) constantly or predominantly stressed, (2) constantly or predominantly unstressed, and (3) optionally stressed. The ranges are as follows:

(−) constantly or predominantly stressed: 100-66%;
(x) optionally stressed: 65-25%;
(∪) constantly or predominantly unstressed: 25-0%.

The selection of ranges was not accidental: they are based on the most typical stressing diapasons on weak and strong syllabic positions of Russian and English iambic pentameter (see Table 1.1). The "non-stress" range is narrower than the "stress" range because the material analyzed shows that non-ictic positions are more sensitive to "extra-metrical" stressing than are ictic positions to the loss of stress.[6]

The analysis of stress profiles from the point of view of types of syllabic positions (−), (∪), and (x) makes it possible to compare the correlation between these three national variants of iambic pentameter verse: its strictest variant (Russian), its loosest variant (Italian), and an intermediate variant (English).

For this comparative study I take four examples of Russian iambic pentameter verse, ranging from a stricter form (Žukovskij, 1812) to a looser form (a contemporary poet, Mežirov, 1955-1962); four examples of Italian verse, two of a stricter type: C form (Alfieri, 1749-1803, and Ariosto, 1474-1533), and two of a looser, more modern type: **B** form (Carducci, 1835-1907, and D'Annunzio, 1863-1938); and six examples of English verse, from a stricter form (Pope) to the loosest form known (Donne's "Satyres") (see Table 1.1 and Figure 1.1). The material in Table 1.1 is arranged in the order of a decreasing value of the "iambic index". Italian verse is compared to its language model of the **A** type and English verse to a speech model of decasyllabic verse constructed from Donne's "Sermons".[7]

Using the data in Table 1.1 and the ranges of values assigned to (−), (x), and (∪), Russian iambic pentameter can be defined:

∪ − ∪ − ∪ − ∪ x ∪ −

Italian hendecasyllabic verse assumes the following form:
B type (Carducci):

x x x x ∪ − ∪ x ∪ −

C type (Ariosto):

∪ x ∪ − ∪ x ∪ x ∪ −

English iambic pentameter assumes the following form:
The Pope-Browning type:

x − ∪ − ∪ − ∪ − ∪ −

Table 1.1

Stress Profile Data for Russian and English Iambic Pentameter, Italian Hendecasyllabic Verse, and Verse Models

Data Sources			Percentage of stress on syllabic positions										Mean of position 1,3,5,7 W	Mean of position 2,4,6,8 S	"Iambic" index S−W
			1	2	3	4	5	6	7	8	9	10			
	Russian:														
1	Zukovskij		--	83.9	--	78.5	--	96.2	--	41.6	--	100	--	75.0	75.0
1	Puškin		--	81.4	--	75.6	--	96.8	--	37.8	--	100	--	72.9	72.9
1	Nekrasov		--	78.2	--	69.5	--	90.9	--	30.5	--	100	--	67.2	67.2
2	Mezirov		--	78.0	--	68.0	--	89.0	--	28.5	--	100	--	65.9	65.9
	Italian:														
3	Alfieri		32.6	44.0	14.6	86.4	12.4	57.2	12.0	83.2	5.0	100	17.9	67.7	49.8
3	Ariosto		19.6	43.0	17.0	67.8	4.2	65.4	16.0	52.0	3.4	100	14.2	57.0	42.8
3	Carducci		34.8	34.4	30.2	59.8	2.6	71.6	17.4	56.4	1.2	100	21.3	55.5	34.2
3	D'Annunzio		21.6	34.2	33.2	49.8	0.8	79.2	8.8	32.8	1.2	100	16.1	49.0	32.9
3	Language model (A) of syllabic verse		20	38	30	29	31	28	25	27	--	100	26.5	30.5	4.0

Table 1.1 (cont.)

English:												
4 Pope	32.3	78.1	12.4	97.8	3.2	74.4	2.4	85.7	1.4	99.0	12.6	84.0	71.4
4 Milton	31.6	75.3	9.6	82.1	9.9	78.5	8.6	81.9	4.6	95.8	14.9	79.4	64.5
4 Shakespeare	27.3	65.8	11.6	90.2	13.1	71.1	11.6	76.0	10.4	94.3	15.9	75.9	60.0
5 Browning	32.0	71.6	16.8	81.4	13.0	80.2	11.7	73.3	12.8	92.1	18.3	72.4	54.1
4 Swinburne	34.1	60.5	29.1	83.6	16.9	70.4	12.3	77.1	11.6	84.7	23.1	72.9	49.8
4 Donne, "Satyres"	39.4	61.2	26.7	80.0	20.0	66.6	24.8	70.7	14.8	78.2	27.7	69.6	41.9
4 Speech model (C) of syllabic verse	21.0	41.4	35.0	45.2	35.2	47.4	35.2	40.2	14.2	82.4	31.6	43.6	12.0

Data Sources:

1. Taranovsky, 1953, Tables IX and XII.
2. Gasparov, 1974, Table 11, p. 102.
3. Gasparov, 1980, Table 3, p. 206.
4. Tarlinskaja and Teterina, 1974, Table I, p. 69; p. 74; Table IV, p. 78.
5. Tarlinskaja, 1976, Table 41, pp. 279-280.

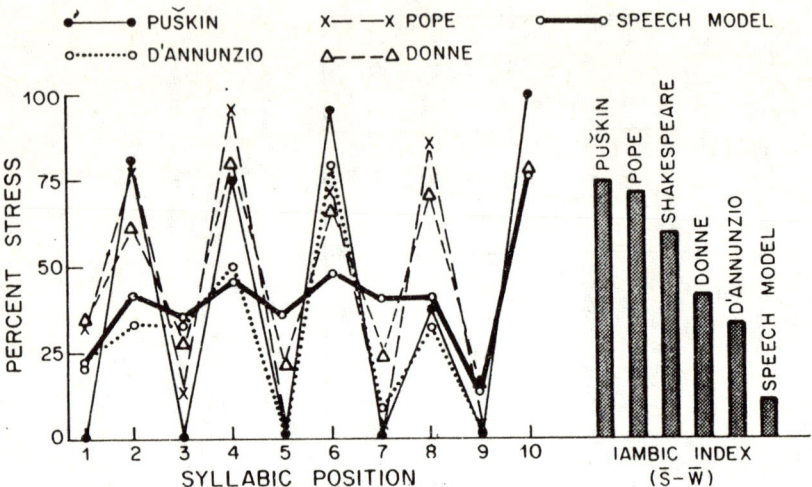

Figure 1.1. Stress profiles and iambic indices representative of Russian (Puškin), Italian (D'Annunzio), and English (Pope, Donne), and speech model C of English syllabic verse. The iambic index of Shakespeare's verse place it mid-way between the extremes of English iambic pentameter.

The Swinburne-Donne type:
$$x\,x\,x\,-\,\cup\,-\,\cup\,-\,\cup\,-$$
The type C speech model of English decasyllabic verse has the following form:
$$\cup\,x\,x\,x\,x\,x\,x\,x\,\cup\,-$$
The Russian pentameter line scheme presents an alternation of obligatorily unstressed (∪) and predominantly stressed (−) metrical positions; only one position, ictus IV, is filled with optionally stressed (x) syllables. The final position is constantly stressed.

The Italian verse of the more syllabic type (**B**) is truly "syllabic" only in the first "hemistich". The second "hemistich" contains only one optionally stressed position: as with the Russian iambic pentameter it is in position 8. Thus, out of ten positions only five are not optionally stressed: two ictic positions (6 and 10) and three non-ictic positions (5, 7, 9).

The more syllabo-tonic type (**C**) of Italian hendecasyllable contains only three optionally stressed positions: 2, 6, and 8. The two stressed positions (predominantly stressed, 4, and constantly stressed, 10) terminate both "hemistichs".

Even the loosest form of Italian hendecasyllabic verse has an iambic tendency: its "iambic index" is 8 times higher than that of the language model (**A**) of purely syllabic verse. The more rigid form is even closer to syllabo-tonic: its "iambic index" is 12 times higher than that of the language model of purely syllabic verse and approaches that of the English iambic pentameter (cf. Alfieri and Swinburne in Table 1.1).

The English iambic pentameter scheme of the most common type (Pope-Browning) presents an alternation of predominantly unstressed (∪) and predominantly stressed (−) metrical positions everywhere in the line except the first non-ictus, which is optionally stressed. So the difference between the most general scheme of the Russian pentameter and the common type of English pentameter lies in the nature of one optionally stressed position: in Russian it is an ictus, in English a non-ictic position. If we examine more closely the difference, we notice that the final ictic position in the Russian verse is constantly stressed, while in the English verse only predominantly stressed. Further, non-ictic positions in Russian verse are close to constantly non-stressed (exceptions are rare: cf. Bailey 1973a) while in English verse they are only predominantly unstressed.

The scheme of the looser form of English iambic pentameter (the Swinburne-Donne type) contains three optionally stressed positions: the whole first "hemistich"[8], except its final ictic position 4, is organized according to a syllabic rather than syllabo-tonic principle. The second "hemistich" is syllabo-tonic.

The C model of English decasyllabic verse is, as is to be expected, mostly filled with optionally-stressed syllables. The three exceptions are position 10, predominantly stressed by definition, position 9, predominantly unstressed by contrast with 10, and position 1 (English phrases often begin "iambically").

The English iambic pentameter verse occupies an intermediate place between the Russian pentameter and Italian hendecasyllabic; in its more commonly used variant the English iambic pentameter approaches the Russian scheme, while in its less conventional, looser form, it comes closer to the Italian scheme, especially the more archaic form of Italian verse: cf. Ariosto and Donne. However, both non-ictic and ictic positions are more strongly stressed in the "Satyres" than in Ariosto's verse; though the general contrast between even and odd positions (the "iambic index") is very close, the Italian and English verse each has its own typological features. The Russian iambic pentameter is the most syllabo-tonic of the three national verse forms analyzed. The most rigid variant of the English verse somewhat approaches the Russian variant, but looser variants of English verse which are more common (Shakespeare-Browning type) move away from it. The even looser "Satyre" type of verse is a mixed form, transitory between syllabo-tonic and syllabic (cf. Tarlinskaja and Teterina 1974).

Thus, the Russian and English variants of iambic pentameter can be defined in the most general way as an alternating sequence of unstressed and stressed syllabic positions. The difference resides in the following features:

(1) In the Russian iamb, the non-terminal ictic positions are only predominantly stressed, and the final ictus is constantly (100%) stressed, while in the English iamb all ictic positions are only predominantly stressed.

(2) Non-ictic positions in the Russian iamb are constantly unstressed, while in the English iamb they are only predominantly unstressed; the anacrusis (the first non-ictic position preceding the first ictus of the line) even tends to be optionally stressed. Non-ictic stresses in the Russian iamb, when they occur at all, are normally restricted to the anacrusis and to monosyllables. Exceptions did not occur before the twentieth century (e.g., Brjusov, Bagrickij, or Čvetaeva); they are relatively numerous only in experimental works like Ivan Aksënov's translations of Elizabethan-Jacobean dramas. For example, the English iambic pentameter line[9] *Slăndĕr (thĕ bĕggăr's sìn), l̆ies (sìn ŏf fŏols)* (Dekker, "The Honest Whore", Part I, I:134) is perfectly normal, while Aksënov's translation of this line, imitating its structure, is absolutely abnormal for the Russian iambic pentameter: *Brănjū (grĕx niščĭx), lòžjŭ (grèx bĕzùmcĕv)* (Aksënov 1938:290; cf. Bailey 1973a:134-135).

(3) An important difference between the two national forms of iambic meter resides in the fact that in Russian iamb it is <u>ictic</u> positions that are <u>more</u> <u>liable</u> to <u>optional</u> <u>stressing</u>, while in English it is <u>non-ictic</u> positions. Since non-ictic positions are more sensitive to accentual "deviations", it is this difference which moves English iambic pentameter towards purely syllabic verse.

Italian syllabic verse, particularly its more archaic type, has a syllabo-tonic tendency which makes it possible to consider Italian hendecasyllable the loosest variant of iambic pentameter (cf. Žirmunskij 1977:375).

Stress profile data can frequently be displayed to advantage graphically. Plotting the percentage of stress by syllabic position leads to a "saw-toothed" pattern, and the more pronounced the pattern, the stronger the accentual alternation of syllables. Figure 1.1 plots representative data from Table 1.1, and we see directly how much more rigidly syllabo-tonic are Puškin's and Pope's verse compared with that of Donne and D'Annunzio. But even these poets on the average markedly alternated the stressing in their lines compared with the averages of many lines of prose (speech model).

Closer examination of the curves reveals certain further interesting details:

1. In comparing Puškin and Pope, we notice that the former constructed pentameter lines with a stress constant on the final ictus and, by contrast, the penultimate ictus, IV, becomes the weakest of all; while in Pope's verse the final ictus is not 100% stressed and the weakest ictus is not IV, but III, a sign of a symmetrical "hemistich" line segmentation (4+6 or 5+5). Notice also the lack of stress on non-ictic positions in the Russian verse of all epochs.

2. The visual analysis emphasizes the difference between the first and second "hemistich" of the Italian verse (D'Annunzio): positions 5 to 10 show the marked syllabo-tonic alternation of stresses, while positions 1 to 4 differ little from prose (cf. speech model).

3. The curve constructed from prose (speech model of English syllabic verse) reveals two basic tendencies of English:

(a) English phrases tend to begin "iambically" (position 1 is stressed only one-half as much as position 2); and
(b) "back-to-back" stressing is avoided in English.

This is shown by the very low average stress on position 9 in contrast with position 10—the prose fragments for the model were chosen to end with a predominant stress (more than 80%), hence the particularly low stress on position 9.

Stress profile data (cf. Table 1.1) also show that verse "metricality/non-metricality" has two aspects: objective and subjective. The objective aspect requires that there be an objective contrast between ictic and non-ictic positions (a non-zero value of the iambic index). The subjective aspect determines whether a particular verse form is acceptable as metrical by contemporary poets and readers. If the second condition is missing, a verse text in which a contrast between strong and weak syllabic positions objectively exists and can be proved statistically, can be judged as unmetrical within a particular literary tradition or by the audience of a particular period. Not only will a Russian poem following the laws of English pentameter (like Aksënov's translations) be estimated as unmetrical by the Russian audience; Shakespeare's verse seemed barbarously unmetrical to Dryden and Pope.

Detailed vertical (stress profile) analyses of Shakespeare's works are the subject of Chapters 2-4. The data are used to follow the rhythmical evolution throughout Shakespeare's canon and to study the poet's skill in making stylistic use of rhythmical variations within the same play.

1.1.5. At lower levels of abstraction, a "horizontal" analysis of separate lines becomes more relevant for comparing metrical subsystems of epochs and individual authors within a national literary tradition, as opposed to interliterary comparison between national variants of meter. However, horizontal analyses of line types can also help compare national variants of meter.

It is well known that an "inversion" of stresses in non-ictic, or weak (W) + ictic, or strong (S) positions caused by a non-oxytonic disyllabic word is unmetrical in the Russian iamb, marginal in German, and perfectly normal in English iambic verse (cf. Tomaševskij 1929:52, Bailey 1973, Bjorklund 1978, Tarlinskaja 1976). For example: the Russian "line" *Brátu prosíl nagrádu dát' (Tomaševskij 1929:52) is unmetrical, the German line Éwig verlornes Lebe! ich grolle nicht (Heine, "Ich grolle nicht. . .", 2; cf. Bjorklund 1978:191) is marginal, while the English line Póinting to each his thunder, rain and wind (Shakespeare, Son. 14:6) is fully acceptable.

Another example: an "inversion" caused by an oxytonic disyllable is acceptable in Russian trochee (e.g. čegó, Kólja, částo xódiš or: V pučók izmotálasja: Trubetskoy 1963,15,17), but unacceptable in English (e.g., *Obscúre rábbits of the forest: Hayes 1985, cf. Tarlinskaja 1976:106). The explanation for this lies in the specific features of trochee in different literary

15

traditions. One of the rules of the Russian meters is "the stabilization of the first ictus after the first metrically weak syllable, i.e., in iambic lines on the second syllable, in trochaic lines on the third" (Taranovsky 1980:20). Therefore in the Russian verse tradition the first foot of both trochee and dactyl is less rigidly metrical than of iamb, amphibrach, and anapest. Tomaševskij (1923:47-49) even suggested that the whole of the first foot of Russian trochee and dactyl should be considered their anacruses. In the English verse tradition another rule is at work: avoidance of clashes of stresses on adjacent weak and strong (or strong and weak) syllabic positions if the clash occurs at the end of a phrase, as in *Hĕr màd lŏoks tō thĕ lĭghtnīng, ānd crīed: "Ēat!"* (Shelley, "The Revolt of Islam" VI,LII:2). The clash is particularly undesirable if the stress on the weak position is phonological, that is, marks a stressed syllable of a polysyllabic word, and the clash of stresses occurs within the same phrase, as in *Ăre bàse pĕoplē. Bĕlĭeve thĕm nòt; thĕy lĭed* (Beaumont and Fletcher, "The Maid's Tragedy" IV,I:44), or *Hăve ĕxcŭsed mŭch, dŏubtĕd; ănd whēn nŏ dŏubt* (Shelley, "The Cenci" I,III:114; cf. Gasparov 1973, Magnuson and Ryder 1970, Tarlinskaja and Teterina 1974, Kiparsky 1975, 1977, Bjorklund 1978, Hayes 1983).

If we want to discover more specific rules of a national variant of meter or find out the differences between metrical subsystems of epochs or styles of individual poets, a more subtle analysis of minute structural features is required. Such an inquiry is based on information invoking not only phonological, but also the grammatical level of the texts. Here is one example. Rhythmical (accentual and word boundary) line types constitute an element of meter, and a national variant of meter can be presented in the form of a finite list of rhythmical line types allowed by the rule of meter in this particular national literary tradition (see 1.1.1). But rhythmical forms of words are correlated with their part-of-speech and, consequently, morphological characteristics. Therefore, particular rhythmical line types "attract" particular parts of speech arranged syntactically in a specific order. In this way specific grammatical patterns accompanying particular line types also become, as it were, an element of meter on a lower level of abstraction. I studied the problem of whether or not rhythmical types of lines in English verse are in any way connected with their characteristic part-of-speech and syntactic composition (Tarlinskaja 1981, 1984). The result showed that there is a reciprocal correlation between rhythmical and grammatical line structures: particular rhythmical line types favored by an epoch call forth particular part-of-speech and syntactic patterns, while particular syntactic patterns favored by an epoch call forth particular rhythmical line types. For example, in the English Classicists' iambic pentameter verse, the rhythmical line pattern $\cup \perp \cup / \perp \cup / - \cup \perp \cup / \perp$ is practically always accompanied by the grammatical pattern modifier + modified + modifier + modified; some examples are:

The silver/Token/and the circled/Green
Of various/Habits/and of various/Dye
With hoary/Whiskers/and a forky/Beard
(Pope, "The Rape of the Lock", I:32, III:84,38)
With honest/anguish/and an aching/Head
(Pope, "To Dr. Arbuthnot:" 38)
The various/Labour/of the silent/Night
Portentous/Thunder,/in the troubled/Sky
(Thomson, "Winter:" 314, 348)
Th'alternate/labours/of their humble/Life
Thy upland/Forest/or thy Valley's/Flood
His tingling/fingers/into gathering/heat
And silken/Kerchief/for the Seaman's/neck
(Crabbe, "The Borough:" 24, 26, 60, 142)

The connecting link between verse rhythm and line syntax is morphology: words of different parts of speech have dissimilar rhythmical structures (cf. Kroeber 1958, Vanvick 1961, Bolinger 1965:157). A typical rhythmical structure of disyllabic adjectives and participles, frequently used as prepositional attributes, is non-oxytonic; on the contrary, disyllabic verbs (not participles) typically have an oxytonic structure. Therefore if the first, polysyllabic, element of a two-word English micro-phrase has a "feminine" ending, there is a good chance that this element is an adjective or a participle, and the whole phrase is attributive. This language tendency is actively used in English iambic meter and was strongly exaggerated in the eighteenth-century verse.

Here is another example of invoking the grammatical level in the definition of meter on a lower level of abstraction. The rhythmical figure "inversion of stress" on S + W (+ S...) syllabic positions of English iambic pentameter is normally caused by two monosyllables, an unstressed form-word on S and a stressed notional word on W. The English language, where the rhythmical tendency of stress alternation is very strong, avoids back-to-back clashes of stress (cf. van Draat 1912, Bolinger 1965:139-180), and English metrical verse avoids such clashes even more strongly. Therefore rhythmical "inversions" on positions SW "prefer" grammatical patterns where the stress of the word on W is subordinate to the following strongly stressed word. The most preferred pattern is attributive: the stress of the monosyllabic attribute on W is weaker than that of the following strongly stressed modified noun; e.g., *And thē hĭgh Dòme re-ecchoes to his Nose* (Pope, "The Rape of the Lock", V:86). The pattern "form-word + subject (+ predicate)" is characteristically avoided because a subject and a predicate normally have equal degrees of phrasal stress. However, this grammatical pattern is relatively frequent in the verse of later Romantic and post-Romantic poets and becomes one of the distinctive features of their rhythmical styles compared to that of Classicist authors. For example: *Ănd thē răck mākes hĭm ŭttĕr, do you think* (Shelley, "The Cenci",

V,II:96); *Ănd thē sŭn mĕlts thĕ snow in high Pamere* (Arnold, "Sohrab and Rustum": 15); *Thŏugh yŏur ĕye twĭnklĕs still, you shake your head* (Browning, "Fra Lippo Lippi": 76).

Thus the metrical characteristics of each epoch are reflected in the frequency with which poets use certain rhythmical and grammatical line types in their verse. Some variants of lines are favored by all poets, others are used sparingly, still others may be used by poets of one period but never occur in the verse of another epoch. The most frequent and typical forms determine the metrical norm of a period. The notion of norm is narrower than the notion of metrical rules (cf. Wimsatt 1970). Metrical rules determine the outer limits of legitimacy. For example, a line like *Nătūre's sĕcrētarў thē Phĭlŏsŏphēr* (Donne, "Satyre I": 6) would be both outside the norm and unmetrical for the iambic pentameter model of Shakespeare's dramas, while a line like *Ŭnclē, ĕven īn thĕ glàssĕs ōf thĭne ĕyes* (Shakespeare, "Richard II", I,III:208) is metrical but still outside the norm. A line like *Hŏlds hīs sŏul lĭght; he dies upon a motion* ("Othello", II,III:170) is within the norm for Shakespeare's dramas but not for Pope's verse, while the line *Clăpp'd hīs glăd wings and sate to view the Fight* (Pope, "The Rape of the Lock", V:54), which contains a trisyllabic "figure" (Bailey 1975:38) rhythmically similar to that of the previous example, is normative for Pope: trisyllabic "deviations" on positions WSW in Pope's verse are normally filled with the grammatical pattern "verb + attribute + noun (usually an object to the verb)", where the attribute is accentually subordinate to the noun.

"Horizontal" analyses of Shakespeare's verse, i.e., rhythmical and grammatical line patterns, are the subjects of Chapters 6 and 7, while Chapter 8 deals with the semantic functions of "rhythmical figures".

1.2 Problems of attribution and chronology

Definitions of rhythmical idiosyncrasy of a poet's style inevitably lead to problems of chronology and authorship, which I consider or touch upon in almost every chapter of this book. I do not have to emphasize what dangers, difficulties, and disappointments face anyone opening this Pandora's box, and what caution is needed before any conclusion at all can be safely ventured (cf. the eight principles cautiously recommended for those who address the problems of authorship in Schoenbaum 1966:163-183). Moreover, attribution is not among the primary aims of this book; the problem, so to say, poses itself to anyone studying individual peculiarities of verse style. It seems proper, therefore, to survey the history and methods used in determining authorship of verse.

The primary subject of the scholars interested in attribution of English verse has almost always been Shakespeare and other Elizabethan-Jacobean playwrights. The main reason was the peculiar conditions of the playwrights' work which stimulated writing in co-authorship. Copyright in the modern sense of the word was practically non-existent and pirating was widespread. Plays, as opposed to non-dramatic verse, were not held in high regard by the poets themselves, except, probably, Ben Jonson, who took great care in publishing his own collection of plays in a 1616 folio; as Suckling wrote in his "Session of Poets", "good old Ben"

> . . . told them plainly he deserved the bayes,
> For his were call'd Works where others' were but Plaies
> ("Session of Poets", II:17-20)

Poets working for competing theatre companies, both public and private, often formed teams to meet the requirements and deadlines of the theatre directors. Methods of Elizabethan-Jacobean literary partnership are studied, for example, in Thorndike 1901, Thompson 1908, Hatcher 1910, Neilson and Thorndike 1922, Oliphant 1927, Appleton 1956, and Jackson 1979. Co-authorship between Fletcher and his main partner, Beaumont, and later with Shakespeare and Massinger, are two of the many examples.

Seventeenth-century dramatic collaboration was not based on the ideal of a conceptually unified dramatic work but rather on a simple principle of a division of labor. Often one of the collaborators was the principal and dictated the terms, reserving for himself the most important or interesting scenes and leaving the routine chores to the partner. After making a fairly detailed outline of the general plot and idea of the project, the play was divided either simply by acts and scenes, or in a more elaborate way, into plot and subplot (cf. Appleton 1956:81-82, Schoenbaum 1966:226). The division could be worked out with reference to the character of the material, one playwright undertaking farcical scenes while another assumed responsibility for tragic episodes. In the Beaumont-Fletcher partnership the relations were evidently balanced, but each co-author had his own habitual preferences. Beaumont, noted for his plot-building abilities, often began the play, while Fletcher stepped in after the action was well under way (Thompson 1908, Hatcher 1910). In his short partnership with Shakespeare, Fletcher's role was evidently subordinate; an example is the scene of Cardinal Wolsey's fall in "Henry VIII" (III,II): its key part, before the exit of the King (the first 202 and a half lines), is believed to belong to Shakespeare, while the second part of the scene, its anti-climax (after the King leaves with his last menacing words ". . . *and then to breakfast with What appetite you have*") was finished by Fletcher (cf. Oras 1953, Law 1959, Mincoff 1961). In Fletcher's collaboration with Massinger the roles were obviously reversed; tragi-comedy had apparently begun to bore Fletcher by that time, and in Massinger he found a useful assistant. Massinger was industrious and evidently willing to follow Fletcher's suggestions. Fletcher's boredom with exposition and conclusion in most cases imposed the task of writing the first and final acts upon Massinger (Oliphant 1927:48, Appleton 1956:82). Fletcher is believed to have taken upon himself the subplots featuring the lower types and characters, scenes with a comic relief, war scenes, and scenes of pathos, leaving female characters to his partners (Oliphant 1927:49-57).

Techniques for determining attribution, both older and simpler ones that began to be applied to Shakespeare and other Elizabethan-Jacobean plays in the middle of the nineteenth century, and modern and more sophisticated ones used by present-day scholars, may be classified in the following way: (1) metrical; (2) grammatical: (a) morphological, entwined with orthographic analysis, and (b) syntactical; (3) lexical; (4) stylistic (i.e., images, rhetorical figures, and stylistic devices).

(1) Metrical tests were one of the first applied to Shakespeare's canon and his apocrypha (Fleay 1874a-d, Spedding 1876, Hickson 1876a,b, Spalding 1876, Ingram 1974, Boyle 1880-1886a, König 1888, Parrott 1919; see Chambers' review: 1930, 2, appendix H; Wentersdorf 1951, Oras 1953, 1960, 1966, Law 1959, Mincoff 1961; Jackson 1979: Chapter V, Tables XV p.208, XVI p.209, XVIII p.210; see the general review in Schoenbaum 1966). The main object of the scholars' interest was the structure of line endings: rhymed and unrhymed, terminating in a weakly stressed or unstressed monosyllable, feminine endings including compound and heavy, as well as run-on lines (enjambment), extra syllables in mid-line and the proportion of alexandrine lines; the ratio and position of splits in the lines as indicated by punctuation and change of speakers (cf. esp. Oras 1960, Suhamy 1984). The correlation between the metrical scheme and stressing in the line, as mentioned above, has only been employed very recently. Oliphant (1927: 30-31), enumerating four directions of approach to the study of the finer details of verse texture, remarked that "the infinite music that permeates it all (the rise and fall of the melody, proceeding one hardly knows whence, but mainly doubtless from the distribution of stresses) . . . is the most subtle, the most elusive, the most insecure, the most perilous of these four means; but its importance is enormous". It is the "rise and fall of melody" proceeding from the "distribution of stresses" that is the primary focus of study in this book.

Scholars of the nineteenth through the first quarter of the twentieth century drew such extravagant and drastic conclusions from the on the whole unsophisticated, one-sided statistical data that metrical tests came into general disrepute, a disrepute in part shared by modern critics and publishers (e.g., Schoenbaum 1966:XIX).

(2) Grammatical tests were introduced by Thorndike (1901) who noticed differences between Shakespeare's and Fletcher's use of the forms "-em—them": "Every one who has read many of Fletcher's plays must have noticed the great frequency with which he uses "em' instead of 'them' -'kill 'em', 'with 'em', etc. This fact led me to count the 'thems' and "ems' in "Henry VIII" and "The Two Noble Kinsmen" with a view of testing the generally accredited divisions of those plays between Fletcher and Shakespeare. The results given

in another place are rather surprising" (Thorndike 1901: 24-25). The skeptical Chambers took into consideration Thorndike's " 'em" and "them" evidence "for all it is worth" (1930, I:497); but later work confirmed the validity of morphological-orthographical tests; cf. for example, Farnham 1916, Partridge 1949, 1964, Hoy 1956-1962, Waller 1966, Jackson 1979. The later authors studied the use of the periphrastic auxiliary verb do, favored by Shakespeare but avoided by Fletcher, -th inflectional endings for the third person singular instead of -s forms (doth and hath versus does and has), colloquial clippings of personal pronouns 'em, ye (y') and contractions 'tis, in't, to't, on't, knew't, i'th, o'th, to th', by th', on's (= on us or on his), in's, cram's, let's, and others (Farnham 1916, Hoy 1956-1962, Partridge 1949, 1964:147-162, Waller 1966, Jackson 1979; cf. also Franz (1939) who studied the use of the periphrastic auxiliary verb do, and Oras (1966) who examined the frequency of -ed forms in Milton). These scholars demonstrated that not only Shakespeare and Fletcher, but various other Jacobean dramatists, differed from one another in their characteristic "linguistic patterns"—in their habits with respect to certain word forms and colloquial contractions—thus formulating idiosyncratic features typical of Middleton, Rowley, Ford, Chapman, Jonson, Massinger, Tourneur, Webster, Shirley and Field, Beaumont, Fletcher, and Shakespeare.

Much insight into Shakespeare's syntactic idiosyncrasy has been offered by Partridge (1949, esp. pp. 27-30, and 1964:147) who has not, however, undertaken any systematic analysis. Comparing syntactic patterns typical of Shakespeare and Fletcher, Partridge wrote about "a Shakespearean peculiarity which is the syntactical difficulty with which he develops his ideas in verse" (Partridge 1949:27). "Since Dryden established syntactical correctness as the classical basis of Augustan writing, the reading eye has learnt to subsist on precise formalities of arrangement that make intelligibility their first aim. But Shakespeare inhabited another world—what Professor Hardin Craig has called a pre-Cartesian, baroque world—and the effect of that ideological environment upon his style is remarkable" (ibid.). Elizabethan English shows the language to be in a highly fluid state; the absence of definite systems of teaching grammar was a drawback, but it was also an advantage: it freed the authors from conventional speech patterns, and, in Partridge's opinion, Shakespeare made a personal use of the language fluidity. Shakespeare's "ideas overlap his syntax;" "Shakespeare tends to lose track of his relative clauses, especially in continuative function and in proximity to participial phrases, or adverbial clauses of time" (Partridge 1964:47 and 1949:29-30); he has a "habit of making participial phrases do duty for temporal and conditional clauses. They tend to clog the meaning, and modern syntax avoids them in complicated sentence structures" (Partridge 1949:30). Fletcher's syntax, on the other hand, is clear and lucid, his syntactical patterns almost anticipating those of Dryden: "Fletcher and Massinger, from the modern prose point of view, are more competent stylists than Shakespeare" (Partridge 1964:147). Most of Partridge's studies on syntax, however, focus on non-Shakespearean verse (Partridge 1953, 1969).

Mincoff, in his sophisticated article of 1961, also mentioned syntax as one of the idiosyncratic features distinguishing Shakespeare from Fletcher in "Henry VIII". The "little rushes and eddies", short appositional phrases coupled with lexical repetitions that characterize Fletcher's style and add to the great number of pauses, break his lines into smaller, constantly recurring units of simple grammatical structure (Mincoff 1961:242,249). These are opposed to Shakespeare's syntax characteristic of his last period. His "sentences form lengthy, sweeping, and very varied units, and every sentence pause comes in the middle of the line" (Mincoff 1961:250; cf. Langworthy 1931, Oras 1960, 1966, and Wright 1983).

One should also mention J. X. Maxwell (1950) who in his short article on "Titus Andronicus" compared the occurrence in Peele and Shakespeare of a grammatical construction incorporating an attributive phrase as an antecedent of an attributive subordinate clause, e.g.:

I am his *first-born son, that was the last*
That ware the imperial diadem of Rome;
Agree these deeds with *that proud brag of thine*,
That saidst, I begged the empire at thy hand
                                                          ("Titus Andronicus" I,I:5-6,306-307)

Baldwin Maxwell (1956:60-61) mentioned the difference with which "parenthetical matter" in the center of a clause is used by Shakespeare and Massinger, on the one hand, and Fletcher on the other (cf. Mincoff 1961).

Josephine Miles' work on the history of style may also give some clues for approaching the problems of authorship and particularly chronology (e.g., Miles 1967). She discovered three typical "modes" of sentence-making favored by each of the major periods of English and American literature: "the predicative, the connective-subordinative, and the adjectival" (Miles 1967:4). The history of literature indicates a rising and falling pattern as the simple predicative mode loses favor at the end of the Renaissance and gains it again in modern times. Kroeber (1958) subjected Miles' techniques and conclusions to further examination. He considered the influence of the state of the language in each period, the poetic forms employed by the poets examined, and other factors that might have influenced the general historical pattern Miles had found. Baker (1967) showed that similar methods can be used in studying the favored poetic syntax of a single poetic period (cf. R. Bailey 1969:229-230). An example of a detailed, "computer-assisted" stylistic study of Shakespeare's syntax in two plays, "Richard II" and "Antony and Cleopatra", is Burton 1968. The author compared the evolution of several syntactic categories (e.g., nominal groups and relative clauses) in early and late Shakespeare, and came to an interesting conclusion that ". . . the clauses, of *Antony and Cleopatra* are simpler than those of *Richard II* . . . The fact that clauses are simpler in themselves while their external nexes (e.g. in hypotactic group complexes) and their internal constituents (e.g. nominal groups) are more cohesive makes it possible for Shakespeare to complicate other levels of syntax without too great a loss of clarity" (Burton 1968:231). Liisa Dahl, who studied nominal sentences in Shakespeare's soliloquies, came to a similar conclusion: the tendency towards shorter and simpler syntactic structures progressed from period one through four, and is particularly striking in "Cymbeline" (Dahl 1969:207). The stylistic function of shorter nominal sentences in soliloquies is probably to give conventional representations of mental processes.

(3) Lexical tests have been based on the frequency counts of words in Shakespeare's verse compared to other Elizabethan-Jacobean poets. G. Sarrazin (1897, 1898), using Schmidt's "Lexicon", picked out Shakespeare's "rare words" and built correspondences between plays, arranging them into four clusters that correspond to a chronological grouping of plays. Hart (1934, 1943a,b) showed that Shakespeare used rare words more freely than his contemporaries. He also studied the occurrence of certain morphological forms of words, e.g., adjectives with the prefix un-, and found their frequency revealing of Shakespeare's periodization.

Bennett (1957), using the technique suggested by G. Udny Yule (1944), applied a statistical vocabulary test to "Julius Caesar" and "As You Like It". He compared repetitiveness of nouns by acts and scenes and came to the conclusion that though frequency indices by acts noticeably fluctuate, the general characteristics of the two plays are much closer than those found by Yule for the works belonging to different authors (cf. Varma 1973).

Jackson (1979), following Sarrazin, studied Shakespeare's rare words in connection with chronology and authorship (cf. Metz 1979). He proposed a "vocabulary index" as "a valuable aid in dating not only Shakespeare's plays, but more importantly perhaps, his sonnets" (Jackson 1979:148). Jackson also examined oaths and exclamations as evidence of individual style as well as the idiosyncratic use of function words (1979, Chapter VII). Slater (1975, 1978) followed word links between Shakespeare's plays and poems. Šajkevič (1968, 1976) showed that grammatical (function) words, such as articles, are stylistically relevant, and that analyses of their frequencies can shed some light on the problems of periodization and authorship (their use also individualizes different *emploi*, such as noble vs. lower personages; see Chapter 4).

A lexical-grammatical approach, viz. the study of recurrent phrases and parallel passages (e.g., Boyle 1880-1886, Parrott 1919, Sykes 1919, 1924, Robertson 1924), was unfortunately typical of another attempt to "disintegrate" Shakespeare's canon (for critiques see M. St. Clare Byrne, 1932, Hill 1957:61, Schoenbaum 1966:65-146). "The identification of authorship through verbal parallels has been tried and found seriously wanting. Verbal parallels may be explained as plagiarism, deliberate or unconscious. And even if one skirts the frightening possibility of mere coincidence, one is faced with the problem of independent derivation from a common source," wrote Hill (1957:61; cf. Schoenbaum 1966:189-193). The nature and causes of rhythmical-grammatical-lexical repetitions in the works of the same or different authors is a fascinating subject, in part discussed in Chapter 8 (see also Žirmunskij 1978 (1924), Kreider 1941, Oras 1953, Mincoff 1961, Altman 1973, Jakobson 1976, Tarlinskaja 1981, 1984).

(4) Finally, tests based on the study of images, rhetorical figures, and other stylistic devices: scholars investigate specific stylistic devices, images, and associative clusters in the poets' texts (cf. Spurgeon 1981 (1935), Armstrong 1946, Mincoff 1952, Prior 1955, Hill 1957, Muir 1960, Jackson 1963, Levin 1969, Metz 1979, Zholkovsky 1980:87-114,205,244; 1984). R.F. Hill's ingenious article in which he studied the stylistics of "Titus Andronicus" is one of the best examples of a stylistic research. Hill composed a list of rhetorical devices and ornamentations based on the scheme given by George Puttenham in "The Arte of English Poesie" and studied 130 rhetorical figures and other stylistic devices, such as alliteration, metaphor, and word-play, used in "Titus Andronicus" and eleven other plays by Shakespeare. Interestingly, he also studied "the vices of the language"—such deficiencies of style as inkhorn terms, malapropisms, bombast, the synonym disease, tautology, and excessive alliteration. The findings led Hill to an important conclusion—that "Titus" is Shakespeare's earliest play, revised by the author himself at the end of 1593 (Hill 1957:69; cf. Metz 1979).

An imagistic test was proposed by Edward Armstrong (1946) who constructed groupings of unconsciously associated words, ideas, and images that recur from one work to another by the same author (cf. Spurgeon 1981 (1935), Rauschenberger 1981). Muir (1960) applied Armstrong's method to Shakespeare's apocrypha and discovered that a typically Shakespearean "cluster" of associations "kite-bed-death-spirits-birds-food" also occurs in Act I scene I of "The Two Noble Kinsmen", where the kite appears as the center of the entire cluster. "As an investigative technique, cluster criticism has the merit of exploiting the psychology of unconscious associative patterns, a factor generally left out of account in stylistic analyses" wrote Schoenbaum (1966:188), cautiously adding, however, that the formation and repetition of clusters may be influenced by general literary models, or caused by an accident (cf. Jackson 1963). Image cluster approach has been instrumental in studying "poetic universes" of two Russian poets, Mandelštam and Pasternak (e.g., Levin 1969, Zholkovsky 1984:135-158).

It goes without saying that studies of authorship and periodization must be based on clear-cut, explicit, and verifiable methodology and that large amounts of text material are required to render the results reliable. It is always easier to give a negative answer (the text was not written by so-and-so) than positive (this text was written by so-and-so); and it is of course easier to confirm or reject somebody else's findings than to produce new data; it is so much easier to work with "Henry VIII" after Spedding demonstrated the Shakespearean and Fletcherian division into scenes, or to make Shakespeare's chronology more accurate after it was outlined by Chambers.

1.3 Links between verse form and meaning

I examine two areas of connection between verse form and verse semantics (Chapters 4 and 8). The problem of links between verse form and meaning (semantics) is one of the most important and complicated in verse theory. The links are several and exist on different levels of verse form, so the problem can be approached from at least three directions. These are the connection between (1) meter and semantics; (2) text rhythm and semantics; and (3) rhythmical (accentual) variations of separate lines and the expressed contents.

The first approach, meter and meaning, is concerned with the historically developed, conventional association of a specific metrical form with a specific repertoire of themes treated in a specific stylistic and emotive way (cf. Jakobson 1979c, Richards 1979:76, Vinogradov 1959:28, Hollander 1966, 1975, Gasparov 1974:35, 1976, 1979, 1982, 1983, Levin 1982, Tarlinskaja and Oganesova 1985). The link is developed not through violation of but rather in conformation with the canon. Thus, Taranovsky (1963) showed that the Russian trochaic pentameter quatrain rhymed **AbAb** (feminine-masculine-feminine-masculine line endings, cross-rhymed) is associated in the Russian poetic tradition with the theme of the "road", in both the direct and metaphorical meanings of the word: life viewed as a road. The theme was introduced in 1841 by Lermontov in his poem "Vyxodu odin ja na dorogu..." which had an enormous influence on both Lermontov's contemporaries and generations of later poets. Gasparov (1976) showed that the Russian trochaic trimeter quatrain rhymed **AbAb** had as a thematic preference "death in a rural setting". Tarlinskaja and Oganesova (1985) studied English lyrical iambic and trochaic tetrameter quatrains rhymed **abab** and **aabb** (eighteenth-nineteenth centuries) and found that each meter and rhyming form had its own set of themes treated in a specific way. For example, the love theme is more typical of iambic than of trochaic poems, and within iambic poems more typical of the rhyme scheme **abab** than **aabb**. A semantic field analysis of the theme "God" in both iambic and trochaic poems rhymed **aabb** showed that in the iambic form the theme is treated in a more elevated, poetic, emotional way, while in the trochaic form in a more "down to earth", prosaic, matter-of-fact manner.

The link between metrical forms (meter, line length, stanza form, types of rhyming) and the thematic and emotive contents of poems is not rigid. The laxity of a link results in homonymy (one form—different thematic spheres) and synonymy (one thematic sphere—different metrical forms). The link is not obvious; it is often obscure and slurred (this is particularly the case with widely used, "omnivorous" forms) and requires special efforts to discover. The poets seldom realize why they choose a particular form for a particular contents; it just seems "more suitable". One example of "self-consciousness" of literature, of its comprehension that there is a connection between a particular verse form and a theme treated in a specific way, is <u>verse parody</u> (Levin 1982:20).

The second approach is "<u>text rhythm and semantics</u>". The poet selects particular accentual and word boundary types of verse lines and combines them to form a text. Such a selection and combination, as pointed out above, is to a certain extent different from epoch to epoch, genre to genre, and author to author, and even from period to period of the same author. All the line types preferred and selected by the poet are within the metrical norm of his national literary tradition and epoch, but their frequency in different epochs and genres is dissimilar. It is the preference for different line types evidenced in early and late Shakespeare and in different genres within each period that is responsible for the dissimilarities in the text rhythm, e.g., in the stress profiles of Shakespeare's early and late plays, or between his chronicles, tragedies and comedies (Chapter 2).

Roman Jakobson several times emphasized that a specific rhythmical variant of meter is more suitable for a specific contents; for example, in his article on Macha, a nineteenth-century Czech poet, he wrote: "A rhythmical analysis of Macha's iambic trimeter shows that the undulatory curve of downbeats is confined to one single wave (see Chart A). Such terseness makes the meter especially appropriate for the motif of <u>instability</u>, fragility, frailty, and hurried coming-into-being and vanishing" (Jakobson 1979b:477); or: "The IAMBIC PENTAMETER, asymmetrical because of its three-membered structure, is closely linked semantically in Macha's poetry with the theme of repeated, generally uncompleted motion and especially wandering" (ibid., 483).

It is fairly obvious that a change of meter in a polymetrical poem can signify a change in the plane of contents, as in Byron's "The Bride of Abydos" or "The Siege of Corinth". Gasparov (1974:285-287), by comparing consecutive segments of text, showed that the change in a poem from one rhythmical variation of the same meter to another variation also signals a change in the semantic plane of the text. In Chapter 4 of this book I compare roles of Shakespeare's personages by extracting and arranging the whole part of each character into a separate text, on the hypothesis that Shakespeare may have used rhythmical variations of meter as an additional means of characterizing and typifying his dramatis personae.

Finally, the third approach is concerned with a possible link between <u>accentual variants of separate lines</u>, or their parts containing "rhythmical figures", and the meaning expressed by words building these "figures", as well as by other words syntactically and semantically connected with the "figure-building" words. The semantic effect in this case is based on the breach of the statistically prevalent alternation of syllable stresses. The breach makes the words appearing in "rhythmical figures" stand out from the context. Points of view as to the possible link between "rhythm and meaning" differ, sometimes polarly. Some scholars deny any connection between rhythm and meaning; the most extravagant denial was expressed by John Crowe Ransom who wrote: "It is not telling the whole truth to say that Shakespeare and other accomplished poets resort to their variations, which are metrical imperfections, because a determinate meaning has forced them into it. The poet likes the variations regardless of the meanings, finding them essential in the capacity of a sound-texture to go with the sound-structure" (Ransom 1972:36). A similar idea was expressed in one of Richards' earlier works (Richards 1954:232).

An opposite equally extreme point of view was formulated by Šervinskij in a study of the rhythmical variations of Puškin's verse. He concluded that rhythm in Puškin's poems always serves some semantic aim: ". . . in the poetry of Puškin rhythm and meaning are facets of the same phenomenon" (Šervinskij 1961,257).

The most commonly held views seem to lie between these poles. They are based on the assumption that "deviations from meter", though having no independent meaning out of context, do not pass unnoticed by the reader and may be used by the poet as a kind of rhythmical italics, or as bearers of some additional semantic information (Stein 1951, 1953, Hamm 1954, Frye 1957, Bobrov 1965, 1966, Levy 1966, Taranovsky 1963:289, Gasparov 1974:36, Xolševnikov 1969, Hollander 1975b, Tarlinskaja 1976:177, Attridge 1982:287-315). The existing views on the semantic functions of line rhythm may be summed up in the following way. (1) The poet emphasizes words important for him in a particular context; in doing so the poet places usually stressed words on metrically weak positions, or usually unstressed words on metrically strong positions; for example: _Swĕets_ wĭth _swĕets_ wăr nŏt, joy delights in joy (Shakespeare, Son. 8:2); Sĭnce _Ī lĕft yŏu_ mine eye is in my mind (Shakespeare, Son. 113:1) (cf. Stein 1951:33). (2) The poet adds, with the help of verse rhythm (and sound patterns), to the lexical meaning of words denoting motion or sound ("iconic", "mimetic", or "metaphoric" effect), for example: _Strŭgglĕ with frosty air and winter snow_ (Wordsworth, "The Old Cumberland Beggar": 174); _Prăttlĕ fantastically on disease_ (Browning, "An Epipstle, Containing the Strange Medical Experience of Karshish, the Arab Physician": 241). (3) The poet conveys, with the help of rhythm or sound patterns, additional semantic and emotive information not expressed in the text explicitly but, in the opinion of the scholar, probably implied. Thus Northrop Frye believed that the rhythm of the line spoken by Claudio, from Shakespeare's "Measure for Measure": _Ay, but to die, and go we know not where_ conveys the emotion of a man "in imminent fear of death" (Frye 1957:XXVI). Another example: analyzing a passage from Donne's elegy "Julia", Stein wrote: "The short u sound first introduced above in Orcus has of course no meaning, or even suggestion, by itself. Still I can believe it possible that that slack and almost formless vowel sound may have put Donne in mind of the idea that carries through the passage. At any rate, that sound, which becomes identified with the idea of formlessness and chaos, precedes the expression of the idea and to that extent anticipates the metaphorical relationship between Julia's hell and Julia's chaos" (Stein 1951:259-260). Case (2) corresponds to Stein's terms "naturalistic imitation" and "contributing metaphor", case (3) to his term "complete metaphor" (Stein 1951:22).

The third approach to the problem "verse form and meaning" (i.e., "rhythmical figures and meaning") is undertaken in Chapter 8. Only cases (1) and (2) will be studied; cases of the third type probably do exist, but obviously, if not commented on by the author, for example, in stage remarks (as in Shelley's "The Cenci": "She enters staggering, and speaks wildly"), their interpretation is extremely subjective, as in the examples cited above (cf. Jarxo 1984:223).

Meter and rhythm are, naturally, not the only elements of verse form that have a link with the contents; there are other elements, for example, the well known phenomenon of sound imitation, or the effect of enjambment (cf. Hollander 1975a, Attridge 1982:304). However the primary object of research in Chapters 4 and 8 is the semantic functions of meter and rhythm: (a) rhythmical variation of meter, which results from a prevalence of certain line types in the text, and its possible use by Shakespeare as an additional means of characterizing and typifying his dramatis personae (Chapter 4), and (b) accentual variation within individual lines ("rhythmical figures") and its link with the word and sentence semantics (Chapter 8).

Notes to Chapter 1

[1] The Russian metrists actually use the word "ritm" (rhythm) in three meanings: (1) an isochronic alternation of events (e.g., rhythm in music, dancing, singing); (2) a variant of meter resulting from the poets' preference for particular line types (cf. "the meter of Russian iambus" with "the rhythm of Puškin's *Boris Godunov*"); (3) accentual and word boundary structure of any particular verse line which, objectively, can be far from isochronic. The last two meanings of "ritm" are conventionally terminological.

[2] The "perceptible" part of the definition is important: a person used to a more rigid form of a meter may fail to identify the alternating principle, while a person raised on a looser metrical form would grasp the principle of alternation. This is true not only of both poets and audience of different national verse traditions but of poets and readers within the same tradition but during different epochs. So, meter has both objective and subjective constituent elements (cf. Jakobson 1979a:77-78). In my analyses I concentrate on the "objective" part.

[3] The "stress profile" analysis introduced by the Russian scholar B.V. Tomaševskij (1929) originated the so-called "Russian method" in studying verse (e.g., Taranovsky 1953, Gasparov 1974, Bailey 1975, Tarlinskaja 1976).

[4] Gasparov (1980:199-200) gave a succinct explanation of how theoretical, language probability models of verse are constructed, and why. His explanation is summarized below.

The sequence of operations in constructing a theoretical, language model of verse according to the method of B. Tomaševskij-A. Kolmogorov requires the following basic data and steps: (1) "the rhythmical vocabulary" is determined, which is calculated from prose (fiction) of the given language (the notion "rhythmical word" refers to lexical, fully stressed words forming a unit with unstressed proclitic and enclitic form-words). The "rhythmical vocabulary" data show what part of the authors' total vocabulary is comprised of one-syllable words, two-syllable words stressed on the first syllable, two-syllable words stressed on the second syllable, and so on; to put it in a different way: the data show the probability of a particular rhythmical type of word in the prose texts analyzed (the number of words of each type divided by the total); (2) the full list of word combinations which are possible in a given verse meter of a given syllabic subtype (e.g., iambic pentameter), i.e., the list of all accentual line variants of the meter (different distribution of stresses), and for each of these accentual line variants the list of all word boundary variants (different distribution of word boundaries). Next (3) we take each of these line variants, consisting of such-and-such word combinations, and multiply the probabilities of the rhythmical types of words that compose each variant of line: this operation calculates the probability of occurrence of each rhythmical type of "line" in a prose text. Next (4) all the products for all possible line variants are summed: the resulting total figure gives us a general probability of a random occurrence in prose of any nugget "line" of the meter analyzed, for example, of iambic pentameter. And finally, (5) we define, in percentage from this general sum, the proportion of each item, or group of items, for example, all "lines" stressed on such-and-such a syllable, or a word boundary after such-and-such a syllable, and so on. These figures are theoretical indices of our meter. The theoretical indices are compared to the actual frequencies of these forms in the verse analyzed. If the theoretical and empirical indices are close, it means that the poets are indifferent to this particular form, and its occurrence is governed only by language laws; if the indices are dissimilar, it means that the given form is preferred, or avoided, by the poet; then we are faced with a specific verse tendency which has to be studied.

[5] The notation used herein is as follows: W stands for a weak (non-ictic) position (1,3,5 . . . .), S stands for a strong (ictic) position (2,4,6 . . . or I,II,III. . .), and an overbar signifies an average value. Values of W and S are determined in percent from the total of lines analyzed for each position. Thus the "iambic index" as used here is $(\overline{S}-\overline{W})$. The final ictus, 100% stressed in Italian and Russian verse, is disregarded.

[6] Gasparov (1974:190-191) suggested that the difference between obligatory non-stress and optional stress can be derived from the language probability of stressing: if a non-ictic position in a verse line is stressed as often as the language probability of its stressing, it should be considered optionally stressed; if a non-ictic position is stressed less frequently than the language probability of stressing, it should be considered obligatorily unstressed. Since no language probability model of English iambic verse has yet been constructed, I must rely on the empirical data from verse analysis.

[7] Tarlinskaja and Teterina (1974) constructed four different speech models of verse. A speech model of verse (or "an experimental model": Proxorov 1984) is a quasi-text constructed of quasi-lines that satisfy the "horizontal parameters" of a meter but occur in prose by pure accident (see Taranovsky 1980, Gasparov 1974:49-53, Tarlinskaja and Teterina 1974). Similarly to the theoretical, or language models of verse, experimental, or speech models are used to discover which features of actual verse are caused by the general language and text characteristics (e.g., the typical structure of a phrase) and which features belong to verse as a specific form of speech.

The speech model used here for comparison is type C, in which fortuitous decasyllabic prose segments had to satisfy two requirements: (a) the quasi-lines had to begin with the beginning of a phrase; (b) they had to end in a predominantly stressed syllable in position 10 in a proportion typical of English verse (over 80% stressed). The comparison of syntagmatic and asyntagmatic prose models of English decasyllabic verse (**A** and **C** models) shows that the "iambic" tendency is already present in syntagmatic "lines" (i.e., "lines" roughly corresponding to phrases) with a stress dominant in position 10; the iambic index of asyntagmatic decasyllabic segments (i.e., "lines" not corresponding to phrases) without a stress dominant in position 10 (model **A**, Tarlinskaja and Teterina 1974:78) is only 3.3% (cf. Gasparov's language model, type **A**); "iambic index" of syntagmatically-constructed "lines" with a stress dominant in position 10 (model **C**) is 12%, or almost 4 times higher than in the model **A**. "Iambic" rhythm in a rudimentary form already exists in English prose phrases but is, naturally, amplified in verse.

[8] There is no constant, metrically relevant caesura (i.e., obligatory word boundary after a certain syllabic position) in English iambic pentameter. However, a tendency for a word boundary to occur after positions 4/5 in a stricter verse, or after positions 6/7 in a looser verse, does exist. It is often accompanied by a syntactic seam and/or a loss of stressing on ictus III (in a stricter verse) or IV (in a looser variant). Therefore the term "hemistich" when applied to English verse loses its conventional meaning. The term is used here to denote the first and the second parts of a line which in one way or another displays a bipartite structure.

[9] The sign ($-$) stands for an ictic position, ($\cup$) for a non-ictus, ($\nearrow$) means a strong stress and ($\diagup$) a weaker stress. When the stress markings are combined with position markings the signs are: strong stress on ictic $\perp$; weak stress on ictic $\top$; strong stress on non-ictic $\in$; weak stress on non-ictic $\ni$. The sign (/) will be used to indicate a word boundary. The sign (/) will be also used in later chapters to indicate a relatively strong syntactic break between sentences or phrases. A weaker syntactic break will be marked by (\), for example:

> Who'er keeps me,/let my heart be his guard;
> Thou canst not then \ use rigour in my gaol:
>
> (Shakespeare, Son. 133:11-12)

The strongest break marked (/) was assumed to take place at the juncture of two independent sentences, between the main sentence and a subordinate clause, between a sentence and an apposition, a parenthesis or a direct address. A weaker link (\) was marked between a subject and a predicate, especially if these are extended; between homogeneous sentence elements; between a verb and its prepositional object or adverbial modifier expressed by a nominal phrase (*And hail* \ *with Musick . . . The Lock, obtained* \ *with Guilt. . .*), between a noun and an of-phrase postpositional attribute, object, or adverbial modifier (*The various off rings* \ *of the World . . . the Rival* \ *of his Beam*); and between any sentence elements that have no immediate syntactic or semantic link (*For when success* \ *a Lover's toil attends*). <u>Close</u> syntactic links occur, for example, between a modifier and a modified noun, a verb and a direct object, or a verb and an adverb, e.g., *his <u>golden</u> <u>Scales</u>; to <u>view</u> the <u>Fight</u>; these Honours shall be <u>snatch'd</u> <u>away</u>* (see Smirnickij 1957:173-193).

Chapter 2

Evolution of Stress Profiles. Periodization

This chapter presents the results of the most general "vertical" analysis: stress profiles of entire dramas and poems. The results show the evolution of Shakespeare's rhythmical style over the whole of his 25-year writing career and contribute to clarification of long-standing questions about the dates of some of his plays. They also disclose epochal trends and reveal some of his idiosyncrasies in comparison with his contemporaries. Almost all texts also show considerable fluctuations in rhythmical structure within themselves, for example, between acts or scenes, and between different personages. These more detailed "vertical" analyses are under taken in Chapters 3 and 4.

The material analyzed for this chapter included all of Shakespeare's 37 dramas, his two poems "Venus and Adonis" and "The Rape of Lucrece", and all of his sonnets. The material taken for comparison included seven dramas by Shakespeare's older and younger contemporaries, all six dramas by Marlowe, and four dramas by Byron. Analyses of Shakespeare's contemporaries provide the epochal background for Shakespeare's canon; Marlowe's and Byron's dramatic cycles were analyzed to show if Shakespeare's rhythmical evolution was typical of a more general literary process, or uniquely idiosyncratic.

2.1 Principles of stressing

2.1.1. Primary "vertical" analysis was directed to the rhythmics of strong (ictic) stresses, but stressing of weak (non-ictic) positions was also studied.

The main, phonologically-relevant differentiation opposes stress and nonstress (e.g., présent—to presént), but there are many phonetical gradations of stress and it is difficult to differentiate between them (cf. Bolinger 1965a). It has become conventional to single out three degrees of stress in English: nonstress, secondary stress, and main stress (Jones 1927, 1964), though sometimes four degrees are singled out: nonstress, tertiary stress, secondary stress, and main stress (cf. Trager and Smith 1951). The correlation of stresses in a word or phrase can be also presented hierarchically; degrees of stress in such a representation acquire only relative values, depending on the immediate context of every syllable (Liberman and Prince 1977). For the general stress profile analysis, however, it is most convenient to differentiate only two absolute degrees: stress and non-stress. The main problem facing a metrist is verse accentuation, i.e., deciding which syllables will be counted as stressed and which as unstressed. The approach must be explicit and consistent, so that it can be verified and compared to the results obtained by other scholars (cf. Taranovsky 1966:174).

Other problems also arise. Phrase semantics might considerably influence stressing of words; even normally unstressed monosyllables may acquire a strong stress in a specific context (cf. Nikolaeva 1982). To what extent should the reader's individual interpretation of a poem influence the text accentuation?

Next comes the problem of phrase rhythm. English words, particularly monosyllables, are subject to speech rhythm: they may lose or gain stress depending on their position in relation to other, adjacent stresses (cf. van Draat 1912, Curme 1914, 1915, Jones 1964, Bolinger 1965b). The rhythmical tendency is particularly strong in verse where the general regularity of stress alternation creates a "meter-formed" inertia in stressing accentually ambivalent monosyllabic words (cf. Chatman 1965): words can be promoted on S and toned down on W, for example: *Whò àrt thou, questioner? I have no father* and *As . . . Whò art thòu? swear to me, ere I die* (Shelley, "The Cenci", III,I:40,56). Should verse rhythm be taken into consideration in stressing verse texts, or should they be treated exactly like prose? The latter approach has been adopted by most linguists who study verse (e.g., Kiparsky 1977, Hayes 1983).

And one more question arises: should the relative prominence of syllables be taken into consideration? How should we, for example, treat an ictic non-stress that is more prominent than the adjacent unstressed syllables, as in <u>and at the</u> rock, and does form a "stress maximum" (Halle and Keyser 1971)? Attridge considers such cases capable of forming an ictic stress: ". . . an unstressed syllable may realise a beat when it is not adjacent to a stress in the same line" (Attridge 1982:168). Should such cases be counted as "stress" or "non-stress" in stress profile analyses? How do we treat subordinate stresses on non-ictic positions when the ictic stress is stronger than both adjacent non-ictic stresses, as in *Blue waves roll* on, and forms a "stress maximum"? The answer to the final question is the shortest , so I shall give it at once: whether or not a syllable on an ictus forms a "stress maximum" (its relative characteristic) was considered irrelevant for verse analysis (cf. Bailey 1973:472). Only absolute, phonological accentual characteristics (stress *vs.* nonstress) were taken into consideration. My principles of verse text accentuation are stated below.

2.1.2 Word and phrase stress in prose and in verse

Any oral speech is characterized by intonation, and phrase stress, or accent (not word stress!) is one of its components. Word stress is only a potential for the phrase accent (Bolinger 1965b:17, Lehiste 1970:150). In verse, the role of word stress is considerably greater than in prose, because word stress in verse tends to "show through" the phrase accent (cf. Tomaševsky 1929:95-96, Beaver 1968, 1969, Bailey 1973). In prose, long segments following an emphatic final phrase accent tend to be fully unstressed; e.g., '*Why don't you like fluorescent lamps?*' '*The húm annoys me*', or: *I have some búsiness to take care of* (Bolinger 1965a:75-76). In verse, loss of phrase accent is compensated by a "showing-through" word stress, which tends to fall on ictic positions: the segment *The ╲hum annoys me* can theoretically occur in any iambic line, while *The ╲hum bothers me* only as the rarest of exceptions, for example, *The wind doubled me up* . . . (Browning, "Fra Lippo Lippi", 87; see also Chapters 6 and 7). The word stress of bothers does not fall on an ictic position and the word itself does not begin a phrase and/or a "hemistich". In the latter case "inversions of stress" are metrical. If word stresses did not "show through" and compensate losses of phrase accent, they would not tend to fall on S, as they almost invariably do.

One should point out here that the effect of syllabic prominence in the English sentence is not achieved only by means of stress, but I shall take into consideration only stress-induced prominence. The main components of the phrase stress, or accent, are the following: a) pitch of tone; b) length of vowel; c) intensity of stress; and d)quality of the vowel. The role of intensity seems to be secondary: "the prominence itself is an *accent*, whose major cue is pitch and whose auxiliary and residual cue is length and—to a minor (and hardly more than "voice-qualifying" or emotional) degree—intensity" (Bolinger 1965b,17). In doubtful cases I took into consideration also the last component.

Losses of phrase accent occur in various speech situations; the most general cause is a strong emphatic accent on the preceding word. Words that follow a strong emphatic accent tend to lose their phrase accent partially or fully and to cling enclitically to the preceding stressed word. Reasons causing an emphatic accent are usually semantic: an emphatic accent on a sentence element is a sign of its particular informative signficance ("the rheme"); all other words that follow the emphatic accent carry less information and can in fact be even omitted: "*Why don't you like fluorescent lamps?*"—"*The ╲hum*" (Bolinger 1965c). Since word stress in verse normally "shows through", cases when it fails to coincide with an ictic position after an emphatic phrase accent are extremely rare. Here are two examples:

   . . . They and the seconds of it
   Are ╲base people. Believe them not; they lied
                    (Beaumont and Fletcher, "The Maid's Tragedy"
                                                        IV,I:43-44)
   Whom ╲thus answered the archfiend now undisguised
                    (Milton, "Paradise Regained" I,357)

An emphatic accent also occurs in cases of semantic contrast. Words that follow emphatic accents tend to weaken or lose their phrase stress; for example: *On thís síde, mý hánd, and on thát síde, thíne* (Shakespeare, "Richard II" IV,I:18); *Myríght hánd would be gloved, lady, My léft hànd would be bare* (Ballad "Tom Lin" 127-128); *I see the dúst flíe. Now I see the Bódy* (Fletcher, "Bonduca" III,III:3).

The semantic weight usually shifts to the first component of traditional combinations of words, such as *móvie théater* vs. *móvie pavílion* (Bolinger 1972:639); the second component of such combinations tends to lose phrase accent. The tendency is even stronger if the whole word combination refers to one notion; cf. *a desígning wòman* (a profession), and *a desìgning wóman* (a woman who is artful) (Bolinger 1965c:70). A similar phenomenon occurs in idiomatic combinations approaching a compound; for example: *Which is kind Junius?—This.—Are you my swéet heart?* (Fletcher, "Bonduca" III,V:31).

Loss of phrase accent also characterizes words of "broad semantics" ("semi-pronouns": Bresnan 1971:271, cf. Bolinger 1972:639), such as man, thing, self; there, then, still, else, cf. *cráwling thìngs* vs. *cráwling ínsects*. Such cases frequently appear in verse: *Be scorned like óld mèn of less truth than tongue; By adding óne thìng to my purpose nothing* (Shakespeare, Son. 17:10;20:12); *Fit for destruction?—Yield, and be a Qúeen stìll; Prithee away, sweet Junius.–Let me síng thèn* (Fletcher, "Bonduca" IV,IV:96; V,II:35) (see also Chapter 6).

Losses of phrase accent after the final strongly stressed sentence element explain the phenomenon of post-positional initially stressed vocatives, which sometimes occur in verse on WS instead of SW; for example: *Lead us to Rome, stráŋgers, and more than so* (Shakespeare, "Titus Andronicus" IV,II:33); *My right hand will be gloved, lády, My left hand would be bare* (Ballad "Tom Lin" 127-128); *Hard by Saint Lawrence, hail féllow, well met* (Browning, "Fra Lippo Lippi" 67). A similar phenomenon occurs in Russian verse: *Ox, net, brátec! . . . šumim, brátec, šumim . . .* (Tomaševskij 1959:145).

Narrators' words following quoted direct speech also tend to lose strong phrase accent; one of the signs of such a loss is a low pitch of the phrase following the quoted utterance; for example: *"Let us be↘gin"— he sáid impátiently*.

Loss or weakening of phrase accent also occurs in postpositional reflexive pronouns following a verb, as in *you forget yourself* and in some postpositional adverbs, such as *enough*, or *again* following adjectives and adverbs (Jones 1964, cf. Bailey 1975), as in *not good enough*, or *got up again*.

The strength of phrase accent borne by a word depends on the syntactic function of the word and its position in a phrase (and in verse also on its place in the verse line). Syntactically subordinate elements which do not terminate a phrase (in verse also a line or a hemistich) are normally more liable to weakening of phrase accent than syntactically dominant phrase elements and/or elements that terminate a phrase (in verse—also a line or a "hemistich"). This is demonstrated by some verse phenomena; here is one example. Full (non-reduced) trisyllabic forms of nouns of the type <u>cardinal</u> or <u>murderer</u> are typical of these words in the function of a subject or an object, particularly at the end of a phrase ("hemistich"), while syncopated, disyllabic forms are typical of the same words in the function of a prepositional attribute in the middle of a phrase ("hemistich"). And syncopation of a word is a sign of its weakened, subordinated phrase accent. Compare *Find out the <u>murther-ers:</u> let them be known*, with: *With <u>murtherer</u> thieves that came to rifle me* ("Arden of Feversham" XIV:408, IV:95). Or: *The <u>Cardinal!</u> Cause we express no scene*, with: *The <u>Cardinal's</u> nephew, madam, Don Columbo* (Shirley, "Cardinal", The Prologue:1, and I,II:94; Tarlinskaja 1976:29).

In these analyses I take into consideration the possibility of word stress combining with, and compensating, phrase accent (cf. Beaver 1968). Bailey tended to consider weakened phrase accent as non-stress: words with a weakened phrase accent "may become enclitics or proclitics in normal speech" (Bailey 1975,25). Here are some examples of his verse accentuation:

A thóusand <u>little</u> sháfts of fláme;
Óne <u>praised</u> her her áncles, óne her éyes;
Though sóme belíeve (sóme <u>even</u> plán);
Dówn, <u>wanton</u>, dówn! Have you nó sháme;
These ácres, álways <u>again</u> lóst
And it has wídth <u>enough</u> for yóu
The tóad who dréams <u>away</u> the pást

(Bailey 1975:25,39,45)

True, a word stress not supported by a strong phrase accent gets weakened and displays specific features in verse. For example, disyllabic oxytonic words usually appear in positions SW if they do not terminate a phrase. Quite frequently they are the first notional (lexical) word of a phrase. Such words are, as a rule, adjectives and verbs. For example:

The life of purity, the <u>supreme</u> fair
    (Shakespeare, "The Rape of Lucrece", 112:3)
Nor draw no lines there with thine <u>antique</u> pen
    (Shakespeare, Son. 19:10)
Encamp their legions, or with <u>obscure</u> wing
    (Milton, "Paradise Lost" II:132)
Our <u>supreme</u> Foe in time may much remit
    (Milton, "Paradise Lost" II:210)
Sir, <u>replied</u> Michael, you mistake; these things
    (Byron, "The Vision of Judgment" 68:1)
The battle <u>became</u> ghastlier—in the midst
    (Shelley, "The Revolt of Islam" VI,XVI:1)
Might <u>create</u> smiles in death—the Tartar horse
    (Shelley, "The Revolt of Islam" VI,XX:5)

But:

> If there must be no response to my cry
> (Shelley, "The Revolt of Islam", Dedication, XIV:2)

In toning Shakespeare's verse one should, of course, also bear in mind pronunciation characteristics of the period, when the language situation was more flexible than in present-day English, and when many words had grammatical and phonetical variants (cf. Schmidt 1875, Bridges 1967, Dobson 1957, Kökeritz 1974, Cercignani 1981). Even in present-day English, disyllabic words of particular morphological structures tend to vary their place of stress under the influence of speech rhythm (Bolinger 1965d). These usually are: (1) disyllabic compound adjectives and numerals used in pre-nominal position; (2) words with prefixes, such as un- or mis- (Householder 1971:265-286, Bjorklund 1977:324). All these words were considered stressed on the syllable which coincides with an ictus, e.g., *As yét unknówn*, but *The únknown danger*.

Oxytonic words of foreign, primarily Romance, origin represent another category which probably allowed vacillation of stress (see above). Many of them are prefixed forms. The non-native origin of such words meant an instability of stress and allowed for recession of accent (note that shifts of stresses from the first to the second syllable in native Germanic words did not occur: the native stress tendency was firm). The most likely candidates for recession of word stress were adjectives and verbs (Bjorklund 1977:331-334), such as obscure, supreme, extreme; pursue, request or regret, i.e., the same words which probably had a weakened phrase accentuation. Part of these words still tend to have two stress variants (see Bolinger 1965d:143-145), sometimes registered by dictionaries, e.g. antique (Oxford English Dictionary). I, on the whole, tended to consider such words oxytonic, particularly if their occurrence on positions WS markedly prevailed over SW (see, e.g., Spevack 1974). They were assumed to bear a phrasal accent. Archaic forms, such as envie, were also considered oxytonic.

Stressing disyllabic auxiliary and semi-auxiliary words is another problem. Most disyllabic prepositions, conjunctions, and relative words, particularly those in which the stress does not fulfill a phonological (sense-differentiating) function, were considered unstressed (into, unto, upon, without, within, until, whoso). Prepositional modal verbs with a negation filling positions SW (cannot move), or blending of two modal verbs, or of a modal and an auxiliary verb (maybe), disyllabic forms of auxiliary and link verbs (having done, being seen) were considered unstressed. Reflexive pronouns after verbs were regarded as stressed (Bailey treated them as unstressed), although in a differentiated system of toning they would be treated as having a weaker stress than after pronouns (compare: *wásh yoursèlf—hé himsélf*).

2.1.3. The problem of stressing monosyllabic words, which are rhythmically flexible and, as is generally accepted, have no sense-differentiating phonological stress, is particularly complicated. The differentiation of stress degrees in monosyllabic words is so gradual and so variable that often it is difficult to determine, for example, whether a word on S has sufficient stress in order not to be registered as a case of a missing ictic stress, or whether some other word has sufficient stress on a non-ictus to be regarded as a case of an extra-metrical stress. The transition from stress to non-stress is gradual; therefore a metrist working with the binary opposition "stress-nonstress" has to resort to conditional simplifications: some words in some syntactic functions and in some metrical positions are to be considered stressed, while some others as unstressed. In this way, a metrist is working not with the actual diversity but with a model of stress, and any model represents a simplification. However, analyses of large amounts of material require a model, both for consistency in analysis and for formulating conclusions.

Extrametrical stresses caused by monosyllables are different than those caused by polysyllabic words (Jakobson 1979a, Bailey 1975). The main reason is that monosyllables have no phonologically relevant word stress and therefore easily lose the phrase accent under the influence of phrase rhythm. However, it is the phrase accent that appears to become sense-differentiating for monosyllabic words. The presence of stress helps to distinguish, for example, compound words from word combinations: a gréen hóuse—a gréenhouse; a gréen horn—a gréenhorn . The presence of stress distinguishes idiomatic phrases and free combinations: a líon's sháre (the share of a lion)—a líon's share (a bulk of something); a snáil's páce (the pace of a snail)—a snáil's pace (a slow progress). A usually stronger stress on the second element in verb-phrases (to gèt úp, to sìt dówn) helps to differentiate them from noun-phrases (a gét ùp, a sít dòwn) stressed on the first element (Trager and Smith 1951:73). Monosyllabic words can produce "stress clashes" in prose (cf. Van Draat 1912, Bolinger 1965d:150-153); I assumed them to be able to produce extrametrical stresses on W in verse (cf. Tarlinskasja 1976, Hayes 1983). Some metrists disregard extrametrical stresses caused by monosyllables which are "essentially without stress" and which "gain a stress feature in the appropriate environment" (Bjorklund 1978:209). Such an approach, however, effaces significant differences not only between national forms of meter (e.g., English and Russian iambic pentameter), but also between individual rhythmical styles of poets within the same national literary tradition (e.g., Shakespeare and Fletcher; see Chapter 6).

The influence of metrical laws on stressing cannot be disregarded. However, a poet does not violate the "linguistic givens", but he chooses a "legal" variant which suits his meter in the best way. This is true of both polysyllables with variable stressing and of ambivalent monosyllables. I assumed that a notional monosyllable on S is always stressed, even if it follows an emphatic sentence stress; in this case it probably loses strong sentence stress, but its word stress "shows through" to satisfy the meter. Hayes (1983,383) completely disregarding the role of verse rhythm considered such words unstressed; for example:

> Another time mine eye is my héart's <u>guest</u>
>
> (Son. 47)
>
> Coral is far more red than her lĭps' <u>red</u>
>
> (Son. 130)

I marked such cases as stressed on both positions 9 and 10. Bailey is inclined to give even more credit to the role of verse rhythm; in reviewing the manuscript of this book, he marked the stressing of the cited lines in the following way: *is mў hèart's gŭest ; than hér lĭps réd* .

In differentiating the stress of monosyllables I took into consideration the following factors: (a) their lexical and part-of-speech peculiarities; (b) their syntactic functions in the sentence; and (c) the frequency of their occurrence on ictic or non-ictic positions of the verse line. In case (a) the principal point was a conditional division of words into notional (words of full lexical meaning) and non-notional, grammatical words, although, as in the case of stress vs. non-stress, the transition from "notional" words to "non-notional" is very gradual. Notional words (nouns, verbs, adjectives, numerals, most adverbs) were regarded practically always as stressed, while grammatical words (articles, prepositions, particles, conjunctions, auxiliary, link and modal verbs not in the construction of a general question) were considered, as a rule, unstressed. I also stressed pronominal nouns.

Personal pronouns on the ictic position terminating a phrase were considered stressed, for example: *But rise, and be not wroth! not wroth am <u>I</u>*; (Arnold, "Sohrab and Rustum", 429). Personal pronouns on S not terminating a phrase were considered unstressed: *And said: O Ruksh! bear Rustum well! — but <u>I</u> (Have never known my grandsire's furrow'd face)* (Arnold, "Sohrab and Rustum", 755). Personal pronouns on W were always considered unstressed.

Pronouns <u>some</u> and <u>such</u> and possessive and demonstrative pronouns were considered unstressed on both W and S, except in cases of emphasis or contrast indicated by context; for example:

> And then believe me, mў love is as fair
> As any mother's child, though not so bright
> As thóse gold candles fix'd in heaven's air:
>
> (Shakespeare, Son. 21:10-12)

(The disyllabic pronoun <u>any</u> was also considered stressed.) The monosyllabic pronouns <u>all</u> and <u>no</u>, which, one feels, have more semantic weight than, for example, <u>some</u>, were regarded as stressed on ictuses and unstressed on non-ictuses. Prepositions on S followed by a personal pronoun on W were considered stressed, prepositions on W preceding a pronoun on S were considered unstressed; for example: . . . *Gŏd fĭghts for ŭs and wĭth us.*

Combinations of verbs and prepositional adverbs were always regarded as stressed, although it is quite possible that the element of this combination which happens to stand on W should be regarded as rhythmically weakened (cf. Trager and Smith 1951:73; Bailey 1975; see Chapters 5, 6 of this book). In a differentiated system of stressing I would regard the elements on W as accentually weakened, but still not unstressed; therefore, in a non-differentiated system of stressing I treat them as stressed.

The word <u>half</u> (<u>half</u> <u>told</u>, just as the first element of the combinations of the <u>so</u> <u>old</u>, <u>too</u> <u>bad</u>), I also consider stressed (in a differentiated system of stressing—as a weakened stress).

I also stress notional verbs in "double predicate" structures like <u>felt</u> <u>tired</u>, <u>looked</u> <u>funny</u>, <u>taste</u> <u>sweeter</u>; the stress differs such verbs from link- verbs in nominal predicates of the type <u>was</u> <u>tired</u>, <u>is</u> <u>funny</u>.

Adjectives on W even when directly preceding their modified noun were considered stressed. In a differentiated system they would be regarded as having a weakened stress: pòor ĕyes, wĭld hĕart.

In doubtful cases I took into consideration the frequency with which words of some classes in some syntactical functions occur on ictic and non-ictic positions. It was assumed that the more often a word is used on S, the more strongly stressed it was for the poet, and *vice versa* (Tarlinskaja 1976:66-70).

In all probability, I tended to overestimate the number of non-metrical stresses. The counting should probably have been done in two variants, maximum and minimum (cf. Bailey 1975:43, Tarlinskaja 1976: Tables 37, 42, and 51); this, however, would have overloaded the text with figures without changing the basic conclusions.

2.2 Background: stress profiles of rigid and loose verse

Before analyzing stress profiles of Shakespeare's work we must know how to evaluate the form of his plays and poems compared to looser and more rigid variants of English iambic pentameter in general, and in relation to the verse of other poets of the Elizabethan-Jacobean epoch in particular.

Earlier analyses of English verse (Tarlinskaja and Teterina 1974, Tarlinskaja 1976; see also Chapter 1) showed that in the English iambic pentameter the most strongly stressed ictuses are usually the final and the second, while the weakest are the first and either the third or the fourth. The main features of stress profiles which vary, and thereby characterize both epochs and different periods of an individual poet's verse style, are: (a) the strength of·stress on the second ictus (position 4), and (b) the correlation between ictuses III and IV (positions 6 and 8). A low stress on ictus III accompanied by a particularly strong stress on ictus II is a sign of a rhythmically and syntactically symmetrical bipartite line structure, typical of a more rigid variant of English iambic pentameter, for example, the standardized verse of the eighteenth-century English Classicism. A low stress on ictus IV reflects an asymmetrical bipartite line structure, or absence of a clear midline boundary, for example, the looser verse of mid-nineteenth-century English post-Romantic poetry. Here are some typical lines of late eighteenth- and mid-nineteenth-century verse (positions of missing ictic stresses underlined and noted in brackets):

A heav'nly Image in the glass appears . . .	(6)
The various off'rings of the World appear . . .	(6)
Thin glitt'ring Textures of the filmy Dew . . .	(6)
The giddy Motion of the whirling Mill . . .	(6)

(Pope, "The Rape of the Lock" I:125,130;II:64,134)

I am poor brother Lippo, by your leave!	(8)
You need not clap your torches to my face.	(8)
Hands and feet, scrambling somehow, and so dropped...	(8)
My stomach being empty as your hat.	(8)

(Browning, "Fra Lippo Lippi", 1,2,65,86)

Notice that unstressed (or weakly stressed) monosyllables fill the sixth position of Pope's lines whose structure is frequently symmetrical not only rhythmically but also grammatically, while they fall on position 8 of Browning's lines, which are both rhythmically and grammatically asymmetrical. Notice also a typically stronger syntactic link between two contiguous notional words with contiguous stresses on S than between two notional words separated by an unstressed monosyllable on S, for example: *Thin glittering Textures \ of the filmy Dew; You need not clap your torches \ to my face.* The link between glittering and Textures, filmy and Dew is stronger than between Textures and filmy: the latter belong to two different phrases. The link between clap and torches is stronger than between torches and face: the latter again belong to two different phrases. The weaker syntactic link coupled with a missing ictic stress makes the symmetrical or asymmetrical bipartite line structure more noticeable.

Another difference in ictic stress between more rigid and looser variants of English iambic pentameter is the degree of opposition between the more strongly and more weakly stressed ictuses. In more rigid pentameter there are larger differences in proportion of stress on ictuses I-II, II-III, and IV-V, while in a looser variant the values are leveled out.

Occasionally in English pentameter stresses appear on non-ictuses (odd positions of the verse line). Normally they are concentrated on the anacrusis (position 1), and their number tends to decrease towards the end of the line. The next "peak" is usually in midline (position 5), after a syntactic break. The contrast between positions 1 and (3,5,7,9) is particularly high in a more rigid variant of pentameter and is much less in a looser variant, where all weak positions tend to receive a fair amount of stress; this moves the verse farther from a pure syllabo-tonic, closer to a syllabic model (cf. Chapter 1). In a looser variant of iambic pentameter there also may appear an absolute increase of stressing on one of the midline non-ictuses (5, 7, or 9), and the looser the verse, the closer to the end of the line appears the absolute maximum of non-ictic stress (see Table 1.1). Here are three examples of non-ictic stress distribution,

(a) in a more rigid and (b,c) two looser variants of English iambic pentameter (positions of "extrametrical" stresses underlined and noted in brackets):

(a) Slíght is the Súbject, but not só the Práise, (1)
Thríce rúng the Béll, the Slípper knóck'd the Gróund (1)
Séem'd to her Ear his wíning Líps to láy (1)
Fáirest of Mórtals, thou distínguish'd Cáre (1)
  (Pope, "The Rape of the Lock" I:5,17,25,27)
(b) (Which the inténse eyes lóoked through) cáme at éve (5,7)
Who wént and dánced and gót mén's héads cút óff! (7,9)
Thére's fór you! Gíve me síx mónths, then gó, sée (1,7,9)
Fórward, púts óut a sóft pálm—'Nót só fást!' (1,3,7,9)
  (Browning, "Fra Lippo Lippi",159,197,345,371)
(c) Y'have héld your héads úp thís dáy: whére's yóung Június? . . . (5,7,9)
Léad úp to th'héad, and líne súre: the Quéenes Báttell (1,7,9)
Bíd him be góne, he díes élse. Shall Róme sáy (1,7,9)
Órder, swéet fríends: fáces abóut nów.— Hére, Sír (1,3,5,9,11)
  (Fletcher, "Bonduca" III,V:110,116;
  IV,III:183,184; II,III:137)

The iambic indices (which compare the averages of ictic vs. non-ictic positions, see Chapter 1, Table 1.1) decrease from the more rigid to looser variants of iambic verse.

To ascertain what tendencies in the structure of English iambic pentameter are caused by the features of the English language and the English phrase and which by specific verse conventions, real verse is compared with its speech model. The speech model of the iambic pentameter is a "text" consisting of segments that fortuitously occur in prose but satisfy the general requirements of the meter analyzed and could "fit" into genuine verse. Figure 2.1 presents stress profiles constructed for the extremes of canonized, rigid (Pope) and decanonized, loose (Browning)variants of English iambic pentameter, together with the speech model. In this presentation the ictic (even) and non-ictic (odd) positions are connected separately (cf. Fig. 1.1) to emphasize the differences and trends in stressing.

Ictic positions of the speech model are stressed less often than in actual verse: the curve of the model is well below even Browning's.[1] The opposition between "weak" (less often stressed) and "strong" (more often stressed) ictuses is smoothed out in the model and in Browning's loose verse but is much greater in Pope's highly canonized pentameter. In general, however, the ictic stress distribution of the model is not unlike actual verse: for example, position 4 ("ictus" II) is stressed more strongly than 2 and 6 ("ictuses" I and III). Thus, actual verse is to a certain extent conditioned by the accentual-syllabic structure of the English phrase. It is obvious that the stress profile of Browning's verse more nearly resembles the stress profile of the model, while Pope is its antipode. Both the model and Brownings' verse display a "dip" in

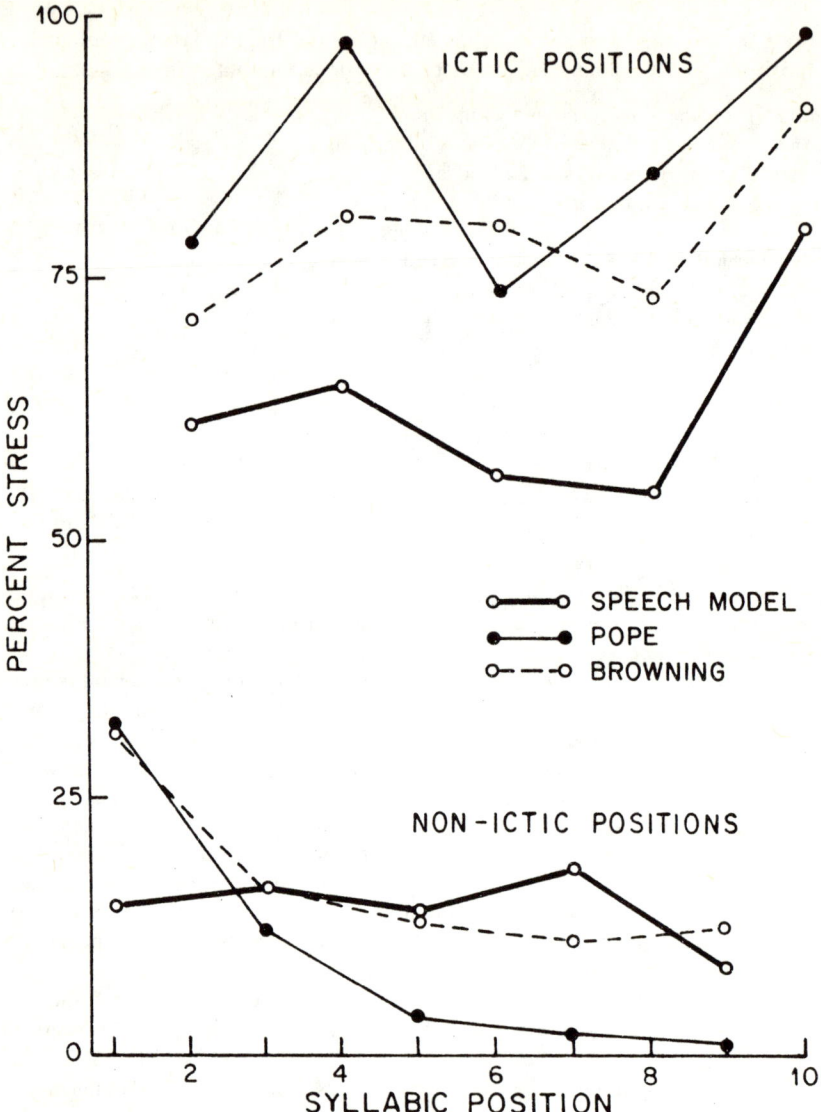

Fig. 2.1. Stress profile of a speech model compared with canonized (Pope) and decanonized (Browning) extremes of English iambic pentameter. In this visualization, even (ictic) and odd (non-ictic) syllabic positions are connected separately rather than sequentially. Connecting positions sequentially gives the sawtooth pattern representative of the actual rhythm (cf. Fig. 1.1) but obscures the important differences and trends in stressing. Speech model data from Tarlinskaja and Teterina (1974: Table IV) and Pope and Browning from Table 1.1.

position 8, not 6. A "dip" in position 8 is a sign of a longer phrase (and longer words) in the first part of the line which spreads over 6-7 syllabic positions. Here are some typical nugget iambic "lines" found in prose:

This was the case at present, and in less . . .
. . . the many declarations I have made . . .
I see no reason why I should object . . .
. . . into a wicked sacrifice to lust . . .
(Fielding, "Tom Jones, A Foundling", Book I
Chapter XII, the first two pages)

A longer first half-line marked by a "dip" in position 8 of the looser, decanonized verse, illustrated in Fig. 2.1 by Browning, brings the verse closer to the tendencies of prose. Poets whose verse is characterized by a looser meter either did not know how to create a stronger opposition to prose tendencies (the earliest metrists) or did not wish any more to oppose their verse to prose so strongly (see below). Pope's verse, on the other hand, illustrates the maximum opposition of verse to prose: note the strong stresses on ictuses II and V and a large "dip" in position 6.

Non-ictic stresses of the speech model are scattered throughout the "line". The stressing of position 1 not only does not exceed position 3, as in actual verse, but is actually less than position 3: English phrases typically begin "iambically" and "anapaestically", with one or two unstressed monosyllables. It follows that the extra-heavy stress in position 1 of actual verse is caused by a conventional law of the meter, not by the influence of the laws of the English phrase.

The strong contrast of stress on the anacrusis to the other non-ictic positions and the decrease of non-ictic stressing from the beginning to the end of the line are signs of traditional English iambic pentameter. Browning's looser verse is again closer to that of the speech model than Pope's canonized iambic pentameter.

In Fig. 2.1 note the maximum of "extra-metrical" stresses on position 7 of the speech model. The "dip" on position 9 reflects the "aversion" to back-to-back stressing of English prose: position 10 in the model is dominantly stressed by definition, therefore position 9 is, by contrast, most often unstressed. Here are some more "iambic lines" selected at random from prose:

. . . the poor lad bore not only the whole smart . . .	(3,9)
. . . are doomed to be in love once in their lives.	(7)
Those who will tell one fib, will hardly stick . . .	(1,5)
. . . the wench hath not been nine months gone away.	(7)

(Fielding, "Tom Jones, A Foundling", Book I
Chapters III, IV, XI)

The looser forms of iambic pentameter at least in part obviously follow the tendencies of non-metrical, prosaic speech, while the more rigid forms tend to deviate from prose tendencies as far as possible, increasing the conventional verse-prose opposition.

The whole history of English pentameter is an alternation of periods of more rigid and looser verse forms. A looser form is the sign of either a canon in the making (e.g., Wyatt) or decanonization (e.g, Fletcher, Browning). Interestingly, the early metrists, unconstrained by any rigid canon, evidently followed the prose tendencies: Chaucer, Lydgate, Hoccleve, Skelton, Henryson, Wyatt, and Surrey all weakened their fourth ictus. Later poets, having created and mastered the canon, moved the weakest ictic stress from ictus four to three (e.g., Spenser, Kyd, Chapman, Drayton), while the younger generation (Jonson, Donne, Beaumont and Fletcher, Webster and Ford), in loosening the canon, moved the weakest ictic stress again to position 8 (Tarlinskaja 1976: Tables 41 and 50, pp. 279,292). Figure 2.2 presents a comparison of generalized stress profiles of Shakespeare's earliest and latest plays (on the basis for dividing Shakespeare's canon into four periods, see section 2.4), and of five plays by other poets: two pre-Shakespearean plays (Norton/Sackville and Kyd), two post-Shakspearean plays (Webster and Ford), and a contemporary play (Ben Jonson). The stress profiles of both non-Shakespearean earlier plays demonstrate many features of a rigid pentameter ("peak" on position 4, a "dip" on 6) while the stress profiles of both later dramas display features of a looser variant (position 4 is stressed about the same as or even less than 6, and position 8 is the weakest of all ictuses). Thus, the dramatic iambic pentameter of the Elizabethan-Jacobean epoch evolved from a more rigid to a looser form. Shakespeare's rhythmical style evolved precisely within his epoch. The verse form of his plays of Period I were almost, but not quite, as canonized as those of his predecessors Norton/Sackville and Kyd, while the form of his last plays (Period IIIb) was markedly loosened, but not yet to the extent of his successors Webster and Ford. Ben Jonson's "Sejanus" coincides in time with Shakespeare's Period IIIa and reflects the degree of "metrical rigidity" acceptable at that time. Two questions that I cannot yet answer are: why, and how, a new trend is born? Was Shakespeare merely following, or originating, the new trend?

The following examples illustrate a tradition in the making (Chaucer), a rigid verse (Kyd), and a looser verse (Beaumont and Fletcher):

    And seyde: 'Lord, to whom Fortune hath yiven
    Victorie, and as a conque<u>r</u>our to liven,   (8)
    Nought greveth us your glorie and <u>your</u> honour;   (8)
    But we biseken mercy <u>and</u> socour.   (8)
    Have mercy on our woe and <u>our</u> distresse.   (8)
        (Chaucer, "The Canterbury Tales, 'The Knightes Tale' ": 915-919)

    With what excuses <u>canst</u> thou show thyself—   (6)
    With what dishonour <u>and</u> the hate of men—   (6)
    From this dishonour <u>and</u> the hate of men,   (6)

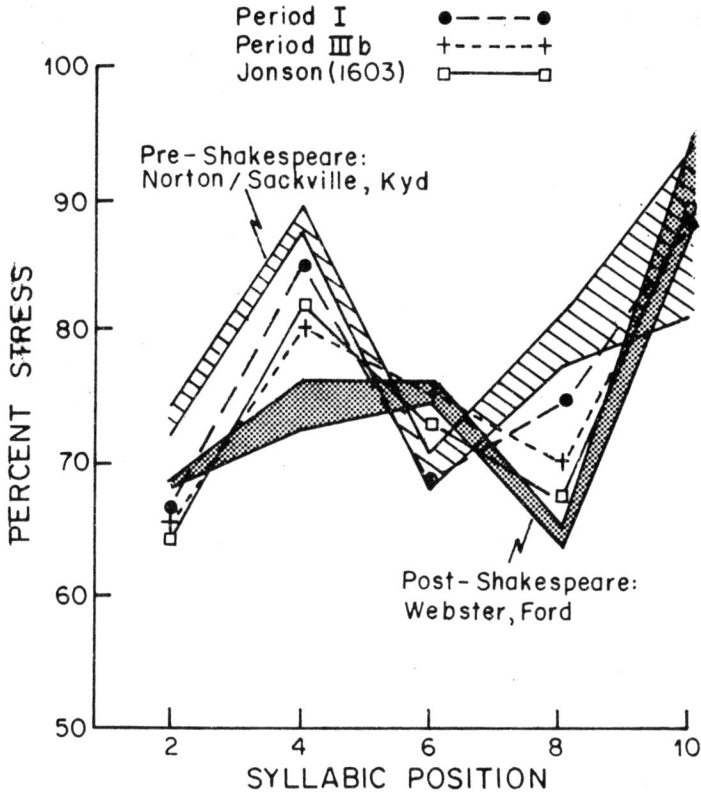

Fig. 2.2. Stress profiles (ictic positions only) comparing Shakespeare's plays with earlier, contemporaneous, and later plays. Pre-Shakespeare curve is a composite of Norton / Sackville and Kyd, and post-Shakespeare of Webster and Ford (data of Table 2.3); Shakespeare data from Table 2.1 and Ben Jonson from Table 2.3. Notice the marked trend over the Elizabethan-Jacobean epoch from a more rigid to looser verse, and how Shakespeare's rhythmical style evolved within the trend. Ben Jonson's "Sejanus" coincides with Shakespeare Period IIIa and precisely reflects the degree of "rigidity" of that time.

Thus to neglect the loss and life of him	
Whom both my letters <u>and</u> thine own belief	(6)
Assures thee to be causeless slaughtered?	
Hieronimo, for shame, Hieronimo,	
Be not a histor<u>y</u> to aftertimes	(6)
Of such ingrati<u>tude</u> un<u>to</u> thy son.	(6,8)
Unhappy mothers <u>of</u> such children then!	(6)
But monstrous fathers <u>to</u> forget so soon	(6)

45

Table 2.1

Shakespeare: stress profiles of ictic positions by periods

Date	Period	Positions						Correlation between:			No. Lines
		2	4	6	8	10	S̄ (2-10)	4-2	4-6	8-6	
1588-1596	Titus Andronicus - King John (13 plays)	66.7	85.5	68.8	74.5	88.4	76.8	+18.8	+16.7	+5.7	28,479
1596-1602	Merchant of Venice - Troilus and Cressida (11 plays)	63.7	83.0	70.4	71.6	88.3	75.4	+19.3	+12.6	+1.2	15,214
1603-1606	Measure for Measure - Macbeth (6 plays)	63.1	82.6	75.1	69.0	93.8	76.7	+19.5	+7.6	-6.1	9,959
1606-1613	Antony and Cleopatra - Henry VIII (7 plays)	65.8	80.5	75.9	70.3	88.5	76.2	+14.7	+4.6	-5.6	14,699

The death of those whom <u>they</u> with care and cost	(6)
Have tended so, thus careless <u>should</u> be lost.	(8)
(Kyd, "The Spanish Tragedy" III,XIII:8-20)	
For all I know, all husbands <u>are</u> like me;	(8)
And every one I talk with <u>of</u> a wife	(8)
Is but a well dissembler <u>of</u> his woes,	(8)
As I am. Would I knew it! <u>For</u> the rareness	(8)
Afflicts me now.	

(Beaumont and Fletcher, "The Maid's Tragedy" III,II:49-53)

The grammatical line structure of a more rigid variant of meter, characterized by losses of stress on position 6, tends to divide the line symmetrically into two phrases with a syntactic seam on the hemistich boundary, between positions 4-5 or 5-6 (*From this dishonour \ <u>and</u> the hate of men; Unhappy mothers \ <u>of</u> such children then*), while the grammatical line structure typical of a looser verse form effaces the bipartite line structure, or moves the syntactic seam to the right, increasing the length of the first "hemistich" and decreasing the second one (*And every one I talk with \ <u>of</u> a wife Is but a well dissembler \ <u>of</u> his woes*).

And now we can turn to Shakespeare's verse.

2.3 Chambers' and Wentersdorf's chronologies

Shakespeare's dramas are arranged in Table 2.2 in the order suggested by Karl Wentersdorf (1951:164-165), who modified the long-accepted chronology of Chambers (1930). Later studies (see below) have confirmed Wentersdorf's modifications. My stress profile and other analyses also in part support the corrected chronology; I must admit that I am venturing to depart from Chambers' chronology for the first time (cf. Tarlinskaja 1983). Here are the dates and sequence of plays accepted by Chambers and Wentersdorf.

	Chambers' chronology	Wentersdorf's chronology
1588-89:		"Titus Andronicus"
1589-90:		"Henry VI", Part 1
1590-91:	"Henry VI", Part 2	"Henry VI", Part 2
	"Henry VI", Part 3	"Henry VI", Part 3
1591-92:	"Henry VI", Part 1	"Taming of the Shrew"
		"Richard III"
1592-93:	"Richard III"	"Two Gentlemen of Verona"
	"Comedy of Errors"	(Non-dramatic poetry)

	Chambers' chronology	Wentersdorf's chronology
1593-94:	"Titus Andronicus" "Taming of the Shrew"	"Love"s Labour's Lost" (Non-dramatic poetry)
1594-95:	"Two Gentlemen of Verona" "Love's Labour's Lost" "Romeo and Juliet"	"Midsummer Night's Dream" "Romeo and Juliet" "Richard II"
1595-96:	"Richard II" "Midsummer Night's Dream"	"King John" "Merchant of Venice"
1596-97:	"King John" "Merchant of Venice"	"Henry IV", Part 1 "Henry IV", Part 2 "Merry Wives of Windsor"
1597-98:	"Henry IV", Part 1 "Henry IV", Part 2	"Much Ado About Nothing"
1598-99:	"Much Ado About Nothing" "Henry V"	"Henry V" "Julius Caesar"
1599-1600:	"Julius Caesar" "As You Like It" "Twelfth Night"	"As You Like It" "Twelfth Night"
1600-01:	"Hamlet" "Merry Wives of Windsor"	"Hamlet"
1601-02:	"Troilus and Cressida"	"Troilus and Cressida"
1602-03:	"All's Well That Ends Well"	
1603-04:		"Measure for Measure" "Othello"
1604-05:	"Measure for Measure" "Othello"	"All's Well That Ends Well" "Timon of Athens"
1605-06:	"King Lear" "Macbeth"	"King Lear" "Macbeth"
1606-07:	"Antony and Cleopatra"	"Antony and Cleopatra"
1607-08:	"Coriolanus" "Timon of Athens"	"Pericles" "Coriolanus"
1608-09:	"Pericles"	"Cymbeline"
1609-10:	"Cymbeline"	"Winter's Tale"
1610-11:	"Winter's Tale"	"Tempest"
1611-12:	"Tempest"	
1612-13:	"Henry VIII"	"Henry VIII"

The more important deviations from Chambers in Wentersdorf's chronology are "Titus Andronicus", moved five theatre seasons earlier; "Merry Wives of Windsor", moved earlier four seasons; "Comedy of Errors" and "Timon of

Table 2.2

Stress profiles of Shakespeare's works (ictic stresses)

Chronology after Wentersdorf	Dramas and Poems	Positions						$\bar{S}$ (2-10)	Correlation between:		No. Lines
		2	4	6	8	10			4-6	8-6	
1588-89	Titus Andronicus	66.4	86.6	69.6	75.0	87.1	76.9	+17.0	+ 5.4	2416
1589-90	Henry VI, 1	65.9	83.9	68.1	72.4	85.0	75.1	+15.8	+ 4.3	2623
	Comedy of Errors	67.9	84.5	67.4	72.5	90.5	76.6	+17.1	+ 5.1	1401
1590-91	Henry VI, 2	69.4	85.1	70.0	74.7	87.9	77.4	+15.1	+ 4.7	2250
	Henry VI, 3	70.0	87.3	70.0	75.5	90.2	78.6	+17.3	+ 5.5	2800
1591-92	Taming of the Shrew	64.9	87.2	68.6	74.3	88.6	76.7	+18.6	+ 5.7	1900
	Richard III	64.7	84.8	68.7	75.3	89.9	76.7	+16.1	+ 6.9	3376
1592-93	Two Gentlemen of Verona	63.6	81.0	67.0	70.3	87.2	73.8	+13.9	+ 3.0	1437
1593-94	Love's Labour's Lost	67.8	86.4	70.7	74.2	89.8	77.8	+15.7	+ 4.2	1300
1594-95	Midsummer Night's Dream	65.5	85.5	68.8	75.0	85.4	76.0	+16.7	+ 6.2	1350
	Romeo and Juliet	65.7	87.2	68.3	75.6	88.5	77.1	+18.9	+ 7.3	2456
	Richard II	68.8	85.2	70.0	75.6	91.0	78.1	+15.2	+ 5.6	2630
1595-96	King John	65.6	85.3	67.7	75.0	88.4	76.4	+17.6	+ 7.3	2540

Table 2.2 (cont.)

	Merchant of Venice	63.4	84.5	70.4	70.9	87.7	75.4	+14.1	+ 0.5	1857
1596-97	Henry IV, 1	65.4	82.8	66.8	74.0	82.4	74.3	+16.0	+ 7.2	1542
	Henry IV, 2	62.5	84.0	67.9	71.9	86.2	74.5	+16.1	+ 4.0	1382
	Merry Wives of Windsor	74.1	80.1	78.5	68.3	91.4	78.5	+ 1.6	-10.2	186
1597-98	Much Ado About Nothing	66.2	82.0	70.2	70.2	86.6	74.9	+11.8	0	650
1598-99	Henry V	63.5	81.7	70.8	71.9	86.9	74.9	+10.9	+ 1.1	1736
	Julius Caesar	62.1	82.5	69.1	72.2	86.2	74.4	+13.4	+ 3.1	1957
1599-1600	As You Like It	60.8	82.4	70.0	72.2	88.4	74.7	+12.4	+ 2.2	930
	Twelfth Night	62.1	83.2	72.5	69.9	91.7	75.9	+10.7	- 2.6	781
1600-01	Hamlet	61.2	81.9	72.5	69.3	92.9	75.6	+ 9.4	- 3.2	2335
1601-02	Troilus and Cressida	67.6	84.6	72.4	72.7	91.9	77.8	+12.0	+ 0.1	1858
1602-03	----									
1603-04	Measure for Measure	62.3	82.9	71.7	65.6	90.4	74.6	+11.2	- 6.1	1382
	Othello	62.3	84.8	72.5	70.9	94.3	77.0	+12.3	- 1.6	2272
1604-05	All's Well That Ends Well	62.5	81.3	75.1	69.5	93.9	76.5	+ 6.2	- 5.6	1350
	Timon of Athens	62.8	82.3	77.4	69.7	93.6	77.0	+ 4.9	- 7.7	1389
1605-06	King Lear	63.9	82.0	77.6	67.8	95.7	77.4	+ 4.4	- 9.8	1915
	Macbeth	65.0	81.8	76.8	69.6	94.5	77.4	+ 4.6	- 7.2	1651
1606-07	Antony and Cleopatra	66.0	79.6	76.5	71.0	88.0	76.2	+ 3.1	- 5.5	2458
1607-08	Pericles	65.9	82.7	73.5	69.5	87.9	75.9	+ 9.2	- 4.0	1318

50

Table 2.2 (cont.)

1608-09	Coriolanus	63.9	80.1	75.5	67.3	88.9	75.1	+ 4.6	- 8.2	2330
1609-10	Cymbeline	67.8	79.7	76.9	72.6	89.0	77.2	+ 2.8	- 4.3	2614
1610-11	Winter's Tale	66.1	79.6	75.1	71.5	87.3	75.9	+ 3.5	- 3.6	2027
1611-12	Tempest	67.9	80.1	77.7	70.4	87.6	76.7	+ 2.4	- 7.3	1378

1612-13	Henry VIII	64.3	81.7	75.6	70.0	89.8	76.3	+ 6.1	- 5.6	2574
	Venus and Adonis	66.5	88.9	74.5	72.8	97.0	80.9	+14.4	- 1.7	1190
	Rape of Lucrece	72.4	89.2	74.2	78.5	92.7	81.4	+15.0	+ 4.3	1855
	Sonnets	66.6	89.1	71.5	75.6	94.3	79.4	+17.6	+ 4.1	2153

Table 2.3

Shakespeare's older and younger contemporaries
(stress profiles of Elizabethan-Jacobean dramas in chronological order)

Author	Drama and date	Strong Positions						Mean	Correlation between positions		
		2	4	6	8	10			4-2	4-6	8-6
Norton, Sackville	"Gorboduc", 1562: all "Gorboduc", acts I-III	72.0 73.4	89.8 89.7	71.2 66.9	81.7 84.6	94.6 93.6		81.9 81.6	+17.8 +16.3	+18.6 +22.8	+10.5 +17.7
Kyd*	"The Spanish Tragedy", 1589	74.4	87,4	70.3	77.8	81.6		78.3	+13.0	+17.1	+ 7.5
Anonym.*	"Arden of Feversham", 1592	70.5	87.9	71.4	76.2	89.3		79.0	+17.4	+16.5	+ 4.8
Ben Jonson	"Sejanus", 1603	64.2	82.3	73.3	67.8	89.8		75.5	+18.1	+ 9.0	- 5.5
Beaumont, Fletcher	"The Maid's Tragedy", 1611: act II sc.II, act IV sc.I, act V sc.I,II	54.3	82.9	75.6	67.3	92.9		74.6	+28.6	+ 7.3	- 8.3
Webster	"The Duchess of Malfi", 1623	68.5	76.8	74.9	65.6	87.7		74.7	+11.7	+ 1.9	- 9.4
Ford	"Perkin Warbeck", 1634	68.7	72.7	76.5	63.9	95.4		75.4	+ 6.0	- 3.8	-12.6

*Source: Tarlinskaja 1976, Table 50, p. 292.

Athens", each moved earlier three theatre seasons; and "Henry VI", Part 1, "Taming of the Shrew", and "Two Gentlemen of Verona", moved earlier two years each. Among the plays moved earlier one theatre season only, I point out specifically "Othello" and "Pericles". The accurate dating of "Titus Andronicus", "Henry VI", Part 1, "Timon of Athens", and "Pericles" is complicated by questions of authorship.

In my analyses in this chapter and in Chapters 3 and 5 I touch upon the chronology of "Timon of Athens". Problems of authorship of "Titus Andronicus", "Pericles", and "Henry VIII" are discussed in Chapters 3, 5, and 6. I shall sum up the existing points of view concerning "Timon of Athens" in this chapter, and in Chapter 3 those concerning "Titus Andronicus", "Pericles", and "Henry VIII".

The date and authorship of "Timon of Athens" has aroused much controversy. Chambers fixed its date as 1608 (Chambers 1930, I:483); however, several scholars had found thematic, stylistic, lexical, and metrical contacts between "Timon of Athens" and "King Lear" written in 1605-6 (e.g., J.C. Maxwell 1968:xii-xiii, Slater 1978). "Timon" was even considered a first sketch of "King Lear", set aside unfinished.

It has long been noticed that "Timon" does indeed look like an unfinished draft yet to be refined stylistically and moulded into poetic shape. It was found, moreover, that not only the style, but even spelling of some names and certain abbreviations differed from scene to scene (cf. Nowottny 1959, Hinman 1963, II:280-285). The authorship of the play was often attributed to Shakespeare and another poet, e.g., Middleton (Wells 1920, Jackson 1979:54-66); it was also suggested that Shakespeare left his own draft unfinished, and it was completed later by Chapman (Parrott 1923).

Vocabulary tests also seem to indicate another hand in "Timon". Similarly with the questionable "Pericles" and "Henry VIII", "Timon" is poorer in vocabulary than other, unquestionably Shakespearean later plays (Hart 1943). The date and authorship of "Timon of Athens" are still open questions.

The striking difference in the datings of "Merry Wives of Windsor" rests mainly on external evidence (Hotson 1931, Wentersdorf 1951:172-173). The play is short and analyses of its verse structure cannot add new insights as to its place in Shakespeare's canon; therefore its chronology is not discussed further.

2.4 Evolution of ictic stresses in Shakespeare

The statistics most revealing of a stress profile evolution are: (a) the degree of stress on ictus II (position 4) and the correlation of stresses between ictuses II and III (positions 4 and 6); (b) the correlation of stresses between ictuses IV and III (positions 8 and 6)termed rigidity index: a positive index (a "dip" on 6) is a proof of a rigid, symmetrical bipartite line structure $4+6$ or $5+5$, while a negative index (a "dip" on 8) is a sign of looser verse, closer to the prose tendency without a clear-cut bipartite line structure, or a division into asymmetrical parts, e.g., $3+7$ or, more often, $6+4$ or $7+3$.

The whole of Shakespeare's dramatic canon was divided into four periods. Shakespeare's dramas, of course, have been grouped into periods before, and the principles of grouping can vary. The division may follow, for example, the facts in Shakespeare's biography, such as his joining the company of Lord Chamberlain (in 1594), the opening of The Globe theatre in 1599, the taking over of the Blackfriars Theatre by the King's men in 1608, and the burning down of The Globe in 1613 (Alexander 1939). The division may be based on the poet's genre preference at different periods, combined with an evaluation of the "ripeness of talent" (Anikst 1963, 109). Then, more formal principles may be employed, for example, occurrence of "rare" words and lexical ties between the dramas (Jackson 1979:149). My division of the canon into periods is mainly based on the evolution of Shakespeare's accentual line structure (see below). The periods are as follows: I (1588-1596, 13 plays); II (1596-1602, 11 plays); IIIa (1603-1606, 6 plays); and IIIb (1606-1613, 7 plays).

Table 2.1 and Fig. 2.3 present the stress profiles of Shakespeare's plays averaged by periods. Shakespeare's ictic stress shows a gradual but very obvious evolution: (1) a progressive decrease of stress on ictus II (position 4) from 85.5 to 80.5%; (2) a "dip" on ictus III (position 6) evolves through a leveling-out of ictuses III-IV to a "dip" on ictus IV (position 8); (3) the opposition between ictuses I-II, II-III, and III-IV decreases from Period I through IIIb; for example, the difference between positions 4-6 decreases, by almost 4 times, from +16.7 to +4.6%.

Thus, evolution of Shakespeare's ictic stressing transformed his verse from a more rigid into a looser metrical form. Shakespeare's evolution is typologically not unlike the change from, for example, eighteenth-century Classicism to the nineteenth-century post-Romanticism (cf. Pope and Browning, Tarlinskaja 1976: Table 41). As already shown in section 2.2, Shakespeare's evolution went within the general trend of Elizabethan-Jacobean verse (cf. Fig. 2.2); so it appears that Shakespeare was very much the son of his time, very much in the mainstream of Elizabethan-Jacobean rhythmical practice. Note in Figure 2.3 how strongly Shakespeare's early pentameter differs from the speech model of verse, and how the tendencies of his later verse begin to resemble the speech model curves. The discovered evolution of Shakespeare's rhythmical style is in itself an indirect proof of the general correctness of the Chambers-Wentersdorf's chronology, though not of the exact dating of plays.

Consider now each of Shakespeare's plays individually (Table 2.2). In spite of the gradual evolution of Shakespeare's rhythmical style throughout the canon, one notices places of more marked change, turning points, as it were, in the process of evolution. These were seasons 1596-1597, between "King John" and "The Merchant of Venice" (in the latter play ictuses III and IV are leveled out for the first time: a new tendency is born), 1601-1602, between "Troilus and Cressida" and "Measure for Measure" (in "Troilus" ictuses III and IV are leveled out for the last time; from now on ictus IV will be always

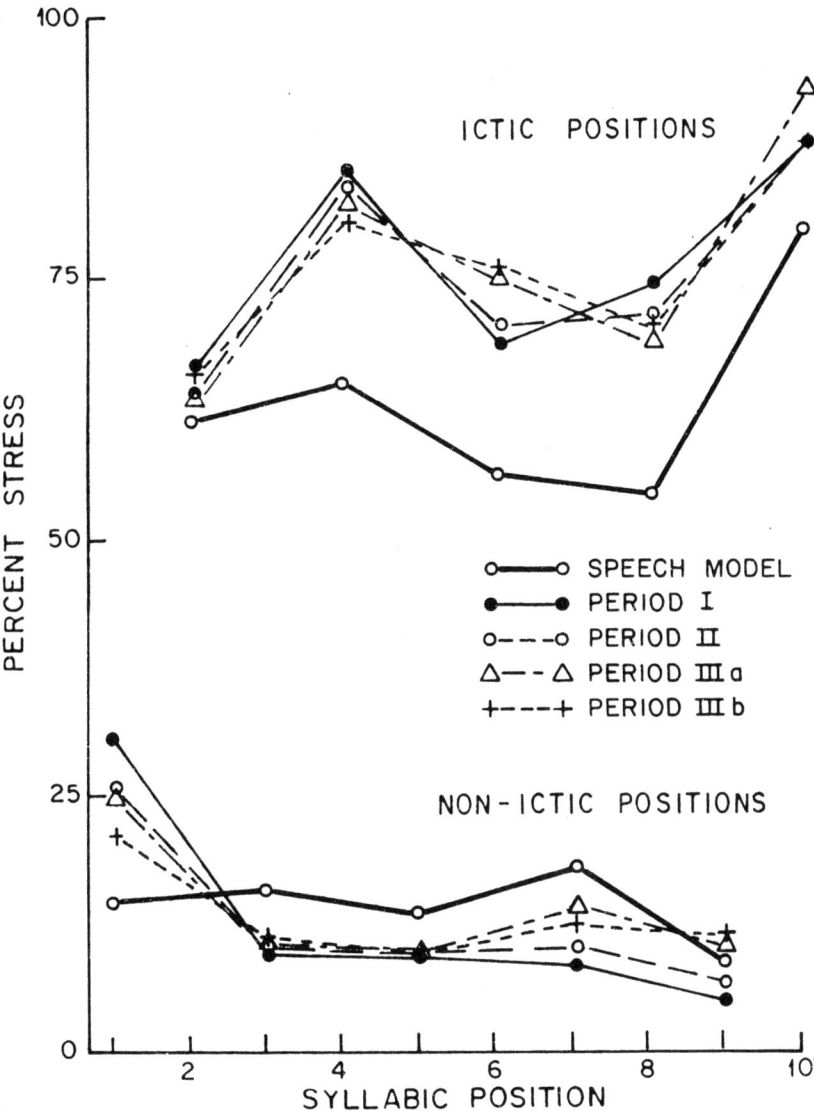

Fig. 2.3. Stress profiles for the four periods of Shakespeare's dramatic canon and speech model of iambic pentameter, with ictic and non-ictic positions connected separately. The trend from rigid to looser form is marked: Period I shows the lowest mid-line ictic stress on position 6 and strongest contrast with position 4; the curve is similar to Pope's (cf. Fig. 2.1) but not quite as rigid. Loosening has begun in Period II -stressing on positions 6 and 8 is nearly equal -and is complete (for Shakespeare) in Period III when the lowest mid-line stress is on position 8, as in the speech model. Non-ictic stresses also show the trend toward the speech model curve. But even the loosest verse still differs significantly from its speech model. (Data from Table 2.1; speech model curve as in Fig. 2.1.)

weaker than III), and 1606-1607, between "Macbeth" and "Antony and Cleopatra" (the latter play, as is well known, is characterized by a sharp increase in the number of missing stresses on the final ictus caused by unstressed monosyllables). These turning points become the boundaries for the sub-division of the canon into periods.

We now consider each period separately.

All thirteen plays of the first period show a "dip" on position 6, i.e., a positive rigidity index: ictus III is weaker than IV. The typical place of the strongest syntactic break within the line is usually after positions 4 or 5. The bipartite line segmentation may be purely syntactical, or purely rhythmical (accompanied by a loss of stress in position 6), or both. Here are typical examples from plays of Period I (the syntactic breaks of various strengths are marked; the figure between the bars indicates the position after which a relatively strong syntactic break takes place; syllabic position of missing stress underlined and given in brackets):

```
My lovely Aaron, /5/ wherefore look'st thou sad,
When every thing \4\ doth make a gleeful boast?
The birds chaunt melody \6\ on every bush,                    (6)
The snake lies rolled \5\ in the cheerful sun,                (6)
The green leaves quiver \5\ with the cooling wind,            (6)
And make a chequered shadow \7\ on the ground
       . . . . . . . . . . . . . . . . . .
Believe me, queen, /4/ your swarth Cimmerian
Doth make your honour \5\ of his body's hue,                  (6)
Spotted, detested, \5\ and abominable.                        (6)
Why are you sequest'red \6\ from all your train,              (6)
Dismounted \3\ from your snow-white goodly steed,
And wondered hither \5\ to an obscure plot,                   (6)
Accompanied \4\ but with a barbarous Moor,                    (6)
If foul desire \4\ had not conducted you?
              ("Titus Andronicus" II,III:10-15,72-79)
Wilt thou be gone? /4/ It is not yet near day.                (6)
It was the nightingale, /6/ and not the lark,                 (6)
That pierced the fearful hollow \7\ of thine ear.
Nightly she sings \4\ on yond pomegranate tree.               (6)
Believe me, love, /4/ it was the nightingale.                 (6)
       . . . . . . . . . . . . . . . . . .
Let me be ta'en, /4/ let me be put to death                   (6)
I am content, /4/ so thou wilt have it so.                    (6)
       . . . . . . . . . . . . . . . . . .
Evermore weeping \5\ for your cousin's death?                 (6)
What, wilt thou wash him \5\ from his grave with tears?       (6)
And if thou couldst, /4/ thou couldst not make him live.      (6)
Therefore have done /4/—some grief shows much of love,
But much of grief \4\ shows still some want of wit.
       . . . . . . . . . . . . . . . . . .
```

```
Indeed I never \5\ shall be satisfied                               (6)
With Romeo /4/ till I behold him—dead—                             (6)
Is my poor heart \4\ so for a kinsman vexed.                       (6)
                        ("Romeo and Juliet" III,V:1-5,17,18,70-74,94-96)
I'll give my jewels \5\ for a set of beads,                        (6)
My gorgeous palace \5\ for a hermitage,                            (6)
My gay apparel \5\ for an almsman's gown,                          (6)
My figured goblets \5\ for a dish of wood,                         (6)
My sceptre \3\ for a palmer's walking-staff,
My subjects \3\ for a pair of carved saints,
And my large kingdom \5\ for a little grave.                       (6)
                                      ("Richard II" III,III:146-152)
```

The maximum numerical difference in stressing between positions 8 and 6 is found in the tragedy "Romeo and Juliet" and in two later chronicles, "Richard III" and "King John", the minimum difference in the comedies "The Two Gentlemen of Verona" and "Love's Labour's Lost" and in the two early chronicles "Henry VI", parts 1 and 2. Though the strength of stressing of the third ictus is somewhat variable, there seems to be a systematic difference between the earlier and later chronicles and between the chronicles and the tragedies and comedies. The opposition of earlier and later chronicles seems to suggest that young Shakespeare at first moved from a slightly less symmetrical to a more symmetrical bipartite line structure, which consolidated in "Romeo and Juliet"; this conclusion is supported by a more detailed rhythmical analysis of "Titus Andronicus" by scenes and acts (see Chapter 3) and by the stress profile of Shakespeare's first poem "Venus and Adonis" (see below). From this point of view the chronological place for "Henry VI", part 1, suggested by Wentersdorf seems to be more logical than the one fixed by Chambers.

The data also oppose comedies to chronicles and tragedies (cf. Chambers 1930:I,253, Wentersdorf 1951:186-187): the symmetrical structure of the early Shakespearean verse is the least obvious in two comedies, particularly in "The Two Gentlemen of Verona", which show a minimum of opposition between strong and weak ictic stresses. A relatively stronger "prosaicness" of the rhythm in the comedies is obviously a peculiarity of comical and satirical genres (cf. Donne's "Satyres": Tarlinskaja and Teterina 1974). Rhythmical "prosaicness" of verse in the comedies is also explained by the occurrence of prose pieces and fragments of non-iambic, doggerel verse. Such insertions interrupt the flow of iambic pentameter verse and loosen its metrical structure.

The stressing of the second ictus is particularly high in the dramas of the first period: it reaches 87%. The maximum difference between the second and the third ictuses is displayed by "Romeo and Juliet"; the opposition between strong and weak ictuses in this drama is particularly striking. The least difference between the second and the third ictuses is predictably found in a comedy, "The Two Gentlemen of Verona". This comedy also displays the lowest mean ictic stress. As far as stress profile analysis is concerned, the two opposite rhythmical tendencies that coexist in the first period, i.e., more rigid and looser variants of iambic pentameter, are best represented by a tragedy ("Romeo and Juliet") and a comedy ("The Two Gentlemen of Verona"). The strength of stress of the first ictus in the plays of 1588-1596, in comparison with later periods, is rather high; it decreases starting with the first play of the second period.

"The Merchant of Venice" (1595-96) marks the first break in the rhythm of ictuses III-IV: in this play they are leveled out. It is not surprising that the change in the correlation between the "key" ictuses III and IV, indicating loosening and prosaization of the meter, begins with a comedy. The period of the leveling-out of ictuses III and IV ends with "Troilus and Cressida" (1601-02). The decreasing difference in stress values between ictuses III and IV reflects the beginning of a transition from a more symmetrical to an asymmetrical "hemistich" line structure, from more uniform to more diverse line grammar, and from a more rigid to a looser variant of iambic pentameter. The place of the strongest syntactic seam begins to shift to the right: it typically occurs not only after positions 4 or 5, as in earlier plays, but also after 6 or 7. For example:

Mislike me not \4\ for my complexion	(6)
The shadowed livery \5\ of the burnished sun,	(6)
To whom I am a neighbour \7\ and near bred.	(8)
Bring me the fairest creature \7\ northward born,	
Where Phoebus' fire \4\ scarce thaws the icicles,	
And let us make incision \7\ for your love	(8)
To prove whose blood is reddest, /7/ his or mine.	

("The Merchant of Venice" II,I:1-7)

The stressing of ictus II, compared to the first period, is much reduced, and the differences between strong and weak ictuses has decreased. The increased stressing of position 10 is explained by a lower number of polysyllabic words not stressed on the last syllable, which was typical of earlier Elizabethan plays; e.g., *To-morrow are they to be márried*; *But such as have upon thine árticles*; *Know, sovereign, I come to sólemnize*; *Come, worthy viceroy and accómpany* (Kyd, "The Spanish Tragedy" III,XII:18,25, 27,36); *Of scythian trumpets! Hear the básilisk!*; *The soldan's daughter, for his cóncubine, And with a troop of thieves and vágabonds*; *While you, faint-hearted, base Egýptians* (Marlowe, "Tamburlaine the Great" IV,I:2,5,6,8); *Tribunes, and me, a poor compétitor*; *Romans, make way! the good Andrónicus, Patron of virtue, Rome's great chámpion*; *From whence at first she weighed her áncorage* (Shakespeare, "Titus Andronicus" I,I:66,67,68,76) (see also Chapter 5).

Here are two more examples of the transitory period II:

(a) ictuses III and IV are leveled (syllabic position of missing stress in brackets):

Urge me no more, I shall forget myself;	(6)
Have mind upon your health, tempt me no further.	(8)
Away, slight man!	
Is't possible? Hear me, for I will speak.	(8)
Must I give way and room to your rash choler?	(8)
Shall I be frightened when a madman stares?	(6)
O ye gods, ye gods! Must I endure all this?	(6)
All this! ay, more: fret till your proud heart break;	(6)
Go show your slaves how choleric you are, etc.	(8)

("Julius Caesar" IV,III:35-43)

Out of the eight full pentameter lines, four contain a missing ictic stress in position 6 and four in position 8.

(b) ictus IV is weaker than III:

Since my dear soul \4\ was mistress of her choice	(8)
And could of men \4\ distinguish her election,	(8)
Sh'hath sealed thee for herself, /6/ for thou hast been	(8)
As one in suff'ring all /6/ that suffers nothing,	
A man that Fortune's buffets \7\ and rewards	(8)
Hast ta'en with equal thanks; /6/ and blest are those	
Whose blood and judgement \5\ are so well co-medled,	(6)
That they are not a pipe \6\ for Fortune's finger	
To sound what stop the please; /6/ give me that man	(8)
That is not passion's slave, /6/ and I will wear him	(8)
In my heart's core, /4/ ay in my heart of heart . . .	(6)

("Hamlet" III,2:65-75)

Out of the eleven cited lines, six contain missing stresses on position 8 and only two on position 6. Only four lines contain a relatively strong syntactic break after positions 4 or 5, and seven lines display a break after positions 6 or 7.

The change in correlations between ictuses III and IV are not completely smooth: there are variations in both directions. Two plays are constructed according to the stress model of the first period; these are "Henry IV", parts 1 and 2 (rigidity indices +7.2 and +4.0), closely followed by "Julius Caesar" (rigidity index +3.1). These facts confirm Wentersdorf's conclusion that historical plays tend to be metrically more regular than other genres: "This is due to the fact that the poetry of the historical works is more formal. During the first half of Shakespeare's career, as Chambers puts it, the poet 'moves more freely in comedy than in history' (Chambers 1930, I:253). In other words, the conception and composition of the historical dramas was more deliberate, in view of the necessity for close adherence to the facts in the chronicles which served the dramatist as his source. This meant less speed, less fluency, and therefore less freedom in writing" (Wentersdorf 1951:186-187). "Julius Caesar", closely following Plutarch's "Lives", also falls into this category.

The plays written according to the new-formed trend of weaker stress on ictus IV are: "The Merry Wives of Windsor" (though the shortness of the verse portion makes its "vertical" analysis of questionable value), "Twelfth Night", and "Hamlet". "Troilus and Cressida", though closer to comedy, follows a more symmetrical line pattern: ictuses III and IV are leveled as in plays written 5-6 years previously (cf. "Merchant of Venice"). "Troilus and Cressida" is stylistically in many respects unusual. It seems to have been written, or adapted, for a special performance, perhaps for an academic audience. This fact could explain a large number of Latin borrowings and rare words as well as suffixes of Roman origin in this play:—ire,—ion,—ure,—ive, —ate, and—ance. It is also possible that "Troilus and Cressida" was a stylistic experiment. By stylizing an "antique" tragi-comedy, Shakespeare made, as it were, a chronological step backward, returning to a more symmetrical verse than what he already used by 1601. The rhythm of Shakepeare's play is unquestionably different from the rhythm of Chaucer's poem "Troilus and Criseyde" which was the main source of the plot for Shakespeare: in Chaucer's poem the fourth ictus is considerably weaker than the third. It is quite obvious that Chaucer's verse was not used by Shakespeare as his metrical model. Here is a typical example from Chaucer's "Troilus and Criseyde":

But ho! no more as now of this matere,	(8)
For-why this folk wol comen up anoon,	
That han the lettre red: lo, I hem here.	(8)
But I conjure thee, Criseyde, and oon,	(8)
And two, thou Troilus, whan thou mayst goon,	(6,8)
That at myn hous ye been at my warninge,	(6,8)
For I ful wel shal shape your cominge.	(8)
(Chaucer, "Troilus and Criseyde", Book III:190-196)	

The seven lines cited above contain six cases of a possible weakening or complete absence of stress on position 8 (ictus IV), and only two lines with a missing stress on position 6 (ictus III).

And here is a typical example from Shakespeare's "Troilus and Cressida":

But value dwells not in particular will:	(6)
It holds his estimate and dignity	(6)
As well wherein 'tis precious of itself	(8)
As in the prizer. 'Tis mad idolatry	
To make the service greater than the god;	(8)
And the will dotes that is attributive	(6)

```
       To what infectiously itself affects,                    (6)
       Without some image of th'affected merit.                (6)
       I take today a wife, and my election                    (8)
       Is led on it the conduct of my will . . .               (8)
                    (Shakespeare, "Troilus and Cressida" II,II:53-62)
```

The ten cited lines contain five cases of missing stress on ictus III (position 6) and four cases of missing stress on ictus IV (position 8).

There is another possible explanation of the metrical peculiarity of "Troilus" being closer to the meter of the earlier plays: it may have been written several years before 1601-02 (cf. Boas 1925:369-370). The supposition that Shakespeare wrote "Troilus" some time before its publication seemed not unlikely to Chambers (1930,I:443). If it was indeed written before "Hamlet", closer to 1598-99, then probably "Troilus and Cressida" can be identified with the mysterious comedy mentioned by Meres in his "Palladis Tamia" as "Loue labours wonne" (Hotson 1949:42).

Beginning with the theater season 1603-04, ictus IV of Shakespeare's dramas is invariably weaker than ictus III: the rigidity index is negative. This season opens the third period of his career. It is convenient, however, to divide this period into two subperiods, (a) and (b), drawing a demarcation between "Macbeth" and "Antony and Cleopatra". The stressing on the second ictus and especially on the final one is sharply reduced compared to period II. The reasons for the weakening of the final ictus, particularly in later dramas, are quite different from those in early plays; they will be analyzed in detail when we consider the structure of line endings (Chapter 5). It is sufficient to mention here a sharp weakening of the final ictus beginning with the season of 1606-07, caused by a high incidence of unstressed monosyllables. Shakespeare loosened his line syntax, and one sign of this loosening is an increased number of run-on lines, e.g., *And the Phoenicians go a-ducking: we (Have used to conquer standing on the earth); His power went out in such distraction as (Beguiled all spies)* ("Antony and Cleopatra" III,VII:64-65,76-77).

In my earlier division into periods (Tarlinskaja 1983)subperiod IIIa contained five plays, and now it contains six: "Timon of Athens", following Wentersdorf, has been moved from 1607-08 to 1604-05. And, indeed, the stress profile of "Timon" resembles those of the period IIIa rather than IIIb: the stressing on the second ictus (82.3%) is closer to the index of "Measure for Measure", "Othello", and "King Lear"; while plays of the period IIIb (except the questionable "Pericles" and "Henry VIII") all have reduced stressing of the second ictus, to 80% or less. Also, the difference between positions 8-6 in "Timon" is too high for Shakespeare's final period, where ictuses tend to be leveled in strength, and the final ictic stress is too strong. The incidence of unstressed monosyllables in position 10 is too low for a post-"Antony and Cleopatra" play, but it is very close to the indices of "All's Well That Ends

Well", "King Lear", and "Macbeth", and this is exactly the position where "Timon of Athens" was placed by Wentersdorf.

The following metrical phenomena are characteristic of the plays of subperiod IIIa, 1603-1606: (1) a progressive lowering of stressing on ictus II (the correlation between positions 4-6 decreases from +12.3 in "Othello" to +4.6% in "Macbeth"); this process continues the progression to the asymmetrical bipartite line segmentation typical of Shakespeare's later plays which began in Period II (the more strongly stressed is ictus II, the more pronounced is a first hemistich comprised of 4-5 syllables); (2) an increased difference between positions 6 and 8: stress on 6 grows and on 8 falls, another sign of an asymmetrical line structure; (3) an increase of stress on the final ictus: losses of stress on position 10 caused by polysyllables of the type <u>murderer</u>, <u>followers</u>, <u>emperor</u>, and <u>massacres</u> occur very seldom, and unstressed monosyllables in position 10 are still used very sparingly. Period IIIa has the strongest final ictus of all Shakespeare's canon; and (4) a further shift of relatively strong syntactic breaks from the midline to the right and particularly to the left. Here are two examples of Shakespeare's period IIIa:

I looked not for you yet, /6/ nor <u>am</u> provided	(8)
For your fit welcome. /5/ Give ear, sir, /7/ <u>to</u> my sister;	(8)
For those /2/ that mingle reason \7\ <u>with</u> your passion	(8)
Must be content to think you old, /8/ and so—	
("King Lear" II,III:230-233)	
They are not yet come back. /6/ But <u>I</u> have spoke	(8)
With one /2/ that saw him die: /6/ who <u>did</u> report	(8)
That very frankly \5\ <u>he</u> confessed his treasons,	(6)
Implored your highness' pardon, \7\ <u>and</u> set forth	(8)
A deep repentance: /5/ nothing <u>in</u> his life	(8)
Became him like the leaving <u>it</u>; /8/ he died	(8)
As one /2/ that had been studied \7\ <u>in</u> his death	(8)
To throw away the dearest thing /8/ he owned	
As 'twere a careless trifle. /7/—There's no art	
To find the mind's construction \7\ <u>in</u> the face:	(8)
("Macbeth" I,IV:3-13)	

There is one play in the period IIIa that seems to deviate slightly from the general tendency: this is "Othello". The stress profile of this play resembles that of "Troilus and Cressida" two years earlier (and "Troilus and Cressida" was also an exception) or "Much Ado About Nothing" six years earlier. As we shall see in Chapters 3 and 4, the more rigid form of "Othello" is explained by a more symmetrical, rigid verse form of acts I-II, determined by the part of Othello himself: harmony in his soul (acts I-II) is emphasized by a more regular structure of his verse, and Othello's part is a dominant portion of the play.

Period IIIb is characterized by the following features: (1) lowering of stress on position 4; (2) decrease of stress on position 10 caused by more unstressed monosyllables; (3)a decreased difference between positions 4-6 and 8-6: the opposition between strong and weak ictuses becomes effaced, and this is a sign of prosaization of verse (cf. prose models of verse: Tarlinskaja and Teterina 1974: Table IV, p. 78); and (4) a further shift of syntactic seams farther from midline. Two plays which do not follow this pattern completely are "Pericles" and "Henry VIII", both generally considered to be of mixed authorship. A more detailed analysis of "Pericles" is undertaken in Chapter 3, and of "Henry VIII" in Chapters 3, 5, and 6. The general stress profiles of these plays viewed against the overall trend of period IIIb already reveal some peculiarities of structure: ictus II is stressed too strongly, particularly in "Pericles" (cf. plays of two to three theatre seasons earlier). The strength of stress on ictus II of "Pericles" reflects the influence of acts I-II, whose rhythm is strikingly different from Shakespearean (see Chapter 3). Here is an example of Shakespeare's period IIIb:

Away, /2/ I do condemn mine ears /8/ that have   (10)
So long attended thee. /6/ If thou wert honourable,   (8)
Thou wouldst have told this tale for virtue, /9/ not   (2)
For such an end thou seek'st, /6/ as base as strange. (2)
Thou wrong'st a gentleman /6/ who is as far   (6,8)
From thy report /4/ as thou from honour,/9/ and   (2,10)
. Solicits here a lady /7/ that disdains   (8)
Thee and the devil alike. /6/ What ho, /8/ Pisanio!   (2)
                    ("Cymbeline" I,VI:140-147)

In these eight lines from "Cymbeline" there are four cases of missing ictic stresses on position 2, three on position 8, two on position 10 (both caused by unstressed monosyllables), and one on position 6: the stressing is markedly more erratic than in earlier dramas. The places of relatively strong syntactic breaks are typically after positions 6, 7, or 8.

Viewed overall, the rhythmical style of Shakespeare's plays shows a smooth evolution over the course of his 25-year writing career, from a more rigid to a looser verse form. A plot of the rigidity index (position 8 minus position 6), one of the main indicators of a rhythmical style, makes this quite apparent (Fig. 2.4). The indices of the early plays, +5 to +7, decrease smoothly over time to the negative values of the late plays, −4 to −8. A least-squares regression line fits the data with a very high correlation, $r = -0.87$.

But within the general evolution we can interpret some details in the evolution of stressing. The first few years Shakespeare was apparently working hard to make his verse form, particularly of the chronicles, more rigid. The trend line for Period I actually has a positive slope, dominated by an increasing rigidity of the chronicles. But approximately mid-way in this early period Shakespeare began also to write the opposing genre of comedies; these became coupled with a looser verse style. A trend line fitted through all "pure" comedy data fits exceedingly well: $r = -0.75$. Thus it was the genre of comedy

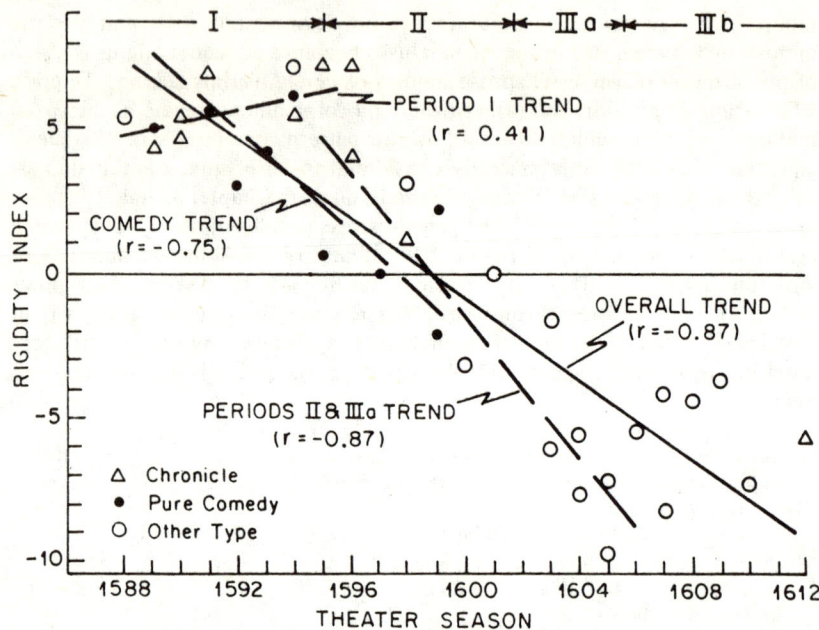

Fig. 2.4. Rigidity indices (stressing of position 8 minus position 6) for Shakespeare's plays plotted by theater season (Wentersdorf's chronology). Chronicles and "pure" comedies are identified separately. Three trend lines (fitted by linear regression: r = correlation coefficient) identify specific details within the generally smooth evolution of Shakespeare's rhythmical style from a more rigid to a looser verse form. Data from Table 2.2; "Merry Wives of Windsor" omitted because of (1) too few iambic pentameter lines and (2) play-within-play.

that led the trend of loosening of his stressing style, which was then followed by all types of plays.

The change in this measure of rhythmical style actually took place over a relatively shorter period of time than the total span of 25 years. A trend line fitted to the data of periods II plus IIIa, a total of 10 years, fits the data as well as the overall line: r = −0.87. Then from 1604-5 onward the negative trend in rigidity index reverses, becoming definitely positive. This means the difference in stressing between positions 8 and 6 is decreasing, these two ictuses becoming more "leveled". This change does not, however, signal a change in evolution; rather, it means the prosaization is continuing, with all ictuses becoming more evenly stressed (the difference between positions 4 and 6 is also a minimum in period IIIb; cf. Table 2.2).

Now let us look once again at period IIIa, when the rigidity index is minimum (reaching −9.8 in "King Lear"). This stressing pattern is not the ultimate in prosaizaton of verse. Rather, this strong "dip" on position 8 actually emphasizes the "*A mayore*" line segmentation, and though typical of a less rigid verse form, can be thought of as a "conventional" pentameter form in its own right. Good examples of an even looser iambic pentameter verse more closely approaching the prose model tendencies are Byron's "The Two Foscari" and "Werner" (Table 2.9): the difference between ictuses is so small that I-II-III-IV are nearly equally stressed. In a yet looser verse the difference between <u>ictuses</u> and <u>non-ictuses</u> decreases, tending to approach the indices of purely syllabic verse (cf. Donne's "Satyres" and the speech model of syllabic verse in Table 1.1).

The relatively smooth evolution of Shakespeare's rhythmical style, which resulted from both conscious and unconscious efforts on Shakespeare's part, is yet another proof of a one-man authorship of Shakespeare's canon. Only one author could have written 37 plays in which the rhythmical evolution is displayed so consistently over the course of 25 years. Neither groups of collaborators nor several independent authors who allegedly wrote fully or partially at least some of Shakespeare's plays (see, for example, the reviews of authorship controversies in Wilson 1953, Churchill 1958, McMichael 1962, Gibson 1962) could have produced such a long cycle in which the evolution developed on the whole so uniformly. This applies even to the earliest dramas: whatever their substrate, Shakepeare's hand must have molded other participants' contributions, even if we admit their existence, because stress rhythm is one of the most individual elements of verse form.

It has been shown that Shakespeare's earlier plays are lexically close to those of Lyly, Marlowe, Greene, and Peele, while the vocabulary of his later plays is closer to Ben Jonson, Chapman, and Fletcher. The hypotheses that Lyly, Marlowe, Greene, or Peele were Shakespeare's "diachronic" or "synchronic" co-authors were mainly based on the similarity of vocabulary and recurring phrases. But common vocabulary and phraseology, just as the resemblance of topical repertoire and plot models, may be a feature of the same epoch, the same school, and the same genre within the same school. It may also be a sign of imitation: the young, immature author reproduced the style of older, experienced playwrights in whose dramas he also probably acted. Rhythm, however, is considerably harder to imitate than the topical repertoire and vocabulary (cf. Tomaševskij 1929:245-250), and though Shakespeare's evolution went within the mainstream of Elizabethan-Jacobean drama, the inner logic of the evolution of a poetic cycle governs the structure of every individual drama within the cycle. Comparing the works of several authors at the same point in time reveals considerable differences in their rhythm. Consider, for example, the stress profiles of Marlowe's "Edward II" and Shakespeare's "Richard III", and of Chapman's "Bussi d'Ambois" and Shakespeare's "Antony and Cleopatra" (Table 2.4). The first pair of plays was written around 1592, the second around 1606.

The rhythmical form of the two non-Shakespearean dramas in both cases

Table 2.4

A synchronic comparison of plays by different authors

Authors and plays	Positions					Correlation between positions	
	2	4	6	8	10	4-6	8-6
Shakespeare "Richard III"	64.7	84.8	68.7	75.3	89.9	+15.2	+5.6
Marlowe "Edward II"	69.6	81.8	74.6	72.1	85.3	+ 7.2	-2.5
Shakespeare "Antony and Cleopatra"	66.0	79.6	76.5	71.0	88.0	+ 3.1	-5.5
Chapman "Bussi d'Ambois"	60.7	87.0	67.3	70.8	92.1	+19.7	+3.5

have nothing in common with the rhythm of Shakespeare's plays of the same years. By 1592 Marlowe had already passed from a symmetrical line with a "dip" on position 6 to an asymmetrical line with a "dip" on position 8 (see also Table 2.6). Shakespeare will evolve into this rhythmical pattern only seven years later (e.g., "Twelfth Night"). In conformity with later Shakespeare, Marlowe's second ictus (position 4) is beginning to lose its stress. Shakespeare's bipartite line structure of the first period is symmetrical, with a "dip" on position 6 and a syntactic seam after positions 5 or 4. However, "Edward II" at the same time displays several features of a more archaic rhythmical style. The first is a high proportion of missing ictic stresses on position 10 caused by unstressed syllables of polysyllabic words (lines like *And with a troop of thieves and vágabonds* are numerous), and the second is the low proportion of feminine endings even in late Marlowe compared to early Shakespeare (see also Chapter 5): lines with masculine endings comprise 99.2% of Marlowe's "Edward II" but only 80.5% of Shakespeares's "Richard III" and only 89.2% of all Shakespeare's plays of the first period. Thus, in its stress profile "Edward II" resembles later Shakespeare, while in the structure of line endings it has no parallel even with the earliest of Shakespeare's plays. Therefore, "Edward II" has no place in Shakespeare's canon; this is an argument against one "anti-Stratfordian" theory that "Shakespeare" was Marlowe's pen-name (Hoffman 1955, Williams 1966; cf. its critique in Churchill 1958, Gibson 1962, Martin 1965).

Chapman's "Bussi d'Ambois" is also very unlike Shakespeare of the same period. Such strong stressing on the second ictus and such enormous difference between ictuses II and III had not been used by Shakespeare for 12 years, since "Romeo and Juliet"; besides, the ends of Chapman's lines are too strongly stressed. But the main thing is that in "Bussi d'Ambois" the weakest midline ictus is not the fourth, which is typical of Shakespeare's already asymmetrical line of the period 1606-07, but the third, which divides the line into two symmetrical parts. Such a structure has not been used by Shakespeare for seven years, since "Julius Caesar".

2.5 Shakespeare's evolution of non-ictic stressing (Tables 2.5-2.7, Fig. 2.3)

We first consider the general stress profiles of non-ictic positions, and then more differentiated data. Non-ictic stresses caused by monosyllables and polysyllables are examined separately, and, within each category, phrase-initial and mid-phrase words.

2.5.1. The most important general features of non-ictic stressing in English iambic meter are: (1) the stress on the first position (the anacrusis): a high stress on position 1 and a sharp decrease of stress on line-internal non-ictuses is a sign of a rigid variant of iambic pentameter; (2) the mean stress on line-internal non-ictuses: the higher the stress, the farther the verse form moves from syllabo-tonic to syllabic; (3) the presence and place of an absolute maximum of stress on one of the midline non-ictic positions: an increase of stress on one of the midline non-ictuses is one of the signs of a bipartite syntactic and rhythmical line segmentation: the second half-line often begins with a new phrase, and its beginning is frequently marked by a non-ictic stress, or both a non-ictic stress and a missing ictic stress in the same foot—an "inversion". For example: *No joyful tongue \ gave him his welcome home* (an "inversion" in positions 5-6: "Richard II" V,II:29); *Th' estate of my poor queen./ Leave me alone* (an "inversion" in positions 7-8: "Henry VIII" V,I:74).

Tables 2.5, 2.6, 2.9, and 2.11 also contain an "iambic index" calculated slightly differently than in Chapter 1 (cf. Table 1.1). There, to enable comparison, I had to follow Gasparov's system designed for the verse of the Russian and Italian types. In English verse, however, the final non-ictic position also receives appreciable extra-metrical stressing and must be included into the calculation of the mean $\bar{W}$. The first position, the anacrusis, must, on the other hand, be excluded: high stressing on position 1 and low stressing on other non-ictuses are signs of a more rigid metrical form, while a lower stressing on the anacrusis and a higher stressing on mid-line non-ictuses are features of a looser meter. These tendencies are countervailing, so that mean values of non-ictic stressing including both position 1 and the other non-ictic positions are less significant in demonstrating the demarcation between a more rigid and a looser form of English iambic pentameter. So for the "iambic index", in calculating $\bar{W}$ I disregarded position 1, and in calculating $\bar{S}$ I disregarded the final ictus, which, though not stressed 100%, still has especially high stressing

Table 2.5

Shakespeare: stress profiles of non-ictic positions by periods

Date	Period	Weak syllabic positions						Mean values $\bar{W}$ (3-9)	$\bar{S}$ (2-8)	Iambic index $\bar{S} - \bar{W}$	No. Lines
		1	3	5	7	9					
1588–1596	Titus Andronicus – King John	30.7	9.4	9.5	8.2	5.1		8.1	73.9	65.8	28,479
1596–1602	Merchant of Venice – Troilus and Cressida	25.4	10.1	10.0	10.3	7.1		9.4	72.2	62.8	15,214
1603–1606	Measure for Measure – Macbeth	24.8	11.2	10.4	13.3	10.2		11.3	72.5	61.2	9,959
1606–1613	Antony and Cleopatra – Henry VIII	21.5	11.7	9.8	12.6	11.2		11.3	73.1	61.8	14,699

Table 2.6

Stress profiles of Shakespeare's works (non-ictic positions)

Dramas and poems	Weak syllabic positions					Mean values		Iambic index
	1	3	5	7	9	$\bar{W}$ (3-9)	$\bar{S}$ (2-8)	$\bar{S} - \bar{W}$
Titus Andronicus	34.1	8.4	8.7	6.9	3.6	6.9	74.4	67.5
Henry VI, 1	33.4	8.1	7.2	5.1	3.6	6.0	72.6	66.6
Comedy of Errors	29.5	8.5	10.3	7.6	5.2	7.9	73.1	65.2
Henry VI, 2	30.6	8.8	7.7	7.9	3.4	7.0	74.8	67.8
Henry VI, 3	31.6	9.1	9.2	7.3	4.1	7.4	75.7	68.3
Taming of the Shrew	30.1	9.1	9.1	7.3	3.7	7.3	73.8	66.5
Richard III	32.3	11.3	9.6	8.3	5.0	8.6	73.4	64.8
Two Gentlemen of Verona	28.9	8.8	7.7	7.2	5.1	7.2	70.5	63.3
Love's Labour's Lost	30.0	12.3	12.2	10.4	7.7	10.7	74.8	64.1
Midsummer Night's Dream	28.2	9.5	10.4	9.3	6.6	9.0	73.7	64.7
Romeo and Juliet	33.2	13.4	13.0	12.3	7.5	8.3	74.2	65.9
Richard II	27.0	11.3	9.4	9.4	5.9	9.0	74.9	65.9
King John	27.5	10.0	9.8	8.4	6.2	8.6	73.4	64.8

Table 2.6 (cont.)

Merchant of Venice	22.6	9.6	10.1	9.0	5.9	8.7	72.3	63.6
Henry IV, 1	21.3	8.4	8.4	8.8	6.4	8.0	72.3	64.3
Henry IV, 2	24.2	11.7	9.8	8.8	7.7	9.5	72.3	62.8
Merry Wives of Windsor	26.9	9.6	14.0	10.2	9.1	10.7	75.3	64.6
Much Ado About Nothing	30.3	10.8	12.4	9.1	6.4	9.7	72.2	62.5
Henry V	25.3	10.1	8.4	10.0	6.5	8.8	72.0	63.2
Julius Caesar	30.6	10.5	11.9	11.7	7.1	10.3	71.5	61.2
As You Like It	26.6	10.2	9.2	9.2	7.5	9.0	71.4	62.4
Twelfth Night	24.9	9.8	10.2	12.3	7.0	9.8	71.9	62.1
Hamlet	24.5	9.2	9.1	11.5	8.2	9.5	71.2	61.7
Troilus and Cressida	26.4	11.4	10.7	11.5	7.4	10.3	74.3	64.0
Measure for Measure	24.0	9.3	9.2	13.3	8.6	10.1	70.6	60.5
Othello	25.8	11.4	10.4	12.9	9.1	11.0	72.6	61.6
All's Well That Ends Well	20.2	10.8	9.2	11.6	8.7	10.1	72.1	62.0
Timon of Athens	26.8	13.5	11.3	14.2	12.5	12.9	73.1	60.2

Table 2.6 (cont.)

King Lear	25.5	11.4	12.0	14.8	11.7	12.5	72.8	60.3
Macbeth	25.7	10.8	9.7	12.9	10.5	11.0	73.2	62.2
Antony and Cleopatra	24.4	11.1	10.2	14.1	11.0	11.6	73.3	61.7
Pericles	22.2	9.0	9.2	10.0	6.0	8.6	72.9	64.3
Coriolanus	20.7	10.4	8.9	12.1	10.7	10.5	71.1	61.2
Cymbeline	19.8	10.9	9.7	12.1	10.8	10.9	74.3	63.4
Winter's Tale	19.3	11.4	9.5	14.1	11.8	11.7	73.1	61.4
Tempest	20.9	14.8	10.5	12.7	14.1	13.0	74.0	61.0
Henry VIII	22.9	14.2	10.5	12.5	13.2	12.5	72.9	60.4
Venus and Adonis	27.9	10.6	9.5	9.3	6.0	9.4	75.7	66.3
Rape of Lucrece	22.3	10.8	8.7	8.3	4.9	8.2	78.6	70.4
Sonnets	23.2	11.2	10.4	9.2	8.6	9.9	75.7	65.8

typical only of the end of the line. Thus, the "iambic index" discussed in Chapter 2 et seq. qualifies the non-initial and non-final part of the line, i.e., reflects the opposition between $\overline{S}$ and $\overline{W}$ inside the line.

Consider first the generalized stress profiles of non-ictic positions by periods (cf. Fig. 2.3). Similarly with ictic stresses, non-ictic stress profiles show a gradual evolution: (1) a decrease of stress on the anacrusis, particularly between periods I-II and IIIa and IIIb; (2) an increase of mean stress from periods I through IIIb; (3) an increase of stress on non-ictuses in the second part of the line (positions 7,9); and (4) no position with a clear maximum of stressing in periods I and II, which changes to an absolute maximum on position 7 in the period IIIa, followed by high, almost equal stressing on positions 7 and 9 in period IIIb. In Period I position 1 receives six times more stress than position 9, while in IIIb the anacrusis gets only 1.9 times more stress than the last W. There is also a slight change in the iambic index: it falls, though not much, from Period I through IIIb: the contrast between ictic and non-ictic positions gets slightly effaced; thus Shakespeare's iambic pentameter moved somewhat closer to a purely syllabic form. Note how the curve of his non-ictic stresses gradually begins to resemble that of the speech model of verse (Fig. 2.3). The stressing of the verse anacrusis, however, never reaches the low index of the speech model of verse even in Period IIIb.

Let us now look at the non-ictic stress profiles of individual plays. Table 2.6 shows in greater detail the evolution of the anacrusis; its indices are particularly high in Period I, especially in the first tragedy, "Titus Andronicus". In addition to a relatively high anacrusis stressing, a relatively low $\bar{W}$ (positions 3,5,7,9) characterizes "Romeo and Juliet" in comparison with other plays of the same time bracket; this tragedy also displays the strongest opposition between strong and weak ictuses (Table 2.2). These features taken together single out "Romeo and Juliet" as Shakespeare's most rigid early play. The most rigid, crystallized iambic form accompanies a tragedy, while the loosest form is typical of comedies; e.g., the highest $\bar{W}$ of the first period is found in "Love's Labour's Lost".

There are two cases in the first period of an absolute maximum of non- ictic stressing in midline, on position 5. The latter is the first non-ictus of the second half-line of a bipartite line composition, 4+5 or 5+5 characteristic of a more rigid verse form ("The Comedy of Errors" and "A Midsummer Night's Dream"). In Period II the absolute maximum begins to shift from position 5 (in "The Merchant of Venice", "The Merry Wives of Windsor", and "Much Ado About Nothing") to position 7 (in "Henry V", "Twelfth Night", "Hamlet", and "Troilus and Cressida"), where it remains throughout Period IIIa and most of IIIb. Then in the two final plays the absolute maximum moves to the end of the line, position 9: the bipartite structure of the line becomes progressively more asymmetrical. Here are some typical examples (positions with non-ictic stresses are underlined and indicated by bracketed figures):

A wretched soul, / <u>bruised</u> with adversity (5)
("The Comedy of Errors" II,I:34)
Whiles it was ours /—<u>so</u> will it fare with Claudio (5)
("Much Ado About Nothing IV,I:222)
Go to their graves like beds, / <u>fight</u> for a plot (7)
("Hamlet" IV,IV:62)
Nor play at subtle games /—<u>fair</u> virtues all (7)
("Troilus and Cressida" IV,IV:87)
By nursing them, my lord. / <u>List</u> a <u>brief</u> tale (7,9)
("King Lear" V,IV:180)
Be free, and fare thou well . . . / <u>Please</u> you \ <u>draw</u> near (7,9)
("The Tempest" V,I:321)
As loud and to as many tunes; / <u>hats</u>, cloaks,— (9)
Deserve our better wishes. /—But, <u>sir</u>, sir (9)
("Henry VIII" IV,I:73, V,I:26)

Thus, in his stressing of non-ictuses Shakespeare's rhythmical evolution shows an even smoother trend than in his stressing of ictic positions.

2.5.2. We now consider more detailed data on the evolution of Shakespeare's non-ictic stressing. I analyze 800 lines from two plays, one of the earliest, "Richard II" (act I fully and act II, scene I, 165 first lines), and his latest, "Henry VIII" (800 lines of the "Shakespearean" portion (see Chapter 3, section 2): act I, scenes I and II, act II, scenes III and IV fully, and the first 19 pentameter lines from act III, scene I). To compare with Shakespeare, I analyze 800 lines from a rhythmically loose nineteenth-century romantic tragedy: Shelley's "The Cenci" (act IV fully and act V, scenes I and II fully, and the 24 first lines of scene III) (Table 2.7).

There is a gradation in the strength of syntactic ties between words in a sentence; therefore some cases referred to the category "phrase-initial extrametrical stresses" are more unquestionable than others. Compare: *In your offence? / <u>Speak</u> truth and the whole truth* and *And I will pass,\ <u>wrapped</u> in a vile disguise* (Shelley, "The Cenci" V,II:4 and V,I:85). In questionable cases I took into account the relative strength of ties between words within a "phrase" and at the "phrase boundary" and expansion/unexpansion of sentence members. For example, expanded subject groups or predicate groups were considered capable of forming separate phrases, while an unexpanded subject plus an unexpanded predicate were treated as one syntactic group. Compare: *<u>I</u> with my words \ <u>killed</u> her and all her kin*, and *Spare me! My <u>brain</u> swims round . . . I cannot speak* (Shelley, "The Cenci" V,II:143,88).

I considered the beginnings of phrases to be formed by the first notional (lexical) word. Therefore, for example, in the line *My God! I did not kill him; I <u>know</u> nothing* (Shelley, "The Cenci" V,I:5); <u>know</u> was considered to begin a phrase. In the line *In which you stand that gives you this <u>pale</u> sickness* (Shelley, "The Cenci" V,I:28) <u>pale</u> was considered a mid-phrase case of non-ictic stressing.

Table 2.7

Differentiated stress profiles of non-ictic positions
(each excerpt 300 lines)

Shakespeare, "Richard I"
Monosyllables

Location in phrase	Type of syntactic relation	Non-ictic positions								
		1		3		5		7		9
Phrase beginning	Proclitic link	67	8.4	6	0.8	23	2.9	7	0.9	2	0.3
	Syntactically more autonomous	85	10.6	3	0.3	14	1.7	9	1.1	--
	Total	152	19.0	9	1.1	37	4.6	16	2.0	2	0.3
Mid-phrase and end of phrase	Proclitic link	67	8.4	17	2.1	42	5.3	25	3.1	--
	Enclitic link	11	1.4	21	2.6	4	0.5	4	0.5	--
	Syntactically more autonomous	--		1	0.2	--		--		--
	Total	88	9.8	39	4.9	46	5.8	29	3.6	--
Monosyllables, total		240	28.8	48	6.0	83	10.2	45	5.6	2	0.3

Polysyllables

	1		3		5		7		9	
Phrase beginning	37	4.6	--		4		1	0.2	--	
Mid-phrase	1	0.1	--		--		--		1	0.2
Polysyllables, total	38	4.7	--		4	0.5	1	0.2	1	0.2
Monosyllables and polysyllables, total	278	34.7	48	6.0	87	10.7	46	5.8	3	0.5

Shakespeare, "Henry VIII"
Monosyllables

Location in phrase	Type of syntactic relation	1		3		5		7		9	
Phrase beginning	Proclitic link	28	3.5	2	0.3	2	0.3	26	3.3	38	4.8
	Syntactically more autonomous	40	5.0	--		8	1.0	26	3.3	3	0.3
	Total	68	8.5	2	0.3	10	1.3	52	6.6	41	5.1
Mid-phrase and end-phrase	Proclitic link	20	2.5	50	6.3	32	4.0	17	2.1	43	5.4
	Enclitic link	--		20	2.5	16	1.8	12	1.5	8	1.0
	Syntactically more autonomous	18	2.3	1	0.1	--		2	0.3	--	
	Total	38	4.8	71	8.9	46	5.8	31	3.9	51	6.4
Monosyllables total		106	13.3	73	9.1	56	7.0	83	10.4	92	11.5

Table 2.7 (cont.)

Polysyllables

Phrase beginning		16	2.0	6	0.8	1	0.1	6	0.8	--
Mid-phrase and end-phrase		13	1.6	--		1	0.1	1	0.1	--
Polysyllables, total		29	3.6	6	0.8	2	0.2	7	0.9	--
Monosyllables and polysyllables, total		135	16.9	79	9.9	58	7.3	90	11.3	92	11.5

Shelley, "The Cenci"

Monosyllables

Phrase beginning	Proclitic link	37	4.6	4	0.5	16	2.0	9	1.2	29	3.6
	Syntactically more autonomous	78	9.8	1	0.1	32	4.0	21	2.6	8	1.0
	Total	115	14.4	5	0.6	48	6.0	30	3.8	37	4.6
Mid-phrase and end-phrase	Proclitic link	9	1.1	87	10.9	25	3.1	17	2.1	33	4.1
	Enclitic link	--		2	0.6	4	0.5	2	0.3	2	0.3
	Syntactically more autonomous	14	118	3	0.4	5	0.7	1	0.1	3	0.4
	Total	23	2.9	92	11.9	34	4.3	20	2.5	38	4.8
Monosyllables, total		138	17.3	97	12.1	82	10.3	50	6.3	75	9.5

Polysyllables

Phrase beginning	26	3.3	1		12	1.5	9	1.2	4	0.5
Mid-phrase and end-phrase	22	2.8	--		3	0.4	3	0.4	--	
Polysyllables, total	48	6.1	1		15	1.9	12	1.6	4	0.5
Monosyllables and polysyllables, total	253	31.6	98	12.2	97	12.1	62	7.8	79	10.0

I also differentiated proclitic and enclitic types of syntactic link within a phrase containing a strongly stressed monosyllable on W (for more detail see Chapters 6 and 7) as opposed to cases where the stressed word on W is more syntactically autonomous. In the first category the stressed monosyllable on W is syntactically linked to the following or, less often, preceding adjacent word with a strong ictic stress. The word on W is often syntactically (and probably accentually) subordinate to the adjacent word with a strong stress on S. Some examples are: *With these w̆eak wŏmen's fears. A noble spirit* (a proclitic link in *w̆eak wŏmen's*); *Such doubts, as false cŏin, from it. The k̆ing lŏves you* (an enclitic link in *false coin* and a proclitic link in *king loves*); *Sir, I desire you do*

75

me right and justice (a syntactically autonomous stressed word Sir on W) (Shakespeare, "Henry VIII" III,II:169,171 and II,IV:13).

Let us now compare the tendencies in non-ictic stressing in early and late Shakespeare; later, comparison of Shakespearean verse with that of the nineteenth century will lead to more general conclusions concerning the tendencies in non-ictic stressing in English dramatic iambic pentameter.

Consider first the monosyllables on W.

The already mentioned decrease of stressing on the anacrusis in the course of Shakespeare's poetic career is mainly caused by monosyllabic words: their number in "Henry VIII" is one-half that in "Richard II". (The number of disyllabic non-oxytonic polysyllables has not decreased so drastically.) The syntactic characteristics of monosyllables in the anacrusis has also evolved: in "Richard II" monosyllables are more often syntactically autonomous, while in "Henry VIII" they are usually syntactically subordinate to the following word; compare: *Join with the present sickness that I have; Live in thy shame but die not shame with thee!*; *Right, you say true—as Hereford's love, so his* ("Richard II" II,I:132,135,145), and: *Made former wonders its. To-day the French*; *Shone down the English; and to-morrow they Made Britain India: every man that stood* ("Henry VIII" I,I:18,20,21). Thus, line beginnings are more strongly marked and more opposed to the prose tendencies in "Richard II" than in "Henry VIII" (cf. Tarlinskaja and Teterina 1974: Table IV, speech models (D) of "quasi" iambic pentameter).

Conversely, the number of extrametrical monosyllables in midline is two times higher in "Henry VIII" than in "Richard II". Their "peak" has moved from position 5 ("Richard II") to 7 and 9: one of the signs of a changed rhythmical-syntactic line segmentation in early and late Shakespeare. This becomes particularly clear if we follow the distribution of phrase-beginning monosyllables on W: their peak is on position 5 in "Richard II" and on 7 (followed by 9) in "Henry VIII". Compare: *There lives or dies \ true to King Richard's throne* ("Richard II" I,III:86) and *Things to strike honour sad. / Bid him recount*; *Out of the Duke of Buckingham. /—Speak freely* ("Henry VIII" I,II:126,131).

Mid-phrase and phrase-final strongly stressed monosyllables on W typically have syntactic ties with an adjacent word with a strong ictic stress. Their number within the line is considerably higher than that of phrase-beginning extrametrical stresses. Strongly stressed monosyllables on W are more evenly distributed along the line of "Richard II" than "Henry VIII". In the latter, extrametrical mid-phrase monosyllables gravitate to position 3; their number decreases from position 3 through 7 and increases in position 9: their relatively low number in position 7 is another sign of a prevailing syntactic line segmentation after positions 6 or 7 (see also Chapter 4). The number of proclitics is everywhere higher than enclitics; the number of enclitics on W has not changed substantially from "Richard II" through "Henry VIII". Their almost unchanged proportion (5-7 cases per 1000 lines) is one of the features of Shakespeare's rhythmical idiosyncrasy (see also Chapter 6).

On the whole, the number of syntactically autonomous strongly stressed monosyllables is much higher in the anacrusis than within the line: syntactically subordinate monosyllables tend to weaken their sentence accent; quite obviously Shakespeare was trying to tone down the rhythm-breaking effect of extrametrical monosyllables used on non-initial W.

The ictic stress profile in "The Cenci" is not unlike late Shakespeare; it is 58.4—79.2—72.1—69.6—89.2 (with a slight "dip" in ictus IV). The non-ictic stressing of monosyllables is not unlike "Henry VIII": the total number of cases is close; the stressing of the anacruses is similar, and differs from the tendency of "Richard II". Both in "Henry VIII" and "The Cenci" strong stresses on W caused by monosyllables are generously distributed among all midline non-ictic positions. In both plays position 9 is frequently stressed, emphasizing the frequent strong syntactic break (often foregrounded by a change of speakers) after position 8: *That enters whistling as in scorn.* Come, follow!; *And more depends on God than me.* Well . . . well . . . ; *To poison and corrupt her soul.*—One, *two* ("The Cenci" IV,III:42, IV,I:43,45). However, the number of monosyllables in position 5, particularly of phrase-beginning ones, is almost five times higher in "The Cenci" than in "Henry VIII": the syntactic seam after positions 4/5 is much stronger in "The Cenci", while in "Henry VIII" it is typically in the second half of the line. A split after 6/7 is not characteristic of "The Cenci"; a more typical syntactic line segmentation is not unlike that in "Richard II", for example: *Be overworn?* Tame her with chains and famine? ("The Cenci" IV,I:8). Both Shakespearean tendencies, earlier and later, occur in Shelley's play at the same time.

Similarly with Shakespeare's verse, the "mid-hemistich" non-ictic positions of "The Cenci" "prefer" syntactically subordinate mid-phrase strongly stressed monosyllables. They are particularly numerous in position 3 and relatively many in 9. If two stressed monosyllables occur in positions 1 and 3 of the same line, the first is typically more syntactically autonomous, while the second syntactically subordinate to the following word, for example: Lífe a wòrse hèll *than that beyond the grave* ("The Cenci" IV,I:48) (see also Chapter 7). Enclitics on W are not typical of Shelley's rhythmical style (1 per 1000 lines). Similarly with Shakespeare's verse, they may form phrase-final extrametrical stresses, which tend to be accentually smoothed, being syntactically linked to the preceding word, for example: *When* hígh Gòd *grants He punishes and prayers,* or: *Like the last thoughts of* sóme dày *sweetly spent* ("The Cenci" IV,I:138 and V,III:3).

Polysyllabic words causing extrametrical stresses on W are typically disyllabic non-oxytones. Their stress, unlike that of some oxytonic words, never shifts onto the other syllable. Such polysyllables cause a more obvious "breach" of the prevailing iambic rhythm and are more restricted in their position within the line, particularly in a more rigid type of verse. Thus, in 800 lines from "Richard II" there occur only 44 cases of non-oxytonic polysyllables causing extrametrical stressing on W. Of these, 42 (or almost 96%) begin a phrase, and 37 (84%) also begin the line, for example: *Further I say, and further will maintain* ("Richard II,I:98). Most midline cases (four out of five) occur in positions 5-6, that is, the beginning of the second "hemistich", for example: *Make pale our cheek, chasing the royal blood* ("Richard II" II,I:118). If the poet had not been conscious of the "hemistich" segmentation of his line, such cases would occur anywhere in the line, provided it was the beginning of a phrase. There are only two cases in the eight hundred lines analyzed when the disyllabic word does not begin a phrase. One of them is a non-oxytonic word in positions 1-2 (absence of a phrase-beginning position is compensated by the line-beginning position of the "offending" word), and the other is an oxytonic word on positions 8-9; a recessive shift of stress in this word is almost a certainty. Here are the two cases: *Farewell, my lord, securely I espy Virtue and valour couched in thine eye* ("Richard II" I,III:97-98) (virtue, a direct object, obviously forms a phrase with the verb in the preceding line); *In wholesome counsel to his unstaid youth?* ("Richard II" II,I:2).

In the looser verse of "Henry VIII" relatively more rhythm-disrupting polysyllables occur in mid-phrases and fewer, compared to "Richard II", at the beginning of the line. Almost half of the line-beginning non-oxytones do not begin a phrase, for example: *And like her true nobility she has Carried herself towards me.—Most gracious sir* ("Henry VIII" II,IV:142-143). However, none of the rhythm-disrupting mid-phrase non-oxytones occur in the middle of the line; they only occur at the beginning. The poet was very conscious of the linear segmentation of his verse (see also Chapter 7).

The place of the phrase-beginning midline non-oxytones, compared to "Richard II", has shifted to the right: six out of seven "rhythm-disrupting" midline non-oxytonic words occur in positions 7-8, emphasizing the late Shakespearean line segmentation. Some examples are: *Another spread on's breast, mounting his eyes,* or: *A thousand pounds a year, annual support* ("Henry VII" I,II:205, II,III:64).

Five out of eight cases of midline "rhythm-disrupting" oxytones are in fact also phrase-beginning: they are the first lexical word of a phrase and occur in positions 2-3, for example: *This compelled fortune! . . .* ; *His confessor, who fed him . . .* ; *My surveyor is false . . .* ; *Can advise me like you* ("Henry VIII" II,III:87, I,II:149, I,I:222,135). The three remaining cases are located in mid-phrase, for example: *Of the duke's confessor, John de la Car* ("Henry VIII" I,I:218). In all probability such words underwent a recessive stress shift and did not, after all, disrupt the prevailing iambic rhythm. If there was a stress shift, however, and if such words did not disrupt the rhythm, why do they appear only in a looser verse (cf. with Shelley's)?

Rhythm-disrupting polysyllables are more typical of "The Cenci" than of

"Henry VIII". Similarly with "Henry VIII", half of the line-beginning non-oxytones do not begin a phrase, for example:

Upon such evidence that justifies
Torture.—What evidence? This man's?—Even so.

("The Cenci" V,I:76-77)

It is significant, however, that only four cases out of the twenty-six mid-phrase "inversions" caused by non-oxytonic lexical words occur in midline (two on positions 5-6, and two on positions 7-8), for example: *If thou hast done murders, made thy life's path* ("The Cenci" V,II:134). Twenty-two cases (over 80%) occur at the beginning of the line: as with Shakespeare, Shelley was conscious of the linear segmentation of his verse.

Of the eight cases of oxytonic words on positions SW (as many as in our 800 lines from "Henry VIII"), only four occur at the beginning of the phrase, e.g., *I demand who were the participators* ("The Cenci" V,II:3) and the other four in mid-phrase, as in *A gulf of obscure hatred* . . . ("The Cenci" IV,IV:100). However such words probably shifted their stress to the first syllable and did not disrupt the iambic rhythm.

In conclusion, we can state that an evolution of non-ictic stressing in Shakespeare is clearly apparent if we consider it in greater detail. Two equally important conclusions are of a more general character and relevant for our understanding of the nature of English iambic pentameter:

(1) There is a considerable difference in the positioning of monosyllables and polysyllables causing extrametrical stresses on W. Even in a looser variant of English iambic pentameter "rhythm-disrupting" polysyllables are positionally more restricted than monosyllables; they gravitate to the beginnings of lines and phrases.

(2) Linear line segmentation is obviously more metrically relevant for the poets than syntactic segmentation into phrases (cf. Hayes' opposite point of view: Hayes 1984; see also Chapter 7).

2.6 Evolution of ictic stresses in Marlowe's and Byron's poetic cycles

To see just how universal are the evolutionary tendencies of Shakespeare's dramatic cycle we now consider the cycles of two other poets: Shakespeare's older contemporary, Marlowe, and a poet of a completely different epoch, Byron. Marlowe, like Shakespeare, wrote for the stage; Byron, like most poets of the nineteenth century, did not write for the theatre but addressed his verse to a reader rather than to a listener-spectator. Marlowe's and Byron's dramatic cycles are short compared with Shakespeare's. Their plays were written during a period of less than ten years, but even so they also show signs of change.

2.6.1 Evolution of rhythm in Marlowe's dramas

Marlowe's dramas were less well preserved than Shakespeare's. Marlowe's Company, "Lord Admiral's Servants", was not as strong and permanent as

Shakespeare's, and Marlowe did not have such devoted friends as did Shakespeare in Heminge and Condell, who carefully collected variants of his plays and, having rejected pieces spoilt by mendings, restored and preserved a genuine author's text. Marlowe's plays are supposed to have been considerably tampered with after his death. It is possible that some parts were lost and restored from memory by actors and directors; maybe they were amended by the introduction of buffoonery and coarse comic scenes which were liked by unsophisticated provincial spectators (see, e.g., Boas 1925:50-52, Wilson 1953:57-75). The middle scenes of "Doctor Faustus" (at the Pope's; and the miracles worked by Faustus with the help of Mephistopheles) were probably written or amended by someone else. In 1602 Henslowe ordered William Bird and Samuel Rowley to prepare some "additions" to the play. It is quite possible that these additions were the middle scenes, in which the verse rhythm is indeed quite different from the rest of the text.

The dating of Marlowe's plays has also been a subject of controversy. In tables 2.8 and 2.9 they are arranged according to Legouis and Cazamian (1971:399-406). In contrast, F.P. Wilson believed that "The Jew of Malta" was Marlowe's second play, while "Faustus" was his last play written after "Edward II" and simultaneously with the first two sestiades of the poem "Hero and Leander".

The rhythmical style of the early Marlowe is characterized by the following features: a) weak stressing on the medium, third ictus (position 6); b) an opposition between strong and weak ictuses; c) a considerable weakening of the final ictus caused by unstressed syllables of polysyllabic words (often in an archaic syllabic form), e.g.:

> Where Sigismund, the King of Hunga<u>ry</u> . . .
> What! shall we parle with the Christi<u>an</u>?
> Proud Tamburlaine, that now in As<u>ia</u> . . .
> Though from the shortest northern paral<u>lel</u> . . .
> ("Tamburlaine" I,I:9,11,16,25)

The last peculiarity explains why in Marlowe's stress profiles the penultimate ictuses are more strongly stressed on the average than the final ones. Weakening of the final ictus by unstressed syllables of polysyllabic words is in general typical of earlier Elizabethan dramas. Such a termination of lines probably helped create a distinct segmentation in the recitation in open theatres (and earlier in inn yards). It might have required a certain special actor's intonation which was simplified in the performance of later dramas and ultimately disappeared. One may recall Hamlet's advice to the actors: he asks them to avoid shouting out their lines like a town-crier, not to split the ears of the groundlings; to act with restraint, and not to saw the air too much with their hands ("Hamlet", act II, scene II).

In none of the earlier dramas, however, is the last ictus ever weaker than the

Table 2.8

Stress profiles of Marlowe's dramas (strong syllabic positions)

Date	Drama	Positions						Mean	Correlation between positions					Mean non-ictus stress	No. Lines
		2	4	6	8	10			4-2	4-6	8-6	10-8		
1587	Tamburlaine	70.2	86.9	66.3	79.7	75.3		75.7	+16.7	+20.6	+13.4	- 4.4	7.2	2185
1588	Doctor Faustus	70.0	86.0	67.0	78.7	75.9		75.5	+16.0	+19.0	+11.7	- 2.8	11.9	1230
1589	The Jew of Malta	66.2	83.8	62.9	73.9	81.0		73.6	+17.6	+20.9	+11.0	+ 7.1	13.2	1786
1589	The Massacre in Paris	70.7	86.7	69.3	73.7	85.1		77.1	+16.0	+17.4	+ 4.4	+11.4	9.5	1029
1590	Dido*	68.5	84.3	74.0	72.1	90.8		77.9	+15.8	+10.3	- 1.9	+18.7	11.4	1706
1592	Edward II	69.6	81.8	74.6	72.1	85.3		76.7	+12.2	+ 7.2	- 2.5	+13.2	12.9	2412

*Finished by Thomas Nash

Table 2.9

Stress profiles of Marlowe's dramas
(weak syllabic positions)

Play	Positions					Mean 3-9	Mean 2-8	Iambic Index S - W
	1	3	5	7	9			
Tamburlaine	24.6	3.9	4.4	3.1	1.1	3.1	75.8	72.7
Doctor Faustus	34.6	6.7	8.3	7.3	2.8	6.3	75.4	69.1
The Jew of Malta	34.3	8.3	9.6	9.3	4.7	8.0	71.7	63.7
The Massacre in Paris	25.8	6.9	7.9	5.2	1.8	5.5	75.1	69.6
Dido	29.5	8.2	8.5	7.5	3.5	6.9	74.7	67.8
Edward II	34.3	8.2	10.1	8.3	3.5	7.5	74.5	67.0

fourth, a rhythmic pattern typical of the earlier Marlowe's verse style. "Doctor Faustus", therefore, could not be the poet's last play: rhythmical peculiarities of this drama place "Doctor Faustus", and not "The Jew of Malta", immediately after "Tamburlaine". The opposition between strong and weak ictuses is less in "Doctor Faustus" and the inversion of stressing between ictuses IV-V is not so striking as in "Tamburlaine", whereas in "The Jew of Malta" this correlation is reversed. The trend continues in the following dramas, and only slightly diminishes in "Edward II". The strength of ictus III grows from drama to drama, while the strength of ictus IV falls; thus the third and the fourth ictuses are practically leveled in "The Massacre in Paris", and ictus IV becomes weaker than ictus III in "Dido, Queen of Carthage" and especially in "Edward II". Therefore, the stress profiles show that "Edward II" was Marlowe's last drama. The leveling-out of the third and the fourth ictuses in the first two sestiades of "Hero and Leander" must be a peculiarity of its genre: the lines in lyrical and narrative poems are more symmetrical than in dramas of the same period (see section 2.7).

We see that even in Marlowe's short cycle of poorly preserved dramas there is an evident evolution in rhythmical style: from a more symmetrical to a less symmetrical line, from more archaic to less archaic structure of line endings. Therefore, Marlowe's cycle, like Shakespeare's, underwent the evolution characteristic of Elizabethan drama. But Marlowe began his career as a playwright five or six years earlier than Shakespeare, which is why his earlier dramas have the traces of an even more archaic rhythmical style. The end of his career came too soon, therefore the evolution of his verse did not go as far as Shakespeare's. Besides, both Marlowe and Shakespeare, naturally, have idiosyncratic individual features (cf. their structure of endings). But the logic and the direction of the evolution is very much alike and corresponds to the tendency of the period; still, the stages (synchronic sections) of individual cycles did not coincide. Thus, the already asymmetrical verse of the late Marlowe existed side by side with the still symmetrical verse of the earlier Shakespeare.

2.6.2 Evolution of rhythm in Byron's dramas (Tables 2.10, 2.11)

Byron's four dramas belong to his late period and were written in a very short space of time (1821-1823). Even the first play analyzed, "Marino Faliero", already has an asymmetrical line structure: the fourth ictus is weaker than the third. Some examples are:

That it should fall to me! / and that my days	(8)
Proud Genoa's prouder rival! / 'Tis to sap	(8)
So let them die the death. /—We are prepared	(8)
Abatement of your punishment, / the Giunta	(8)
("Marino Faliero" V,I:6,17,20,23)	

Earlier Byron, heir to the eighteenth-century classical traditions, began with a more rigid, more symmetrical verse, with a "dip" on position 6. Some examples from earlier Byron are:

What goodly prospects \ o'er the hills expand!	(6)
But man would mar them \ with an impious hand:	(6)
On sloping mounds, / or in the vale beneath,	(6)
Thy fairy dwelling \ is as lone as thou!	(6)
("Childe Harold's Pilgrimage" I,XV:4-5, XXII:1, XXIII:4)	

The stressing (in percentage) of the third and the fourth ictuses in "Childe Harold" is 76.8 and 78.2%, while in "Beppo" and "Don Juan" is, respectively, 75.4-65.7 and 76.2-69.7% (Tarlinskaja 1976: Table 41, p. 279). Then also the strength of ictus II decreases from drama to drama and the opposition between strong and weak ictuses on the whole levels sequentially: the difference between ictuses II and III (positions 4 and 6) falls from "Marino Faliero" through "Werner" in the following way: +11.2, +9.7, +6.9, +2.4 (Table 2.10). The mean non-ictic stressing (positions 3,5,7,9) increases from 8.8 to 12.1% (Table 2.11). Thus, even in a short group of dramas written in a short space of time and in a period quite different from Elizabethan reveals a similar evolutionary tendency: a greater prosaization of rhythm and a decrease in "verse-prose" opposition.

The inner logics of the evolution from piece to piece within a verse cycle generally goes in the direction of a decreased "verse-prose" opposition and a movement closer to prose tendencies. An evolution from a more rigid to a looser form seems to be in general characteristic of individual poets' styles. An

Table 2.10

Stress profiles of Byron's dramas (strong syllabic positions)

Drama	Positions					Mean	Correlation between positions			No. Lines
	2	4	6	8	10		4-2	4-6	8-6	
Marino Faliero	64.9	76.1	71.6	66.4	89.0	73.6	+11.2	+4.5	-5.2	3486
Sardanapalus	67.2	76.9	73.7	68.1	88.4	74.9	+ 9.7	+3.2	-5.6	2834
The Two Foscari	67.9	74.8	71.4	68.3	82.0	72.9	+ 6.9	+3.4	-3.1	1989
Werner	71.0	73.4	73.4	66.3	83.4	73.5	+ 2.4	0	-7.1	3225

Table 2.11

Stress profiles of Byron's dramas
(weak syllabic positions)

Play	Positions					Mean 3-9	Mean 2-3	Iambic index S - W
	1	3	5	7	9			
Marino Faliero	21.8	10.9	8.4	7.8	9.0	8.8	69.6	61.0
Sardanapalus	23.34	13.0	11.5	10.4	11.9	11.7	71.4	59.7
The Two Foscari	20.5	14.5	10.4	10.1	11.0	11.5	70.6	59.1
Werner	22.6	13.7	10.0	11.8	12.1	11.9	71.0	59.1

evolution was discovered even in Pope's poems (Tarlinskaja 1976: Table 41; see also below). This process resembles the evolution of one's handwriting from the beginning to the end of a letter. An opposite process is less typical. I can think of only two examples: Chaucer's verse evolved from tonic to syllabo-tonic, and Wyatt's from syllabic to syllabo-tonic (cf. Wright 1985). The verse of these poets, then, are examples of a canon in the making.

2.7 Shakespeare's non-dramatic verse

The dramatic and non-dramatic verse of the same poet do not always develop in a uniform and parallel way. Thus the stress profiles of Shakespeare's two poems, "Venus and Adonis" and "The Rape of Lucrece", do not correspond to the stress profiles of his dramas of the same period (Tables 2.2, 2.6). The strength of the second ictus in both poems and particularly in the sonnets is higher than in any play of Period I; it approaches 90%, a point never reached in the dramatic verse. The almost constant strength of the final ictus (93-97%) has no parallel in any drama of the period. Such a high stress is approached only in "King Lear", written 8 to 14 years later than the sonnets and the poems. The mean ictic stress and the "iambic index" are also very high, particularly in "The Rape of Lucrece". And last but not least, the correlation between ictuses III and IV in the first poem is not typical of the period: the fourth ictus in "Venus and Adonis" is a little weaker than the third. In "The Rape of Lucrece" and in the sonnets the correlation is more typical of the period: ictus III is noticeably weaker than IV (cf. with "Henry VI", part 1). An impression is formed that in his non-dramatic verse Shakespeare varied his rhythmical style, only gradually moving to the hemistich line segmentation so typical of his earlier dramas. A longer first hemistich (*"A mayore"*) occurs in the Italian hendecasyllabic verse line, while a shorter first hemistich ("*A *minore"*) characterizes the French decasyllabic verse. It is quite possible that Italian verse form influenced the structure of Shakespeare's early non-dramtic verse, while in his later non-dramatic verse the poet followed the already consolidated inertia of his own dramatic verse. Here are some examples of missing ictic stresses on the eighth position typical of "Venus and Adonis", which help to form "*A mayore*":

"Thrice fairer than myself",/thus she began
If thou wilt deign this favour,/for they meed
A thousand honey secrets \ shalt thou know
Courageously to pluck him \ from his horse
Each leaning on their elbows \ and their hips
Now doth she stroke his cheek,/now doth he frown,
He burns with bashful shame;/she with her tears.
Doth quench the maiden burning \ of his cheeks, etc.
                    ("Venus and Adonis" 7,15,16,30,44,45,49,50)

The asymmetric bipartite line segmentation, typical of "Venus and Adonis", is also obvious in the lines without missing midline ictic stresses, e.g.:

Even as an empty eagle,/sharp by fast
Tires with her beak on feathers,\ flesh and bone, etc.
                    ("Venus and Adonis" 55,56)

With the exception of the hypothetical earlier substrate of "Titus Andronicus" (see Chapter 3), Shakespeare began his earlier plays with the "*A minore*" type of first "hemistich". This was probably more convenient for the actors and easier for the audience: ta-tá ta-tá (stop) ta- ta-ta-tá ta-tá , or: ta-tá ta-tá -ta (stop) ta-ta-tá ta-tá.

The fact that the "hemistich" structure "*A mayore*" did not strike root in the rigid variant of English pentameter, but is characteristic of both the archaic, early, still forming verse and of the later, looser verse approaching prose (Tarlinskaja 1976: Table 41, pp. 279-280), may be explained in the following way. A longer first "half-line" and the missing stress on the eighth position are typical of the prose model of English iambic pentameter (see above)which is the consequence of longer words in prose than in rigid verse, and of the particular distribution of word and phrase boundaries in an English sentence. In the periods of a rigid verse form and a strong verse-prose opposition, the poets preferred a syntactic break after positions 4/5; they avoided a longer first "half-line" and concentrated missing ictic stresses on position six. In the periods of looser form, when the "verse-prose" opposition was still weak or already beginning to decrease, the first half-line was long (the syntactic break occurred after positions 6-7), its volume approached that of a phrase in prose, and the maximum of missing ictic stresses moved along the line to position eight.

The marked rhythmical divergence between Shakespeare's dramatic and non-dramatic verse clearly shows that it is erroneous to draw a direct parallel between the genres and to attribute Shakespeare's earlier plays on the ground of their resemblance to his poems: genre differences between Shakespeare's dramatic and non-dramatic verse are considerable and take place not only at the level of rhythm but on other levels of verse structure as well.

Thus we have seen there is both a marked chronological and a marked genre variation of accentual structure in Shakespeare's canon of iambic pentameter verse, as well as a marked evolution of certain rhythmical parameters.

2.8 Evolution of the syllabic structure in Shakespeare's verse

The primary aim in this chapter has been to formulate the most general characteristics of the accentual structure of Shakespeare's verse. The "vertical", stress profile analyses of Shakespeare's canon have helped to discover an evolution of his rhythmical style over the whole of his 25-year writing career. But accentual peculiarities of metrical verse do not encompass the full scope of a poet's rhythmical style, particularly within the English literary tradition— there is also a syllabic aspect.

The model of iambic pentameter theoretically requires that every ictic and non-ictic position be filled with only one syllable. The English literary verse, however, influenced by a long-standing tradition of syllabic variability in its medieval and folk poetry (cf. Tarlinskaja 1973, 1974a, 1976: Chapter 4) allows, within certain limits, "deviations" from this general rule. Non-ictic positions of iambic pentameter, particularly in the dramatic genre, may, to an accepted, "non-offensive" proportion, be filled with two syllables, usually in the anacrusis (position 1) or on the hemistich boundary (positions 5 or 7). Less frequently a syllable may be missing from a non-ictic position (usually 1 or 5) and even less frequently, from an ictus (cf. Tarlinskaja 1976:160-164). Some examples are as follows. Disyllabic non-ictic positions: **one**: *Bŭt thĭs nĭght, sweet Alice, thou hast killed my heart*; **five**: *I cannot ĕat, bŭt Ĭ'll sĭt for company* (Anonymous, "Arden of Faversham" I:63,360); **seven**: *A good night be it thĕn, ănd ă lŏng one, madam* (Beaumont and Fletcher, "The Maid's Tragedy" V:I,10). Missing syllables: position **one**:_ _ _ *With a truth.—If 'twere to do again*; **seven**: *But they are all as ill._ _ _ This false smile*; **six**: *And every Ill. But_ _ _ stay, stay, my friend* (Beaumont and Fletcher, "The Maid's Tragedy III,I:94; II,II:51; III,I:58).

In analyzing the syllabic structure of English verse one has to decide how to treat certain doubtful, ambiguous cases. The difficult cases fall into four main groups: (1)polysyllables which may or may not have had a syncopated form, e.g., heartily, dignity, Imogen; (2) words where a sonorant preceded by a consonant may have either been syllabic or non-syllabic, as in noble, people, prison, heaven, haven, uncle, discomfortable, unseasonable; (3) cases where the so-called triphthongs [aiə] and [auə] might have been either monosyllabic

87

or disyllabic, as in <u>fire</u>, <u>violent</u>, <u>flower</u>, or <u>power</u>; and (4) instances of hiatus, when two syllables belonging to two different words contain two "colliding" vowels, or a vowel and an [h], and occupy the same syllabic position as in *Nay, that's a mŏck:Ĭ hăve sĕen a lady's nose*, or *Give me. the bòy, Ĭ ăm glàd you did not nurse him* (Shakespeare, "The Winter's Tale" II,I:14,56). Should the latter cases be treated as elisions not leading to disyllabic combinations on a W, or should they be considered two independent syllables filling one and the same non-ictic position? Differences in interpreting cases (1)-(4) cause discrepancies in the percentages of lines containing disyllabic combinations between adjacent ictuses; therefore I shall give a resume of the principles that guided my evulation of the syllabic length of words.

In the analysis I was guided not only by the general rules of Modern English phonology (the syllable-forming properties of sounds) but also by the way the questionable cases are typically used in Elizabethan verse. Thus, I not only proceded "from language to verse", but also "from verse to language". Turning to verse itelf in order to find answers to linguistic problems is, of course, not new; this approach has been often used, for example, by students of Slavic and Germanic languages; e.g., Ellis 1871, König 1888, Košutic 1919, Scholl 1944, Kökeritz 1953, Sprott 1953, Dobson 1957, 1967, Panov 1967, Sipe 1968, Grigorjev 1971, Halle and Keyser 1971, Tarlinskaja 1976, Bjorklund 1978, Cercignani 1981, Hayes 1983. Verse as a specific speech structure has peculiarities of its own; poets sometimes make a wide use of forms which, though "legitimate", rarely appear in non-poetic speech, but happen to suit the needs of the meter (cf. Halle and Keyser 1971, Tarlinskaja 1974). However, on the whole the same general language laws operate both in verse and prose.

Comparison of the frequency of <u>full and syncopated</u> forms of such words as <u>heartily</u> or <u>Imogen</u> in the Elizabethan-Jacobean poetry shows that on the whole full forms dominate over reduced ones, particularly in the earlier, Elizabethan verse. A reduction of the middle vowel usually occurs: (a) before sonorants [l,m,n,r] (which can compensate the loss of a vowel) more often than before other types of consonants; that is why such words as <u>heartily</u>, <u>cardinal</u>, <u>murderer</u> are more easily syncopated than words like <u>majesty</u>, <u>negligent</u>, <u>covetous</u>; (b) in common nouns more often than in proper names, such as <u>Mortimer</u>, <u>Pericles</u>, <u>Imogen</u> (c) in words used in the middle of a phrase, especially in an attributive function, more often than in syntactically more independent words terminating a phrase, and particularly <u>both</u> a phrase <u>and</u> a verse line (cf. Scholl 1944, Fussell 1954, Kökeritz 1953: esp. p. 521, Tarlinskaja 1976:20-39). Here are four "clusters" of examples illustrating the occurrence of full and syncopated forms of four words:

1. (a) fully syllabic: *Yonder is Edward with his <u>flatterers</u>*; (b) syncopated: *No, Edward, no; thy <u>flatterers</u> faint and fly* (Marlowe, "Edward II" XI:195,200), or: *As fear or <u>flattering</u> words may make him false* (Kyd, "The Spanish Tragedy III,II:83);

2. (a) fully syllabic: *With these, O, these accursed <u>murderers</u>* (Kyd, "The

Spanish Tragedy" IV,III:161), or: *Find out the murtherers; let them be known* (Anonymous, "Arden of Faversham" XIV:408); (b) syncopated: *Forgive the murderers of thy noble son* (Kyd, "The Spanish Tragedy" IV,II:33), or: *With murtherer thieves that came to rifle me* (Anonymous, "Arden of Faversham" IV:95);

3. (a) fully syllabic: *Crown him, and say, "Long live our emperor!*, or: *Lord Saturninus Rome's great emperor*; (b) syncopated: *And say 'Long live our emperor Saturnine*, or: *That thou create our emperor's eldest son* (Shakespeare, "Titus Andronicus" I,I:232,235,236,227);

4. (a) fully syllabic: *The Cardinal! Cause we express no scene*; (b) syncopated: *The cardinal's nephew, madam, Don Columbo* (Shirley, "The Cardinal", Prologue:1 and I,II:94).

On the basis of these observations I tended to consider every word terminating a phrase and/or a line as fully syllabic; but one can be particularly certain of the full syllabic form of words not containing the consonants [m,n,r,l] after the middle vowel, and also of proper names: these are almost certainly fully syllabic. Fully syllabic forms of such words occupying a reduced number of syllabic positions were considered capable of forming disyllabic inter-ictic intervals; for example: *I have a bird more beautiful.—Try the sound on't* (Webster, "The Duchess of Malfi" II,IV:62).

The problem of syllabic vs. non-syllabic sonants requires another decision. In Modern English a sonant preceded by a consonant can form a syllable. The syllable-forming property of sonants depends upon several factors (cf. Jones 1927, 1964, 1966; Kenyon 1950; Gimson 1962; J.C. Wells 1965):

(1) the quality of the preceding consonant: a sonant preceded by a plosive invariably forms a syllable (marble, uncle), a sonant preceded by a fricative is syllabically ambivalent (the words prism or prison may be either monosyllabic or disyllabic), while a sonant preceded by another sonant is usually non-syllabic (film, realm); however, [l] preceded by a nasal sonant may form a syllable, as in channel, tunnel (Kenyon 1950:92,70);

(2) the location of the consonant + sonant in a word: a sonant in the final position of a word forms a syllable more often than in the middle, e.g., *his gentle heart*, but *the gentleman usher*, or: *the prison of their bones*, but *The prisoner of the Goths*;

(3) the length of the word: a sonant forms a syllable in short words more often than in long polysyllables, cf: *With many fair and noble ornaments*, and *Why, 'tis impossible thou canst be so wicked* (Middleton and Rowley, "The Changeling" I,I:224, III,IV:122);

(4) the function of a word with a sonant in the sentence and its place in a phrase: a sonant more easily loses its syllable-forming capacity in syntactically subordinate words in the middle of a phrase (usually attributes) than in syntactically more independent elements terminating a phrase and particularly a verse line; for example: *A strange invisible perfume hits the sense* ("Anthony and Cleopatra" II,II:212), or *And skills in Neptune's deep invisible paths*

(Chapman, "Bussy d'Ambois" I,I:21), but: *That you will be more mild and* tractable ("Titus Andronicus" I,I:473);

(5) the character of the initial sound of the following word: if the latter begins with a vowel or [h], the final sonant of the preceding word may fail to form a syllable, even if preceded by a plosive consonant, e.g., (1) *Titus Andronicus, the* people of *Rome*, but: *The* people *will accept whom he admits* ("Titus Andronicus" I,I:182,225); (2) *Lose not so* noble *a friend on vain suppose*, but: *Thanks, gentle tribune,* noble *brother Marcus* ("Titus Andronicus" I,I:443,174); (3) *And let the emperor* dandle him *for his own*, but: *My hand hath been but* idle*, let it serve* ("Titus Andronicus" IV,II:162, III,I:172).

The syllable-forming capacity of sonants has obviously grown in time. For example, the word "peple" (people) as used by Chaucer is regularly monosyllabic if the next word begins with a vowel or [h] (*And to the* peple *he seyd in this manere*; *Unnethe the* peple *hir knew for hir fairnesse*; *Was ofte vertu hid, the* peple *him helde* ("Canterbury Tales": "The Clerke's Tale" 368,384,425). In the Elizabethan verse, as we have seen, the sonant preceded by a plosive consonant most often does form a syllable; exceptions (that can also be interpreted as disyllables, forming a disyllabic W) are rare; e.g., *And tell me, would the* rebels *deny me that?* (Marlowe, "Edward II" XI:101); *Of the abashed* oracle*, that, for fear* (Chapman, "Bussy d'Ambois" V,III:51).

The word haven is invariably disyllabic in Elizabethan verse, while heaven is ambivalent; for example: *O* heavens*, can you bear a good man groan* (disyllabic), but: *Revenge the* heavens *for old Andronicus!* (monosyllabic) ("Titus Andronicus" IV,I:124,130). The monosyllabic form of heaven seems to prevail. The word spirit is usually monosyllabic. In the much later twentieth-century syllabo-tonic verse, however, the words spirit and heaven are invariably disyllabic. Even the reduced forms of auxiliary verbs with a negation (doesn't, wasn't) containing a sonant preceded by a fricative [z] are regularly disyllabic, e.g., *I wonder why he* doesn't *marry her*; *Such as it is. It* isn't *worth the mortgage* (Frost, "The Housekeeper": 84,97). Sonants preceded by plosive sounds are now invariably disyllabic even if the next word in the same phrase begins with a vowel or [h]: *"Let* people *in that I can keep them out"* (Frost, "The Housekeeper": 4). In Elizabethan times, however, the combinations of a sonant with a preceding consonant were syllabically very ambivalent. My decisions therefore were mainly based on the evidence provided by verse itself; if the word heaven, for example, was used on one syllabic position only, it was considered monosyllabic, not forming a disyllabic non-ictus.

Elizabethan poets obviously took advantage of the ambiguous syllabic characteristics of various sounds and sound combinations. Still, one can trace some "preferences" and tendencies. The syllabic feature of the so-called triphthongs [aiə] and [auə] are usually related to the morphological structure of words and their etymology, their length, the syntactic function of the words, and their place in a phrase. Jones (1927) considered words like hire, dire, and flour monosyllabic, while higher, dyer, and plougher as disyllabic: [haie]-[hai-e], [flaue]-[plau-e] Indeed, native English words in which the monophthong vowel has gone through a shift (as in fire), or Romance borrowings where in place of the triphthong there was originally one vowel sound (as in dire) tend to be treated in Elizabethan verse as monosyllables, while borrowings, where in place of the triphthong there were originally two vowels (as in dial), tend to be disyllabic (cf. Kökeritz 1953:286-291).

The triphthongs tended to be monosyllabic in longer words, particularly if the latter are syntactically subordinate and occupy a non-terminal position in a phrase: otherwise they tended to be disyllabic; cf. monosyllabic: *Their violent shot resembling th'ocean's rage (Kyd, "The Spanish Tragedy" I,I:48); Must go upon their knees. Come, violent death* (Webster, "The Duchess of Malfi" IV,III:249), and disyllabic: *Blows up with sudden violence and horror* (Chapman, "Bussy d'Ambois" V,II:19); *Nor shall you do mine ear that violence* ("Hamlet" I,II:171). In Shakespeare's verse words like flower, hour, and tired are syllabically ambivalent: they are used in both monosyllabic and disyllabic forms, e.g., monosyllabic: *An hour before the worshipp'd sun peer'd forth*, or: *Within this hour my man shall be with thee* ("Romeo and Juliet" I,III:11, II,IV:188) and disyllabic: *And that you'll say, ere half an hour pass*, or: *One hour's storm will drown the fragrant meads* ("Titus Andronicus" III,II:192, II,IV:54). The disyllabic form of the word hour seems to be more archaic; the monosyllabic variation is more frequent, particularly in Shakespeare's later works (cf. Spevack 1974: 604-606). Some more examples: monosyllabic: *Tired with all these, for restful death I cry* (Son. 66:1); disyllabic: *The beast that bears me, tired with my woe* (Son. 50:5); or: *Weeds among weeds, or flowers with flowers gathered* (Son. 124:4); the word flower is treated as a monosyllable and a disyllable in the same line. König (1888:50-53), Partridge (1964:100), Scholl (1944), and Sprott (1953: Chapter VI, esp. pp. 55-56) all mentioned the ambivalent quality of the triphthongs in the sixteenth-seventeenth centuries (Sprott believed them to be intermediate between monosyllables and disyllables: "hypermonosyllables"); either variant could be used to suit the needs of verse form. In the final position of the verse line the choice of variant depends on the reader's taste (Partidge 1964:100). In my analysis of the Elizabethen verse I generally considered simple, root words of the fire and dire type as monosyllables; but I also took into account the number of syllabic positions these words occupied. Suffixed forms (like higher) and Romance borrowings of the dial and trial type were usually considered disyllabic.

Faced with the ambivalent syllabic character of some words discussed above and the possibility of elisions at the juncture of two words, the first ending in a vowel and the second beginning with a vowel or an [h], I ended up making three separate counts of the number of lines likely to contain disyllabic combinations in their non-ictic positions (usually not more than one per line). The minimum count included only the most indisputable cases, when two syllables not ending or beginning with a vowel belong to two adjacent words and occupy the same metrical position (*Bŭt this night, sweet Alice...*). The middle count included, in addition to such cases, also polysyllables not containing sonorants [m,n,l,r] after the central vowel (as in <u>majesty, beautiful, Imogen</u>) but occupying two, instead of three, syllabic positions. The third, maximum, count, in addition to all these cases, included also instances of two syllables of two adjacent words with "colliding" vowels, or a vowel and an [h], occupying the same syllabic position (*<u>I have</u> done those follies . . . <u>She</u> awoke at dawn...*). Such cases most probably underwent elision and did not form disyllabic non-ictuses, particularly in plays. In Italian verse such cases would most certainly be treated as elisions, but in English verse I could not be so certain.

Table 2.12 presents the incidence of lines containing (a) a disyllabic combination on W according to the three separate counts outlined above; (b) an omission of a syllable either on W or on S (a "zero-syllabic position"); and (c) both a disyllabic and a zero-syllabic position (the data are extracted from Tarlinskaja 1976: Table 47).

English verse drama was syllabically most irregular during the late Elizabethan-early Jacobean epoch, culminating in Webster's "Duchess of Malfi" (published in 1623, but probably produced as early as 1613-14). Later Jacobean plays, as if foreseeing the new post-Restoration trend, were gradually becoming syllabically more regular, e.g., Ford's "Perkin Warbeck". The post-Restoration and nineteenth-century plays never went back to the syllabic variability of the Jacobean verse. In fact, the accentual looseness of Shelley's dramatic iambic pentameter is accompanied by its extremely rigid syllabic structure.

Shakespeare's dramatic verse is representd here by three plays: the earliest ("Titus Andronicus"), mid-career ("Hamlet"), and one of the latest ("Cymbeline)"). There is a marked evolution in the syllabic structure of his lines. The evolution went parallel with the general evolution of dramatic verse of his epoch; it accompanied other evolutionary tendencies in the meter of his dramas, i.e.,stress profiles and line endings (see Chapter 5). The number of lines with disyllabic W approximately <u>doubled</u> from "Titus" to "Hamlet" and from "Hamlet" to "Cymbeline". The most typical place of a disyllabic W is, first and foremost, the anacrusis. Next comes the non-ictic position which separates two half-lines. Similarly to a strong syntactic break and an extrametrical stress, the disyllabic W is a marker of a bipartite line structure. In earlier Elizabethan verse the most typical place of a disyllabic W was position 5, while in later verse it became position 7. Some examples are: position **five**: *I cannot eat, / <u>but</u> I'll sit for company* (Anon. "Arden of Faversham", I:360); *Then cursed she <u>Richard</u>, / <u>then</u> cursed she Buckingham* ("Richard II" III,II:17). Position **seven**: *Is breach of all. I am ill, / <u>but your</u> being by me; This bloody man, the care <u>on't</u>. / <u>I</u> hope I dream* ("Cymbeline" IV,II:111,237).

Table 2.12

Syllabic Structure of Dramatic Verse (in percentage of lines containing the feature from the total number of lines analyzed)

Poet and drama	With a disyllabic position			With a zero-syllabic position	With both a disyllabic and a zero-syllabic position
	Minimum count	Medium count	Maximum count		
Norton, Sackville, "Gorboduc"	0.1	0.6	0.8	--	--
Kyd, "The Spanish Tragedy"	1.6	2.5	2.9	0.3	--
Anon., "Arden of Faversham"	7.8	8.6	12.0	6.1	0.1
Marlowe, "Edward II"	2.9	4.6	5.4	1.4	--
Shakespeare, "Titus Andronicus"	0.8	2.4	3.5	0.1	--
Ben Jonson, "Sejanus"	1.3	3.3	3.3	0.1	--
Shakespeare, "Hamlet"	4.5	5.1	8.0	0.6	--
Chapman, "Bussi D'Ambois"	0.8	4.1	4.5	0.5	0.1
Shakespeare, "Cymbeline"	6.7	9.9	14.9	0.8	--
Webster, "The Duchess of Malfi"	14.7	17.0	24.3	3.3	0.8
Middleton, Rowley, "The Changeling"	9.1	10.7	13.0	4.5	0.9
Ford, "Perkin Warbeck"	0.3	1.6	2.2	0.5	--
Shirley, "The Cardinal"	2.9	4.8	9.6	1.1	0.1
Dryden, "All for Love"	0.3	0.6	2.1	--	--
Shelley, "The Cenci"	--	1.1	1.9	0.1	--

Thus, a loosening of Shakespeare's iambic pentameter, evidenced in various aspects of his verse, is very obvious both in its accentual ("stress profile") and syllabic structures.

Note to Chapter 2

[1] Each "line" of the speech model could be found in genuine verse, but the frequency of different line types in the "text" of the model and in real verse is dissimilar; this explains the lower range of the ictic stresses in the model.

Chapter 3

Homogeneous and Heterogeneous Plays: Authorship, Style

3.0 Preliminary notes

So far we have compared the stress profiles of plays and poems considering each as a whole, and thereby derived certain conclusions regarding the authorship and chronology of Shakespeare's canon and how his work fits within the framework of English verse in general. But the indices used for comparison efface the complexity and heterogeneity of the inner structure of the individual works. Each play consists of scenes and acts, and these subsections are not necessarily rhythmically homogeneous. Also, each play is composed of utterances of numerous characters. A stylistical differentiation of characters, both idiosyncratically and typologically (*emploi*), has already been suggested (cf. Warnken 1964; Šaikevič 1976:358), and it seems not unlikely that the author's individualization of personages can extend into other levels of the text structure; for example, specific variations of the iambic pentameter could be used to oppose character types such as monarchs vs. commoners or heroes vs. villains. Finally, the part of each character consists of at least three kinds of verse utterances, to say nothing of prose segments: short cues, longer utterances, and monologues or soliloquies. It is plausible that the iambic pentameter of short utterances frequently constituting quick repartees, and of monologues or soliloquies, which conventionally represent orations, reasoning, meditations, and inner speech, has specific rhythmically distinctive features.

In this and the next chapter we will investigate the verse rhythm of separate plays in greater detail, dividing the texts first into acts and scenes (Chapter 3) and then into the parts of different personages and utterances of various lengths (Chapter 4). It is of course obvious that the shorter the portion of text, the greater the probability of a large variance in the stress profile values which would make comparisons statistically insignificant. Therefore in this chapter I usually limit my analysis to whole acts. In Chapter 4 only the verse rhythm of leading characters with long parts is studied.

The comparison of acts and scenes shows the range of rhythmical fluctuation within a play. It has been postulated that the greater the rhythmical similarity between acts, the more reason to suppose that the play was written by one author within a short period of time; the broader the range of rhythmical divergence of the acts, the more reason there is to suspect that the play was rewritten by its own author at some later date, or tampered with by some other poet, or written by two collaborators simultaneously. Fluctuation of rhythm by acts and scenes may, of course, have also other causes due to, for example, the peculiarities of plot development, and the number and types of characters involved in the scenes. The degree of fluctuation of rhythm by acts also depends on the length of the play: the longer the acts, the more homogeneous will the play appear statistically. This is one of the reasons why comedies (usually shorter plays) demonstrate more heterogeneous rhythm than, for example, chronicles (long plays).

3.1 Rhythm variation by acts

3.1.1. Evolution tendencies in Shakespeare.

We first consider the stress profiles of ictuses in separate acts or longer scenes. In some plays acts were united to provide sufficient verse material (e.g., "Love's Labour's Lost", acts II and III) and three plays with insufficient verse in their acts were excluded ("The Merry Wives of Windsor", "Much Ado About Nothing", and "Twelfth Night").

To see if evolutionary tendencies are observed in the stress profiles of separate acts the thirty-four plays were arranged chronologically (Table 3.1). As we remember, Period I is characterized by a strong stress on ictus II (position 4), supporting the first half-line, and by a decreased stress (a "dip") on ictus III (position 6), dividing the line into two symmetrical "hemistiches", $4+6$ or $5+5$. In the following periods, stress decreases a little on position 4 and increases on 6, such that the difference between 4 and 6 is lessened, while ictuses III and IV become leveled; this transitory stage passes to a marked "dip" on position 8 (ictus IV) in the final seven plays after "Macbeth". The separate acts, however, particularly in the plays before "Measure for Measure", sometimes deviate from the leading tendency of the period. Figure 3.1 shows stress profiles of acts I, III, V of four plays, and deviations, particularly in the comedies, are obvious (see below). In the first thirteen dramas, from "Titus Andronicus" through "The Merchant of Venice" (1588-1596), the most typical stress profile scheme by acts predictably displays a "dip" on position 6; the most striking exceptions are: "Titus Andronicus", act I; "Henry VI", 2, act II; "A Midsummer Night's Dream", acts IV and particularly V; and "The Merchant of Venice", act V: the "dip" is on ictus IV (position 8). The reasons may be as follows:

(a) <u>chronological</u> (the "pre-first-period", archaic style of "Titus", act I, or the already changing style in "The Merchant of Venice");

(b) <u>genre</u> (cf. the leveled stressing of ictuses III and IV in acts II-IV of "The Comedy of Errors");

Table 3.1

Stress profiles of separate acts in Shakespeare's dramas, arranged chronologically. Minima in midline ictic stressing are underlined.

Chronology	Drama	Acts	Positions					Lines	Correlations between positions			
			2	4	6	8	10		4-2	8-6	4-6
1588–1589	Titus Andronicus	I	66.9	82.7	72.3	70.6	82.5	490	+ 15.8	− 1.7	+ 10.4
		II	69.4	84.5	73.5	76.7	88.8	510	+ 14.1	+ 3.2	+ 11.0
		III	64.2	88.9	69.0	79.8	90.7	377	+ 24.7	+ 10.8	+ 19.9
		IV	69.4	89.4	72.5	72.1	85.4	479	+ 20.0	− 0.4	+ 16.9
		V	62.2	88.1	61.3	76.4	88.6	560	+ 25.9	+ 15.1	+ 26.8
1589–1590	Henry VI,1	I	63.5	79.6	69.9	70.2	84.9	583	+ 16.1	+ 0.3	+ 9.7
		II	65.4	84.3	66.7	72.2	86.0	477	+ 18.19	+ 5.5	+ 17.6
		III	67.6	85.0	72.8	73.4	81.9	459	+ 17.4	+ 0.6	+ 12.2
		IV	66.0	86.2	69.1	73.7	88.4	549	+ 20.2	+ 4.6	+ 17.1
		V	69.5	84.7	62.8	72.1	83.2	554	+ 15.2	+ 9.3	+ 21.9
1589–1590	Comedy of Errors	I	63.8	86.9	58.7	74.2	91.1	259	+ 23.1	+ 15.5	+ 28.2
		II	67.6	85.6	69.2	70.0	92.0	250	+ 18.0	+ 0.8	+ 16.4
		III	62.7	87.4	68.7	68.7	91.6	166	+ 24.7	0	+ 18.7
		IV	67.7	80.1	72.7	72.7	89.4	322	+ 12.4	0	+ 7.4
		V	73.0	84.7	67.1	74.3	89.6	404	+ 11.7	+ 7.2	+ 17.6
1590–1591	Henry VI,2	I	70.0	87.2	65.5	73.8	83.0	400	+ 17.2	+ 8.3	+ 21.7
		II	73.2	82.9	73.7	70.6	91.2	350	+ 9.7	− 3.1	+ 9.2
		III	70.1	86.5	69.6	77.5	86.5	800	+ 16.4	+ 7.9	+ 16.9
		IV	69.0	82.5	73.2	73.2	90.5	400	+ 13.5	0	+ 9.3
		V	62.7	83.7	69.0	75.3	90.7	300	+ 21.0	+ 6.3	+ 14.7

Table 3.1 (cont.)

1590–1591	Henry VI,3	I	69.6	87.7	75.8	70.2	88.6	550	+ 18.1	+ 5.6	+ 17.5
		II	70.6	89.3	77.6	69.2	92.9	700	+ 18.7	+ 8.4	+ 20.1
		III	69.1	87.5	75.5	67.5	90.5	550	+ 18.4	+ 8.0	+ 20.0
		IV	67.7	85.1	72.6	70.0	88.0	550	+ 17.4	+ 2.6	+ 15.1
		V	73.4	86.7	77.4	76.0	90.8	450	+ 13.3	+ 1.4	+ 10.7
1591–1592	Taming of the Shrew	Induction	62.2	85.9	74.9	65.7	88.6	227	+ 23.7	+ 9.2	+ 20.2
		I	65.5	83.0	70.2	68.0	88.6	375	+ 17.4	+ 2.2	+ 15.0
		II	62.8	89.5	77.3	70.0	88.2	373	+ 26.7	+ 7.3	+ 19.5
		III	60.4	88.5	70.8	70.4	84.7	260	+ 28.1	+ 0.4	+ 18.1
		IV	68.8	88.5	76.1	67.3	89.9	477	+ 19.7	+ 8.8	+ 21.2
		V	67.6	87.6	76.1	71.3	91.0	188	+ 20.0	+ 4.8	+ 16.3
1591–1592	Richard III	I	64.9	85.1	73.3	67.3	89.5	950	+ 20.2	+ 6.0	+ 17.8
		II	64.0	89.5	73.3	68.5	89.0	400	+ 25.5	+ 4.8	+ 21.0
		III	65.6	82.0	75.6	70.0	89.4	750	+ 16.4	+ 5.6	+ 12.0
		IV	65.9	86.2	76.4	67.7	91.2	836	+ 20.3	+ 8.7	+ 18.5
		V	59.9	90.1	78.8	68.2	88.3	434	+ 30.2	+ 10.6	+ 21.9
1592–1593	Two Gentlemen of Verona	I	65.3	84.0	71.7	70.7	87.0	300	+ 18.7	+ 1.0	+ 13.3
		II	65.0	85.0	72.7	67.3	86.4	300	+ 20	+ 5.4	+ 17.7
		III	59.2	81.0	69.7	61.7	89.9	316	+ 21.8	+ 8.3	+ 19.6
		IV	62.5	78.3	67.5	66.5	85.2	304	+ 15.8	+ 1.0	+ 11.8
		V	66.9	74.7	70.6	70.0	85.3	217	+ 7.8	+ 0.6	+ 4.7
1593–1594	Love's Labour's Lost	II,III	70.0	82.7	71.3	71.3	92.0	150	+ 12.7	+ 11.4	+ 11.4
		IV	71.5	85.5	72.5	64.0	87.5	200	+ 14.0	+ 8.5	+ 21.5
		V, a	72.0	87.7	78.3	72.3	88.9	350	+ 15.7	+ 6.0	+ 15.4
		V, b	65.0	86.3	71.7	71.7	92.0	300	+ 21.3	0	+ 14.6
		V all	62.0	87.3	69.0	72.0	89.3	300	+ 25.3	+ 3.0	+ 15.3
			63.5	86.9	70.3	71.9	90.7	600	+ 23.4	+ 1.6	+ 15.0
1594–1595	Midsummer Night's Dream	I	66.8	86.0	82.8	59.6	81.6	250	+ 19.2	+ 23.2	+ 26.4
		II	62.3	86.6	73.5	66.9	86.9	350	+ 24.3	+ 6.6	+ 19.7
		III	64.7	88.0	76.9	70.2	87.2	450	+ 23.3	+ 6.7	+ 17.8
		IV	64.7	80.7	71.4	74.0	82.0	150	+ 16.0	− 2.6	+ 6.7
		V	67.4	79.4	63.4	78.7	86.7	150	+ 12.0	− 15.3	+ 0.7

Table 3.1 (cont.)

Year	Play	Act									
1594–1595	Romeo and Juliet	I	67.5	89.0	68.9	71.9	91.6	571	+21.5	+ 3.0	+20.1
		II	62.6	86.7	69.9	74.1	88.1	435	+24.1	+ 4.2	+16.8
		III	64.0	87.7	68.3	79.3	86.3	706	+23.7	+11.0	+19.4
		IV	66.3	85.3	69.9	74.1	90.7	332	+19.0	+ 4.2	+15.4
		V	68.9	85.9	64.6	77.1	86.4	418	+16.0	+12.5	+21.3
1594–1595	Richard II	I	67.1	85.1	68.7	74.3	89.1	650	+18.0	+ 5.6	+16.4
		II	69.7	85.2	73.0	76.9	89.2	600	+15.5	+ 3.9	+12.2
		III	69.1	84.4	71.1	71.2	90.6	550	+15.3	− 0.1	+13.3
		IV	66.3	86.0	67.4	74.7	92.0	300	+19.7	+ 7.3	+18.6
		V	70.8	85.9	68.6	75.8	93.0	516	+15.1	+ 7.2	+17.3
1595–1596	King John	I	63.0	82.7	70.7	73.3	87.1	300	+19.7	+ 2.5	+12.0
		II	66.2	84.6	68.6	73.2	87.7	570	+18.4	+ 4.6	+16.0
		III	63.4	87.8	66.9	76.4	88.8	600	+24.4	+ 9.5	+20.9
		IV	65.1	82.8	66.6	79.5	88.6	550	+17.7	+12.9	+16.2
		V	66.9	85.6	67.1	71.8	87.3	520	+18.7	+ 4.7	+18.5
1595–1596	Merchant of Venice	I	64.3	86.0	71.3	72.7	83.4	300	+21.7	+ 1.4	+14.7
		II	64.5	84.0	70.3	73.3	87.0	400	+19.5	+ 3.0	+13.7
		III	66.0	83.4	68.5	71.2	89.6	450	+17.4	+ 2.7	+14.9
		IV	60.3	86.3	69.8	70.8	88.5	400	+26.0	+ 1.0	+16.5
		V	61.4	82.4	73.4	65.7	90.0	300	+21.0	− 7.7	+ 9.0
1596–1597	Henry IV,1	I	61.7	80.5	64.9	75.9	79.8	415	+18.8	+11.0	+15.6
		II	71.6	81.1	67.4	74.8	87.4	95	+ 9.5	+ 7.4	+13.7
		III	62.2	82.7	67.2	75.8	82.4	375	+20.5	+ 8.6	+15.5
		IV	68.7	83.4	68.3	71.7	82.7	300	+14.7	+ 3.4	+15.1
		V	68.6	85.2	67.0	71.8	83.8	357	+16.6	+ 4.8	+18.2
1596–1597	Henry IV,2	I	61.8	87.8	71.8	67.7	89.0	319	+26.0	− 4.1	+16.0
		II,III	64.4	83.7	67.8	74.1	84.7	208	+19.3	+ 6.3	+15.9
		IV, a	67.4	80.1	68.9	76.0	82.9	350	+12.7	+ 7.1	+11.2
		IV, b	63.8	84.6	69.3	73.9	88.2	345	+20.8	+ 4.6	+15.3
		V	62.5	83.8	65.6	70.6	85.0	160	+21.3	+ 5.0	+18.2

Table 3.1 (cont.)

1598–1599	Henry V	Prologues	62.9	88.2	66.4	70.8	85.7	202	+ 25.3	+ 4.4	+ 21.8
		I	59.5	81.0	70.0	73.5	86.8	400	+ 21.5	+ 3.5	+ 11.0
		II	62.2	81.5	70.1	68.9	89.5	344	+ 19.3	− 1.2	+ 11.4
		III	67.9	79.4	71.8	70.7	90.2	184	+ 11.5	− 1.1	+ 7.6
		IV	67.5	81.0	73.6	72.7	88.3	458	+ 13.5	− 0.9	+ 7.4
		V	69.6	80.4	70.3	75.7	84.5	148	+ 10.8	+ 5.4	+ 10.1
1598–1599	Julius Caesar	I	60.4	81.4	68.2	72.0	84.4	436	+ 21.0	+ 3.8	+ 13.2
		II	59.4	81.9	62.5	73.3	86.7	480	+ 22.5	+ 10.8	+ 19.4
		III	66.3	83.3	70.7	71.4	87.9	430	+ 17.0	+ 0.7	+ 12.6
		IV	60.7	84.0	73.6	70.5	86.0	356	+ 23.3	− 3.1	+ 10.4
		V	65.1	81.9	70.2	73.7	85.5	255	+ 16.8	+ 3.5	+ 11.7
1599–1600	As You Like It	I	50.7	87.3	64.7	72.7	88.7	150	+ 36.6	+ 8.0	+ 22.6
		II, a	61.5	81.0	70.5	76.5	86.0	200	+ 19.5	+ 6.0	+ 10.5
		II, b	66.0	82.5	74.5	71.5	87.5	200	+ 16.5	− 3.0	+ 8.0
		III	62.0	84.0	76.0	68.5	91.0	200	+ 22.0	− 7.5	+ 8.0
		IV	61.2	83.3	62.3	71.7	88.3	180	+ 22.1	+ 9.4	+ 21.0
1600–1601	Hamlet	I	61.5	82.1	74.3	70.5	92.2	765	+ 20.6	− 3.8	+ 7.8
		II	61.4	80.0	73.0	69.5	93.3	369	+ 18.6	− 3.5	+ 7.0
		III	65.4	83.1	71.9	71.2	93.7	480	+ 17.7	− 0.7	+ 11.2
		IV	59.8	81.2	72.8	69.9	94.0	415	+ 21.4	+ 2.9	+ 8.4
		V	60.8	86.3	72.9	67.7	94.8	306	+ 25.5	+ 5.2	+ 13.4
1601–1602	Troilus and Cressida	I	66.6	81.7	72.7	70.1	92.4	487	+ 15.1	− 2.6	+ 9.0
		II	66.4	85.2	68.8	68.2	90.9	330	+ 18.8	− 0.6	+ 16.4
		III	68.9	84.3	67.3	71.9	93.8	324	+ 15.4	− 4.6	+ 17.0
		IV	67.2	86.1	75.3	76.1	89.7	417	+ 18.9	+ 0.8	+ 10.8
		V	70.3	86.7	77.7	76.7	93.0	300	+ 16.4	− 1.0	+ 9.0
1603–1604	Measure for Measure	I	59.6	80.3	70.4	64.8	88.4	250	+ 20.7	− 5.6	+ 9.9
		II	61.5	84.0	72.2	65.5	90.8	400	+ 22.5	− 6.7	+ 11.8
		III	66.7	84.7	72.7	70.0	91.4	150	+ 18.0	− 2.7	+ 12.0
		IV	62.0	85.0	71.0	64.5	90.5	200	+ 23.0	− 6.5	+ 16.0
		V	63.1	81.4	71.8	64.9	90.8	382	+ 18.3	− 6.9	+ 9.6

Table 3.1 (cont.)

1603-1604	Othello	I	61.5	82.7	70.2	69.7	94.5	542	+ 21.2	- 0.8	+ 12.5
		II	64.2	86.4	72.2	72.7	93.3	374	+ 22.2	+ 0.5	+ 14.2
		III	60.1	86.3	69.3	69.6	93.2	585	+ 26.2	- 0.3	+ 17.0
		IV	60.5	84.1	75.9	72.0	95.8	357	+ 24.6	- 3.9	+ 8.2
		V	65.2	84.8	77.6	72.3	95.2	414	+ 19.6	- 5.3	+ 7.2
1604-1605	All's Well That Ends Well	I	66.4	78.0	70.8	64.4	93.6	250	+ 11.6	- 6.4	+ 7.2
		II	62.3	79.5	75.8	70.5	86.3	400	+ 17.2	- 5.3	+ 3.7
		III	62.0	80.4	76.4	73.2	94.0	250	+ 18.4	- 3.2	+ 4.0
		IV	60.0	86.7	75.3	68.0	95.3	150	+ 26.7	- 7.3	+ 11.4
		V	61.0	83.7	76.7	70.0	95.7	300	+ 22.7	- 6.7	+ 7.0
1604-1605	Timon of Athens	I	61.9	79.9	78.4	66.4	96.4	278	+ 18.0	- 12.0	+ 1.5
		II	61.6	80.5	81.2	66.5	91.5	164	+ 18.9	- 14.7	- 0.7
		III	58.9	81.2	74.6	69.6	89.3	197	+ 22.3	- 5.0	+ 6.6
		IV	65.3	84.5	80.0	71.1	92.9	450	+ 19.2	- 8.9	+ 4.5
		V	62.7	83.0	72.0	72.3	93.4	304	+ 21.3	+ 0.3	+ 11.0
1605-1606	King Lear	I	61.8	80.5	78.5	68.8	94.0	400	+ 18.7	- 9.7	+ 2.0
		II	64.0	82.6	73.8	68.4	95.5	442	+ 18.6	- 5.4	+ 8.8
		III	66.7	83.2	80.2	63.0	95.6	273	+ 16.5	- 17.2	+ 3.0
		IV	62.0	82.0	81.0	69.8	97.5	400	+ 20.0	- 11.2	+ 1.0
		V	65.5	82.2	76.5	67.8	95.8	400	+ 16.7	- 8.7	+ 5.7
1605-1606	Macbeth	I	63.9	81.9	73.3	67.7	93.1	393	+ 18.0	- 5.6	+ 8.6
		II	68.6	79.5	80.6	71.7	95.4	258	+ 10.9	- 8.9	- 1.1
		III	63.2	82.3	76.3	68.9	94.6	350	+ 19.1	- 7.4	+ 6.0
		IV	66.3	79.2	81.4	65.8	93.7	350	+ 12.9	- 15.6	- 2.2
		V	67.3	83.7	73.0	75.3	96.0	300	+ 16.4	+ 2.3	+ 10.7
1606-1607	Antony and Cleopatra	I	65.3	80.4	74.2	69.9	91.6	368	+ 15.1	- 4.3	+ 6.2
		II	66.2	80.0	76.4	69.1	90.0	550	+ 13.8	- 7.3	+ 3.6
		III	63.4	81.1	76.5	72.2	86.5	672	+ 17.7	- 4.3	+ 4.6
		IV	67.8	77.0	77.8	75.0	86.4	500	+ 9.2	- 2.8	- 0.8
		V	69.1	78.8	77.2	67.2	85.9	368	+ 9.7	- 10.0	+ 1.6

101

Table 3.1 (cont.)

1607–1608	Pericles	I	69.0	95.3	73.5	70.3	91.3	400	+ 16.3	− 3.5	+ 11.8
		II	64.1	84.4	72.2	70.0	86.3	320	+ 20.3	− 2.2	+ 12.2
		III	64.7	82.8	71.9	68.9	89.3	167	+ 18.1	− 3.0	+ 10.9
		IV	67.5	79.2	79.8	66.9	90.2	163	+ 11.7	− 12.9	− 0.6
		V	63.5	79.5	71.3	69.4	82.6	268	+ 16.0	− 1.9	+ 8.2
1607–1608	Coriolanus	I	63.8	80.0	77.9	65.8	87.7	535	+ 16.2	− 12.1	+ 2.1
		II	66.5	75.4	77.6	68.9	88.1	371	+ 8.9	− 8.7	− 2.2
		III	60.5	83.9	73.3	65.9	91.0	546	+ 23.4	− 7.4	+ 10.6
		IV	66.8	81.5	72.0	70.2	88.0	400	+ 14.7	− 1.8	+ 9.5
		V	63.6	82.0	76.4	66.4	88.9	478	+ 18.4	− 10.0	+ 5.6
1608–1609	Cymbeline	I	64.9	79.6	74.3	68.2	87.2	493	+ 14.7	− 6.1	+ 5.3
		II	66.6	76.0	78.3	69.7	87.5	350	+ 9.4	− 8.6	− 2.3
		III	67.9	80.4	76.6	74.0	88.7	626	+ 12.5	− 2.6	+ 3.8
		IV	69.3	80.7	79.7	73.2	91.8	462	+ 11.4	− 6.5	+ 1.0
		V	69.3	80.3	76.6	75.6	89.8	683	+ 11.0	− 1.0	+ 3.7
1609–1610	Winter's Tale	I	66.5	79.8	76.5	70.9	86.5	450	+ 13.3	− 5.6	+ 3.3
		II	59.9	80.5	73.3	70.8	88.7	434	+ 20.6	− 2.5	+ 7.2
		III	67.0	76.3	71.5	73.2	83.2	291	+ 9.3	+ 1.7	+ 4.8
		IV	69.5	79.8	77.4	72.7	87.1	476	+ 10.3	− 4.7	+ 2.4
		V	68.4	77.9	75.3	70.3	89.1	376	+ 8.5	− 5.0	+ 2.6
1610–1611	Tempest	I	68.1	80.0	74.9	71.6	86.5	450	+ 11.1	− 3.3	+ 5.1
		II	68.1	78.6	83.1	69.4	90.0	219	+ 10.5	− 13.7	− 4.5
		III	65.6	80.0	79.2	65.2	87.6	250	+ 14.4	− 14.0	+ 0.8
		IV	63.8	81.6	79.3	67.8	84.5	174	+ 17.8	− 11.5	+ 2.3
		V	70.5	84.2	76.1	75.1	89.5	285	+ 13.7	− 1.0	+ 3.1
1612–1613	Henry VIII	I	67.4	77.0	75.8	67.6	88.6	500	+ 9.6	− 8.2	+ 1.2
		II	63.8	81.2	76.4	71.2	85.7	707	+ 17.4	− 5.2	+ 4.8
		III	62.8	81.4	75.4	68.2	90.9	606	+ 18.6	− 7.2	+ 6.0
		IV	63.0	87.7	76.7	71.7	90.3	300	+ 24.7	− 5.0	+ 11.0
		V	64.3	83.9	73.7	72.0	89.5	464	+ 19.6	− 1.7	+ 10.2

102

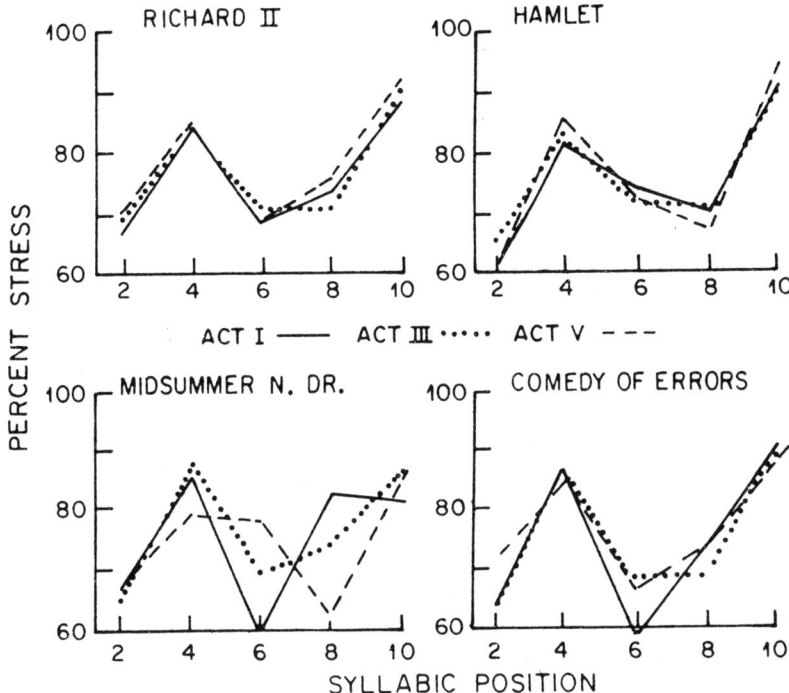

Fig. 3.1. Stress profiles of acts I, III, and V of four plays. The two comedies illustrate the marked heterogeneity by acts of this genre. "Richard II" is typical of the more homogeneous nature of chronicles and tragedies; "Hamlet" is the most rhythmically homogeneous play of Shakespeare's canon. Data from Table 3.1.

(c) questionable authorship (as in "Titus Andronicus" or "Henry VI", 2);

(d) development of the plot: the scenes and acts of climax or anticlimax may have rhythmical characteristics of their own, e.g., act V of "Midsummer Nights's Dream" which contains the tail end of the framing plot about Theseus, Duke of Athens, and his betrothed, Hippolyta, Queen of Amazons. (It also contains a comical interlude about Pyramus and Thisby, approximately 50 lines only; its stress profile is similar to the rest of act V);

(e) more general laws that govern the structure of a complex whole. As we shall see below, verse units of various length and complexity, such as: a canon analyzed by periods; a separate play analyzed by acts and scenes; a poem analyzed by stanzas; a stanza analyzed by lines; and even a line analyzed by hemistiches and "metrical words" (Gasparov 1974:145) seem to have their own inner, specific laws of composition (cf. Taranovsky 1966b, Tarlinskaja 1980, G.S. Smith 1981). In the fourteen first plays (Table 3.1) considered by acts, it is act IV that provides most of the exceptions to the general rule of

Period I: it contains a "dip" in position 6 less frequently than other acts. Of the first three acts, Act I and particularly II display the most rigorous stress profile (cf. Fig. 3.1): twelve plays of fourteen have a "dip" in position 6 in Act II. The same is true of leveled ictuses III and IV: most of the cases occur in the second half of the plays, the fewest cases in the first two acts. It appears as though the form of plays usually becomes looser from acts I-II through IV-V.

A similar tendency is apparently at work in the following thirteen plays, 1596-1606, beginning with "Henry IV", 1, through "Macbeth". The general tendency of stress profiles has already changed, the place of the "dip" has shifted to position 8; but Act IV displays this tendency most fully (in nine plays out of thirteen) while Act I has the highest number of cases with the "dip" in position 6, the sign of a more rigid iambic pentameter form; see also the rhythmically constrained "Prologue" in "Henry V". A notable exception is "Timon of Athens" (Table 3.1): it is Act II that displays the most decanonized stress profile of all: ictus III is untypically stronger than II, and the rigidity index is particularly low: −14.7%. Act V, on the other hand, is the most "canonized" of the whole play: positions 8 and 6 are leveled and position 4 (ictus II) is relatively strong.

However, "Timon of Athens" is a controversial play (see Chapters 2 and 5). The manuscript supplied by Heminge and Condell gave a version of a rough-hewn play which abounds in prose fragments and verse undivided into lines. In Chambers' opinion, "Timon" is an unfinished draft consisting of rough notes hastily jotted down to be worked on later (Chambers 1930:1,481-486). A number of scholars, however, believed that "Timon" is the result of collaboration. Nowottny, who found traces of what she thought was a non-Shakespearean hand in several parts of the play, felt that the last act definitely belongs to another author: ". . . the area of my bafflement on the authorship question is, precisely, from IV.III.464 (the entry of Flavia, after the thieves' exit) to the end of the play" (Nowottny 1959:497). Jackson, however, believed that the non-Shakespearean parts, which he attributed to Middleton, embrace Act I scene II, Act III, and one or two other places which are "as like Middleton's" as they are "unlike Shakespeare's" (Jackson 1979:48). Thus the whole of acts III and V are suspected of not belonging to Shakepeare. Stress profiles of "Timon of Athens" by acts (Table 3.1) suggest the following groupings of similar acts: the first and the second; the third and the fourth; and the fifth, which differs from the rest of the play. There may be other, compositional, character-changing, or plot-evolving reasons for this difference, but a possible cause of the fifth act deviating from the rest might indeed be another hand.

The frequency of stress on position 4 (ictus II) gradually decreases and on position 6 (ictus III) gradually increases from Period I through III-b. In some acts of the final period we come across an untypical correlation: position 6 is stressed more strongly than 4, for example, in acts II and particularly IV of "Macbeth", and in Act II of "Coriolanus", "Cymbeline", and "The Tempest". Such a gradual increase of strength from ictus I through III is not uncommon in later Jacobean dramas (e.g., Ford, "Perkin Warbeck": Tarlinskaja 1976: Table 50, p. 292); it was also discovered in separate acts of Byron's plays (see Table 3.4). In "Werner", Act III, there is an even more unusual correlation: both positions 2 and 6 are stressed more strongly than 4: ictus I > ictus II < ictus III: the reverse of the traditional scheme of pentameter where ictus I < ictus II > ictus III. Some examples from "Werner":

> Infects me <u>to</u> my shame: but <u>as</u> all feelings . . .
> Will live but <u>on</u> the atmosph<u>ere</u>; your feasts . . .
> My spirit—<u>I'm</u> a fores<u>ter</u> and breather . . .
> My father, <u>I</u> salute you, <u>and</u> it grieves me, etc.
> (Byron, "Werner" IV,I:204,223,225,235)

Missing stresses on positions 4 and 8 emphasize the loosened structure of the English dramatic pentameter by shifting rhythmical and syntactical seams to the left or to the right of positions 4/5—away from the traditional mid-line seam of a rigorous pentameter form. The line variation with missing stresses on positions 4 and 8 (ictuses II and IV) is typical of the Russian iambic pentameter, and appears even in translations of Shakespeare's plays, e.g., by Kozlov or Veinberg (Taranovsky 1953: Tables XI and XII): regressive dissimilation of strong and weak feet starting from the last one and decreasing towards the beginning of the line is obvious in all the Russian material analyzed by K.F. Taranovsky (1953: Tables IX-XII).

The strongest stress on position 4 in the final seven dramas by Shakespeare is displayed in Acts I and II of "Pericles" (particularly in Act I: 95% stressed, unseen anywhere else in Shakespeare's canon), and in Acts IV and V of "Henry VIII" (particularly in Act IV, attributed in its entirety to Fletcher). Thus, Acts I and II of "Pericles" and Act IV of "Henry VIII" display some stress profile peculiarities decidedly atypical of late Shakepeare (see below).

3.1.2. Homogeneous and heterogeneous plays: typology.

Consider now the diapasons by acts of stress variation on ictic positions of Shakespeare's thirty-four longer plays. This variation was examined in two ways. (1) I superimposed the stress profiles of all five acts of every drama upon each other (see, for example, Fig. 3.1) and calculated the difference between the maximum and minimum indices on every ictic position of every play; thus I found out the <u>maximum range of dispersion</u> (RD) of ictic stressing by acts (Tables 3.2, 3.3, and 3.5). (2) I also calculated the <u>mean deviation</u> (MD) of ictic stresses of acts from the general stress profile of the play (Table 3.6, Fig. 3.2). Though these statistics are both measures of the homogeneity / heterogeneity of plays, they tell us different things: RD indicates the maximum variation of stressing, and is a better index for identifying re-working or co-authorship, while MD is an estimator of internal homogeneity, and is a better index for, e.g., genre differentiation.

The RDs range between 1.6% (position 4 in "Richard II") and 19.4% (position 8 in "A Midsummer Night's Dream" (Table 3.2)). The ten percent index was taken to be a threshold between "narrow" and "wide" ranges. Broad RDs (over 10%) are almost all discovered in the plays of the first two periods (1588-1602), particularly in Period I: seven plays of the thirteen. Four of these are comedies ("The Comedy of Errors", "The Two Gentlemen of Verona", "Love's Labour's Lost", and "A Midsummer Night's Dream"); the remaining three plays all belong to the earliest years of Shakespeare's career, and all have been suspected of not having been written entirely by Shakespeare: "Titus Andronicus" and "Henry VI", parts 1 and 2. These facts seem to suggest that a greater heterogeneity of rhythm occurs (1) in the earliest plays of a poet, whose rhythmical style is only in the making: the sign of an uncertain hand of a young dramatist; (2) in plays perhaps based on an earlier substrate or worked on by another author; (3) in comedies: uneven rhythm is probably a sign of the genre.

The rhythmical heterogeneity of the comedies is also probably the result of large portions of prose and of the so-called doggerel verse which interrupt the flow of the main, iambic text ("The Comedy of Errors", "Love's Labour's Lost"); the author, as it were, "forgets" the rhythmical inertia of the preceding iambic pentameter text. The rhythmic heterogeneity of comedies may also be explained by heterogeneity of their style and plot. High and low styles clash in "Love's Labour's Lost", and reality and a fairy tale plot within yet another plot exist side by side in "A Midsummer Night's Dream".

In Period II, RD indices over 10% occur in two comedies ("As You Like It" and "Troilus and Cressida" - actually a tragi-comedy) and in "Henry V" and "Julius Caesar". But in both latter plays, RDs on other ictic positions are so small that the mean indices of rhythmical variation are in both plays quite low; thus, the relatively high index on one of the ictic positions in the plays might be simply fortuitous (cf. Table 3.6).

Periods IIIa and IIIb both contain plays of relatively homogeneous rhythm; the only exception is "Henry VIII", position 4: ictus II is a clashing point of two tendencies: late Shakespeare style with its weak stress on position 4 and Fletcher's with his strong marking of position 4.

The broadest RDs (14% and over) are displayed by three comedies: "The Comedy of Errors", "A Midsummer Night's Dream", and "As You Like It". "A Midsummer Night's Dream" stands out: its first and fifth acts demonstrate in fact opposite tendencies (Fig. 3.1), with a deep "dip" first on position 6 (Act I) and then on 8 (Act V). In general, the broadest RDs all occur on these two metrically relevant midline positions, six and eight. Conversely, the most stable positions are 4 and particularly 10—the end of the first "hemistich" and the end of the line, the metrical footholds of English iambic pentameter. The variable midline ictuses III and IV are the first to be affected by changes of epoch or style.

Let us now make a more general comparison of the plays by acts. In Table

Table 3.2

Range of rhythm variation by acts (RD) of 34 Shakespearean plays, arranged by period. Ranges exceeding 10% are underlined.

Period	Drama	Positions					Mean
		2	4	6	8	10	
I	Titus Andronicus	7.2	6.7	12.2	9.2	8.2	8.7
	Henry VI,1	6.0	6.6	10.0	3.5	6.5	6.5
	Comedy of Errors	10.3	7.3	14.0	5.6	2.6	7.9
	Henry VI,2	10.5	5.7	8.2	6.9	7.7	7.8
	Henry VI,3	5.7	4.2	8.5	5.0	4.9	5.7
	Taming of the Shrew	8.4	6.5	5.6	7.1	6.3	6.8
	Richard III	6.0	8.1	2.7	5.5	2.9	5.0
	Two Gentlemen of Verona	7.7	10.3	9.3	5.2	4.7	7.4
	Love's Labour's Lost	10.0	5.0	8.3	13.7	4.5	8.3
	Midsummer Night's Dream	5.1	8.6	19.1	19.4	5.6	11.6
	Romeo and Juliet	6.3	3.7	5.3	7.4	5.2	5.6
	Richard II	4.5	1.6	5.6	2.6	3.9	3.6
	King John	3.9	5.1	4.1	7.7	1.7	4.5
II	Merchant of Venice	5.7	3.9	4.9	7.6	6.6	5.7
	Henry IV,1	9.9	4.7	3.4	4.2	7.6	5.9
	Henry IV,2	5.6	7.7	6.2	8.3	6.1	6.8
	Henry V	10.1	1.6	3.6	6.8	5.7	5.5
	Julius Caesar	6.9	2.6	11.1	3.2	3.5	5.4
	As You Like It	15.3	6.3	13.7	8.0	5.0	9.7
	Hamlet	5.6	6.3	2.4	3.4	2.2	4.0
	Troilus and Cressida	3.9	5.0	10.4	8.5	4.1	6.4
III-a	Measure for Measure	7.1	4.7	2.3	5.5	3.0	4.5
	Othello	5.1	3.7	8.3	3.3	2.5	4.6
	All's Well That Ends Well	6.4	8.7	5.9	8.8	9.4	7.8
	Timon of Athens	7.4	4.6	9.2	5.9	7.1	6.8
	King Lear	4.9	2.7	7.2	6.8	3.5	5.0
	Macbeth	5.4	4.5	8.1	9.5	2.9	6.1
III-b	Antony and Cleopatra	5.7	4.1	3.6	7.8	5.7	5.3
	Pericles	6.4	6.1	8.5	3.4	8.7	6.6
	Coriolanus	6.3	8.5	5.9	4.4	3.3	5.7
	Cymbeline	4.4	4.7	5.4	7.4	4.6	5.3
	Winter's Tale	9.6	4.2	5.9	2.9	5.9	5.7
	Tempest	6.7	5.6	8.2	9.9	5.5	7.2
	Henry VIII	4.6	10.7	3.0	4.4	5.2	5.6

3.3 Shakepeare's plays are arranged in order of increasing mean values of RD. For comparison, thirteen non-Shakespearean dramas and one poem are included; these are: Norton and Sackville's "Gorboduc", Ben Jonson's "Sejanus; His Fall", Beaumont and Fletcher's "Maid's Tragedy", five plays by Marlowe, four plays by Byron, Shelley's "The Cenci", and "Hero and Leander", a poem by Marlowe and Chapman (analyzed by sestiades). Shakepearean and non-Shakespearean plays with similar indices are arranged in parallel. It must be emphasized that indices of homogeneity do not much help to establish chronology of plays, as there are several different reasons that might cause a broad range of rhythm within a play; the order of plays in Table 3.3 is not chronological but structural.

The data suggest subdivision of the material into three groups: (1) with low ranges of variation (3.6-5.9%); (2) with medium ranges (6.0- 6.9%); (3) and with high ranges (7.0-11.6%). Plays of the first group may be defined as relatively homogeneous and plays of the third group as heterogeneous, while the second group is transitional (a clash of tendencies?).

Three-quarters of Shakespeare's dramas display a high and medium degree of homogeneity (low and medium range of variation). The indices of eighteen plays by Shakespeare with a high degree of homogeneity correspond with six non-Shakespearean plays unquestionably written by a single author (Shelley, Byron, Ben Jonson). Indices of seven of Shakespeare's plays that place them in the transitory or heterogeneous categories either correspond to the indices of works unquestionably written by two authors (Beaumont and Fletcher, Marlowe and Nash, Marlowe and Chapman, Norton and Sackville) or to Marlowe's dramas whose texts have been supposedly tampered with during the companies' tours in the provinces, particularly "The Jew of Malta" and "Faustus" (cf. Wilson 1953:63,75).

Consider in more detail the RDs in non-Shakespearean dramas as compared to Shakespeare's plays (Tables 3.4 and 3.5). The zone of homogeneous rhythm covers Shelley's "The Cenci", all the dramas by Byron, and Ben Jonson's "Sejanus; His Fall". Individual authorship of these dramas has never been disputed, and each of them, at least the nineteenth-century plays, was written within a short period of time. This strongly suggests that the indices below 6% are, indeed, indicative of dramas with a more homogeneous rhythmical structure resulting from their individual authorship and absence of serious later reworking.

The RDs of acts is particularly small in "The Cenci", in "Marino Faliero", Byron's earliest play in our material, and in Ben Jonson's "Sejanus" (Ben Jonson took special pains in perfecting the style of his poetical works). The homogeneous structure by acts of the nineteenth-century plays is, in a way, quite unexpected: all the dramas of the nineteenth century analyzed, and particularly "The Cenci", display considerable loosening of the iambic meter; a number of lines are metrically marginal, and would in fact be evaluated as

Table 3.3

Comparison of mean values of Range of Dispersion (RD) of Shakespearean plays with selected other plays. Arranged in order of increasing heterogeneity.

Shakespearean plays		Non-Shakespearean plays	
Richard II	3.6		
Hamlet	4.0	Shelley, "The Cenci"	4.0
King John	4.5	Byron, "Marino Faliero"	4.5
Measure for Measure	4.5		
Othello	4.6	Ben Jonson, "Sejanus"	4.7
Richard III	5.0		
King Lear	5.0		
Anthony and Cleopatra	5.3		
Cymbeline	5.3		
Julius Caesar	5.4		
Henry V	5.5		
Henry VI,3	5.6		
Romeo and Juliet	5.6		
Henry VIII	5.6		
Merchant of Venice	5.7		
Coriolanus	5.7	Byron, "The Two Foscari"	5.7
Winter's Tale	5.7	Byron, "Sardanapalus"	5.8
Henry IV,1	5.9	Byron, "Werner"	5.8
Macbeth	6.1	Marlowe, "Edward II"	6.2
Troilus and Cressida	6.4		
Henry VI,1	6.5		
Pericles	6.7	Beaumont/Fletcher, "The Maid's Tragedy"	6.7
Taming of the Shrew	6.8	Marlowe/Nash, "Dido"	6.8
Henry IV,2	6.8		
Timon of Athens	6.8		
Tempest	7.2	Marlowe, "Tamburlaine"	7.2
Two Gentlemen of Verona	7.4		
Henry VI,2	7.8		
All's Well That Ends Well	7.8		
Comedy of Errors	7.9		
Love's Labour's Lost	8.3		
Titus Andronicus	8.7	Norton/Sackville, "Gorboduc"	8.9
		Marlowe/Chapman, "Hero and Leander"	9.1
		Marlowe, "The Jew of Malta"	9.6
As You Like It	9.7		
		Marlowe, "Faustus"	11.0
Midsummer Night's Dream	11.6		

Table 3.4

Stress profiles of separate acts (scenes)
in thirteen non-Shakespearean dramas

Author and Drama	Act (scene)	Positions					Lines	Correlations between positions			
		2	4	6	8	10		4-2	4-6	8-6	10-8
Norton, Sackville "Gorboduc"	I	74.2	88.2	68.2	84.5	92.5	450	+ 14.0	+ 20.0	+ 16.3	+ 8.0
	II	72.0	92.0	62.2	86.4	92.8	250	+ 20.0	+ 29.8	+ 24.2	+ 6.4
	III	72.4	89.2	68.4	82.0	96.0	258	+ 16.8	+ 20.8	+ 13.6	+ 14.0
	IV	66.3	91.5	80.2	80.5	97.0	400	+ 25.2	+ 11.13	+ 0.3	+ 16.5
	V	73.8	88.2	72.8	76.0	94.8	416	+ 14.4	+ 15.4	+ 3.2	+ 18.8
Marlowe "Tamburlaine"	I	65.9	87.8	64.9	81.1	73.1	513	+ 21.9	+ 22.9	+ 16.2	− 8.0
	II	71.2	87.0	66.9	79.7	75.3	375	+ 15.8	+ 20.1	+ 12.8	− 4.4
	III	68.7	87.3	65.2	80.3	71.3	447	+ 18.6	+ 22.1	+ 15.1	− 9.0
	IV	70.9	81.8	70.0	82.6	76.9	350	+ 10.9	+ 11.8	+ 12.6	− 5.7
	V	73.8	89.4	64.6	76.2	80.2	500	+ 15.6	+ 25.0	+ 11.6	+ 4.0
Marlowe "Faustus"	I	70.0	85.2	59.6	70.8	74.8	250	+ 15.2	+ 25.6	+ 11.2	+ 4.0
	II	72.0	85.2	66.0	72.0	82.4	250	+ 13.2	+ 19.2	+ 6.0	+ 10.4
	III	68.8	87.2	68.8	88.0	64.8	250	+ 18.4	+ 18.4	+ 19.2	− 23.2
	IV	70.0	86.4	72.8	82.4	74.0	250	+ 16.4	+ 13.6	+ 9.6	− 8.4
	V	69.9	85.7	67.8	80.4	83.9	230	+ 16.1	+ 17.9	+ 12.6	+ 3.5
"Faustus" segmented according to plot structure	(1) before the scene with the Pope	71.0	85.2	62.8	71.6	78.6	500	+ 14.2	+ 22.4	+ 8.8	+ 7.0
	(2) at the Pope's; scenes with Helen	68.9	85.5	70.9	88.3	64.3	350	+ 16.6	+ 14.6	+ 17.4	− 24.0
	(3) the end	70.5	87.4	68.9	79.5	82.9	380	+ 16.9	+ 16.5	+ 10.6	+ 3.4

Table 3.4 (cont.)

Marlowe "Jew of Malta"	I	70.7	82.8	57.8	79.1	76.7	550	- 12.1	+ 25.0	+ 21.3	- 2.4
	II	61.2	82.5	67.7	71.9	84.0	445	+ 21.3	+ 14.8	+ 4.2	+ 13.1
	III	64.9	86.5	65.9	66.7	86.9	252	+ 21.6	+ 20.6	+ 0.8	+ 20.2
	IV	62.5	85.8	63.5	68.8	88.3	189	+ 23.3	+ 22.3	+ 5.3	+ 19.5
	V	68.6	82.0	62.3	76.3	75.5	350	+ 13.4	+ 19.7	+ 14.0	- 0.8
Marlowe, Nash "Dido"	I	70.8	85.0	77.2	67.7	95.3	294	+ 14.2	+ 7.8	+ 9.5	+ 7.6
	II	66.7	80.8	72.4	72.7	84.4	333	+ 14.1	+ 8.4	+ 0.3	+ 11.7
	III	70.3	85.5	71.9	70.7	93.4	420	+ 15.2	+ 13.6	+ 1.2	+ 22.7
	IV	69.6	84.4	75.4	75.9	91.6	345	+ 14.8	+ 9.0	+ 0.5	+ 15.7
	V	64.7	85.4	73.9	73.3	88.9	314	+ 20.7	+ 11.5	- 0.6	+ 15.6
Marlowe "Edward II"	I	70.6	81.2	71.0	67.8	85.0	500	+ 10.6	+ 10.2	- 3.2	+ 17.2
	II	69.0	81.4	70.6	74.0	81.0	500	+ 12.4	+ 10.8	- 3.4	+ 7.0
	III	68.2	81.6	79.4	71.8	86.0	500	+ 13.4	+ 2.2	- 7.6	+ 14.2
	IV	69.0	85.5	79.1	67.1	86.5	310	+ 16.5	+ 6.4	- 12.0	+ 19.4
	V	70.3	80.5	74.4	70.0	87.7	600	+ 10.2	+ 6.1	- 4.4	+ 17.7
Ben Jonson "Sejanus"	I	65.9	82.4	77.9	65.4	89.0	580	+ 16.5	+ 4.5	- 12.5	+ 23.6
	II	63.4	83.6	73.2	71.2	90.4	500	+ 20.2	+ 10.4	- 1.0	+ 19.2
	III	63.2	81.8	71.5	66.6	87.6	750	+ 18.6	+ 10.3	- 4.9	+ 21.0
	IV	61.9	84.9	72.6	68.7	90.6	522	+ 23.0	+ 12.3	- 3.9	+ 21.9
	V	66.0	82.8	72.0	67.6	91.8	782	+ 16.8	+ 10.8	- 4.4	+ 24.2
Beaumont, Fletcher "The Maid's Tragedy"	I	68.3	84.3	67.3	70.7	92.7	300	+ 16.0	+ 17.0	+ 3.4	+ 22.0
	II	61.5	83.8	70.8	66.2	93.0	400	+ 22.3	+ 13.0	- 4.6	+ 26.8
	III	65.8	81.6	69.2	74.2	91.0	500	+ 15.8	+ 12.4	+ 5.0	+ 16.8
	IV	60.4	80.4	74.4	64.7	92.0	550	+ 20.0	+ 16.0	- 9.7	+ 27.3
	V	59.1	86.2	72.5	67.6	91.6	450	+ 27.1	+ 13.7	- 4.9	+ 24.0
Shelley "The Cenci"	I	58.4	78.5	73.2	70.7	89.4	413	+ 20.1	+ 5.3	- 2.5	+ 18.7
	II	60.5	78.8	74.3	72.9	89.0	354	+ 18.3	+ 4.5	- 1.4	+ 16.1
	III	60.8	77.5	70.6	66.9	89.6	480	+ 16.7	+ 6.9	- 3.7	+ 22.7
	IV	57.5	79.8	71.6	65.7	89.9	475	+ 22.3	+ 8.2	- 5.9	+ 24.2
	V	57.9	80.9	71.9	73.7	88.5	593	+ 23.0	+ 9.0	+ 1.8	+ 14.8

Table 3.4 (cont.)

Byron "Marino Faliero"	I	67.1	75.4	72.1	65.1	92.8	622	+	8.3	+	3.3	− 7.0	+ 27.7
	II	67.2	77.1	69.9	67.3	86.8	716	+	9.9	+	7.2	− 2.6	+ 19.5
	III	63.1	74.3	72.7	66.2	89.4	660	+ 11.2	+	1.6	− 6.5	+ 23.2
	IV	65.8	78.2	72.3	69.0	89.2	664	+ 12.4	+	5.9	− 3.3	+ 20.2
	V	62.0	75.4	71.3	64.2	88.5	824	+ 13.4	+	4.1	− 7.1	+ 24.3
Byron "Sardanapalus"	I	65.2	77.3	72.5	66.9	92.3	713	+ 12.1	+	4.8	− 5.6	+ 25.4
	II	61.0	79.8	73.5	67.5	86.3	600	+ 18.8	+	6.3	− 6.0	+ 18.8
	III	68.0	75.1	75.1	70.8	87.4	437	+	7.1	+	0	− 4.3	+ 16.6
	IV	71.3	75.0	74.9	68.2	88.2	584	+	3.7	+	0.1	− 6.7	+ 20.0
	V	71.6	76.2	72.8	67.8	85.2	498	+	4.6	+	3.8	− 5.0	+ 17.4
Byron "The Two Foscari"	I	66.3	75.0	69.5	67.4	83.7	380	+	8.7	+	5.5	− 2.1	+ 16.3
	II	69.1	69.1	75.0	65.0	80.0	440		0	−	5.9	− 10.0	+ 15.0
	III	67.8	77.5	71.1	70.6	78.4	435	+	9.7	+	6.4	− 0.5	+ 7.8
	IV	68.1	75.9	70.9	69.8	84.6	357	+	7.8	+	5.0	− 1.1	+ 14.8
	V	67.8	76.4	69.4	68.8	84.2	372	+	8.6	+	7.0	− 0.6	+ 15.4
Byron "Werner"	I	71.5	72.8	72.3	67.2	84.4	750	+	1.3	+	0.5	− 5.1	+ 17.2
	II	65.6	75.0	71.9	66.8	82.4	773	+	9.4	+	3.1	− 5.1	+ 15.6
	III	70.5	75.3	71.8	68.5	81.1	600	−	4.8	−	3.5	− 3.3	+ 12.6
	IV	74.6	70.4	76.9	64.2	82.7	550	−	4.2	−	6.5	− 12.7	+ 18.5
	V	74.6	72.6	75.1	64.4	86.7	550	−	2.0	−	2.5	− 10.7	+ 22.3

112

Table 3.5

Range of Dispersion (RD) of stressing by acts of dramas taken for comparison with Shakespeare's

Author and drama	Positions					Mean
	2	4	6	8	10	
Norton/Sackville, "Gorboduc"	7.9	3.8	18.0	10.4	4.5	8.9
Marlowe, "Tamburlaine"	7.9	7.6	5.4	6.4	8.9	7.2
Marlowe, "Faustus"	3.2	2.0	13.2	17.2	19.1	11.0
Marlowe, "Jew of Malta"	9.5	4.5	9.9	12.4	11.6	9.6
Marlowe/Nash, "Dido"	5.1	4.7	5.3	8.2	10.9	6.8
Marlowe, "Edward II"	2.6	5.0	8.8	6.9	6.7	6.0
Ben Jonson, "Sejanus"	4.1	3.1	6.4	5.8	4.2	4.7
Beaumont/Fletcher, "The Maid's Tragedy"	9.2	5.8	7.1	9.5	2.0	6.7
Shelley, "The Cenci"	3.3	3.4	3.7	8.0	1.4	4.0
Byron, "Marino Faliero"	5.2	3.9	2.8	4.8	6.0	4.5
Byron, "Sardanapalus"	10.6	4.8	2.6	3.9	7.1	5.8
Byron, "The Two Foscari"	2.8	8.4	5.6	5.6	6.2	5.7
Byron, "Werner"	9.0	4.9	5.1	4.3	5.6	5.8

"unmetrical" if considered from the point of view of a more traditional form of iambic pentameter (cf. Kiparsky's 1977 definition of iambic pentameter, or Hayes' 1983 statements; see also Tarlinskaja 1985a,b). And yet the nineteenth-century poets managed to stay within a narrow range in their individual rhythmical variation throughout the long plays with their complicated plots and obvious oppositions of various characters.

It is interesting to note the way Byron's three dramas following "Marino Faliero" increase slightly in rhythmical heterogeneity and form a cluster with almost identical indices (5.7-5.8%). Byron's dramas display an increased loosening of meter with time (as with Shakespeare and almost all other poets); however, a broadening of the RD, which is probably one of the consequences of this loosening, remains within the limits evidently characteristic of his individual style.

The transitory zone of medium range of dispersion, which supposedly reflects a clash of tendencies (indices 6-7%), covers two plays by Marlowe: "Edward II" and "Dido Queen of Carthage", the latter written together with Nash, and "The Maid's Tragedy" by Beaumont and Fletcher. Two of these three plays are of mixed authorship. Consequently, the transition category reflects different tendencies coexisting in one play.

Finally, the category of heterogeneous rhythm covers five works. Two of them are of unquestionably mixed authorship: the drama "Gorboduc" by Norton and Sackville and the poem "Hero and Leander" by Marlowe and Chapman (for further discussion, see 3.2).

Three other non-Shakespearean pieces with large values of RD are plays by Marlowe: "Tamburlaine", "The Jew of Malta", and "Doctor Faustus". Marlowe's plays in general, and the latter two in particular, have been poorly preserved, and they apparently were substantially reworked after the poet's death. The second part of "The Jew of Malta" and the middle scenes of "Faustus" (Faustus' miracles worked with Mephistopheles' help, particularly the scenes at the Pope's) are believed to have been supplied, or at least significantly refurbished, by another author. Some scholars trace Dekker's hand in the additions of 1604. Apparently the serious parts of the play had been cut, with an enlargement of the spectacular and comic scenes of conjuring and dancing that appealed to the cruder tastes of the provincial spectators. In 1602 Henslowe paid William Bird and Samuel Rowley for more "additions" to the play which were presumably included in the enlarged edition of 1616 (Baskervill, Heltzel and Nethercot 1965:308). In any case, the aesthetic level of the scenes at the Pope's and with Helen of Troy, the peculiarities of their style and, as we now know, of their verse rhythm, markedly differ from the scenes generally attributed to Marlowe. Diapasons of rhythmical variation on individual ictic positions of "Gorboduc" and several plays by Marlowe (particularly in "Faustus") can only be compared to Shakepeare's "A Midsummer Night's Dream": such broad diapasons are not displayed even by the questionable plays of Shakespeare's canon.

Thus, RDs that exceed 7% are indeed signs of a strongly heterogeneous verse structure and suggest a multiple authorship, in the poets' lifetime or posthumously. And indeed, at least five plays by Shakespeare located in groups two and three (Table 3.3) have been suspected of not having been written by Shakespeare alone. These are: "Henry VI", 1; "Pericles"; "Henry VI", 2; "Timon of Athens"; and "Titus Andronicus". It seems that the range of dispersion of stressing in a play may be used as one argument for distinguishing its single or multiple authorship (see section 3.2).

There are, however, at least seven more reasons for a heterogeneous verse structure of a play, apart from a hypothetical co-authorship.

(1) The yet unformed style of a young poet: most of Shakespeare's earlier dramas display a heterogeneous verse structure by acts, for example, "Henry VI", 1 and 2, "Titus Andronicus", "The Comedy of Errors" (see above); Shakespeare's later plays, even though rhythmically looser and asymmetrical in their line structure, are more homogeneous by acts ("Hamlet", "Othello", "King Lear", "Antony and Cleopatra"): the poet has mastered his technique and is writing with a firm hand. The similarity of Shakespeare's early plays to

the style of his older contemporaries such as Peele, Greene, or Marlowe may be explained not only by a possible co-authorship; the young poet who probably also acted in these plays imitated their rhythm.

(2) Later reworking of the text by Shakespeare himself, for example, "A Midsummer Night's Dream". "A Midsummer Night's Dream" was probably not written at once (Chambers 1930:I,358-360). It is generally believed that the play was first drafted in 1592 and then reworked (possibly twice) for the celebration of a society wedding, either of William, Earl of Derby, to Elizabeth Vere at Greenwich on 26 January 1595, or of Thomas Berkley to Elizabeth Carey at Blackfriars on 17 February 1596. Chambers favored the second wedding and dated the play 1595-96, while Wentersdorf was inclined to believe that the play had been written for the forthcoming marriage of the Earl of Derby, i.e., in the late autumn of 1594 (Wentersdorf 1951:170). Wentersdorf also noted that Queen Elizabeth, who is obviously flattered in the play, was definitely present at the Derby wedding, whilst it is not known whether she attended the nuptials of Thomas Berkley. The heterogeneous structure of "Midsummer Night's Dream" is a possible indicator of the poet's reworking it for a special occasion.

(3) Insertions of prose and doggerel into the main body of iambic pentameter, which might have broken the poet's iambic "inertia".

(4) Stylistic peculiarity of comedy as a genre (see below): of the nine heterogeneous plays by Shakespeare, only two are not comedies (both are early plays and both of questionable authorship: "Titus" and "Henry VI", 2). Comedy and "satyre" as a genre traditionally seemed to require crude verse (cf. Donne's "Satyres" and his other genres: Tarlinskaja and Teterina 1974).

(5) A combination of genres, as in "Love's Labour's Lost" or "A Midsummer Night's Dream", where lyrical drama, folklore-like fairy-tale, and burlesque are interlaced in one text; or insertions of a play in play, as in "Hamlet" or "The Merry Wives of Windsor;" or rhetorical prologues and epilogues which rhythmically and even metrically differ from the main text: cf. Prologue and Epilogue in "Henry V" spoken by a chorus, or Gower's monologues which open and close "Pericles:" the prologue is in iambic tetrameter and the epilogue in rhymed pentameter.

(6) The specific features of text composition, of the plot structure, the types of personages involved in different acts, and character development (see Chapter 4). Even in rhythmically homogeneous plays one act is often unlike the others; in rhythmically heterogeneous plays which combine different, sometimes opposing tendencies one act as a rule is particularly dissimilar to the rest. Generally, this is either the first or the fifth act, less frequently both the first and fifth. For example, in "Hamlet", "The Merchant of Venice", "Titus Andronicus", and "Timon of Athens" it is Act V; in "Measure for Measure", "All's Well That Ends Well", and "The Comedy of Errors" it is Act I; while in "A Midsummer Night's Dream" it is the first and the fifth acts that provide two opposing rhythmical tendencies and account for the highest rhythmical

variation index found in Shakespeare's plays. This phenomenon may be explained in at least two ways: compositional laws of verse structure, and compositional laws of plot evolution.

The frequent opposition between the first and the last acts is probably explained by the composition laws of the plot evolution: plotting of the intrigue, its climax and its denouement evidently call forth idiosyncratic kinds of rhythm.

There also seem to be more general laws of verse structure which cause isomorphism of different levels of verse texts. In the first act of a play the poet does not yet follow a firm rhythmical "momentum"; his starting point and his background "thesaurus" are his own preceding works or the verse of his contemporaries in the same or different genres. The poet is still working out a rhythm which will be further molded and confirmed in the following acts. That is, hypothetically, why the first act sometimes differs from the following ones, where the rhythmical style becomes formed and firmed up.

It is noteworthy that in the English iambic verse, both pentameter and tetrameter, the first line of a poem and of a stanza differs from the rest of the text: its form is usually looser than that of other lines (see Fig. 7.3). Inside verse lines, the beginnings of the line, "hemistich" and phrase also display a looser structure than other parts of these units (cf. Bjorklund 1978:243 and Hayes 1983). This structural rule of verse units seems to be at work not only inside a drama, but even within a canon: Shakespeares's early dramas, the beginning of his canon, display the most rhythmical variety, while later plays are much more homogeneous. We can draw a parallel between later plays of a canon and the second line of a quatrain stanza (see Chapter 7, Tables 7.4 and 7.5) which is usually more regular than the first line.

The idiosyncrasy of Act V might be explained by the same factors which explain the difference of the end of a line from its beginning, of the last line in a stanza from its other lines, of the first line of a poem from the rest of its text, and of the last stanza from other stanzas of a poem (cf. B.H. Smith 1968, Gasparov 1974:100; see also Chapter 7). Preparation of the finale changes the form of verse segments on different levels. Possibly, preparation for the denouement changes the form of the final act. Thus, isomorphism of tendencies seems to exist not only on different levels of a text, such as, for example, parts of a verse line—the whole verse line—a stanza—the whole poem, but seem to be also at work in dramas and in the whole dramatic canon. The first acts display their own rhythmic features, as do the final acts; early plays are the least homogeneous rhythmically (as are the final plays: cf. "Henry VIII"); Shakespeare's mid-canon plays are by and large the most homgeneous of all.

(7) The length of the texts: the shorter the acts (as in most comedies), the more heterogeneous the play appears statistically.

Consider how the mean deviation (MD) of ictic stresses of acts from the general stress profile. Arranged in the increasing order of MD, the dramas form the following sequence:

Hamlet	1.12
Measure for Measure	1.30
Richard II	1.38
King Lear	1.46
Henry VI, 3	1.48
King John	1.53
Richard III	1.59
Cymbeline	1.59
Henry VIII	1.61
Othello	1.63
Antony and Cleopatra	1.67
Merchant of Venice	1.68
Henry VI, 1	1.70
Julius Caesar	1.70
Winter's Tale	1.71
Romeo and Juliet	1.71
Coriolanus	1.83
Henry IV, 1	1.89
Pericles	2.04
Henry IV, 2	2.05
Henry V	2.05
Macbeth	2.09
Timon of Athens	2.13
Troilus and Cressida	2.13
Taming of the Shrew	2.14
All's Well that Ends Well	2.14
Tempest	2.14
Two Gentlemen of Verona	2.28
Comedy of Errors	2.35
Henry VI, 2	2.40
Love's Labour's Lost	2.58
As You Like It	2.65
Titus Andronicus	2.96
Midsummer Night's Dream	3.55

The arrangement of the plays is not unlike that in Table 3.3. The same 18 dramas display internally heterogeneous rhythm; "Hamlet", however, has changed places with "Richard II" and is the most homogeneous play. The number of truly heterogeneous plays (a threshold was assumed between 2.14 and 2.28) has decreased from nine (Table 3.3) to seven. The most heterogeneous plays are again "A Midsummer Night's Dream" and "Titus Anronicus", together with four comedies and a chronicle of possibly mixed authorship ("Henry VI", 2). Heterogeneous rhythm, as noted above, is a possible indication of mixed authorship (see section 3.2). Even more obviously, heterogeneous rhythm is particularly typical of the genre of comedy.

Consider Table 3.6 in which the plays are divided into five genres: (1) Chronicles, (2) Pure Comedies, (3) Dark Comedies ("Merchant of Venice" has been included in Dark Comedies), (4) Tragedies, and (5) Romances. The genres arranged in the increasing order of mean MD form the following sequence:

Chronicles	1.77
Dark Comedies	1.81
Tragedies	1.83
Romances	1.86
Pure Comedies	2.59

The main genre differentiation opposes the pure comedies to all other genres. This is shown graphically in Fig. 3.2 where the MDs of the plays plotted chronologically are identified by genre: all but one of the pure comedies lie well outside Shakespeare's norm of act stress variation (we note that the early tragedy and early chronicle outside the norm are "Titus" and "Henry VI", 2). Pure comedies are most strongly opposed to chronicles. Prior to 1600, 80% of Shakespeare's plays were either one or the other of these genres, so it was during the first half of his career when he resorted to the largest variations of internal rhythm, quite obviously opposing the genres "chronicle-comedy". But all other genres are like chronicles, therefore there is really no trend in

Table 3.6

Mean Deviation of Ictic Stressing by Acts (MD), arranged by genre

		Syllabic Position					
		2	4	6	8	10	Mean
Chronicles							
1589	Henry VI, 1	1.0	1.8	2.8	1.0	1.9	1.70
1590	Henry VI, 2	2.4	2.0	26	2.0	3.0	2.40
1590	Henry VI, 3	1.5	1.1	1.9	1.4	1.5	1.48
1591	Richard III	1.4	2.9	0.9	1.8	0.9	1.59
1594	Richard II	1.5	0.5	1.9	1.6	1.4	1.38
1595	King John	1.4	1.7	1.3	2.5	0.7	1.53
1596	Henry IV, 1	3.5	1.4	0.9	1.8	1.9	1.89
1596	Henry IV, 2	1.8	1.8	1.7	2.8	2.2	2.05
1598	Henry V	4.0	1.0	1.2	2.1	2.0	2.05

Table 3.6 (cont.)

Year	Play						
1612	Henry VIII	1.3	2.7	0.8	1.8	1.4	1.61
	MEAN	2.0	1.7	1.6	1.9	1.7	1.77

Pure Comedies

Year	Play						
1589	Comedy of Errors	3.0	2.2	3.5	2.0	1.0	2.35
1591	Taming of the Shrew	2.8	1.9	1.6	2.8	1.6	2.14
1592	Two Gentlemen of Verona	2.4	3.2	2.8	1.5	1.5	2.28
1593	Love's Labour's Lost	3.7	1.4	2.2	4.0	1.6	2.58
1594	Midsummer Night's Dream	1.6	3.0	5.5	5.3	2.4	3.55
1599	As You Like It	3.5	1.8	4.8	1.9	1.3	2.65
	MEAN	2.8	2.3	3.4	2.9	1.6	2.59

Dark Comedies

Year	Play						
1595	Merchant of Venice	1.9	1.4	1.3	2.0	1.8	1.68
1601	Troilus and Cressida	1.3	1.5	3.4	3.1	1.3	2.13
1603	Measure for Measure	1.8	1.8	0.7	1.4	0.8	1.30
1604	All's Well that Ends Well	1.7	2.8	1.6	2.4	2.2	2.14
	MEAN	1.7	1.9	1.8	2.2	1.5	1.81

Tragedies

Year	Play						
1588	Titus Andronicus	2.1	2.5	3.7	3.7	2.8	2.96
1594	Romeo and Juliet	2.1	1.2	1.5	2.4	1.7	1.78
1598	Julius Caesar	2.6	0.9	2.9	1.1	1.0	1.70
1600	Hamlet	1.1	1.7	0.7	1.1	1.0	1.12
1603	Othello	1.7	1.2	2.9	1.4	0.9	1.63
1604	Timon of Athens	1.7	1.6	3.1	2.1	2.0	2.10
1605	King Lear	1.7	0.7	2.4	1.7	0.8	1.46
1605	Macbeth	2.0	1.5	3.2	2.8	0.9	2.09
1606	Antony and Cleopatra	1.7	1.2	0.9	2.4	2.2	1.67
	MEAN	1.9	1.4	2.4	2.1	1.5	1.83

Romances

Year	Play						
1607	Pericles	2.0	2.2	2.3	0.9	2.8	2.04
1607	Coriolanus	1.9	2.4	2.2	1.7	1.0	1.84
1608	Cymbeline	1.4	1.2	1.5	2.4	1.4	1.59
1609	Winter's Tale	2.6	1.3	1.9	1.1	1.7	1.71
1610	Tempest	2.0	1.5	2.6	2.9	1.7	2.14
	MEAN	2.0	1.7	2.1	1.8	1.7	1.86

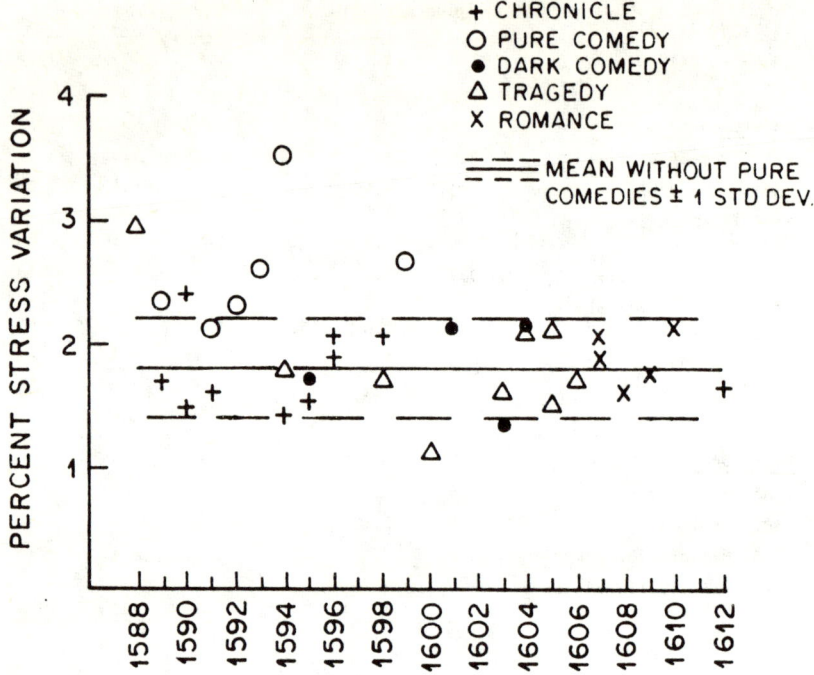

Fig. 3.2. Mean percent stress variation by acts (MD) plotted chronologically, and identified by genre. At this level of internal stress variability, all Shakespeare's plays except pure comedies lie within a limited range of act heterogeneity, centered at 1.8% variation of stressing on ictic positions. The genre of pure comedy stands out as having much more variable stressing. Data from Table 3.6.

internal rhythmical variation by acts over his whole career, even though there are definite trends in many other rhythmical parameters.

It is interesting to contrast the most homogeneous play, "Hamlet", and the most heterogeneous play, "A Midsummer Night's Dream". "Hamlet" is, of course, Shakespeare's most intellectual and most philosophical play. "A Midsummer Night's Dream" can certainly not be qualified as the least sophisticated play of Shakespeare's canon, but the opposition "serious, meditative—comical, active" which can be applied to "Hamlet" and "A Midsummer Night's Dream" (and other comedies) is echoed in the rhythmical structure opposition "homogeneous—heterogeneous" (compare the stress profiles of these plays in Fig. 3.1). In Chapter 4 we will see this same opposition: different rhythmical styles are used to contrast serious, meditative, and non-active characters with comical and active personages: one more obvious link between verse form and meaning!

3.2 Contrast between groupings of acts or scenes in three questionable or stylistically heterogeneous plays

To study further the significance of rhythmical heterogeneity within plays, we analyze three "questionable" dramas, dividing each into two groupings of acts or scenes, "Shakespearean" and "non-Shakespearean". These are: "Titus Andronicus", "Pericles", and "Henry VIII".

Henslowe's record of a performance of "Titus Andronicus" by Sussex's on January 24, 1594, is marked "ne" (new); but if this means that the piece was then completely new it seems unlikely that Shakespeare was the original author. In Wentersdorf's opinion, a master poet who had produced "Midsummer Night's Dream" in the fall of 1594 could not have written—however carelessly—such a crude drama as "Titus" at the same time (Wentersdorf 1951:165). More likely, Henslowe's record means that the play was a <u>new production</u> of an older drama, reworked by Shakespeare. The question is then: did Shakespeare rework somebody else's or his own play? Earlier scholars believed that the author of the source play belonged to a pre-Shakespearean school; in their opinion, parallels in thought and phrasing suggested that the author of the original melodrama was Peele (e.g., Parrott 1919:23,25). Parrott analyzed line endings of separate scenes and claimed that those with a higher proportion of feminine endings (later substrate) had been reworked or written by Shakespeare, while scenes with a lower proportion of feminine endings (early substrate) pointed to Peele. As we shall see below, this may not necessarily be proof of another author's hand, but merely the sign of an earlier date of the scenes.

J. C. Maxwell compared specific grammatical constructions of the two susbstrates of "Titus" and came to the conclusion that even if Act I had indeed been written by another author, the "stylometric test" "pointed away from Peele" (J.C. Maxwell 1950:558).

Still other scholars are inclined to believe that "Titus" shows signs of a painstaking but inexperienced juvenile effort. The stylistic peculiarities of the play, in Hills' opinion, reveal immaturity, "naivete and uncertain grasp of method such as one might expect in a dramatist of five-and-twenty" (Hill 1957:69). Scholars who studied word links between "Titus" and other plays and poems by Shakespeare (Slater 1975), or the use of rare words in these works (Jackson 1979:152-158), are also inclined to suppose that the whole of "Titus Andronicus" looks like Shakespeare, but part of it belongs to a very early date (Jackson 1979:153). Jackson, however, did not reject outright the possibility that part of "Titus" is the work of another author—Peele.

Analysis of line endings of "Titus Andronicus" by scenes reveals that the latter fall into two groups: (1) with a low proportion of feminine endings (as low as 2.3% in Act I, scene II) and (2) with a relatively high proportion of feminine endings (up to 18% in Act V, scene I) (see Chapter 5, Table 5.5; cf. Parrott 1919:37). A low proportion of feminine endings is a sign of earlier Elizabethan verse (Timberlake 1931, Tarlinskaja 1976: Table 47). The scenes with the lowest proportion of non-masculine endings (below 5% of all lines) can be grouped into the following cluster: I,I; II,I-II; IV,I (773 lines), while the scenes with the highest proportion of feminine endings (beginning with 11%) into the following cluster: II,III; III,II; IV,II-III; V,I and V,III (1005 lines). The first cluster includes primarily the scenes from the first two acts and the second cluster mainly the scenes from the last two acts of the play. The stress profiles of Groups 1 and 2 are as follows:

	Syllabic Positions					Difference	
	2	4	6	8	10	4–6	8–6
Group 1	67.4	83.7	72.8	71.4	84.9	+10.9	−1.4
Group 2	68.7	85.6	69.9	75.2	88.0	+15.7	+5.3

Here are some typical examples from the two groups of scenes:
Group 1:

Noble patricians, patrons <u>of</u> my right,	(8)
Defend the justice <u>of</u> my cause with arms;	(6)
And, countrymen, my loving followers,	
Plead my successive title <u>with</u> your swords:	(8)
I am his first-born son, that <u>was</u> the last	(8)
That ware the imperial dia<u>dem</u> of Rome;	(8)
. . . .	
Friends, that have been thus forward <u>in</u> my right,	(8)
I thank you all, and here dismiss you all,	
And to the love and favour <u>of</u> my country	(8)
Commit myself, my person, <u>and</u> the cause.	(8)
("Titus Andronicus", I,I:1-6,59-62)	

Group 2:

Out on thee, murde<u>rer</u>! thou kill'st my heart;	(6)
Mine eyes are cloyed with view of tyranny:	
A deed of death done <u>on</u> the innocent	(6)
Becomes not Titus' brother: get thee gone;	
I see thou art not <u>for</u> my company.	(6)
. . . .	
O, take this warm kiss <u>on</u> thy pale cold lips,	(6)

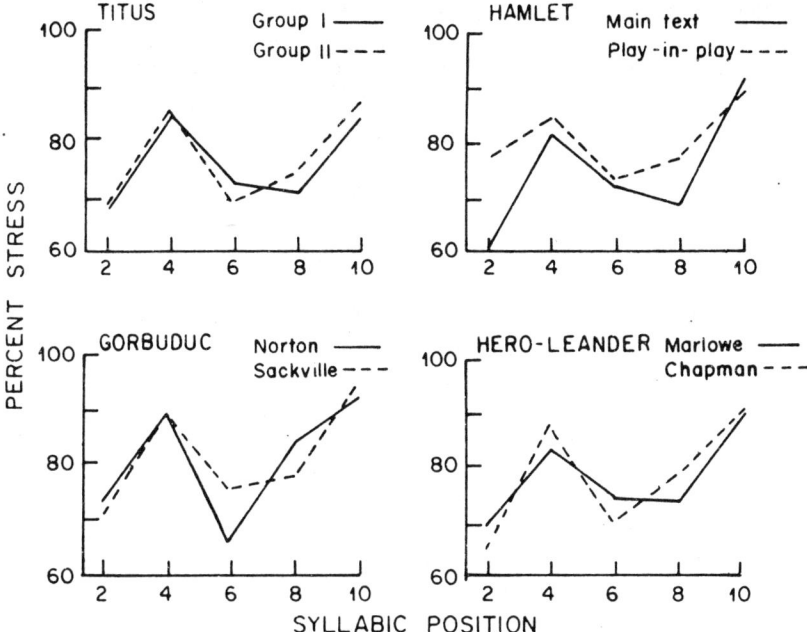

Fig. 3.3. Stress profiles (ictic positions only) of four texts, each divided into two groups. Division of "Titus Andronicus" is based on line endings, and Group I represents the earlier substrate; the stress profile supports this conclusion. The "play-in-play" profile of "Hamlet" illustrates its much more rigid verse structure vis-a-vis the main text. The profiles for "Gorboduc" and "Hero and Leander" illustrate the markedly different rhythmical styles that can occur in co-authored plays.

Those sorrowful drops up<u>on</u> thy blood-stained face, (6)
The last true duties <u>of</u> thy noble son! (6)
("Titus Andronicus", IV,I:54-8 and V,III:153-155)

Stress profiles of the two groups are graphed in Fig. 3.3. Group 2 displays a stressing tendency typical of Shakespeare's first period: there is a "dip" in position 6 (a rigidity index of +5% is characteristic of the theatre seasons 1588-1596), and ictus II (end of the first "hemistich") is strongly opposed to III (cf. Tables 2.1 and 2.2). Group 1, on the other hand, shows a different tendency: ictus IV is slightly weaker than III, and the difference between positions 4 and 6 is lower than in any play of the first period. A smaller opposition between strong and weak ictuses, and the absence of a "dip" on position 6 is a sign of a less rigid canon: the canon has either not crystallized yet, and the verse form is still not strict enough, or the verse form has already begun to loosen (cf. Periods II and IIIa, Table 2.1). In "Titus Andronicus" the first cause must be the case; the scenes of the first group display signs of a more archaic rhythmical style than do those of the second group. This might be either a sign of Shakespeare's own earlier efforts or of an earlier substrate reworked by Shakespeare. As shown below, leveling of positions 6 and 8 does occur in some acts of Shakespeare's early plays (see Table 3.1) and a slight "dip" in position 8, exactly as in the scenes of Group 1 in "Titus", was observed in "Venus and Adonis". Interestingly, Slater's word link test also showed a strong correlation between "Titus" and "Venus and Adonis" (Slater 1971:160-161). The stress profile data can be taken as an indication of Shakespeare's own authorship of "Titus Andronicus", but at a very early date. The difference between the two groups of scenes, however, is significant enough to postulate either a mixed authorship of the play or a considerable time interval between the earlier and the reworked variants. The variation of rhythm in "Titus Andronicus" between act groupings is very reminiscent of Shakespeare's variation by period (Chapter 2), as if quite a number of years separated Act I from the rest of the text. The stress profiles of "Titus" divided into the two substrates (Fig. 3.3) strongly support this contention. Combined with the line-ending evidence, one is really tempted to attribute "Titus" to two different authors; probably Shakespeare did rework an earlier, substrate play.

"Pericles" is another play that has raised doubt as to Shakespeare's sole authorship. The play was not included in the first folio; a possible indication that Heminge and Condell did not consider it Shakespeare's. The difference in style between various parts of the play led Chambers to divide it into four segments: (a) acts I-II; (b) acts III-V; (c) the brothel scenes in Act IV, scenes II,V,VI, written mainly in prose; and (d) Gower's prologues and epilogues (Chambers 1930,I:525-526). The stylistic difference between acts I-II and III-V had been noticed long before Chambers; in 1874 Fleay published an article on "Pericles" in which he presented a table with the absolute number of rhymed lines, "double endings", Alexandrines, and short lines in both parts (Fleay 1874c:195). Fleay's interpretation of the data seems today absurd; but the fact of a discrepancy between the two parts remains. Commenting on the stylistic dissimilarity between acts I-II and III-V, Chambers admitted that only acts III-V resemble the style of Shakespeare's later plays, while acts I-II are quite unlike Shakespeare. Gower's texts also struck Chambers as non-Shakespearean. He suggested that the probable author of the non-Shakespearean fragments might have been George Wilkins who, in 1608, published a prose version of "Pericles", and who had been connected with The King's Men (see also Alexander 1938:222, Muir 1960:56-96).[1] The stylistic difference betweeen acts I-II and III-V made Kenneth Muir assume that "Shakespeare based his play on the work of another dramatist, making few alterations in the opening acts and completely rewriting the last three" (Muir 1960:77; cf. also 78).

The stress profiles of acts I-II (720 lines) and III-V (598 lines) are as follows:

	Syllabic Positions									
Acts	1	2	3	4	5	6	7	8	9	10
I-II	22.1	66.8	9.3	<u>85.0</u>	9.2	73.2	7.6	70.2	3.8	89.0
III-V	22.0	64.9	8.5	80.1	9.2	73.8	<u>12.9</u>	68.6	8.5	86.5

Acts	$\bar{S}$ (2-8)	$\bar{W}$ (3-9)	Iambic Index ($\bar{S} - \bar{W}$)
I-II	73.8	7.4	66.4
III-V	71.8	9.8	62.0

The general stress tendencies of the two portions are not unlike; but there are some relevant differences: (1) position 4, the end of the first "hemistich", is noticeably more strongly stressed in acts I-II than in III-V and stronger than in Shakespeare's other plays of the last period. Such a strong stress in position 4, indicating a break after position 4 (5), was last observed in "Othello" (1604-05) which in its turn was an exception; (2) non-ictic stresses have no absolute maximum in the middle of the line in acts I-II but display a maximum on position 7 in acts III-V, similarly with all other Shakespearean dramas beginning in at least 1599-1600 ("Twelfth Night", Table 2.5); (3) the iambic index of acts III-V is close to those of all other plays of periods II and IIIa,b, while in acts I-II it is untypically high; such a high iambic index is found only in Period I (e.g., "Romeo and Juliet", "Richard II"); an iambic index exceeding 65% has not occurred in Shakepeare's canon for 13 years, since 1594-95. So the stress profile of acts I-II of "Pericles" does indeed suggest a non-Shakespearean hand.

The structure of line endings (Chapter 5), the proportion of lines split between two characters, and the typical location of the split in the lines (Chapter 4) also suggest a possible non-Shakespearean origin (or an earlier date; or both) of acts I-II.

The play "Henry VIII", a fascinating object of study, has long been, and still is, the cause of controversy among scholars. Presumably Shakespeare's final play, it was acted by The King's Men on June 29, 1613, a year after Shakespeare had retired. But he evidently from time to time came to London and was still connected with the company (Thorndike 1901:37). The only external evidence that the play is Shakespeare's is its place in the folio of 1623. True, the folio editors certainly included some other plays not wholly Shakespeare's and omitted others in which he had a part, e.g., "The Two Noble Kinsmen" (Mincoff 1952); they did not, however, include any play in which Shakespeare did <u>not</u> have a share. "In 1623, if no other part of the play was by Shakespeare his fellow actors must have known it, and there is no reason to imagine that they would have placed it in the folio" (Thorndike 1901:39).

In August 1850 James Spedding, Esq., published an essay in "Gentleman's

Magazine" under the title "Who wrote Shakspere's Henry VIII?", which was reprinted in 1874 in "Transactions of the New Shakspere Society" (Spedding 1874). Stylistic idiosyncrasies of "Henry VIII" had been earlier observed by Tennyson, who in a conversation with Spedding several years previously expressed the view that the style in some portions of "Henry VIII" resembled Fletcher's (Schoenbaum 1966:34). Spedding came to the conclusion, supported by Hickson (1978), Fleay (1974f: *23), and Spalding (1876), that the portion of Shakespeare in "Henry VIII" was limited to I:I,II; II:III,IV; III:II (the first 202 and a half lines, until the exit of the King), and V:I. The rest of the play was attributed to Fletcher. The attribution was based on the structure of line endings: "the proportion of redundant syllables" at the end of the line in certain parts of the play, which is twice as high "as in any other play of Shakspere's", and "the number of passages in which the lines are so run into each other that it is impossible to separate them in reading by the slightest pause at the end of each" (Spedding 1874: *2; cf. Nicolson 1922). This opinion, confirmed in 1901 by Thorndike's "them—'em" test (Thorndike 1901:35-44), was accepted even by such an authority and opponent of "disintegrators" as Chambers (1930: I,496) (the "disintegrators" have gone so far as to exclude Shakespeare from "Henry VIII" altogether and to substitute for him Massinger; cf. Boyle 1880-1886: 443-488, Sykes 1919:18-47).

In later years, however, voices were raised in defense of Shakespeare's sole authorship of "Henry VIII". Baldwin Maxwell (1939), while accepting in principle the probability of Fletcher's hand in "Henry VIII", questioned Neilson's and Thorndike's statement that "after making a fairly detailed outline, each writer took certain scenes, and to all intents, completed these scenes after his own fashion" (Neilson and Thorndike 1922:160). He found the style of the allegedly Fletcherean portion of the play unlike that of Fletcher's individual plays and suggested "that the scenes assigned to Fletcher had not been written by him alone 'after his own fashion'. They suggest that, if indeed he had a hand in the play at all, his participation was limited: either he was revising another's work, or the peculiarities of his style and method were modified by a collaborator" (Baldwin Maxwell 1939:63). Other scholars, e.g., Alexander (1931:85-119 and 1938:219), Craig (1945), and Foakes (ed., 1957:XVII-XXVI), completely denied Fletcher's participation in "Henry VIII". Peter Alexander, trying to explain the high incidence of feminine endings in "Henry VIII", pointed out that they occur in all of Shakespeare's later plays. A metrical test, in his opinion, "can carry no weight by itself, since Shakespeare's later plays show an increase in the use of double endings that might well have developed in *Henry VIII*" (Alexander 1938:219). Thus, according to Alexander, the striking frequency of feminine endings in parts of "Henry VIII" does not suggest that Fletcher wrote these parts but that a tendency already noticeable in Shakespeare's late romances became intensified—admittedly to a very marked extent, but no more, he claims, than could be expected of a writer whose versification had already undergone a rather sudden transformation during 1606/7, in "Antony and Cleopatra" (cf. Oras 1953:198). Alexander did not try to explain, and probably did not realize, that the incidence of such endings is almost two times higher in some scenes of "Henry VIII" than in others and that there are also other important stylistic discrepancies between separate scenes of "Henry VIII". These differences in style and rhythm appear and reappear without reference to the subject matter, the logic of plot development, or individual idiosyncrasies of personage; for example, why would "...the conversation in I.I. be in one style, and the very similar conversation in I.III. in the other, or why should Katharine defend herself at Blackfriars in one style, and before the legates in another?" (Mincoff 1961:245).

Three articles published between 1953 and 1961, which present detailed linguistic analyses of "Henry VIII" (Oras 1953, Law 1959, and Mincoff 1961, cf. Mincoff 1952 on "The Two Noble Kinsmen"), give new proof of a Shakespeare-Fletcher collaboration in the play; a detailed outline of the articles is given in Chapter 5. Here it is sufficient to say that their findings seem to me convincing and are supported by my own data (see Chapters 5 and 6).

Let us begin by comparing stress profiles of "Shakespeare's" and "Fletcher's" portions of the play. To compare with Fletcher's presumed portion of "Henry VIII" consider the stress profile of 757 lines from Fletcher's "Bonduca" (1614): act III scenes 1-5, act IV scenes 1-3.

Syllabic Positions

	1	2	3	4	5	6	7	8	9	10
Shak "HVIII"	20.7	64.9	11.0	79.2	8.0	75.6	10.5	67.4	13.0	86.9
Flet "HVIII"	24.5	63.7	16.6	83.6	12.3	75.7	13.3	71.9	13.2	92.0
Flet "Bond"	32.0	65.3	14.9	88.2	12.8	79.9	20.1	74.4	18.6	95.7

	$\bar{S}$ (2-10)	$\bar{W}$ (1-9)
Shak "HVIII"	74.8	12.6
Flet "HVIII"	77.4	16.0
Flet "Bond"	80.7	19.7

The general tendency of both portions from "Henry VIII" are not unlike: both clearly represent a later Elizabethan-Jacobean rhythmical style with a "dip" on position 8, particularly low in "Shakespeare's" text. There are, however, a number of relevant discrepancies.

(1) A high incidence of stress on positions 4 and 10 in Fletcher's portion of "Henry VIII" and particularly in "Bonduca"; these are signs of a rhythmical-

127

syntactical break after position 4 (5) and of "end-stopped", syntactically complete lines. A "dip" in position 8 and a relatively strong non-ictic stress on 7 and/or 9 indicate another rhythmical-syntactic break after positions 6, 7, or 8. Such a three-part line segmentation into relatively simple sometimes structurally recurrent, grammatical phrases is characteristic of Fletcher (cf. Partridge 1949:27-30, Mincoff 1961:249). Some examples from Fletcher's "Bonduca" are:

> I doe not fear.-/My good boy.-/I know, Uncle,
> Yes, my sweet boy./-Mine Aunt too,/and my Cosins?
> All, my good childe./-No Romans, Uncle?-/No, boy.
> I warrant thee;/come cheerfully.-/And boldly.
> ("Bonduca" IV,II:2,9,10,72,89)
> Desperate and strange./-'Tis won, Sir,/and the Britains
> I am glad of this,/I have found ye.-/In my belly
> O how it tumbles?/-Ye good gods,/I thank Ye.
> ("Bonduca" IV,IV:154,158,159)
> Look, Uncle, look,/these multitudes/that march there
> Now dry thine eyes,/my boy.-/Are they all gone?
> ("Bonduca" V,I:22,91)
> Run, run, ye Rogues,/ye precious Rogues,/ye rank Rogues
> ("Bonduca" IV,II:72)
> cf.: O, very mad,/exceeding mad,/in love too;
> ("Henry VIII", I,IV:28)

(2) A strong mean stress on ictuses; and

(3) Greater stressing of non-ictuses: Fletcher's verse abounds in extrametrical stresses which occur in a phrase not only "proclitically", as in Shakespeare's texts, but also "enclitically" (see Chapter 6). Some examples of proclitic stresses are: . . . *a nobler sir* \ *ne'er líved*; *For whom my heart* \ *dròps blood* / *and my false spírits* ("Cymbeline" V,V:145,148). Some examples of enclitic stresses are: *His many thousand ways* \ *to lèt òut* / *soul; Thou art a Souldier:* /*strìke hóme,* \ *hóme; have at ye* ("Bonduca" III,V:103,158). The syntactical and rhythmical structure of Fletcher's verse make it sound much "heavier" than Shakespeare's.

The rythmical differences between the Shakespearean and Fletcherean portions of "Henry VIII" seem to be another indication of the dual authorship of the play. Plays written solely by Shakespeare are rhythmically much more homogeneous than is "Henry VIII". Consider, for example, stress profiles of acts I-III and IV-V of "Cymbeline":

				Syllabic Positions					
Acts	1	2	3	4	5	6	7	8	9	10
I-III	20.0	66.6	10.1	79.0	8.9	76.2	10.6	71.0	11.7	86.5
IV-V	19.7	69.3	12.0	80.5	10.8	77.8	14.2	74.4	10.0	90.6

Both ictic and non-ictic positions of the two portions are stressed in similar ways and resemble each other closely. In contrast, stress profiles of portions of dramas hypothetically written by two authors display much greater differences, as we found with all three plays analyzed above.

To make this point more convincing I analyzed stress profiles of two works that we know positively were written by two authors: "The Tragedy of Gorboduc" by Thomas Norton and Thomas Sackville, and "Hero and Leander" by Marlowe and Chapman.

"The Tragedy of Gorboduc" is the first regular English tragedy-chronicle and the first English play to be written in blank verse. It was acted by the Gentlemen of the Inner Temple during their Christmas festival in 1561-62 and again before Queen Elizabeth at Whitehall Palace, January 18, 1562. The title-page of the edition of 1565 informs us that three acts were by Thomas Norton and the last two by Thomas Sackville (Baskervill, Heltzel and Nethercot 1965:77). Here are the stress profiles of the two portions:

Syllabic Positions

Acts	1	2	3	4	5	6	7	8	9	10
Norton I-III	20.4	73.4	7.3	89.7	7.2	<u>66.9</u>	5.4	84.6	0.4	93.6
Sackville IV-I	22.4	70.5	7.4	90.0	9.9	<u>76.1</u>	7.0	78.2	2.3	95.6

Correlation between:	4-6	8-6
Norton I-III	+22.8	+17.7
Sackville IV-V	+13.9	+ 1.1

The opposition of strong and weak ictuses is clearly marked in Norton's portion but is dramatically less in Sackville's part of the play; the "hemistich" line segmentation 4 + 6/5 + 5 is more pronounced in Norton's first two acts with their "dip" in position 6. Non-ictic stresses are somewhat stronger in Sackville's portion, particularly in the second half of his line. Some typical examples are:

Norton:
Shall stretch the thread \ of <u>your</u> prolonged days   (6)
Too soon he clamb \ in<u>to</u> the flaming car,   (6)
Whose want of skill \ did set the earth on fire.
Time and example \ <u>of</u> your noble grace   (6)
Shall teach your sons \ both <u>to</u> obey and rule.   (6)
("Gorboduc" I,II:329-333)

Sackville:
I pray to Jove / that <u>we</u> may rather wail   (6)
Such hap in them / that witness <u>in</u> ourselves   (8)

    Eke fully with the duke \ my mind agrees,
    Though kings forget \ to govern a̲s̲ they ought,   (8)
    Yet subjects must obey / as t̲h̲e̲y̲ are bound.   (8)
                                              ("Gorboduc" V,I:39-43)

The more marked rhythmical bipartite segmentation of Norton's portion is accompanied by a more marked syntactic segmentation. I calculated the proportion of syntactic breaks after positions 1-9 of Norton's and Sackville's acts. The highest number of breaks occurs in both portions at the juncture of "hemistichs", after positions 4 (5) (*A minore*): about 75% of all strong and medium breaks in the lines. But Sackville's acts display another relative maximum of syntactic breaks after position 6. Thus, Norton's line is almost always structured 4+6 or 5+5, while Sackville's displays one more, competing tendency: *A mayore*, a longer first half-line, 6+4 line structure (cf. Shakespeare's "Venus and Adonis").

Obviously, the rhythm of stresses and of the syntactic segmentation of the lines in the portions belonging to two co-authors of the same play are different even in "Gorboduc", a considerably constrained drama, which at first glance seems rhythmically homogeneous and monotonous.

A second example of the difference in authors' rhythmical styles is found in the poem "Hero and Leander", the first two sestiades of which were written by Marlowe (818 lines) and the last four (after Marlowe's death) by Chapman (1592 lines). The stress profiles of ictuses in Marlowe's and Chapman's portions are:

	Syllabic Positions					Difference between positions:		
	2	4	6	8	10	4-2	4-6	8-6
Marlowe	69.8	84.3	75.4	75.4	90.6	+14.5	+8.9	0
Chapman	64.2	88.3	71.0	78.7	91.7	+24.1	+17.3	+7.7

The different structure of Marlowe's and Chapman's half-lines is striking: in the first two sestiades, ictuses III and IV are leveled as in "Edward II" (cf. Table 2.6), while in the last four sestiades the midline ictus III (position 6) is particularly weakened as in "Bussi d'Ambois" (Tarlinskaja 1976: Table 50). An opposition of strong and weak ictuses and a symmetrical bipartitite segmentation of the line is very typical of Chapman's rhythmical style.

A clear rhythmical division between co-authors' styles is seen when the stress profiles of each author's text are superimposed (Fig. 3.3). Norton and Chapman each used in these works notably more canonized verse (in the English poetic tradition) than did their respective co-authors. We note that it is the large differences in stressing on ictuses III and IV that are the cause of the large values of range of dispersion (RD; secton 3.1.2).

Here are some additional particulars of Marlowe's and Chapman's verse rhythm: the frequency of occurrence of the "rhythmical figure" SW (a missing stress on S followed by a strong stress on W): for example: *ănd thē brĭ́ght flăme*, or *ănd thē hĕ́ll rèeks* (see Chapters 7-8). This rhythmical figure occurs 45 times per 1000 lines in Marlowe's portion of "Hero and Leander" and 138 times per 1000 lines in Chapman's portion, or three time more frequently. A poet's rhythmical idiosyncrasy is obviously displayed on various levels of verse structure.

3.3 Play-in-play

Consider now a particular stylistic function of verse rhythm displayed in the opposition "a play within the play" versus "the main text".

The device of a play within a play was widely used by the Elizabethan-Jacobean authors. The "play in play" could be either a short insertion (as in "Hamlet") or constitute the main body of the drama (as in "Taming of the Shrew" and "A Midsummer Night's Dream"). We shall compare the rhythmical structure of "play in play" with the main text in "Hamlet" and "The Merry Wives of Windsor".

The deliberate stylization of verse in the "play in play" is noticeable at once. They are written in rhymed couplets and consist of end-stopped lines not split between speakers. The language of the "plays" is pompous and bombastic, which produces a comic effect. The style of the plays in plays "estranges" them, and makes them sound more theatrical than the background verse of the main text. The contrast is not unlike that between verse and prose in other parts of Shakespeare's dramas.

This deliberate stylization by the poet penetrates still other layers of the verse form. Here are the stress profiles of the main texts and the "plays in plays" (the stress profiles for "Hamlet" are plotted in Fig. 3.3):

	Syllabic Positions					Difference	No.
	2	4	6	8	10	(8-6)	Lines
"Hamlet" Main text	61.2	81.9	72.5	69.3	92.9	−3.2	2335
Play-in-play	77.2	85.7	74.3	78.6	90.0	+5.4	70
"Merry Wives" Main text	74.1	80.1	78.5	68.3	91.4	−10.2	186
Play-in-play	74.2	96.0	72.0	86.0	84.0	+14.0	50

The stress profile structure of "plays in plays" is strikingly different from that of the main texts: (1) The mean ictic stress in the "plays" is 4-5% higher than in the main text. (2) The contrast between more strongly and more weakly stressed ictic positions is greater. (3) Position 4, the end of the *A minore* first "hemistich", is particularly strongly stressed, especially in the "play in play" of "The Merry Wives;" this indicates a strongly symmetrical (4+6 or 5+5) bipartite line composition. (4) In the main texts of both dramas, there is a "dip" on position 8: this "asymmetrical" profile is typical of later Shakespeare. In "plays in plays" there is a "dip" on position 6 which is more weakly stressed than 8, particularly in the rhymed couplets of "The Merry Wives". This is another indication of a deliberately stylized, symmetrical bipartite line composition of the "plays in plays". Here are two examples. (Syntactic breaks after positions 4-5 are marked.)

(1) "The Merry Wives of Windsor"

The main text:
Fenton: Good Mistress Page,/for that I love your daughter (6)
In such a righteous fashion as I do, (8)
Perforce, against all cheeks, rebukes and manners,
I must advance \ the colours of my love, (8)
And not retire../Let me have your good will. (6,8)
Anne: Good mother, do not marry me to yond fool. (8)
("The Merry Wives of Windsor", III,V:79-84)

The "play in play":
Fairy-Queen: Strew good luck, ouphs,/on every sacred room,
That it may stand \ till the perpetual doom, (6)
In state as wholesome/as in state 'tis fit, (6)
Worthy the owner,/and the owner it. (6)
("The Merry Wives of Windsor", V,V:60-63)

(2) "Hamlet"

The main text:
Polonius: It shall do well./But yet do I believe (2,8)
The origin and commencement of his grief (4,8)
Spring from neglected love . . . How now, Ophelia? (2)
You need not tell us \ what Lord Hamlet said, (6)
We heard it all . . . /My lord, do as you please (8)
But if you hold it fit, after the play, etc. (2,8)

"The Mouse-trap" (play in play):
Player Queen: So many journeys \ may the sun and moon (6)
Make us again \ count o'er ere love be done! (2)
But woe is me,/you are so sick of late, (6)
So far from cheer,/and from your former state, etc. (6)
("Hamlet", III,I:178-183, and III,II:166-169)

In his "plays in plays", particularly in "The Mouse-trap", Shakespeare was obviously parodying the more archaic style of earlier Elizabethan dramas. Manipulation of the stressing served Shakespeare as one more way of creating a particular stylistic effect, opposing the conventional, artificial verse of "play in play" to a more prose-like background verse of the main text.

Note to Chapter 3

[1] There is another point of view: Wilkins' prose version of "Pericles" published in 1608 echoes Shakespeare's play, which was based on an old drama of unknown authorship (e.g., Wentersdorf 1951:176).

Chapter 4

How Personages Speak: Rhythmical Differentiation of Characters

4.0 Preliminary remarks

Rhythmical dissimilarity of acts and scenes (Chapter 3) is only one aspect of heterogeneity in a dramatic verse text. A dramatic text is spoken by different characters—male and female, kings and commoners, heroes and clowns, noble personages and villains. The characters' text in a play consists of long monologues and soliloquies, shorter utterances, and repartees, sometimes less than a line long. Monologues and soliloquies are usually associated with scenes of pathos or are meditations (conventionalized inner speech), while repartees are more typical of rapid give-and-take scenes, sometimes between lower characters in everyday, genre situations. My first aim in this chapter is to see if there is a connection between the type of utterance, indirectly reflecting the semantic, emotive, and situational type of scene, and the verse rhythm used by the poet in these utterances. The second aim is to find out if the author's individualization of characters, apparent on various levels of the text, for example, lexical and stylistic (cf. Warnken 1964), can be traced on the level of verse rhythm (cf. Čudovskij 1914).

In this chapter I segment the dramatic texts in two different ways: (a) form-oriented segmentation: utterances of different length; and (b) character-oriented segmentation: parts of various dramatis personae. A more content-oriented and situation-oriented segmentation, for example, into scenes of solemn pathos, emotional love scenes, scenes of violence and battle, comic and farcical scenes, or genre scenes of everyday life, might possibly seem more exciting. However, such a segmentation, though rich with possibilities and promising for further research, was not carried out because the principles of classifying scenes into various types, particularly in plays belonging to different genres, are not yet clear; the danger is subjectivity, though there <u>might</u> be some indicators of scene differentiation in the texts themselves (cf. Jarxo's principles of classifying dramatic genres, or measuring the degrees of "liveliness" in a play: Gasparov 1969:510).

4.1 Formal analysis of utterances

4.1.1 Lines split between speakers

We begin with lines split between personages into two (rarely three) parts. Calculations were made of the percentage of split lines from all iambic pentameter lines of each play and the places of the split (the final syllabic position of the preceding utterance), and comparisons were made between the stress profiles of split lines and the general stress profile of the play (Tables 4.1-4.4, Fig. 4.1).

4.1.1.1. The <u>number of split lines</u> shows an evolution over the course of Shakespeare's dramatic canon (Table 4.1). The number is negligible in the early plays and increases, reaching nearly one-fifth of all lines in the final dramas. Figure 4.1 (upper panel) plots the percentage of split lines in each drama by theater season (Wentersdorf's chronology), and the trend line shown, fitted by linear regression, has a very high correlation (r = 0.90). When the data are divided into four periods as in Table 4.2 (the principles for division into periods differs somewhat from those used in Chapters 1 and 5, and are discussed below), the mean proportion of split lines increases in the ratio 1.5—4.5—13.7—14.9, from 1588 through 1613.

The evolution, however, does not proceed smoothly. We can identify several factors that cause deviations from the mean trend.

(1) Split lines are relatively less frequent in the genre of historical plays (chronicles) compared with tragedies and, particularly, comedies (cf. also the stress profile data, Chapter 2, Tables 2.2 and 2.5). The mean proportion of split lines in the first nine chronicles (1588-1599: "Henry VI",1—"Henry V") is 1.7%, while in the first nine comedies (1589-1600: "The Comedy of Errors"—"Twelfth Night") it is twice as great: 3.5%. Split lines are, of course, a sign of a livelier action and of a faster speech tempo; no wonder they are more numerous in comedies. If we take the incidence of split lines to be an index of liveliness of action, then Shakespeare's comedies are two times livelier than the chronicles, the least lively of all genres (cf. Wentersdorf 1951:186-187).

My results are, interestingly enough, close to those of Boris Jarxo (1889-1942), a Russian literary critic and medievalist and an enthusiastic advocate of scientific methods in literary research. His works are still, unfortunately, largely unpublished (however, see Jarxo 1984). Trying to find objective criteria for genre differentiation, Jarxo calculated "indices of liveliness" of Corneille's tragedies and comedies. His "index of liveliness" was the correlation between the number of utterances and the total number of lines in a play. The "index of liveliness" of Corneille's comedies is 1.8 times higher than of his tragedies (Gasparov 1969:510).

(2) Split lines are less typical of monocharacter plays and/or plays with fewer personages than of plays with two main characters and/or plays with a great number of personages; cf. "Richard II", a monocharacter play, and "Romeo

Table 4.1

Places of utterance junctures in Shakespeare's dramas
(juncture follows the position; in percent of all split lines)

Chronology	Drama	1	2	3	4	5	6	7	8	9	Mean position	Number of split lines	% of split lines
1588-89	Titus Andronicus	–	–	10.5	36.8	26.3	21.0	5.3	–	–	4.7	19	0.8
1589-90	Henry VI,1	–	6.2	–	37.5	12.5	25.0	12.5	6.2	6.2	5.1	16	0.6
	Comedy of Errors	–	–	–	30.7	53.8	15.4	–	–	7.7	5.5	13	0.9
1590-91	Henry VI,2	–	–	–	66.6	–	33.4	–	–	–	4.6	6	0.2
	Henry VI,3	–	–	14.3	43.0	–	28.6	14.3	–	–	4.8	7	0.2
1591-92	Taming of the Shrew	–	–	2.4	48.8	26.8	21.9	7.3	2.4	2.4	5.6	41	2.1
	Richard III	–	8.0	6.0	58.0	12.0	18.0	–	2.0	–	4.7	50	1.4
1592-93	Two Gentlemen of Verona	–	6.9	6.9	62.1	10.3	10.3	3.4	6.9	3.4	5.0	29	2.1
1593-94	Love's Labour's Lost	–	3.7	–	44.5	24.1	18.5	9.3	–	–	4.8	54	4.2
1594-95	Midsummer Night's Dream	–	5.5	–	25.5	35.2	25.5	8.3	–	–	5.0	36	2.6
	Romeo and Juliet	–	1.2	–	29.4	29.4	24.7	12.9	2.3	–	5.2	85	3.5
	Richard II	–	2.5	2.5	32.5	22.5	25.0	15.0	–	–	5.1	40	1.4
1595-96	King John	1.5	4.4	1.5	31.3	41.6	10.4	11.9	1.5	1.5	5.2	65	2.5
	Merchant of Venice	–	1.2	1.2	20.0	32.5	26.2	18.3	–	–	5.2	80	4.3
1596-97	Henry IV,1	–	2.6	2.6	26.3	21.3	34.2	13.2	2.6	–	5.4	38	2.5
	Henry IV,2	–	–	–	23.8	28.5	19.0	26.2	2.4	–	5.5	42	3.0
1597-98	Much Ado About Nothing	–	–	–	23.5	20.5	35.5	20.5	–	–	5.5	34	5.2
1598-99	Henry V	–	3.4	3.4	20.7	27.6	31.0	13.8	–	–	5.2	29	1.6
	Julius Caesar	–	1.7	3.5	26.9	30.4	22.6	19.1	1.7	–	5.5	118	6.0

Table 4.1 (cont.)

1599-1600	As You Like It	–	–	3.3	12.1	27.0	36.4	17.9	3.3	–	5.6	33	3.5
	Twelfth Night	–	2.0	2.0	20.4	28.5	28.5	18.6	–	–	5.4	49	6.2
1600-01	Hamlet	–	1.1	0.6	25.8	24.2	35.4	14.6	1.6	1.1	5.6	178	7.6
1601-02	Troilus and Cressida	–	0.7	0.7	31.3	26.7	22.1	13.7	3.8	0.7	5.3	131	6.9
1603-04	Measure for Measure	–	–	–	16.0	14.1	38.4	28.8	2.7	–	5.9	125	9.0
	Othello	0.9	0.4	2.3	26.1	21.5	32.5	20.2	0.9	1.3	5.7	218	3.5
1604-05	All's Well That Ends Well	–	–	1.4	13.1	13.6	44.3	24.8	1.4	1.4	5.9	145	10.7
	Timon of Athens	–	3.8	1.5	10.8	17.7	42.3	22.3	3.8	3.1	6.1	130	9.3
1605-06	King lear	–	0.5	0.5	16.2	17.1	38.6	26.7	2.4	–	5.9	212	11.1
	Macbeth	–	0.4	–	16.3	14.1	48.4	24.9	4.7	0.4	6.4	233	14.0
1606-07	Antony and Cleopatra	0.2	0.4	0.9	13.5	16.0	41.8	24.8	4.2	3.7	6.3	450	18.2
1607-08	Pericles	–	–	–	17.6	12.9	35.3	23.5	8.2	2.3	6.0	85	6.4
	Acts I-II	–	–	–	30.8	7.7	38.5	7.7	15.4	–	5.7	13	1.8
	Acts III-V	–	–	–	15.2	13.9	34.7	26.4	7.0	2.7	6.0	72	12.0
	Coriolanus	–	0.2	0.5	10.5	12.1	30.5	32.1	5.5	3.9	6.4	380	17.0
1608-09	Cymbeline	0.2	0.2	0.5	13.4	18.5	37.1	23.4	6.1	2.5	6.0	393	15.4
1609-10	Winter's Tale	–	0.3	0.6	14.8	15.2	39.5	23.3	6.5	1.8	6.0	322	15.8
1610-11	Tempest	–	0.9	0.4	11.9	14.2	40.7	28.4	4.1	3.2	6.3	218	15.8
1612-13	Henry VIII	0.2	1.0	0.8	10.1	14.2	26.1	35.5	13.4	3.6	6.6	386	14.9
	"Shakespeare"	0.6	–	0.6	9.1	13.6	34.6	35.2	6.2	6.1	6.6	176	15.8
	"Fletcher"	–	1.9	0.9	10.9	14.7	19.0	35.7	19.1	2.4	6.6	210	14.5

Table 4.2

Places of utterance junctures (splits) in Shakespeare's dramas: generalized for four periods (% from all split lines)

Chronology	Drama	Positions of splits									Mean position*	Number of split lines	% of split lines
		1	2	3	4	5	6	7	8	9			
1586-95	Titus Andronicus - Richard II	-	3.0	2.6	41.1	21.7	20.4	8.1	1.8	1.3	4.9	372	1.5
1595-1602	King John - Troilus and Cressida	0.1	1.6	1.4	24.9	28.0	26.1	15.7	1.6	0.6	5.3	851	4.5
1603-1611	Measure for Measure - Tempest	0.1	0.4	0.7	14.0	15.2	38.9	24.5	4.0	2.2	6.0	3022	13.7
1612-13	Henry VIII	0.2	1.0	0.8	10.1	14.2	26.1	35.5	13.4	3.6	6.6	2574	14.9

*The mean position of the split was calculated in the following way: the index for each position was multiplied by the number of the position, the results were added and divided by 100.

Table 4.3

Places of utterance junctures in Byron's dramas
(% from all split lines)

Drama	Position of cue juncture									Mean position	Number of split lines	% of split lines
	1	2	3	4	5	6	7	8	9			
Marino Faliero	1.3	6.2	3.7	14.7	14.3	22.2	21.6	15.4	6.2	6.2	292	8.4
Sardanapalus	2.3	6.6	9.1	16.5	20.1	18.4	19.2	13.3	8.4	6.3	563	19.8
The Two Foscari	2.4	7.9	8.9	16.0	18.8	16.2	19.3	14.2	9.7	6.2	492	24.7
Werner	1.3	8.2	9.3	14.4	14.2	21.1	18.2	15.4	9.7	6.4	739	23.0

Table 4.4

Stress profiles of the whole text (wh.t.) and of split lines (s.l.) in Shakespeare's dramas

Drama	Types of lines	Ictic positions						Mean	Non-ictic positions					Mean
		2	4	6	8	10		1	3	5	7	9	
Richard III	wh.t.	64.7	84.8	68.7	75.3	89.9	76.7	32.2	11.2	9.6	8.3	5.0	13.3
	s.l.	72.0	100	74.0	78.0	98.0	84.4	56.0	14.0	20.0	18.0	0	21.6
Romeo and Juliet	wh.t.	65.7	87.2	68.3	75.6	88.5	77.1	32.4	10.7	13.5	10.9	7.3	14.9
	s.l.	70.5	87.2	82.1	70.6	92.3	80.5	50.0	11.5	19.2	23.1	10.5	22.9
Julius Caesar	wh.t.	62.1	82.5	69.1	72.2	86.2	74.4	31.5	10.3	12.0	10.1	8.5	14.5
	s.l.	61.1	86.5	78.8	78.0	90.7	79.2	43.2	10.2	21.2	19.5	9.3	20.3
Hamlet	wh.t.	61.2	81.9	72.5	69.3	92.9	75.6	28.4	8.1	11.2	12.0	6.7	13.5
	s.l.	65.2	83.2	86.5	71.4	98.4	81.9	35.4	13.4	19.1	18.0	11.8	19.5
Othello	wh.t.	62.3	84.8	72.5	70.9	94.3	77.0	30.3	12.1	11.1	14.7	11.3	15.9
	s.l.	66.1	84.0	85.8	78.0	96.8	82.1	30.7	12.8	17.9	32.1	17.4	22.2
King Lear	wh.t.	63.9	82.0	77.6	67.8	95.7	77.4	25.4	12.5	11.9	13.9	13.2	15.4
	s.l.	62.9	81.8	88.2	72.7	98.1	80.5	31.1	13.2	17.0	33.0	19.3	22.7
Antony and Cleopatra	wh.t.	66.0	79.6	76.5	71.0	88.0	76.2	23.2	11.6	10.3	13.2	12.0	14.0
	s.l.	68.4	78.9	87.9	78.5	92.7	81.3	25.0	13.9	13.5	23.8	17.5	18.7
Cymbeline	wh.t.	67.8	79.7	76.9	72.6	89.0	77.2	23.3	10.7	11.5	13.4	12.5	14.3
	s.l.	69.5	80.9	86.2	78.9	95.2	82.1	20.9	10.1	13.2	20.1	15.2	15.9

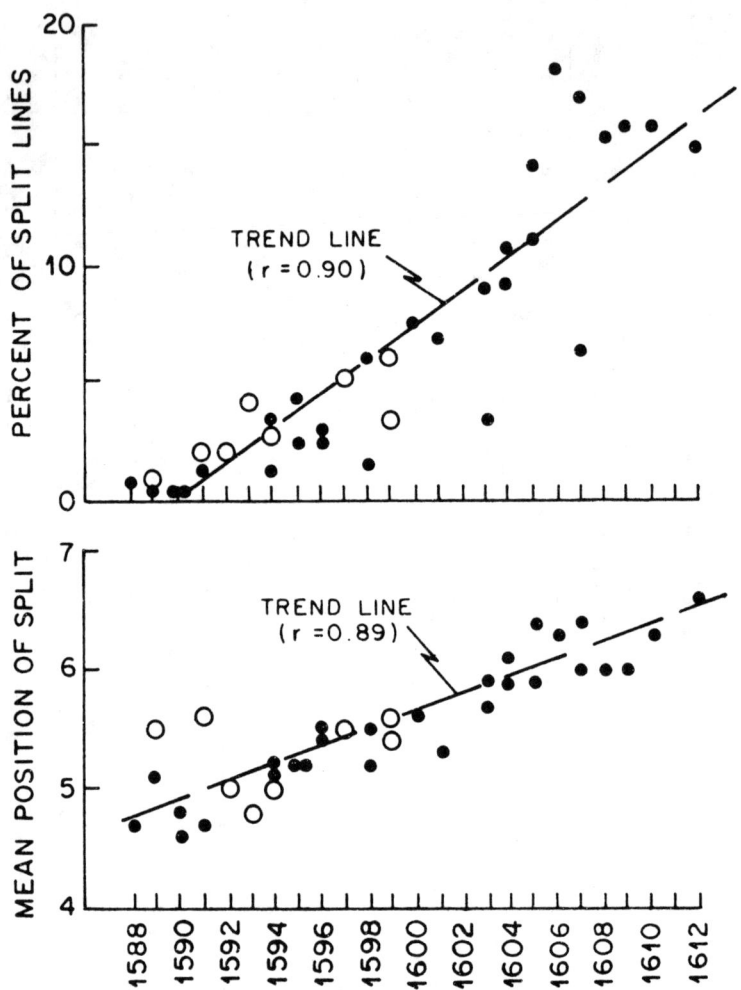

Fig. 4.1. Percentage of split lines (upper) and mean position of split (lower) plotted by theater season (Wentersdorf's chronology). Open circles identify pure comedies. There is a marked evolution toward a more frequent use of split lines together with the movement of the position of split toward the end of the line. Data from Table 4.1.

and Juliet'', a play with two main characters (the number of split lines in "Romeo" is 2.5 times higher than in "Richard II"), or "Antony and Cleopatra" on the one hand and "King Lear" or "Macbeth" on the other (Table 4.1).

(3) Split lines are less frequent in plays with long prose insertions. In such

dramas verse, as it were, tends to oppose itself to prose, to maintain a verse identity; and split lines undoubtedly add prose-like features to verse, effacing the verse-prose opposition. Large insertions of prose seem to account (in part) for a relatively low proportion of split lines in the verse of such dramas as, for example, "Henry V" and "Timon of Athens". If "Timon of Athens" is dated according to Chambers, the divergence is even more striking: according to Chambers, "Timon" (9.3% of split lines) follows "Coriolanus" (17% of split lines); the proportion of split lines in "Timon" is almost two times lower than in "Coriolanus". This fact lends support to Wentersdorf's dating of "Timon of Athens" three theatre seasons earlier, placing it before "King Lear".

Another exception is "Pericles;" the number of split lines calculated for the whole play is three times lower than in other plays of the same period. The difference is even more striking in acts I-II, generally suspected of having not been written by Shakespeare (see Chapters 2, 3, and 5). The proportion of split lines in acts I-II is only 1.8%, as low as in "Henry V" eight years earlier, and "Henry V" was also an exception. In acts III-V the proportion of split lines increases almost seven times and comes much closer to the chronological neighbors of "Pericles", particularly before "Antony and Cleopatra" and after "Coriolanus", two plays with the highest proportion of split lines in Shakespeare's canon (18% in "Antony and Cleopatra"). In Byron's four plays analyzed (Table 4.3) the proportion of split lines varies between 8.4-24.7% ("Marino Faliero" —"The Two Foscari") displaying "signs of liveliness" unseen in Shakespeare's canon.

The data on "Henry VIII" are also revealing and shed some additional light on the authorship controversy: the proportion of split lines in "Shakespeare's" scenes is identical to that of the three preceding plays, "Cymbeline", "Winter's Tale", and "The Tempest", while in "Fletcher's" scenes it is somewhat lower, closer to "Macbeth" seven years earlier.

Judging from the proportion of split lines, "Troilus and Cressida" again looks as though it were written earlier than "Hamlet" (cf. its stress profile, Chapter 2, Tables 2.2 and 2.4); but this may also be the result of the peculiar stylistics of "Troilus". Another play exhibiting stylistic idiosyncrasy is "Othello:" the proportion of split lines is almost three times smaller than in its chronological neighbors "Measure for Measure" and "All's Well that Ends Well". True, both latter plays are closer to comedy; therefore a smaller proportion of split lines in the tragedy "Othello" is predictable; but the index of "Othello" is two times lower than even in "Hamlet" written three theatre seasons previously. The unexpected peculiarity of style is also noticeable in the stress profiles of "Othello" (cf. Tables 2.2 and 2.4). We will return to this play in 4.1.1.2.

4.1.1.2. The <u>place of the split</u> in the lines also shows a smooth evolution. The most frequent position of the juncture of utterances moves from after <u>four</u> in Shakespeare's earlier plays (the masculine ending of the first "hemistich") to after five (the feminine ending of the first "hemistich") in the plays written between 1595-1602, to after six in the later plays (another sign of an asymmetrical line segmentation; cf. with stress profiles, Table 2.1 and 2.4), and to nearly seven in "Henry VIII" (Table 4.2). The mean position of the split evolves, accordingly, from 4.9 to 6.6. This smooth evolution is shown graphically in Fig. 4.1 (lower panel), where the mean split positions for each play are plotted chronologically. The trend line fitted by linear regression shows the same high correlation as the percentage of splits ($r = 0.89$). Thus both the increased use of split lines and the shifting of the position of the split toward the end of the line evolved simultaneously over Shakespeare's dramatic career.

In Byron's plays the splits are placed more freely along the line and are concentrated in its second half; consequently, the mean position of splits is closer to the end of the line than in most of Shakespeare's dramas and resembles the index for "Henry VIII" (Table 4.3).

Here are examples of splits after each of the positions 1-10:

Position 1:
Peace! -/Hear the crier.—What the devil art thou?
$$\text{("King John" II,I:134)}$$
Ha! -/O, beware, my lord, of jealousy;
Lie -/With her?—With her, on her; what you will.
$$\text{("Othello" III,III:166; IV,I:34)}$$
What! -/I am fearful: wherefore frowns he thus?
$$\text{("Henry VIII" V,I:87)}$$

Position 2:
Mark me. -/I will.—My hour is almost come.
Farewell. -/How now Ophelia, what's the matter?
$$\text{("Hamlet" I,V:2; II,I:71)}$$
How now? -/An't please your grace, the two great cardinals
Was dead? -/Yes, madam; but I think your grace,
$$\text{("Henry VIII" III,I:15; IV,II:7)}$$

Position 3:
Who art thou? -/Who thou wilt: and if thou please,
$$\text{("King John" V,VI:9)}$$
What, Brutus! -/Pardon, Caesar; Caesar, pardon:
O Caesar -/Hence! wilt thou lift up Olympus?
Great Caesar -/Doth not Brutus bootless kneel?
$$\text{("Julius Caesar" III,I:55,74,75)}$$

Position 4:
Daughter, well met. -/God give your graces both
Strike up the drum. -/I prithee, hear me speak
$$\text{("Richard III" IV,I:5; IV,IV:180)}$$
Rise up, good aunt. -/Not yet, I thee beseech.
Good aunt, stand up. -/Nay, do not say "stand up";
$$\text{("Richard II" V,III:92,111)}$$

Position 5:
Some misadventure. -/Tush, thou art deceived.
("Romeo and Juliet" V,I:29)
To undeservers. -/I an itching palm!
Than such a Roman. -/Brutus, bay not me,
What, durst not tempt him? -/For your life you durst not
("Julius Caesar" IV,III:12,28,62)
Position 6:
Who put my man i' th' stocks? -/What trumpet's that?
Out, varlet, from my sight! -/What means your Grace?
("King Lear" II,III:180,185)
Be bounteous at our meal. -/Give me thy hand
Will answer as a law. -/Caesar, I go.
In every power that moves. -/Caesar, I shall.
("Antony and Cleopatra" IV,II:10;III,XII:33,36)
I so much thirst to see. -/Now, good Camillo,
Be born another such. -/My good Camillo,
("The Winter's Tale" IV,IV:518,584)
Position 7:
Transform us not to women. -/Ho, ho, ho!
Be comforted, dear madam. -/No, I will not:
She's dead too, our sovereign. -/Lady! Madam!
Thou mean'st to have him grant thee. -/What's thy name?
That rids our dogs of languish? -/Cleopatra,
As plates dropped from the pocket. -/Cleopatra -
("Antony and Cleopatra" IV,II:36;
IV,XV:2,69; V,II:11,42,92)
Position 8:
In this our fabric, if that they -/What then?
May give you thankful sacrifice! -/Thy news?
("Coriolanus" I,I:119; I,VI:9)
I thought you would not back again. -/Most like,
Then not in Britain must you bide. -/Where then?
Cam'st thou from where they made the stand? -/I did.
Though you, it seems, come from the fliers? -/I did.
("Cymbeline" III,IV:118,137; V,III:1,2)
Position 9:
The people are incensed against him. -/Stop,
("Coriolanus" III,I:32)
Is Lucius general of the forces? -/Ay.
("Cymbeline" III,VII:11)
Your grace must wait till you be called for. -/So.
I shall remember this bold language. -/Do.
("Henry VIII" V,II:7, V,III:84)
Position 10:
Be comforted, dear madam, gentle Queen! -/Oh!

(construct)

145

As an aside, the examples also demonstrate the following regularity: the shorter an utterance, the more often it is constructed according to definite repeated syntactic patterns which are sometimes filled by identical or similar lexical units, for example: *Now, good Camillo—My good Camillo*; *Caesar, I go—Caesar, I shall*; *What then? - Where then?*; *I did—I did* (see Chapter 8).

Byron's plays are in many ways similar to the Elizabethan-Jacobean dramas, but they display a greater freedom and variety in the splitting of lines: utterance junctures are distributed along the line in a more unconstrained way than in the seventeenth-century dramas, and there are cases (though infrequent) of an unstressed monosyllable in position 10 following an utterance juncture in position 9. Such cases are absent even from "Henry VIII". Two examples from Byron:

I shall not need so many seconds. -/We
Will now retire.
An hour ago I should have felt it. -/And
Will you not now resent it?

("The Two Foscari" V,I:35-36,88-89)

We now examine more closely the evolution of Shakespeare's principle of splitting lines between two or more characters.

The most typical place of split in the dramas of the first period is after position 4. There are two exceptions, both comedies: "The Comedy of Errors" and "A Midsummer Night's Dream". A loosening of the rigid 4+6 bipartite structure begins in the genre of comedy: cf. Tables 2.1 and 2.4. In Fig. 4.1 (lower) the first two comedies lie markedly above the trend line.

"King John" is the first play of the canon where the "split maximum" occurs after position 5: "King John", therefore, conventionally begins a new period, which ends with "Troilus and Cressida". The latter play not only contains fewer split lines than its chronological neighbors, but the position of maximum split moves back to four, as in "Richard II" seven years previously. This is yet another sign of a possibly earlier date of "Troilus and Cressida". "Hamlet", on the other hand, displays another sign of a later play: the "split maximum" has moved to the right and occurs after position six.

The next twelve plays, beginning with "Measure for Measure" and ending with "The Tempest", all display a "split maximum" following position six: a masculine ending of the first part of the line, "*A mayore*" type (6+4). The second most common place of split is following position seven, a feminine ending of the "*A mayore* hemistich". The only exception is again found in "Othello": the second maximum occurs after position 4, a clear trace of the 4+6 "hemistich" segmentation. Once again "Othello" displays idiosyncratic signs of a more canonized verse form.

And finally, "Henry VIII": both in "Shakespeare's" and particularly in

"Fletcher's" scenes the "split maximum" occurs after position 7. Position 8, however, differentiates "Shakespeare's" and "Fletcher's" scenes more strikingly: utterance junctures occur after position 8 three times more frequently in "Fletcher's" than in "Shakespeare's" portions of the play. The proportion of splits after position 8 in Byron's plays resembles Fletcher's scenes of "Henry VIII", while the percentage of splits after position 9, particularly in "The Two Foscari" and "Werner", is considerably higher than anywhere in "Henry VIII". One feels that Byron manipulated utterance junctures with greater abandon than did Shakespeare; but is it possible that Shakespeare's more conventional line segmentation was easier for the actors to handle?

4.1.1.3 Stress profiles of split lines

Consider now the stress profiles of split lines (Table 4.4). Both ictic and non-ictic positions in split lines are stressed more strongly than in whole lines. The stress is particularly high on the last ictus of the preceding utterance and on the first non-ictic position of the following utterance, immediately after the juncture. There is also an increase of stress on the anacrusis. These facts are explained by the compositional laws of English verse: the beginnings of verse units on various levels of verse structure, such as the beginning of a poem, of a stanza, and of a couplet in rhymed verse, of lines, "hemistichs", and/or phrases, are characterized by more rhythmical variety (a loosening of metrical rules) than the middle portions of the units (see Chapter 7). The constituent following a split begins a new phrase uttered by a new speaker; "rhythmical inversions" and extrametrical stresses on W often signal this change. The first part of the line is also frequently an independent utterance marked by an "inversion". The end of each utterance is "supported" by a strong ictic stress. Here are some examples:

Caesar. $\underline{W\overset{\varepsilon}{e}lcŏme\ t\breve{o}\ R\grave{o}me}$.
Antony. $\underline{Th\overset{\varepsilon}{a}nk\ you}$.
Caesar. $\underline{S\overset{\varepsilon}{i}t}$.
Antony. $Sit,\ \underline{s\vec{i}r}$.
Caesar. $N\breve{a}y,\ \underline{th\vec{e}n}$.
                                       ("Antony and Cleopatra" II,II:28)
Enobarbus. $\underline{Menas},\ I'll\ not\ on\ shore$.
Menas. $\underline{No,\ to\ my\ cabin}$.
                                       ("Antony and Cleopatra" III,I:133)

The location of a particularly strongly stressed midline ictus and of the midline non-ictic position bearing an increased extrametrical stress depends on the typical place of the split in the lines of the period (cf. Tables 4.1 and 4.4). In "Richard III", for example, most splits occur after position 4; consequently the strongest midline ictus (stressed 100% of all cases) in the split lines is position four, and the most strongly stressed midline non-ictic position is, predictably, five. In "Antony and Cleopatra" most splits occur after position

6, therefore the most strongly stressed midline ictus in the split lines is six, and the strongest midline non-ictic position is seven.

4.1.2 Utterances of different lengths

All utterances containing non-split lines were grouped in the following way: short utterances, 1-4 lines long; medium utterances, 5-10 lines long; and long utterances: monologues and soliloquies, 11 and more lines long (Table 4.5).

The length of the text of a role is limited. In my choice of roles for analysis I was guided by the role's importance in the play and the number of its lines. The following role texts were selected for a differentiated analysis of utterances: Richard III; Romeo, Juliet; Richard II, Bolingbroke; King John, Bastard, King Philip ("King John"); Brutus, Antony, Cassius ("Julius Caesar"); Hamlet, King Claudius; Othello, Iago, Desdemona; King Lear; Macbeth; Antony, Cleopatra, Caesar Octavius ("Antony and Cleopatra"); Imogen, Posthumus, the Queen, Jachimo ("Cymbeline"). Role texts shorter than 200 lines were usually excluded, the only exception is the part of King Philip (187 lines). Still, in the role texts selected there are three groups of utterances each less than 50 lines long, and 18 groups of utterances with a line volume of each group less than 100; that is why the dispersion of frequencies in stress profiles of the utterances in the text of a role is sometimes considerable.

For initial examination, stress profiles (ictic positions only) were constructed for long and short utterances by averaging ictic positions for all role texts analyzed. Figure 4.2 shows the profiles. We see a definite regularity: shorter utterances are on the average strongly opposed to long utterances. They exhibit a much less rigid verse form, with a noticeable "dip" on position 8, in contrast with a more rigid verse form of long utterances with the "dip" on position 6.

Examined in closer detail (Table 4.5), shorter utterances are again rhythmically opposed to longer ones. Shorter utterances display hardly any accentual symmetry in their line structure; opposition between strong and weak ictuses is barely noticeable. Longer utterances, on the other hand, as a rule display marked signs of accentual symmetry, and their strong and weak ictuses are usually opposed to each other. In Shakespeare's early dramas with their symmetrical, rhythmically rigorous verse structure, the short utterances sometimes even display an asymmetrical tendency charcteristic of much later plays, their medium utterances just begin to show signs of accentual symmetry, typical of Shakespeare's early works, while long utterances emphasize an accentual symmetry even more noticeably than was observed in the mean stress profiles of the early plays. Thus, in the short utterances of the role text of Richard II the third ictus is more strongly stressed than the fourth, similar to much later plays (the difference between positions 8 and 6, the rigidity index (RI) is −10%; see Chapter 2); medium utterances bear signs of the early

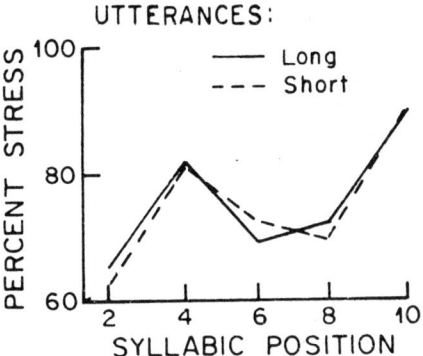

Fig. 4.2. Comparison of stress profile (ictic positions) of long versus short utterances. Values are the means of all role texts of Table 4.5. Long utterances (more than 11 lines) are notably more canonized than short utterances (four lines or less).

Shakespeare tendency towards accentual symmetry: the third ictus is somewhat weaker than the fourth (RI = +0.9%); and finally, long utterances fully display the symmetric tendency: the third ictus is considerably weaker than the fourth (RI reaches +7.0%). Some examples are:

K. Richard.
What must the king do now? must he submit? (8)
The king shall do it/: must he be deposed? (8)
The king shall be contented: must he lose
The name of king?/a God's name let it go:
I'll give my jewels \ for a set of beads: (6)
My gorgeous palace \ for a hermitage: (6)
My gay apparel \ for an almsman's gown: (6)
My figured goblet \ for a dish of wood: (6)
My sceptre for a palmer's walking-staff:
My subjects for a pair of carve'd saints,
And my large kingdom \ for a little grave, (6)
A little little grave, an obscure grave,
Or I'll be buried \ in the king's highway, (6)
Some way of common trade, where subjects' feet
May hourly trample \ on their sovereign's head; (6)
("Richard II" III,III:143-157)

Of the fifteen lines, seven contain a missing ictic stress on position 6 while only two lines on position 8; and nine lines contain syntactic seams of various strength after positions 4/5. Syntactical parallelism of lines 144-145, 147-153,

149

and 155,157 and lexical repetitions emphasize the rhythmical parallelism in this highly symmetrical, rhythmically rigid text.

K. Richard.
But now the blood \ of twenty thousand men
Did triumph in my face, and <u>they</u> are fled: (8)
And till so much blood \ thither come again,
Have I not reason \ <u>to</u> look pale and dead? (6)
All souls that will be safe, fly <u>from</u> my side (8)
For time hath set a blot up<u>on</u> my pride. (8)
("Richard II" III,II:76-81)
Aumerle. Good mother, be content—it <u>is</u> no more (8)
Than my poor life must answer.
Duchess.   <u>Thy</u> life answer! (8)
York. Bring me my boots, I <u>will</u> un<u>to</u> the king. (6,8)
Duchess. Strike him, Aumerle. Poor boy, thou <u>art</u> amazed. (8)
Hence, villain! never more come <u>in</u> my sight. (8)
("Richard II" V,II:82-86)

Thus we see that King Richard's shorter utterance, and particularly the colloquial exchange between secondary characters in a comic scene, are characterized by frequent loss of stress on position 8.

A similar phenomenon is observed in the dramas of the transitory Period II. For example, the short utterances of Brutus are the least symmetrical (the RI is only $+0.6\%$), while medium utterances display a much greater symmetry (RI $= +8.4\%$).

The opposition between shorter and longer utterances extends through Shakespeare's late dramas: long utterances are notably less asymmetrical than medium and short ones. Thus, the whole role text of Antony ("Antony and Cleopatra") displays the accentual asymmetry typical of the later plays. But in Antony's short utterances the fourth ictus is particularly weak while the third is particularly strong (RI $= -14.4\%$); in the medium utterances the fourth ictus is slightly stronger and the third ictus weaker (RI $= -6.2\%$), while in his monologues the third ictus almost equals the fourth (RI is only -3.0%). Antony's short, medium, and long utterances are clearly opposed to each other. The same phenomenon is observed in the rhythmically quaint, affected role text of Jachimo ("Cymbeline"). The rigidiy indices are as follows: short utterances -24.1%; medium utterances -14.9%; long utterances -5.4%.

Of the twenty-four roles compared, an increasing accentual symmetry from short to medium to long utterances was discovered in thirteen parts (Juliet, Richard II, Bolingbroke, King John, King Philip, Brutus, Antony from "Julius Caesar", Hamlet, Othello, Iago, Macbeth, Antony from "Antony and Cleopatra", Jachimo). In nine more parts, an opposition between longer and shorter utterances was observed in at least two types of utterances (Richard III, Romeo, Bastard, King Claudius, Desdemona, Cleopatra, Caesar Octavius, Imogen, Posthumus). Five times out of nine, it is the <u>medium</u>-length utterances that deviate from the general tendency (in the roles of Richard III, Romeo, Bastard, Cleopatra, Caesar Octavius); short and long utterances deviate from the general tendency in only two role texts each (short utterances: the role texts of Claudius and Imogen; long utterances: the texts of Desdemona and Posthumus). One can only guess why it is the medium utterances that deviate particularly often (a clash of tendencies?). However, this deviation only emphasizes the prevailing regularity: development of a rhythmical opposition between the less symmetrical verse of short utterances and the more symmetrical verse of monologues and soliloquies. This opposition occurs in 22 role texts out of 24, i.e., in 92% of cases. By the way, though short utterances show almost level stressing on the third and fourth ictuses in Imogen's text (in her medium utterances and monologues the fourth ictus is invariably weaker than the third), they also level the second and the third ictuses. Such a general leveling of the stressing on ictic positions is a sure sign of the rhythmical prosaization of short utterances; but as this sign does not involve the main opposition between ictuses III and IV, I disregard it and assume that Imogen's short utterances deviate from the main tendency.

Two roles deviate completely from the main tendency; these are King Lear and Cassius. The tendency in Cassius' text is opposite to the main one: his monologues are the least symmetrical while his short utterances display the most symmetry.

Why this happens is hard to say, but it is tempting to make a guess. Probably in his shorter utterances, in faster exchanges with other characters, Cassius is trying to curb his passions and to seem more sophisticated and reasonable, while in longer utterances he speaks with more abandon, revealing his basic trait: aggressive impatience.[1]

King Lear's verse is "mad" indeed. First, his third ictus is stronger than the second in both short and long utterances (the same tendency as in Ford's "Perkin Warbeck"). Secondly, King Lear's three types of utterances do not coincide with the main correlations: his medium utterances are the most symmetrical; they deviate both from the period and from the main trend (in the role texts where medium utterances deviate from the main tendency, they usually are the most asymmetrical, as in Richard III), while his short utterances and monologues are almost equally asymmetrical (rigidity indices are -14.2 and -17.0%, respectively). However, even King Lear's "mad" verse displays a greater prosaization of short utterances as compared to monologues and soliloquies, but on another level of verse structure: the level of line endings. The number of non-masculine (mainly feminine) endings decreases from short utterances towards monologues. (A similar phenomenon was observed in "Timon of Athens".) The indices are as follows: short utterances 31.1%, medium utterances 25.3%, long utterances 21.8% of non-masculine endings.

Thus it is the verse of long utterances that displays maximum symmetry and structural rigorousness; the verse of the longest utterances, monologues and soliloquies, is particularly strongly opposed to prose. In contrast, the verse of the shortest utterances is the closest to prose, showing the least verse-prose opposition.

Monologues and soliloquies are, of course, more characteristic of scenes of pathos and heroic scenes, of oratories and meditations, while short utterances are more typical of comic scenes and scenes of everyday life; they often occur in repartees of secondary characters, in fast give-and-take exchanges. This means that a more symmetrical, more canonized verse form was typically used by Shakespeare for scenes of pathos, heroic scenes, oratories and meditations, while a loosened verse form seemed to him more suitable for more colloquial speech of ordinary exchanges: another link between verse form and meaning.

4.2 Character study

4.2.1 Differentiation of characters through rhythm

A stylistic differentiation of dramatic characters in a verse play can be accomplished in several ways. The most obvious opposition of Shakespeare's characters is observed when the author has certain dramatic types speak only, or mostly, in prose and others in verse. Prose-speaking personages are, for example, commoners and servants, clowns, fools and madmen, villains, and other lower characters. Some examples are: Launce and Panthino ("The Two Gentlemen of Verona"), Fool ("King Lear"), Cloten ("Cymbeline"), Hamlet feigning madness, and Iago in his scenes with Roderigo (e.g., I,III:301-380). Verse-speaking personages are, for example, noble heroes and kings.

A less obvious, indirect differentiation of character is accomplished by varying the length of utterances. The characters' preference for various length utterances gives us the first glimpse of character individualization via verse form (Table 4.5). Of the twenty-four roles compared, fifteen (62.5%) "prefer" long utterances. The latter are particularly numerous in the texts of Antony ("Julius Caesar"), Hamlet, King Claudius, and Posthumus (but Posthumus is a small part): monologues and soliloquies comprise 61.6-65% of their whole role texts. In three of four cases these are mainly meditative soliloquies, while in Antony's role they are mostly orations. Many long utterances are also found in the parts of Richard II (58.5%) and Philip the Bastard ("King John") (54.4%). It is remarkable that long and short utterances occur about equally in the part of Richard III (40.6 and 33.8%). This even distribution corresponds to the peculiarities of his character: Richard III plots his intrigues in soliloquies and carries them out in dialogues.

Other roles have a more equal proportion of all three types of utterances. Still, monologues and soliloquies slightly prevail in the parts of Juliet (38.8%), Bolingbroke (47.1%), King Philip (43.9%), Cassius (41.7%), Iago (46.3%), King Lear (46.4%), Imogen (47.5%), and Jachimo (43.9%). Medium utterances prevail in five parts: King John (38.1%), Romeo (39.0%), Macbeth (42%), Antony from "Antony and Cleopatra" (46.1%), and Caesar Octavius (46.0%).

Table 4.5

Stress profiles of short, medium, and long utterances in 24 role texts of Shakespeare's plays

Personage	Length of utterance (in lines)	2	4	6	8	10	Number of lines and their % of the role text	
Richard III	1-4	63.1	82.8	71.7	71.9	87.2	360	33.8
	5-10	56.9	83.2	67.6	63.8	87.8	262	25.6
	11 and more	66.8	86.3	66.1	75.3	92.4	433	40.6
Romeo	1-4	63.2	87.5	69.5	68.8	92.4	144	28.6
	5-10	62.0	85.8	71.6	66.5	89.4	197	39.0
	11 and more	68.3	83.6	67.1	78.7	88.5	164	32.4
Juliet	1-4	69.2	86.6	69.4	70.9	87.3	134	27.0
	5-10	61.1	87.8	64.4	79.1	86.1	172	34.7
	11 and more	56.3	87.4	64.3	74.8	88.4	190	38.3
Richard II	1-4	64.3	85.7	75.7	65.7	95.7	70	10.2
	5-10	63.4	84.1	72.8	73.7	89.2	213	31.2
	11 and more	67.5	83.5	67.8	74.8	91.5	400	58.5
Bolingbroke	1-4	68.3	79.8	71.2	75.0	87.5	104	28.6
	5-10	61.4	88.6	67.1	70.5	87.5	88	24.3
	11 and more	64.3	88.9	59.7	77.8	90.0	171	47.1
King John	1-4	67.9	79.3	71.7	75.5	84.9	106	28.1
	5-10	61.8	85.4	72.9	73.7	86.8	144	38.1
	11 and more	64.6	78.0	63.8	77.2	85.0	127	33.8
Bastard	1-4	64.2	82.6	65.4	75.3	93.8	81	16.1
	5-10	61.2	81.9	75.8	68.5	89.9	149	29.5
	11 and more	67.2	83.2	63.2	75.2	85.8	274	54.4

Table 4.5 (cont.)

King Philip	1-4	63.2	77.8	68.4	68.4	92.1	38	-	20.3
	5-10	50.8	85.1	65.7	71.7	80.6	67	-	35.8
	11 and more	72.0	87.8	58.6	78.1	90.3	82	-	43.9
Brutus	1-4	61.2	80.3	68.9	69.5	89.1	193	-	35.1
	5-10	61.1	77.9	70.1	74.3	82.1	167	-	30.3
	11 and more	62.6	84.2	64.3	72.7	86.3	190	-	34.6
Antony ("Julius Caesar")	1-4	50.0	88.5	63.5	65.4	88.5	52	-	17.2
	5-10	59.7	87.1	63.0	64.5	93.6	62	-	20.6
	11 and more	66.0	85.7	70.2	77.1	84.1	188	-	62.2
Cassius	1-4	62.0	79.3	70.7	71.3	89.3	150	-	36.3
	5-10	58.3	79.1	71.5	70.4	82.5	91	-	22.0
	11 and more	55.8	77.9	69.2	67.5	89.6	172	-	41.7
Hamlet	1-4	63.9	83.5	77.4	71.2	94.9	97	-	14.2
	5-10	60.0	85.8	74.9	75.5	94.2	155	-	22.6
	11 and more	62.5	82.9	71.0	69.9	93.8	431	-	63.2
King Claudius	1-4	55.7	76.6	65.7	78.1	85.9	64	-	14.9
	5-10	55.8	81.5	72.1	65.2	96.6	86	-	20.1
	11 and more	65.2	81.3	70.6	68.7	93.6	278	-	65.0
Othello	1-4	61.2	81.7	69.3	66.7	94.5	180	-	33.3
	5-10	63.5	85.9	69.4	71.2	91.8	170	-	27.9
	11 and more	60.5	79.1	65.9	69.1	93.2	220	-	38.8
Iago	1-4	59.7	90.4	76.9	62.9	96.2	156	-	26.2
	5-10	58.8	87.9	72.2	69.1	95.9	165	-	27.5
	11 and more	60.1	87.5	70.2	68.8	95.7	278	-	46.3
Desdemona	1-4	57.7	86.5	71.3	69.5	92.4	118	-	52.4
	5-10	62.8	82.4	74.5	82.4	96.0	51	-	22.7
	11 and more	64.3	82.2	71.4	62.5	92.9	56	-	24.9

Table 4.5 (cont.)

King Lear	1-4	60.4	78.3	82.1	67.9	93.4	106	-	23.3
	5-10	63.1	81.2	68.8	78.3	97.8	138	-	30.3
	11 and more	63.1	77.8	83.4	66.4	93.9	211	-	46.4
Macbeth	1-4	67.8	82.2	76.3	69.0	92.4	118	-	22.3
	5-10	64.4	84.7	72.6	68.0	94.0	222	-	42.0
	11 and more	68.6	78.2	73.4	70.8	94.8	188	-	35.7
Antony ("Antony	1-4	62.8	79.1	81.1	66.7	91.5	153	-	25.8
and Cleopatra")	5-10	63.3	81.3	77.9	71.7	88.2	272	-	46.1
	11 and more	61.1	80.3	76.1	73.1	91.0	167	-	28.1
Cleopatra	1-4	60.6	83.7	76.4	73.4	92.1	203	-	45.8
	5-10	68.3	82.0	78.3	63.4	85.7	161	-	36.2
	11 and more	75.0	81.2	72.5	78.8	86.7	80	-	18.0
Caesar Octavius	1-4	64.6	75.8	77.4	62.9	88.7	62	-	23.7
	5-10	63.7	77.5	67.8	71.0	83.8	124	-	46.0
	11 and more	62.9	74.9	68.9	67.1	83.6	81	-	30.3
Imogen	1-4	62.5	73.9	74.8	74.8	85.2	88	-	21.4
	5-10	64.1	82.8	75.0	72.7	89.9	128	-	31.1
	11 and more	67.2	80.5	74.8	75.9	89.2	195	-	47.5
Posthumus	1-4	61.6	76.9	74.4	76.9	94.9	39	-	13.2
	5-10	62.2	79.7	69.0	74.3	93.3	74	-	25.2
	11 and more	73.5	86.2	76.8	71.4	94.5	181	-	61.6
Jachimo	1-4	72.4	79.3	77.6	52.5	92.4	58	-	21.4
	5-10	66.0	65.6	71.3	56.4	86.2	94	-	34.7
	11 and more	72.3	75.6	79.9	74.0	83.2	119	-	43.9

It turns out that the impulsive Romeo is more abrupt and more "communicative" than the sophisticated Juliet, while Antony the lover in "Antony and Cleopatra" is livelier and more "communicative" than Antony the statesman in "Julius Caesar". King John is more communicative than his opponent King Philip and the Bastard. Short utterances prevail in only two parts, both feminine: Desdemona (52.4%) and Cleopatra (45.8%). Both female parts, then, are characterized by laconic expression: they mainly speak as partners in dialogues. Brutus makes almost equal use of all three types of utterances: long 35.1—medium 30.3—short 34.6%. The same tendency is revealed in the parts of Cassius (36.3—22.0—41.7%), Othello (33.7—27.9—38.4%), and Richard III (33.8—25.6—40.6%). Short utterances are very scarce with Richard II, Posthumus, Hamlet, King Claudius, Bastard, and Antony the statesman ("Julius Caesar"): 10.2-17.2% of their parts. The opposition between Richard II and Richard III is particularly interesting: a passive personage vs. an active personage. On the whole, long utterances are more typical of meditating or plotting characters, both heroes and villains, of sophisticated and lyrical personages, of monarchs and orators, while short utterances characterize either lively, communicative types (they talk themselves, and make others talk, like Cleopatra) or uncommunicative, reserved ones (they speak only when spoken to, like Desdemona). Short utterances are, of course, more typical of secondary personages as opposed to the main characters.

Another means of differentiating characters is lexical: colloquialisms, vulgarisms, and concrete nouns are more typical of lower characters and villains (e.g., Iago), while poetic vocabulary and abstract nouns are more characteristic of noble heroes, such as Othello of the first two acts (cf. Warnken 1964).

Shakespeare also differentiates his personages grammatically. For example, there are characters whose speech abounds in indefinite articles; these are: servants, citizens, comic personages, wits and their victims, simpletons, and fools. Opposing characters whose speech contains a lower number of indefinite articles are lyrical and noble heroes, other "serious people", and monarchs (Šajkevič 1976:358). Šajkevič found it hard to interpret his findings; but they seem to be connected with the higher number of concrete nouns referring to countable objects in the speech of lower characters, and the prevalence of abstract, uncountable nouns in the texts spoken by monarchs and noble heroes.

There may be yet other ways of individualizing and typifying characters stylistically, for example, through the use of a different rhythmical verse structure of their parts: different types of characters probably use different variants of iambic pentameter. This phenomenon, which is another possible link between "verse form" and "meaning", has not gone unnoticed by sensitive and experienced scholars. Oliphant, for example, comparing Massinger to his more talented contemporaries and co-authors, remarked that in Massinger's dramas "outbursts of anger are illustrated by the same dignified verse that he employs for the portrayal of a state of happy contentment . . .

The words are those of Massinger, not of his characters" (Oliphant 1927:60-61). Mincoff (1961:245), trying to prove the double authorship of "Henry VIII", pointed out that two different verse styles appear in the play in identical situtations. Thus he implied that identical situations would normally be in the same style, while different situations might require dissimilar verse styles. However, the rhythmics of verse spoken by different dramatis personae has practically never been studied before. Čudovsky (1914) wrote about different rhythmical line variants (though he did not use these terms) of iambic pentameter spoken by different characters in Puškin's drama "Rusalka [The Mermaid]": its lyrical heroine, the miller's daughter, speaks in "paeons" (that is, her verse contains many cases of missing ictic stresses). Another attempt to find a link between line rhythm and different dramatic characters and situations in Gribojedov's "Gore ot Uma [Woe from Wit]" was made by Filipov (1925). Both Čudovsky and Filipov had more ear than method and their articles seem today naive; but they were moving in the right direction.

In this section I present the results of stress profile analysis of twenty-six leading parts, comparing characters of the same play, and typologically grouping personages whose parts reveal similar tendencies (Table 4.6). Two parts have been added to the 24 parts analyzed in section 4.1, viz. Lady Macbeth and the Queen from "Cymbeline". The nine longest parts cover 23.8-31.5% of their respective dramas (between 455 and 1064 verse lines). The gigantic part of Richard III, equaling in length some of the shorter plays by Shakespeare, heads the list. The second place is taken by the long parts of Richard II and Hamlet (683 iambic pentameter lines each); these cover 26.0 and 29.2% of the verse text of their plays (Hamlet's part also contains prose fragments). The third place belongs to Iago: 599 verse lines, 26.0% of "Othello". Then, in order of decreasing length come the parts of Antony ("Antony and Cleopatra"), Othello, Brutus, Macbeth, and King Lear. The part of Macbeth is relatively long: it covers one-third of the drama (32.0% of all lines); those of Othello, Brutus, and King Lear comprise about one-fourth of the verse text of their plays (23.8-28.1%). Other parts cover 4.3-21.1% of their dramas. There are only three short parts in the whole collection: King Philip from "King John": 187 lines, Lady Macbeth: 164 lines, and the wicked Queen from "Cymbeline": 114 lines.

The stress profile of Richard III closely resembles that of the whole play "Richard III" (Table 4.6). As we remember, separate acts of this long drama also displayed similarity (Chapter 3). Still the role text of Richard III and the whole drama "Richard III" display a discrepancy in stressing on position 8, the fourth ictus: the difference between the third and fourth ictuses (positions 6 and 8) in the role text of Richard III is considerably less than in the whole play. This means that the part of Richard III is less symmetrical in its rhythmic structure than the drama as a whole. Accentual line rhythm largely depends on its syntax; and indeed Richard's utterances are often composed asymmetrically on the syntactic level, too, or fail to display any bipartite structure.

Table 4.6

Rhythmical characteristics of 26 personages against the background of the whole drama

Personage and drama	Positions					Correlation between positions 8-6	Number and % of lines	
	2	4	6	8	10			
Richard III	63.4	84.6	68.7	71.6	89.6	+ 2.9	1065	(31.5)
Drama "Richard III"	64.7	84.8	68.7	75.3	89.9	+ 6.6	3376	
Romeo	64.4	85.6	69.5	71.1	90.1	+ 1.6	505	(20.5)
Juliet	61.5	87.3	65.8	75.2	87.3	+ 9.4	496	(20.2)
Drama "Romeo and Juliet"	65.7	87.2	68.3	75.6	88.5	+ 7.3	2456	
Richard II	65.9	83.9	70.1	73.6	91.3	+ 3.5	683	(26.0)
Bolingbroke	64.8	86.3	64.8	75.3	88.8	+10.5	363	(13.9)
Drama "Richard II"	68.8	85.2	70.0	75.6	91.0	+ 5.6	2630	
King John	64.5	81.2	69.5	75.1	85.5	+ 5.6	377	(14.8)
Bastard	65.5	82.8	67.3	73.3	88.3	+ 6.0	504	(19.8)
Drama "King John"	65.6	85.3	67.7	75.0	88.4	+ 7.3	2540	
Brutus	61.7	80.9	67.7	72.0	86.0	+ 4.3	550	(28.1)
Antony	61.9	86.6	67.6	72.6	86.0	+ 5.0	302	(15.4)
Cassius	58.6	78.7	70.2	69.5	87.9	- 0.7	413	(21.1)
Drama "Julius Caesar"	62.1	82.5	69.1	72.2	86.2	+ 3.1	1957	

Table 4.6 (cont.)

Hamlet	62.1	83.6	72.8	71.4	94.0	− 1.4	683	(29.2)
King Claudius	61.7	80.9	70.1	67.1	93.0	− 3.1	428	(18.3)
Drama "Hamlet"	61.2	81.9	72.5	69.3	92.9	− 3.2	2335	
Othello	61.4	81.9	69.5	68.9	93.2	− 0.6	569	(25.0)
Iago	59.6	88.4	72.5	67.3	95.8	− 5.2	599	(26.3)
Desdemona	60.5	84.4	72.0	70.7	93.4	− 1.3	225	(9.9)
Drama "Othello"	62.3	84.8	72.5	70.9	94.3	− 1.6	2272	
King Lear	62.5	78.9	78.7	69.7	95.0	− 9.0	455	(23.8)
Drama "King Lear"	63.9	82.0	77.6	67.8	95.7	− 9.8	1915	
Macbeth	66.7	81.9	73.7	69.4	93.9	− 4.3	528	(32.0)
Lady Macbeth	62.0	84.4	73.9	66.5	87.6	− 7.4	161	(9.7)
Drama "Macbeth"	65.0	81.4	76.8	69.6	94.5	− 7.2	1651	
Antony	62.4	80.5	78.3	69.1	89.9	− 9.2	592	(24.1)
Cleopatra	66.0	82.7	76.4	70.8	88.8	− 5.6	444	(18.1)
Caesar Octavius	62.9	74.9	68.9	67.1	83.6	+ 1.8	267	(10.8)
Drama "Antony and Cleopatra"	66.0	79.6	76.5	71.0	88.0	− 5.5	2458	
Imogen	65.3	79.8	75.0	74.7	88.6	− 0.3	411	(15.7)
Posthumus	69.8	83.4	74.5	72.8	91.9	− 1.7	294	(11.2)
Queen	64.9	78.9	75.5	68.4	86.0	− 7.1	114	(4.3)
Jachimo	73.8	76.4	76.4	63.5	86.0	−12.9	271	(10.3)
Drama "Cymbeline"	67.8	79.7	76.9	72.6	89.0	− 4.3	2614	

Here are some examples of rhythmically and syntactically symmetrical utterances of other personages:

Hastings.
Woe, woe for England!/not a whit for me;
For I, too fond,\ might <u>have</u> prevented this. (6)
Standley did dream/the boar did raze his helm,
And I did scorn it,\ <u>and</u> disdain to fly: (6)
("Richard III" III,IV:79-82)

Buckingham.
Madam, good hope;/his grace speaks cheerfully.

Queen Elizabeth.
God grant him health!/Did <u>you</u> confer with him? (6)
("Richard III", I,III:34,35)

Rivers.
Were you well served,/you <u>would</u> be taught your duty (6)

Queen Margaret.
To serve me well,/you all should do me duty.
("Richard III" I,III:250,251)

And here are examples of Richard's utterances. They are syntactically asymmetrical and seldom break into 4 + 6 or 5 + 5 parts; the syntactic and linear text segmentation sometimes fail to coincide.

So dear I loved the man,/that <u>I</u> must weep. (8)
I took him for a plainest harmless creature
That breathed upon this earth a Christian . . .
. . . .
Yet had not we determined/<u>he</u> should die, (8)
Until your lordship came to see his end,
Which now the loving haste of <u>these</u> our friends, (8)
Somewhat against our meanings,\ <u>have</u> prevented: (8)
Because, my lord \ I <u>would</u> have had you hear (6)
The traitor speak \ and timorous<u>ly</u> confess (8)
The manner and the purpose <u>of</u> his treasons; (8)
That you might well have signifi<u>ed</u> the same (8)
Unto the cit<u>i</u>zens,/who haply may (6)
Misconster us in him and wail his death.
("Richard III" III,V:23-25, 51-60)

All these peculiarities of verse structure turn Richard's utterances into an unbroken torrent of words; they were probably meant to quicken the actor's recitation. How much of it was a conscious effort on the part of the poet? Did Shakespeare know what he was doing to verse rhythm, or was he only working on his line syntax, with a peculiar rhythm merely the result? One can only guess.

Consider now the stress profiles of Romeo and Juliet, comparing them with each other (Fig. 4.3A) and with the whole play (Table 4.6). In comparison with

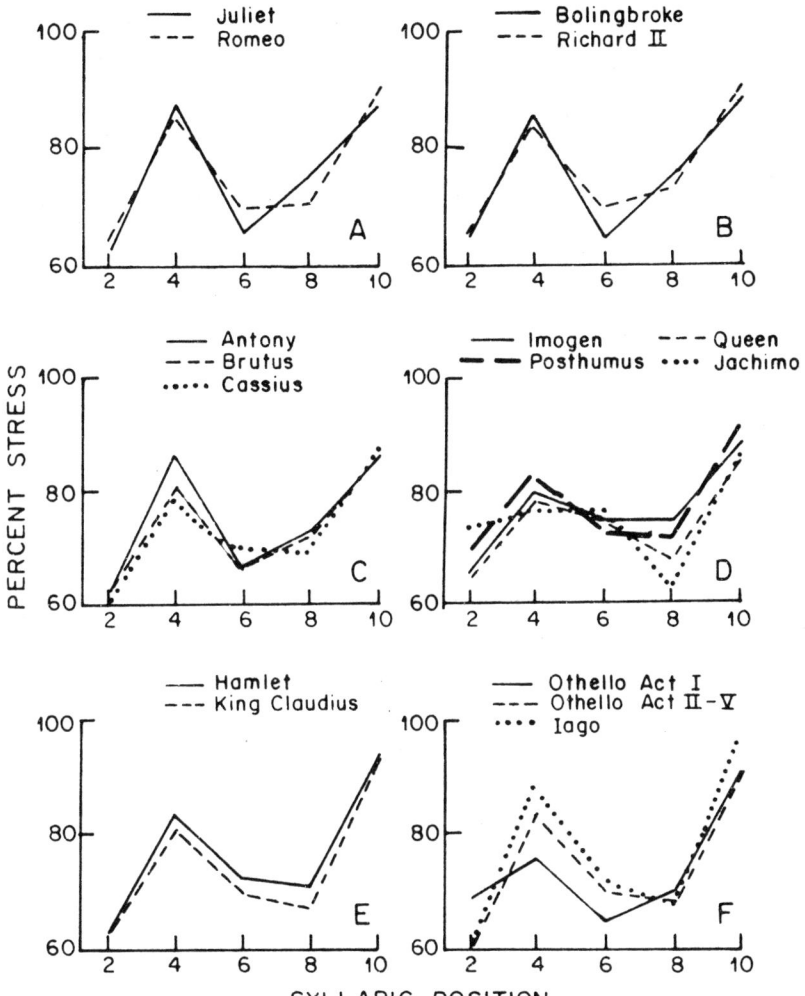

Fig. 4.3. Stress profiles (ictic positions) of some major character roles. (A) illustrates the female (more rigid form)—male (less rigid form) opposition, as well as that of emotionally stable—unstable. (B) illustrates the hero (more rigid form)—villain (less rigid form) opposition. (C) illustrates how Cassius was definitely cast by Shakespeare as a lower character. Note the strong peak on position 4 of Antony's profile, marking him as an orator. (D) contrasts both female-male and hero-villain in the characters of "Cymbeline". (E) The contrast between Hamlet's and King Claudius' characters is marked even in the most rhythmically homogeneous of all Shakespeare's plays. (F) illustrates Othello's marked character evolution toward Iago. Data from Table 4.6.

the general stress profile of the drama, Romeo's stress profile is less symmetrical, while that of Juliet is, on the contrary, more symmetrical: the rigidity index (position 8 minus 6) of Romeo's part is only +1.6%, in the general stress profile of the play it is +7.3%, while in Juliet's part it is as high as +9.4%. Romeo's part also displays a relatively low stress on the second ictus, supporting the first "hemistich." This means that Romeo's part is definitely more decanonized than Juliet's who speaks in a more rigorous verse, strongly opposed to prose. Possibly, the rhythmic-syntactic composition of Romeo's part was designed to make it into an unbroken stream of lines, to quicken the tempo of the actor's recitation, while the composition of Juliet's role text was to prompt a more distinct recitation emphasizing the line and "hemistich" verse structure. The text peculiarities of the two main parts correspond to their characters (cf. Anikst 1963). Romeo displays more fervor and impulsiveness than Juliet. He is more inclined to go over from one extremity to another: fits of temper, transports of joy, and gusts of despair freely follow one another. Impulsiveness is one of his most typical features. In a fit of rage Romeo kills Tybalt, bringing misfortune on Juliet and himself; in a gust of despair he helplessly sobs at Father Lawrence's while Juliet is planning a secret meeting for them both.

Juliet's spiritual maturity and willpower are remarkable. She is wiser and more sophisticated than Romeo; she is not only passionate, but can precisely analyze her emotions and the situation. Juliet's wisdom and her ability to think intelligently in highly dramatic circumstances are emphasized throughout the play. We recall, for example, Juliet's verbal duel with Paris; her behavior after she has learned about Tybalt's death; and the episode in which Juliet takes Father Lawrence's sleeping drug after she overcomes her hesitation and fear of death. The structure of Juliet's symmetrical, canonized verse and of Romeo's, comparatively asymmetrical and decanonized, clearly emphasize this opposition of their characters.

Juliet's verse text becomes more strictly canonized after she has learned of Tybalt's death. She, as it were, grows up before our eyes, becomes older and wiser; and her verse changes, becomes more symmetrical.

Here is an example of Romeo's verse:

Speakest thou of Juliet?/How is it with her?	(8)
Doth not she think me an old murderer,	(6)
Now I have stain'd the childhood of her joy	(8)
With blood removed but little from her own?	(8)
Where is she? and how doth she? and what says	(8)
My conceal'd lady to our cancelled love?	(6)

("Romeo and Juliet" III,III:93-98)

Romeo's verse text contains not only fewer cases of clear bipartite line segmentation, but also more cases of enjambment, than Juliet's. Enjambments undoubtedly also add to a quicker recitation tempo.

Here is an example of Juliet's verse:

But wherefore, villain,\ didst thou kill my cousin?	(6)
That villain cousin would have killed my husband.	(6)
Back, foolish tears,/back to your native spring!	(6)
Your tributary drops belong to woe	
Which you, mistaking,\ offer up to joy.	
My husband lives,/that Tybalt would have slain,	(8)
And Tybalt's dead/that would have slain my husband:	(6)
All this is comfort;/wherefore weep I then?	
Some word there was,\ worser than Tybalt's death,	(6)
That murd'red me./I would forget it fain,	(6)
But oh, it presses \ to my memory	(6)
Like damned guilty deeds to sinners' minds—	
'Tybalt is dead/and Romeo banished'.	

("Romeo and Juliet" III,II:100-112)

The 4+6 or 5+5 bipartite line segmentation and the frequently missing stresses on position 6 produce a rhythmical variant of iambic pentameter obviously different from Romeo's.

Here is another illustrative example:

Juliet.

Wilt thou be gone?/It is not yet near day.	(2,6)
It was the nightingale,\ and not the lark,	(2,6)
That pierced the fearful hollow of thine ear.	(8)
Nightly she sings \ on yond pomegranate tree.	(2,6)
Believe me, love,/it was the nightingale.	(6)

Romeo.

It was the lark,/the herald of the morn;	(2,8)
No nightingale./Look, love, what envious streaks	(4)
Do lace the severing clouds in yonder last.	
Night candles are burnt out, and jocud day	(4)
Stands tiptoe on the misty mountain tops.	(4)

("Romeo and Juliet" III,V:1-10)

Juliet's five lines are all end-stopped and, except one, all contain a syntactic seam after positions 4 or 5. Four lines out of five (three, if the demonstrative yond is considered stressed) contain a missing ictic stress on position 6. In Romeo's reply (the first five lines) there are two cases of enjambment (typical of his verse), and only two lines contain syntactic breaks after positions 4 or 5. Not a single line has a missing ictic stress on position 6.

One could, of course, find different examples: symmetrical lines in Romeo's part and asymmetrical in Juliet's; but the general stress profiles of their texts (Fig. 4.3A) suggest that the extracts cited above are representative of the rhythmical structure of their respective parts.

In the drama "Richard II" Richard's text stress profile is less symmetrical, and the ictuses are leveled more, than in the stress profile of the whole play. The role text of Bolingbroke, Richard's antagonist, on the contrary, displays a more symmetrical stress profile than that of the whole play; strong and weak ictuses are most opposed in Bolingbroke's role text. Thus, the second ictic stress in the general stress profile of the play is 85.2%, in King Richard's text 83.9%, while in Bolingbroke's it is 86.3%. The rigidity index of the general stress profile is +5.6%, in Richard's part +3.5%, in Bolingbroke's +10.5%. This means that Bolingbroke speaks in a "heroic", canonized pentameter while Richard II in a less symmetrical, more decanonized verse. The stress profiles of the two characters, clearly illustrating this opposition, are superimposed in Fig. 4.3B. And indeed, as it is seen from the plot, Richard II is most unstable in his feelings and moods, passing from one extremity to another. Richard's emotional instability and capriciousness are displayed not only in his private life and personal relations; he also demonstrates these features as the King and head of the state. He is unable to act purposefully, to plan ahead and gain his ends; first he is nearsighted and care-free, later unwisely desperate:

> My lord, wise men ne'er sit and wail their woes
> But presently prevent the ways to wail.
> To fear the foe, since fear oppresseth strength,
> Gives in your weakness strength unto your foe —

says Carlisle (III,II:178-181).

Shakespeare draws the character of Richard II in this particular way to show that he is not fit to rule and therefore does not deserve to be a king.

Bolingbroke, on the other hand, is exactly Richard's opposite. All the character traits of Richard II inexorably bring him to his failure; all of Bolingbroke's aspects assure his victory. Bolingbroke's success is a logical result of his strong will and integrity of purpose. Bolingbroke is regally full of self-respect and pride; he never hesitates to form independent opinions and to speak his mind. He is a courageous person who refuses to submit, intent upon fighting for his rights. He is a shrewd and clever politician who knows how to defend his own prerogatives, and at the same time to consider other people's needs and aspirations. It is this opposition of the two personages, Richard's weak ill and capricious impulsiveness, and Bolingbroke's intensity of purpose, brighter intellect, and strong will, that are obviously conveyed not only by the content of their texts, but also by their verse form. It is worth noting that, similarly with the first pair of personages studied (Romeo and Juliet), in this pair, too, a more impulsive, emotionally unstable personage is characterized by a relatively less symmetrical verse, while a more sophisticated, strong-willed and active personage is characterized by a more symmetrical, more strictly canonized verse.

In "King John" the stress profiles of the two leading characters (whose parts are also the longest), King John and Philip Faulconbridge the Bastard, display much similarity; however, they were never planned as opponents: Faulconbridge takes King John's side and faithfully serves him. The character opposition shows up elsewhere: King John, a mean and worthless monarch, is opposed to the worthy and just King Philip of France, whose verse is markedly symmetrical. Thus the rigidity index in King John's verse part is +5.6% and in King Philip's text twice as great: +10.7%. True, King Philip's part is not long and the stress indices might be fortuitous, but unmistakeable rhythmic and syntactic symmetry can be noticed in King Philip's regal speech even without the stress calculations. The symmetry of the bipartite line structure is of course meant to convey a regal solemnity and importance of judgement.

Here are some examples of King Philips' part:

Peace be to England, / if that war return	(6)
From France to England, / there to live in peace:	
England we love, / and for that England's sake	(6)
With burden of our armour here we sweat:	
. . . .	
This little abstract \ doth contain that large	(6)
Which died in Geffrey; / and the hand of time	(6)
Shall draw this brief \ unto as huge a volume:	(6)
That Geffrey was thy elder brother born,	
And this his son: / England was Geffrey's right,	(6)
And this is Geffrey's \ in the name of God:	(6)
How comes it then / that thou art call'd a king,	(6)
When living blood \ doth in these temples beat,	(6)
Which owe the crown, / that thou o'ermasterest?	(6)

("King John" II,I:89-92,101-109)

Rhythmical characteristics of the personages in "Julius Caesar" are particularly interesting (Fig. 4.3C). Stress profiles of Brutus' and Antony's parts are much alike, only in Antony's verse the second ictus is more strongly stressed. This is probably explained by the general oratorical style of Antony's utterances; a strong second ictic stress emphasizes the bipartite structure of his short utterances and particularly of his monologues. The third ictus in Brutus' and particularly Antony's parts is somewhat weaker than in the whole play, which is a sure sign of a more symmetrical rhythmic and syntactic structure of their texts.

In contrast, Cassius' part is rhythmically opposed to both Brutus' and Antony's. Cassius' verse is strongly decanonized: the RI is negative, as in later plays (−0.7%), while in the whole play it is positive (+3.1%) and in Brutus' and Antony's parts even higher (+4.3 and +5.0%, respectively). The second ictus in Cassius' text is rather weakly stressed, 78.7%, while in the general stress profile of the play it is 82.5%, and in Antony's text as high as 86.6%. This means that Cassius' verse text is the loosest. It displays the same relative tendency (modified by the rhythmical idiosyncrasy of the period) as was discovered in the parts of Romeo or Richard II. Both Romeo and Richard II, though naturally different in many ways, were characterized by impulsiveness; both were inclined to fits of passion. Probably the rhythm of Cassius's verse text also adds to his general characteristic as a fervent, active person: he is the mainspring of the anti-Caesar plot. There is no vulgar simplification or mystery in a parallel between rhythm and character traits: in order to make an active, impulsive personage speak in keeping with his character, the author constructs his part rhythmically and syntactically in such a way that the text runs swiftly, in an unbroken, continuous flow.

Brutus, in contrast to Cassius, is not a man of action; he is a philosopher, a man of wisdom and sophistication. Like Hamlet, he is almost exceptional among Shakespeare's leading characters: he is not merely intelligent, but is a thinker by vocation. Being a philosopher, he is not inclined to an active fight and takes part in the anti-Caesar plot only in the name of an idea. His philosophical cast of mind, his steadiness, and his tendency to reason and meditate rather than act seem to be reflected in his manner of speaking, in the rhythmic-syntactic balance of his utterances.

Another interpretation is also possible. As we have already seen in the character of Richard III, and as we shall see over and over again, there exists a rhythmical opposition in Shakespeare's dramas of elevated and low personages, of virtuous and villainous characters, and the villains' verse text is always composed less symmetrically than the more rigid verse of virtuous personages. We know that Brutus is virtuous. But is Cassius a low character? Both in Plutarch's "Lives", where Shakespeare borrowed his plot (cf. Plutarch 1969:264-389) and in Shakespeare's "Julius Caesar" Cassius is an unpleasant person. He is selfish and in his fight against Caesar he is mainly guided by personal motives. He is an aristocrat and does not want to be anybody's servant; he desires personal freedom above all. He is also envious. He remembers the time when Caesar and himself were equal in position; Caesar then acted as a weakling, a coward, and now he is raised high and wants to order Cassius about. Cassius finds it hard to bear and is impatient to put an end to the situation. Caesar has guessed what passions storm in Cassius' soul: *Yond Cassius has a lean and hungry look; He thinks too much; such men are dangerous.* Cassius is not very particular as to his means and methods, as long as they are effective in his fight. He is the soul of the plot, Caesar's actual murderer; he insists that Antony should also be killed, because he is afraid that Antony will revenge Caesar's assassination. Cassius unscrupulously supports the republican army by illegal extortions and does not disdain to resort to pillage. Brutus, on the contrary, is an idealist and believes that a noble deed must be done with clean hands. Brutus wants to act, remaining at the same time morally pure, while Cassius cynically believes it to be impossible.

If we compare Brutus and Cassius in Plutarch and in Shakespeare we come to the conclusion that Shakespeare has more strongly polarized these two characters, and has more sharply contrasted them than did Plutarch. The rhythmical opposition of their verse in Shakespeare's drama probably reflects the opposition of an elevated character (Brutus) to a lower character (Cassius); Brutus is particularly elevated and idiolized.

However, no matter what the interpretation, the fact remains: Brutus and Cassius were evidently planned by Shakespeare as counterposed characters, and this opposition is conveyed rhythmically, too.

Here are examples of Brutus' mainly canonized, 4 + 6 and 5 + 5 bipartite line segmentation (short utterances and fragments of monologues and soliloquies):

The games are done, / and Caesar is returning.
("Julius Caesar" I,II:178)

I will do so: / but, look you, Cassius
The angry spot \ doth glow on Caesar's brow,
And all the rest \ look like a chidden train:
("Julius Caesar" I,II:182-184)

'Tis very like: / he hath the falling-sickness.
("Julius Caesar" I,II:256)

The exhalation \ whizzing in the air
Give so much light / that I may read by them.
"Brutus, thou sleep'st: / awake and see thyself.
Shall Rome, etc. / Speak, strike, redress . . . "
("Julius Caesar" II,I:44-47)

People and senators, / be not affrighted;
Fly not; stand still: / ambition's debt is paid.
("Julius Caesar" III,I:82,83)

He greets me well. / Your master, Pindarus,
In his own change, \ or by ill officers,
Hath given me some worthy cause to wish
Things done undone: / but if he be at hand,
I shall be satisfied.
("Julius Caesar" IV,II:6-10)

Judge me, you gods; / wrong I my enemies?
And, if not so, / how should I wrong a brother?
("Julius Caesar" IV,II:38,39)

Examples of Cassius' mainly asymmetrical, colloquialized verse:

I know that virtue to be in you, Brutus,
As well as I do know your outward favour.
Well, honour is the subject of my story . . .
("Julius Caesar" I,II:90-92)

I was born free as Caesar, so were you;
We both have fed as well, and we can both
Endure the winter's cold as well as he.
For once, upon a raw and gusty day,
The troubled Tiber \ chafing with her shores,

        Caesar said to me / 'Dar'st thou, Cassius, now
        Leap in with me \ into the angry flood
        And swim to yonder point? Upon the word, ...
                                  ("Julius Caesar" I,II:97-104)
        Why, man, he doth bestride the narrow world
        Like a Colossus, / and we petty men
        Walk under his huge legs and peep about
        To find ourselves dishonourable graves.
                                  ("Julius Caesar" I,II:135-138)
        Well, Brutus, thou art noble; yet, I see
        Thy honourable metal may be wrought
        From that it is disposed: therefore, it is meet
        That noble minds \ keep ever with their likes;
                                  ("Julius Caesar" I,II:310-313)
        That you have wrong'd me / doth appear in this:
        You have condemned and noted Lucius Pella
        For taking bribes here on the Sardians;
                                  ("Julius Caesar" IV,III:1-3)

As to a possible interpretation of the rhythm of Antony's part, it is quite probable that Antony and Cassius are juxtaposed on some different plane, e.g., as Caesar's best friend and worst enemy.

The next pair of characters is Hamlet and King Claudius. "Hamlet" is one of the most rhythmically homogeneous plays; little wonder, therefore, that stress profiles of both parts display much similarity and strongly resemble that of the whole play (Fig. 4.3E). Still, there is some significant difference. Claudius' rhythmics in fact mirrors that of the whole play, while Hamlet's verse text is accentually more canonized and has a more distinct bipartite structure: cf. the rigidity indices and ictus II in Hamlet's and Claudius' parts (Table 4.6). The difference is not great; but even the difference between the most rigorous and the loosest iamb in the same national tradition has a comparatively narrow range of variation, so that statistically a small difference is still relevant for verse structure. Hamlet's text is obviously rhythmically opposed to Claudius'; this is probably an opposition between an elevated and a low character, between a hero and a villain, an abstract thinker and a pragmatic plotter. Possibly the name Claudius itself is a semantic key to his verse rhythm; the name means "lame".

The opposition between a noble hero and a low villain is even more distinct in "Othello". Othello's verse, as compared to that of the whole play, is organized symmetrically and its bipartite structure is evident; the third and the fourth ictuses are practically leveled; in the first two acts, as we shall soon see, the symmetry is even stronger. Here is an example of Othello's text (syntactic breaks after positions 4 or 5 are marked):

        My Desdemona \ must I leave to thee: (6)
        I prithee, let thy wife attend on her;

And bring them after \ in the best advantage.	(6)
Come, Desdemona, / I have but an hour	(6,8)
Of love, of worldly matters and direction,	(8)
To spend with thee; / we must obey the times.	(6)
("Othello" I,III:295-300)	

Othello's syntax breaks the line into rhythmically symmetrical constituents: the word boundary after positions 4-5 usually coincides with a syntactic seam between phrases and sentences. Othello's part is analyzed in more detail below.

The stress profile of Desdemona's verse is close to that of the whole play. However, the rhythm of her part is semantically not neutral: similarly with Othello's, Desdemona's rhythm presents her as a "high personage" and as such she is opposed to Iago. Desdemona's part is not long (Othello's and Iago's parts are more than twice as long) and consists mainly of short utterances (Desdemona is a quiet, short-spoken person); that is why I did not look for evolution in her verse rhythm. In contrast with both Othello and Desdemona, Iago's verse is markedly asymmetrical (RI = −5.2%), and the midline juncture is shifted to the right, to the left, or is missing altogether. Here are some examples of Iago's verse:

The Moor already changes with my poison:	(8)
Dangerous conceits \ are in their nature poisons	(6)
Which at the first \ are scarce found to distaste,	(8)
But, with a little act upon the blood,	(2,8)
Burn like the mines of sulphur./ I did say so:	(2,8)
Look where he comes! / Not poppy, nor mandragora,	(2,8)
Nor all the drowsy syrops of the world	(8)
Shall ever medicine thee to that sweet sleep	(8)
Which thou owedst yesterday.	
("Othello" III,III:327-335)	
I see, sir, / you are eaten up with passion:	(4)
. . . .	
And may; / but how? / how satisfied, / my lord?	(8)
Would you, / the supervisor, / grossly gape on -	
. . . .	
It were a tedious difficulty, / I think,	(2,8)
To bring them to that prospect; / damn them, then,	(4)
If ever mortal eyes do see them bolster	
More than their own! / What then? / how then?	(2)
("Othello" III,III:393,396-397,399-402)	

Both the syntax and stress distribution in Iago's part make its line structure asymmetrical and efface the canonized bipartite line segmentation. Iago's lines often have non-masculine endings: feminine "light" and "heavy" (see Chapter 5), as in . . . *I did sáy sò,* . . . *grossly gápe òn,* and dactylic (*mandrăgora*). Non-masculine line endings are also a sign of a loosening of form, of a

169

prosaization in the English iambic verse. The lexical and syntactic style of Iago's utterances is also typical of colloquial prose; for example, *Look, where he comes . . . ; And may; but how? how satisfied, my lord? . . . damn them, then.* Or in other scenes: *Why, how now, general!* (III,III:336); *Zounds! hold your peace* (V,II:222); *Villainous whore!* (V,II:232), and others. It is clear that Iago's speech is stylistically lowered on many levels; some of them, such as choice of words and images, are more obvious (cf. Warnken 1964), and to these we can now add verse rhythm.

In the tragedy "King Lear" only the main part was analyzed. It has been shown above that Lear's short utterances and monologues are almost unique in their structure: ictus III is stronger than II. His medium utterances, contrary to the general tendency, follow the rigorous pentameter canon: ictus II is stronger than III, the third ictus is weaker than the fourth and segments the line into two symmetrical "hemistichs". The unusual character of the stress profiles of Lear's short utterances and monologue affects his overall stress profile: the second and the third ictuses are leveled and deviate from the stress profile of the whole play which is more traditional and corresponds to the general norm of the period IIIa. Here, too, the character's traits are laid bare by his speech rhythm: a "mad" verse rhythm, as it were, emphasizes King Lear's eccentric character and final madness.

The next tragedy analyzed is "Macbeth", in which two characters are compared: Macbeth and Lady Macbeth. Lady Macbeth's part is constructed less symmetrically than that of her husband. Of the two villains, Lady Macbeth is undoubtedly more heinous; she pleads with the murdering spirits to fill her with *direst cruelty*, to *make thick her blood*, and *stop the access and passage to remorse*. She leads on Macbeth who is, to her mind, infirm of purpose, too soft, too *full o' the milk of human kindness To catch the nearest way . . . .* The opposition "more active—less active", "more villainous—less villainous" is revealed in the verse structure of the two personages. There is also one more aspect to the opposition of their characters which is discussed below.

Now comes "Antony and Cleopatra". Comparison of the general stress profile of the play with the stress profiles of its main characters reveals the following peculiarities. The most symmetrical verse text belongs to Caesar Octavius, where the third ictus is weaker than the fourth. Octavius' relatively symmetrical bipartite line structure is particularly noticeable against the background of general asymmetry of late Shakespeare. It is true that the second ictus in Octavius' text seems too weak for a rigorous pentameter but, after all, this is late Shakespeare; on the whole it is clear that Octavius speaks not unlike King Phillip ("King John"): there is a regal solemnity in the relatively balanced verse rhythms of the two monarchs.

Antony's part is more asymmetrical than Cleopatra's. The second ictus in Cleopatra's verse is more strongly stressed than in Antony's and in the whole play (82.7—80.5—79.6%, respectively); the rigidity index is negative, as it should be for a late Shakespeare play, but the difference is smaller than in

Antony's part: Cleopatra's RI = −5.6%, Antony's RI = −9.2%. Antony's verse is slightly looser than Cleopatra's. A similar opposition was observed in an earlier couple: Romeo and Juliet; thus, both female parts are characterized by a comparatively more symmetrical (for their period) verse form. It is well known that Shakespeare's male and female characters are stylistically opposed to each other on other levels; now we see they are clearly opposed on the level of their verse rhythm, too.

And finally, the last drama in our analysis, "Cymbeline". The four characters studied have dissimilar stress profiles (Fig. 4.3D); the two "positive" characters, Imogen and Posthumus, display a more symmetrical bipartite line structure, the two "negative" characters, the Queen and Jachimo, a more asymmetrical structure. The rigidity indices are: −0.3% in Imogen's part and −1.7% in Posthumus', but −7.1% in the Queen's part and −12.9% in Jachimo's.

Here are some examples of character opposition in "Cymbeline". Imogen's verse:

A father cruel / and a step-dame false;
A foolish suitor \ to a wedded lady
That hath her husband banished. O, that husband,
My supreme crown of grief, and those repeated
Vexation of it! / Had I been thief-stol'n,
As my two brothers, / happy; but most miserable
Is the desire / that's glorious. Blest be those,
How mean soe'er, / that have their honest wills,
Which seasons comfort. / Who may this be? Fie!
("Cymbeline" I,IV:1-9)

Thou told'st me, when we came from horse, the place
Was near at hand. / Ne'er longed my mother so
To see me first / as I have now. Pisanio, man,
Where is Posthumus? / What is in thy mind,
That makes thee stare thus? / Wherefore breaks that sigh
From the inward of thee? / One but painted thus, ...
("Cymbeline" III,IV:1-6)

In evaluating these lines we should bear in mind that this is late Shakespeare's rhythmical style with all its rhythmic-syntactic characteristics. Still, a syntactic break seam of varying strength after the first, "A minore hemistich" (positions 4-5) occurs in twelve lines out of fifteen, and in two more lines the boundary is found after position 6. Features of late Shakespeare are also displayed by the type of ending of the first "hemistich": in most cases they are feminine. However, the fifteen lines are undoubtedly composed symmetrically. A particular symmetry is observed in the two first lines. They contain almost identical word boundary forms in both parts of the line and fully identical parallel, morpho-syntactic patterns: in the first line these are Noun + Modifier + Noun + Modifier, while in the second line they are Modifier +

Noun + Modifier + Noun (see Chapter 7). And here are examples of Jachimo's text:

> It cannot be i' th' eye—for apes and monkeys,
> 'Twixt two such shes, / would chatter this way <u>and</u>
> Contemn with mows the other; nor i' th' judgement -
> For idiots, in this case of favour <u>would</u>
> Be wisely definite; / no i' th' appetite -
> Sluttery, to such neat excellence opposed,
> Should make desire / vomit emptinesss, . . .
>
> ("Cymbeline" I,VI:38-44)
>
> Not he: but yet heaven's bounty towards him <u>might</u>
> Be used more thankfully. In himself 'tis much;
> In you, which I account his, beyond all talents.
> Whilst I am bound to wonder, I am bound
> To pity too
> . . . .
> I was about to say, enjoy your—<u>But</u>
> It is an office of the gods to venge it,
> Not mine to speak on't.
>
> ("Cymbeline" I,VI:77-81,90-92)

A rhythmical and syntactic midline seam after positions 4-5 can be distinguished in two pentameter lines out of fourteen. Most lines contain asymmetrical phrase constituents or have no bipartite structure at all. Besides, there are several cases of a strong enjambment: syntactic and line segmentation do not coincide; lines often end in an unstressed monosyllable (<u>and</u>, <u>would</u>, <u>might</u>, <u>but</u>). There are cases of disyllabic interictic intervals (*In you which I account his beyond all talents*), which are very rare in Imogen's part. It is quite clear that Jachimo, as compared to Imogen, speaks in a quicker tempo and is stylistically closer to colloquial prose.

Interestingly enough, female characters are opposed to male both in the "virtuous" and the "villainous" pairs: the male parts are more asymmetrical than the female. This is the fourth case in our gallery of characters in which this opposition occurs. The only exception has been the "Macbeth-Lady Macbeth" pair, but this exception has a logical explanation. Lady Macbeth is not only a more active villain; she also takes upon herself the male functions. She pleads with the *murdering ministers* to *unsex her*: *Come to my woman's breasts, And take my milk to gall, you murdering ministers*. Macbeth, in her opinion, is *too full o' the milk of human kindness* . . . . "Milk", a sign of the female, is associated with Macbeth, not Lady Macbeth.

To sum up and rationalize the results of this analysis, let us arrange the twenty-six characters in two opposing columns (in one case opposed to a whole play). The left-hand column contains characters whose stress profiles indicate a relatively more rigid pentameter form, the right-hand column those with a comparatively looser form.

The whole play "Richard III"	— King Richard III"
Juliet	— Romeo
Bolingbroke (Henry IV)	— Richard II
King Philip	— King John
Brutus, Antony	— Cassius
Hamlet	— King Claudius
Othello, Desdemona	— Iago
Macbeth	— Lady Macbeth
Cleopatra, Caesar Octavius	— Antony
Imogen, Posthumus	— The Queen, Jachimo
Imogen	— Posthumus
The Queen	— Jachimo

The rhythmical opposition of characters is noticeably consistent in plays of all periods. The characters are typologically opposed in several different ways.

(a) The most frequent opposition is "hero—villain". This characterization opposes: Hamlet—Claudius; Othello and Desdemona—Iago; Imogen, Posthumus—Queen, Jachimo. This group also includes opposition of all the personages of the chronicle "Richard III" to Richard III himself, the main villain of the play. This opposition also seems to emphasize "degrees of villainy": Macbeth—Lady Macbeth.

(b) A good (worthy) King—a bad (worthless) King, or King—no King: Bolingbroke (at the end of the play he becomes Henry IV)—Richard II; King Philip—King John; Octavius Caesar—Antony.

(c) An elevated personage—a lower personage: Brutus—Cassius.

(d) A wiser, more sophisticated personage—an impulsive, whimsical personage: Juliet—Romeo, Imogen—Posthumus, Bolingbroke—Richard II.

(e) Female—male personages: Juliet—Romeo, Cleopatra—Antony, Imogen—Posthumus, Queen—Jachimo.

A number of personages are opposed along several lines, e.g., Juliet—Romeo: female—male, and at the same time a wiser, more sophisticated character *versus* an impulsive, whimsical one; Bolingbroke—Richard II: a worthy king—a poor king, and at the same time a wiser and more judicious personage *versus* an impulsive and capricious one; Brutus—Cassius: a philosopher, a meditator, *versus* a man of action, and at the same time an elevated personage *versus* a lower character guided by his passions. The first member of all opposing pairs is characterized by a relatively more rigid verse form, while the second member by a relatively looser verse form. Shakespeare obviously used different rhythmical variants of the iambic pentameter to differentiate types of personages (*emploi*); Shakespeare's verse form has a strong link with a generalized specific meaning, thus acquiring a semiotic value.

4.2.2 Evolution of characters

Verse rhythm is also a means of achieving an evolution in character of a dramatic personage. Consider two major roles: Richard III and Othello.

Richard's role was divided into two parts—Richard Gloucester (acts I-II) and King Richard III (acts IV-V). Here are the stress profiles of the two parts:

	Syllabic Positions					
	2	4	6	8	10	RI
Richard Gloucester:	65.2	84.2	66.7	73.6	88.2	+6.9
Richard III:	60.0	85.0	71.8	68.5	92.0	−3.3

The character evolution is quite obvious: the stress profile of the first part corresponds to the rhythmical style of early Shakespeare (ictus III is weaker than IV)while the rhythm of the second part of the role is quite unlike the data on early Shakespeare and the whole text of the chronicle: ictus IV, as in many of his later plays, is weaker than III (cf. Table 2.1). This is the result of Shakespeare's creating a dynamic portrait of Richard III, changing him in the course of the play from a high-spirited, self-confident character into one who is entrapped in bloody murders, tortured by nightmarish visions, losing confidence in himself (*Up with my tent there! here will I lie to-night: But where to-morrow?...*), knowing what fate has in store for him (*... let us to't pell-mell; If not to heaven, then hand in hand to hell*). The structure of the final five lines of Richard's part is also remarkable; the four first lines are both rhythmically and syntactically asymmetrical; the final line, as with the four previous ones, contains a missing stress on ictus IV, but it has a syntactic break after the "*A minore*" first "hemistich" (position four). Such a structure is typical of concluding lines, e.g., in a sonnet (cf. 7.6.1.2).

Slave, I have set my lief up<u>o</u>n a cast,	(8)
And I will stand the hazard <u>of</u> the die.	(8)
I think there be six Richmonds <u>in</u> the field;	(8)
Five have I slain to-day instead of him.	
A horse! a horse! / my Kingdom <u>for</u> a horse!	(8)
	("Richard III" V,IV:9-13)

The syntax of these lines, their asymmetrical rhythmical structure (missing or weak stresses on position 8), and places of the word boundaries in the first three lines clearly differentiate them from the main text of this early chronicle. Stress profiles for Othello are:

	Syllabic Positions					
	2	4	6	8	10	RI
Othello, act I:	69.0	76.2	65.1	70.7	91.3	+5.6
Othello, acts II-V:	59.4	83.6	70.7	68.4	89.3	−2.3

At the beginning of the play we see Othello as a war hero. He is used to curbing his passions with his reason. In his love for Desdemona, Othello has acquired inner peace and harmony. This inner harmony is reflected in the verse structure of his part in the first act (RI is strongly positive); and the verse rhythm is more metrically rigorous than in the whole play and the verse of the whole period (cf. Table 2.1). The rigorous structure of Othello's verse in act I is largely conditioned by his famous long monologues in which Othello tells the story of his and Desdemona's love for each other. An example:

I ran it through, / even from my boyish days	(6)
To th' very moment / that he bade me tell it:	(6)
Wherein I spake \ of most disastrous chances,	
Of moving accidents \ by flood and field,	(6)
Of hair-breadth 'scapes \ i' th' imminent deadly breach,	
Of being taken \ by the insolent foe, . . .	(6)
	("Othello" I,III:132-137)

When Iago, however, has succeeded in poisoning Othello's love with jealousy, when his inner harmony is replaced with inner chaos, Othello's part changes not only stylistically (colloquialisms and vulgarisms creep in) but also rhythmically. His verse becomes markedly looser and more asymmetrical:

Committed! O thou public commoner!	(10)
I should make very forges of my cheeks,	(2,8)
That would to cinders burn up modesty,	(2,10)
Did I but speak of deeds. / What committed !	(2)
Heaven stops the nose at it,/ and the moon winks, . . .	(6,8)
	("Othello" IV,II:74-78)

The syntactical and rhythmical break after positions 4-5 disappears; lines without any bipartite boundary (meant to be spoken as an unbroken stream of words) or with a seam after positions 2-3 and/or 6-7 become more and more numerous. Missing stresses shift from ictus III to earlier (ictus II) and later (ictus IV). Cases of syllabically incomplete lines or lines with one syllable missing (a syllable in position 7 before *What committed* in above example) also become fairly frequent. The loss of inner harmony in a dramatic personage is manifested by Othello's increasingly disharmonious verse. Figure 4.3F, which superimposes stress profiles of Othello early (Act I) and later (acts II-V) on that of Iago, shows graphically the evolution of his role text. Stresses on both ictuses II and III increase markedly and decrease on ictus IV, creating a much looser form from an originally quite canonized pattern. The stress profiles of later Othello and Iago are practically identical: Othello is acquiring features of a villain. The fact that Othello gradually assumes the character traits of Iago is also supported by the data of a lexical and stylistic analysis, which shows an evolution of verbal patterns and images used in the parts of these characters (Warnken 1964).

Thus, the semiotic function of verse rhythm goes even deeper than emphasizing typological similarity of some characters and opposing other characters as different types (*emploi*). Verse rhythm can be used to develop characters dynamically, and analysis of the rhythm helps us understand the subtleties of the poet's own interpretation of his personages. The results of such an analysis may be of interest not only to literary critics but also to actors in their interpretation of roles.

Note to Chapter 4

[1] The idea of a character pretending to be someone he really is not was suggested to me by Prof. George T. Wright.

Chapter 5

Line Endings: Accentual and Syllabic Structure

5.1 Problem; principles of analysis

The structure of line endings in Elizabethan-Jacobean verse has been subjected to detailed study for more than a hundred years (e.g., Spalding 1876, Spedding 1874, Hickson 1874, Ingram 1874, Fleay 1874, König 1888, Parrott 1919, Oliphant 1927, Timberlake 1931, Wentersdorf 1951, Oras 1953, Law 1959, Mincoff 1961, Jackson 1979:150-153, and others; see the extensive bibliography in Schoenbaum 1966:231-256). It is a well-trodden path, probably because endings are the most noticeable feature of verse lines. Shakespeare's line endings are the main object of my study, but they are compared with those of his older and younger contemporaries and with the verse of later poets. The results are also compared with those obtained by earlier scholars (though there is some difference in the classification of endings adopted here compared to some earlier works).

In analyzing the structure of line endings one has to distinguish between (1) the accentual structure and (2) the syllabic structure. Accentual structure of line endings is in part connected with one more problem—that of the syntactic characteristics of verse: phrase and line correspondence. If a line ends in an unstressed or weakly stressed monosyllable, the end of the line does not correspond with the end of a phrase thus producing the effect of a strong enjambment: the line syntactically and intonationally "runs on" the following line. Enjambments may also occur when a line ends in a fully stressed word. The majority of scholars who analyzed the types of endings in Shakespeare's dramas differentiated weakly stressed ("light") from unstressed ("weak") monosyllables, including among the former, for example, modal verbs and personal pronouns, and among the latter, prepositions and conjunctions (cf. the definitions given by Chambers 1930,I:265). Here is an example:

> The gods throw stones of sulphur on me, if
> That box I gave you was not thought by me
> A precious thing; I had it from the queen.
>
> ("Cymbeline" V,V:240-242)

Me illustrates a "light" line ending, and if is an example of a "weak" ending.

Oliphant, discussing Philip Massinger's idiosyncrasy of style, used yet another term for an even weaker final syllable: "feeble terminations" (Oliphant 1927:590), expressed by, for example, an article:

> Whatever is, or can be wished, in the
> Idea of a woman! O, what service . . .
> (Massinger, "The Maid of Honor" IV,III:75-76)

Both "light" and "weak" — but not "feeble" — types of endings are characteristic of later Shakespeare and result from a changed syntax of his line (Oras 1960, esp. p. 88; Wright 1983). However, a missing ictic stress may also be caused by an unstressed syllable of polysyllabic words, such as miracle, murderer, Hieronimo. This rhythmical type of ictic non-stress was widely used in the early Elizabethan verse (see also Chapter 2); it accompanied the end-stopped syntactic tendency of the period and probably had something to do with the prevailing mode of oral presentation of verse. Here I do not differentiate between "light" and "weak" monosyllables but draw a line between missing final ictic stress caused by unstressed syllables of polysyllabic words and by unstressed or weakly stressed monosyllables, because the former are more characteristic of early Shakespeare while the latter of Shakespeare's final period. Some examples from early Shakespeare are:

> What counsel, lords? Edward from Belgia,
> With hasty Germans and blunt Hollanders, . . .
> My sovereign, with the loving citizens . . .
> Well-minded Clarence, be thou fortunate!
> Farewell, sweet lords; let's meet at Coventry.
> ("Henry VI" 3, IV,VIII:1,2,19,27,32)

Line endings typical of later Shakespeare are:

> And that most venerable man which I (Did call my father. . .)
> And pray'd me oft forbearance; did it with (A prudency so rosy. . .)
> Or less,—at first?—perchance he spoke not, but (Like a full-acorn'd boar. . .)
> The kings your ancestors, together with (The natural bravery. . .)
> Our ancestor was that Mulmutius which (Ordained our law. . .)
> ("Cymbeline" II,V:3,10,15; III,I:17,55)

The analysis of the syllabic structure of non-masculine endings distinguishes simple and compound subtypes, that is, endings formed by one or more than one word (cf. Law 1959). Compound endings are further classified into compound light and heavy. Following earlier approaches (e.g., Boyle 1880-1886:453; Oras 1953:203; Mincoff 1961:241,247) I consider words with an almost certain weakening of strong phrase accent as stressed if they are perceived as somewhat heavier than fully unstressed words. Oras marked as "heavier, but still not very heavy" the negative not, the pronominal one after an adjective (a gŏod òne), the vocative sir (. . . your l̆eave, Sìr), and prepositions following a verb, but not followed by a noun, e.g., he d̆ies fòr't, to r̆ise in. Oras considered the following groups of words to have a somewhat heavier stress: adverbs of vague or broad semantics, such as hence, thus, yet, so, then, there, here, now, as in: to d̆ie sò; Awăy thèn; dispătch thère; where's your l̆ove nòw?; auxiliary and link verbs—substitutes for the repeated predicate, as in: . . . be kindlier moved than thŏu ạrt; lest she suspect, as hĕ does . . . ; the nominal pronoun this (and c̆all thịs), and nouns of broad semantics, such as way, time, year, man (the făir wạy, no ĭll mèn) (Oras 1953:203-205). Boyle also considered cases like a grĕat òne, shrĕwed ònes, ăre sò, stăte sò, make shŏw òf, "heavier than unstressed" (Boyle 1880-1886:453). Consider, for example, (1) He that advances one foot higher d̆ies fòr't, and (2) Though in your mutinies, I dare not h̆ate you (Fletcher, "Bonduca" II,I:71,90). The compound feminine ending in the first line is perceived to be heavier than in the second. If we disregard such "heavier but still not very heavy" cases, we risk bypassing an important feature of stylistic idiosyncrasy typical of some Jacobean poets (see below). And indeed, if adverbs like too, so, else, now, then, yet, nouns like man, thing, or way, and monosyllabic vocatives were fully devoid of stress, they would be used more freely and equally by all poets of the epoch that favored compound feminine endings; but this, as we shall see, is far from being the case. This means that the difference between complete non-stress and a slight accentual promotion "heavier than non-stress" was a very real thing for the poets. I considered the latter cases "stresses".

Here is the brief outline of my accepted syllabic and accentual classification of line endings.

Masculine: Stressed: *When dying clouds contend with growing light*. Unstressed: *To whom God will, there be the victory!* ("Henry VI" 3, II,V:2,15); *Ready in gibes, quick-answered, saucy and* ("Cymbeline", III,IV:160).

Feminine: Simple: *So I might live one hour on your sweet bosom* ("Richard III" I,II:124). Compound: Light: (a) position 10 stressed: *In your despite, upon your purse—revenge it* ("Cymbeline" I,VI:136); (b) position 10 unstressed: *To more convenient lodgings, and it shall be* (*My care to cherish you*) (Massinger, "The Maid of Honor" IV,IV:105). Heavy: *Those articles, my lord, are in the king's hand* ("Henry VIII" III,II:299). *Is this an hour for temporal affairs, ha?* ("Henry VIII" II,II:72).

Dactylic: Simple: *I cannot rightly say. But since King Pericles* ("Pericles" III,IV:7). Compound: Light: *And she will be your scholar: therefore look to it* ("Pericles" II,V:39). Heavy: *How doe you like her, John?—As well as y̆ou, Frĕdrick* (Fletcher, "The Chances" II,III:76).

Hyperdactylic: Simple: *To who shall find them.—Sir, my c̆ircumstances* ("Cymbeline" II,IV:61). Compound: Light: *Of your king's sorrow.—Sit, sir, I will rec̆ount it to you* ("Pericles" V,I:62). Heavy: *Time, and the wars together* *make me stóop, gèntlemen* (Fletcher, "The Loyal Subject" I,III:43) (the last example is borrowed from Oliphant 1927,33).

Some lines with both dactylic and hyperdactylic endings are ambivalent: they can be interpreted as iambic hexameter. The "pentameter" interpretation was supported by a stronger stress on position 10 than on 12, or by a stress on position 11 instead of 12, and got "the benefit of the doubt."

Conditions taken into account in estimating the strength of stress on monosyllables were listed in sections 2.1.2 and 2.1.3. Here I just re-state my attitude to the so-called ambivalent words. Ambivalent words, such as, for example, pronouns or modal verbs, are sometimes stressed and sometimes unstressed, depending on their rhythmical environment, their location on either a weak or a strong metrical position in a verse line, and their place in a phrase. Since this chapter discusses the final ictic position of the line, the ambivalent words filling this position are considered stressed if they terminate a phrase; otherwise they are regarded as unstressed. Examples:

(1) *Or she that bore you was no queen, and you (Recoil from your great stock)* ("Cymbeline" I,VI:128);

(2) *To keep her chamber.—There is gold for you; (Sell me your good report.)* ("Cymbeline" II,III:84). The first *you* is considered unstressed, the second stressed.

Interpreting the syllabic length of some words, as was discussed in Chapter 2, presents another problem. The questionable cases were summed up in 2.8. I add a few points here which are relevant for the analysis of line endings.

In analyzing syllabically ambivalent words forming the ends of lines I usually chose the longer variant, because a longer form is more typical of non-attributive sentence elements at the end of a phrase.

All polysyllabic words of the type murderer, venison, irrespective of the quality of the consonant following the central vowel, were considered unsyncopated and capable of forming dactylic endings if their stressed syllable fell on position 10 (such words are practically never syncopated at the end of a phrase). Some examples are: *And that she hath all courtly parts more èxqŭisīte; I should woo hard but be your groom. In hònĕstў; How deeply you at once do touch me! Imŏgĕn; But that of coward hares, hot goats, and vènisŏn; Our chariots and our horsemen be in rĕadĭnĕss; Thy favour's good enough. Some jay in Itălў* ("Cymbeline" III,V:72; III,VI:69; IV,III:4; IV,IV:37; III,V:23; III,IV:50).

Words containing a sonant preceded by a plosive sound invariably form feminine, dactylic, and hyperdactylic endings, for example: *Of space had pointed him sharp as my nĕedlĕ* ("Cymbeline" I,IV:19): feminine; *As my two brother, happy! but most mĭserăblĕ* ("Cymbeline" I,VI:6): dactylic; *So long attended thee. If thou wert hònŏurăblĕ* ("Cymbeline" I,VI:141): hyper-dactylic. The words heaven and spirit at the ends of the line were regarded as disyllables capable of forming feminine endings.

The word flower at the end of the Elizabethan verse line was treated as a disyllable, because this variant prevailed at the phrase terminations. In rhymed verse, when rhymed with hour, flower was considered monosyllabic. Hour was considered monosyllabic, because this was by far its most typical form. Root forms like fire were considered monosyllabic, while suffixed forms like higher were considered disyllabic, capable of constituting feminine endings. In rhyming pairs (aspire—higher) the monosyllabic variant of the triphthong [aie] was assumed for both elements.

The syllabic ambivalence of many sounds and sound combinations in Elizabethan verse and their possible different syllabic interpretation explains some discrepancy between Parrott's and my own figures characterizing the syllabic structure of line endings in "Titus Andronicus". Probably we interpreted in different ways such words as flower, deflower, briers, prison, showers, prayers, powers, and heaven (cf. Parrott 1919:37; Table 5.5).

5.2 General evolution of line endings in Shakespeare

Tables 5.1 and 5.2 present the structure of line endings by periods and in individual plays. Figure 5.1 shows graphically there is a marked evolution in both the accentual and syllabic features of line endings over Shakespeare's dramatic career.

Accentual forms of the final ictus generally evolved in the following way. Losses of stress caused by unstressed syllables of polysyllabic words such as destiny, emperor, or murderer are particularly numerous in the first two periods. This phenomenon is in keeping with the general trend of early Elizabethan verse: polysyllabic words with an unstressed final syllable at the end of the line were evidently in fashion (cf. Table 5.3, "Tamburlaine"). This line type probably required a particular style of declamation and a specific intonation. Here are some examples of such lines:

> And all the saints do sit soliciting
> For vengeance on those cursed murderers
> What, would you have us play a tragedy?
> Why, Nero thought it a disparagement
>   (Kyd, "The Spanish Tragedy" III,XII:33-34,84-85)
> Their scourge and terror tried on emperors.
> Smile stars, that reigned at my nativity . . .
> Disdain to borrow light of Cynthia!
>   (Marlowe, "Tamburlaine the Great" Part I,IV,II:32-33,35)
> And here in sight of Rome to Saturnine,
> King and commander of our commonweal,
> The wide world's emperor, do I consecrate
> My sword, my chariot, and my prisoners
>   ("Titus Andronicus" I,I:249-252)

Table 5.1

Generalized structure of line endings averaged by periods in Shakespeare's dramas
(in percent of total lines)

Chronology	Period	Accentual		Masculine Total	Syllabic					
		Loss of stress caused by:			Non-masculine					Dactylic*
		monosyl-lables	polysyl-lables		Total	Feminine				
						Total	Simple	Compound		
								Light	Heavy	
1588-1596	I Titus Andronicus – King John	0.5	11.1	89.2	10.8	10.6	9.1	1.4	0.1	0.3
1596-1602	II Merchant of Venice – Troilus and Cressida	0.9	10.6	81.6	18.4	18.1	15.4	2.6	0.2	0.3
1603-1606	IIIa Measure for Measure – Macbeth	1.2	4.9	73.1	26.9	26.3	21.2	4.7	0.4	0.7
1606-1613	IIIb Antony and Cleopatra – Henry VIII	5.5	5.8	67.1	32.9	32.2	25.1	6.1	0.9	0.8

*The exceptional cases of hyperdactylic endings in later dramas are added to dactylic endings.

Table 5.2

Structure of line endings in Shakespeare's dramas
(in percent of total lines)

Chronology after Wentersdorf	Dramas	Accentual Loss of stress caused by:		Masculine Total	Syllabic						
		monosyl-lables	polysyl-lables		Total	Non-masculine					Dactylic*
						Total	Feminine		Compound		
							Simple	Light	Light	Heavy	
1588-89	Titus Andronicus	1.0	11.9	92.5	7.5	7.3	6.2	1.1	0.0	0.2
1589-90	Henry VI,1	0.5	14.5	92.6	7.4	7.2	6.5	0.7	0.0	0.1
1590-91	Comedy of Errors	0.5	8.6	85.9	14.1	14.0	10.6	3.3	0.1	0.1
1590-91	Henry VI,2	0.3	12.0	88.2	11.8	11.5	9.8	1.4	0.1	0.3
1590-91	Henry VI,3	0.2	9.6	86.1	13.9	13.5	10.7	1.4	0.1	0.4
1591-92	Taming of the Shrew	0.4	11.4	80.7	19.3	18.8	16.6	2.0	0.2	0.5
1591-92	Richard III	0.4	9.9	80.5	19.5	18.9	16.3	2.5	0.1	0.7
1592-93	Two Gentlemen of Verona	0.2	12.7	81.5	18.6	18.1	14.1	3.5	0.5	0.5
1593-94	Love's Labour's Lost	0.8	10.2	94.6	5.4	5.4	5.1	0.3	--	--
1594-95	Midsummer Night's Dream	0.4	13.8	95.4	4.6	4.6	3.8	0.7	0.1	--
1594-95	Romeo and Juliet	0.7	10.8	92.5	7.5	7.4	6.7	0.7	0.0	0.0
1594-95	Richard II	0.8	8.7	90.2	9.8	9.5	8.8	0.7	--	0.2
1595-96	King John	0.8	11.2	94.8	5.2	5.1	4.5	0.6	--	0.1
1595-96	Merchant of Venice	1.0	11.1	83.3	16.7	16.4	13.3	2.8	0.3	0.3
1596-97	Henry IV,1	1.3	16.1	95.2	4.7	4.6	3.5	1.0	0.2	0.1
1596-97	Henry IV,2	0.8	12.8	85.7	14.3	13.9	12.7	1.2	--	0.4

Table 5.2 (cont.)

1597-98	Much Ado About Nothing	0.3	12.9	78.9	21.1	20.9	18.3	2.5	0.2	0.2
1598-99	Henry V	0.6	12.4	80.5	19.5	19.2	17.5	1.5	0.1	0.3
	Julius Caesar	1.2	12.7	81.3	18.8	18.5	16.1	2.4	0.0	0.2
1599-1600	As You Like It	1.2	10.4	76.8	23.2	23.0	19.5	3.3	0.2	0.2
	Twelfth Night	0.9	7.3	78.7	21.3	21.0	15.9	4.9	0.3	0.3
	Hamlet	0.4	5.7	77.5	22.5	22.0	18.4	3.5	0.2	0.4
1601-02	Troilus and Cressida	0.7	7.2	77.0	23.0	22.4	19.1	3.2	0.1	0.6
1603-04	Measure for Measure	0.8	8.9	73.8	26.2	25.1	21.4	3.4	0.3	1.0
	Othello	0.2	5.3	73.0	27.0	26.5	22.8	4.9	0.7	0.5
1604-05	All's Well That Ends Well	1.9	4.4	74.2	25.8	25.3	18.5	6.3	0.4	0.5
	Timon of Athens	2.1	4.9	74.2	25.8	25.1	13.4	5.6	0.1	0.7
1605-06	King Lear	0.9	3.2	71.8	28.2	27.4	22.6	4.5	0.3	0.8
	Macbeth	2.1	3.6	74.8	25.2	24.9	20.6	3.8	0.5	0.4
1606-07	Antony and Cleopatra	5.2	6.1	73.1	27.0	26.3	21.9	4.3	0.2	0.6
1607-08	Pericles	3.0	8.9	79.1	20.9	20.3	15.4	4.2	0.7	0.7
	Coriolanus	5.9	5.1	69.8	30.2	29.6	22.6	6.4	0.6	0.6
1608-09	Cymbeline	6.3	4.2	69.7	30.4	29.4	23.7	5.0	0.7	0.3
1609-10	Winter's Tale	6.7	5.2	66.9	33.1	32.3	26.0	5.9	0.4	0.9
1610-11	Tempest	6.6	6.3	65.0	35.0	34.5	26.9	7.3	0.3	0.5
1612-13	Henry VIII	4.1	6.1	51.7	48.3	47.5	34.9	9.4	3.1	0.9

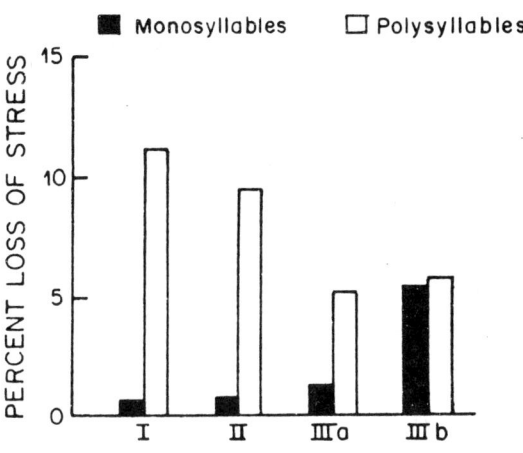
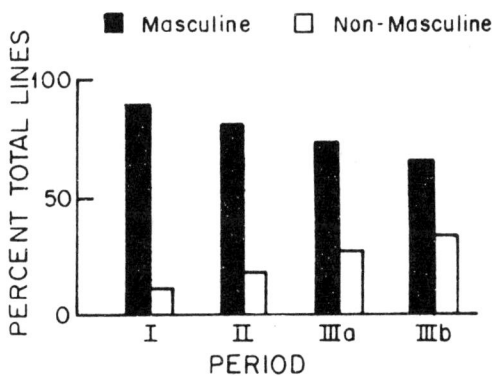

Fig. 5.1. Evolution of features of line endings in Shakespeare's dramatic works, generalized by periods. (A) Accentual: percent (from total lines) of loss of stress caused by monosyllables and polysyllables. (B) Syllabic: percent (from total lines) of masculine vs. non-masculine endings. Data from Table 5.1.

The proportion of such lines steadily decreases from period I to IIIa (there are, of course, some deviations, for example "Henry IV",1 with its 16% of unstressed syllables of polysyllabic words in position 10) and remains relatively low throughout Shakespeare's final period. On the whole, the proportion

Table 5.3

Structure of line endings in Marlowe's dramas

Chronology	Drama	Accentual structure: loss of stress caused by		Syllabic structure: masculine endings (% of total lines)
		monosyl-lables	polysyl-lables	
1587	Tamburlaine	0.4	24.3	98.5
1588	Doctor Faustus	0.3	23.8	97.5
1589	The Jew of Malta	0.6	18.5	96.6
1589	Massacre in Paris	0.6	14.3	96.4
1590	Dido	0.4	14.3.	95.0
1592	Edward II	0.1	11.0	99.2

of unstressed syllables of polysyllabic words in position 10 decreased twofold from Period I through IIIb.

Missing final ictic stresses caused by unstressed monosyllables generally evolve in the following way: beginning with only exceptional cases in Period I their number slowly increases through Period IIIa, then grows almost five times in the final period. A "leap" occurs between 1606 and 1607, in "Antony and Cleopatra;" but it is presaged already in "Macbeth". On the whole, from the first through the last period the number of unstressed monosyllables in position 10 increases <u>ten</u> times.

The period between 1599 through 1606 is worth noticing: the proportion of unstressed syllables of polysyllabic words on the final ictus is already low, while the ratio of unstressed monosyllables is not yet very high. Therefore, most dramas of this period have the strongest final ictic stress of the whole canon, e.g., "Hamlet", "Othello", "King Lear", and "Macbeth" (Table 5.2; cf. Tables 2.1 and 2.2).

Two examples of unstressed monosyllables in position 10:

Which is our honour, bitter torture <u>shall</u> (Winnow the truth from falsehood. . .)
Be called Posthumus Leonatus, <u>and</u> (Be 'villain' less than 'twas!. . .)
("Cymbeline" V,V:133,224)

Unstressed monosyllables in position 10 are, of course, a sign of syntactically incomplete lines. This syntactic line structure of later Shakespeare is one of his idiosyncratic features; it differentiates his verse style from that of almost all of his contemporaries and immediate followers. For example, the proportion of unstressed monosyllables in the final ictic position of Webster's "Duchess of Malfi" (1623) and Ford's "Perkin Warbeck" (1634) is 1.9 and 1.6%, respectively. One poet who is very close to Shakespeare in the number of strong enjambments is Massinger: weak and "feeble" terminations, that are so common in his verse (Oliphant 1927,59), make his style resemble Shakespeare's; they were one of the reasons why the non-Fletcherean scenes of "Henry VIII" were extravagantly attributed by Boyle to Massinger (Boyle 1880-1886:579-628). However, other elements of Massinger's style including other features of line endings are quite unlike Shakespeare's. Here are some examples of Massinger's "feeble line terminations:" *Whatever is, or can be wished, in the* (*Idea of a woman!* . . .); *Such a dominion o'er you. Yet, ere I* (*Deliver the demands*. . .); *By a solemn contract bind yourself, when she* (*Requires it.* . . .) (Massinger, "The Maid of Honor" IV,III:75,80,86).

What are the possible causes of this evolutionary trend, a decrease of unstressed syllables of polysyllabic words in the final ictus and an increase in the number of unstressed monosyllables, in Shakespeare's canon? As mentioned earlier, unstressed monosyllables in position 10 are a sign of non-correspondence between syntactic and intonational segmentation of a verse text and its metrical (line) segmentation, which results in enjambment. Possible reasons for an increased amount of enjambment and a decrease in the number of polysyllabic words with an unstressed final syllable in position 10 are the following. (a) Changed conditions of recitation: the companies transferred from roofless public theatres where the actor had to articulate his text loudly and distinctly, separating each line from the next for the audience to hear them better, to roofed, mostly private, theatres with better acoustics, where the audience could hear the parts better and the actors no longer had to shout out each line and separate it from the next. Such a change of acoustic conditions might have quickened the recitation tempo, possibly influencing even the modes of intonation. (b) A change in the tastes of both the audience and the poets. The fashionable public had wearied of stilted plays full of long dialogues and soliloquies; it required more dynamic action, a more colloquial, prose-like style, a quicker exchange of repartees, a faster tempo of declamation. A change in taste could have caused a genre change: blood tragedies of revenge and "drum-and-trumpet" chronicles were gradually replaced by tragicomedies and romances (Thorndike 1901:99-108, Appleton 1956:55). This genre change could have caused a change in verse style. (c) A change in the verse sophistication of the audience: people became used to verse, could hear it better, and could recognize verse where they would have failed to do so some ten years previously.

All these are external reasons; there must be some internal reasons as well. There seems to be some inner logic of evolution in a verse cycle, which usually proceeds from a greater towards a smaller opposition between verse and prose, from a stricter towards a looser verse form (cf. Chapter 2). A similar conclusion can be reached on the basis of the analysis of line endings. Thus, an evolution is traced even in Marlowe's short dramatic cycle (Table 5.3). His dramatic verse displays a low number of unstressed monosyllables on the final ictus; a slight increase from "Tamburlaine" to "Massacre in Paris" is replaced by their complete disappearance in the final ictus of "Edward II" (in "Richard III", Shakespeare's play of the same year, their number is relatively high). However, there is a significant evolution in the ratio of unstressed syllables of polysyllabic words on the final ictic position: from 24.3% in "Tamburlaine" to 11.0% in "Edward II". There is a break between "Doctor Faustus" and "The Jew of Malta" ("Faustus" is an early play closely related to "Tamburlaine") and another break between "The Jew of Malta" and "The Massacre in Paris". "The Jew of Malta" is, as it were, a connecting link between early and late Marlowe. Thus in its own way Marlowe's dramatic cycle also displays an evolution from a more rigid to a slightly looser verse form (cf. the stress profiles of his dramas, Table 2.6) and a decrease of unstressed syllables of polysyllabic words at the ends of his lines.

An evolution from a more rigid to a looser rhythm can be also observed in the sequence of plays of another poet who belonged to a completely different epoch and school: Byron. His four dramas undergo the following evolution in the proportion of unstressed monosyllables on the final ictus: "Marino Faliero" 5.6% (lower than in later Shakespeare); "Sardanapalus" 7.6%; "The Two Foscari" 12.8%; "Werner" 12.3% (twice as much as in later Shakespeare: "Tempest" 6.6%). A loosening of verse form, manifested, among other ways, by an increase in the proportion of final unstressed monosyllables, is apparently a usual occurrence within a verse cycle.

The <u>syllabic</u> structure of line endings in Shakespeare's plays generalized by periods evolves in the following way (Table 5.1, Fig. 5.1). The proportion of non-masculine endings gradually increases from period I through IIIb; the percentage of non-masculine endings in the final period is <u>three</u> times higher than in the first period. Shakespeare began his career using a higher proportion of feminine endings than his older contemporaries, in whose verse the percentage of non-masculine endings did not exceed 4% (cf. Timberlake 1931, Tarlinskaja 1976:Table 55; see also Table 5.3), but he ended with a lower percentage of non-masculine endings than his younger contemporaries; for example, in Fletcher's "Bonduca" only 29.6% of all line endings are masculine.

It is important to note that in Shakespeare's verse the increase in the number of feminine endings proceeded side by side with the increase in number of unstressed monosyllables in the final ictic position; this tendency contrasted with the verse of most Jacobean poets (e.g., Fletcher, Webster, or Ford) and of the later, post-Restoration dramatists (Otway) where the high proportion of feminine endings accompanied a high proportion of end-stopped lines (Tarlinskaja 1976:Tables 51 and 55). The one exception was Massinger, who, similar to Shakespeare, widely used both lines with feminine endings and lines with masculine endings terminating in unstressed monosyllables.

Table 5.4

Syllabic structure of line endings in Byron's dramas
(in percent of total lines)

Drama	Masculine	Feminine		Compound		Dactylic
		Totally	Simple	Light	Heavy	
Marino Faliero	67.2	32.5	26.4	5.1	1.1	0.3
Sardanapalus	66.5	33.2	25.6	6.2	1.5	0.3
The Two Foscari	68.4	30.9	23.0	6.1	1.9	0.7
Werner	68.3	30.5	22.8	5.8	1.9	1.2

The correlation between simple and compound feminine endings is also period-specific: the proportion of compound feminine endings gradually increases from Period I through IIIb. Simple feminine endings are six times more frequent than compound ones in Period I, but only about three times more frequent in the final period. Particularly striking is the increased number of heavy feminine endings: they are practically nonexistent in the earliest plays, but their number approximately <u>doubles</u> in each succeeding period.

Heavy feminine endings were evidently fashionable with Jacobean playwrights; but they are particularly typical of Fletcher's style. The high proportion of heavy feminine endings found in Fletcher's verse is almost unique. Ford, for example, in his "Perkin Warbeck" with as many as 45.6% feminine endings has only 0.8% heavy ones. Only Massinger (e.g, "The Maid of Honor") and Middleton and Rowley (e.g., "The Changeling") resemble Fletcher in the proportion of heavy feminine endings, for example, 3.7% in "The Changeling;" but this is almost three times less than in Fletcher's "Bonduca" with 9.4%. The Restoration playwrights (e.g., Dryden) anticipating, as it were, eighteenth-century Classicism, seemed reluctant to use feminine line endings. Otway is the only exception: the number of feminine endings in his play "Venice Preserv'd" reaches 46.7%; however, the proportion of heavy feminine endings does not reach even 2% (Tarlinskaja 1976:Table 55).

In Byron's plays (Table 5.4) the indices of syllabic structure of line endings are not unlike those of both Shakespeare in his final period and of the later Jacobean poets; cf., for example, the percentages of masculine and compound feminine endings in Tables 5.1, 5.2, and 5.4, especially "Sardanapalus" and "The Two Foscari". The number of unstressed monosyllables in the final ictic position, particularly in "Werner", is almost twice as great as in later Shakespeare. In Byron's verse two tendencies stemming from Shakespeare's and later Jacobean plays are amplified: (1) a large number of weakly stressed monosyllables in position 10 of lines with masculine endings resulting in strong enjambment, and (2) a large number of lines with feminine endings, particularly compound, both light and heavy. Loss of the final ictic stress caused by weakly stressed monosyllables (prepositions, modal or auxiliary verbs) in lines with feminine endings also occur, though infrequently; but such lines never occurred in Shakespeare's verse and were exceptional even for Massinger. So here again Byron is amplifying a specific, though exceptional, tendency of the Jacobean verse system. Some examples are:

And when I beg of any one, it shall be
Of him who was the first to offer what
Few can obtain by asking. Pardon me.
. . . .
Would please him better than the table, after
His soaking in your river: but for fear
. . . .
My own from his, not to alarm him into
Suspicion of my plan. Why did I leave
                    (Byron, "Werner" I,I:221-223,270-271,494-495)

5.3 Some particulars of the evolution of line endings

Consider now the structure of line endings in individual plays (Table 5.2). Two points appear: (a) the structure of the line endings is to some extent genre-specific; and (b) Wentersdorf's periodization of Shakespeare's canon is more convincing than Chambers'.

The evolution of line endings, on the whole regular and gradual, fluctuates and deviates in separate plays. The most marked "leaps" - sharp increases in the number of non-masculine endings—usually occur in the comedies: "The Comedy of Errors", "The Taming of the Shrew", "The Merchant of Venice", "Much Ado About Nothing", and "As You Like It". The only non-comedy in which this occurs is "Henry VIII;" but this is yet another indication of Fletcher's possible co-authorship in the play (see also 5.4).

There are three cases of an exceptional decrease in the number of non-masculine endings: "Love's Labour's Lost", "Henry IV",1, and "Pericles". The latter is relatively easy to explain: the low proportion of non-masculine endings in "Pericles", compared to its chronological neighbours "Antony and Cleopatra" and "Coriolanus", seems to be one more indication of a non-Shakespearean hand in this play (cf. Chapters 2 and 3; see 5.4).

The sharp decrease in the number of non-masculine endings in "Love's Labour's Lost" (more than three times compared to the preceding comedy "The Two Gentlemen of Verona") is probably explained by the stylistic peculiarities of the play. "Love's Labour's Lost" is considered a poke-fun at pedantry, a gibe against pompous artifice and a "Euphuistic" parody of Lyly's manner (e.g., Yates, 1936; cf. *The Complete Works of William Shakespeare*, 1980: "Love's Labour's Lost:" "Introduction", p. 166). The pompous-archaic object of Shakespeare's effervescent parody may explain the sharp increase in the number of masculine line endings in the parodying text.

The decrease in the proportion of non-masculine endings in "Henry IV", Part 1, is harder to understand even if we make allowance for the genre of the play (as mentioned earlier, chronicles are more constrained in structure than other genres). The greater number of masculine endings in "Henry IV",1 is undoubtedly connected to some degree with a high proportion of missing ictic stresses caused by unstressed syllables of polysyllabic words; these occur only in lines with masculine endings. Still, this does not seem to be a complete explanation for the phenomenon.

A sort of momentum develops in the sequence: "Love's Labour's Lost" opens a whole series of plays with a low proportion of non-masculine endings; five plays altogether: "Love's Labour's Lost" through "King John". It is possible to include "Henry IV", 1 in this cluster, its tail-end; this would also help explain its line-ending peculiarities. Only in "The Merchant of Venice" does Shakespeare go back to the proportion of non-masculine endings already reached in six earlier plays ("The Comedy of Errors" through "The Two Gentlemen of Verona").

The proportion of compound, particularly heavy, feminine endings is also genre-specific: they are more frequent in comedies and the least typical of chronicles (and of "Love's Labour's Lost"), e.g., "Richard II" and "King John". The predictable exception is "Henry VIII" (see 5.4).

This comparative survey of the syllabic structure of line endings in individual plays justifies Wentersdorf's changes in Chambers' chronology (see 2.3). Thus, Period I plays with a particularly low proportion of non-masculine endings are distributed in Chambers' periodization less logically than in Wentersdorf's. If arranged according to Wentersdorf's chronology, a low proportion of non-masculine endings is displayed (a) by the two earliest dramas, "Titus Andronicus" and "Henry VI", Part 1, and (b) by the cluster of plays following "Love's Labour's Lost". "Richard III", an earlier play according to Chambers, displays a puzzling increase of non-masculine endings if it is assumed to follow "Henry VI",1; but "Richard III" has a predictable proportion of non-masculine endings if it is assumed to follow "The Taming of the Shrew", as Wentersdorf suggested. The same is true of "Timon of Athens:" the proportion of non-masculine endings in this play suggests its chronological place not after "Coriolanus", but three theatre seasons earlier, before "King Lear."

"Troilus and Cressida" and "Othello", whose stress profiles display features of a stricter rhythmical form, do not deviate from their period expectations in the proportion of non-masculine endings: in "Othello" it is even slightly higher than in other plays of Period IIIa, except "King Lear". The style of a play is, of course, a complex system of interacting distinctive features; which of them are more relevant for resolving periodization problems must be judiciously decided in every case.

5.4 Line endings of acts and scenes in four controversial plays

In sections 5.2 and 5.3 we concentrated on the general evolution of Shakespeare's accentual and syllabic structure of line endings, which demonstrated a relatively gradual, though not always smooth, transition from certain leading tendencies in early Shakespeare to different tendencies in later Shakespeare. The characteristics of the inner structure of plays, analyzed by acts and scenes, show sometimes considerable variations. The variation of line endings by scenes and acts in four plays of Shakespeare's canon ("Titus Andronicus", "Timon of Athens", "Pericles", and "Henry VIII") is outlined below (more data on the heterogeneous structure of these plays are given in Chapters 2 and 3). The variation of indices in separate acts and particularly scenes raises several questions; the main questions are those of chronology and authorship, but also of a probable link between verse form and plot development and genre of scenes.

The controversy concerning the dating and authorship of "Titus Andronicus" has already in part been touched upon (Chapters 2 and 3). Most earlier scholars came to the conclusion that Shakespeare had revised an older play dated apparently between 1584 and 1589; the play was produced by Shakespeare's company and published in its revised form in 1594 (Parrott 1919:17,20). Some believe the author of the source-play to be Peele (Parrott 1919, J.X. Maxwell 1950). Others hold that "Titus Andronicus" was Shakespeare's earliest play, later revised by the poet himself (Wentersdorf 1951, Hill 1957).

Line endings of "Titus Andronicus" analyzed by scenes (Table 5.5; cf. Parrott 1919:37) reveal a considerable range in the percentage of feminine endings: 2.3-15.2% [the rare cases of dactylic endings, as in *We are beholding to you, good Andronicus* (V,III:33), were added to feminine]. As we already know, early Shakespeare used more feminine endings than other Elizabethan playwrights at the end of the sixteenth century (cf. Tables 5.2 and 5.3; see also Timberlake 1931). Shakespeare's dramas of 1590-1596, except for "Love's Labour's Lost" and "A Midsummer Night's Dream", each contain not less than 7% of non-masculine endings. The non-masculine endings in "Titus Andronicus" by scenes can be grouped into two clusters: 2.3-6.4% (I.I, II.I, II.III, II.IV, IV.I, V.II) and 7.2-18.0% (II.III, III.I, III.II, IV.II, IV.III, IV.IV, V.I, V.III). The first cluster includes primarily scenes of the first two acts of the play while the second cluster contains mainly scenes of acts III-V. The mean index for the first group of scenes is 4.1% feminine endings (42 cases in 1030 lines), for the second group 11.4% (160 cases in 1400 lines). The second index is much closer to those in the majority of Shakespeare's plays during the

Table 5.5

Feminine endings in acts and scenes of "Titus Andronicus"

Act and Scene	Number of lines	Number of fem. endings	Percentage of fem. endings	(Parrott's data of fem. endings)
I.I	495	19	3.8	(3.6)
II.I	129	3	2.3	(2.3)
II.II	26	1	3.8	(4.1)
II.III	302	34	11.3	(11.6)
II.IV	55	3	5.6	(5.5)
III.I	293	21	7.1	(6.4)
III.II	80	10	11.3	(11.6)
IV.I	123	3	2.4	(2.4)
IV.II	169	19	11.2	(9.5)
IV.III	92	14	15.2	(11.7)
IV.IV	105	9	8.6	(8.0)
V.I	162	29	18.0	(20.7)
V.II	202	13	6.4	(5.9)
V.III	197	24	12.5	(13.6)

first period and is almost identical to the mean percentage of non-masculine endings of this period (10.8%, see Table 5.1). Many scholars have commented on the more archaic style of certain scenes of "Titus Andronicus", both those scholars who claimed that Shakespeare had reworked an earlier play by Peele (e.g., Parrott 1919, J.C. Maxwell 1950) and those who believed "Titus" to be the earliest play by Shakespeare himself written at the end of the eighties and reworked by the author in 1593/94 (Alexander 1938:77; Wentersdorf 1951; Hill 1957; Oras 1960:88; Jackson 1979:148-156). The stress profiles of the two groups of scenes also indicate a more archaic style in the first group (Chapter 3).

Act I seems especially archaic in style. One element of this archaic trait is a particularly low number of feminine endings, including feminine compound ones. The latter are very infrequent everywhere, but particularly so in the first half of the play; compare, for example, one case in each of I.I and III.I (129 and 293 lines respectively), but five cases in each of IV.II (169 lines) and V.I (162 lines). Another feature of a more archaic style in the first half of the play, and particularly of Act I, is the incidence of missing final ictic stress caused by

193

unstressed syllables of polysyllabic words. The percentages of missing stresses are particularly high for I.I, IV.III, and IV.IV (16.0, 18.5, and 19.9%, respectively), and particularly low for III.I (6.1%).

The more archaic style in the first part of the play can, however, also be explained stylistically: scenes of more pathos, consisting mainly of longer monologues and orations by heroic characters (mainly Titus himself) contain more lines in the "archaic" style (with archaic phonetical word variants) than conversational scenes consisting primarily of repartees between lower or negative characters. In I.I Titus, victorious, returns from the wars with the Goths and is triumphantly welcomed by his countrymen (*Romans, make way! the good Andronicus, Patron of virtue, Rome's best champion . . . Thou great defender of this Capitol; With burial among their ancestors*, etc.: 66,67,80,87). After the burial of Titus' sons slain by the Goths, the tribune Marcus informs Titus that the people of Rome have elected him Rome's emperor. Titus, however, declines the honor and advises that Saturninus become emperor instead. The Romans take this advice: "(. . . *we create) Lord Saturninus Rome's great emperor, And say 'Long live our Emperor Saturnine!'* " (232-233). In IV.III, which is relatively short, the main incidences of unstressed final ictuses caused by polysyllables occurs in Titus' first monologue (*Then, when you come to Pluto's region; And that it comes from old Andronicus; Ah, Rome! Well, well; I made thee miserable What time I threw the peoples suffrages:* 13,16,18,19). In IV.IV most of the lines of the type analyzed occur in Saturninus' opening monologue (1-26) and his two following long utterances (50-60 and 69-77); stylistically such lines are probably meant to convey a stately, weighty speech of an emperor (*See, here's to Jove, and this to Mercury* (14); *But if I live, his feigned ecstasies* (21); *Have by my means been butchered wrongfully* (55); *Nor age nor honour shall shape privilege* (57); *That Lucius' banishment was wrongfully* (76), and others).

The lowest index of missing final ictic stress occurs in III.I: first, Titus pleads with the tribunes for his sons' lives as they are being led to the "palace of execution:" a fast speech tempo is very probable here. Next, Lavinia, raped and maimed, is brought by Marcus, and Titus in vain keeps asking her who had done that outrage; at that moment Aaron the Moor comes telling Titus that the emperor had decided to spare the lives of Titus's sons in exchange for his chopped hand; a quick repartee between Titus, Marcus, and Lucius follows in which each offers his hand to be chopped; Titus cunningly sends them off to fetch an axe and hurriedly asks Aaron: "*Lend me thy hand, and I will give thee mine;*" and finally, a Messenger comes with two heads and a hand telling Titus that he had been deceived; Titus, who has "*not another tear to shed*", sends Lucius off: "*Hie to the Goths, and raise an army there*". The quick tempo of the scene seems to explain a low incidence of the lines of the type analyzed; such lines not only slow down the tempo but evidently also required a specific, solemn declamation style.

Thus, the varying proportions of different line endings in certain scenes may have a stylistic explanation. Nevertheless, we cannot rule out the possibility that the higher mean percentage of missing final ictic stresses for the first group of scenes (13.2%) than for the second group (10.2%) reflects a more archaic style in the first group of scenes, particularly of I.I.

"Timon of Athens" is another play of questionable authorship (see also Chapter 3). In the opinion of some scholars (e.g., Nowottny 1959:497, Edwards 1968:134, W. Wells 1920, Jackson 1979:54-66,213-215) "Timon of Athens" is the product of collaboration between Shakespeare and Middleton. MacD.P. Jackson's grammatical and lexical tests led him to believe that the style of I.II,III "and one or two other patches of *Timon* is as like Middleton as it is unlike Shakespeare's . . . Now I should be happy to try to explain away this linguistic evidence of Middleton's hand in *Timon* were it not for the fact that of all the candidates put forward by earlier scholars for the position of 'collaborator' or 'reviser' or 'original author' of the play Middleton is the one dramatist for whom a serious case was made out" (Jackson 1979:58). Nowottny (1959) felt that it was the end of Act IV and Act V that probably did not belong to Shakespeare. The stress profile of act V also indicates a different rhythmical style which is further evidence of a different hand (see Table 3.1).

The structure of line endings of acts I (277 iambic pentameter lines), II (162 lines), III (231 lines), IV (500 lines), and V (276 lines) looks as follows (in percent):

Act	Accentual: Loss of stress caused by		Mascul. (Total)	Syllabic: Non-masculine			
	Monosyl.	Polysyl		(Total)	Feminine		Dactylic
					Simple	Comp.	
I	1.8	2.9	70.4	29.6	22.4	6.5	0.7
II	2.5	4.3	71.6	28.4	21.0	6.8	0.6
III	2.2	8.7	75.3	24.7	16.9	6.9	0.9
IV	0.8	5.0	79.2	20.8	15.4	4.4	1.0
V	1.0	4.8	77.5	22.5	16.3	5.1	1.1

In spite of the fact that the text of "Timon" looks more like a draft than a finished play and that it abounds in long passages of prose and in deviating, faulty verse lines (flagrantly non-pentameter lines were excluded from my analysis), its line endings by acts display more similarity than could be expected when compared with the stress profiles by acts (Table 3.1). However, the dynamics of line endings repeats, in a way, the dynamics of the stress profiles. The first two acts with a high proportion of missing ictic stresses on position 8 (the type of stress profile conventionally associated with a looser variant of iambic pentameter) also display a high proportion of non-masculine line endings—another sign of loosening (decanonization) of verse form, while the last act, which displays a leveled stress on positions 6 and 8, has a lower proportion of non-masculine line endings, a sign of a more rigorous, canonized verse form.

On the whole, the proportion of non-masculine endings decreases in "Timon of Athens" from the beginning through the end of the play. The proportion of non-mascline endings in acts III or V (the two "questionable" acts) gives little support to the hypothesis of mixed authorship of the play. This obvious evolutionary tendency that develops throughout the text, corrupt as it is, lends another argument in favor of a single authorship of the play: mixed authorship is usually accompanied by much more mixed rhythmical tendencies and little "rhythm" or logic of evolution (for a comparative example, see "Henry VIII" below).

Line endings analyzed by scenes, however, display a somewhat wider range of variation, which seems to be connected with the development of the plot and the stylistic particularities of the scenes. For example, Scene I of Act IV, which consists of Timon's meditative soliloquy, contains only 12.5% of non-masculine line endings. In contrast, Scene III (the setting is "woods and cave near the sea shore" where Timon has retreated) consists mainly of dialogues between Timon and various people who come to prey on him, and whom Timon with curses drives away. This scene contains 21.9% of non-masculine line endings, with quite a number of compound endings among them. Some examples, illustrating the more colloquial style of scene III, are:

> What is thy name? Is man so hateful tó thee?
> I know thee too, and more than that I know thee . . .
> Noble Timon, what friendship may I dó thee?
> Be a whore still; they love thee not that use thee;
> ("Timon of Athens" IV,III:51,57,70,84)

"Pericles" is another play that has raised doubts as to Shakespeare's sole authorship. Commenting on the stylistic differences between acts I-II and III-V, Chambers admitted that only acts III-V resemble the style of Shakespeare's later plays, while acts I-II are quite unlike Shakespeare (cf. Chapter 3). Gower's texts also struck Chambers as non-Shakespearean.

The differences in the structure of line endings of acts I-II and III-V of "Pericles" is as follows (in % of the total number of lines):

	Accentual:			Syllabic:				
	Loss of stress caused by			Non-masculine				
			Masc.		Feminine			Others
Acts	Monosyl.	Polysyl.		Total	Simple	Light	Heavy	
I-II	1.7	8.9	84.0	16.0	11.1	3.2	0.8	0.9
III-V	5.2	8.4	72.7	27.3	20.7	5.3	0.5	0.7

The most striking differences between acts I-II and III-V are the incidence of unstressed monosyllables in position 10 and the proportion of non-masculine line endings. The incidence of unstressed and weakly stressed monosyllables in the final ictic position in acts III-V is three times higher than in I-II; this is a sign of a more frequent occurrence of end-stopped lines in the first two acts of the play. The index for acts III-V is close to that for all other plays of the same period ("Antony and Cleopatra" 5.2, "Coriolanus" 5.9, "Cymbeline" 6.3). Thus the line-ending data definitely show that acts I-II are not only different from acts III-V but from Shakespeare's other plays of the same period. Another point of difference is the proportion of non-masculine endings in both parts of "Pericles". The percentage for acts III-V (27.3%) seems to refer this play to the first half of Period IIIb, between 1606 and 1610 (Table 5.1); the percentage for acts I-II (16.0%) suggests either an impossibly early date, somewhere close to "Henry V" and "Julius Caesar" (1598-1600), or the presence in "Pericles" of another hand.

Let us ask a question: suppose the differences in verse style in "Pericles" is a sign of an evolution of rhythm within a play? We have already seen that any author's verse style can vary through the course of a drama. This variation may be caused by an evolution of the plot, by the predominance of solemn monologues or colloquial repartees in certain acts or scenes, or by the specific rhythmical characteristics of different personages (cf. Mincoff 1961:250, 252,258; see also Chapter 4). However, the more generalized rhythmical characteristics of a play definitely written by one author within a short period of time always indicate a more homogeneous rhythm or a smoother evolution than is observed in plays written in collaboration or reworked at a later date. To prove this point I divided "Cymbeline", an unquestionably Shakespearean play, into two portions, acts I-III and IV-V (cf. Chapter 3). The indices of the line endings are as follows (in percent):

Acts	Loss of stress caused by		Masculine endings	Non-masculine endings
	Monosyl.	Polysyl.		
I-III	7.7	4.6	69.1	30.9
V-V	5.2	3.7	70.5	29.5

The two parts are certainly much more homogeneous than acts I-II and III-V of "Pericles".

Taking all the evidence together, it appears that the first two acts of "Pericles" were indeed written by another, probably earlier author.

"Henry VIII" has long been one of Shakespeare's most controversial plays. Analysis of its line endings by scenes has always provided the main argument for discriminating the Shakespeare-Fletcher partnership in the play (see Chapter 2). R.A. Law (1959) based his argument on the incidence of compound feminine endings formed by a verb followed by an unstressed pronoun, which are four times more frequent in the scenes attributed to Fletcher than in those attributed to Shakespeare. Law obtained similar indices for the allegedly Fletcherean and Shakespearean portions of "The Two Noble Kinsmen". In addition, Law also studied the stylistic idiosyncrasies of images used in the Shakespearean and Fletcherean scenes of "Henry VIII" and the difference in handling the source material (Holinghed's chronicle) by the two hypothetical co-authors: Fletcherean scenes, as opposed to Shakespearean, exhibit a "lack of dexterity in handling source material" (Law 1959:484).

Mincoff took into account thirteen "objectively measurable and essentially independent indicators" of style (Mincoff 1961:159). Of these, four characterize the verse form: double (that is, feminine) endings, run-on lines, weak (unstressed or weakly stressed) endings, and the extra monosyllable before a "pause;" one indicator is lexical (Hart's vocabulary test); and four are grammatical (discussed by A.C. Partridge). Mincoff introduced three more indicators: sentence structure; the high concentration of "fletcherisms" in Fletcher's scenes; and "alliterative humor" typical of Fletcher. Mincoff admitted that Fletcherean scenes in some ways do differ in style from the plays written by Fletcher alone, such as "Bonduca" or "Valentinian" (cf. Baldwin Maxwell 1939:54-63), but he attributed the difference, as in "The Two Noble Kinsmen", to the leading role of Shakespeare in the collaboration. Both in "Henry VIII" and in "The Two Noble Kinsmen" ". . . Fletcher rises so far above his usual level in poetics and dramatic imagination. . ." that it "seems hard to avoid the conclusion that he was working here under the influence of Shakespeare himself" (Mincoff 1952:115). As we shall see in Chapter 6, the influence was in fact reciprocal: minute stylistic peculiarities, generally typical of Fletcher, also occur in Shakespearean scenes, but they tend to decrease in number from the beginning to the end of each author's scene. This fact seems to reveal the dynamics of the creative process: one co-author initially consciously or subconsciously imitates the manner of the other, then drops into his more usual style as he warms to his task and is carried away by the theme (cf. Mincoff 1961:259; Mincoff, however, noticed such a reversal only in the Fletcherean scenes).

In his article of 1953 Ants Oras, with his typical deep inquiry into the subtleties of the text structure (cf. Oras 1960:1966), analyzed the feminine endings in separate scenes of "Henry VIII", paying close attention to heavy feminine endings and particularly to their parts of speech. Fletcherean scenes in "Henry VIII" were compared with plays written by Fletcher alone; for example, "Bonduca", "Valentinian", and "Monsieur Thomas". Oras singled out morphological patterns, such as adjective + noun (*Nor build their evils on the graves of gréat mèn*: II,I:67), possessive + noun (*These articles, my lord, are in the Kíng's hànd*: III,II:299), numeral + noun (*A Marshalsea shall hold ye play these twó mònths*: V,IV:90), or monosyllabic past participle used as an extra monosyllable (*Spirits of peace, where are ye? Are ye àll gòne?*: IV,II:83). Oras also registered the occurrence of once more; verb + most; verb + none; of adverbs hence, there, then, too, else, and out, and of vocative nouns such as sir, lord, and lords; for example: *A good digestion to you all! and ónce mòre* (I,IV:62); . . . *do wéll, lòrd* (I,IV:87); *Can you thínk, lòrds* (III,I:83); ". . . agréed, lòrds*" (V,III:91). Apart from typically Fletcherean adverbs, such as too, so, else, then, and now, an idiosyncrasy of Fletcher's style is the morphological diversity of heavy feminine endings, and a genuinely heavy stress on the extra monosyllable, which is often a fully notional word. The heavy stress on the extra monosyllable may be enhanced by a syntactic break between the tenth and eleventh syllables: *Is this a time for temporal affairs? há?* (II,II:73); cf. *Shame tread upon thy heels: all's lost, all's lóst, héark* (Fletcher, "Bonduca" III,V:153). In Shakespeare's scenes, as in the rest of his later plays, the heavy feminine endings are seldom fully stressed. Such endings never occur in groups, while Fletcher is obviously "fond of repeating the same final monosyllables in close succession, often in lengthy series: a tendency which is one of many manifestations of his passion for parallelism" (Oras 1953:211). Oras also noted, in passing, the occurrence of "dangling" midline monosyllables in Fletcher's scenes: Fletcher uses stressed monosyllables in unstressed positions in midline in much the same way as in line endings (cf. Chapter 6), distorting "the normal speech rhythm" (Oras 1953:208,212).

My main contributions to solving the controversy are stress analyses (Chapters 2, 3) and analysis of phrase endings (Chapter 6). However, before we finish with the structure of line endings, here are my data on the Shakespearean and Fletcherean scenes (in % of total lines):

	Accentual			Syllabic				
	Loss of stress caused by:			Non-masculine				
					Feminine			
				Non-masc. Total	Fem. Total	Simple	Compound	
	Monosyl.	Polysyl.	Masc.				Light	Heavy
Shak.	8.2	4.7	67.2	33.8	32.8	27.5	4.6	0.8
Flet.	1.0	7.2	40.6	59.4	58.7	40.6	13.2	4.9

The incidence of unstressed monosyllables, a sign of acute run-on lines, is almost nine times more frequent in Shakespeare's than in Fletcher's scenes (cf. "The Winter's Tale" —6.7%; "The Tempest" — 6.6%). It is hard to conceive that Shakespeare, who had been moving in the direction of an ever-increasing freedom of line syntax, should have returned, in some scenes only, to the index of "King Lear", written seven years before "Henry VIII". Rather, the index 8.2 seems to be a logical development of the process already at work in "The Winter's Tale" and "The Tempest", while the low figure 1.0 must certainly be an indicator of another poet's hand.

The percentage of non-masculine endings is also revealing. The index in the Shakespearean scenes is close to that of "The Tempest" (34% and 35%, respectively), while in the Fletcherean scenes of "Henry VIII" it is almost two times higher: about 60%; cf. "Bonduca:" about 70%, and the four "Fletcherean" scenes from "The Maid's Tragedy:" about 48%. The higher figure in "Bonduca" can be explained by the fact that the tragedy, written by Fletcher alone, was not influenced by the style of a co-author. The lower figure in "The Maid's Tragedy" may be explained both by an earlier date of the play, and by the influence of Beaumont's style: the mean index for feminine line endings in presumably Beaumont's scenes of "The Maid's Tragedy" (Oliphant 1927:182) is only 12.2%. The differences between acts in the plays written by one author alone are slight compared to those between acts and scenes in plays written in co-authorship. For example, the frequency of non-masculine line endings in five acts of Fletcher's "Bonduca" is 73.5 —68.6—67.7—68.2—74%, respectively, a range of about 6%, while in Beaumont and Fletcher's "The Maid's Tragedy" the lowest index (II.I: 8.7%) is more than six times less than the highest (IV.I: 54.5%).

The differences between Shakespearean and Fletcherean scenes of "Henry VIII" in terms of compound feminine endings is even more revealing: the index for compound light endings is three times higher in the Fletcherean than in the Shakespearean scenes, and the index for compound heavy endings is more than six times higher. .

A more detailed accentual, grammatical, and semantic analysis of "heavy" feminine line and phrase endings is undertaken in the next chapter.

Note to Chapter 5

[1] The total number of pentameter lines in "Timon of Athens" in Table 2.2 is 57 lines less than here: my selection of lines for a stress profile analysis was stricter than for the analysis of line endings.

Chapter 6

Phrase Endings: Aspects of Rhythm; Authors' Idiosyncrasy

6.1 The problem

So far, by studying the accentual and syllabic structure of line endings we have stayed within a traditional frame of verse analysis and have not looked closely inside the line. A verse line, however, is a rhythmical and grammatical/phonological unity which divides into smaller groups of syntactically linked words—syntagmas, or phrases.[1] The latter have a complex relationship with the phonological phrase, on the one hand,[2] and with the metrical line structure on the other, for example its bipartite composition or its accentual and word boundary types (cf. Langworthy 1931, Oras 1960, 1966, Tarlinskaja 1981, 1984, Hayes 1983, 1984, Wright 1983). The structure of line endings, then, becomes part of a more general question: the structure of phrase endings in verse. In this chapter we examine the quantitative correlation and the qualitative, grammatical, and semantic characteristics of specific two-element phrasal combinations of words found in verse (micro-phrases). One element of these combinations, or its stressed syllable, falls on an ictic, or strong (S) syllabic position of the verse line, while the other element falls on a non-ictic, weak (W) syllabic position, either preceding or following S. In the former case the word on W becomes, as it were, a proclitic, in the latter case an enclitic to the stressed word on S. For example: *Or whàt stro̊ng hànd* (proclitic) *can hold his swi̇ft fo̊ot* (enclitic) *back* (Son. 65:11), or: *Where nothing but trůe jȯy is* (proclitic).—*That's a gòod wḛnch* (enclitic) (Fletcher, "Bonduca" IV,IV:108).

Several questions arise here. (1) What phrases, proclitic or enclitic, better correspond with the typical tendencies of English speech rhythm? (2) What part-of-speech and syntactic structures are more characteristic of the enclitic phrases in contrast with the proclitic ones, and what are the general semantic "preferences" of enclitic vs. proclitic elements? (3) Which phrases are more numerous and more normative for English iambic pentameter in general, viewed as a national variant of iambic meter? (4) What phrases are more typical of specific epochs and individual authors, constituting one aspect of stylistic idiosyncrasy? The problem, then, has several aspects relevant for linguistics, verse theory, history of national literature, and the idiosyncrasies of individual poets and of Shakespeare in particular.

6.1.1 Linguistic aspect

Placement of monosyllables on weak and strong positions of verse lines reflects the semantic weight and degree of stress these words normally have in "ordinary", non-poetic speech. The study of proclitic and enclitic microphrases helps to differentiate and explain cases of a stronger accent on either the first or the second component of two-word phrases. Thus one might say that such a study opens a "metrical window" into the linguistic, phonological structure (cf. Hayes 1983:388).

Stressing of words in a phrase is determined by the semantic and grammatical (morphological and syntactic) features of words, by their position in a phrase or sentence (sentence perspective), and by their correlation with other stressed or unstressed syllables in the phrase (phrase rhythm).

The so-called notional (lexical) words are usually stressed, while the so-called form-words (grammatical words) are generally unstressed. Within the category of notional words, nouns, for example, are on the whole stressed more regularly than adverbs, and words of full lexical meaning are stressed more regularly than words of broader and vaguer semantics (cf. Bresnan 1971:271, Bolinger 1972:639).

The degrees of stress, however, are even more conditioned by the grammatical and semantic situation in the utterance (sentence). Phrasal accentuation strongly depends on the place of the notional word in a phrase or sentence: in non-emphatic speech the strongest sentence accent normally shifts to "the last stressable constituent" (cf. Chomsky and Halle 1968: "Nuclear Stress Rule:" "the intonational reality is . . . that the speaker will put the main accent as far to the right as he dares, when assertive pressure is high; and he frequently dares to put it on a syllable . . . farther to the right than the recognized lexical stress" [Bolinger 1972: 644]). This means that proclitic structures in verse are obviously more in keeping with the general speech accentuation tendency in English than are enclitic (cf. also Eitrem 1901:69; van Draat 1912:514; Curme 1914; Jones 1964, 1966, Kenyon 1950:88).

Speech reality, however, is diverse, and the placement of the strongest sentence accent may frequently shift from the final lexical element of the sentence or phrase to the left. The main reason is, in Bolinger's opinion, "semantic and emotional highlighting. Syntax is relevant indirectly in that some structures are more likely to be highlighted than others" (Bolinger 1972: 644; an opposing, syntactic explanation of stress placement was proposed by Bresnan 1971, 1972, while a syntactic-semantic explanation is given by Berman and Szamosi 1972:309).

"Exceptions" from the Nuclear Stress Rule, when the strongest stress does not fall on the final sentence (phrase) notional word, can be classified in the following ways relevant for the verse analysis undertaken in this chapter (some points are repeated from Chapter 2, but approached and classified differently):

(1) In cases of post-positional vocatives. This "exception" explains such instances of stress shifts from W to S as *We are not sáfe, Clārènce, we are not safe* (Shakespeare, "Richard III" I,I:70), or *Quick, qùick, Ūnclè, I have it . . .* (Fletcher, "Bonduca" V,III:125).

(2) In cases of an accentual emphasis (cf. Nikolajeva 1982) on a non-final sentence (phrase) notional word. This "exception" explains the legality of seemingly "unmetrical" lines (cf. Hayes 1983) in which a disyllabic word realizing an "inversion" occurs at the end of a phrase, for example: (*They and the seconds of it*) *Are bàse pēoplè. Believe them not; they lied* (Beaumont and Fletcher, "The Maid's Tragedy" IV,I:44); *Whom thùs ānswēred the archfiend now undisguised* (Milton, "Paradise Regained" I:357).

(3) In cases of semantic contrast, for example: *On thīs sìde, mȳ hànd, and on thàt sìde, thīne* (Shakespeare, "Richard II" IV,I:183).

(4) In cases of different semantic weight of elments in two-word microphrases (cf. Bolinger 1972:639). The more predictable and, consequently, less informative final component may receive less stress than the penultimate one. This phenomenon is typical, for example, of cases when the second component is a word of broad semantics (cf. "semi-pronouns:" Bresnan 1971:271), such as thing, self, body, man. This accentual phrase variant sometimes appears in verse, for example: *Thou of thyself thy swēet sèlf dost deceive; As testy sīck mèn, when their deaths be near* (Shakespeare, Son. 4:10 and 140:7); *By ōne màn's disobedience lost, now sing; Winning by conquest what the fīrst màn lost* (Milton, "Paradise Regained" I,2:154).

In traditional phrases or idiomatic combinations of words the stress frequently shifts to the first word, for example in *trūe lòve* (a traditional folk-verse phrase) vs. *trùe knīght* (a free combination), or *māre's nèst* (an idiom) vs. *spàrrow's nēst* (a free combination). This "exception" explains such cases as the following: *O, lest your trūe lòve may seem false in this* (Shakespeare, Son. 72:9).

(5) There are also purely rhythmical reasons why an enclitic structure can be used in verse instead of a proclitic one. In Beaver's opinion, the Nuclear Stress Rule may be substituted by another, optional rule of English, which Beaver termed "Stress Exchange Rule" (Beaver 1971:602). According to the latter, if a syllable with a primary stress appears on some strong position of the line, the Stress Exchange Rule working leftwards from the primary stress reverses the Nuclear Stress Rule assignments, so that in Beaver's example *So let the blūe lùmp poise between my knees, blūe lùmp* changes into *blùe lūmp*. True, the "nuclear-stress-rule" accentuation is more typical of English; therefore cases like *Why, that's wèll sāid* (Fletcher, "Bonduca" IV,I:15) are more frequent in verse than *You're wèll mèt once again* (Shakespeare, "Henry VIII" IV,I:1), but the rhythm-caused cases of the second type are perfectly "legitimate" (cf.

also Eitrem 1903:74, van Draat 1912, Jones 1964, or Gimson 1962). Many poets, particularly of certain epochs, made use of this option in their verse.

The linguistic aspect of proclitic *versus* enclitic phrase endings boils down to the following: proclitic structures are on the whole more typical of English speech tendencies, but enclitic structures are well within the law. When used in verse, they do not "distort the normal speech rhythm", as Ants Oras (1953:212) assumed. Their existence in ordinary speech, explained semantically, syntactically, and phonologically, justifies their appearance in verse, albeit, as we shall see, they are more frequent in some periods and with some authors. A closer study of proclitic and enclitic phrases used in verse contributes to a better understanding of the linguistic bases of enclitic two-word combinations.

6.1.2 Verse theory aspect

Meter is understood here as a set of phonological and phonetical (accentual and word boundary) restrictions and rules, obligatory for verse in different degrees, ranging from absolutely compulsory to optional (see Chapter 1; cf. Gasparov 1974:4, 1984b; Xolševnikov 1984).[3] These rules can be outlined both in terms of a system (e.g., English iambic meter as opposed to Russian iamb) and of a process (e.g., changes in English iambic meter in its dynamics, for example, from Classicism through post-Romanticism). The most common rules constitute the general norm, while less common rules fall outside the general norm (cf. Wimsatt 1970). The rhythmical system of a certain poet (e.g., Donne, Fletcher, Shelley, Hopkins) may include phenomena which are within the norm for this poet, but not for the whole system of national meter in a given epoch, because these phenomena are on the periphery of the rhythmical systems of most of the poets of the epoch. The general norm (e.g., of the English iambic pentameter) incorporates and generalizes individual rhythmical norms, abstracting from their minute idiosyncratic particulars.

How can we discover which features of a poet's idiosyncratic subsystem are within the general norm and which are normative only for this particular poet and are therefore on the "metrical periphery"? One possible indicator of the degree of "metricality" ("normality") is the frequency of occurrence of rhythmic-syntactic structures. If a structure occurs frequently in the verse of all poets of all epochs, this is a sign of its high metricality: it is thus within the most general norm. If a structure occurs only during certain epochs, or in the verse of only certain poets, it may be normative for these poets, but outside the general norm viewed as a whole. The study of grammatical composition and frequency of proclitic and enclitic phrases helps to evaluate them in their relation to the norm of the English iambic system of verse and provides the background against which to view Shakespeare's rhythmical style.

6.1.3 The aspect of epochs and individual styles

Different rhythmical-grammatical patterns have different degrees of "metricality" when viewed as a part of the whole national system of meter; they may also have different degrees of "normality" in different epochs. A pattern normative for one epoch may seem unacceptable to poets of a later period. It is well-known how Dryden, nearly a century after Shakespeare, tried to "improve" Shakespeare's verse which, regarded from the point of view of changed norms, seemed "barbarous" to pre-Classicist and Classicist poets. Norms are flexible, within certain limits, and vary from epoch to epoch, tending to recur, not unlike fashions, in a wave-like pattern (Taranovsky 1953, Tarlinskaja 1976).

What seems to be an idiosyncratic individuality of a poet often turns out to be the sign of an epoch (cf. Kiparsky 1975, 1977, Hayes 1983). Kiparsky compared Shakespeare and Milton to two bears on a mountain, each having his own domain, not crossing over to the other's territory. The opposition, however, is not so much between the two poets as between the two epochs. As we shall see, the rhythmical-grammatical variant of the type *Resembling stróng yóuth īn his middle age*, considered idiosyncratic of Shakespeare by both Kiparsky (1975, 1977) and Hayes (1983) ("Shakespeare I rule"), is characteristic of the whole Jacobean epoch and is far more typical of other poets than of Shakespeare. In fact, it is most typical of Fletcher and is an important feature of his very peculiar individual style. Apparently in Fletcher's view of "metricality" the pattern was more normal, and therefore more acceptable, than in Shakespeare's. The study of grammatical composition (consequently— correlation of accents) and frequency with which proclitic and enclitic phrases appear in the verse of Shakespeare, his older and younger contemporaries, and later poets helps to single out individual authors' idiosyncrasies and adds another indicator to the whole set (cf. Mincoff 1961:259) used by scholars addressing the complicated problem of verse attribution.

6.2 Material

The main materials analyzed for the specific problems discussed in this chapter are as follows:

(1) Marlowe, "Tamburlaine the Great" (written before 1590), acts IV, V: 863 lines; the play represents the style of earlier Elizabethan dramas;

(2) Shakespeare, "Titus Andronicus", an earlier and a later substrate. The earlier substrate (A): act I sc.I, act III sc.I,II,IV; act II sc.I, act IV sc.I, act V sc.II: 1344 lines. The later substrate (B): the rest of the play (except act IV sc.II, in which there is a clash of tendencies): 1002 lines;

(3) Shakespeare's Sonnets: 2154 lines;

(4) Shakespeare, "Richard II", act IV sc.I, act V sc.I,II: 553 lines;

(5) Shakespeare, "The Winter's Tale", act I sc.II, act V sc.I,III: 613 lines;

(6) Shakespeare, "Henry VIII:" "Shakespeare" (A): act I sc.I,II; act II

sc.III,IV; act III sc.II (the first 203 lines); act V sc.I: 1167 lines; "Fletcher" (B): the rest of the play, 1593 lines (cf. Spedding 1876);

(7) Chapman, "Bussy D'Ambois:" act IV sc.I,II; act V sc.I-IV: 1002 lines. Chapman (born in 1559) was five years older than Shakespeare. "Bussy D'Ambois", possibly written in 1598 and revised for publication in 1607, was analyzed for a contemporary comparison with Shakespeare;

(8) Beaumont and Fletcher, "The Maid's Tragedy" (apparently produced in 1611). Beaumont (born in 1584) and Fletcher (born in 1579), Shakespeare's younger contemporaries, were chosen to represent the style of Jacobean dramas. "Fletcher" (B): act II sc.II, act IV sc.I, act V sc.I,II: 590 lines. Out of "Beaumont's" portion (A) I analyzed act II sc.I and act IV sc.II: 662 lines (cf. Oliphant's (1927) attribution of the scenes; pp. 309-314);

(9) Fletcher, "Bonduca" (1614), act III sc.V; acts IV and V fully: 1157 lines. The play was chosen to illustrate Fletcher's style not influenced by collaborators;

(10) Massinger, "The Maid of Honor" (1622), act III sc.I-III, act IV sc.I-IV: 828 lines. Massinger (born, like Beaumont, in 1584) was Fletcher's later co-author. Massinger's style in some ways resembles Shakespeare's (he was an epigon of Shakespeare); some scholars claimed that it was Massinger rather than Shakespeare who cooperated with Fletcher in "Henry VIII" (e.g., Boyle 1880-1886; cf. Oliphant 1927:60-61, Partridge 1949:38-40);

(11) Milton, "Paradise Regained" (1671), fully (2070 lines);

(12) Pope, Epistle IV: "To Richard Boyle, Earl of Burlington" (1731) and "An Epistle to Dr. Arbuthnot" (1735): 623 lines;

(13) Byron, "Werner" (1824), Act II fully and Act III, sc. I, the first 230 lines: 1000 lines.

(14) Browning, "An Epistle, Containing the Strange Medical Experience of Karshish, the Arab Physician" and "Fra Lippo Lippi:" 692 lines.[4]

Milton's, Pope's, Byron's, and Browning's verse represents tendencies of later epochs.

6.3 Grammatical types of proclitic and enclitic phrases. General information

The two-word combinations fall into two major groups: a smaller one with a syntactic seam between the two elements, and a larger one without a seam. Only the second category actually constitutes "micro-phrases"—syntactically and semantically linked words.

Two-word groups of the first type do not exceed 20% of all proclitic or enclitic combinations (for example, postpositional vocatives in Fletcher's "Bonduca", used by this poet more frequently than by any other, constitute only 16.4% of all his enclitic structures), and in most cases amount to only a few percent. Grammatical isolation does not necessarily cause an intonational isolation of an element, such as a vocative or an interjection. The latter may become intonationally fused with the adjacent word. However, a syntactic break between two words provides a basis for their possible intonational isolation. That is why the number of such cases in verse is everywhere relatively low.

Typical grammatical forms of the first, syntactically isolated element of proclitic phrases are as follows:

(a) Exclamations, interjections, "yes" and "no" utterances, for example: *Puffe, there it flies* . . . (F.B, III,V:89); *Sworn!—Ay.—How? Sworn, Evadne?* (BF.MT, II,I:155); *Yes, madam, to your grief* (BF.MT, II,III:4); *Fie, sister, fie* . . . (F.B, IV,IV:98).

(b) Imperative verbs, for example: *Come, let me pour Romes blessing on ye* . . . ; *Come, chicken, let's go seek some place of strength* (F.B, IV,V:119, IV,II:82);

(c) Isolated homogeneous sentence elements: *Hares, fearful Hares* . . . (F.B, III,V:149).

(d) Vocatives. Used proclitically and adjoining a fully stressed word on S, vocatives are very infrequent; e.g., *Sir, spare your threats* . . . (Sh.WT, III,II:92). Much more frequent are attributes on W followed by a vocative on S, as in *Good sirs* . . . , *Dear Captain* . . . , or vocatives on W followed by an unstressed word on S (see Chapter 7), for example: *Sir, I may tell it you* . . .; *Charles, I will play no more to-night* . . . ; *Sir, I have brought my lord the archbishop* (Sh.HVIII, V,I:42,56,80). Evidently the clash between two strong stresses, one of them a vocative on W, is avoided.

Typical grammatical forms of the second, syntactically isolated element of enclitic phrases are as follows:

(a) The most typical grammatical element here is a vocative; for example: *I have, boy.—Am not I your kinsman?—Yes*; *Quiet, and cast his sting, boy?—Dead, Petillius*; *Awake, sir*; *yet the Roman bodie's whole*; *Famine is faln upon me, uncle.—Come, Sir* (F.B, IV,II:45, IV,I:13, III,V:90, IV,II:50). Postpositional vocatives, often serving as markers indicating the end of an utterance by a dramatic personage, are liable to a loss of sentence accent; they follow the final phrase element marked by a falling tone, and are low in pitch, e.g., *Come, Sir* (↘.).

(b) An adverbial modifier to the whole sentence, often expressed by an adverb of broad semantics. Such words are also undoubtedly liable to partial or full loss of phrasal accent. Examples are: *My honour falls no farther. I am well, then* (BF.MT, IV,I:275); *The king, that gave it.—It must be himself, then* (Sh.HVIII, III,II:251).

(c) Imperatives, interjections, "yes" and "no" utterances: these grammatical elements, which are so typical of proclitic structures, appear very infrequently as enclitics. Obviously, isolated enclitic elements are better tolerated by verse if their stress is at least partially reduced. Some examples of the (c) subtype are: *Shame tread upon thy heels: all's lost, all's lost, heark* (F.B, III,V:153); *How tastes it? is it bitter? forty pence, no*; *Is this an hour for temporal affairs, ha? And let him cry "Ha!" louder!—But, my lord* (Sh.HVIII, II,IV:89, II,II:72, III,II:62).

Two-word combinations without a syntactic seam between the elements are prevalent both among proclitic and enclitic structures.

Before classifying the grammatical types of two-word phrases organized proclitically and enclitically, I must clarify my principle for segmenting three adjacent notional words into two-word phrases. A decision was necessary: either to refer the word on W to the following stressed element and consider the phrase proclitic, or to refer the word to the preceding stressed element, thus treating the phrase as enclitic. Consider, for example, such a line: *Give my love fame faster than Time wastes life* (Sh.Son 100:13). Which of the two possible ways of segmentation to accept: *Time wastes*, or *wastes life*? My guiding principle was the relative strength of syntactic ties between pairs of words; words united by a stronger tie were assumed to form the phrase.

There is a hierarchy of strength of syntactic junctures in an English sentence (cf. Chomsky, Halle, and Lukoff 1956:67, Smirnickij 1957:173-184). The conventionally accepted differentiation of syntactic junctures between adjacent words is listed below. Breaking up strings of words into two-word micro-phrases naturally involves decisions concerning immediate constituents and hierarchy of syntactic links; for example: *My most true mind* (Sh.Son 113:14): *most true*, not *true mind*, was assumed to constitute a two-word syntactic unit.

Types of syntactic junctures between adjacent words:

(1) Between two adjacent words not connected syntactically and semantically: the loosest juncture, as in *My deepest sense, how hard \ true sorrow hits* (Sh.Son 120:10): *hard* and *true* have the weakest syntactic link. Cf. also: *And Death once dead, there's no more dying then* (Sh.Son 146:14): *once dead*, not *Death once*, was considered a phrase, because the former contains a stronger tie. *Let him have time to mark how slow time goes* (Sh.RL, 142:3): *time goes* rather than *slow time* were assumed to have a stronger link and, consequently, to form the phrase. The relationship can be represented arboreally:

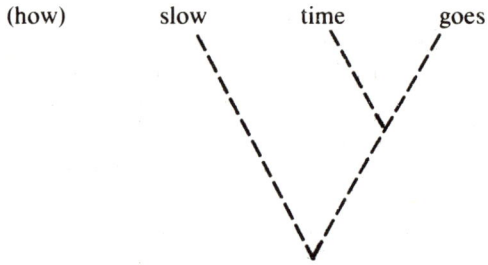

(2) Between a subject and a predicate: as it follows from the examples above,

this type of link was considered stronger than type (1); some further examples are: *Triumph in love; flesh stays no further reason* (Sh.Son 151:8), or: *And will, thy soul knows, is admitted there* (Sh.Son 136:3).

(3) Between an adverbial modifier of time or place and the word to which it is tied syntactically and semantically. As it follows from the example cited in (1) (*And Death once dead...*), type (3) juncture was considered stronger than (1), consequently *once dead*, rather than *Death once*, form a phrase.

(4) Between a verb and a prepositional adverb (*to let out life*), between a verb and an adverbial modifier of attending circumstances expressed by an adverb (*why that's well said*), between a verb and an adjective, both forming a predicate (*make pale our cheek*), between an adverb qualifying another adverb or an adjective (*most true*). Some more examples: *For since each hand hath put on nature's power* (Sh.Son 127:5); *Love is a babe; then might I not say so* (Sh.Son 115:3) (compare *say so* with another example illustrating a weaker tie between *so* and an adjacent word with which the adverb is not linked syntactically and semantically: *So \ Ladies in Romance assist their Knight*: P.RL, III:129). Evaluation of the hierarchy of junctures can be illustrated by the following example: *That music hath a far more pleasing sound* (Sh.Son 130:10): *far more* rather than *more pleasing*; the relationship between the three words can be represented arboreally:

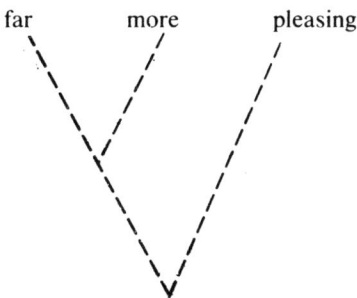

(5) Between a verb and its direct object; this link is particularly strong in a phraseological unit, e.g., *give ear*. Some examples: *We sicken to shun sickness when we purge* (Sh.Son 118:4); *The Pow'rs gave Ear, and granted half his Pray'r* (P.RL, II:45): *gave Ear* rather than *Pow'rs gave*. *Give my love fame faster than Time wastes life* (Sh.Son 100:13): *wastes life* rather than *Time wastes*.

(6) An attributive tie, for example: *Bare ruined choirs, where late the sweet birds sang* (Sh.Son 74:4): *sweet birds* rather than *birds sang* constitute the phrase. *The French king's sister ...* (Sh.HVIII, II,II:41): *French king's*, not *king's sister*; the relationship can be presented arboreally:

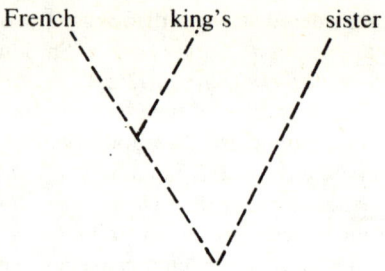

cf. The _Club's black Tyrant_ . . . (P.LR, III:69): <u>black</u> <u>Tyrant</u>, not <u>Club's</u> <u>black</u>; or arboreally:

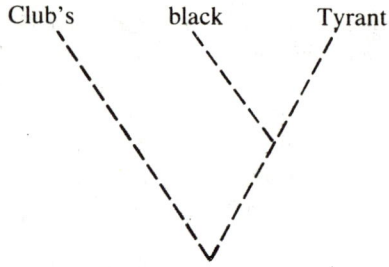

Similarly with heavy feminine endings terminating verse lines, enclitic elements of two-word mid-line phrases are obviously accentually weakened. However, these words were evaluated as stressed in contrast with unquestionably fully unstressed form-words; cf: (a) _Ye tell me what ye wish <u>for</u> \ both, my ruin_, and (b) _Mend 'em <u>for</u> shame, my lords. Is this your comfort?_ (Sh.HVIII, III,I:98,105). Boyle (1880-1886:451,455) also registered cases of the (a) type as stressed. Adverbs of "broad semantics" (<u>so</u>, <u>too</u>, <u>then</u>, <u>else</u>) and the pronoun <u>one</u> were also considered capable of forming heavy feminine phrase endings because they are noticeably more prominent than fully unstressed light feminine endings. Cf.: (a) _My life is like a souldier.— You will seek <u>then</u>_ and (b) _Thou shalt live still I hope Boy. Shall I draw <u>it?</u>_ (F.B, V,III:92,143) (see also Boyle 1880-1886:453) The difference in prominence between <u>then</u> and <u>it</u> is beyond doubt. As we shall soon see, his preference for the former type of feminine endings differentiates Fletcher's verse style from that of his co-authors. Some more examples with enclitic adverbs of broad semantics are: _Bid him be gone, he dies <u>else</u>. Shall Rome say; I'll tickle your young tail <u>else</u>. —I defie thee; Continue so <u>still</u>. The Lord general; Pray bring your dish <u>then</u>. Hearty knaves: more meat <u>there</u>_ (F.B, IV,III:183, IV,II:52, IV,III:51, II,III:80). Nouns of broad semantics were also counted as stressed (no matter how weakly) and capable of forming enclitic elements of phrases; e.g., _By_

adding one thing to my purpose nothing (Sh.Son 20:12); *Thy of thyself thy sweet self dost deceive* (Sh.Son 4:10).

Proclitic components of two-word micro-phrases may also lose their phrasal accent partially or fully. These are: appositional titles (*King Richard, Queen Katharine*) and prepositional adjectives and adverbs, particularly those of broad semantics: e.g., *Incertainties now crown themselves assured* (Sh.Son 107:7); *And, like unletter'd clerk, still cry 'Amen'* (Sh.Son 85:6); *That thou in losing me shall win much glory* (Sh.Son 88:8). Notional verbs used as link-verbs, and verbs of broad semantics requiring a complement also tend to lose stress: *Make answer, Muse* . . . (Sh.Son 101:5); *And sweets grow common* . . . (Sh.Son 102:12); *My love looks fresh* . . . (Sh.Son 107:10). However, all these words were considered stressed to some degree and capable therefore of forming proclitic phrases; so were interrogative and exclamatory words, such as *how, what*, and others; for example: *Why write I still all one, ever the same* . . . *?* (Sh.Son 76:5); *How careful was I, when I took my way* . . . *!* (Sh.Son 48:1).

I distinguished the following most commonly occurring part-of-speech and syntactic two-word structures, occupying S and either of the adjacent W:

(1) **Subject + predicate**: (a) proclitic: *Death rides in triumph, Drusus* . . . (F.B, III,V:101); (b) enclitic: *My frozen soul melts. May each sin thou hast* (BF.MT, IV,I:258); *As shall appear when time calls.—That's wel, down with 't* (F.B, II,II:67);

(2) **Modifier + modified**: (a) proclitic: *Sweet love, renew thy force*; (b) enclitic: . . . *where late the sweet birds sang* (Sh.Son, 56:1 and 73:4);

(3) **Verb + adverb** (adverbial modifier) or **adjective** (part of predicate); (a) proclitic: *Sink down to earth* . . . (Sh.Son 45:8); *Make pale our cheek* . . . (Sh.RII, II,I:118); (b) enclitic: *I'll point a thousand wounds to let out life* (BF.MT, II,I:280); *It looks ill on't; how long is't, pretty soul?* (F.B, III,V:32);

(4) **Adverb + verb**: (a) proclitic: *Why, that's well said* (F.B, IV,I:15); (b) enclitic: *You're well met once again* (Sh.HVIII, IV,I:1);

(5) **Adverb + adverb (adjective)**: (a) proclitic: *Grows fairer than at first, more strong, far greater* (Sh.Son, 119:12); (b) enclitic: *They are, as all my other comforts, far hence*; *Have I lived thus long—let me speak myself* (Sh.HVIII, II,IV:90,125);

(6) **Verb + object**: (a) proclitic: *Give salutation to my sportive blood* (Sh.Son 121:6); (b) enclitic: *And never take note of the female more* (BF.MT, III,I:228); *A man to rule men, to have thousand lives* (F.B, IV,III:100); *I do not think he fears death.—Sure, he does not* (Sh.HVIII, II,I:37);

(7) A word (usually an **adverbial modifier**, typically an adverb) loosely connected with the adjacent word (usually a noun): (a) proclitic: *So \ fare you well, my little good lord cardinal* (Sh.HVIII, III,II:394); (b) enclitic: *I'll be a wolf \ first. 'Tis, to be thy brother* (BF.MT, IV,I:59); *What would you live to be?—A whore \ still.—Mercie* (F.B, IV,IV:99);

(8) **Apposition** (usually a title) + **noun**: (a)proclitic: *Be now produced and*

heard. — *Lord Cardinal* (Sh.HVIII II,IV:69); (b) enclitic: *My Lord Sands, you are one will keep 'em waking* (Sh.HVIII I,III:23).

Most of these structures particularly often constitute proclitic micro-phrases with a stronger second accent. However, some structures form enclitic phrases relatively often, while others only in the rarest of exceptions. Three examples of relatively frequent enclitic structures are the grammatical patterns modifier + modified, verb + adverb (adjective), and subject + predicate; two examples of rare enclitic structures are apposition + noun and verb + object. These facts reflect the semantic and grammatic correlation between the components and their typical accentuation pattern in non-metrical speech, for example, the semantic, grammatical, and accentual parity of subject and predicate, and the higher semantic and accentual weight of the object than of the preceding verb.

6.4 General analysis of proclitic and enclitic phrases: rhythm and the authors' idiosyncrasy (Table 6.1, Figure 6.1)

The total percentage of enclitic structures calculated from all proclitic and enclitic phrases varies between 5 and 37% and the percentage of proclitic structures between 63 and 9%. The prevalence of proclitic structures is explained by the prevailing tendency of English speech to stress the last notional word of a phrase (sentence) particularly strongly. But since, for semantic or rhythmical reasons, other tendencies of stressing are also possible, poets make use of them in their verse, though to a different extent. The number of enclitic micro-phrases per 1000 lines of text varies between 13 and 295 (Marlowe's "Tamburlaine" — Fletcher's "Bonduca"). Enclitic phrases are "normative" for only certain periods and individual authors. The enclitic tendency was evidently not characteristic of early Elizabethan verse (cf. Marlowe), and Shakespeare during his whole career kept to the more traditional, proclitic tendency: the proportion of enclitic phrases did not change significantly from his earlier to later works (disregarding the low index for the questionable earlier substrate of "Titus Andronicus"), while other features of his style changed very markedly. Shakespeare's use of enclitic phrases is more conservative than Chapman's, his senior by five years: in this regard, Chapman is closer to the younger poet Beaumont than to his contemporary, Shakespeare, though there are other features of Chapman's style that mark it as Elizabethan rather than Jacobean. For example, Chapman's line particularly often terminates in a polysyllable which causes a frequent loss of stress on position 10 (a more archaic tendency: cf. with Kyd and Marlowe, see Table 2.3). Here is a line illustrating the two idiosyncrasies of Chapman's rhythmical style, viz. (a) relatively frequent enclitic phrasing, and (b) relatively frequent polysyllables at the end of his lines causing losses of the final ictic stress: *What new flame breaks out of the firmament* (Ch.BDA, V,I:160).

The low percentage of enclitic phrases in "Titus Andronicus", particularly

Table 6.1

Proclitic and enclitic phrases

Author and title	Proportion of proclitic and enclitic phrases (in percentage)		Number of enclitic phrases per 1000 lines
	Proclitic	Enclitic	
Marlowe, "Tamburlaine"	94%	6%	13
Shakespeare, "Titus Andronicus":			
Early substrate	94%	6%	21
Later substrate	89%	11%	47
Shakespeare, Sonnets	86%	14%	59
Shakespeare, "Richard II"	86%	14%	58
Shakespeare, "The Winter's Tale"	82%	18%	73
Shakespeare, "Henry VIII":			
"Shakespeare"	85%	15%	58
"Fletcher"	63%	37%	201
Chapman, "Bussi D'Ambois"	73%	27%	125
Fletcher, "Bonduca"	59%	41%	295
Beaumont and Fletcher, "The Maid's Tragedy":			
"Beaumont"	75%	25%	92
"Fletcher"	64%	36%	220
Massinger, "The Maid of Honor"	64%	36%	152
Milton, "Paradise Regained"	91%	9%	28
Pope, "Richard Boyle", "Dr. Arbuthnot"	95%	5%	18
Byron, "Werner"	67%	33%	135
Browning, "Karshish", "Fra Lippo Lippi"	68%	32%	175

in the early substrate, seems to serve as another proof of an earlier date for the play (particularly of the early substrate), but not of its authorship: the early substrate could just as well have been written by an older poet as by Shakespeare himself earlier in his career.

The proportion of enclitic phrases strongly differentiate Shakespeare's and Fletcher's styles in "Henry VIII:" enclitic phrases are over three times more frequent in Fletcher's than in Shakespeare's scenes. The use of enclitic phrases also differentiates Shakespeare from Massinger (Massinger did not write Shakespeare's scenes of "Henry VIII"!) and Beaumont from Fletcher: in "The Maid's Tragedy" Fletcher used enclitic phrases 2.5 times more fre-

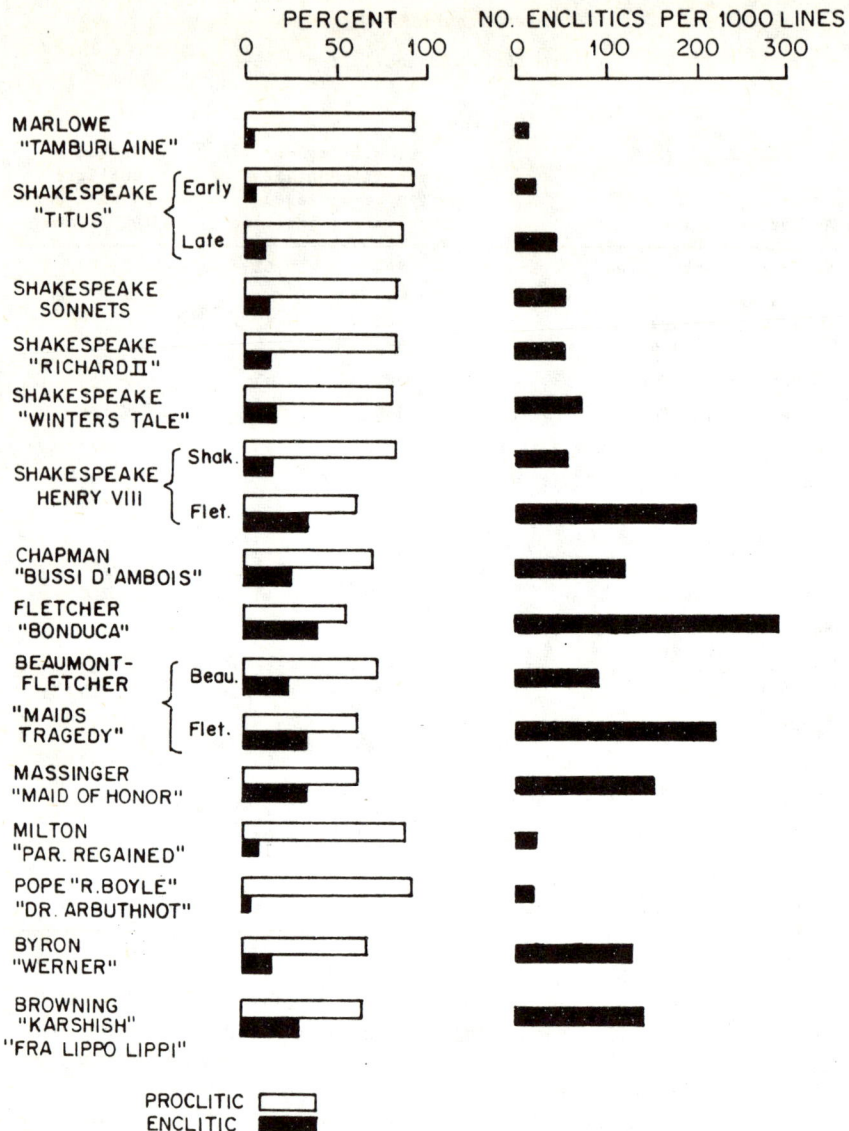

Fig. 6.1. The proportion (in percent) of proclitic to enclitic micro-phrases in the texts analyzed, and the incidence of enclitic phrases per 1000 lines of text.

quently. The more conservative Beaumont differs from his co-author Fletcher more than he does from Shakespeare. But the highest number of enclitic phrases appears in Fletchers' verse when he is writing all by himself: their frequency in "Bonduca" is particularly high. Enclitic phrases in "Bonduca" appear five times more frequently than in Shakespeare's Sonnets, "Richard II", or Shakespeare's scenes in "Henry VIII", and three times more frequently than in Beaumont's scenes of "The Maid's Tragedy". In the plays written in collaboration, Fletcher consciously or unconsciously "toned down" his own style, and the proportion of enclitics is lower than in the play written by Fletcher alone. The influence of co-authors is reciprocal. The data from "Henry VIII" show that not only Shakespeare influenced Fletcher, but Fletcher influenced Shakespeare (cf. Thorndike 1901, Appleton 1956). Consider, for example, the first scene of act III, written, as everybody seems to agree, by Shakespeare. In lines 16-39 (the beginning of the scene, excluding the song and non-pentameter lines) there are 10 cases of enclitic phrases, for example: *To come near. What can be their business; But all hoods make not monks* . . . ; *The full cause of our coming* . . . ; *Could speak this with as free a soul as I do*; *My lords, I care not, so much I am happy* (19,23,29, 32,33). In lines 112-136 (the middle of the scene) there are only four cases of enclitic phrases (e.g., *And all the fellowship I hold now with him*; *Have I lived thus long - let me speak myself*; *And am I thus rewarded?* *'tis not fair, lords*: (121,125,133), and in the final 24 lines (161-184)there are only two enclitic phrases; e.g., *Such doubts, as false coins, from it. The king loves you* (171). At the beginning of the scene Shakespeare seems to "hear" Fletcherian rhythm in his head, but as the scene proceeds he lapses into his own, "proclitic" rhythm.

In his partiality to enclitic phrase endings Fletcher was practically unique: his habit of "riding to death" a favored stylistic device is known (cf. Mincoff 1961:250). But the enclitic rhythmical tendency was obviously fashionable with Jacobean poets (e.g., Massinger), though each of them, even epigons like Massinger, had specific idiosyncrasies of style. Massinger's style, for example, brings together features of both Shakespeare's and Fletcher's rhythmical subsystems: his enclitic phrase composition is not unlike Fletcher's, while his frequent run-on lines, ending in an unstressed monosyllable, remind us of late Shakespeare (Fletcher's lines, as is well-known, are predominantly end-stopped; cf. Mincoff 1961:247,249). Here are some lines illustrating Massinger's stylistic idiosyncrasies:

That I yet live, my weak hands fasten on (Hope's anchor. . .)
                (Massinger, "A New Way to Pay Old Debts" IV,III:3-4)
You must not think yourself so.—I am what (You'll please to have me. . .)
                (Massinger, "The Maid of Honor" III,III:70-71)

The enclitic tendency evidently ebbed away in the verse of post-Restoration poets: the index of Milton's "Paradise Regained" reminds us of the early substrate of "Titus Andronicus". The tendency was at its lowest in the Classicists' verse: Pope's enclitic indices resemble Marlowe's in his "Tamburlaine". Enclitically formed phrases began to be normative again in the poetry of certain Romantic authors, e.g., Byron's "Werner" which stylistically in many ways resembles Jacobean dramas. The indices of enclitic phrases in post-Romantic poetry of Browning are even closer to the Jacobean proportions.

If we calculate the mean number of enclitic phrases per 1000 lines of verse for all of Shakespeare's texts analyzed (excepting the questionable early substrate of "Titus Andronicus") and for the three Elizabethan-Jacobean poets whose treatment of enclitic phrases is not dissimilar (Chapman; Fletcher, 3 texts; and Massinger), the evolution of the enclitic tendency in the English iambic pentameter becomes even more obvious:

Marlowe	:	13
Shakespeare	:	59
Beaumont	:	92
Chapman, Fletcher, Massinger	:	172
Milton	:	28
Pope	:	18
Byron	:	135
Browning	:	175

The enclitic tendency came and went in a wave-like pattern: typological similarities between rhythmical styles, not unlike fashion, recur every other epoch, while adjacent epochs show features of stylistic dissimilation (see, for example, Taranovsky 1953, Gasparov 1974, Tarlinskaja 1976). So, indeed, the enclitic rhythm is relatively more characteristic of Shakespeare than of Milton; but Shakespeare and Milton look almost like twins when compared in this respect with Shakespeare's younger contemporaries, the Jacobean poets, or with later, Romantic and post-Romantic verse. The "Shakespeare I rule" of Kiparsky (1977) and Hayes (1983) does not so much apply to Shakespeare himself as to Fletcher, Byron, and Browning.

The enclitic tendency, even when at its lowest, never completely disappeared from English iambic verse. This is one of the features that differentiate the English and the Russian variants of the iambic meter. In the Russian eighteenth-century poetry of Lomonosov, Sumarokov, and particularly Trediakovskij, enclitic phrases were part of the metrical norm; for example: *Primér zrím v nášix vremenáx* (Lomonosov); *Blažén múž, kto, merzjá ne vxódit* (Sumarokov); *Daét bóg domočádcev v dom* (Trediakovskij)

Table 6.2

Proportion of proclitic vs. enclitic attributive phrases arranged in order of decreasing percent of enclitic. In parentheses is the proportion of attributive enclitic phrases of all enclitic phrases.

Fletcher, "Henry VIII"	60-40%	(41%)
Byron, "Werner"	61-39%	(42%)
Fletcher, "The Maid's Tragedy"	63-37%	(38%)
Browning, "Karshish", "Fra Lippo Lippi"	65-35%	(40%)
Fletcher, "Bonduca"	66-34%	(29%)
Chapman, "Bussi D'Ambois"	69-31%	(49%)
Massinger, "The Maid of Honor"	71-29%	(29%)
Beaumont, "The Maid's Tragedy"	73-27%	(28%)
Shakespeare, Sonnets	77-23%	(70%)
Shakespeare, "Richard II"	78-22%	(69%)
Shakespeare, "Titus Andronicus", later substrate	79-21%	(55%)
Shakespeare, "Henry VIII"	79-21%	(51%)
Milton, "Paradise Regained"	84-16%	(65%)
Shakespeare, "The Winter's Tale"	86-14%	(24%)
Shakespeare, "Titus Andronicus", earlier substrate	90-10%	(48%)
Pope, "Richard Boyle", "Dr. Arbuthnot"	90-10%	(82%)
Marlowe, "Tamburlaine"	96- 4%	(18%)

(Taranovsky and Proxorov 1982:151-153). However, this practice was discarded by later poets, and nineteenth-century authors practically never used enclitic phrases; the line *Stojál On*, \ *dúm velíkix póln* was pointed out by Tomaševskij as exceptional (Tomaševskij 1929:128, cf. Taranovsky and Proxorov 1982). In contrast, enclitic "rhythmical figures" remained acceptable throughout the English iambic canon (they always stayed within the general "rule"), but in some epochs the practice came closer to the "norm" while in others it retreated to the periphery of the acceptable.

Table 6.3

Proportion of proclitic vs. enclitic phrases of the type <u>verb + adverb (adjective)</u>, arranged in order of decreasing percent of enclitic. In parentheses is the proportion of <u>verb + adverb (adjective)</u> phrases of all enclitic phrases.

Fletcher, "Henry VIII"	44-56%	(21%)
Fletcher, "Bonduca"	55-45%	(23%)
Byron, "Werner"	58-42%	(26%)
Browning, "Karshish", "Fra Lippo Lippi"	60-40%	(23%)
Fletcher, "The Maid's Tragedy"	68-32%	(15%)
Chapman, "Bussi D'Ambois"	69-31%	(18%)
Massinger, "The Maid of Honor"	69-31%	(23%)
Shakespeare, "The Winter's Tale"	70-30%	(37%)
Beaumont, "The Maid's Tragedy"	76-24%	(21%)
Shakespeare, "Richard II"	77-23%	(22%)
Shakespeare, "Henry VIII"	79-21%	(21%)
Marlowe, "Tamburlaine"	82-18%	(45%)
Shakespeare, "Titus Andronicus", later substrate	84-16%	(15%)
Shakespeare, Sonnets	87-13%	(11%)
Milton, "Paradise Regained"	88-12%	(17%)
Pope, "Richard Boyle", "Dr. Arbuthnot"	93- 7%	(9%)
Shakespeare, "Titus Andronicus", earlier substrate	94- 6%	(11%)

6.5 Particular grammatical patterns of proclitic and enclitic phrases: grammatical and semantic aspects of rhythm

Consider now the most frequently occurring, or stylistically particularly relevant, grammatical patterns in more detail (Tables 6.2 and 6.3).

<u>Modifier + modified</u> is one of the most frequent micro-phrases appearing in

both proclitic and enclitic structures. Table 6.2 shows the relative proportion of proclitic and enclitic attributive phrases and the percentage of attributive structures from all enclitic phrases. The predominance of the attributive phrase in Shakespeare's Sonnets and Milton's "Paradise Regained" is explained by the genre characteristics of the texts. However, they are also very typical of Shakespeare's dramas, particularly "Richard II", which resembles the sonnets in its style. The total number of enclitic phrases in Pope's verse is extremely low; however, out of the eleven cases discovered in the 623 lines analyzed, nine are attributive structures. This fact seems to indicate the accentual ambivalence of their components.

The highest relative percentage of enclitically built attributive phrases is found in Fletcher's, Byron's, and Browning's texts, the lowest in Marlowe's and Pope's. The difference in the indices again opposes Shakespeare's and Fletcher's scenes of "Henry VIII:" attributive phrases are on the whole more numerous in Shakespeare's scenes, but enclitic patterns are considerably more frequent in Fletcher's. The difference between Beaumont's and Fletcher's scenes of "The Maid's Tragedy" is also noticeable, but less so than between Fletcher and Shakespeare in "Henry VIII". There is some difference between the earlier and the later substrates of "Titus Andronicus".

Close as Shakespeare's and Milton's use of proclitic attributive phrases seems to be in terms of quantity, there is some marked qualitative difference. The modified noun in Milton's enclitic attributive phrases is usually a word of broad semantics (such as sake, sort, way (= means of doing something), and particularly thing and man): 27 cases out of 37, or 73%. In Shakespeare's Sonnets, for example, there are 85 cases of enclitic attributive phrases, but only 24 (28%) of the phrases contain semantically "empty" nouns; these are man /men—9, thing—4, self—4, time (= instance) preceded by a numeral—3, sake—2, and turn (= service: *good turns*)—2; and two more cases are a traditional combination (*trúe lóve*). Nouns of broad semantics and second elements of traditional phrases semantically close to compounds tend to lose their phrasal accent partially or fully (cf. Curme 1914, Bolinger 1972). That brings the total of enclitic phrases with a weakly stressed or unstressed modified noun to 30.6% of all enclitic attributive structures. The figure is probably even higher: of the remaining 59 phrases, six contain modified nouns referring to abstract notions of space and time, sometimes preceded by a numeral (hour, day, time, year; world, sides); the second element of such phrases (e.g., *óne hóur míne*) could probably also lose some accent (cf. Oras 1953:206). A further analysis of the attributive enclitic phrases found in the Sonnets shows that they appear particularly often when the first element bears a strong semantic contrast (e.g., *thís màn's art* vs. *thát màn's scope*, and *súch wèalth . . . that* in Son.29, . . . *dressing óld wòrds new* in Son.76, . . . *what dárk dàys seen* in Son.97, . . . *to make thy lárge "Wíll" more* in Son.135, or *Suns of the world may stain when héaven's sún staineth* in Son.33). The second element of such phrases should probably also be considered not fully

221

stressed. Still it is obvious that Milton avoided the syncopated enclitic rhythm more strongly than did Shakespeare.

Even Fletcher, however, frequently used words of broad semantics and the final components of traditional and idiomatic phrases as the second element of his enclitically built attributive structures. The total number of enclitic attributive phrases in the 1157 lines from "Bonduca" is 97. Twenty-four of these cases (almost 25%) contain words of broad semantics, such as man (13), sake (*for héaven's sáke, for Fáme's sáke*) (5), one (3), part (*my ówn párt*), means (*by nó méans*), and self (*his wíse sélf*). Eight more cases are traditional or idiomatic combinations approaching compounds, so the second element has partially or fully lost its accent: *swéet héart, lóve sòng, máre's nèst, crówes nèst, fóul plày, fáir plày, góod gòds*. This brings the total of the attributive phrases with an accentually weakened second element to 32 (33%: almost identical to the index of the Sonnets). Of the remaining 65 cases, eight include modified nouns referring to abstract notions of space (way in the meaning of "direction", and side) and five to notions of time (time; day and hours, usually modified by numerals). The second element of these phrases could probably also lose some sentence stress (*o' bóth sìdes; on the léft sìde; turn thís wày; within these thrée hòurs; within these twó hòurs*) (cf. Oras 1953:206). That leaves us with only 52 cases (about 54%) where the second element can be assumed to retain a relatively strong degree of phrasal accent; for example: *Their gílt cóats shine like Dragons scales . . .* (III,V:96); *A tóugh hén puls their teeth out, tyres their souls* (IV,I:36); *To whip these próud théeves from our kingdom. Heark* (IV,II:30); *Run, run, ye Rogues, ye precious Rogues, ye ránk Rógues* (IV,II:72); *Which is far baser, Hanging? 'tis a dógs déath* (IV,III:134). In most of these cases the modifier is emphasized and consequently bears a contrastive stress; therefore the modified noun, though a word of full lexical meaning, probably does lose its phrasal accent, at least partially.

A similar tendency is observed in Byron's and Browning's verse. Out of the fifty-eight enclitic attributive phrases found in 1000 lines of Byron's "Werner", thirteen contain a modified word of broad semantics, such as man or thing, in nine more cases the modified noun belongs to the semantic field "time" (*thrée mònths sínce, a féw hòurs móre*), and four more enclitic nouns are at the same time proclitic modifiers of the following word, e.g., *For yóur Lórd's lòsses, his lást nìght's slúmber*. This brings the number of enclitic modified nouns of full lexical meaning to thirty-two, or 55% of all modified nouns used enclitically: the figure is very close to Fletcher's. Some examples are: *The bare knife in your hand . . . ; My worst foe, Stralenheim . . . ; Watch him!—as you would watch the wild boar when . . .* (By.W, II,II:119,131,368). The last example contains a "rhythmical figure" (Bailey 1975) relatively frequent in Byron's dramas: a strong stress on position 9 and an unstressed monosyllable in the final ictic position.

Of the forty-three enclitic attributive phrases found in Browning's poems, ten contain a modified word of broad semantics (e.g., man, thing, time =

"instance", way = "manner"), in eight more cases the first element is a numeral and the second a countable noun belonging to the semantic field "time" (year, month, week, day): thrée dáy's sléep, síx mònths sínce, éight yèars óld, and others. This brings the total of the enclitic attributive phrases with the accentually weakened second element to nineteen, while the number of presumably fully stressed enclitic nouns is twenty-four; they occur in about 55% of enclitic attributive phrases: very much like in Fletcher's and Byron's verse. In one more line a semantic contrast and a strong emphatic stress on the modifier justifies a weakening of stress on the modified noun: Lèft fóot and rìght fóot, go a double step (Br.FLL: 206). This means that even in the most "enclitically-oriented" verse style the poets preferred a more weakly stressed element in an enclitic position. In a "proclitically-oriented" style the tendency is even more obvious: of the nine enclitic attributive phrases found in Pope's Epistles, four contain words of broad semantics (man, time = "instance", and sake), and the remaining five phrases are combinations of numerals (or pronouns substituting numerals) with countable nouns belonging to the semantic field "time:" tén yèars' slander, áll dày long, a whòle wèek's war.

Fletcher's verse, like Byron's and Browning's, does not, of course, "distort the normal speech rhythm" (Oras 1953:212), but Fletcher indeed made extensive use of an accentual pattern not very typical of English phrasal accentuation: enclitic attributive phrases occur 86 times per 1000 lines in Fletcher's "Bonduca", 62 times per 1000 lines in Browning's poems, 58 times per 1000 lines in Byron's "Werner", only 41 times per 1000 lines in Shakespeare's Sonnets, 18 times per 1000 lines in Milton's "Paradise Regained", and only 14 times per 1000 lines in Pope's Epistles (cf. proclitic attributive structures: they occur, for example, 169 times per 1000 lines in "Bonduca", 140 times per 1000 lines in the Sonnets, 130 times per 1000 lines in Browning's verse, 124 times per 1000 lines in Pope's Epistles, and 96 times per 1000 lines in Milton's "Paradise Regained").

The general scarcity in the English iambic pentameter, viewed as a whole, of cases like *Resembling strong youth in his middle age* is probably explained linguistically rather than metrically. Such "rhythmical figures" are scarce in verse because enclitic phrase rhythm, though "legitimate", is not typical of English speech, and not because such cases constitute "misbracketing" — a violation of a feet boundary (Kiparsky 1977). This does not mean, however, that I am denying the poets' possible awareness of "feet;" simply in this particular case a linguistic explanation seems more justified.

Next in frequency is the enclitically built structure verb + adverb (adjective) (Table 6.3). Micro-phrases of this grammatical type form enclitic structures more readily than modifier + modified, particularly in Fletcher's texts, where they sometimes outnumber proclitic structures. The percent correlation between proclitic and enclitic structures verb + adverb (adjective) in Byron's and Browning's verse resembles Fletcher's, but the absolute indices are much lower: enclitic structures verb + adverb occur in Fletcher's "Bonduca" 67 times per 1000 lines, while in Byron's "Werner" only 31 times and in Browning's Epistles only 35 times per 1000 lines. Byron's and Browning's rhythmical tendency is not unlike Fletcher's, but on the whole their verse is considerably smoother than that of the Jacobean dramatists.

Shakespeare's style is again more "proclitic" than that of his contemporaries; in fact, the data of the Sonnets and Milton's "Paradise Regained" are almost identical. The difference in indices opposes Fletcher's and Shakespeare's scenes of "Henry VIII" even more strongly than in the case of attributive phrases: Fletcher used enclitic phrases verb + adverb almost three times more frequently than Shakespeare. The stylistic difference between Fletcher and Beaumont in "The Maid's Tragedy" is also strong: here again Beaumont is closer to Shakespeare than to his own collaborator Fletcher.

The question arises: why do the poets use the enclitic pattern verb + adverb relatively more often than modifier + modified? Let us look at Fletcher's enclitic phrases verb + adverb (adjective) more closely. There are 78 cases altogether; out of these, 31 are verb + prepositional adverb (máde úp, be snátched óut, lét óut, sít dówn; páid for 't, belóng to 't), and 35 are verb + adverb of broad semantics (tóo, thére, thén, yét, só, stíll, élse, hére, nów, and thús). In all these cases the verb has much more semantic information than the adverb; the latter loses its phrasal accent partially or fully. Thus, at least in 66 cases out of 78 (almost 85%) the adverbial element of the enclitic phrase has little or no stress. However, such cases cannot be disregarded altogether: they do constitute enclitic phrases. If it were not so, patterns of this kind would be more widely used by Shakespeare and Milton, but both of these poets avoid them. This is a proof of the enclitic, syncopating effect of the phrases like *To cóme dówn, and be taken . . . ; Now márch ón, Souldiers . . .; . . . the multitudes that márch thére . . .; I yéeld thén; and even . . . will cóme ón't.* Here are some examples of the verbal phrases where the second element, adverb or adjective, is a word of full lexical meaning and obviously strongly stressed: *Live, and lead Armies all: ye bléed hárd.—Best* (F.B, III,V:120); *Thou art a Souldier: stríke hóme, hóme; have at ye* (F.B, III,V:159); *Dwindle away, because a woman díes wéll* (F.B, V,II:81).

The tendency to use a semantically empty or broad word as the second element of enclitic adverbial phrases is even more obvious in Byron's and Browning's verse; for example, of 24 cases of enclitic phrases verb + adverb in Browning's Epistles, twenty-three contain an adverb of broad semantics or a prepositional adverb: *I starved there, God knows how . . . ; But see, now— why, I see as certainly; . . . we're made so that we love; We get on fast . . .* (Br.FLL, 83,271,300,332).

The same rule works with the combinations noun + adverb (usually a verb-adverb or an adverbial modifier to the whole sentence) particularly in "enclitically oriented" texts; the absolute numbers of proclitic vs. enclitic structures of this type in some texts analyzed are as follows: Sonnets: 3-1; Beaumont, "The Maid's Tragedy": 0-12; Fletcher, "The Maid's Tragedy":

1-20; Fletcher, "Henry VIII": 2-32; Shakespeare, "Henry VIII": 1-3; Fletcher, "Bonduca": 2-43; Milton, "Paradise Regained": 5-0; Byron, "Werner": 3-11; Browning, Epistles: 10-14. Again Fletcher differs from both his collaborators; again Milton is Fletcher's antipode; and again Shakespeare's Sonnets and Milton's "Paradise Regained" show typological similarity. However, out of Fletcher's record-breaking figure 43 ("Bonduca"), 13 cases are prepositional adverbs (the nouns on S separate them from the verb), and 4 cases are adverbs of broad semantics, such as too, still, else, yet, and then. This means that at least 37 cases out of 43 (almost 80%) have semantic reasons for loss of phrasal accent, partially or fully. Some examples: *And take their skin off where they are tasted; shun 'em* (F.B, IV,I:38); *I'll tickle your young tail else. - I defie thee* (F.B, IV,II:52); *Ye draw away my soul then. I would live* (F.B, V,III:144).

The grammatical pattern subject + predicate is, as mentioned earlier, relatively more often built enclitically than verb + object, even in Fletcher's texts. For example, the proportion of proclitic and enclitic phrases of the subject + predicate pattern in "Bonduca" is 49-51%, while of the pattern verb + object it is 86-14%. In Byron's "Werner" the proportion of proclitic and enclitic phrases subject + predicate is 62-38%, while the proportion of proclitic and enclitic phrases verb + object is 83-17%. In Browning's verse the indices are 58-42% for subject + predicate and 84-16% for verb + object. Evidently, the second element of the word combination subject + predicate has relatively less informative value than of the phrase verb + object; consequently, the former is more liable to accentual weakening than the latter. Similarly to the patterns modifier + modified and verb + adverb/adjective, the second component (on S) of proclitic phrases subject + predicate and verb + object is a word of full lexical meaning, while in the enclitic phrases it is frequently a word of broad or weakened lexical meaning. Some more examples of proclitic phrases are as follows.

Verb + object: *We'll offer a reward; move heaven and earth* (By.W, II,I:64); *Frankfurt; post notices in manuscript* (By.W, II,I:66).

Subject + predicate: *Fools deem me knave* ... (By.W,II,II:193); *If the judge ask'd me, I would answer "No"* (By.W, II,II:288).

Here are some more examples of enclitic phrases, with the second element either a word of full lexical meaning or of weakened or broad meaning.

Verb + object: *The wound snares round me?* ... (By.W,II,II:144); *thought;—Must I bear this? - Pshaw! We all must bear* (By.W, II,II:275); *Let's sit and set things straight now, hip to haunch* (Br.FLL: 44); *Not thieves. The dead, who feel nought, can lose nothing* (By.W, II,II:427).

Subject + predicate: *'Sayeth', the same bade, 'Rise', and he did rise* (Br.K: 101); *How say I?—nay, which dog bites, which lets drop* (Br.FLL: 122); *I starved there, God knows how, a year or two* (Br.FLL: 83).

Shakespeare's texts are again typologically not unlike Milton's: for example, the proportion of proclitic to enclitic phrases subject + predicate is 89-11% in

"Richard II" and 93-7% in "Paradise Regained", while the correlation between proclitic and enclitic phrases verb + object is 94-6% in Shakespeare's Sonnets and 98-2% in Milton's "Paradise Regained" (cf. 83-17% in Massinger's "Maid of Honor;" 86-14% in Chapman's "Bussy D'Ambois").

6.6 Resumé: grammar and word semantics as aspects of rhythm

A quantitative correlation between proclitic and enclitic micro-phrases, a grammatical differentiation of enclitic phrases, and a semantic study of the enclitic elements reveal subtle but relevant peculiarities of individual rhythmical styles; their differentiation is essential for a deeper study of the English iambic pentameter. The syntactic and semantic features, determining the accentual structure of the phrase, are important components of English iambic meter.

Analysis of proclitic and enclitic micro-phrases provides another proof of the Shakespeare-Fletcher division of authorship of "Henry VIII", and of two substrates, one early and one late, in "Titus Andronicus".

6.7 Postscript: Word Boundary Rhythm and the Epoch

In my later work, after this book was finished and being prepared for typesetting, I studied the rhythm of word boundaries in English iambic hexameter and septameter (heptameter), and the link between the structure of word endings and their grammatical (part-of-speech and syntactic) characteristics. It turned out that the Jacobean epoch was not only the time of looser verse and syncopated rhythm of "heavy feminine" phrase endings, not only a period of feminine endings of lines, but also an epoch of feminine endings of words.

The correlation between phrasal and word stresses and the metrical scheme of the iambic line constitutes the primary rhythm of iambic verse. However, there are some elements of line structure that form the secondary rhythm. Prevalence of word endings of particalar types is an important constituent of secondary rhythm (cf. Jakobson 1979a: 28-30, 1979d:586-598, Tarlinskaja 1984).

I distinguished the following rhythmical types of word endings or word boundaries: (1) **masculine** (*That burn / from year /to year/*); (2) their rare variant- **dactylic** (*to register /thy fame*); (3) **feminine** (*but slowly /fled; countless /and swift*); (4) their almost unique variant—**hyperdactylic** (*immeasurable /wings*). Rhythmical structure of word endings is not to be confused with line endings; for example the line ending of *On night- black columns poised- one hollow hemisphere!* (Shel. R.I. I,LII:9) is masculine but the rhythmical structure of the final word ending is dactylic.

My hexameter and septameter material included four sixteenth- and seventeenth- and two nineteenth-century poets. I analyzed 500 hexameter lines from

each of the three following authors: Spenser's "The Faerie Queene", Drayton's "Poly-Olbion", and Shelley's "The Revolt of Islam". My septameter material included 477 lines from all of Surrey's poems written in "poulter's measure", 500 lines from Chapman's translation of Homer's "Iliad", and Tennyson's "The May Queen" and "Conclusion" (104 lines).
Here are my results on word boundary rhythm in a nutshell.

Hexameter. In Spenser's and Shelley's verse, masculine ("feet-emphasizing") word-boundaries prevail over feminine. They are not only a constant or predominant feature at the juncture of lines and hemistichs (positions 12 and 6), but also mark other even syllabic positions. In Spenser's verse these are specifically positions 4 and 8. This preference reflects Spenser's peculiar tendency towards a tripartite line segmentation of his "Iambicum Trimetrum" (Spenser, "Of Reformed Versifying", in Elizabethan Critical Essays 1971, vol.I:90). Spenser was obviously influenced by the structure of ancient Greek iambic trimeter (cf. Allen 1973:304, 314). In Shelley's hexameter, "peaks" of masculine endings occur in the first hemistich, after positions 2 and 4.

In contrast to Spenser and Shelley, Drayton prefers the "feet-effacing" feminine rhythm for his word boundaries. In his verse the latter form "peaks" after positions 5 and 3 of the first hemistich and position 9 of the second. Here are examples of lines typical of the three hexameter texts (masculine word boundaries are underlined in Spenser's and Shelley's lines, feminine word boundaries in Drayton's. Notice in the second example a curious phenomenon found occasionally in Spenser's verse: absence of a conventional, caesura-forming word boundary after position 6).

The wood / is fit / for beasts,/the court / is fit / for thee /
Into the world / to guide him / backe,/ as he him brought.
                    (Spenser, "The Faerie Queene" II,III,30:9,II,VII,65:9)
Like mind / while yet / it mocks / the all-devouring / grave./
To thrones / on Heaven / or Earth,/ such destiny / may know./
                    (Shelley, "The Revolt of Islam" VII,XXVIII:9,VIII,XII:9)
In Neptunes / agèd /armes,/ to Neptune /seeming /chast,
But, courting /Dyffren / Cluyd, / her beautie /doth prefer.
                    (Drayton, "Poly-Olbion",X:58,63)

Drayton also uses occasional "heavy feminine" phrasal endings, e.g.:

From prodigal expense can no way / keepe his wife;
As strong men / when they meet, contending for the path
                    (XV:22;X:79)

Septameter. A similar difference in word boundary rhythm was found in the septameter material.

Preference for masculine word boundaries not only at the line and hemistich junctures (positions 14 and 8), but also within the hemistichs, particularly within the first, gives Surrey's verse the notorious "jog-trot" effect, for example:

> From war / to peace,/ from truce /to strife,/and so / again / return
> Far off / I burn;/ in both / I waste,/ and so /my life / I lese.
> (Surrey, "Description of the Fickle Affections . . . :"16,42)

Word boundaries after even syllabic positions also predominate in Tennyson's "May Queen", though not all of them are masculine (cf. the repeating vocative *mother* which occupies WS positions). The chief way Tennyson uses to vary the rhythm of his line is shifting the rhythmical-syntactic seam from position 8 (hemistich boundary) to the left and to the right. Here are two typical lines:

> But sit / beside / my bed,/ mother, /and put /your hand / in mine
> They say / his heart / is breaking, / mother / - what / is that / to me?
> (Tennyson, "Conclusion" :23, "The May Queen" :22)

In contrast to Surrey and even Tennyson, Chapman strongly prefers the "feet-effacing" feminine rhythm of word boundaries within both hemistichs. Similarly to other Jacobean poets, Chapman often uses "heavy feminine" phrase endings. Two typical lines are:

> This Slaughter'd / issue. / Hector's /dart / shook Eioneus / dead.
> That this day / no more / mortal / wounds / may either / side / envade.
> (Chapman, Homer's "Iliad", VII:11,26)

The prevailing structures of word and phrase endings are obvious at the ends of lines, less obvious at the junctures of hemistichs, and take special research to discover inside hemistichs. Yet these structures are an important factor of secondary rhythm in English iambic verse. They differentiate both "preferences" of epochs and individual poets' style.

Notes to Chapter 6

[1] The term "phrase" has different meanings in the Russian and American/English linguistic traditions. For an English-language linguist, "the phrase" is more or less equivalent to a syntactic word combination, though it can have various degrees of complexity (. . . sings old ballads, for example, is a verb-phrase incorporating a noun-phrase old ballads; cf. Newmeyer 1983). For a Russian linguist, "the phrase" is a more autonomous syntactic-intonational unit, sometimes equaling a sentence or at least a clause (cf. Peškovskij 1938:40,410-411; Nikolaeva 1982:12). I am using the term "phrase" the way it is accepted in the English-language linguistic literature. In this meaning "phrase", or "micro-phrase", is analogous to "syntagma" or "micro-syntagma" ("slovosočetanije"): a syntactic combination of adjacent words forming a semantic "whole". In this chapter I analyze two-word "micro-phrases" in their correlation with meter.

² Hayes (1983) claimed that the main structural unit of English verse is not the line or hemistich but the phonological phrase. Even if we assume that a phonological phrase usually corresponds to a syntactic phrase (cf. Peškovskij 1938:410-411), Hayes' claim does not seem to be valid. True, English words are short and the dominant meter, iambic pentameter, generates longer lines (in Russian the reverse is true: words are long and the line is short, because the dominant meter is iambic tetrameter). Therefore, syntactic segmentation does play a greater role in English than, say, in Russian (cf. Jakobson 1979:585). However, segmentation of English verse into its own, "verse-specific" units—lines and "hemistichs"—is highly relevant, and poets are very conscious of this conventional segmentation. I have already approached this controversy in Chapter 2; here are some more arguments. Shelley's verse represents one of the loosest forms of English iambic pentameter. In his drama "The Cenci" (2327 lines) there are 198 cases of "inversions" of stresses on positions WS caused by non-oxytonic disyllabic words. Of these, 139 (70%) begin the line and 59 (30%) are not line- initial. In the first group, 35 (one quarter) do not begin a phrase, and 8 are even phrase-final, for example:

Aye . . . Rocco and Cristofano my curse
Strangled: and Giacomo, I think, will find . . .
                                                            (IV,I:46-47)

Earth, in the name of God, let her food be
Poison, until she be encrusted round . . .
                                                            (IV,I:128-129)

Are you resolved?—Is he asleep?—Is all
Quiet?—I mixed an opiate with his drink.
                                                            (IV,II:29-30)

In the second group (59 cases), 19 (almost one-third) are not phrase-initial, and 5 are even phrase-final; some examples:

Rightfullest arbiter!—If the lightning
Of God has e'er descended to avenge . . .
                                                            (III,I:179-180)

If thou hast done murders, made thy life's path
Over the trampled laws of God and man . . .
                                                            (V,II:134-135)

Who yet remain stubborn.—I overrule
                                                            (V,II:185)

Dead! The sweet bond broken!—They come! let me . . .
                                                            (V,IV:137)

The correlation between phrase-initial "inversions" that at the same time begin a line and those that are not line-initial is 104-40 (72-28%), the correlation between non-phrase-initial "inversions" at the beginning of the lines and elsewhere is 35-19 (65-35%): nearly identical tendencies. These facts suggest that the line as a metrical unit is a very real thing even for an author of metrically "looser" verse: if it were not so, non-phrase-initial "inversions" would occur at the beginning of lines as frequently as elsewhere, or probably even less frequently than in other parts of the line.

The conclusion that the poet is not only line-conscious, but also conscious of half-lines, can be drawn from the following facts. Non-phrase-initial "inversions" occur on positions 5-6 (the beginning of the second hemistich) even more readily than phrase-initial ones: of 41 phrase-initial mid-line "inversions" in "The Cenci", 23 (a little more than one-half) occur on positions 5-6, while out of 19 non-phrase-initial "inversions" as many as 15 (almost 80%) occur on positions 5-6. The fact that Shelley was obviously conscious of the half-line as a specific verse unit is particularly revealed if we consider the position in the verse line of those sentence elements realizing the non-phrase-initial "inversion" that are especially closely tied syntactically to the preceding word, for example, a direct object preceded by a verb. In "The Cenci", direct objects realizing non-phrase-initial "inversions" inevitably occur on positions 5-6, the beginning of the second half-line. For example:

Could but despise \ danger and gold and all

(II,II:130)

If thou hast done \ murders, made thy life's path

(V,II:134)

The position of the "inversion" at the beginning of the second half-line implies, as it were, a break before the word, and the break tones down the "deviation". The same phenomenon explains why Shakespeare uses a non-phrase-initial disyllabic word, an object, in his Sonnet 107, line 8: the word appears on positions 5-6, at the beginning of the second "hemistich", and there is an implied break before it: *And peace proclaims \ olives of endless age*. Early Shakespeare was very conscious of 4 + 6 bipartite structure of verse lines (cf. Oras 1960, Tarlinskaja 1983, Suhamy 1984).

[3] Grammatical (part of speech and syntactic) correlates of the accentual and word boundary line structure are metrically more relevant for English iambic verse with its shorter words, typically longer lines and their more diverse rhythmical variation than, for example, for the Russian iamb with its typically shorter lines and longer words (cf. Jakobson 1979d:585).

[4] Abbreviations accepted in this chapter, used from now on, are: Shakespeare, "Titus Andronicus": Sh.TA; Sonnets: Son; "Richard II": RII; "The Winter's Tale": WT; "Henry VIII": HVIII; Chapman, "Bussi D'Ambois": Ch.BDA; Fletcher, "Bonduca": F.B; Beaumont and Fletcher, "The Maid's Tragedy": BF.MT; Massinger, "The Maid of Honor": M.MH; Milton, "Paradise Regained": Mil.PR; Pope, "The Rape of the Lock": P.RL; Byron, "Werner": By.W; Browning, "Karshish": Br.K; Browning, "Fra Lippo Lippi": Br.FLL.

Chapter 7

Rhythmical Figures: Structural Types, Grammatical Features, and Compositional Functions

7.1 Preliminary remarks. Aim and material.

In Chapters 1 through 5 analyses were focused mainly on the general trends in the distribution of stressed and unstressed syllables among strong (ictic) and weak (non-ictic) syllabic positions of the verse line. The study largely concentrated on the "stress profiles", which were derived from all the lines of a text, or selected portions, such as acts or roles of dramatis personae. This kind of general analysis is termed "vertical" (see Chapter 1).

In Chapter 6 I studied "extrametrical" strongly stressed monosyllables as elements of phrases, disregarding the complexity of any "rhythmical figure" that they might be part of; interest was centered on the syntactic function of these monosyllables and their position in a phrase in relation to the adjacent word with which they usually have a syntactic tie. Chapters 7 and 8 present the study of "rhythmical figures" in all their syllabic size and structural complexity: monosyllabic, disyllabic, trisyllabic, and the occasional longer figures, containing both "extrametrical" stresses on W and losses of stress on S. I will concentrate on the rhythmical and grammatical structure of the figures themselves and investigate their euphonic, compositional, semantic, and stylistic functions in verse of different epochs, genres, and poets. This kind of more detailed analysis made with special attention to minute particulars of line structure is termed "horizontal" (see Chapter 1).

Following a study of the monosyllabic figure W ("extrametrical" strong stresses on non-ictic positions), attention is paid to their disyllabic combinations with adjacent unstressed syllables on ictic positions (S) preceding or following the "extrametrical" strong stress, and then to even longer chains of syllables whose stress (or stresses) fails to correspond to the general metrical scheme. These chains of syllables break the prevailing rhythmical momentum "weak-strong-weak-strong..." which develops in iambic verse and are therefore more noticeable to the readers; but the readers, or listeners, recognize these forms as something they have frequently seen or heard before and have learned to expect as part of English iambic verse. These forms, then, are accepted through common usage as a "legitimate" part of poetic tradition; they not only represent a substantial element of English iambic meter, but are frequently well within its norm, i.e., constitute the most frequent forms typical of all periods of English poetic tradition. That is why it is actually misleading to term these phenomena "deviations" (though strictly speaking some of them are, though not from the meter, but from the prevailing tendency), and I generally try to avoid this term. The term "inversions of stress" is usually also avoided for the following reasons: (a) to eliminate associations with the notion of feet, a notion which seems today to upset many students of poetics (e.g., Attridge 1982:49); and (b) to be able to analyze accentual combinations of syllables longer than a "foot" and crossing the "feet boundaries". Instead, I use the neutral term "rhythmical figure" introduced by James Bailey ("Certain patterns of non-metrical stressing are acceptable to poetic tradition because of common usage, while others are rarely utilized and therefore are less acceptable. These patterns will be termed 'rhythmical figures'." James Bailey 1975:38). We shall investigate the disyllabic, trisyllabic, and the (exceptional) longer chains of adjacent syllables forming all types of "rhythmical figures" appearing in English iambic verse by Shakespeare and other poets.

7.1.1 The main aims and order of analysis in chapters 7 and 8 are as follows. (1) The incidence of the various types of rhythmical figures in Shakespeare's verse of different genres and periods is determined and compared with the verse of later poets. (2) Grammatical characteristics of different rhythmical figures are investigated: we will try to find out if different figures "prefer" words of particular parts of speech of particular morphological forms in specific syntactic structures. (3)The compositional functions of rhythmical figures in rhymed verse is studied. (4) The semantic functions of these figures are explored. If semantic functions are discovered, we shall try to elucidate which figures, of what grammatic structures, have specific semantic functions, and how often these functions are materialized in the verse of different genres and periods. An important question is whether the semantic role of rhythmical figures is dictated each time by the specific needs of the individual context (e.g., "rhythmical italics" of words important for the poet in a specific situation) or whether there are semantic categories that are regularly coupled in the English poetic tradition with one or several rhythmical figures of certain syntactic composition. Stated in another way, can a link between rhythmical figures ("rhythm") and certain semantic categories ("meaning") be in some way generalized and typified? (5) Another aim is to find out which functions and semantic categories are coupled with rhythmical figures of various types, which functions and semantic categories prevail, and to what extent. A reasonable assumption is that rhythmical figures do not always have a semantic load and are used not solely for semantic purposes, but also for others, such as euphonic or compositional. (6) Did Shakespeare make the same semantic use of his rhythmical figures in different genres at different periods of his career? (7) Yet another aim is to see if the semantic functions of verse rhythm evolved in quantity and quality within the English literary tradition following

Shakespeare. Narrative and dramatic verse of three later poets is compared with Shakespeare's to see if their rhythmical figures have the same semantic functions as Shakespeare's. It seems probable that the hypothetical link between certain semantic categories ("meaning") and certain rhythmical figures ("rhythm") became more conventional with the passage of time and was materialized more often in the works of later poets. In other words, two questions are posed: (i)Was Shakespeare's handling of the rhythm-meaning link in any way different from other poets'? (ii) Did the poetic skill in using rhythm for semantic purposes evolve through the centuries?

7.1.2 The main material for these analyses and the accepted abbreviations are as follows: Shakespeare's poem "The Rape of Lucrece" (Sh.RL): 1855 lines; all of his sonnets (Sh.Son): 2154 pentameter lines; and four plays, representing all genres and periods: a chronicle, "Richard II" (Sh.RII): 2630 lines; a comedy, "As You Like It" (Sh.AYLI): 930 lines; a tragedy, "Othello" (Sh.Oth): 2272 lines; and a lyrical drama, "The Winter's Tale" (Sh.WT): 2027 pentameter lines. The three authors of the eighteenth-nineteenth centuries and their works selected are: Pope, all of his "The Rape of the Lock" (P.RL) and the first 120 lines from his two epistles, "To Richard Boyle, Earl of Burlington" (P.RB) and "To Dr. Arbuthnot" (P.DA): a thousand lines altogether; Shelley's poem "The Revolt of Islam" (Shel.RI), Dedication and Cantos I-III and VI-VIII: 2547 lines; his tragedy "The Cenci" (Shel.C): 2327 lines; and Arnold's narrative poem "Sohrab and Rustum" (A.SR): 892 lines; a grand total of 18,634 iambic pentameter lines. There are also some examples for specific cases selected from the works of other eighteenth and nineteenth century poets: Crabbe, Erasmus Darwin, Gay, John Arbuthnot, Johnson, Thomson, Wordsworth, Byron, and Keats. For the analysis of the compositional function of rhythmical figures I also analyzed, in addition to "Lucrece" and the sonnets, Shakespeare's "Venus and Adonis" (Sh.VA) and 95 iambic tetrameter lyrical poems by 26 authors.[1]

7.2 Types of "rhythmical figures" in English iambic verse: general characteristics

The metrical norm of the English iambic pentameter permits seven main types of monosyllabic, disyllabic, and trisyllabic rhythmical figures; several others are borderline or outside the norm and appear as exceptions (Bailey 1975, Tarlinskaja 1976).

7.2.1 Monosyllabic

There are two kinds of monosyllabic "figures". The first is formed by an unstressed syllable, instead of a stressed one, on a strong (ictic) syllabic position of the verse line. The loss of stress may be caused by an unstressed or weakly stressed monosyllable or an unstressed syllable of a polysyllabic word.

The sign used hereafter to indicate this type of rhythmical figure is S, that is, a strong syllabic position with a missing stress. Two examples are: *'Twas He had summon'd to her silent Bed* (P.RL I:21); *Of thousand bright Inhabitants of Air* (P.RL I:28).

The second figure is a strongly stressed monosyllable on a weak (non-ictic) position. The sign used for this figure is W, that is, a weak syllabic position bearing a strong stress. The strongly stressed monosyllable is usually accentually subordinate either to the following, or, much less often, to the preceding word with a strong ictic stress; or, less frequently, not subordinated by any other word at all. Examples: *Smooth flow the Waves, the Zephyrs gently play* (P.RL II:51); *The wise Man's Passion, and the vain Man's Toast* (P.RL V:10); *Sighs,\ Sobs, and Passions, and the War of Tongues* (P.RL IV:84).

I want to emphasize that here and hereafter a syllabic position, not the degree of stress, is used as the basis of the nomenclature. (In Gasparov's opinion, the differentiation of the notions "syllable" and "position" was a major step forward in the twentieth-century theory of verse: Gasparov 1984b:174.) Thus, S means a missing stress on a strong syllabic position, W means a strong stress on a weak syllabic position, WS means stress-nonstress on weak plus strong syllabic positions, SW stands for nonstress-stress on positions strong plus weak, and so on.

7.2.2 Disyllabic

These figures are combinations of a loss of stress on a strong syllabic position (S) coupled with an extrametrical strong stress on either of the adjacent weak positions (W), to the left or to the right of S:

WS and SW. Both WS and SW may be of two general subtypes: (a) formed by two monosyllables (a loss of stress on S may be also caused by an unstressed syllable of a polysyllabic word), and (b) formed by a polysyllable (usually a disyllabic word). Subtypes (a) are designated WS-1 and SW-1, subtypes (b) WS-2 and SW-2. Subtypes WS-1, WS-2, and SW-1 are within the metrical norm for English verse, while subtype SW-2 is on the border or, for the eighteenth-century verse, outside the norm (see below). As we shall soon see, both WS and SW (particularly WS) are more acceptable at the beginning of a phrase/line (or half-line), less so in mid-phrase, and exceptional at the end of a phrase. In case of the figure SW, the stressed element on W is often the first notional (lexical) word of the line/phrase (see also Chapters 2 and 6). Examples of the figures are:

WS-1: *Chang'd to a Bird* . . . (P.RL III:123); *Falls undistinguish'd by the victor Spade* (P.RL III:64);

SW-1: *You should live twice* . . . (Sh.S 17:14); *That in black ink* . . . (Sh.S 65:14); *Nor shall Death brag* . . . (Sh.S 18:11);
WS-2: *Seeing such emulation in their woe* (Sh.RL 259:2); *Sudden he view'd, in spite of all her art* (P.RL III:143).
SW-2: *Have excused much, doubted; and when no doubt* . . . (Shel.C I,III:114); *Will arise thence, where every other one* (Shel.C III,I:205).

The most typical morphological component on W of the figure WS-1 is the verb; a frequent element forming the figure WS-2 is also a verb, a non-oxytonic disyllabic form (see below). For example: *Lay on our royal sword your banished hands*; *Banished this frail sepulchre of our flesh* (Sh.RII I,III:179,196).

The most typical morphological component on W in SW-1 is an adjective, syntactically an attribute. Next in frequency come an adverb and a noun in the possessive case used as an attribute (cf. Tarlinskaja 1976:149-151 and 171-174, Bailey 1975:40, Kiparsky 1977). Such components are syntactically and accentually subordinate to the following word with a strong ictic stress: this "metrical subordination" (Attridge 1982:230, cf. Tarlinskaja 1981) is accompanied by grammatical and accentual subordination. English iambic verse definitely avoids sharp, back-to-back collisions of two stresses in the middle of the line preceded by a loss of an ictic stress; therefore the figure SW-1 "avoids" syntactic breaks after W; cases like *And holding his breath*, *died* (Shel.C V,II:183), or *And they fled, scattering—lo!* . . . (Shel.RI VI,XIX:2) are exceptional. Even the structure subject (on W) plus predicate (on the following S) is scarce (e.g., *And the rack makes him utter* . . . : Shel.C V,II:96): the components of this syntactic structure, which is the backbone of the sentence, are not syntactically subordinate to each other, and the accentual subordination of the subject to the following predicate seems less likely than, for example, in a "modifier + modified" pattern, e.g., *In the clear Mirror of thy ruling Star* (P.RL I:108) (see 7.4).

The figures SW-2 formed by a disyllabic word with its stress on the second syllable, if not subject to a stress shift, are avoided even more: such words break the iambic rhythm so sharply that this figure is essentially outside the norm of the English iambic verse (Gasparov 1973:415, Tarlinskaja and Teterina 1974, Bjorklund 1978:119). Poets of certain epochs (Classicism) never used it at all; even among those who did (e.g., Shelley), its use is clearly exceptional. Thus, in "The Cenci" the figure WS-2 in the middle of a line occurs 51 times, while SW-2 occurs only 19 times, almost three times less frequently. Even more revealing is the correlation between SW-1 and SW-2: they occur in "The Cenci" in the ratio 357 to 19, or 95 to 5% of the total, while the correlation between WS-1 and WS-2 (only those occurring in the middle of Shelley's lines) is 107 vs. 51, or 68 vs. 32%.

The syntactic structure of line-internal WS-1 shows again that even the authors of the loosest iambic verse avoided violent breaks in the rhythmical momentum. There are two conventional ways, both syntactical, for smoothing or relieving the breach of iambic alternating rhythm caused by a line-internal WS-1: (a) introducing a syntactic break between W and S: the element on W ends a phrase and is enclitically subordinate to the preceding word with a strong ictic stress, while the element on S begins a new phrase; for example: *I, who have white hairs \ and a tottering body* (Shel.C II,II:39); (b) the element on W begins a new phrase and is syntactically, and by an implied pause, separated from the preceding strongly stressed word on an ictic position, as in *O that the earth would gape! / Hide me, O God!* (Shel.C II,I:111). In both examples the clash between two stresses is relieved, in (a) by an accentual subordination of the strongly stressed noun on W to the preceding attribute (*white hairs*), and in (b) by a syntactic break and a possible pause between the verb on W and the preceding sentence.

The figures WS-2 in internal positions of the line are normally limited to the beginning of a phrase (cf. Hayes 1983); cases like *Who yet remain stubborn* ..., or *Dead! The sweet bond broken!* ... (Shel.C V,II:185; V,IV:137), constructed for very clear stylistic reasons, are practically outside the English iambic norm. However, they are not "unmetrical", as Beth Bjorklund or Hayes thought; cf. Bjorklund's "unmetrical" construct * *O'ersnowed beauty and bareness everywhere* (Bjorklund 1978:96) and a very real line *Are base people. Believe them not; they lied* (Beaumont and Fletcher, "The Maid's Tragedy" IV,I:44) (see also 6.1.1).

The syntactic functions of disyllabic non-phrase-initial words constituting rhythmical figures WS-2 seem to determine the "degrees of acceptability" of the figure; some syntactic functions are obviously less permissible than others. For example, modified nouns (*Are base people*) are really very infrequent; slightly more common are direct objects following a verb, for example: *And peace proclaims olives of endless age*; *Have I not seen dwellers on form and favour* (Sh.Son 107:8 and 125:5); even more common are predicates or their parts, post-positional (predicative) attributes or adverbial modifier participles, for example: *When lofty trees I see barren of leaves* (Sh.Son 13:7); *Sate one waving a sword* (Shel.RI VI,XIX:7); *Who yet remain stubborn* (Shel.C V,II:185). The frequency of a disyllabic syntactic element on positions WS obviously depends on the strength of the syntactic tie between this element and the preceding word: the stronger the tie, the less probable is the occurrence of a WS figure formed by the element (see below).

The most typical position for the figures WS is the beginning of lines. Next in frequency are positions 5-6 in metrically more rigorous verse, or 7-8 in verse of a looser form: the beginning of the second "hemistich". Note that both examples above from Shakespeare's sonnets of a disyllabic direct object constituting the figure WS-2 occur on positions 5-6, after the canonized "caesura" (cf. Gascoigne 1971 (1575):54). The implied "caesura", as it were, implies a break after position 4, thus creating more favorable conditions for the figure WS-2.

The beginnings of the line are preferred by both WS-1 and particularly WS-2 for the following obvious reasons. (1) The figures occur after the strongest syntactic break (between two lines), so there is no preceding stressed syllable and no back-to-back clash between two stresses (back-to-back stresses are avoided not only specifically in verse, but in English non-poetic everyday speech as well; cf. van Draat 1912, Bolinger 1965). (2) The rhythmical momentum, already formed in the middle of the line, is not yet strong at the beginning, even if the line is not the first in the text (cf. Jespersen 1966:117). As we shall soon see, it is the very first line of English iambic poems that has the highest number of initial WS variations; second in frequency are in lines opening a new stanza.

7.2.3 Trisyllabic and polysyllabic figures

Three adjacent syllables, stressed contrary to the metrical positions they fill (WSW and particularly SWS), seem to be marginal for the norm of English iambic pentameter (Tarlinskaja and Teterina 1974). In other literary traditions the length and structure of normative rhythmical figures may, naturally, differ from English. In Russian iambic verse, for example, the marginal length of rhythmical figures is only two syllables, and the normative structure contains an obligatory word boundary between W and S; the figure is formed by a stressed monosyllable on W plus an unstressed syllable of a polysyllabic word on S. On the other extreme is Italian hendecasyllabic verse, which still is "twice closer to the syllabo-tonic than to the syllabic model" (Gasparov 1980:217; see also Chapter 1), where the marginal length of strings of syllables constituting "rhythmical figures" is at least twice greater than in the English iambic pentameter. In the English pentameter four and more adjacent syllables stressed contrary to the metrical positions they occupy occur at only certain periods of English literature, and only in certain genres, for example, in the poetry of later Elizabethan-Jacobean authors; specifically in Donne's verse, and particularly in his "Satyres" (Tarlinskaja and Teterina 1974), for example: *Pérfĕct Frénch, ānd Ĭtălĭan; I replyed* (Donne, "Satyre I" 103). Fairly long polysyllabic rhythmical figures are also found in Jacobean dramatic verse, for example: *Thắt's thē grḗatēst tŏrtūre sŏuls fĕel ĭn hĕll* (Webster, "The Duchess of Malfi" IV,I:69): a hexasyllabic figure SWSWSW. In Shakespeare's dramatic verse the longest figures are tetrasyllabic. They occur very infrequently (being obviously outside Shakespeare's norm) and usually belong to two different syntactic phrases separated by a syntactic seam, for example: *Unclē,/gĭve mē your hand, nay, dry your eyes* (Sh.RII III,III:202). The polysyllabic figures are often marked by a specific intonation and are followed by a pause, as they frequently contain a vocative, as in the example above, and the pause obviously neutralizes stress. If unbroken syntactically and not marked by a specific intonation, polysyllabic rhythmical figures practically always play a specific stylistic and semantic role (see Chapter 8); for example: *Ŏ, shĕ's gōne ăgāin! Thḗre thē cŏrds ŏf lĭfe brŏke* (Webster, "The Duchess of Malfi"

IV,II:371), or *Ĭ hāve tālked sōme wĭld wòrds, but will no more* (Shel.C III,I:66).

Three adjacent syllabic positions normally allowing rhythmical variations are in the overwhelming majority of cases WSW, rather than SWS. One of the obvious reasons is the fact that most of the figures WSW occur at the beginning of the line and are therefore more numerous than the figures SWS, which can only occur in mid-lines. The difference in number of the figures WSW and SWS is usually considerable. In all of Shakespeare's sonnets there occur 41 cases of WSW and only two cases of SWS, which are in part relieved by a syntactic seam between the first S and the following group WS: *Nătĭvĭtȳ, ŏnce ĭn thĕ māin ŏf līght; Admit impĕdĭmĕnts. Lŏve ĭs nŏt lòve* (Son. 60:5, 116:2). In "The Winter's Tale" there are 65 figures of the WSW type, and only one SWS, also with a syntactic seam in the middle: *Ĭ māy bĕ nĕglĭgēnt, fŏolīsh ănd fĕarfŭl* (S.WT I,II:250). Even in Shelley's "The Cenci" there are only 6 cases of SWS to 67 cases of WSW. For example: *Rightfullest arbiter!—Ĭf thē lĭghtnīng (Of God has e'er descended to avenge)* (Shel.C III,I:179). Particularly avoided are the figures SWS in which the positions WS are filled by polysyllabic words stressed on the first syllable, not isolated syntactically from the unstressed monosyllable on the first S of the figure, as in the last example above; cf. also Beth Bjorklund's (1978:18) "unmetrical" constructs *Shall Ĭ lĭken thee to a summer's day*, or *Shall I compare thee tŏ sŭmmer's fair day*.

The cases of the figure WSW are of two main subtypes: (a) all three syllables are monosyllabic words, as in *Plŭck the kĕen tĕeth from the fierce tiger's jaws* (Sh.Son 19:3); (b) the first two syllables are a non-oxytonic disyllabic word as in *Crŭel, cŏld, fŏrmal măn . . .* (Shel.C V,IV:108). There is also, but used only exceptionally, one more subtype, formed by a monosyllable and a disyllabic oxytonic word, as in *Lĕss appĕar sŏ, in cŏmforting your ĕvils* (Sh.WT II,III:56). This subtype is also strongly avoided because the disyllabic word filling the second and the third positions of the figure does not begin a phrase and fills a W with a syllable marked by a phonological stress.

The frequent occurrence of specific types of rhythmical figures and avoidance of others lead to the following conclusion: "inversions of stress" both on positions SW and WS realized by a polysyllabic word not beginning a phrase are outside the norm of English iambic verse. The avoidance of a phonological stress on W in the sequence SW has been noticed several times previously: cf. Magnuson and Ryder 1970:811, Gasparov 1973:415, Tarlinskaja and Teterina 1974, Kiparsky 1977:202, Chisholm 1977:147; but it was Bjorklund (1978:18) and Hayes (1983:373) who pointed out that the same was true of the sequence WS, unless the polysyllabic word realizing the "inversion" began a phrase. Thus, <u>syntactic word grouping predetermining a specific intonation contour is a relevant constituent of the English meter</u> (cf. Jakobson 1979:585).

Four and more adjacent syllables stressed contrary to the metrical positions they fill are exceptional; they lie on the border or outside the metrical norm. Even in "The Cenci" there are only 5 cases in 2327 lines: *Retire tŏ yōur* chămbĕr, ᴇinsōlĕnt gìrl! (Shel.C I,III:145); *I hāve tălked sōme w³ĭld wòrds but will no more* (Shel.C III,I:66); *Earth, in the name ŏf Gòd, lᴇ̄t hĕr fōod bē (Poison...)* (Shel.C IV,I:128); *But shakes ĭt nòt.—Mᴇūrdĕr! Mᴇūrdĕr! Mᴇūrdĕr!* (Shel.C IV,IV:52) (cf. *Never, never, never, never, never!* : Shakespeare, "King Lear" V,IV:308); *If thou hăst dòne mᴇūrdĕrs, măde thȳ l³ĭfe's pàth (Over the trampled laws of God and man...)* (Shel.C V,II:134). Even here there is only one case without a syntactic break and implied pause; however, his line (*Ĭ hāve tălked sōme w³ĭld wòrds...*) does not contain a single disyllabic word, and monosyllables are phonetically ambivalent and at least theoretically can lose or acquire a phrasal accent to better fit the general rhythm. In each of Shakespeare's dramas analyzed there are 1 to 4 cases of tetrasyllabic figures; some examples: *Ūnclᴇ̄, g³ĭve mē yŏur hànd ...; Ūnclē, ᴇēven īn the glasses of thine eyes; When Bòlingbrōke rŏ̄de ōn r³òan Bàrbărȳ; The King hăd cùt off mȳ hᴇ̄ad wīth my brother's* (Sh.RII III,III:202; I,III:208; V,V:78; II,II:103); *Prithee, nŏ mòre: lᴇ̄t hīm cōme whēn hĕ wìll; Lᴇ̄t hīm spᴇ̄ak līke yŏursèlf, and lay a sentence* (Sh.Oth III,I:76; I,III:199); *Thīs wās sŏ̄, ānd nŏ slŭmbĕr ... Dreams are toys* (Sh.WT III,III:39). All of the cases either contain a phrase juncture in the middle or are composed of monosyllables. Lines like *Nătūre's Sᴇ̄crētarȳ, thē Phĭlòsŏphĕr* (Donne, "Satyre I" 6) are definitely outside Shakespeare's norm (Tarlinskaja and Teterina 1974:73).

Disyllabic and polysyllabic figures must have been employed by the poets more deliberately than monosyllabic variations. These figures are less conditioned by the characteristics of the language material and more by the poets' choice: the abundance in English of strongly stressed monosyllables can at least partially explain the frequent occurrence of the monosyllabic figure W, but not of disyllabic and polysyllabic figures. Because the poets obviously use them more deliberately, the disyllabic and longer figures are more likely to have an additional stylistic or semantic function. However, both monosyllabic figures, particularly strong stresses on W, evidently are also capable of playing an occasional semantic role, as Pope illustrated in his "Essay on Criticism" (*When Ajax strives some rock's vast weight to throw, The line too labours, and the words move slow*: II:370-371). The following questions arise: how often do extrametrical stresses play a semantic role, compared, for example, with the disyllabic rhythmical figures? Do they play the same role in different genres? What use did Shakespeare make of them? I shall try to answer these questions in Chapter 8.

7.3 Incidence of different rhythmical figures in Shakespeare's verse and in the verse of later poets (Table 7.1)

The number of strong stresses on W in "Lucrece" and "Richard II" equals the total of disyllabic and longer rhythmical figures together. The number of polysyllabic figures decreases from disyllabic, formed by two monosyllables,

Table 7.1

Incidence of the Types of Polysyllabic Rhythmical Figures
(in percent from the total)

Types of figures	Shakespeare						Pope	Shelley		Arnold
	Lucrece	Sonnets	Rich.II	As You	Othello	W.Tale	Rape Lock	Islam	Cenci	Sohrab
SW	36.6	37.9	31.1	32.8	34.1	42.0	20.8	43.9	40.0	<u>50.6</u>
WS	<u>55.5</u>	<u>55.8</u>	<u>60.8</u>	<u>56.5</u>	<u>54.9</u>	45.9	<u>63.0</u>	<u>51.2</u>	<u>51.7</u>	43.2
(WS-1	31.2	37.3	42.5	41.0	41.3	23.4	45.8	30.7	32.3	21.0)
(WS-2	24.3	18.5	18.3	15.5	13.6	13.5	17.2	20.5	19.4	22.2)
Trisyllabic	7.9	6.3	8.1	10.7	11.0	12.1	14.2	4.9	8.3	6.2
Total	440	633	684	271	675	563	197	873	931	338

to trisyllabic figures. The prevalence of WS over SW is particularly marked in Pope's verse, while the reverse is true of Arnold's poem: thus the figure SW appears to have become more "fashionable" in the nineteenth century. Shakespeare's verse in this respect went through an evolution, from a strong prevalence of WS over SW in the earlier material to their almost equal occurrence in "The Winter's Tale". A wider use of SW seems to be a sign of a less rigorous verse form in the English iambic tradition. As will be shown below, the nineteenth-century poets not only began to use the figure SW more freely, but they also changed its part-of-speech and syntactic composition and gave it a heavier semantic load than in earlier poetry.

Trisyllabic and the exceptional polysyllabic figures are relatively the least frequent in Shakespeare's Sonnets and Arnold's poem and, surprisingly, relatively the most frequent in Pope's texts. This, in my opinion, goes to prove Pope's deliberate use of these "deviations". The highest absolute number of trisyllabic figures per line was discovered in dramatic verse: "The Winter's Tale", "Othello", "As You Like It", and in "The Cenci" (31 to 34 cases per 1000 lines of text). Probably, polysyllabic figures are less "offensive" when heard in an oral presentation than when seen in the text by a reader.

7.4 Consider now in greater detail the **grammatical characteristics of rhythmical figures**. The questions are whether the different figures have specific part-of-speech preferences in all, or some texts analyzed, and whether our poets coupled them with particular syntactic functions and patterns.

7.4.1 Morphology

The relative frequencies of the parts of speech occurring in rhythmical figures (viz. nouns, verbs, adjectives, and adverbs, which in the overwhelming majority of cases constitute the figures or their stressed parts) were compared with their occurrence (a) in verse, minus its rhythmical figures, and (b) in prose. For the latter comparison, the entire prose texts of "Othello" and "The Winter's Tale" were analyzed, as well as 2500 monosyllabic and disyllabic words from each of three texts: Swift's "Gulliver's Travels", Fielding's "The History of Tom Jones, A Foundling", and Austen's "Pride and Prejudice". Note that in the comparative material I did not take account of a category of words called "others", while in the analysis of rhythmical figures there is reference to such words, which include pronouns, interjections, numerals, or interrogative words, for example: <u>Some</u>, *as she sipp'd, the fuming Liquor fann'd*; <u>This</u> *just behind Belinda's Neck he spread*; *Then thus address'd the Pow'r*—<u>Hail</u>, *wayward Queen! And thus broke out—My Lord,* <u>why</u>, *what the devil?* <u>Z-ds!</u> *damn the Lock! 'fore Gad, you must be civil!* (P.RL III:113,133; IV:127,128). In the interpretation of results I make allowance for this difference.

Table 7.2

Part-of-Speech Correlation Between Monosyllabic Strongly Stressed Words on W (the whole texts) and S (600 lines from each text) in Shakespeare's "The Rape of Lucrece" and "Richard II" (in percent from the total)

	In rhythmical figure		Outside rhythmical figures, on ictic positions	
Part of speech	Lucrece	Richard II	Lucrece	Richard II
Nouns	15.4 (75)	15.2 (102)	41.4	48.4
Verbs	30.0 (142)	29.0 (194)	31.8	29.0
Adjectives	25.3 (122)	15.4 (103)	12.9	10.7
Adverbs	21.9 (105)	24.5 (164)	13.9	11.9
Others	7.4 (35)	15.9 (106)	Not considered	
Total	479	669	1553	1389

7.4.1.1 Consider first the part-of-speech correlation between notional words in the rhythmical figures containing monosyllabic words. The part-of-speech correlation in the monosyllabic figure W—an extrametrical stress on a non-ictic position—is shown in Table 7.2; the part-of-speech correlation in disyllabic figures SW-1 and WS-1 is given in Tables 7.3 and 7.4. The correlation between nouns, verbs, adjectives, and adverbs in verse outside rhythmical figures and in prose is presented in Tables 7.2, 7.6 and 7.7. These results are generalized in the following correlation scheme, in which a plus sign indicates a prevalence of a part of speech in the particular figure, and two pluses a great prevalence. The results are also shown graphically in Fig. 7.1.

Monosyllabic Rhythmical Figure: Part-of-Speech Correlation
[+ equals prevalence in figure, + + equals great prevalence]

	Rhythmical figures					In verse, minus rhythmical figures	In prose
				WSW-1			
	W	SW-1	WS-1	Wa	Wb		
Noun						+ +	+
Verb	+		+ +	+ +		+	+
Adj	+	+ +			+ +		
Adv	+		+				

242

Table 7.3

Part-of-Speech Correlation Between Monosyllabic Stressed Components on W in the Figure SW-1
(in percent of the total)

Part of speech	Shakespeare			Pope	Shelley		Arnold
	Lucrece	Sonnets	Dramas	Rape Lock	Islam	Cenci	Sohrab
Nouns	5.0 (8)	16.6 (39)	7.4 (57)	2.5 (1)	10.5 (39)	12.6 (45)	16.7 (27)
Verbs	9.4 (15)	15.0 (35)	28.3 (217)	2.5 (1)	10.8 (40)	19.5 (69)	16.0 (26)
Adjectives	66.7 (106)	52.0 (122)	45.1 (346)	72.5 (29)	70.7 (263)	52.7 (186)	55.5 (90)
Adverbs	17.1 (27)	13.6 (32)	17.5 (134)	12.5 (5)	4.6 (17)	10.5 (37)	6.8 (11)
Others	1.8 (3)	2.8 (7)	1.7 (13)	10.0 (4)	3.4 (13)	4.5 (16)	5.0 (8)
Total	159	235	767	40	372	357	162

Table 7.4

Part-of-Speech Correlation Between Monosyllabic Stressed Components
on W in the figure WS-1 (in percent of the total)

Part of speech	Shakespeare			Pope	Shelley		Arnold
	Lucrece	Sonnets	Dramas	Rape Lock	Islam	Cenci	Sohrab
Nouns	15.3 (21)	13.7 (34)	11.0 (95)	11.0 (10)	12.3 (33)	7.3 (22)	8.6 (6)
Verbs	46.0 (63)	32.7 (81)	45.5 (390)	42.2 (38)	44.0 (118)	48.7 (147)	45.2 (31)
Adjectives	0.7 (1)	3.6 (9)	3.4 (19)	6.6 (6)	4.5 (12)	3.0 (9)	8.6 (6)
Adverbs	22.0 (30)	25.0 (62)	21.1 (182)	26.6 (24)	29.5 (79)	17.7 (53)	30.4 (21)
Others	16.0 (22)	25.0 (62)	19.0 (174)	13.6 (12)	9.7 (26)	23.3 (70)	7.2 (5)
Total	137	248	860	90	268	301	69

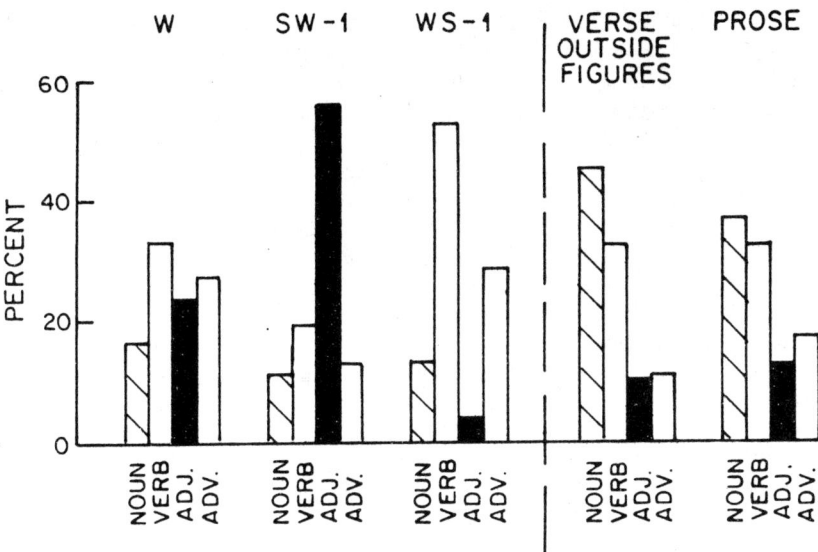

Fig. 7.1. Morphological characteristics of the three main rhythmical figures formed by monosyllables: proportions (in percent) of four main parts of speech (nouns, verbs, adjectives, adverbs; "others" were disregarded). For comparison, the incidences of the same parts of speech in verse outside of rhythmical figures and in prose are shown. Note the marked preference of rhythmical figures for certain parts of speech in contrast with their normal distribution in prose, particularly of WS-1 for verbs and SW-1 for adjectives. Data from Tables 7.2, 7.3, 7.4, 7.6, and 7.7.

The most frequent strongly stressed monosyllabic words in prose are nouns and verbs, with adverbs and particularly adjectives two to three times less frequent (Table 7.7).

In verse minus rhythmical figures, nouns markedly prevail, while verbs occupy second place, and their proportion is identical in verse and prose. Adverbs slightly prevail in prose, otherwise the proportion of adjectives and adverbs in verse minus rhythmical figures and in prose is not dissimilar.

In the rhythmical figures the part-of-speech correlation is warped, but in different figures in different ways. Their part-of-speech deviation from both prose and verse minus rhythmical figures increases from the simplest, most frequent figure, W, through WS-1 to SW-1 (WSW-1 combines features of both WS-1 and SW-1). The only aspect common to all rhythmical figures is their avoidance of nouns. The decrease of nouns in cases of extrametrical stresses on W is accompanied by an increased usage of adjectives and adverbs, by about 10-15% each, as compared with prose and with verse minus rhythmical figures. The ratio of verbs on W is similar to that in prose and verse without

245

rhythmical figures. In general, words on W are those that constitute nonterminal parts of phrases, i.e., verbs, adjectives, and adverbs, while words on the following ictic position, already outside the figure, that usually terminate the phrase are as a rule nouns. Here are typical, proclitic part-of-speech structures that contain the monosyllabic figure W: <u>Fair</u> torch, / <u>burn out</u> \ thy light . . . <u>Blind</u> muffled bawd! / <u>dark</u> harbour \ for defame! Do wounds \ <u>help</u> wounds, / or grief \ <u>help</u> grievous deeds? (Sh.RL 28:1, 110:5, 261:2); <u>Brought</u> hither \ Henry Herford . . . Until the heaven, envying earth's \ <u>good</u> hap; <u>Speak</u> truly, \ on thy knighthood, and thy oath (Sh.RII I,I:3; I,I:23; I,III:14) (see also Chapter 6).

The nouns on W are typically either titles, or attributes in the possessive. They are accentually subordinate to the following or, less frequently, preceding word. Some typical examples: <u>Lord</u> marshal; <u>King</u> Richard; What says <u>King</u> Bolingbroke? ("Richard II"); . . . <u>love's</u> modest snow-white weed; Against <u>love's fire</u> . . . ("Lucrece").

In WS-1 the preference is markedly for verbs, particularly if WS-1 begins the line, while the most avoided part of speech is the adjective. In contrast, the figures SW-1 just as markedly prefer adjectives; verbs and particularly adverbs are much less frequent, an exception being in Shakespeare's dramatic verse, where the proportion of verbs is relatively high, though adjectives still prevail. In Shelley's "The Cenci" the proportion of verbs in SW-1 is also higher than in his narrative poem "Revolt of Islam;" obviously an increased use of verbs in SW-1 is characteristic of dramatic verse. Nouns in SW-1 are usually in the possessive and function as attributes: the figure SW-1 "prefers" syntactically and accentually subordinated elements that do not disrupt the general rhythmical momentum of the iambic verse too strongly.

Some examples of the most typical and less typical part-of-speech realizations of the figures WS-1 and SW-1 are as follows.

WS-1, verbs: the most frequent part of speech in the figure (half of all the cases). The most typical positions of the verbal WS-1 are 1-2 (beginning of the line), next come 5-6 and 7-8 (beginnings of the second "hemistich"): <u>Show me</u> the strumpet that began this stir; But Tarquin's shape \ <u>came in</u> her mind the while (Sh.RL 211:1, 220:3); To stand in thy affairs, \ <u>fall by</u> her side (Sh.Son 151:12).

WS-1, nouns: a less typical part of speech for the figure. The most typical syllabic positions of the nominal WS-1 are again 1-2 and either 5-6 in a more canonized verse, or 7-8 and 3-4 in a looser variant: <u>Lord of</u> my love to whom in vassalage (Sh.Son 26:1); Resembling strong <u>youth in</u> his middle age (Sh.Son 33:14); Your colt's <u>tooth is</u> not cast yet?—No, my lord (Sh.HVIII I,III:48); You'll find a most unfit <u>time to</u> disturb him (Sh.HVIII II,II:60).

SW-1, adjectives: the most frequent part of speech in this figure: When your <u>sweet</u> issue your <u>sweet</u> form should bear (Sh.Son 13:8); At <u>thy great</u> glory, Look not to the ground (Sh.RII III,II:87); They have been absent: 'tis <u>good</u>

speed; fortells (Sh.WT II,III:199); *On her white Breast a sparkling Cross she wore* (P.RL II:7); *For life, in the hot silence of the air* (Shel.RI X,XXIII:5).

Examples of other, less frequent parts of speech in SW-1: *To be death's conquest and make worms thine heir* (Sh.Son 6:14); *Save bidding farewell to so sweet a guest* (Sh.RII II,II:8); *Though in the trade of war I have slain men* (Sh.Oth I,II:1); *Slide giddily as the world reels . . . My God!* (Shel.C III,I:12); *Or that men gave it him, to swell his fame* (A.SR 614); *And they stood wide with horror; and he seized* (A.SR 699).

The trisyllabic figure WSW-1 combines WS-1 and SW-1; this combination is also seen in the morphological structure of WSW-1. The most frequent part of speech in the first W is the verb, in the second W the adjective. The scheme below shows the ratio of verbs and adjectives in the first (a) and the second (b) non-ictic positions of the figure WSW-1 (the number of words filling each W separately is taken for 100%).

Author and work	Wa, verbs	Wb, adjectives
Shakespeare, "Lucrece"	68.0	48.0
Sonnets	50.0	50.0
Dramas	62.4	30.3
Pope, "The Rape of the Lock"	61.0	65.0
Shelley, "The Revolt of Islam"	69.0	69.0
"The Cenci"	66.0	34.0
Arnold, "Sohrab and Rustum"	50.0	50.0

A verb is usually second in frequency in Wb. In Shakespeare's dramas, however, verbs occupy not the second, but the first place in Wb (almost 42% of the cases), while adjectives come only second. There is also a decrease in the percentage of adjectives in the second W in "The Cenci". The same tendency was observed in SW-1. An increased use of verbs in SW-1 and in the second W of WSW-1 seems to be typical of dramatic verse. Here are some examples of the two typical morphological structures of the figure WSW-1:

(a) **verb + adjective**: *Feeds thy light flame . . . Pluck the keen teeth . . .* (Sh.Son 1:6, 19:3); *Spreads his black Wings . . . Clapp'd his glad Wings . . .* (P.RL IV:88, V:54); *Lull'd by soft Zephyrs . . . Fed with soft Dedication . . .* (P.DA 42,233); *Mock the fierce peal . . . Wound his long arms . . .* (Shel.RI VI,XLV:7; VII,IX:7); *Slake their parch'd throats . . . Rent the tough plates . . .* (A.SR 166, 493).

(b) **verb + verb**: *Rouse him, make after him . . . Seems to cast water . . . Cough, or cry hem . . .* (Sh.Oth I,I:69; II,I:14; IV,II:29); *Shall we go, coz? . . . I'll ask him what he would . . . Did you call, sir?* (Sh.AYLI I,II:241,246).

Here are examples of less typical morphological combinations in WSW-1:

Sol thro' white curtains . . . (P.RL I:13); *White, with eyes closed* (A.SR 849); *Sweets with sweets war not* . . . (Sh.Son 8:2).

7.4.1.2 Consider now disylllabic and trisyllabic figures containing a disyllabic word. The frequency of the four main notional (lexical) parts of speech with the accentual-syllabic structure ($\perp -$) that form the figure WS- 2 is shown in Table 7.5. Cases of WS-2 formed by disyllabic prepositions or conjunctions were disregarded because these words have practically no sentence accent. Table 7.8 shows the proportion of disyllabic non-oxytonic nouns, verbs, adjectives, and adverbs in verse without rhythmical figures, while Table 7.9 shows the part-of-speech correlation in prose.

In prose the dominating notional words of the ($\perp -$) structure are nouns and verbs. Shakespeare's prose is slightly more "verbal" than that of the other authors: this reflects the general features of dramatic verse and the stylistic particulars of certain dramatis personae: prose usually belongs to the lower characters, such as villains, rogues, and clowns, who use fewer adjectives and more verbs in their dynamic vernacular texts.

In verse without rhythmical figures nouns markedly prevail. The frequency of adjectives is much greater, almost double that of prose. It was shown earlier (Tarlinskaja 1984) that the iambic meter actively "selects" adjectives of the ($\perp -$) structure; these adjectives constitute most of the "feminine" word boundaries in the iambic texts. Therefore the number of verbs, and particularly adverbs, of the form ($\perp -$) is on the whole lower in verse than in prose. In the rhythmical figure WS- 2, conversely, verbs prevail almost everywhere, particularly in Shakespeare's non-dramatic verse. Their lower frequency in Shakespeare's dramas, accompanied by an increase in nouns, results from the abundance of nouns in the vocative; for example: *Cousin of Hereford, what dost thou object; Marshal, demand of yonder champion; Harry of Hereford, Lancaster and Derby; Norfolk, for thee remains a heavier doom* (Sh.RII I,I:28; I,III:6; I,III:35; I,III:148). Prevalence of nouns in the figure WS-2 in Arnold's "Sohrab and Rustum" also reflects the poet's extensive use of the exotic proper names of his two main characters: *Sohrab alone, he slept not* . . . *Rustum he loves no more* . . . (A.SR 5,226), and so on. The data from Pope's verse are insufficient to draw a conclusion for the figure WS-2.

The prevalence of disyllabic verbs in WS-2 is all the more remarkable, because disyllabic verbs of the non-oxytonic form ($\perp -$) are as a rule less frequent in prose and in verse as a whole than the oxytonic ($- \perp$) form (cf. Kroeber 1958:312-313, Vanvik 1961:55). In the prose from Shakespeare's dramas the correlation between the two forms of disyllabic verbs, ($\perp -$) and ($- \perp$), is 41 and 59%. In the eighteenth-century prose, verbs of the ($\perp -$) form constitute only 12-16% of non-oxytonic disyllabic nouns, verbs, adjectives, and adverbs, while among these same parts of speech of the oxytonic ($- \perp$) structure, verbs reach 60-64% of the total. In Pope's verse the contrast is even stronger: verbs constitute only 7% among ($\perp -$) forms, and 73% among

Table 7.5

Part-of-speech Correlation Between Disyllabic Strongly Stressed Words Forming the Figures WS-2 (in percent of the total)

Part of speech	Shakespeare			Pope	Shelley		Arnold
	Lucrece	Sonnets	Dramas	Rape Lock	Islam	Cenci	Sohrab
Nouns	19.6 (21)	15.4 (18)	33.4 (112)	44.1 (15)	29.6 (53)	29.3 (53)	40.5 (30)
Verbs	58.9 (63)	57.3 (67)	38.2 (128)	11.8 (4)	43.0 (77)	41.4 (75)	32.4 (24)
Adjectives	13.1 (14)	16.2 (19)	13.1 (44)	17.1 (6)	17.3 (31)	18.8 (34)	12.2 (9)
Adverbs	7.5 (8)	10.3 (12)	10.4 (35)	20.6 (7)	10.1 (18)	9.7 (17)	14.9 (11)
Others	0.9 (1)	0.8 (1)	4.9 (13)	5.9 (2)	--	1.1 (2)	--
Total	107	117	335	34	179	181	74

Table 7.6

Correlation Between Monosyllabic Nouns, Verbs, Adjectives, and Adverbs in Verse, Outside Disyllabic or Polysyllabic Rhythmical Figures (600 lines from each text; "The Rape of the Lock" the whole text) (in percent of the total)

Part of speech	Shakespeare			Pope	Shelley		Arnold
	Lucrece	Sonnets	Dramas	Rape Lock	Islam	Cenci	Sohrab
Nouns	43.4	43.2	42.0	51.5	51.7	41.1	41.6
Verbs	32.4	31.5	34.6	29.1	28.5	37.5	37.8
Adjectives	11.0	12.6	9.4	8.1	10.9	9.7	8.7
Adverbs	13.2	12.7	14.0	11.3	8.9	11.7	11.8
Total	1463	1278	4912	2087	1403	1179	987

($-\perp$) forms. These data show that the preference of verbs by WS-2 is extremely specific and deviates strongly from English speech.

What morphological forms of verbs prevail in WS-2? It is the <u>participles</u>, mainly the present participles. They constitute 80% of disyllabic verbs in the figure WS-2 in "Lucrece", 90% of WS-2 verbs in the Sonnets, and over 50% of WS-2 verbs in Shakespeare's dramas. The explanation for the lesser number in the dramas lies in a more simple syntax of the dramatic verse: most participles in Shakespeare's non-dramatic verse are adverbial modifiers of attending circumstances, which appear in longer and more complicated syntactic periods of his rhymed poems. All the four cases of WS-2 verbs in Pope's 1000 lines are present participles; this morphological verb form constitutes almost 64% of WS-2 verbs in Shelley's "Islam" and over 50% of the WS-2

Table 7.7

Incidence of Monosyllabic Nouns, Verbs, Adjectives and Adverbs in Prose (in percent of the total)

Part of Speech	Shakespeare Othello and Winter's Tale	Swift Gulliver's Travels	Fielding Tom Jones	Austen Pride and Prejudice
Nouns	35.9	43.8	36.6	33.2
Verbs	38.1	27.1	31.5	35.0
Adjectives	9.3	14.9	13.6	14.6
Adverbs	16.7	14.2	18.3	17.2
Totals	2562	930	906	834

Table 7.8

Correlation Between Disyllabic Nouns, Verbs, Adjectives, and Adverbs of the [́ _] Form in Verse, Outside Rhythmical Figures (600 lines from each text) (in percent of the total)

Parts of speech	Shakespeare			Shelley		Arnold
	Lucrece	Sonnets	Dramas	Islam	Cenci	Sohrab
Nouns	49.4	46.0	55.0	47.3	50.8	51.6
Verbs	11.4	15.6	10.5	9.1	13.4	10.4
Adjectives	34.7	34.8	28.0	40.2	26.4	33.1
Adverbs	4.5	7.4	6.5	3.4	9.4	4.9
Total	571	526	2201	569	478	384

verbs in "The Cenci". Similarly to Shakespeare, the frequency of present participles in the function of the adverbial modifier is lower in Shelley's dramatic than in his non-dramatic verse: another genre feature on the morphological level. Participles (-ing forms) constitute 70% of disyllabic verbs in the figure WS-2 in Arnold's "Sohrab and Rustum". Here are some typical examples from "The Rape of Lucrece":

Reckoning his fortune at such high-proud rate (3:5)
Braving compare, disdainfully did sting (6:5)

Table 7.9

Correlation Between Disyllabic Nouns, Verbs, Adjectives, and Adverbs of the [́ _] Form in Prose (in percent of the total)

Part of speech	Shakespeare	Swift	Fielding	Austen
	"Othello" and "Winter's Tale"	"Gulliver's Travels"	"Tom Jones"	"Pride and Prejudice"
Nouns	58.3	52.0	53.3	59.6
Verbs	13.6	14.0	16.7	12.2
Adjectives	16.8	22.0	19.1	14.0
Adverbs	11.1	12.0	10.9	14.2
Total	374	636	684	844

<u>Proving</u> from world's minority their right (10:4)
<u>Hiding</u> base sin in plaits of majesty (14:2)

Conversely, in the prose text of "Othello" out of 51 disyllabic verbs of the non-oxytonic (⊥−) structure there are only 7 present participles, about 14%. These data show once more that the rhythmical figure WS-2 actively "selects" the morphological form of present participles.[2] The compositional function of this morphological verb form is discussed in 7.4.2.

The <u>figure SW-2</u>, as it was mentioned in 7.2.2, is practically outside the metrical norm of English iambic verse (cf. Bjorklund 1978:119). The highest number of SW-2 was discovered in Shelley's "The Cenci", but there are only 19 while the total number of WS-2 is 181, a proportion of 9.5 to 90.5%. If we compare the number of SW-2 with the number of only non-initial WS-2, the absolute figures are 19 and 51, or 27 and 73%, respectively. This correlation, interestingly enough, corresponds to the correlation between (−⊥) and (⊥−) verb forms in "The Cenci" excluding the rhythmical figures, which is 22.5 and 77.5%, respectively. So Shelley's use of verbs in his figures SW-2 and WS-2 is about the same as that in his verse in general. At least in "The Cenci" Shelley does not specifically avoid the figure SW-2; but "The Cenci" <u>is</u> an exception, and the other poets analyzed undoubtedly avoided the figure SW-2. The exceptional cases of SW-2 in Shakespeare's verse are practically always formed by verbs with the accentually ambivalent prefixes <u>in</u>- and <u>un</u>-; these verbs probably had an accentual variant with the stress on the first syllable (cf. Kökeritz 1974:33,337-338,393). Other words infrequently used by Shakespeare in SW-2 are verbs, such as <u>become</u>, <u>beguile</u>, <u>begin</u>, and <u>deserve</u>, and adjectives, such as <u>supreme</u>, <u>extreme</u>, <u>forlorn</u>, <u>obscure</u>, and <u>divine</u>. Most of the latter are of foreign, primarily Romance origin; their non-native etymology probably "meant an instability of stress and allowed for recession of accent" (Bjorklund 1978:328). Note what Kökeritz wrote about these words: "Such words when adopted into English had a system of accentuation other than that of the native Germanic words. The inevitable conflict between two different stress-systems gave rise to considerable vacillation in ME and NE, which eventually led to a reaccentuation of many Romance words according to native English principles, though others retained their original stress or continued to waver between the two systems. This accentual instability, still noticeable in a good many Romance words, was quite marked in Shakespeare's English" (Kökeritz 1953:333). Some people would use non-oxytonic rhythmical variants of such words even today. The probable stress-shifts in verbs and adjectives relieves the rhythm-breaking effect of the figures SW-2 in Shakespeare's verse.

Cases of the <u>figure WSW-2</u> are relatively infrequent; there are only nine cases in "The Rape of Lucrece", only 8 cases in all of Shakespeare's Sonnets, 15 in the whole of "Richard II", 12 in "Othello", and 10 in "The Winter's Tale". There are only 7 cases in the 2547 lines analyzed of Shelley's "Islam" and only 12 cases in all of "The Cenci". Undoubtedly it is their scarcity that makes WSW-2 so hard to generalize. Their second W is treated much like that in the figure WSW-1: the second W "prefers" adjectives and verbs. The first element of the WSW-2, a disyllabic word on WS, displays no noticeable preference. However, if WS is a noun, it tends to be a vocative or an exclamation, particularly in dramas; if a verb, it tends to be an imperative or a present participle; the preferred adverbs are ever, never, and only. Some examples: *"Lucrece", quoth he* . . . *"Daughter, dear daughter* . . . (Sh.RL 74:1, 251:1); *Treason! foul treason!* (Sh.RII V,II:72); *Gilding pale streams* . . . *Uttering bare truth* . . . (Sh.Son 33:4, 69:4); *Never lack'd gold* . . . ; . . . *never loved Cassio* (Sh.Oth II,I:151; V,II:62).

More infrequent morphological types of WSW-2: *Roses have thorns* . . . *Cupid laid by* . . . (Sh.Son 35:2, 153:1); *Chloe stepp'd in* . . . *Nourish'd two Locks* . . . (P.RL V:68, II:20); *Cruel, cold, formal man* . . . (Shel.C V,IV:108).

7.4.2 Syntax

We now will examine recurring syntactic structures typical of the notional parts of speech forming various rhythmical figures. We will also look for cases relevant for a specific intonation potential of various figures, e.g., presence or absence of a syntactic break (implying a pause) before, after, or in the middle of the figure, or a specific tone with which they might be articulated. Some parts of speech are analyzed in greater detail; these are verbs and nouns: their various syntactic functions are highly relevant both for their articulation with a certain intonation, and for the semantic load each rhythmical figure is capable of bearing. Adjectives, on the other hand, so numerous in the figures W, SW-1, WSW-1 and WSW-2 (the second W of the trisyllabic figures), are almost exclusively used in the function of a prepositional attribute and therefore require no specific syntactic study. Adverbs are as a rule also proclitically tied to the following word with a strong ictic stress; besides, they are the least semantically loaded elements of the figures, most of them being "empty" words such as so, too, thus, and then.

7.4.2.1 Consider the syntactic functions, in their relation to the possible degree of stress, of monosyllabic nouns and verbs on W in "The Rape of Lucrece" and "Richard II". These words were conventionally differentiated into two categories: (1) syntactically connected with, or subordinate to, words on the adjacent ictic positions, and (2) syntactically more or less independent of the adjacent words. In the first case accentual subordination was considered more plausible than in the second.

Nouns on W syntactically connected with the following word and belonging with it in the same phrase are relatively frequent; they are mainly appositions and attributes clinging proclitically to the following word and liable to accentual weakening (see Chapter 6); examples are: *Lord marshal*; *King Richard*; *King Bolingbroke*; *A king, woe's slave* . . . ; *Against love's fire fear's frost hath dissolution* (Sh.RL 51:5). Nouns on W syntactically connected with the preceding word of the same phrase are less frequent (cf. Chapter 6); they are usually modified by the word on the preceding ictic position and cling to the latter enclitically, as in *Such shadows are the weak brain's forgeries* (Sh.RL 66:5); *The wise Man's Passion, and the vain Man's Toast* (P.RL V:10). This type of subordination, as it were, from the right to the left, does not occur in the verse of all English poets in the same quantity; as it was already noted in Chapter 6, it is more typical of Fletcher than of Shakespeare, of Shakespeare than of Milton, and of Byron than of Shelley. Some more examples are: *To breathe a full hour longer; not a thought! To let his foul soul out.—Here I swear it; To press my poor heart thus. Can I believe* (Beaumont and Fletcher, "The Maid's Tragedy" IV,I:163,167,210); *To give me refuge for a few hours, well—; Should aid each other.—It is a damn'd world, sir* (Byron, "Werner" III,I:2,42).

A noun on W followed by an element with which the noun has no syntactic connection, or by a predicate, should theoretically retain a strong phrasal accent (subject and predicate belong to different phrases and may not be accentually subordinate to each other). If, however, a noun on W is preceded by an attribute on S, the noun seems liable to an accentual subordination to the preceding attribute, as in *The wolf hath seized the prey, the poor lamb cries* (Sh.RL 97:5) (cf. Chapter 6). That is why a noun on the anacrusis is usually more strongly stressed than in midline: it is not preceded by any attribute with an ictic stress; cf. *Birds never limed no secret bushes fear* and *The adder hisses where the sweet birds sing* (Sh.RL 13:4, 125:3).

Nouns believed to be less liable to accentual subordination and full or partial loss of stress belong to the following general syntactic categories. (1) In an isolated position, for example, in direct address, in cases of homogeneous sentence elements ("enumeration"), or when followed by a predicative apposition or attributive group; for example: *Boy, let me see the writing* (Sh.RII V,II:69); *Wrath, envy, treason, rape, and murder's rages* (Sh.RL 130:6); *Dogs, easily won to fawn on any man!* (Sh.RII III,II:130). (2) When preceded or followed by words with which the noun is not tied syntactically; cf. two combinations of words: *blue blood* (blue is an attribute to the following noun), and *slow time* (slow is a modifier to the verb following the noun time): *Her blue blood changed to black in every vein* (Sh.RL 208:5), and *Let him have time to mark how slow \ time \ goes* (Sh.RL 142:3). The noun on W in the first example seems to be more liable to an accentual weakening than in the second, where it is not syntactically connected with the preceding word; the strong stress on the word time, not weakened for syntactic reasons, undoubtedly plays a semantic role ("the slow passage of time"). (3) When followed by a predicate or predicative element; for example: *Pain pays the income of each precious thing* (Sh.RL 48:5); *Joy absent, grief is present for that time* (Sh.RII I,III:259).

Cases where nouns on W are liable to a possible weakening of phrasal accent prevail both in "Lucrece" and "Richard II", but in "Lucrece" more markedly so: nouns that for syntactic reasons may weaken their stress constitute about 75% of all cases of W in "Lucrece" and less than 64% in "Richard II". Already these figures begin to suggest that the rhythm in the poem is smoother than in the play. This difference is caused not only by the number of nouns on W, but by their syntactic functions.

A similar phenomenon is observed with <u>verbs</u> on W. As a rule, verbs on W are syntactically linked with the <u>following</u> word marked by an ictic stress. The most typical cases are: (a) verb + adverb (adverbial modifier): *But who cómes hḗre? . . .* ; (b) verb + noun (object): *Ádd prŏof into mine armour . . .* ; and (c) verb + adjective (the verb is either part of a double predicate or approaches a link element in a nominal predicate): *The soul hŏlds dĕar . . . ; . . . màke pále our cheek*. Both in "Lucrece" and "Richard II" the three cases cover over 70% of verbs on W. Verbs in these cases are proclitic components of a two-word syntactic combination within the same phrase and are probably liable, in different degrees, to some weakening or loss of phrasal accent. A different approach to two-word syntactic combinations of the type verb + adverb is observed in later, Jacobean verse: the adverb often is placed on W and is enclitically subordinate to the preceding word: *I gŏ thùs from thee, and will never cease*; *It must not bĕ sò. Stay. Mine eyes would tell* (Beaumont and Fletcher, "The Maid's Tragedy" III,II:203,205); cf. *And all the fellowship I hŏld nòw with him*; *To gĭve ùp willingly that noble title*; *They will'd me sǎy sò, madam.—Pray their graces To cŏme nèar. What can be their business?* (Shakespeare, "Henry VIII" III,I:121,140,18,19) (see also Chapter 6).

Imperatives syntactically isolated from the following word are considered more strongly stressed than verbs not isolated from the following element on S; cf. *Go bear this lance to Thomas, Duke of Norfolk* and *Go, Bushy, to the Earl of Wiltshire straight* (Sh.RII I,III:103; II,I:215). Notional verbs on W in the function of a predicate followed by a subject on S are also believed to be strongly stressed; e.g., *Sits Sin, to seize the souls that wander by him* (Sh.RL 126:7).

Imperatives are, predictably, more characteristic of dramatic verse: over 40% of all monosyllabic notional verbs on W in "Richard II" are imperatives, while in "Lucrece" only about 13% are. On the whole, cases with a syntactic break after the verb, particularly in the imperative, are more typical of "Richard II" than of "Lucrece:" 12% and 5% of all the notional verbs on W, correspondingly, are followed by a syntactic break. We discover again that syntax resulting in particular intonation contours and phrasing adds more smoothness to the stressed elements on W in the poem than in the drama.

7.4.2.2 What are the <u>syntactic word combinations typical of the disyllabic rhythmical figure SW-1</u>? The stressed word on W is preceded by a loss of stress on S, while the stress on W is followed by another stress, on the adjacent S; this clash of back-to-back stresses considerably increases the "rhythm-breaking" effect of the figure. This explains why, compared to the monosyllabic figure W, the disyllabic SW-1 has a much lower frequency of nouns and particularly verbs (both parts of speech tend to have a strong phrasal stress) and an increased incidence of adjectives (which usually are syntactically and accentually subordinate to the following word with an ictic stress). The elements occupying the W in the SW-1, even if they are not adjectives or possessive nouns, usually occur in the non-terminal positions of a phrase; they are, for example, an adverb qualifying a verb, or a verb followed by an object or an adverbial modifier. The elements on W tend to be accentually subordinate to the following word with an ictic stress. Cases with no syntactic and accentual subordination are rare; they are usually a noun on W plus a verb on the following ictic position. Their syntactic functions are as a rule <u>subject + predicate</u> (see below). It is this structure that is the most strongly loaded semantically (see Chapter 8). Some examples: *Heaven stops the nose at it, and the moon winks* (Sh.Oth IV,II:78); *I have tremor cordis on me: my heart dances* (Sh.WT I,II:110); *And his hoofs ground the rock to fire and dust* (Shel.RI VI,XX:1).

The syntactic functions of <u>adjectives</u> are clear—they are usually prepositional attributes. The most typical syntactic structures of <u>verbs</u> in SW-1 are three: (1) predicate plus adverbial modifier, or the adverb <u>not</u>: (2) the verbal part of a compound predicate plus its adjective component; (3) predicate plus an object or, less frequently, a subject. (In cases like *The strings of a known sorrow . . .* the participle was considered an adjective.) Examples: (1) *Well, do it, and be brief; I will walk by* (Sh.Oth V,II:31); *The armies are drawn out, and stand at gaze* (A.SR 210); (2) *Honest Iago, that look'st dead with grieving* (Sh.Oth II,III:173); *And they stood wide with horror; and he seized* (A.SR 699); (3) *For I fear Cassio with my night-cap too* (Sh.Oth II,I:310); *So said he, and dropp'd Sohrab's hand, and left* (A.SR 94). In the verse of Shakespeare and the other poets, the correlation of these prevailing structures is not dissimilar. Here are the proportions of the three verb structures in SW-1 in all of Shakespeare's material and in Shelley's "The Cenci" and "Islam":

Structures	Shakespeare	Shelley
V + Adv	38.0	40.2
V + Adj	21.0	16.8
V + N	40.0	38.3
Others	1.0	5.7
Total (cases)	100% (261)	100% (107)

The main difference is a higher proportion of V + Adj in Shakespeare's texts and of "others" in Shelley's verse; verbs in V + Adj are verbal parts of a nominal or double predicate: elements that tend to weaken or lose their phrasal stress; "others" are mainly cases with a syntactic break after the verb. The quantitative divergence shows a difference in approach to the figure SW-1 by Shakespeare and Shelley: the latter displayed more freedom in breaking the prevailing rhythmical inertia with verbal figures SW-1 than did Shakespeare. Some examples of a strong syntactic break after the phrase-terminal verb in SW-1: *I'll see before I doubt; when I doubt, prove* (Sh.Oth III,III:193); *Her mad looks to the lightning, and cried: "Eat!"* (Shel.RI VI,LII:2). Verbs followed by a syntactic break are exceptional for the monosyllabic figure W (12% of all the verbs on W in "Richard II", and only 5% in "Lucrece"); and they are even less frequent in the SW-1: one case in the whole of "Richard II", and one in "Othello" (about 1% of the verbs in SW-1). Thus, a close syntactic link with the following word with an ictic stress appears to be much more rhythmically relevant for the stressed element in SW-1 than in W.

In combinations like stone seat I conditionally consider the first element an adjective, so nouns used as attributes are mostly possessive. The two most characteristic syntactic structures of SW-1 with a noun on W are: (1) noun-attribute, and (2) noun-subject, with its verb-predicate on the following S (less frequently the noun and verb are elements of a complex object). It was assumed that noun-attributes or appositives are susceptible to accentual weakening, while noun-subjects are fully stressed. This means that nouns in SW-1 in the syntactic structure subject + predicate disrupt the general rhythmical momentum more strongly than in other syntactic structures. The correlation between the two syntactic functions of nouns in SW-1, those of an attribute and of a subject, changed both within Shakespeare's canon, and in nineteenth-century verse compared to Shakespeare's. In all genres of Shakespeare's early works nouns used as attributes or appositives prevail; nouns as subjects are infrequent. In all of the Sonnets, for example, there are 23 cases of noun-attributes in the possessive to 9 cases of nouns as subjects (62% and 24% of all nouns in the figure SW-1, respectively), and in "Richard II" the correlation is 50% to 12%. In "Othello" and "The Winter's Tale", however, the correlation changes: the number of noun-attributes equals that of the subjects; examples:

> May the winds blow till they have waken'd death!
> Heaven stops the nose at it, and the moon winks;
> When your eyes roll so. Why I should fear I know not
>   (Sh.Oth II,I:185; IV,II:78; V,II:41)
> I have tremor cordis on me: my heart dances;
> But my heart bleeds; and most accursed am I;
> And his pond fished by his next neighbour . . . ;
> Whiles other men have gates, and those gates opened
>   (Sh.WT I,II:110; III,III:52; I,II:195; I,II:197)

Here is a rare example of a phrase-terminal noun on W, separated by a syntactic break from a verb on the following S:

>   With the Moor, say'st thou? Who would be a father!
>   (Sh.Oth I,I:165)

In Shelley's SW-1 the frequency of nouns coupled with a verb is higher than in Shakespeare's; in "The Cenci" the number of noun-attributes and noun-subjects in SW-1 is equal, in "Islam" the structure noun + verb prevails even more strongly (56% of all nouns in SW-1 are followed by a verb with an ictic stress), while in Arnold's "Sohrab and Rustum", where the figure SW-1 is particularly frequent, the structure noun + verb (usually subject + predicate) embraces 82% of all nouns in this rhythmical figure! Some examples are:

> When the church fell and crushed him to a mummy;
> If a priest wins her. Oh, fair Beatrice!
> Slide giddily as the world reels . . . My God!
> And holding his breath, died . . .
> (Shel.C I,III:60; II,II:128; III,I:12; V,II:183)

(notice a syntactic seam between the object and the following predicate in the last example);

> Parted and quivered; the tears ceased to break;
> Which thy breath kindled, Power of holier name!
> Such were my thoughts, when the tide gan to flow;
> And the winds bore me—through the darkness spread
> (Shel.RI I,XVIII:3; I,XXXII:5; I,XXII:7; III,V:4)
> When the frost flowers the whiten window-pane
> Lithe as a gliding snake, and the club came;
> And then the gloom dispersed, and the wind fell;
> And his knees totter'd, and he smote his hand
> (A.SR 36,418,522,662)

It is obvious that the nineteenth-century poets handled the figure SW-1 with greater confidence, and they made a conscious use of the syntactic structure subject + predicate, with the subject filling the W of the figure SW-1. The semantic potential of this rhythmic-syntactic structure is discussed in Chapter 8.

7.4.2.3 Consider now the syntactic combinations typical of the disyllabic rhythmical figure WS-1 (Table 7.10.). The most frequent part of speech here, as we remember, is the verb. The typical syntactic functions of the verb in the figure analyzed are three: (1) predicate or its component; (2) in the form of participles—postpositional (predicative) attribute or adverbial modifier; (3) imperatives. Some examples: (1) *Ah, yet doth beauty, like a dial-hand, Steal from his figure, and no pace perceived* (Sh.Son 104:9-10); *Think'st thou I'ld make a life of jealousy* (Sh.Oth III,III:179); (2) *For there it is, cracked in a hundred shivers* (Sh.RII IV,I:289); *We passed the isles borne by the wind and*

Table 7.10

Incidence (in percent) of the Syntactic Functions of Monosyllabic Verbs in the Figure WS-1

Functions	Shakespeare			Pope	Shelley		Arnold
	Lucrece	Sonnets	Dramas	Rape Lock	Islam	Cenci	Sohrab
Predicate, direct word order	50.8	28.8	22.1	50.1	72.3	27.9	58.1
Predicate, inverted word order	4.7	20.0	16.0	7.9	3.4	22.4	3.2
Adverbial modifier	15.9	10.0	8.1	28.9	19.3	8.2	16.1
Imperative	28.6	41.2	53.8	13.1	5.0	41.5	22.6
Total	63	80	393	38	119	147	31

storm (Shel.RI VIII,III:1); (3) <u>Call him</u> *a slanderous coward, and a villain*; <u>Call</u> <u>it</u> *not patience, Gaunt, it is despair* (Sh.RII I,I:61; I,II:29).

The difference between authors and, particularly, genres is marked by the syntactic variants of figure WS-1 much more strongly than SW-1. Imperatives are, not surprisingly, more typical of dramatic verse, and they are more frequent in Shakespeare's dramas than in Shelley's "The Cenci". What is unexpected is the <u>increase of imperatives</u> from Shakespeare's earlier to later plays (a more colloquial style? the peculiarities of plot?); the percentage of the imperatives from the total number of verbs in WS-1 in Shakespeare's plays is as follows: "Richard II" 47.3%, "As You Like It" 51.2%, "Othello" 58.1%, "The Winter's Tale" 60%. Imperatives are in general very markedly tied to the rhythmical figure WS-1. In Shakespeare's "Winter's Tale", for example, imperative forms comprise 60% of monosyllabic verbs in the WS-1, but only 13% of monosyllabic verbs outside the rhythmical figures (57 to 430 in 600 lines), in Shelley's "The Cenci" imperatives constitute 41.5% of monosyllabic verbs in the WS-1, but only 8.4% of all monosyllabic verbs outside rhythmical figures (37 to 442 in 600 lines).

Non-dramatic verse tends to avoid imperatives. Our texts arranged in increasing order of imperatives in the figure WS-1 form the following sequence: "The Revolt of Islam" 5.0%; "The Rape of the Lock" 13.1%; "Sohrab and Rustum" 22.6%; "The Rape of Lucrece" 28.6%; Shakespeare's Sonnets 41.2%; "The Cenci" 41.5%; Shakespeare's plays 53.8%. Long narrative poems are at one pole and dramatic verse at the opposite, with lyrical poems (the sonnets) taking an intermediate place, unexpectedly closer to the dramatic verse than to the narratives.

Predicate verbs in the direct word order occurring in the line-initial WS-1 are not phrase-initial: their subject remains in the preceding line. The enjambment has an emphasizing function—it underlines the rhematic role of the predicate. For example: (. . . *the old man's* sword) *Falls from my withered hand . . . (Will* none *among this noble company)* Check the *abandoned villain? . . . (And the calm innocent* sleep *in which he lay,)* Quelled me. *Indeed, indeed, I cannot do it* (Shel.C I,I:128; I,III:92; IV,III:13).

Predicates in the line-initial WS-1 in inverted order usually form questions. Their incidence, similarly with imperatives, is highest in the Sonnets and the dramatic verse of both poets, and lowest in the narrative poems.

Thus the syntactic functions of monosyllabic verbs in the figure WS-1 clearly differentiate the three genres analyzed: narrative poems and dramatic verse are markedly opposed, while the lyrical verse (the sonnets) occupies a place between the two, but is much closer to dramatic verse.

The most typical syntactic functions of line-initial nouns are: vocative (particularly in dramatic verse) and subject; for example: *Sir, she can turn and turn, and yet go on* (Sh.Oth IV,I:257); *Suns of the world may stain when heaven's sun staineth* (Sh.Son 33:14). If the line-initial WS-1 contains a mid-phrase noun (cases of an enjambment) the noun is often an object with a strong rhematic function: (. . . *I thought I saw)* Blood on *the face of one . . . What if 'twere fancy?* (Shel.C V,IV:124-125).

Midline WS-1 incorporating a noun have, as mentioned above, two rhythmical-syntactic variants. In the first variant the noun begins a phrase; a syntactic break occurs before the noun on W; for example: *Mock with thy tickling beam \ eyes that are sleeping* (S.RL 156:5); *Sticks me at heart . . . / Sir, you have well deserved* (Sh.AYLI I,II:235); *Behold her topped?—Death anddamnation! O!*; *Good night, good night. /* Heaven me *such uses send* (Sh.Oth III,III:398; IV,III:107).

In the other syntactic variant the noun on W is a phrase-final element, and the unstressed monosyllable on the following S begins a new phrase; a strong syntactic break occurs after the noun on W; for example: (1) *Swear to thy blind* soul / that *I was thy "Will"* (Sh.Son 136:2); (2) *Better becomes the grey* cheeks \ of *the east* (Sh.Son 132:6). The strength of the syntactic juncture between the noun on W and the following strongly stressed word varies; it depends on the type of syntactic relationship between the elements. For example, the break between the noun and the following syntactic element is stronger in (1) than in (2): in the first case the juncture separates the main sentence and a subordinate clause, while in the second it falls between elements of the same sentence. In both cases, however, the noun on W is more strongly tied to the preceding word, its attribute, with which it forms a syntactic micro-phrase.

The non-phrase-initial syntactic variant of WS-1 is typical of only certain epochs of English poetic tradition and of particular authors. As already shown in Chapter 6, enclitic rhythmical-syntactic phrases are especially characteristic of Jacobean poets, particularly of Fletcher, while in certain other epochs this rhythmic-syntactic variant is almost completely avoided, e.g., Classicism (cf. Kiparsky 1977, Hayes 1983).

Line-internal WS-1 figures containing a noun typically appear in positions 5-6 (in a more canonized verse with a 4+6 or 5+5 bipartite structure and a "dip" in position 6) or 7-8 and, less frequently, 3-4 (in a looser verse form with a "dip" in position 8 and either a bipartite composition 6+4 or 7+3 or no bipartite segmentation at all). Some examples of line-internal non-phrase-initial figures WS-1 are as follows:

3-4:
The sixth part of his substance, to be levied;
(Sh.HVIII I,II:58)

The wild sea of my conscience, I did steer
(Sh.HVIII II,IV:200)

A French song and a fiddle has no fellow
(Sh.HVIII I,III:41)

5-6:
Resembling strong youth in his middle age;
(Sh.Son 7:6)

That did my ripe thoughts in my brain unhearse
(Sh.Son 86:3)

As testy sick men, when their deaths be near
(Sh.Son 140:7)

7-8:
He stretched him, and with one hand on his dagger
(Sh.HVIII I,III:204)

I would not be a young count in your way
(Sh.HVIII II,III:41)

Madam, you wrong the king's love with these fears
(Sh.HVIII III,I:81)

The distribution (in percentage) of non-phrase-initial nominal WS(W)-1 in positions 3-4, 5-6, and 7-8 in Shakespeare's Sonnets[3] and "Shakespeare's" and "Fletcher's" scenes of "Henry VIII" is:

	Positions				Total No.
	3–4	5–6	7–8	10–11	
Sonnets	—	66.7	33.3	—	21
"H VIII", Shak.	43.8	6.2	43.8	6.2	16
"H VIII", Flet.	41.0	33.3	25.7	—	39

The tendencies in a more rigid and in a looser verse form are obviously different: the figures WS-1 coupled with a monosyllabic noun on W preceded by an attribute and followed by an unstressed monosyllable on S concentrate (but not in a hundred per cent of the cases!) in positions 5-6 of the Sonnets with their more rigid form and a "dip" in position 6, but shift to positions 3-4 and 7-8 in Shakespeare's scenes of "Henry VIII". This change mirrors the looser iambic form and the "dip" in stress on position 8 of Shakespeares' later verse. Note that the proportion of WS-1 in positions 5-6 is greater in Fletcher's scenes than in Shakespeare's; this fact reflects a more frequent 4+6 or 5+5 bipartite line variant in Fletcher's than in Shakespeare's scenes, confirmed also by the general stress profile data of the two portions (cf. 3.1.1).

In this connection I cannot bypass a strong and sweeping statement made by Beth Bjorklund (1978:180): ". . . the adjective-noun sequence in the even-odd relationship [i.e., "strong-weak"] is limited to positions 4-5 [i.e., is non-occurring in 2-3, 6-7, 8-9, and 10-11]". This conclusion is by no means general for the English iambic pentameter, even for its more rigid variant, and definitely does not apply to a looser iambic pentameter form.

7.4.2.4 The most typical morphological components of the trisyllabic figure WSW-1 are: verb on the first W plus adjective on the second W; less frequent is another verb in the second W (in Shakespeare's dramas). The figure WSW-1 rhythmically, morphologically, and syntactically incorporates both WS-1 and SW-1. The verb on the first W is usually a predicate or an imperative, while the adjective on the second W is an attribute: *Feed'st thy light flame . . . Pluck the keen teeth . . .* (Sh.Son 1:6; 19:3). In cases of two verbs on both weak positions, their syntactic functions typically are: components of a question or of an imperative, or two independent imperatives; for example: *Shall we call back Northumberland and send* (Sh.RII III,III:129); *Cough, or cry hem, if anybody come* (Sh.Oth IV,II:29).

7.4.2.5 Consider now the disyllabic figure WS-2 formed by disyllabic or, exceptionally, trisyllabic words. Verbs that prevail in WS-2 are most frequently used as participles; it is not surprising, therefore, that the most frequent syntactic functions of verbs in the figure WS-2 are those of attributes or adverbial modifiers of attending circumstances, as in *Women, and babes and men, / slaughtered confusedly; But she was calm and sad, / musing alway* (Shel.RI VI,XLVI:9; VII,IV:4) (see Table 7.11).

The figure WS-2 is particularly frequent in Shakespeare's Sonnets and in "Lucrece", the least frequent in his dramas; these facts reflect the more complex syntactic structure of lyrical and narrative verse compared with dramatic verse. Similarly with monosyllabic verbs in WS-1, imperatives of disyllabic verbs in WS-2 are particularly typical of dramatic verse and, again, of Shakespeare's more than Shelley's. However, the imperative function is two times more typical of monosyllabic verbs in WS-1 than of disyllabic verbs in WS-2. The function of a predicate is also more typical of dramatic than non-dramatic verse, which, as far as the figure WS-2 is concerned, displays less dynamics than in the dramas.

The most typical functions of nouns in the figure WS-2 in Shakespeare's

Table 7.11

Incidence (in percent) of the Syntactic Functions of Disyllabic Verbs in the Figure WS-2

Part of speech	Lucrece	Shakespeare Sonnets	Dramas	Pope Rape Lock	Shelley Islam	Cenci	Arnold Sohrab
Predicate or its part	14.3	4.5	17.2	--	31.5	22.7	20.8
Attribute or adverbial modifier	76.2	89.5	56.3	100.0	68.5	58.7	70.8
Imperative	9.5	6.0	26.5	--	--	18.6	8.4
Total	63	67	128	4	73	75	24

dramatic verse are those of vocatives, exclamations, and questions. These functions embrace up to 66% of all disyllabic nouns in WS-2 (in "Richard II"). For example: *Cousin*, *I am too young to be your father* (Sh.RII III,III:204); *Patience, I say; your mind perhaps may change* (Sh.Oth III,III:453). Not only nouns, but also adjectives qualifying a noun used in the vocative function or in a question tend to be coupled with the rhythmical figure WS-2; for example: *Impudent* *strumpet!—By heaven, you do me wrong* (Sh.Oth IV,II:82). Shelley's drama contains considerably fewer vocative nouns in WS-2 than Shakespeare's plays. The latter also contain more imperatives; these peculiarities seem to add to the conversational form of Shakespeare's plays.

Nouns in both the line-initial and mid-line WS-2, particularly in the non-dramatic genres, are often syntactically isolated; for example: *Poison*, *a snake in flowers, beneath the veil*; *Cythna*, *(for, from the eyes whose deepest light . . .)*; *Dungeons* *wherein the high resolve is found* (Shel.RI I,XXIX:5; VI,XXIV:5; VIII,XXXVI:7); *Haman*, *who next to Peran-Wisa ruled*; *Rustum*; *his morning meal was done, but still*; *Oxus*, *forgetting the bright speed he had* (A.SR 108,196,886). Similarly with vocatives, syntactically isolated nouns constituting the figure WS-2 are probably meant to be pronounced with a specific intonation. Thus, the figure WS "prefers" syntactic isolation and implies a particular intonation and a pause after the break, while the figure SW "avoids" syntactic breaks and "prefers" accentual subordination to the following word with an ictic stress.

In nineteenth-century verse there develops another typical syntactic function of line-initial nouns coupled with the figure WS-2: an object, with its governing verb in the preceding line. The phenomenon of enjambment emphasizes the rhematic function of the object, which, in terms of sentence perspective, expresses the most valuable semantic information of the utterance; for example:

> The careless slave of that dark power which brings
> <u>Evil</u>, like blight, on man, who, still betrayed;
> . . . .
> That one in Argolis did undergo
> <u>Torture</u> for liberty, and that the crowd . . .
>
> (Shel.RI II,XXXIII:7-8; IV,IX:7-8)

However, even the subject emphasized by the figure WS-2 may acquire a rhematic function: <u>Cassio shall have my place</u>. And, sir, tonight (Sh.Oth IV,I:265).

Questions, vocatives, exclamations, and nouns in syntactic isolation accompany the rhythmical figure WS-2 particularly often. These syntactic functions probably call for a specific intonation which seems to fit the ways in which words forming the figure WS-2 tend to be pronounced. This is true not only of English but also of Russian verse, where the exceptional cases of disyllabic words in WS-2 appear in questions and are pronounced with a rising tone: <u>Tájna?</u> Ax, vot čto . . . (Tomaševskij 1929:195, Gasparov 1974:203). The non-initial vocative nouns that cling enclitically to the preceding word tend to lose their strong sentence accent both in English and in Russian. That is why disyllabic nouns stressed on the first syllable but used in the function of a direct address may occur in WS in the middle and even at the end of the English iambic or trochaic verse line, for example: *We are not safe, Clárence; we are not safe* (Shakespeare, "Richard III" I,I:70); *He is dead and gone, lády, He is dead and gone, At his head a grass-green turf, At his heels a stone* (Shakespeare, "Hamlet" IV,V:29-32); *O peace, móther, O peace, móther, Your weeping doth me grieve* (Ballad "The Seven Virgins", 21-22) (see also Chapters 2 and 6).

The same is true in Russian verse; disyllabic non-oxytonic nouns in a direct address lose a strong phrasal accent and cling enclitically to the preceding word and may, particularly in dramatic verse in the part of a comic or low personage, occur on non-initial WS positions, for example: *Ox, nét, brátec! u nás rugájut . . . šumím, brátec, šumím* . . . (Tomaševskij 1959:145).

7.4.2.6 Since the figures <u>WSW-2</u> are not numerous, it is more difficult to find repeating patterns in their <u>syntactic structures</u>. Disyllabic nouns and verbs are the most typical components of the initial WS and monosyllabic adjectives and verbs of the last W. Therefore, vocatives, exclamations, and imperatives are characteristic syntactic elements of the first two positions of the figure, while attributes or monosyllabic verbs, usually in the imperative mood, prevail in the second W. For example: <u>Norfolk, throw</u> down we bid, there is no boot; <u>Cousin, throw</u> up your gage, do you begin; <u>Treason! foul</u> treason! villain! traitor! slave! (Sh.RII I,I:164,186; V,II:71); "<u>Daughter, dear</u> daughter", old Lucretius cries (Sh.RL 251:1). There are a few variations of the general pattern, sometimes with almost identical morphological components: <u>Lintot, dull rogue!</u> will think your price too much; <u>Ammon's great</u> Son one shoulder had *too high* (P.DA 63,117); *Sancho's dread Doctor and his Wand were there* (P.RB 160). Another pattern: *Cupid laid by his brand and fell asleep* (Sh.Son 153:1); *Chloe stepp'd in, and kill'd him with a frown* (P.RL V:68); *Sohrab came forth, and eyed him as he came* (A.SR 301). When the figure WSW-2 is coupled with the syntactic structure subject + predicate, as in the last three examples, the rhythmically emphasized subject seems to acquire a rhematic function.

The rhematic role of a disyllabic word in WSW-2 is also seen in other syntactic functions; the rhematic role of a disyllable is frequently emphasized by an inversion: *Sohrab men call him, but his birth is hid* (A.SR 226).

7.5 Rhythmical-grammatical patterns

In our morphological and syntactical analysis of various rhythmical figures we have discovered repeated rhythmical-grammatical patterns, occurring again and again not only in the same text, but throughout all the material analyzed. These patterns sometimes embrace only the rhythmical figure and one or two adjacent words; for example, **WS-2**: *Justice and Truth* . . . ; *Glory and joy* . . . ; *Mother and soul* . . . ; *Pity and Peace* . . . *Wisdom and Love* . . . ; **WSW-1**: *Feeds the light flame* . . . ; *Pluck the keen teeth* . . . ; *Spreads his black Wings* . . . ; *Bears his own ills* . . . ; *Tempt thy wild thoughts* . . . ; *Drops the light drip* . . . ; *Burst in far peals* . . . ; *Locked in stiff rings* . . . . Sometimes, however, repeated rhythmical-grammatical patterns cover whole lines, in which an accentual and word boundary form, coupled with a particular part-of-speech and syntactic pattern, recurs within the same or different poems by different authors. Some examples of various patterns:

(1) Rouse the wild Game, and strain the guiltless Grove
(Thomson, "Winter", 105)
Dart the quick taunt, and edge the piercing gibe?
(Samuel Johnson, "The Vanity of Human Wishes" 62)
Shake the red cloak, and poise the ready brand
(Byron, "Childe Harold" I,LXXVIII:6)
Bent his thin head to seek the brazen rein
(Shelley, "Islam" VI,XLIII:4)

(2) Caps on their Heads, and Halberds in their Hand
(Pope, "The Rape of the Lock" III:42)
Pain at her side, and Megrim at her Head
(Pope, "The Rape of the Lock" IV:24)
Fire in each eye, and Paper in each hand
(Pope, "Dr. Arbuthnot" 5)
Law in his voice, and fortune in his hand
(Samuel Johnson, "The Vanity" 100)
Fears of the brave, and follies of the wise
(Samuel Johnson, "The Vanity" 316)

> Fire from the mind, as vigour from the limb
>
> (Byron, "Childe Harold" III,VIII:8)
>
> Chains in his eye, and menace in his ear
>
> (Byron, "The Island" IV,IV:6)
>
> Speed on her prow, and terror in her tier
>
> (Byron, "The Corsair" III,XV:12)
>
> Bowls on the board, and banners on the wall
>
> (Byron, "Lara" I,I:6)
>
> Cf.: Knocks at my heart, and whispers in mine ear
>
> (Shakespeare, "Venus and Adonis" 110:5)

This line contains the same accented and word boundary "matrix" as pattern (2) above, but the first word of each "hemistich" is not a noun, as in the examples above, but a verb; the line is, as it were, a homonym of pattern (2). Here is a word boundary variant of pattern (2) with a feminine ending to the first "hemistich:"

> Wreck to the seaman, tempest to the field
>
> (Shakespeare, "Venus and Adonis" 76:4)

The correlation between verse rhythm and line grammar is reciprocal: verse rhythm seems to both predetermine the grammatical structure of verse and is predetermined by it. On the one hand, the favored rhythmical line types call forth particular part-of-speech and syntactic line patterns; on the other hand, particular semantic "starters" of lines and particular part-of-speech and syntactic patterns favored by an epoch or genre call forth particular line types (on rhythmical-grammatical patterns see Brik 1927, Taranovsky 1963:289, Jakobson and Rudy 1977:14, Žirmunskij 1978:239, 307-308, Tarlinskaja 1981, 1984). The correlation between rhythmical-grammatical line patterns and repeating semantic elements and lexical units will be further discussed in Chapter 8 (8.7).

7.6 Compositional function of rhythmical figures in rhymed verse

To introduce this subject, I shall explore in more general terms the compositional function of extrametrical stresses on W and losses of stress on S. To do so I return to stress profile analysis, but this time grouping the material by lines of the stanzas: all the first lines, all the second, and so forth. For this analysis the texts are: (1) Shakespeare's "The Rape of Lucrece" (rhyme royal: **ababbcc**); (2) his Sonnets (three quatrains and a couplet rhymed **ababcdcdefefdd**); (3) the rhymed pairs of lines inserted into "Richard II;" and (4) for comparison, a simple stanzaic form widely used in English lyrics: iambic tetrameter quatrains rhymed **abab** and **aabb**. I analyzed 60 poems by 15 authors (262 stanzas, 1048 lines) rhymed **abab** and 35 poems by 16 authors (171 stanzas, 684 lines) rhymed **aabb**. The texts belong to 27 authors of the late eighteenth-nineteenth centuries, both major and minor poets.

7.6.1 Tables 7.12 and 7.13 present the stress profiles by lines in the stanzas of "The Rape of Lucrece" and the Sonnets and Tables 7.14 and 7.15 the stress profiles of the tetrameter quatrains **abab** and **aabb**.

7.6.1.1 Consider first the stress profile of non-ictic positions in the stanza of "The Rape of Lucrece" (Table 7.12). As expected, the ratio of extrametrical stresses decreases everywhere from the anacrusis to the final non-ictic (ninth) position (cf. Bailey 1975, Tarlinskaja and Teterina 1974). It is important to note the high proportion of stresses on the anacrusis of lines 1, 3, and 5, particularly the heavy stress on position 1 of line one. This extra-heavy stress on the anacrusis of the first line is, as it were, a signal of the beginning of the text. Relatively strong stresses on the first position of lines 1, 3, and 5 give the first suggestion that the law of rhythmical dissimilation of adjacent lines in a stanza and similarity of every other line, discovered in Russian verse (cf. Taranovsky 1966b, G.S. Smith 1981), is probably also true in English verse. The same phenomenon is observed in the iambic tetrameter quatrains of the later poets (cf. Tables 7.14 and 7.15), particularly in their cross-rhymed variant (Table 7.14). In quatrains with both types of rhyming schemes the anacrusis of the first line is stressed especially heavily, particularly in **abab**; thus a heavy stress on the anacrusis of the first line tends to mark the beginning of a verse text. The heavier the stress on the anacrusis of a line, the more assurance there is that the line begins a metrically and syntactically more autonomous part of the text. The syntactic composition of the English quatrain tends to break the stanza into two couplets; this bipartite syntactic structure is emphasized by the system of rhyming (which is obvious) and by the structure of the anacrusis (which is not so obvious without special analysis). Some examples are:

"Never shall woman's smile have power (a)
To win me from those gentle charms!" (b)
So swore I, in that happy hour, (a)
When Love first gave thee to my arms. (b)
                (Thomas Moore, "Tibullus to Sulpicia" 1-4)
Comrades and friends! with whom, where'er (a)
The fates have willed thro' life I've roved, (b)
Now speed ye home and with you bear (a)
These bitter words to her I've loved. (b)
                (Thomas Moore, Carm.11, 1-4)
Oh! bring me one sweet orange-bough, (a)
To fan my cheek, to cool my brow; (a)
One bough, with pearly blossoms drest, (b)
And bind it, mother! on my breast! (b)
                (Felicia Dorothea Hemans, "The Orange-Bough" 1-4)
Lie here, my darling, on my breast (a)
For so, methinks, I love thee best; (a)

Table 7.12

Stress Profiles for Each Line of "The Rape of Lucrece"
(1855 total lines)

Line and rhyming	Ictic positions						Non-ictic positions				
	2	4	6	8	10	Mean	1	3	5	7	9	Mean
1 (a)	75.5	86.0	74.4	76.6	92.9	81.8	32.0	9.0	7.1	7.1	4.5	12.0
2 (b)	69.8	88.7	67.6	78.5	91.3	79.2	18.1	11.3	8.3	10.2	4.1	10.4
3 (a)	69.8	91.3	76.0	74.0	93.6	80.9	23.8	11.3	9.4	6.8	6.8	11.6
4 (b)	78.8	86.7	83.0	79.2	79.2	84.0	15.1	5.7	6.4	6.0	3.4	7.3
5 (b)	70.6	89.1	74.0	75.9	93.2	80.6	29.0	12.8	9.4	11.7	4.1	13.4
6 (c)	69.4	90.6	67.6	83.8	95.1	81.3	19.2	13.2	12.4	7.5	7.1	12.0
7 (c)	72.8	92.1	77.0	81.9	90.2	82.8	19.2	12.4	7.9	8.7	4.5	10.5
Mean	72.4	89.2	74.2	78.5	92.7	81.4	22.3	10.8	8.7	8.3	4.9	11.0

Table 7.13

Stress Profiles for Each Line of Shakespeare's Sonnets

Line and rhyming	Ictic positions							Non-ictic positions					
	2	4	6	8	10	Mean		1	3	5	7	9	Mean
1 (a)	62.1	79.7	67.3	64.7	95.4	73.8		37.2	10.4	7.8	11.8	9.8	15.4
2 (b)	63.2	89.5	75.0	77.0	92.8	79.5		19.1	9.8	7.2	7.2	7.2	10.1
3 (a)	67.4	88.2	71.9	75.2	95.4	79.6		22.9	13.7	11.1	9.8	10.4	13.6
4 (b)	67.3	90.9	68.6	76.5	90.2	78.8		17.0	11.8	11.1	9.8	7.8	11.5
5 (c)	66.7	88.2	71.9	73.9	95.4	79.2		33.3	11.1	11.1	11.8	7.8	15.0
6 (d)	70.0	90.2	68.6	73.9	94.8	79.5		21.6	11.8	5.2	8.5	5.9	10.6
7 (c)	66.7	91.5	74.5	74.5	96.1	80.6		18.9	8.5	9.1	8.5	6.5	10.3
8 (d)	68.6	92.8	71.9	77.1	88.2	79.7		20.9	7.2	11.8	7.8	7.8	11.1

Table 7.13 (cont.)

9 (e)	60.8	88.9	67.3	70.6	92.2	76.0	37.2	13.1	9.1	13.1	11.8	16.9
10 (f)| 64.1	88.9	72.6	77.8	92.8	79.2	11.7	12.4	11.7	11.1	5.9	10.6
11 (e)| 65.1	85.5	72.4	75.0	94.1	78.4	19.1	11.8	6.6	8.5	6.6	10.5
12 (f)| 75.7	90.8	69.7	82.9	94.7	82.7	17.1	14.5	14.5	7.9	4.6	11.7
13 (g)| 64.5	89.5	77.6	75.7	98.0	81.1	29.6	10.5	12.5	7.2	12.5	14.5
14 (g)| 69.8	93.4	71.7	84.2	99.4	83.7	19.1	19.7	16.4	16.4	15.1	17.3
Mean	66.6	89.1	71.5	75.6	94.3	79.4	23.2	11.2	10.4	9.2	8.6	12.5

Table 7.14

Stress Profiles for Each Line of 262 Iambic Tetrameter Stanzas
Rhymed abab

Line	Ictic Positions					Non-ictic Positions				
	2	4	6	8	Mean	1	3	5	7	Mean
1	75.5	89.6	88.9	99.6	88.4	<u>38.5</u>	8.7	2.6	3.0	<u>13.2</u>
2	86.2	85.8	91.2	98.9	<u>90.5</u>	11.0	6.4	3.0	1.5	5.5
3	83.2	84.1	87.4	97.7	88.1	<u>28.2</u>	5.7	6.5	2.3	<u>10.7</u>
4	84.0	83.2	85.5	<u>90.0</u>	<u>85.6</u>	12.6	8.4	5.3	3.0	7.3
Mean	82.2	85.6	88.2	96.6	88.1	22.6	7.3	4.4	2.5	9.2

<u>Look</u> at me with thy glances mild (b)
And play about me as a child. (b)
    (Arthur Hugh Clough, "Lie Here, my Darling, on my Breast" 1-4)

Cf. the same phenomenon in a quatrain where the first three lines are iambic tetrameter and the fourth line is iambic trimeter:

<u>Birds</u> warbled round me—every trace (a)
Of inward sadness had its charm; (b)
"<u>Kilve</u>", said I, "was a favourite place, (a)
And so is Liswyn farm." (b)
    (Wordsworth, "Anecdote for Fathers", 21-24)

Table 7.15

Stress Profiles for Each Line of 171 Iambic Tetrameter Stanzas
Rhymed aabb

Line	Ictic Positions					Non-ictic Positions				
	2	4	6	8	Mean	1	3	5	7	Mean
1	76.0	87.0	88.3	99.5	87.7	<u>33.3</u>	8.2	8.2	2.4	<u>13.0</u>
2	89.5	81.9	88.9	<u>97.0</u>	89.3	17.5	6.4	6.4	1.8	8.0
3	77.2	86.0	86.0	98.8	87.0	<u>20.0</u>	7.0	4.7	3.5	8.8
4	84.8	83.0	80.1	<u>97.0</u>	<u>86.2</u>	14.6	8.8	7.0	2.4	8.2
Mean	81.9	84.4	85.8	98.1	87.5	21.4	7.6	6.6	2.5	9.5

Cf. also in longer stanzas:

<u>Give me</u> more love, or more disdain:	(a)
The torrid or the frozen zone	(b)
<u>Brings</u> equal ease unto my pain;	(a)
The temperate affords me none:	(b)
<u>Either</u> extreme, of love or hate,	(c)
Is sweeter than a calm estate.	(c)

(Thomas Carew, "Mediocrity in Love Rejected" 1-6)

<u>Tell me</u>, ye zephyrs! that unfold,	(a)
While fluttering o'er this gay recess,	(b)
<u>Pinions</u> that fanned the teeming mould	(a)
Of Eden's blissful wilderness,	(b)
Did only softly-stealing hours	(c)
There close the peaceful lives of flowers?	(c)

(Wordsworth, "A Flower Garden" 1-6)

The syntactic and rhyming composition of the quoted stanzas is also marked by the distribution of extrametrical stresses on position 1 or "inversions" (WS) on positions 1-2. "Inversions" tend to mark the <u>first</u> line, while extra metrical stresses on the anacrusis (W) gravitate to line three. Thus, a longer, and therefore more noticeable, rhythmical figure is chosen by the English poets as a marker of the beginning of a text (in Russian verse, in contrast, the first line is traditionally the most regular: cf. Bajevskij 1972:22-36).

In this connection it is interesting to note a relatively heavy stress on the anacrusis of line five in "Lucrece". The rhyme scheme of the poem is **ababbcc**, and one would expect the strongest break before the final couplet; but on the contrary, the break occurs after line four, in this way showing that the first four lines, actually a quatrain rhymed **abab**, form a certain unity, and that line five begins a more autonomous part of the stanza. Indeed, stanzas with a syntactic break after line four are quite frequent in "Lucrece". Line five is often syntactically isolated from both the following, and particularly the preceding text, while the final couplet, with its low stressing of the anacrusis and high stressing of all other non-ictic positions, forms a unity of its own. One typical example:

"<u>So</u>, so", <u>quoth</u> he, "<u>these</u> lets attend the time,
Like little frosts that sometime threat the spring,
To add a more rejoicing to the prime,
And give the sneaped birds more cause to sing.//
<u>Pain</u> pays the income of each precious thing;/
  <u>Huge</u> rocks, <u>high</u> winds, <u>strong</u> pirate, shelves and sands,
  The merchant fears, ere rich at home he lands."

("The Rape of Lucrece" 48:1-7)

Now consider the non-ictic stresses of the Sonnets (Table 7.13; Fig. 7.2). The heaviest anacruses mark lines 1, 3, 5, 7, 9, 13 (all the odd lines except 11,

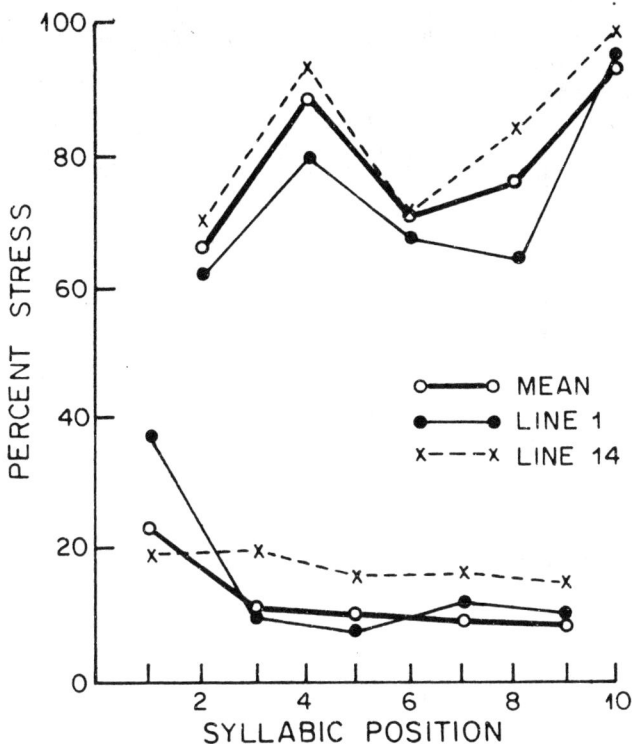

Fig. 7.2. Stress profiles of the first and last lines of Shakespeare's sonnets contrasted with the mean; ictic and non-ictic positions connected separately. Salient features are (1) line 1 shows a marked asymmetrical bipartite structure ("dip" in position 8) compared with symmetrical final lines ("dip" in position 6); (2) the final line is structured differently from all other lines, with a very heavy stressing on non-ictic positions 3, 5, 7, 9, marking the ends of the texts; and (3) a particularly strong stressing on the anacrusis of line 1, marking the beginnings of the texts.

and even here the anacrusis is relatively more frequently stressed than that of the adjacent even lines, particularly the preceding). Especially frequently stressed are the anacruses of lines 1, 9, 5, and 13, which mark the beginnings of the text itself (line 1, cf. Fig. 7.2), of the third quatrain (line 9), of the second quatrain (line 5), and of the final couplet (line 13). These results show that the stanzaic composition of the sonnets is marked by extrametrical stresses on the anacruses. Absence of dissimilation between adjacent lines in terms of their anacruses in quatrains two and three seems to be an indicator of their more complex syntactic composition, hence less marked segmentation into couplets, while the first quatrain still shows the signs of a bipartite structure: **ab/ab**. Most of Shakespeare's sonnets increase in syntactic complexity towards their middle.

A frequent stress on the anacrusis of line one of Shakepeare's sonnets is not a specifically Shakespearean phenomenon. For example, out of 92 sonnets by Wordsworth under the general title "Miscellaneous Sonnets", 41 (or 44.6%)/ have an extrametrical stress on the anacrusis and 24 (26.1%) display an "inversion" (the WS figure) in the first two positions of line one; some examples of the first lines of Wordsworth's "Miscellaneous Sonnets" are:

<u>Happy</u> the feeling from the bosom thrown . . .
<u>Calm is</u> the nature as a resting wind . . .
<u>Bard of</u> the Fleece, whose skilful genius bright . . .
<u>Grief, thou</u> hast lost an ever-ready friend . . .
<u>Lady</u>! the songs of spring were in the flowers . . .
<u>Lady</u>! I rifled a Parnassian cave . . . ,

and others.

The non-ictic positions of the <u>final</u> couplet of Shakespeare's Sonnets, particularly of the final line (cf. Fig. 7.2), bear many extrametrical stresses, more, in fact, than in "Lucrece"; the poet, as it were, still had a lot to say, but the form of the sonnet restricted him to 14 lines. The phenomenon of a heavy ending in a poem is on the whole not typical (as shown below, poems and stanzas usually tend to end in a lighter, sometimes shorter line; cf. B.H. Smith 1968:58-70, Gasparov 1974:323, Table 2). A heavy ending occurs in poems with a "conclusion", a moral, a maxim, an afforism, or a statement (in a narrative poem) relevant to the plot.[4] In the case of Shakespeare's Sonnets, the concluding, summing-up, and theme-formulating function of the final couplet is obvious. Here are some typical couplets:

<u>So</u> long as men can breathe or eyes can see,
<u>So</u> long <u>lives</u> this, and this <u>gives</u> life to thee.

(Sh.Son 18:13-14)

O, him she stores, to show what wealth she had
In days <u>long</u> since, before <u>these</u> last <u>so</u> bad.

(Sh.Son 67:13-14)

<u>Take</u> heed, <u>dear</u> heart, of this <u>large</u> privilege;
The hardest knife <u>ill</u> used doth lose his edge.

(Sh.Son 95:13-14)

<u>Give</u> my <u>love</u> fame <u>faster</u> than Time <u>wastes</u> life;
<u>So</u> thou prevent'st his scythe and crooked knife.

(Sh.Son 100:13-14)

Incapable of more, replete with you,
My most <u>true</u> mind <u>thus</u> maketh mine untrue.

(Sh.Son 113:13-14)

<u>Came</u> there for cure, and this by that I prove,

Love's fire heats water, water cools not love.

(Sh.Son 154:13-14)

A similar phenomenon was observed in "Lucrece", but more weakly expressed. This is understandable: the concluding function of the final couplet in a sonnet is stronger than in the final stanza of a long poem.

7.6.1.2 Consider now the stress profiles of ictic positions in "Lucrece" and the Sonnets (Tables 7.12 and 7.13; Fig. 7.2).

In general, the most relevant formal features of the end of a poem or stanza are: (a) a shortening of the final line (cf. B.H. Smith 1968:58-70); (b) in accentual verse, a decrease in the number of disyllabic intervals between adjacent ictic stresses (Tarlinskaja 1976:324, cf. with Russian verse: Gasparov 1974:324); and (c) in syllabo-tonic, iambic verse, a decrease of stressing of the final line (cf. Taranovsky 1966b), particularly (in English verse) of the final ictic position, except in poems with a moral, a maxim, or a resume. "Lucrece" has extra-light final ictic positions, while in the Sonnets the final positions are extra-heavy (cf. Fig. 7.2).

In "Lucrece" the most marked decrease of final ictic stressing occurs in lines four and seven. Line four is the end of the quatrain **abab**: a frequent loss of stress on the final ictus of line four emphasizes the structural autonomy of the first four lines. The completeness of this quatrain, as noted earlier, is also marked by an increase of non-ictic stresses on the anacrusis of line five. So structurally the stanzas of "Lucrece" break into components **abab + bcc**, or **abab + b + cc**, rather than **ababb + cc**. Here are some examples of a typical accentual structure of the final couplet of "Lucrece":

And fellowship in woe doth woe assuáge,
As palmers' chat makes short their pílgrimage.
(113:6-7)

Which by him tainted shall for him be spént,
And as his due writ in my téstament.
(169:6-7)

But the mild glance that sly Ulysses lént
Show'd deep regard and smiling góvernment.
(200:6-7)

And with my knife scratch out the angry éyes
Of all the Greeks that are thine énemies.
(210:6-7)

Her winged sprite, and through her wounds doth flý
Life's lasting date from cancell'd déstiny.
(247:6-7)

The same general tendency is clearly seen in the rhymed couplets that occur in "Richard II". Some examples:

> And those his golden beams to you here lént,
> Shall point on me, and gild my bánishment.
>
> (I,III:146-147)
>
> Plucked four away. Six frozen winters spént,
> Return with welcome home from bánishment.
>
> (I,III:211-212)
>
> Thou canst help time to furrow me with áge,
> But stop no wrinkle in his pílgrimage.
>
> (I,III:229-230)
>
> Where'er I wander boast of this I cán,
> Though banished, yet a trueborn Énglishman.
>
> (I,III:308-309)
>
> Banish us both, and send the king with mé.
> That were some love, but little pólicy.
>
> (V,I:83-84)

The tendency to lighten the final ictic position of a concluding line is clearly seen in the tetrameter quatrains (Tables 7.4, 7.5), particularly in the **abab** rhyming scheme (Fig. 7.3). The dissimilation of stress on the final S of odd and even lines of the **aabb** variant is a hint of its internal couplet structure (**aa + bb**). Some typical examples of the final stanzas, **abab**:

> He loves to sit and hear me sing,
> Then laughing, sports and plays with me;
> Then stretches out my golden wings,
> And mocks my loss of líberty.
>
> (W. Blake, Song "How Sweet I Roamed...", 13-16)
>
> An angel, wandering from her sphere,
> Who saw this bright, this frozen gem,
> To dew-eyed Pity brought the tear,
> And hung it on her díadem!
>
> (Th. Moore, "The Tear", 9-12)
>
> Farewell! I did not know thy worth,
> But thou art gone, and now 'tis priz'd:
> So angels walk'd unknown on earth,
> But when they flew were récogniz'd!
>
> (Th. Hood, "To an Absentee", 9-12)

Cf. a longer stanza, **abab//cc**:

> For oft when on my couch I lie
> In vacant or in pensive mood,
> They flash upon that inward eye
> Which is the bliss of sólitude,//
> And then my heart with pleasure fills,
> And dances with the dáffodils.
>
> (Wordsworth, "I wondered lonely as a cloud...", 19-24)

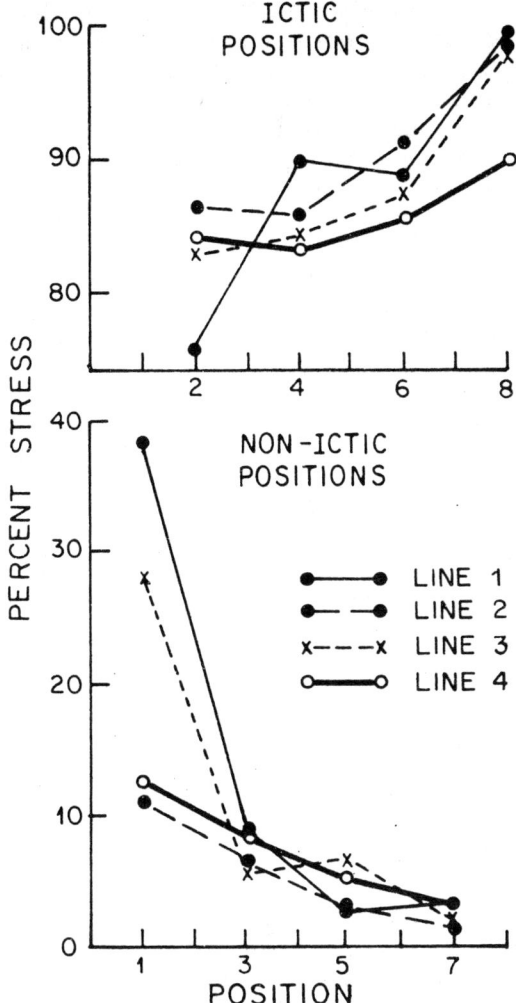

Fig. 7.3. Stress profiles for each line of 262 iambic tetrameter stanzas rhymed **abab** (data from Table 7.14). Ictic and non-ictic positions are connected separately. Notable features are (1) heavy stressing on the anacruses of odd lines (beginnings of couplets) and particularly on line 1 (beginning of stanza); (2) stressing on ictic positions increases and on non-ictic positions decreases systematically from beginnings to ends of lines, indicating a marked increase in regularity towards the ends of lines; and (3) stanzas tend to end more lightly stressed, as indicated by the much lower stressing of the final ictus of line 4.

The tendency for ending a verse text with a non-oxytonic stressed polysyllable may be explained not only from the standpoint of its role in verse composition, but probably also semantically: polysyllables are notional, semantically loaded words, and since in speech the end of a sentence is usually a position of emphasis (the place of the rheme), it is natural to fill it with the semantically most informative elements, such as *daffodils* in Wordsworth's famous poem. Such elements commonly end a poem or stanza (cf. Bjorklund 1978:242).

In Shakespeare's Sonnets both tendencies for ending a stanza are observed. The stress on the last ictic position falls in the final lines of the first two quatrains (lines four and eight), in the third quatrain the last ictic positions of lines eleven and twelve are stressed in the same way, and the degree of stress on the final ictic position keeps growing from line twelve through fourteen. The final line of the Sonnets is the heaviest of all: both its ictic and non-ictic positions are stressed particularly often; this makes the final statements particularly "weighty" (cf. Fig. 7.2).

In spite of the heavy mean ictic stressing of line fourteen, there is a strong contrast between a relatively weak stress on position 6 and strong stresses on both adjacent ictic positions, 4 and 8. A "dip" in position 6 accompanies a canonized bipartite line segmentation 4+6 or 5+5. Thus, the final line is broken into "hemistichs" more markedly than the preceding line. This clear-cut symmetrical bipartite rhythmical structure of line fourteen also adds to the general effect of its finality. Some examples:

> To give away yourself keeps yourself still;
> And you must live,/drawn <u>by</u> your own sweet skill.
>
> ·(Sh.Son 16:13-14)

> For that same groan doth put this in my mind;
> My grief lies onward,/<u>and</u> my joy behind.
>
> (Sh.Son 50:13-14)

> For we, which now behold these present days,
> Have eyes to wonder,/<u>but</u> lack tongues to praise.
>
> (Sh.Son 106:13-14)

In contrast with the Russian verse tradition, where the first line is the most "metrical", in the English iambic verse the reverse seems to be true: the highest number of extrametrical stresses on the anacrusis and the lowest mean ictic stressing both occur in the <u>first</u> line of all texts (cf. Tables 7.13, 7.14, 7.15; Fig. 7.3). This is an example of isomorphism of verse structure: rhythmical variations usually decrease in number both <u>horizontally</u>, from the beginning of the line or "hemistich" to its end (the stress on ictic positions increases and on non-ictic positions decreases), and <u>vertically</u>, from the first line of a poem or a stanza to the last line (cf. Bjorklund 1978:243). <u>Both the beginnings and the ends of the English verse texts have their own specific compositional markers.</u>

7.6.2 Now let us turn to the distribution along the verse lines of the disyllabic rhythmical figures of three subtypes: WS-1, WS-2, and SW-1. Both WS types are compositionally more relevant than SW because they usually occur at the very beginning of the lines, where they stand out and are more obvious. The lines of Shakepeare's Sonnets displaying the relative maxima ("peaks") of each of the three subtypes of disyllabic figures are generalized below. The peaks are marked with a cross, and especiallly high peaks are marked with two crosses.

	Lines of the sonnets													
Figs.	1	2	3	4	5	6	7	8	9	10	11	12	13	14
WS-1	++		+		++		+		++		+			
WS-2						+		+				+		
SW-1				+										

The figure WS-1 marks the beginning of the text and the first line of every quatrain (lines 1, 5, 9); in a milder way this figure also marks the beginnings of the second couplets of the quatrains (lines 3, 7, 11). Here are some examples of how the rhythmical figures WS-1 (WSW-1) mark the first lines of the Sonnets: L̆ook in the glăss . . . (Son.3); L̆o, in the ŏrient . . . (Son.7); Ŏ, that you were yoursĕlf! . . . (Son.13); L̆ord of my l̆ove . . . (Son.26); L̆et me confĕss . . . (Son.36); S̆in of self-l̆ove . . . (Son.62); T̆ired with all thĕse . . . (Son.66); Th̆us in his chĕek . . . (Son.68); S̆ay that thou didst forsăke . . . (Son.89); L̆ove is my s̆in . . . (Son.142); L̆o, as a căreful housewife . . . (Son.143); L̆ove is tŏo y̆oung . . . (Son.151). The figure WS-2 is more typical of the even lines; this rhythmical figure occurs in the middle of quatrains, particularly often in the second and third quatrains, where the syntax is relatively more complicated than in the first. As noted above, the figures WS-2 are mainly formed by verbs, as a rule by participles in the syntactic function of adverbial modifiers. One example:

To win me soon to hell, my female evil
<u>Tempteth</u> my better angel from my side,
And would corrupt my saint to be a devil,
<u>Wooing</u> his purity with her foul pride.

(Sh.Son 144:5-8)

So, in a way, the figures WS-2 are also compositional markers of the Sonnets, only they mark the middle rather than the beginning of a quatrain.

The figure SW-1 has practically no compositional function at all; this rhythmical figure is scattered all over the texts. Still, a "peak" does occur in line four, where other figures are less frequent. The most frequent preference of one of the three figures in a line almost seems to exclude the others. Looked at from another angle, one can say that the rhythmical figures of different types complement each other.

Very similar tendencies were discovered in "Venus and Adonis" and "The Rape of Lucrece" (with rhyming schemes **ababcc** and **ababbcc**, respectively). The line-initial figures WS-1 display a maximum in the first lines of the stanzas. The second peak occurs in line five, marking the compositional break between the quatrain **abab** and the rest of the stanza. Figures WS-2 have a peak in line three of "Lucrece", repeating the tendency of WS-1, and in line two of "Venus and Adonis:" the same tendency as in the Sonnets, where the figure WS-2 served as a marker of the even lines of the quatrains. Similarly to the Sonnets and "Lucrece", the grammatical realization of the figure WS-2 in "Venus and Adonis" is the present participle. Some examples:

What is the body but a swallowing grave,
<u>Seeming</u> to bury that posterity . . .

(127:1-2)

This said, she hasteth to a myrtle grove,
<u>Musing</u> the morning is so much o'erworn . . .

(145:1-2)

'If he be dead,—O no, it cannot be,
<u>Seeing</u> his beauty, thou shouldst strike at it;

(157:1-2)

It shall be sparing and too full of riot,
<u>Teaching</u> decrepit age to treat the measures;

(192:1-2)

The cause of the difference between the Sonnets and "Venus and Adonis", on the one hand, and "Lucrece", on the other, in the distribution of the figures WS-2 lies in their differing syntactic structures. This subject requires more study.

The figure SW-1 is scattered practically throughout the stanzas of "Venus" and "Lucrece;" its minimum in "Venus and Adonis" occurs in lines one and five where the figure WS-1 (in line five also WS-2) is particularly frequent. We see again how rhythmical figures of different types seem to complement each other. Each figure has idiosyncratic preferences for particular lines in a stanza, and in this way plays a stylistic, text-organizing role in rhymed verse.

7.7 Chapter 7 (as with 8 to follow) has dealt with so many minute phenomena and contains so many different bits of information that a shorter synthesis and generalization must be done preliminarily to the concluding Chapter 9. <u>Summing up</u> the information and various conclusions of Chapter 7, one can <u>emphasize the following points</u>.

7.7.1 The most common types and subtypes of rhythmical figures which are not only "<u>metrical</u>", but definitely lie within the <u>norm</u> of English iambic verse, are as follows: S (loss of stress on a strong position); W (extrametrical stress on a weak position); WS-1 (combination of two monosyllables, or of a monosyllable on W plus an unstressed syllable of a polysyllabic word on S); WS-2 (formed by a disyllabic non-oxytonic word); WSW-1 (formed by three monosyllables); WSW-2 (the disyllabic word usually fills the WS rather than the SW positions); and SW-1 (formed by two monosyllables). "Metrically" marginal are the following figures: SW-2 (formed by an oxytonic disyllable); SWS of all subtypes; and tetrasyllabic figures WSWS, particularly those which contain no syntactic break in the middle: WS/WS are much closer to the norm. Longer rhythmical figures should obviously be considered abnormal, or "unmetrical", similarly to occasional "ungrammatical" uses in fiction (for stylistic effects), or in oral speech.

7.7.2 Rhythmical figures display specific preferences for particular parts of speech and syntactic structures. All figures seem to avoid nouns, the most frequent part of speech in both prose and verse without rhythmical figures. The figure SW-1 "prefers" adjectives, both WS-1 and WS-2 "favor" verbs, while the WSW are partial to verbs plus adjectives. Nouns, generally avoided in line internal WS-1, are subject to syntactic and metrical constraints.

The figure WS-2 "prefers" verbs in the imperative mood and in the form of participles. Typical syntactic functions of nouns in the figure WS-2 in dramatic verse are those of vocatives and exclamations; both in the dramatic and non-dramatic texts line-initial nouns in WS-2 tend to be syntactically isolated. These specific syntactic properties of verbs and nouns in WS-2 evidently call for a specific intonation that goes well with the rhythmical figure. Not only nouns-objects (the result of an enjambment) but also nouns-subjects in WS-2 have a marked rhematic function (semantic foregrounding of the word), emphasized sometimes also by an inverted word order.

Particular rhythmical figures regularly coupled with particular morphological components and syntactic patterns tend to produce rhythmical-grammatical "formula-clichés" recurring in the verse of different poets. Rhythmical-grammatical clichés sometimes spread beyond rhythmical figures and embrace the whole line. These clichès bind verse rhythm to the higher levels of the language and text.

7.7.3 Many particulars of rhythmical figures display their genre and epoch partiality, as well as the authors' idiosyncrasies. For example, the figures SW-1, WS-1 and WS-2, WSW-1, and WSW-2 contain more verbs, particularly imperatives, in the dramatic than in non-dramatic verse, while participles in the WS-2 are particularly typical of non-dramatic verse, and the least typical of dramas. The syntactic functions of monosyllabic nouns and verbs on W in Shakespeare's "Lucrece" and "Richard II" show that the rhythm of a lyrical poem is smoother than that of a drama, and that this smoothness is achieved by syntactic means. The difference in epochs and authors is most strikingly demonstrated by the evolution of the figure SW-1: first, the relative proportion has increased in the verse of the nineteenth century compared to that of the earlier epochs; secondly, the syntactic structures coupled with this figure have changed; the structure <u>subject</u> (on W) <u>plus predicate</u> (the following word with an ictic stress), almost exceptional in early Shakespeare (only two in the whole of "Richard II"), increases in number in later Shakespeare (eight cases in "The Winter's Tale"), reaches 42% of all nominal SW-1 in Shelley's "The Cenci" (19 cases out of 45 nominal SW-1), rises to 56% in "The Revolt of Islam" (22 cases out of 39 nominal SW-1), and skyrockets to 81.5% in Arnold's "Sohrab and Rustum" (22 cases out of 27 SW-1 formed by nouns). The semantic consequences of these syntactic changes are discussed in Chapter 8.

7.7.4 Rhythmical figures have specific compositional (text-organizing) functions, particularly in rhymed verse, both tetrameter and pentameter. The compositional functions of rhythmical figures can be considered as part of their stylistic potential (see Chapter 8).

<u>Beginning</u>. Figures W and WS-1 mark particularly strongly the beginnings of English poetic texts, in a lesser way the beginnings of every stanza, and in a yet lesser way the beginnings of every second couplet in a quatrain.

<u>Middle</u>. Figure WS-2, particularly present participles, usually marks even lines of the quatrain, in a way reflecting its tendency to fall into two couplets.

<u>End</u>. The ends of poems, and to a lesser degree ends of stanzas, are marked in two different ways. The prevailing way is a loss of the final ictic stress in the last line of the poem or stanza. A less typical finale, characteristic of poems with a resume, a moral, or a maxim (e.g., sonnets), is an extra-heavy final line, bearing a higher proportion than normal of stresses on both ictic and non-ictic positions.

The final line of Shakespeare's Sonnets, not only heavier than the preceding line, tends to oppose a lighter position 6 to heavier positions 4 and 8, thus rhythmically emphasizing its syntactic bipartite structure. Such a structure gives more weight to the final statement of the Sonnet.

A more typical finale, characteristic of both ends of poems and stanzas, is a lighter line, with a missing ictic stress on the final S.

A general increase of regularity in an English verse text both <u>horizontally</u>, from the beginning to the end of the line, and <u>vertically</u>, from the beginning to the end of a stanza and poem, is another structural marker of verse text composition.

The first syllabic position of a poem tends to be extra-heavy (the "extrametrical" stresses on the anacrusis of line one), while the final syllabic position is often extra-light (the missing ictic stresses on the last S). The general verse composition tendency "heavier at the beginning, lighter at the end" seems to be working diagonally, too.

The systematic use of rhythmical figures for compositional needs shows that

Shakespeare and other poets were fully cognizant of the figures and that the text-organizing function of verse rhythm became widely accepted in the English poetic tradition.

Notes to Chapter 7

[1] Iambic tetrameter poems analyzed and their authors are:

abab

William Blake, Song (*How sweet I roamed from field to field...*); Robert Bloomfield, Aeolus (*Oh, breeze, where sleep'st thou? Come, oh come...*), A Word to Two Young Ladies (*When tender rose-trees first receive...*), To General Loyd (*We soldiers of the western hill...*), Visitor! whoe'er thou art ... ; G.G. Byron, Stanzas to a Lady (*This votive pledge of fond esteem...*), To Caroline (*Think'st thou I saw thy beauteous eyes...*), To D·... (*In thee I fondly hoped to clasp...*), To E ... (*Let Folly smile, to view the names...*); Thomas Campbell, Fifth Sunday in Lent (*Oh Thou whom neither time nor space...*), Fifth Sunday after Trinity (*Creater of the rolling flood!*), First Sunday after Trinity (*The feeble pulse, the gaping breath...*), On Heavenly and Earthly Hope (*Reflected on the lake I love...*), Translation from German (*Take here the tender harp again...*); S.T. Coleridge, Homesick ('*Tis sweet to him who all the week...*), Separation (*A sworded man whose trade is blood...*); George Darley, The Enchanted Spring (*O'er golden sands my waters flow...*), The Luring-On (*When westering winds the ocean soothe...*), The Meermaiden's Vesper-hymn (*Troop home, to silent grots and caves!*); Ebenezer Elliott, Song (*They say I'm old, because I'm grey...*), Song (*With hair grown grey, we look behind...*), The Winter Speedwell (*Ye wintry flowers, whose pensive dyes...*), Reginald Weber, Septuagesima Sunday (*The God of Glory walks His round...*), St. John the Evangelist's Day (*Oh God! who gav'st Thy servant grace...*), Third Sunday in Advent (*Oh Savior, is Thy promise fled?*); Thomas Hood, As it Fell Upon a Day (*Oh! What's befallen Bessy Brown...*), Autumn (*The autumn skies are flushed with gold...*), Song for the Nineteenth (*The morning sky is hung with mist...*), The Careless Nurse Mayd (*I sawe a Mayd sitte on a Bank...*), The Streamlet (*Still glides the gentle streamlet on...*), To an Absentee (*O'er hill, and dale, and distant sea...*); Thomas Moore, Anacreontic (*I filled to thee, to thee I rank*), Carm.11 (*Comrades and friends! with whom, where'er...*), Carm.29 (*Sweet Sirmio! thou, the very eye...*), Carm.70: To Lesbia (*Thou told'st me, in our days of love...*), Elegiac Stanzas (*When wearied wreatches sink to sleep...*), Here, at thy Tomb (*Here, at thy tomb, these tears I shed...*), On the Death of a Lady (*Sweet spirit! if thy airy sleep...*), The Resemblance (*Yes, if 't were any common love...*), The Tear (*On beds of snow the moonbeam slept...*), The Wonder (*Come, tell me where the maid is found...*), Tibullus to Supicia (*Never shall woman's smile have power...*), To.... (*Come, take thy harp—'t is vain to muse...*), To.... (*Sweet lady, look not thus again...*), To a Lady (*Thy song has taught my heart to eel...*), To Julia (*I saw the peasant's hand unkind...*), To Miss.... (*I'll ask the sylph who round thee flies...*), To....'s Picture (*Go then, if she, whose shade thou art...*), To Rosa (*And are you then a thing of art...*), Variety (*Ask what prevailing, pleasing power...*), Woman (*Away, away—you're all the same...*); Samuel Rogers, A Farewell (*Adieu! A long, a long adieu!*), A Wish (*Mine be a cot beside the hill...*), On .... Asleep (*Sleep on, and dream of Heaven awhile...*); Percy B. Shelley, Song VII: Hope (*And said I that all hope was fled...*); Horace Smith, Song to

283

Fanny (*Nature! thy fair and smiling face...*); Henry Kirke White, A Ballad (*Be hushed, be hushed, ye bitter winds...*), The Star of Bethlehem (*When marshalled on the night by plain*); W. Wordsworth, By the Side of the Grave some Years After (*Long time his pulse hath ceased to beat...*), Dirge (*Mourn, Shepherd, near thy old grey stone...*).

aabb

Matthew Arnold, Longing (*Come to me in my dreams, and then...*), Urania (*I too have suffered; yet I know...*); G.G. Byron, Translation of a Romantic Love Song (*Ah! Love was never yet without...*); Bryan, To the Gentian (*Thou blossom bright with autumn dew...*); Arthur Hugh Clough, Come, Pleasant Thought, Sweet Thought, at Will..., Green Fields of England! Wheresoe'er..., Lie Here, my Darling, on my Breast..., O Happy Morning, Far Away..., Old Things Need Not be Therefore True..., That Out of Sight is Out of Mind..., Upon the Water, in the Boat..., Were I with You, or You with Me..., Were You with Me, or I with You...; S.T. Coleridge, Tell's Birth-Place (*Mark this holy chapel well!...*), To a Primrose (*Thy smiles I note, sweet early Flower...*); Barry Cornwall, Stanzas ("*Farewell!*" "*Farewell!*" - *that was the word...*); George Crabbe, Ye Gentle Gales, that Softly Move..., My Birth-Day (*Through a dull tract of woe, of dread...*); Robert Stephen Hawker, The Eyes that Melt, the Eyes that Burn...; Reginald Heber, Lines (*I see them on their winding way...*); Felicia Dorothea Hemans, Impromptu Lines (*Ye tell me not of birds and bees...*), The Orange-Bough (*Oh! bring me one sweet orange-bough...*), The Stranger's Heart (*The stranger's heart! Oh! wound it not!*), The Wanderer (*I come down from the hills alone...*), Translation from Camoens: Part of Eclogue 15 (*If in thy glorious home above...*); William Jones, Extempore Opinion of Native Talent (*Ah! but too well, dear friend, I know...*); Walter Savage Landor, To Mrs. West (*Stiffly I rise from this arm-chair...*); James Montgomery, Two Lovely Sisters Here Unite...; Thomas Moore, From the High-Priest of Apollo to a Virgin of Delphi (*Who is the maid, with golden hair...*), The Meeting of the Ships (*When o'er the silent seas alone...*); Winthrop Mackworth Praed, Enigma (*In other days, when hope was bright...*), To Helen (*Give Crabbe, dear Helen, on your shelf...*), To Helen (*When some grim sorceress, whose skill...*); Henry Kirke White, Solitude (*It is not that my lot is low...*), To Love (*Why should I blush to own I love?*).

[2] The "partiality" of English verse to participles and other -ing forms in the positions WS goes back to Middle English poetry. Under the influence of French borrowings, alongside the original, Germanic stress rule, there developed a Romance stress tendency (Halle and Keyser 1971:101) which affected not only words of French and Latin origin, but also native English words. The words most affected were those which had a long vowel or a "heavy" suffix in their post-tonic syllable, such as -i (lady, only, truly), -ou (fellow, follow, yellow), -dom and -hud (hood)(Dobson 1968:830-848), -ing (felyng, sweryng) (Halle and Keyser 1971:106-109, Tarlinskaja 1974). In this way many disyllabic and trisyllabic words acquired accentual doublets, with and without a secondary stress on the second syllable; "... and though it was not the 'popular' one, the mode of pronunciation which retained secondary stress and full vowels and diphthongs should not be regarded as merely artificial, imitative of French, or 'literary' (as Luick, 466, tends to consider it); the stress-pattern (⌣́) in two-syllabled words was by no means foreign to the native system" (Dobson 1968:831). Middle English poets widely used disyllabic accentual doublets at the ends of their lines, rhyming their second syllables with

monosyllabic words; this practice is one of the proofs that such disyllabic words had, indeed, some kind of stress on the second syllable. Participles and verbal nouns with the suffix -ing were used in the final position particularly often. Some examples are:

Tak nu her this gold ring
(God him is the dubbing)
                                                    ("King Horn" 567-568)
Jesus that is of hevene king,
Yeve us alle His swete blessing
                                                    ("King Horn" 1541-1542)
When Orfeo herd that tiding
Never him nas were for no thing.
                                                    ("Sir Orfeo" 73-74)
That he ne shall ther seen som thing
That shal him lede into loving.
                    (Chaucer, "The Romaunt of the Rose" A:1607-1608)
To dele with other mennes thing,
That is to me a gret lyking.
                    (Chaucer, "The Romaunt of the Rose" C:6979-6980)
Of this dreynte Seys the king,
And of the goddess of sleping . . .
                    (Chaucer, "The Book of the Duchesse" 229-230)
That ye to me assente as in this thing.
Shewe now your pacience in your werking.
            (Chaucer, "The Canterbury Tales; E. The Clerkes Tale" 494-495)

Throughout the fifteenth century Chaucer's epigons widely used disyllabic forms ending with an -ing in the way Chaucer did, at the end of their lines; however, the verse of later poets (e.g., Henryson) shows two "peaks:" disyllabic -ing forms concentrate both at the end of the lines (old tendency) and at the line beginning (new tendency) (Tarlinskaja 1974:125, Fig. 3). The non-poetic language seemed to be avoiding disyllabic forms with an end-stress more and more, and in verse they must have become more of a convention: Wyatt is still using them at his line-ends, not unlike Chaucer, while Surrey seems to have broken with the convention: his disyllabic -ing forms, similarly to other disyllabic words of both Germanic and Romance origin, appear mainly at the beginning of his verse lines, as has been traditional ever since (Tarlinskaja 1974:125, Fig. 3). Disyllabic words normally stressed on the first syllable are now encountered at line ends only in ballads and their literary imitations. Some examples:

As I walked out one May morning,
    When May was all in bloom,
O there I spied a bold fisherman,
    Come fishing all alone
                                        (7. "The Royal Fisherman" 1-4)
When she cam to Carterhaugh,
    Tam Lin was at the well,
And there she fand his steed standing,
    But away was himsel.
                                        (23. "Tam Lin" 15-18)
Quoth she, I have loved thee, Little Musgrave,

285

Full long and many a day;
So have I loved you, fair <u>lady</u>,
Yet never word durst I say.
(36. "Little Musgrave and Lady Barnard" 18-21)

From a rhyming convenience function that -ing forms seemed to serve in the Middle English verse, disyllabic verb-forms turned into a text-organizing, rhythm-varying, and semantic device (see Chapter 8) in Modern English verse.

An alternative interpretation, that the words retained their original stressing on the first syllable, thus forming "inversions of stress" (figures WS-2), seems to be the less likely: (a) it would result in two back-to-back stresses which are avoided in English verse, particularly in mid-phrase, so close to the end of the line; (b) it would result in a feminine line-ending, infrequent in ballads, and the feminine ending would correspond to a masculine ending in the structurally parallel line of the stanza: such cases do occur, but they are practically outside the norm of the English verse.

[3] The full list of non-phrase-initial nominal WS(W)-1 of the Sonnets is as follows:

Positions 5-6
To eat the world's <u>due, by</u> the grave and thee	(1)
Resembling strong <u>youth in</u> his middle age	(7)
Be scorned like old <u>men of</u> less truth than tongue	(17)
By adding one <u>thing to</u> my purpose nothing	(20)
And trouble deaf <u>heaven with</u> my bootless cries	(29)
Who can mine own <u>praise to</u> my own self bring	(39)
As this; mine eye's <u>due is</u> thine outward part	(46)
Shall neigh—no dull <u>flesh in</u> his fiery race	(51)
O, lest your true <u>love may</u> seem false in this	(72)
That did my ripe <u>thoughts in</u> my brain inhearse	(86)
Which on thy soft <u>cheek for</u> complexion dwells	(99)
Swear to thy blind <u>soul that</u> I was thy "Will"	(136)
And to this false <u>plague are</u> they now transferred	(137)
As testy sick <u>men when</u> their deaths be near	(140)

Positions 7-8
Thou of thyself thy sweet <u>self dost</u> deceive	(4)
And every fair with his <u>fair doth</u> rehearse	(21)
And then believe me, my <u>love is</u> as fair	(21)
Suffering my friend for my <u>sake to</u> approve her	(42)
And for myself my own <u>worth do</u> define	(62)
Better becomes the grey <u>cheeks of</u> the east	(132)
Who'er keep me, let my <u>heart be</u> his guard	(133)

[4] Similar results were obtained by my graduate student Almira Safarova in 1981. Her dissertation has not been published.

Chapter 8

Rhythm and Meaning

8.0 Preliminary remarks

Finally we have reached the stage of studying the stylistic and semantic functions of rhythmical figures. This chapter concentrates on two hypothetical functions of rhythmical figures: they either <u>emphasize</u> ("italicize", foreground) syntactic patterns and words whose meanings are important for the poet in a given situation, or iconically (metaphorically) <u>imitate</u> the physical (kinetic, visual, acoustic) or psychic images already expressed, at least in part, lexically. The possible metaphoric function of verse rhythm, the addition of information or the creation of an image not explicitly expressed in the text lexically but probably implied by the whole situation, or by a broader context, will not be studied. The interpretation of such cases, even presuming their very existence, is unavoidably subjective. It does not seem improbable that such cases exist. As an example, consider a line from Shelley's "The Cenci" uttered by the boy Bernardo who has just learned that his sister and their stepmother are to be executed and that the executioners have already arrived. He finds it hard to believe that he will soon see his loved ones dead, and that the bond between him and his sister will be broken: $D\acute{\bar{e}}ad!$ $Th\bar{e}$ $sw\acute{\bar{e}}et$ $b\grave{o}nd$ $br\acute{\bar{o}}k\bar{e}n!$ $Th\breve{e}y$ $c\grave{o}me!$ $L\acute{\bar{e}}t$ $m\bar{e}$ (Kiss those warm lips before their crimson leaves Are blighted . . . white . . . cold . . .) (Shel.C V,IV:137). The line, so masterfully built in terms of its rhythm and syntax, contains semantic elements "death, destruction", "love", "link", "motion", "finality" (the latter component is expressed grammatically by the past participle form: "broken"), but it does <u>not</u> contain lexically expressed, explicit components "despair" or "sobbing". However, it follows from the whole context that the boy <u>is</u> desperate, and it is not hard to imagine that he is sobbing or choking while uttering his final, rhythmically broken lines. But since these components are not expressed lexically, the suggestion that they exist can only be speculative and therefore are not amenable to objective analysis.

In approaching the problem of semantic foregrounding by rhythm, I tried to see if cases of emphasis can be semantically and emotively classified, and if particular semantic and emotive categories are tied to particular rhythmical figures. If no generalization is possible, it means that the poets use the figures *ad hoc*, to emphasize a word or words important to them in each individual context only, or do not use them for emphasis at all.

In studying the cases of iconic imitation, I posed the following questions: (a) What physical (kinetic, visual, acoustic) or psychic (joy, fury, fear, despair, and others) qualities are enhanced by rhythm? (b) How often do such cases occur in different genres and periods of Shakespeare's texts, compared with other poets and epochs? (c) Is there any difference between the different rhythmical figures and the intensity and frequency of their link with meaning, or any difference in the "image repertoire" of different figures? (d) If differences in intensity and frequency occur, are they in any way connected with the part-of-speech and syntactic composition of the figure?

The hypothesis that the semantic function of rhythmical figures may be genre conditioned is based on the fact that dramatic and non-dramatic verse are intended for different kinds of perception: mainly acoustic for dramatic verse and mainly visual for non-dramatic, even though the reader usually, in some way, also "hears" the verse. The visual and acoustic perception of rhythmical figures is quite different, as is well known to anyone who has, for example, read Shakespeare's plays and listened to their performance on stage. Many subtleties of form and rhythmical nuances are lost in an oral dramatic performance and are not caught by the audience. The rhythmical difference between genres has been noticed earlier (cf. Hamm 1954:696-697, Tarlinskaja 1976); probably the semantic load on rhythmical figures is also unequal in various genres.

8.1. We begin with a more general stylistic analysis of the monosyllabic figure W: stressed notional (lexical) words on metrically weak positions of the line. As was mentioned earlier, primary attention is directed to disyllabic and polysyllabic figures on the assumption that these were more unquestionably used by the poets consciously and with a particular aim in mind, while monosyllabic figures could be merely due to the features of English vocabulary; for example, the abundance in English of notional monosyllabic words explains frequent cases of "extra-metrical" stresses in weak positions of English syllabo-tonic verse. It seems logical to assume that the probability of an additional semantic or stylistic load increases with the increased length of the figure: the less language-conditioned and more noticeable a rhythmical figure, the more ground there is to suppose that the poet used it with some aim in mind, probably for euphonic, compositional, semantic, or stylistic reasons.

First, a stylistic analysis of the words forming the monosyllabic figure W was carried out on Shakespeare's poem "The Rape of Lucrece" (1593) and his chronicle "Richard II" (1595-96); both were written during the period of the Sonnets (1592-98) and are of unquestionably high artistic merit. "Richard II" is considered a precursor of Shakespeare's great tragedies; it ". . . discloses a range of stylistic mastery, unprecedented in Shakespeare's career before 1595 . . .; it offers a clear prognosis of the mature . . . style of Shakespeare" (Baxter 1980:55).

The first stage was a comparison of the number of alliterating stressed monosyllables on W and their part-of- speech preference, and the second stage was a comparison of the ratio of monosyllabic adjectives on W with positive, negative, or neutral connotations.

It goes without saying that alliteration in English verse tends to mark a word, making it stand out from the context and attract the reader's attention. The ratio of notional monosyllables on W alliterating with other words of the same line was calculated for "Lucrece" and "Richard II". In "Lucrece" over 20% of all stressed monosyllables on W alliterate with other words of the same line (97 cases out of 479), while in "Richard II" less than 7% (46 cases out of 669). This is one indication that strongly stressed notional monosyllables on W are more noticeable (and were meant to be noticed) in the poem than in the play. To see whether the alliterative effect had a preference for a particular part of speech, the proportion of the four main parts of speech marked by alliteration was calculated from the total of each part of speech occurring on W (in percent):

Part of speech	"Lucrece"	"Richard II"
Nouns	21.3 (16 of 75)	3.0 (3 of 102)
Verbs	18.3 (26 of 142)	9.2 (18 of 194)
Adjectives	35.3 (43 of 122)	13.6 (14 of 103)
Adverbs	7.6 (8 of 105)	6.0 (10 of 164)
Others	11.4 (4 of 35)	0.9 (1 of 106)

Both in "Lucrece" and "Richard II" it is the adjective that is most often marked by alliteration. However, the ratio of alliterating adjectives on W is almost three times higher in the poem than in the play; this is not only a sign of genre difference but also a clue to a more important semantic and emotive role played by adjectives (epithets) in the non-dramatic text. Some examples of alliterating adjectives on W: *Rude ram, to batter such an ivory wall*; *And death's dim look in life's mortality*; *When, patterned by thy fault, foul sin may say*; *Sad sounds are slain in merry company* (Sh.RL 67:2, 58:4, 90:6, 159:4); *Free speech and fearless I to thee allow*; *Will rain hot vengence on offender's head*; *Is pale cold cowardice in noble breasts*; *The sly slow hours shall not determinate* (Sh.RII I,I:123, I,II:8,34, I,III:150). Here are some examples of other parts of speech on W with alliteration.

Noun: *Pain pays the income of each precious thing*; *To keep thy sharp woes waking, wretched I* (Sh.RL 48:5, 163:2); *We make woe wanton with this fond delay* (Sh.RII V,II:101).

Verb: *Sits Sin, to seize the souls that wander by him*; *Great grief grieves most at that would do it good* (Sh.RL 126:7, 160:4); *Feed not thy sovereign's foe, my gentle earth* (Sh.RII III,II:12).

Adverb: *So sober-sad, so weary and so mild*; *Here manly Hector faints, here Troilus swoons* (Sh.RL, 221:2, 213:2); *That's as York thrives to beat back Bolingbroke* (Sh.RII II,II:146).

It is, of course, not surprising that a lyrical poem should have more alliterating words than a play; but it is also a possible sign of a different stylistic role and heavier semantic load assigned to words on W in the poem than in the play. To demonstrate this point, another test was made. All adjectives on W were classified into three groups, with positive, negative, and neutral connotations. Examples of adjectives with a positive connotation are: <u>dear</u>, <u>free</u>, <u>best</u>, <u>fair</u>, <u>sweet</u>, <u>true</u>, and <u>pure</u>. Examples of adjectives with a negative connotation are: <u>black</u>, <u>foul</u>, <u>blind</u>, <u>false</u>, <u>sad</u>, <u>faint</u>, <u>pale</u>, <u>weak</u>, <u>cold</u>, and <u>sore</u>. Most adjectives with a neutral connotation are usually words denoting belonging (<u>own</u>), size, distance quantity, and material: <u>wide</u>, <u>vast</u>, <u>much</u>, <u>brief</u>, <u>short</u>, <u>Greek</u>, <u>stone</u>. Colors were on the whole assumed neutral, except for <u>black</u> and <u>grey</u> which, together with <u>dark</u>, <u>dim</u>, and <u>pale</u>, were considered negative. <u>Red</u>, <u>white</u>, <u>green</u>, and <u>blue</u> were considered neutral, though in a specific context they may acquire an emotive coloring.

"Positive" or "negative" adjectives may in different contexts have different degrees of emotive intensity. For example, <u>dear</u>, <u>good</u>, or <u>sweet</u> in "Richard II" fail to have the same strong positive emotive charge as in "Lucrece" or in the Sonnets. Compare: *<u>dear</u> lord*, *<u>good</u> uncle*, *<u>sweet</u> York* in "Richard II" with *Unmask, <u>dear</u> dear, thy moody heaviness*, or *A little harm done to a great <u>good</u> end*, or *Entombs her outcry in her lip's <u>sweet</u> fold* in "The Rape of Lucrece" (229:6, 76:3, 97:7). These degrees of emotive intensity were disregarded in the emotive classification of adjectives, which naturally impoverishes the results; still the quantitative correlation between the three groups of adjectives on W in the poem and the play is revealing:

Connotation of adjectives on W (in percent)

	Positive	Negative	Neutral	Total
"Lucrece"	32.2	46.8	21.0	122
"Richard II"	42.0	28.0	30.0	103

The ratio between the positive and negative adjectives in the poem and the chronicle is the reverse: in this respect "Lucrece" is more "tragic" than "Richard II". The ratio of neutral adjectives on W is considerably higher in "Richard II" than in "Lucrece". At the same time, positive and negative adjectives in the chronicle are on the whole closer to neutral than in the poem. It follows that adjectives on W play a more important stylistic role in the poem than in the play.

Let us compare the emotive charge of adjectives in the monosyllabic figure, W, with adjectives in the disyllabic figure, SW-1, where adjectives prevail (examples: *Ĭn thē ŏld ăge . . . Ĭn thĕir pūre rănks . . . Bŭt bȳ fāir sĕqŭence . . .*). Figure 8.1 presents the proportions of positive, negative, and neutral

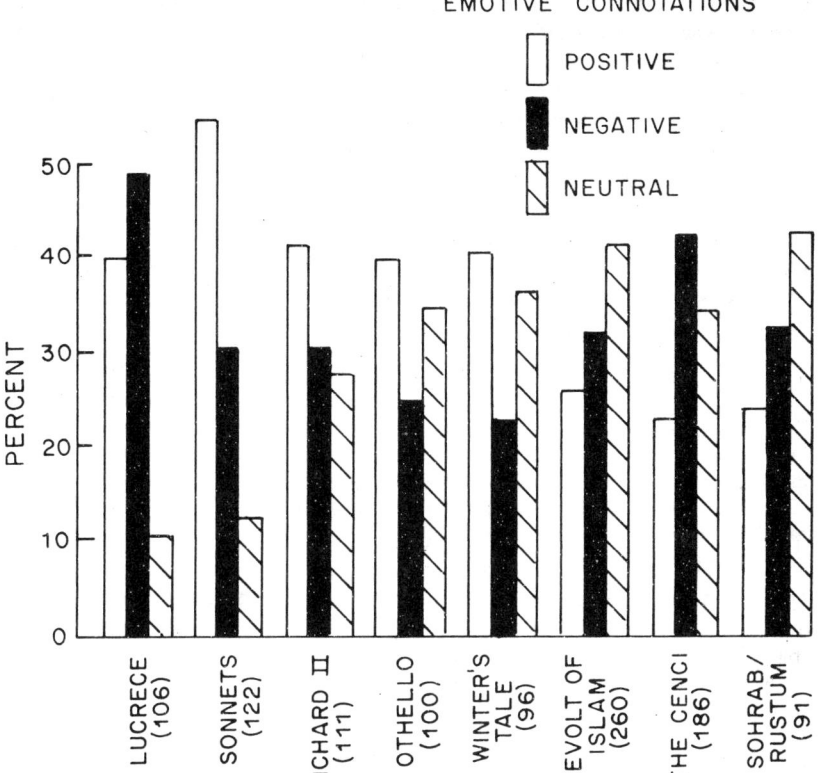

Fig. 8.1. Proportion (in percent) of the emotive connotations of adjectives in the SW-1 rhythmical figure in texts of Shakespeare, Shelley ("The Revolt of Islam" and "The Cenci"), and Arnold ("Sohrab and Rustum"). The use of adjectives with a neutral connotation is genre specific: it is the least in lyrics (Sonnets) and the most in narrative poetry ("The Revolt of Islam"). The total of SW-1 figures containing adjectives is given in brackets.

emotive connotations in the figure SW-1 for "Lucrece", the Sonnets, and three Shakespearean plays, a poem and a play by Shelley, and a play by Arnold.

If we compare the proportion of <u>neutral</u> adjectives in W and <u>SW-1</u>, we notice that in "Lucrece" the figure is two times lower for the disyllabic SW-1 (10.6%) than for the monosyllabic W (21.5%); this might be an indication that the stylistic charge of the disyllabic figure SW-1 is higher than that of the monosyllabic figure W, which is less noticeable and probably more language-conditioned. In "Richard II", however, the proportion of neutral adjectives is

291

practically identical in both W (29.0%) and SW-1 (28.0%). This phenomenon may be explained by the general low degree of emotive intensity of adjectives with non-neutral connotations in "Richard II" (_sweet_ York, _sweet_ Richard, as compared, for example, to _sweet issue_, _sweet form_, _sweet odour_, _sweet deaths_, _sweet'st friend_ of the Sonnets); this trait decreases the stylisic potential of the figure SW-1 in the verse of the chronicle.

The preliminary conclusions we have reached so far about the monosyllabic figure W are: (a) the stylistic charge of stressed words on W in Shakespeare's non-dramatic verse is stronger than it is in his drama of the same period; (b) the stylistic charge of stressed words on W, at least in Shakespeare's non-dramatic verse, is weaker than in the disyllabic figure SW-1.

8.2. Consider now the disyllabic rhythmical figure SW in more detail.

8.2.1. Adjectives are the most frequent part of speech in SW-1. As they are syntactically and accentually subordinate to the following word, they do not break the prevailing rythmical inertia too strongly.

The difference in the proportion of neutral adjectives forming the figures SW-1 in Shakespeare's dramatic and non-dramatic verse is striking: neutral adjectives are two to three times more frequent in the dramas than in the Sonnets and the lyrical poem (Fig. 8.1). Surprisingly, the proportion of neutral adjectives is lower in "Richard II" than in the later plays; the impression is that "Richard II" is in some ways stylistically closer to the earlier non-dramatic genres than "Othello" or "The Winter's Tale", where the proportion of neutral adjectives in the figure SW-1 is identical with Shelley's "The Cenci". It is also significant that alliteration is almost entirely absent from Shakespeare's later dramas. There appears to be a general decreasing trend in Shakespeare's use of alliteration throughout his writing career, which is only in part genre conditioned.

Figure 8.1 makes it clear that the smallest proportion of adjectives with neutral connotation in the material analyzed was found in Shakespeare's lyrical verse, the highest in the narrative poems (Shelley's and Arnold's), while dramatic verse (Shakespeare's and Shelley's) is intermediate.

The high proportion of neutral adjectives in the narrative poems is understandable: these adjectives usually denote size, distance, quantity, or material, and are typical even of a romantic text. A tentative conclusion is that while adjectives with a strong positive or negative connotation help the rhythmical figure SW-1 to play a stylistic role of emphasis, the neutral adjectives in the SW-1 may reduce the latter to a mere means of varying the prevailing rhythmical momentum. It is in such cases that the rhythmical figures tend to become, in Stein's terminology, "an abstract vehicle" (Stein 1951:22), appearing in the text because ". . . the poet likes the variation" (Ransom 1972:36). Indeed, reading, for example, Shelley's "The Revolt of Islam", one gathers the impression that the poet formed a kind of habit, almost constantly using the figure SW-1, particularly in positions 2-3; for example: *From the wide multitude: that lonely man*; *If our own will as others' law we bind*; *Of the broad earth, and feeding from one breast*; *And my young friend was near, and ardently* (V,XXIX:6, XLIX:1, L:2; VI,X:6). On the other hand, of course, their very occurrence in the rhythmical figure emphasizes and adds semantic value even to the most neutral words.

Another way of studying the semantic and stylistic functions of adjectives in the figure SW-1 is a comparison of the frequency of individual words in the SW-1 with their frequency in the text excluding all disyllabic and trisyllabic rhythmical figures. Consider, as an example, the frequency of individual adjectives in Shakespeare's Sonnets. The total number of adjectives forming the SW-1 is 122, while the number of lexical units is less than half that (56): this is, of course, a sign of reoccurrence. The most frequently repeating adjective in the figure SW-1 is sweet—19 times, almost 16% of all the cases, while in the text excluding the rhythmical figures sweet comprises only about 6% of monosyllabic adjectives. Clearly the figure SW-1 "prefers" the adjective sweet. Other adjectives "preferred" by the figure SW-1 are true, poor, fair, and dear. The adjective sweet, so essential for the "sugared sonnets", is clearly foregrounded by its frequent position in the SW-1. The epithets dear and fair, like sweet, help to form the images of the addressees of the sonnets; true and poor refer usually either to the poet himself or to his verse. Thus, all adjectives used extensively in the rhythmical figure SW-1 are not only emotionally charged but also semantically essential for the "poetic universe" of the sonnets. Interestingly enough, the most frequently repeated nouns, which occur in SW-1 relatively more often than in the rest of the text, are death, time, heart, and particularly love. These are, of course, key words of the sonnets, emphasized by their placement in the rhythmical figure SW-1.

8.2.2. The most reasonable way to approach the semantic functions of noun- and verb-formed rhythmical figures seemed to be a kind of componental semantic analysis[1] of the micro-text corresponding to a micro-situation. It is impossible to evaluate the semantic function of a rhythmical figure if we analyze the meaning of only one or two notional words that form it; rhythm often emphasizes, or imitates, meanings of words that are outside the figure but are syntactically and semantically tied with the words that compose it. This is true of all parts of speech, but particularly of adverbs and adjectives. For example: *Ănd thē brĭght sŭn broke forth, and melted all* (*The cloud* . . .) (A.SR, 523). The figure SW-1 (*the bright*) contains an adjective which qualifies the noun *sun* that *broke forth*; it is the motion of "breaking forth" that is emphasized and imitated rhythmically (also with the help of onomatopoeia— the repeating plosive consonant [b]), but the verb itself is not part of the rhythmical figure. The micro-text corresponding to a micro-situation covers, as a rule, only a part of the verse line and is restricted to it, except in cases of an enjambment.

Some examples of the micro-text analysis: (1) *Ănd Ī lay̆ strŭgglĭng as its whirlwinds passed* (Shel.RI III,I:8). The figure SW-1 includes one notional word, lay, while the micro-context also includes the participle struggling; thus, the semantic components of the micro-text are: "lie", "uneven motion", "fight". (2) *Ănd thē răck măkes him utter, do you think* (Shel.C V,II:96). The figure SW-1 contains one notional word, the noun rack, while the micro-context is *the rack makes him* (*utter*); its components are: "torture", "pain", "to force" ("sound of speech"). (3) *Stăbbed wĭth ōne blŏw my everlasting soul* (Shel.C V,II:123). The figure WSW-1 includes the words *stabbed with one*, while the micro-context also includes the word *blow*; the semantic components of the micro-text relevant for our analysis are: "sharp point", "to strike", "to wound", "to kill". (4) *Măkes hīm spēak fŏndly̆ like a frantic man* (Sh.RII III,III:185). The figure WSW-1 covers the first three words, while the micro-text is, in fact, the whole line, *fondly* and *frantic* being its important semantic elements. The semantic components relevant for our analysis are: "to force", "sound of speech", "mental confusion", "emotion: despair".

After identifying all specific semantic components of the micro-texts, the former were then classified into semantic groups. One meaning of a word may contain several semantic components, semes[2], and a micro-text may, naturally, contain even more. That is why a micro-text may contribute to several semantic groups. The groups derived were then hierarchically arranged into subgroups, classes, and subclasses in a way not unlike Roget's *Thesaurus*. For example: (a) "speaking", with subtypes "speaking normally", "whispering", "shouting;" (b) "motion", with subtypes "upward, downward, forward, backward, away", "slow, quick", "flying, sailing, crawling, kneeling, bringing or taking something away", "smooth or uneven: quivering, stumbling, checked;" (c) "physical suffering and death", with subgroups "sickness, pain;" "wounding, torturing;" "causing death and dying;" (d) "emotions", with two subgroups: "negative (fear, shame, fury)" and "positive (joy, bliss, exultation);" (e) "state of mind" (usually unbalanced): "drunk, confused, amazed, mad;" (f) "changes of facial expression (usually resulting from emotions and unbalanced state of mind) and changes of color:" "winking, yawning, laughing, sobbing, smiling, turning red or pale;" (g) "actions connected with breathing:" "breathing, sighing, suffocation;" (h) "changes in the lighting:" "lightening;" "getting dark", and others. It is not hard to see that the classification is strongly affected by the material analyzed. That is why the categories singled out are often asymmetrical; for example, there is a category "sickness, pain" but no category "health, well-being;" there is a cateogry "unbalanced state of mind" but no category for "mental balance, stability". The lopsided classification is clearly leaning towards, as it were, the marked member of each pair, which has a negative connotation.

Next I calculated the percentage of micro-texts with a particular semantic component, for example, "pain, torture, death", from all micro-texts coupled with a particular rhythmical figure, for example, SW-1, containing a particular part of speech, for example, the verb. If a micro-text contained several semantic components, for example, three, it became a part of three semantic groupings of micro-texts. (That is why some examples below illustrate several semantic categories.) The semantic groupings of micro-texts were then arranged in the order of their decreasing size. Their ranking showed the role of each semantic category in each figure formed by each notional part of speech. The results were compared with those of other notional parts of speech, other rhythmical figures, other texts by the same author, and other texts by other authors. I shall not report all the resulting data, but they helped me to establish correlations between various semantic components and identify the most frequently repeating ones.

8.2.3. We shall first consider the semantic characteristics of SW-1 containing a verb. At a preliminary stage I calculated the proportion of verbs (1) with broad or vague meaning, and (2) with a component termed "extra". Verbs of broad or vague meaning are those (a) that are close to link-verbs, such as grow, look, or make, for example, *yĕt hē lŏoks săd; ănd shē'll rŭn măd; Ŏthĕllŏ shăll gŏ măd*; and those (b) that require an obligatory complement, such as give, or have, for example: *Tĭll yōu gĭve jŏy*, or *Fŏr shē hăd ĕyes, and chose me*. Verbs with the component "extra" denote an extra high or extra low intensity or speed of an action; an action detailed; or have an added stylistic connotation, for example, whispering or exclaiming as opposed to saying; crawling or running as opposed to coming or going; words like to slay, or to kill, that have a strong emotive charge; poetic or vernacular (low) vocabulary: *Damn her, lewd minx*!

Verbs of vague or broad meaning comprise about 43% of all verbs in SW-1 of Shakespeare's Sonnets, 40% of the SW-1 verbs in all the four Shakespeare's plays analyzed, 22.5% of all verbs forming the figure SW-1 in Shelley's poem "The Revolt of Islam", 20% of the SW-1 verbs in Shelley's tragedy "The Cenci", and only 8% of all the verbs forming the figure SW-1 in Arnold's narrative poem "Sohrab and Rustum". The data indicate that the nineteenth-century poets, though using verbs in the figure SW-1 as sparingly as Shakespeare (this seems to be a general tendency of the English poetic tradition), clearly do so with more confidence, and with a stylistic and semantic aim in mind. In Shakespeare's texts, however, the verb-formed figures SW-1 are frequently not loaded with any semantic or stylistic information and often seem to serve mere rhythm-varying purposes: they create a mild "ripple", modulating the flow of the verse. The semantic tie between certain classes of verbs and the figure SW-1 seems to have crystallized in the verse of later authors and is particularly strong in Arnold's poem, where practically every verb in the figure SW-1 is loaded with intense and specific meaning, emphasized or imitated rhythmically. Verbs with the component "extra" constitute only 6% of the verb-formed figures SW-1 in Shakespeare's dramas, 8% in his Sonnets, but over 15% in Shelley's "The Cenci", 20% in his "Revolt of Islam", and over 35% in Arnold's "Sohrab and Rustum:" nine verbs out of the total 26 in the figure SW-1 have "extra" as a feature of their semantic structure. The percentage of verbs constituting the figure SW-1 is not higher in "Sohrab and Rustum" than in Shakespeare's Sonnets, but their stylistic charge and semantic load is more than four times stronger. Evidently the semantic and stylistic potential of the rhythmical figure SW-1 was fully recognized only by later poets.

The virtually boundless ocean of different semantic components seemed at first almost hopeless to generalize; but as I proceeded, distinguishable semantic groups kept recurring in texts by different authors, in different genres and different epochs.

The most noticeable and frequently repeated component of the verb-formed figures SW-1 is motion, with its recurring subtypes: forward, backward, away; upward, downward (often kneeling); a broken, uneven, trembling motion. The highest proportions of this component were found in the two narrative poems by Arnold and Shelley: out of 26 verb-formed micro-contexts in the figure SW-1 in "Sohrab and Rustum", 13 (50%) contain the semantic component "motion", while in "The Revolt of Islam" it is 16 cases out of 40 (40%). In the dramatic verse and the Sonnets the percentage of the component "motion" in the verbal SW-1 is lower: 28% in Shakespeare's Sonnets, 26% in his four dramas (57 verbs out of 217), and only 22% in Shelley's "The Cenci". It is not surprising that the incidence of verbs of motion is relatively low in the Sonnets; but their comparatively low incidence in dramatic verse seems at first glance unexpected. However, this is nonetheless logical: dramas as a genre show motion rather than describe it, while narrative poems describe motion, doing this with the help of verbs (or combinations of verbs with other words) which have motion as part of their semantic structure.[3]

The most typical kind of motion that accompanies the rhythmical figure SW-1 is "forward;" next comes "backward". [In the following examples not only the rhythmical figure but also adjacent words which are part of the micro-text / micro-situation are underlined.] Examples: *Long after fearing tŏ crēep fòrth again* (Sh.VA 173:4); *Thŏu hāst pàss'd bỳ the ambush of young days*; *For I am shamed by that whĭch Ī brĭng fòrth*; *Alas, 'tĭs trŭe Ĭ hăve gŏne hĕre and there*; *Ĭf thŏu tŭrn bàck and my loud crying still* (Sh.Son 70:9, 72:13,110:1, 143:14); *Ănd dāres hĭm tŏ sĕt fòrwărd to the fight*; *Sound, trumpets, ănd sĕt fòrwărd, combatants* (Sh.RII I,II:109,117); *O, here it is. Uncle, Ĭ mŭst cŏme fòrth*; *As well to see the vessel thăt's cŏme ĭn*; *I ne'er might say before. Whĕn Ĭ cŏme bàck* (Sh.Oth V,II:257, II,I:37,II,III:232); *Whĕn Ĭ wălked fòrth upon the glittering grass*; *Ĭt mĭght wălk fòrth to war among mankind*; *Whĕn Ĭ gŏ fòrth alone, bearing the lamp* (Shel.RI Dedication III:5 and V:6,II,XLIV:2); *Whĭch wŏuld bŭrst fòrth into the wandering air*; *Have swallowed up the vapours thĕy sĕnt fòrth*; *Stop for God's sake! Ĭ wĭll gŏ* bȧck and kill him (Shel.C III,I:28, IV,III:41,34); Ănd hē ra⁼n fo⁻rward, and embraced his knees; Whĭch ĭt sĕnt flȳĭng wĭde;— then Sohrab threw; Bŭt cȯurteȯuslȳ drȇw bȧck, and spoke, and said (A.SR 341,405,426).

"Off, away (abrupt leaving, quitting)": Which with such gentle sorrow he shook off; Before I have shook off the regal thoughts; If then we shall shake off our slavish yoke (Sh.RII V,II:31, IV,I:163, II,I:291); Will have cast off the impotence that binds (Shel.RI II,XLVI:7); O, that the hour when present had cast off; He has cast nature off which was his shield; I am cut off from the only world I know (Shel.C V,I:5, III,I:286, V,IV:85).

"Up and down": And interchangeably hurl down my gage (Sh.RII I,I:146); And ever still our comrades were hewn down; And he knelt down upon the dust, alway (Shel.RI VI,IX:8, X,XXXIX:7); I have knelt down through the long sleepless nights; The drawbridge is let down, there is a tramp; To be nailed down into a narrow place (Shel.C I,III:117, IV,IV:59, V,IV:51); So said he, and dropp'd Sohrab's hand, and left; And his head swam, and he sank down to earth (A.SR 94, 693); But let thy spiders that suck up thy venom (Sh.RII III,II:14); Of rest, and I heaped up the courser's bed (Shel.RI VI,XXVI:8); Under the penury heaped on me by thee; I will pile up my silver and my gold (Shel.C III,I:295, IV,I:56).

Less frequent but definitely noticeable are such characteristics of motion as "uneven, quivering" and "to be restricted, stopped, confined". Some examples: Her honour is ta'en prisoner by the foe (Sh.RL 230:5); Or like a cunning instrument cased up (Sh.RII I,III:163); You have tripped since.—O my most sacred lady (Sh.WT I,II:76); That he shuts up himself—imagine me (Sh.WT IV,I:19); Before I have shook off my regal thoughts; If then we shall shake off our slavish yoke (Sh.RII IV,I:163, II,I:291); And I lay struggling as the whirlwinds passed; And I lay struggling in the impotence; Sons of the glorious dead, have ye lain bound (Shel.RI III,I:8, III,VI:1, II,XIII:2); Where we sit shut from the wide gaze of day; To be nailed down into a narrow place; I am cut off from the only world I know (Shel.C II,II:90, V,IV:51,85).

Other recurrent semantic components in the verb-formed SW-1 are as follows: bearing or inflicting pain, wounds, torture, death, destruction; closely connected with the previous group, but milder: bearing sadness, grief; negative emotions, such as anger, fury, fear; physical demonstration of emotions: crying, sobbing, breathlessness, suffocation, changing facial expression or color; mental disorder: being drunk, frantic, going mad; intellectual activity, and particularly wavering, doubting; both sounds of speech and lack of words, speech stopped. Some examples of these other semantic groups and subgroups:

"Grief; pain, wounds; destruction, death": This cancer that eats up Love's tender spring; The purple tears that his wound wept, was drenched (Sh.VA 110:2, 176:4); Till his breath breatheth life in her again (Sh.VA 79:6); For they breathe truth that breathe their words in pain; That blood already, like the pelican, Hast thou tapped out and drunkenly caroused (Sh.RII II,I:8,126-127);

297

The wretched animal heaved forth such groans; Than *to die well, and not my master's debtor*; That *can do hurt* . . . (Sh.AYLI 0I,I:36, II,III:76, III,V:27); Though in the trade of war I *have slain men*; Honest Iago, *that look'st dead with grieving*; And *she died* singing it; *that song to-night*; And he grows angry. Now, whether *he kill* Cassio; He *that lies slain* here, Cassio; Though *I lost twenty lives.* Help! help, ho! help! (Sh.Oth I,II:1, II,III:173, IV,III:31, V,I:18, V,II:103,169); The bastard *brains* with these my proper hands Shall *I dash out*. Go, take it to the fire (Sh.WT II,III:140- 141); And ever still our comrades *were hewn down* (Shel.RI VI,IX:8); Till *it wind out your life* and soul? Away!; *To be nailed down into a narrow place* (Shel.C V,I:11, V,IV:51); Which never tender lady *hath borne* greater (Sh.WT II,II:24); *I have borne much*, and kissed the sacred hand; Who *have borne deeper wrongs*. In truth, if he (Shel.C I,III:111, II,I:2).

"Emotions (fury, fear, and others) and their physical display: crying, sobbing, breathlessness, change of facial expression or color." Some examples: *For I fear Cassio with my night-cap too*; And *he grows angry* . . . (Sh.Oth II,I:310, V,I:18); Who *should weep* most, for daughter or for wife (Sh.RL 256:7); *I could weep*, madam, would it do you good; For *they breathe* truth that breathe their words in pain (Sh.RII III,IV:22, II,I:8); The wretched animal *heaved forth* such groans (Sh.AYLI II,I:36); What *he breathes out his breath drinks up again* (Sh.RL 238:7); For *they weep* not; and Widsom had unrolled (Shel. RI I,XXXVIII:3).

"Mental disorder; not smooth process of thinking (doubting); lack of knowledge": *For, if I should despair, I should grow mad* (Sh.Son 140:9); As he shall smile, Othello *shall go mad*; I'll see before I doubt; when *I doubt*, prove (Sh.Oth IV,I:100, III,III:192); It was returned unanswered. *I doubt not*; Of Marzio *I know* nothing . . . My God! I did not kill him; *I knew* nothing (Shel.C II,II:62, III,II:70, V,I:5).

"Speech; lack of words, speech stopped, muteness; mocking": And *she speaks* for you stoutly; From this time forth I never *will speak word* (Sh.Oth III,I:45, V,II:306); Have eyes to wonder, *but lack tongues* to praise (Sh.Son 106:14); That matter of the murder *is hush'd up*; Shall *thou strike dumb* the meanest of mankind; What *might make dumb things speak* . . . (Shel.C I,I:1, II,I:119,172); O mistress, villainy *hath made mocks* with love! (Sh.Oth V,II:154); Is that when selfishness *mocks* love's delight (Shel.RI VII,VI:2).

To generalize: the most typical semantic groups of verbs and verbal combinations of words coupled with the figure SW-1 are those that refer to physical actions: motion, and the physical display or consequence of emotions. Other recurring semantic components refer to sounds and mental states or activity. Words with a strong, usually negative, connotation, such as pain and death (as well as actions causing them), are also characteristic of the figure SW-1. The emphasized semantic components are "downward"; "uneven, unbalanced"; "restricted or interrupted"; "ruinous"; "psychologically horrible". Thus the verbal figures SW-1 serve for emphasis and, even more so, metaphorical imitation of action: breach of rhythm accompanies words denoting broken actions.

It must be pointed out that the specific "preference" of the figure SW-1 for certain semantic classes of words is not fully explained by the overall prevalence of such words in the whole text (cf. with the adjective sweet in the Sonnets). The proportion of some semantic groups was also calculated for monosyllabic words outside all rhythmical figures. It turned out that the proportion of these semantic groups outside rhythmical figures was considerably lower than in the SW-1. For example, the percentage of verbs of motion in Shakespeare's dramas outside rhythmical figures is about 16%, while in the figure SW-1 it is 26%; in "The Cenci" the data are 15 and 22% respectively, in Arnold's "Sohrab and Rustum", 40 and 50%. The qualitative difference between semantic groups of words within and outside the rhythmical figures is even more striking; for example, the verbs lack and mock, or the word combination go (run) mad are almost exclusively coupled with the figure SW-1.

8.2.4. Semantic characteristics of nouns in SW-1 are greatly conditioned by their syntactic functions. The most frequent syntactic functions of nouns in the figure SW-1 are those of an attribute and, coupled with the following verb with an ictic stress, of a subject. Both components, noun-subject and verb-predicate, have equal syntactic weight and (at least theoretically) equal sentence accent. The semantic potential of this part-of-speech/syntactic structure, coupled with the figure SW-1, is very strong. Practically no words of vague or broad semantics occur in this rhythmical-grammatical pattern; words with the component termed "extra" occur in 70-90% of the figures SW-1 coupled with the syntactic structure "subject + predicate (or predicative element)".

The most noticeable semantic groups are two: "motion" and "suffering (pain, torture, wounds, sickness, destruction, death)". The incidence of the component "motion" is 40-55% of all rhythmical-syntactic structures "SW-1/ subject + predicate or predicative element" in Shakespeare's dramas, Shelley's "Islam", and Arnold's "Sohrab and Rustum"; only in Shelley's romantic tragedy "The Cenci" is the component "motion" less frequent than "torture, death".

The most characteristic features of motion in the rhythmical-grammatical structure "SW-1/subject + predicate" are: (a) forward, upward, or downward; (b) uneven, vibrating, shaky; (c) flying, floating, streaming (winds, floods, tears, boats, birds); (d) movement coupled with force (striking, piercing, delivering a blow); (e) strong workings of one's face, mimics. Some examples are:

"Forward, upward, downward": *Whiles other men have gates, and these gates opened; Lead on to some foul issue . . . We all kneel* (Sh.WT I,II:197, II,III:153); *While the sun clomb Heaven's eastern step . . .* (Shel.RI VI,XII:7);

When the church fell, and crushed him in a mummy (Shel.C I,III:60); *As his foe fell; then, like a serpent, coiled* (Byron, "The Island" IV,XII:56); *And the fog rose out of the Oxus stream*; *With his head bowing to the ground, and mane* (A.SR 2,731).

"Vibrating, uneven": *Beating her bulk, that his hand shakes withal* (Sh.RL 67:5); *I have tremor cordis on me: my heart dances* (Sh.WT I,II:110); *After its tumult, his heart vibrating* (Shel.RI II,XXIX:6); *Slide giddily as the world reels . . .* (Shel.C III,I:12); *And his knees totter'd, and he smote his hand*; *And his head swam, and he sank down to earth* (A.SR 661,693).

"Flying, floating": *No cause, but company, of her drops spilling* (Sh.RL 177:4); *May the winds blow till they have waken'd death!* (Sh.Oth. II,I:185); *And the winds bore me—through the darkness spread*; *And the wind bore that tumult to and fro*; *Such were my thoughts, when the tide gan to flow* (Shel.RI III,V:4, V,XLI:5, I,II:7); *When the sun melts the snow in high Pamere*; *Over the fighters' heads; and a wind rose*; *And then the gloom dispersed, and the wind fell* (A.SR 15,483,522).

"Delivering a blow:" *A killing rain of fire,—when the waves smite*; *When its shafts smite - while yet his bow is twanging*; *And his hoofs ground the rocks to fire and dust* (Shel.RI VI,VII:8, XVII:3, XXII:1); *Lithe as the gliding snake, and the club came*; *His covering shield, and the spear pierced his side* (A.SR 418,520).

"Mimics": *Heaven stops the nose at it, and the moon winks*; *When your eyes roll so . . .* (Sh.Oth IV,II:78, V,II:41); *Parted and quivered; the tears ceased to break* (Shel.RI I,XVIII:3).

The component "suffering, pain, sickness, destruction, death", the most frequent in "The Cenci" (almost 40% of all cases of the pattern), keeps recurring in the other texts, too. Examples: *Nor shall Death brag thou wander'st in his shade*; *From hence your memory death cannot take* (Sh.Son 18:11, 81:3); *That my youth suffered. My story being done* (Sh.Oth I,III:158); *O, cut my lace, lest my heart, cracking it*; *But my heart bleeds . . . . 'Fore your queen died, she was more worth such gazes* (Sh.WT III,II:174, III,III:52, V,II:225); *Mine eyes and my heart ached . . . . With the flesh clinging to the roots, was strewed* (Shel.RI VI,LII:6, VI,XV:7); *Slide giddily as the world reels . . . . Is changed to vapour such as the dead breathe*; *My God! I never knew what the mad felt*; *And the rack makes him utter . . . . And holding his breath, died . . . .* (Shel.C III,I:12,15,24, V,II:96,183); *And his sobs choked him . . . . And his soul set to grief . . . .* (A.SR 704,616).

Another repeating component is "speech" (elements of deceit and mocking are emphasized), or any "other sound". Examples: *When my love swears that she is made of truth* (Sh.Son 138:1); *That my poor life must answer.—Thy life answer!*; *What my tongue speaks my right drawn sword may prove* (Sh.RII V,II:83, I,I:46); *For I am falser than vows made in wine* (Sh.AYLI III,V:73); *With the Moor, say'st thou? . . .* (Sh.Oth I,I:165); *Speak thou! Whence come ye? A youth made reply*; *And a voice said:—"Thou must a listener be . . ."*

(Shel.RI VIII,XXIII:1, I,LVIII:5); *As the tongue dares not fashion into words; The house-dog moans, and the beams crack: nought else* . . . . (Shel.C II,II:85, III,II:79).

Yet another component is "getting light or dark", "play of reflection": . . . *till the stars gan to fail* (Shel.RI XVIII,XXVI:5); *When the sun melts the snow* . . . . *When the dew glistens on the pearled ears*; *When the frost flowers the whiten window-panes*; *And the sun sparkled on the Oxus stream*; *Shall the lake glass her, flying over it* (A.SR 15,155,306,488,570).

Other components are less frequent, but we have already encountered some of them earlier, and will find more later, in our analysis of other rhythmical figures. These are: (a) "breathing, choking, sobbing", for example: . . . *as the dead breathe*; *And holding his breath, died* (Shel.C III,I:15, V,II:183); *Which thy breath kindled* . . . *Parted and quivered; the tears ceased to break* (Shel.RI I,XXXII:5, I,XVIII:3); *And his sobs choked him* . . . . (A.SR 704); and (b) "going mad", "feeling giddy:" *Slide giddily as the world reels* . . . . *I never knew what the mad felt* . . . . (Shel.C III,I:12,24); *And his head swam* . . . . (A.SR 693).

8.2.5. In 8.2.1 we analyzed adjectives from the point of view of their connotative (emotive) charge. Viewed in a broader semantic context, adjectives forming the figure SW-1 can be analyzed from another point of view: do they, coupled with a rhythm-varying figure, add to the semantic information of the micro-text (micro-situation) corresponding to one line (or in case of an enjambment, two lines)? All the ninety adjectives forming the figure SW-1 in Arnold's "Sohrab and Rustum" were analyzed in a wider context of the micro-situation they help to create. It turned out that 39 adjectives (43.3%) appeared in a situation dominated by action: movement forward or downward, quivering or flowing motion; eight adjectives appeared in a situation dominated by the motive of dying and death; seven adjectives in a situation dominated by the motive of sound; and four by the motive of getting light, and shining. Situations dealing with crying and swallowing also include one adjective each. Thus, only 30 adjectives out of ninety appearing in the rhythmical figure analyzed were not directly motivated by the semantics of a broader context, while two-thirds of the adjectives were loaded with additional semantic information, mainly, as in cases of verbs and nouns, that of motion. These data show that the iconic potential of the rhythmical figure SW-1 to imitate motion is exploited not only with the help of verbs, but also adjectives which usually have little semantic connection with the idea of motion. Verse-form, as it were, induces an additional component of meaning that normally is not found in the semantic structure of an adjective: a good example of an increased semantic volume of words in verse (cf. Tynjanov 1924:48-120, Levin 1966, Appendix:213-215). Here are some examples.

"Motion": *Through the black tents he passed* . . . (16); *From their black tents, long files of horses, they stream'd* (110); *Who with numb blacken'd*

fingers makes her *fire* (304); *Then*, with weak hasty *fingers, Sohrab* loosed (*His belt* . . .) (669); *And* with fond faltering *fingers* stroked *his cheek* (696); *Regretting* the warm *mansion which it* left (855); *As* that poor *bird* flies home . . . (573); . . . *and* that proud *horsehair plume* (*Never till now defiled,* sank to the dust) (497-498).
    "Death": *On* the mown, dying *grass* . . . (638).
    "Sound": *That* the hard iron corslet clank'd aloud (664).
    "Getting light": *And* the bright sun broke forth . . . (523).

8.2.6. At this stage of analysis, some preliminary conclusions about the semantic characteristics of rhythmical figures can already be drawn.

(1) Repeated semantic components coupled with the rhythmical figure SW-1 definitely exist. They are primarily motion (particularly forward and downward), or emotions resulting in a movement or change of facial expression (fear, trembling, joy, heart dancing, fury, eyes rolling). Other repeating components may be generalized in the following way: (a) events or notions with a strong negative connotation (suffering, death); these events are also often preceded or followed by a kinetic action (suffocation, strangulation, delivering a blow, torturing on a rack, piercing one's side); (b) an action, or process, or sound broken or stopped; being restricted, imprisoned; (c) an unbalanced mental state. It is hard to draw a line between merely emphasizing and actually imitating an action; however, it is clear that the broken rhythm of the figure SW-1 does accompany situations where action, particularly uneven and interrupted, is described, thus iconically (even though conventionally) representing or adding to the action.

(2) Not only are semantic components repeated, but the actual words and word combinations that express them are, too; these combinations of words, forming particular syntactic structures coupled with the rhythmical figure SW-1, tend to become "clichés" (cf. 8.3). Repeated are, for example, the verbs lack and mock and the nouns head, hand, and heart. Some examples with the noun heart: but his heart granteth—which my heart knows—my heart dances — lest my heart, cracking it—but my heart bleeds—though the heart triumphs —and my heart knew repose. Some examples of the verbal "clichés": is to let forth—I must come forth—it might walk forth—when I walked forth— which would burst forth; to be nailed down—I have knelt down —and he knelt down —and he sank down—our comrades were hewn down; before I have shook off —if then we shall shake off—which with such gentle sorrow he shook off; as I lay struggling as its whirlwinds passed—and I lay struggling in impotence. Some more "clichés:" who with numb blacken'd fingers—and with fond faltering fingers—then, with weak hasty fingers; and many, many others.

(3) The semantic and stylistic function of the figure SW-1 largely depends on its part-of-speech and syntactic composition. Different morphological and syntactic structures coupled with the SW-1 have a different semantic and stylistic potential.

(4) The semantic and stylistic potential of the figure SW-1 is realized in different ways in different genres (cf. lyrical vs. narrative vs. dramatic verse).

(5) The semantic and stylistic potential of the figure SW-1 seems to have increased from Shakespeare to the later poets, who apparently were more aware of its semiotic function, consolidated by the literary tradition.

8.3. Consider now the disyllabic figure WS-1 (e.g., C*ŏ*me tō ărrèst thĕ cŭlprĭt . . .). The incidence of the WS-1 figures in earlier verse is about the same as those of SW-1 (except in Pope's texts, where WS-1 figures outnumber SW-1 two to one) while in later verse, particularly in Arnold's, the figures WS-1 are less frequent than SW-1. The difference in the compositional function of both types of figures was discussed in Chapter 7. The prevalence of the figure WS-1 at the beginning of verse lines, its accentual structure (stress followed by two unstressed syllables), its part-of-speech composition (prevalence of verbs), and typical syntactic functions of the components (imperatives and predicates) have a direct connection with the typical semantic properties of words filling the figure.

Since almost half of the notional words forming the figure WS-1 are verbs (and over another one-fourth are less expressive adverbs), our attention is directed to the semantic properties of the verbs.

Verbs in WS-1 are usually used in two moods, indicative and imperative, while verbs in the indicative appear in the forms of affirmation or questions. Link-verbs (e.g. to be), auxiliary verbs (to do, to have), and modal verbs (e.g., must, can), as well as let (in the function of an auxiliary), may get a stress in the imperative mood, especially when followed by unstressed syllables (*Lĕt me dismiss the guests!* . . . Shel.C I,III:92), or in the form of questions (*Wăs it for this you took such constant Care* . . .? P.RL IV:97). Such cases, in which verbs, assumed stressed and capable of forming the figure WS-1, have practically no lexical meaning and are used for purely grammatical purposes, were extracted from the total number of verbs forming the figure; thus the number of verbs analyzed from the point of view of their semantic and stylistic properties was a little less than the total: for example, in Shakespeare's four dramas it was 390—65 = 325. Notional verbs used as link-verbs (go, grow, get, turn) and verbs like do, make, have, which have a broad and vague meaning without an object or an adverbial modifier, were not excluded but formed a group of words "with broad or vague meaning".

8.3.1. Let us examine first the general stylistic (expressive) characteristics of the verbs. The proportions of verbs with broad or vague meaning and with the component "extra" (verbs of quick motion, loud sounds, strongly expressive lexical meaning, or with a strong expressive connotation) used in the figures SW-1 and WS-1 is compared below. Here are some examples of verbs without and with the component "extra": (a) Without "extra": *Come to arrest the culprit . . . Find the disguise to hide me . . . Made it unutterable . . . Think, we shall be in Paradise* . . . (Shel.C IV,IV:22, V,I:103, V,III:81, V,IV:77); (b) With "extra:" *Die in despair* . . . *Yet wake him not, I pray, spare me awhile; Spare me! My brain swims round* . . . *Drag him away to torments* . . . (Shel.C IV,I:50, IV,IV:5, V,II:88,160). The data for "Lucrece" are given only for WS-1 because there are too few verbs in SW-1 (only 15). [Note that the categories "broad or vague meaning" and "extra meaning" do <u>not</u> embrace all verbs of the rhythmical figures.]

Proportion of verbs with broad or vague meaning (in percent of the total of verbal rhythmical figures)

	SW-1	WS-1
"Lucrece"		7
Sonnets	43	10
Dramas	40	9
"Islam"	22	3
"The Cenci"	20	6
"Sohrab and Rustum"	8	0

Proportion of verbs with the component "extra" (in percent of the total of verbal rhythmical figures)

	SW-1	WS-1
"Lucrece"		45
Sonnets	8	41
Dramas	6	14
"Islam"	20	70
"The Cenci"	15	50
"Sohrab and Rustum"	35	88

The ratio of verbs with a <u>vague meaning</u> is many times less in WS-1 than in SW-1, where accentual subordination of the verb on W to the following word with an ictic stress comes easier if the verb is semantically and syntactically dependent (*Othello will go mad* . . .). The ratio of "vague" verbs forming the figure WS-1, as with the trend in SW-1, declines from Shakespeare to later poets and again is the lowest in Arnold's "Sohrab and Rustum". The frequency of verbs with the intensifying component "extra" is two to five times greater in the figure WS-1 than in SW-1: the poets put much more expressive load on their verbs in WS-1 than in SW-1.

The ratio of verbs with the component "extra" in the figure WS-1 is the lowest in Shakespeare's dramatic verse (where "extra" verbs are almost exceptional); in his lyrical verse, however, the proportion of such verbs is three times greater and approaches the proportions characterizing the nineteenth-century texts. The proportion of "extra" verbs within the figure WS-1 in the nineteenth-century works is 50-88%, and is, predictably, the highest in Arnold's dynamic poem. The difference between Shelley's dramatic and narrative verse reveals the same tendency as in Shakespeare's dramas and his non-dramatic poetry: the proportion of verbs with vague and broad meaning is higher in "The Cenci", while the ratio of verbs with the component "extra" is higher in "The Revolt of Islam". These facts indicate that different genres do indeed employ the semantic potential of verse rhythm in different ways; the difference may be caused not only by the difference in function, but also by the difference in perception (aural vs. visual) of dramatic and non-dramatic verse.

To generalize: the data so far reveal (a) substantial difference in the semantic load conventionally accompanying the rhythmical figures WS-1 and SW-1 (greater in WS-1 than in SW-1); (b) a genre difference in the semantic functioning of both figures (the semantic load accompanying both figures is lower in dramas and higher in non-dramatic verse); and (c) some period difference in the semantic functioning of both figures (the semantic load increased from Shakespeare's time to the nineteenth century).

8.3.2. The semantic characteristics of verbs in the figure WS-1 are as follows.

The most frequent semantic component is, by far, that of motion. Consider the frequency of this semantic component in verbs (a) outside disyllabic and trisyllabic rhythmical figures; (b) in the figure SW-1; and (c) in the figure WS-1.

Verbs with the component "motion" (in percent of all verbs in each case; the total number of verbs is in brackets)

	Outside Figures	In SW-1	In WS-1
"Lucrece"	19% (474)		26% (58)
Sonnets	13% (402)	28% (35)	27% (59)
Dramas	16% (1702)	26% (217)	36% (325)
"Islam"	35% (400)	40% (40)	48% (118)
"The Cenci"	15% (442)	22% (69)	31% (110)
"Sohrab and Rustum"	40% (373)	50% (26)	6% (31)

The incidence of the semantic component "motion" is the least in the monosyllabic verbs outside rhythmical figures and is generally greater in WS-1 than in SW-1. The observed differences suggest that (a) both figures, which disrupt the prevailing rhythm, are associated in the poets' minds with the idea of motion; and (b) the figure WS-1 is more closely associated with motion than

SW-1. These conclusions explain why the figure WS-1 not only contains more verbs than SW-1 but also more verbs of motion. Evidently the figure WS-1 breaks the prevailing alternating rhythm more strongly than SW-1, at least when the W in the latter is filled with a verb; when the W in the figure SW-1 is filled with a noun (usually a subject) syntactically linked with the following verb with an ictic stress (usually a predicate), the breach of rhythm is stronger than in the verbal SW-1, and the semantic load of the figure increases, as does the proportion of the component "motion" (see 8.2.4).

The most typical motions associated with the figure WS-1 are "forward" and "away"; verbs with the component "extra" keep recurring. The figure WS-1 definitely "prefers" verbs expressing extra-quick rather than extra-slow motion. The former (run, rush, fly, flee, spring, burst, and shoot) exceed the latter (creep, crawl, or drag) by almost two times. Some examples of the figure WS-1 coupled with the verbs or word combinations with the meaning "motion forward" or "away:" *And unperceived fly with the filth away; Who, angry that the eyes fly from their lights* (Sh.RL 145:2, 66:6); *All souls that will be safe, fly from my side* (Sh.RII III,II:80); *Run from her guardage to the sooty bosom; Fled from her wish and yet said "Now I may"* (Sh.Oth I,II:70, II,I:152); *Ran on the green-sward . . . Fled from his father . . .* (Sh.WT IV,IV:157, V,I:183); *And laughing babes rush from the well-known door!* (Shel.RI VIII,IV:5); *Rush to my heart, and fell into a trance; Fled from your presence, as you now from mine; Fly ere I spurn thee . . .* (Shel.C II,I:41,114, IV,I:172).

Another recurrent verb that tends to form a rhythmical- grammatical-lexical "cliché" is to bear (borne); some examples: *Borne by the trustless wings . . .* (Sh.RL 1:2); *Borne on the bier . . .* (Sh.Son 12:8); *Borne on the storm . . . ; Borne on all winds . . . ; Borne by those slaves . . . ; We passed the isles, borne by the wind . . .* (Shel.RI II,XLV:8, VI,XLIV:6, VII,III:8, VIII,III:1).

One more case of preference by the figure WS-1 is "motion downward"; as with the verbs in SW-1, the incidence of the component "downward" is several times greater than "upward". The verbs sink and particularly fall recur in almost every text (with the figure SW-1 the most noticeable verb was kneel). The preference for the use of fall in the figure WS-1 is illustrated in Shakespeare's Sonnets, where this verb occurs three times (cf. Spevack 1974:387), twice in the WS-1 figure and once outside any figure: *Who lets so fair a house fall to decay* (13:9); *To stand in thy affairs, fall by thy side* (151:12); *Her "love" for whose dear love I rise and fall* (151:14). The verb to fall keeps recurring in the figure WS-1 in the verse of every English poet; its frequency in the figure evidently exceeds the language probability of the verb and its frequency in the verse text outside rhythmical figures; this supposition must be verified, however, on broader material. Here are some examples: *Fall like amazing thunder on the casque; Fall to the base earth from the firmament* (Sh.RII I,III:81, II,IV:20); *He calls us back; my pride fell with my fortunes* (Sh.AYLI I,II:245); *Falls undistinguish'd by the victor Spade!* (P.RL III:64); *Fall from the Conduit prone to Holborn Bridge* (Swift, "A Description of a

City Shower" 60); *Fell on* the ground; and the small mountain birds (Wordsworth, "The Old Cumberland Beggar" 19); *Fall from* his hand, his idle scimitar (Byron, "Childe Harold" IV,XVI:7); *Fall like* a dew of balm upon the world (Shelley, "Queen Mab" VI:53); *Fell to* the sea, while o'er the continent; So that a dizzy trance *fell on* my brain; *Fell on* the pale oppressors of our race; Of blood, from mortal steel *fell o'er* the fields like rain; *Fell, like* a shaft loosed by the bowman's error (Shel.RI I,XIV:7, I,XLVIII:2, Dedication,XIII:6, VI,VI:9, X,XXVI:3); *Falls from* my withered hand. But yesterday; *Fell from* my lips, and who with tottering steps (Shel.C I,I:128, II,I:113); *Fall; and* thy spear transfix'd an unarm'd foe (A.SR 550).

Some other verb-formed WS-1 figures with the component "motion downward" (sink is particularly frequent): *Stoop with* oppression of their prodigal weight (Sh.RII III,IV:32); *Knelt for* his mercy whom they served with blood (Shel.RI XII,IX:6); *Drops like* a plummet; Sohrab saw it come (A.SR 402); On the rich quilt *sinks with* becoming woe; *Sunk in* Thalestris' arms the Nymph he found (P.RL IV:35,89); *Sunk in* a gulf of scorn from which none may him rear!; *Sunk in* my heart, and almost wove a chain (Shel.RI V,XXXI:9, XI,VII:3); He first *sank to* the bottom—like his works (Byron, "The Vision of Judgment" CV:1); Never till now defiled, *sank to* the dust; He reeled, and staggering back, *sank to* the ground (A.SR 498,521).

Cases with the component "up" are somewhat less frequent in the material analyzed. Some examples: *Stands on* his hinder legs with listening ear (Sh.VA 117:2); *Rose at* an instant, learned, played, eat together (Sh.AYLI I,III:74); *Lifts from* the earth to the great Father of all (Shel.C I,III:23); But soon *rose to* the surface—like himself (Byron, "The Vision of Judgment" CV:2).

Why does the figure WS-1 "prefer" the component "downward" more noticeably than the SW-1? Probably the explanation lies in the accentual-syllabic structure of the figures and the adjacent text: the structure of the figure WS-1, as it blends into the text, is a stress followed by two unstressed syllables, while the structure of the SW-1 and its immediate surrounding is two unstressed syllables plus a reduced stress plus a strong stress; probably the effect of the former is more easily associated with a motion downward than the latter.

Other typical semantic components of the verbs of motion in the figure WS-1 are as follows: (a) a large group characterized by the elements "aggression", "force", and "heaviness" (delivering a blow, breaking or crushing); (b) uneven, unsteady, trembling motion, mixing and twining; (c) seizing, clutching, clinging tight; (d) a gliding, flowing motion (water, tears; wind, storm); (e) motion broken or stopped. Some examples of these semantic tendencies are:

"Aggression; force; heaviness": *Knock at* my heart . . . (Sh.VA 110:5); *Beat at* thy rocky and wreck-threatening heart; *Stone him* with harden'd hearts, harder than stone; Ay me! the bark *peel'd from* the lofty pine; The wind *wars with* his torch to make him stay (Sh.RL 85:2, 140:5, 167:5, 45:3); With a foul traitor's name *stuff I* thy throat; *Pierced to* the soul with slander's venomous spear; <u>Plucked from</u> my arms perforce and given away; <u>Bores through</u> his castle wall . . . ; For there it is, <u>cracked in</u> a hundred shivers; <u>Strike him</u>, Aumerle. Poor boy, thou art amazed (Sh.RII I,I:44,171, II,III:121, III,II:170, IV,I:289, V,II:85); <u>Scratch thee</u> but with a pin . . . (Sh.AYLI III,V:21); I had rather have my tongue <u>cut from</u> my mouth; <u>Beat a</u> Venetian and traduce the state (Sh.Oth II,III:217, V,II:356); <u>Clipp'd from</u> the lovely Head where late it grew (P.RL IV:136); <u>Stab her</u>, or give her bread! . . . ; <u>Stabbed in</u> their sleep, trampled in treacherous war; <u>Pierce like</u> reposing flames . . . (Shel.RI V,XXVII:2, V,VI:8, XII,V:9); <u>Pierced by</u> the shaft of banded nations through (Byron, "Childe Harold" III,XVIII:7); The gathering waves <u>rent the</u> Hesperian gate; <u>Wrought from</u> that bitter woe, had wildered her; <u>Smote on</u> the beach beside a tower of stone; <u>Strike with</u> her shadow, shrinks in fear awhile (Shel.RI VII,XII:6, III,VIII:6, IV,I:2, VI,XL:8); <u>Strike in</u> thine envy those life-darting eyes (Shel.C IV,I:135); <u>Prick'd; as</u> a cunning workman, in Pekin, <u>Pricks with</u> vermillion some clear porcelain vase (A.SR 672-673); With Time's injurious hand, <u>crush'd and</u> o'erworn; My mistress, when she walks, <u>treads on</u> the ground (Sh.Son 63:2, 130:12); <u>Tread on</u> each other's kibes . . . ; <u>Trod on</u> the trembling senate's slavish mutes (Byron, "Childe Harold" I,LXVII:5, IV,CXIII:8); Be as a mark <u>stamped on</u> thine innocent brow (Shel.C V,IV:151).

"Uneven, trembling, unsteady motion; mixing, twining": Her hair, like golden threads, <u>play'd with</u> her breath (Sh.RL 68:1); <u>Rub him</u> about the temples . . . (Sh.Oth IV,I:52); <u>Swayed in</u> the air . . . <u>Twined within</u> limb . . . <u>Mixed with</u> mine own . . . <u>Woven into</u> one . . . <u>Shakes with</u> the sleepless surge . . . <u>Shook with</u> the sullen thunder . . . <u>Waved by</u> the wind . . . (Shel.RI III,XVI:3, VI,XXXVI:3, VI,XLII:3, VII,III:3, VII,IX:6, VI,XLV:5, VIII,XXX:4); <u>Stir and</u> be quickened . . . <u>Stirred in</u> his sleep . . . (Shel.C IV,I:189, IV,III:18); But yet success <u>sways with</u> the breath of Heaven (A.SR 387).

"Seizing, clutching, clinging": My tongue <u>cleave to</u> my roof within my mouth (Sh.RII V,III:31); In vision or in dream <u>clove to</u> my breast; But its own kindred leaves <u>clasps while</u> the sunbeams smile; <u>Clasp the</u> relentless knees . . . <u>Seized, and</u> each sixth, thus armed, did now present; <u>Clung to</u> their hoary hair . . . (Shel.RI II,XV:6, VI,XL:9, IV,XXVII:9, VI,XIII:7, IX,XVI:4); <u>Clung to</u> the body stubbornly . . . (Shelley, "Queen Mab" VIII:162); <u>Linked with</u> each lasting circumstance of life; <u>Clings to</u> the mass of life; yet clinging, leans (Shel.C III,I:62, III,I:253).

"Gliding, flowing, floating": (Many a dry drop seem'd a weeping tear) <u>Shed for</u> the slaughter'd husband by the wife; <u>Borne by</u> the trustless wings of false desire (Sh.RL 197:3-4, 1:2); <u>Rained from</u> the wounds of slaughtered Englishmen (Sh.RII III,III:44); Blow me about in winds! . . . <u>Wash me</u> in steep-down gulf of liquid fire! (Sh.Oth V,II:282-283); <u>Flowed with</u> her beauty once . . . (Sh.WT V,I:101); <u>Waft on</u> the breeze, or sink in Clouds of Gold (P.RL II:60); <u>Ebbs o'er</u> the western forest . . . <u>Glide o'er</u> its dim and gloomy strand . . . <u>Poured on</u> the earth . . . <u>Pour on</u> these evil men . . . <u>Flowed at</u> a hundred *feasts . . . Sweeps in the shadow . . . Stream through the city . . . Stream through the gates like waterfalls; Swam in our mute and liquid ecstasies; Borne on the storm . . . Borne on all winds . . . . . . borne by the wind and stream; Waved by the wind . . .* (Shel.RI I,XLIX:5, II,VII:4, II,IX:7, IV,XXVIII:4, IX,XVII:2, VI,XIX:9, X,XI:8, VI,IV:6, VI,XXXIII:7, II,XLV:8, VI,XLIV:6, VIII,III:1, VIII,XXX:4); *Stream over Casbin and the Southern slopes; Flowed with the stream . . .* (A.SR 113,842); *Streams from his flank the crimson torrent clear; Flows from the eternal source of Rome's imperial hill; Floats o'er this vast and wondrous monument* (Byron, "Childe Harold" I,LXXVI:7, III,CX:9, IV,CXXIX:2).

"A motion checked, stopped": *With a foul traitor's name stuff I thy throat* (Sh.RII I,I:44); *The wingless boat paused where an ivory stair; (The Tartar horse) Pause, and I saw the shape . . . (. . . the steed that panted) Paused, might be heard the murmur of the motion; Pause ere it wakens tempests . . . Paused as I spake . . .* (Shel.RI I,LI:3, VI,XX:6, VI,XXIII:3, VII,XXII:7, V,XXXV:2); *Of life and death, pause ere thou answerest me; Check the abandoned villain . . . Checked his unnatural pride . . . Stay, I command you . . .* (Shel.C V,II:116, I,III:92, II,I:44,115).

Other semantic components repeated frequently are: (a) speech, very typical of the figure WS-1 where there are many verbs such as say, tell, swear, plead, and bid, often in the imperative (verbs of speaking reach 20% of all verbal WS-1); (b) emotions and their physical display (weeping, yawning, smiling, laughing); (c) breathing and suffocation; (d) pain, suffering, and death; (e) getting light or dark, shining, fading. Some examples:

"Speech": *Pleads in a wilderness where are no laws* (Sh.RL 70:5); *Bid him repair to us to Ely House* (Sh.RII II,II:216); *Dost thou in conscience think—tell me, Emilia* (Sh.Oth IV,III:61); *The trumpet any more . . . Pray you. Emilia; Lest she should be denied.—Tell her, Emilia* (Sh.WT II,II:35,51); *Plead with awakening earthquake . . .* (Shel.C V,IV:103).

"Emotions and their physical display": *And the red rose blush at her own disgrace; And the dank earth weeps at thy languishment; Which makes the maid weep like the dewy night* (Sh.RL 69:3, 163:3, 176:7); *And play the mother's part, kiss me, be kind* (Sh.Son 143:12); *Fear and be slain, no worse can come to fight; Feared by their breed, and famous by their birth* (Sh.RII III,II:183, I,I:52); *Therefore these stops of thine fright me the more* (Sh.Oth III,III:123); *Fear you the tyrannous passion more, alas?* (Sh.WT II,III:28); *"Fear it!" she said with brief and passionate cry; Laughs o'er the grave in which his living hopes are laid; Laughed in those looks . . . Vexed into whirlpools by the chasm beneath; Vexed the inconstant waves with my perpetual moan; Smiled on the flowery grave in which were lain* (Shel.RI I,XLVII:2, II,XXXIII:9, III,XXVI:7, VII,VII:6, VII,XXIII:9, VII,XXXIII:7); *For thy decree yawns like a Hell between; Quelled me. Indeed, indeed, I cannot do it* (Shel.C III,I:133, IV,III:13); *(. . . his dreadful eyes) Glared, and he shook on high his menacing spear* (A.SR 515).

"Breathing and suffocation": *With a foul traitor's name* stuff *I thy throat;* Breathe I *against thee, upon pain of life;* (cf. also the noun breath: *'Tis breath thou lack'st, and that* breath wilt *thou lose*) (Sh.RII I,I:44, I,III:153, II,I:30); Breathes in *prophetic dreams of day's uprise; Soon I could hear the leaves* sigh, and *could see;* Choked with *his country's dead:—his footsteps reel* (Shel.RI VII,XXXVII:6, III,XXIV:5, X,VIII:4); (*Long flocks of travelling birds dead on the snow,*) Choked by *the air* . . . (A.SR 164-165).

"Pain, suffering, death" (another sizeable group): *Stone him with harden'd hearts . . . Ay me! the bark* peel'd from *the lofty pine* (Sh.RL 140:5, 167:5); Kill me *with spites . . .* Die to *themselves . . .* Feeds on *the rarities . . . With time's injurious hand* crush'd and *o'erworn;* Kill me *outright . . .* (Sh.Son 40:14, 54:11, 60:11, 63:2, 139:14); *Strike him, Aumerle . . .* Plucked from *my arms perforce . . .* Pierced to *the soul . . .* (Sh.RII V,II:85, II,III:121, I,I:171); *I had rather have this tongue* cut from *my mouth;* Blow me *about in winds!* roast me *in sulphur!* Wash me *in steep-down gulf of liquid fire!;* Burn like *the mines of sulphur . . .* Beat a *Venetian . . .* (Sh.Oth II,III:217, V,II:282- 283, III,III:331, V,II:356); Scratch thee *but with a pin . . .* (Sh.AYLI III,V:21); Clipp'd from *the lovely Head . . .* (P.RL IV:136); Groaned with *the burden of a new despair* (Shel.RI X,XVII:5); Killed in his sleep *. . .* Tame her *with chains and famine . . .* Strike in *thine envy . . .* Drag him *away to torments . . .* Die in *despair . . .* (Shel.C V,III:11, IV,I:8,135, V,II:160, IV,I:50). Cf. other parts of speech of the same semantic class: Death and *damnation! . . .* (Sh.Oth III,III:398); *Long flocks of travelling birds* dead on *the snow* (A.SR 164).

"Lightening, shining": Shone like *the moon in water seen by night* (Sh.VA 82:6); Shone through *the plumes . . . And earth and sky* shone through *the atmosphere;* Shone through *the woodbine wreaths . . . (. . . the fourth morn)* Burst o'er *the golden isles . . .* Shone on *her awful frenzy . . .* Shone through *my sleep . . .* Shone in *a hundred human eyes . . .* (Shel.RI I,IX:5, I,XV:2, I,XL:9, III,XXII:2, VII,VI:7, VII,XXXII:9, XI,XXV:4).

The regular (though infrequent) recurrence of the verbs change and mock is worth remembering for our final conclusions. Here are some examples: *Change the complexion of her maid-pale face* (Sh.RII III,III:98); *Changed to a Bird . . .* (P.RL III:123): cf. *Colours that change . . .* (P.RL II:68); *Changed to a mockery . . .* (Shel.C V,III:33); Mock with *thy tickling beams . . .* (Sh.RL 156:5); Mocks thee *in visions . . .* (Shel.C III,II:87).

Some conclusions concerning the semantic characteristics of the figure WS-1 can be drawn at this point. They are:

(1) As with the figure SW-1, words and word combinations in the figure WS-1 display recurring semantic components. They are, primarily, motion and speech. The most frequent subtypes of motion are: forward and particularly downward; an aggressive, heavy motion applied with force, often in the form of a blow; uneven, vibrating motion; flowing, gliding; seizing, holding tight; and the end, or cessation of motion. Other repeated semantic components are: physical display of emotions; change of state; suffering and death and their

physical manifestations: suffocation, crushing, cutting, piercing. To generalize even more: the repeated semantic components (semes) are: intensive action combined with heaviness and force; change (e.g., from action to non-action, from life to death). These semantic features of the language material coupled with the figure WS-1 seem to "support" its physical characteristics: breach of rhythm of a particular kind. Again as with the figure SW-1, it is hard to draw a line between mere emphasis and iconic (conventional) imitation of action by the WS-1 type of rhythm breach, but the fact that most words in the figure WS-1 are verbs, and most verbs are of particular types of motion, lend support to the iconic, metaphoric hypothesis.

(2) Even more noticeably than in the figure SW-1, not only semantic components but words and word combinations keep recurring within the figure WS-1. Throughout the examples listed above are numerous repetitions involving such verbs as come, go, rush, run, fall, bear, pause, fear, weep, shine, and change. Repetitions of words coupled with the rhythmical figure WS-1 are more noticeable in later verse (e.g., Shelley's): the link between particular words and the figure WS-1 has apparently become stronger and more conventionalized with time.

Recurring patterns of word combinations that accompany the rhythmical figure WS-1 create, as it were, "construction blocks" used by the same or different poets. Some examples of these are:

(a) *Yield to my hand . . . —Yield to my love . . .*
("Lucrece" 173:6 and 96:3);

(b) *Look in thy glass . . . —Look in your glass . . .*
(Sonnets 3:1 and 103:6);

(c) *Love is my sin . . . .—Love is a babe . . . —Love is not love . . .*
(Sonnets 142:1, 115:13, 116:2);

(d) "*Give me my hand*" -*saith he;* "*why dost thou feel it!*"—"*Give me my heart*", *saith she,* "*and thou shalt have it*" (Sh.VA 63:1-2); *Support him by the arm . . . Give me your hand* (Sh.AYLI II,VII:202)—*Give me your hand; this hand is moist, my lady* (Sh.Oth III,IV:36)—*I saw his heart in's face . . . Give me thy hand—Give me that hand of yours to kiss . . .* (a variant: *Give me the boy. . .*) (Sh.WT I,II:447, V,III:46, II,I:56)—*When no man was his own.— Give me your hands*("The Tempest" V,I:214).

(e) *Dost thou in conscience think,—Tell me, Emilia* (Sh.Oth IV,III:61)—*The trumpet any more . . . Pray you, Emilia—Lest she should be denied.—Tell her, Emilia* (Sh.WT II,II:35,51).

(f) *Falls undistinguish'd by the victor Spade* (P.RL III:64)—*Sunk undistinguish'd by one common fate* (Lady Mary Wortley Montagu, "Verses Written in the Chiosk of the British Palace, at Pera, Overlooking the City of Constantinople, Dec. 26, 1717", 66) (notice the almost identical rhythmical-grammatical parallelism of the last two lines).

Similar part-of-speech/syntactic structures combined with one and the same rhythmical (accentual, word boundary) pattern and used in similar semantic (plot) situations evidently tend to produce repeated patterns that recur in the verse of the same poet, or different poets of the same or different epochs. In the case of different poets the problem is to differentiate "everybody's material" ("the wide world's common place") from borrowings, allusions, and reminiscences.

(3) The semantic and stylistic potential of the figure WS-1 is realized differently in different genres; at different epochs of English literature; and at different periods of an author's career.

(4) In comparison with each other, the semantic and stylistic potential of the two figures, SW-1 and WS-1, show both differences and similarities. Features of <u>differences</u> are (a) a generally stronger stylistic charge (but probably not potential) of the WS-1 (the number of verbs with the component "extra" is much higher in the WS-1); (b) a stronger link of the WS-1 with the component "motion", particularly fast, heavy, and directed downward.

Features of <u>similarity</u> between the two figures are conditioned by the fact that they both physically break the prevailing rhythmical momentum, drawing at the same time the reader's attention to the words forming the figures. Some examples of the features of similarity are: (a) prevalence of words and word combinations conveying the idea of motion, often violent and uneven, generated with force and ending in a blow; (b) the idea of a process or an action changed, interrupted, or stopped; (c) the idea of emotions accompanied by their physical display; (d) the idea of suffering and death: words and events that have a strong negative connotation; the notion of "death" has also the accompanying connotations of "change" and "stop". Both figures link a specific rhythmical form with a specific "bundle" of meanings closely related to each other. Consequently both rhythmical figures seem to have acquired in the course of English literary tradition a <u>semiotic function</u>.

(5) In contrast with the trend of increased use of the semantic potential of the figure WS-1 in the course of the English literary tradition, Shakespeare seems to have decreased semantization of this rhythmical figure WS-1 not only from the lyrics to drama, but also from earlier to later works. For example, the number of the WS-1 which are semantically "empty" or occur for purely syntactic reasons are higher in "The Winter's Tale" than in "Richard II". Did Shakespeare come to realize that rhythmical subtleties evade the listener during their on-stage presentation? Or was he growing more hurried and careless towards the end of his career? Probably both.

8.4. Consider now the <u>trisyllabic figure WSW-1</u>, which may be regarded as WS-1 and SW-1 partially imposed on each other. The number of cases is nowhere high, so we shall consider them all together, without classification by parts of speech. The most frequent part-of-speech combination in the WSW-1 is "verb + adjective" (*Wŏund hīs lŏng ȁrms* . . .); this in many ways determines the semantic characteristics of the figure.

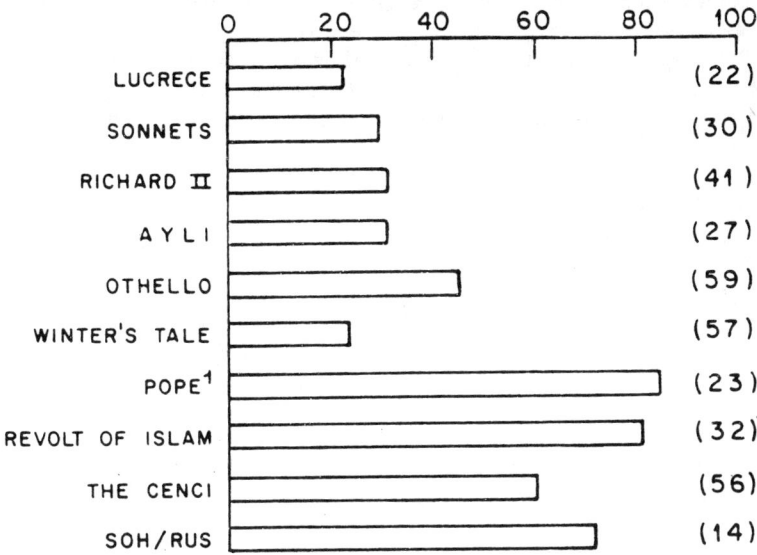

Fig. 8.2. Percentage of WSW-1 rhythmical figures with a semantic loading (total number of WSW-1 figures given in brackets). Notice the much greater use of the figure for semantic purposes by the later poets.

The incidence of semantically "loaded" figures as opposed to semantically "empty" ones is shown graphically in Fig. 8.2. The statistics are tentative, because the number of the cases is relatively low, and the semantic differentiation was made more or less subjectively. However, the results are instructive; they are not unlike those obtained earlier for the disyllabic figures SW-1 and WS-1.

The first thing that strikes us is a much stronger semantization of the figure WSW-1 in the verse of later poets (in this material beginning with Pope) than in Shakespeare's. A similar phenomenon was observed with the figures SW-1 and WS-1. In Shakespeare's texts the incidence of semantic use of the figure WSW-1 increases from "Lucrece" to "Othello" and then drops in "The Winter's Tale" to half the index of "Othello". Here are four examples of (a) "empty" and (b) semantically loaded figures WSW-1 occurring in Shakespeare's verse: (a) semantically empty: <u>Will you take</u> eggs for money? . . . <u>Are you so fond?</u> . . . . (b) semantically loaded: <u>Throw your vile</u> guesses in the devil's teeth; <u>Wrench his sword</u> from him . . . (Sh.WT I,II:161,164; Oth.

313

III,IV:188, V,II:290). In the verse of later poets the lowest percentage of the semantically loaded figures WSW-1 is discovered in the dramatic verse of "The Cenci". This can be explained by a relatively high incidence of "purely syntactic" WSW-1, such as questions and imperatives, in a drama.

What are the typical semantic components found in this trisyllabic figure? These are again: (a) motion, often uneven, unsteady, fluttering; flowing, streaming; directed upward or downward; seizing, clutching; associated with heaviness, weight; (b) pain, torture, death; and (c) speech or other sounds. Less frequent but recurring components, already familiar to us, are: breathing/breathlessness; madness; mockery. Here are some examples.

"Motion": *Pluck the keen teeth* . . . (Sh.Son 19:3); *Lurked like two thieves* . . . (Sh.VA 181:6); *Fetch from false* Mowbray . . . *Go to Flint* castle . . . *Swell'st thou, proud heart?* . . . (Sh.RII I,I:97, III,II:209, III,III:140); *Limped in pure* love . . . (Sh.AYLI II,VII:131); *Come, my dear love* . . . *Shore his old thread* . . . *Wrench his sword from him* . . . (Sh.Oth II,III:8, V,II:209,290); *Take the boy* to you . . . *Bear the boy hence* . . . (Sh.WT II,I:1,59); *Shrink his thin essence* . . . *Clapp'd his glad Wings* . . . *Spreads his black Wings* . . . *Weighs the Men's Wits* . . . (P.RL II:132, V:54, IV:88, V:72); *Seiz'd and ty'd down* . . . (P.DA 33); *Shut the church doors* . . . (John Byrom, "On Clergymen Preaching Politics" 16); *Load some vain Church* . . . (P.RB 29); *Trod the pure*, virgin, Snows . . . (James Thomson, "Winter" 11); *Clasped that bright Shape* . . . *Locked in stiff* rings . . . *Wound his long arms* . . . *Bent his thin head* . . . *Fell, like bright* Spring . . . *Left the torn* human heart . . . *And through the cleft streamed in one* cataract (Shel.RI XII,XXIII:2, I,XII:4, VII,IX:7, VI,XLIII:4, Dedication,VII:2, XIII:9, VII,XXXVIII:5); *Climb with swift* wings . . . *Touched the loose* wrinkled throat . . . *Bow thy white* head . . . *Stabbed with one* blow . . . (Shel.C I,II:85, IV,III:17, I,III:157, V,II:123); *Hiss'd, and went* quivering down into the sand; *Rent the tough* plates, but failed to reach the skin; *His breast heav'd, his lips foamed* . . . (A.SR 404,493,455).

"Pain, torture, death": *Claps her pale* cheek . . . *Strike the wise dumb* . . . (Sh.VA 78:6, 191:6); *Pluck the keen teeth* . . . ; *For precious friends hid in death's dateless night*; *Gored mine own thoughts* . . . (Sh.Son 19:3, 30:6, 110:3); *The king had cut off my head* with my brother's (if my is assumed unstressed, the figure here is SWSW-1: Sh.RII II,II:103); *Shore his old thread in twain* . . . *Wrench his sword from him* . . . (Sh.Oth V,II:209,290); *If I prove honey-mouthed, let my tongue blister* (Sh.WT II,II:33); *Be thy soul choked* . . . . . . *Warp those fine* limbs; *Stabbed with one blow* . . . *Makes the rack cruel* . . . *Dead! the sweet bond broken!* . . . (Shel.C IV,I,74:133, V,II:123, V,III:52, V,IV:137); *Rent the tough* plates . . . *White, with eyes* closed . . . (A.SR 493,849).

"Speech and other sounds": *Cries to catch her* . . . (Sh.Son 143:6); *Right, you say true* . . . ; *Makes him speak* fondly like a frantic man (Sh.RII II,I:145, III,III:185); *Cough, or cry hem* . . . (Sh.Oth IV,II:29); *Cry the man* mercy . . .

(Sh.AYLI III,V:61); <u>Beats the strong heart</u> . . . (Byron, "Lara" II,XXII:16); <u>Burst in far peals</u> . . . (Shel.RI I,II:2).

Other recurring and familiar semantic components are: "breathing/ breathlessness", "mocking", "mental disorder", and changes of facial expression. Some examples are: <u>Draws the sweet infant breath</u> of gentle sleep (Sh.RII I,III:133); <u>Sigh'd in low Whispers</u> . . . (James Thomson, "Winter" 78); <u>Slake their parch'd throats</u> . . . <u>So the pale</u> Persians held <u>their breath</u> in fear; His breast <u>heaved, his lips foamed,</u> and twice his voice Was choked with rage . . . (A.SR 166,169,454); <u>Mock the fierce peal</u> . . . (Shel.RI VI,XLV:7); <u>I have talked some wild words,</u> but will no more (the figure here is SWSW-1: Shel.C III,I:66); <u>Makes him speak</u> fondly, like a frantic man (Sh.RII III,III:185); <u>Worse than tears drown</u> . . . (Sh.WT II,I:112); <u>Kiss those warm</u> lips . . . (Shel.C V,IV:138).

Some conclusions about recurring rhythmical-grammatical-semantic patterns almost invite themselves here, too; segments like *Clapp'd his glad Wings—Spreads his black Wings, Bent his thin head—Bow thy white head* are particularly striking; but we shall come back to them after the description of all rhythmical figures is completed.

8.5. Consider <u>the disyllabic figure WS-2</u>. This figure is formed predominantly by disyllabic <u>verbs</u> (mainly participles) and, in Shakespeare's dramas, nouns in the vocative function. The incidence of words with insignificant semantic loading is everywhere less than in the figures SW-1 and even WS-1: the figure WS-2 is almost invariably used with a semantic purpose. Still, in Shakespeare's verse the semantic load of the figures WS-2, similarly with the other figures examined previously, is again lower than in the texts of later authors. Here are some examples of verbs coupled with the figure WS-2 that seem to have only a small semantic load: <u>Making</u> a complement of proud compare (Sh.Son 21:5); <u>Showing</u> an outward pity . . . (Sh.RII IV,I:240). In contrast, here are some cases where the figure WS-2 seems to have a fuller semantic load: <u>Shorten</u> my days thou canst with sullen sorrow; For Sorrow's eye <u>glazed</u> with blinding tears; <u>Broken</u> his staff of office and dispersed (Sh.RII I,III:227, II,II:16, II,III:27).

8.5.1. The most frequently repeated semantic components discovered in the WS-2 <u>verbs</u> are again: "motion", "emotions and their physical display (sweating, rolling of eyes, kissing, crying, smiling, laughing);" "suffering and death;" "sounds;" "getting light or dark".

"<u>Motion</u>" is, predictably, the most frequent semantic component accompanying the figure WS-2 and has a wide variety of types. It must be emphasized that this semantic component is more typical of the disyllabic verbs coupled with the rhythmical figure WS-2 than of disyllabic non-oxytonic verbs (<u>an</u>swer, <u>car</u>ry, or <u>bu</u>ry) which occur in the verse texts outside rhythmical figures. For example, in "The Rape of Lucrece" verbs of motion constitute 25% of all verbs in WS-2 (16 out of 63) but only 11% of disyllabic non-oxytonic verbs outside the rhythmical figures (7 out of 65 in the 600 lines analyzed for this purpose). In "Sohrab and Rustum" the incidence of verbs of motion in WS-2 is 54% (13 out of 24) while outside rhythmical figures it is only 37% (15 out of 40 non-oxytonic disyllabic verbs in 600 lines).

The kinds of motion coupled with the figure WS-2 are again familiar to us; these are: uneven, trembling, broken, stopped; less frequently flowing, floating, flying; around, upwards, and particularly often downward. Repeated from text to text are not only semantic components, but again (similarly with SW-1, WS-1, and WSW-1) particular words. Such verbs (usually participles) as circling, floating, waving, quivering, and particularly trembling recur in different texts by different authors. Here are some examples:

"An uneven, trembling, checked, or stopped motion". The verb tremble is the most typical: Tremble at patience . . . You, my lord, best know (Sh.WT III,II:33); Tremble, and start at wagging of a straw ("Richard III" III,V:7); Trembled and shook; for why, he stamped and swore ("The Taming of the Shrew" III,II:166); Trembling even at the name of Mortimer ("Henry IV", Part I, I,III:145) [actually, the figure here is tetrasyllabic: WS-2 plus WS- 1]; Find out their enemies now. Tremble, thou wretch ("King Lear" III,II:51); Trembling, begins the sacred Rites of Pride; Trembling, and conscious of the rich Brocade (P.RL I:138, III:116); Trembles before her look, though it be strong; Trembled, as with a zone of ruin bound (Shel.RI IV,XXI:5, X,IV:8); And stood erect, trembling with rage; his club (A.SR 449). It is no surprise to me now to open a book of English poetry at random and find trembling coupled with the figure WS-2: Trembling beneath the scourge of Turkish hand (Byron, "Childe Harold" II,LXXIV:8); (The lady's cheek) Trembled: she nothing said, but, pale and meek (Keats, "Lamia", Part two, 65); Trembles no less, and the fond yielding maid (William Somerville, "Hobbinol:" "On the Village Green" 38);

> Trembling and poor, I saw the light
> New waking from unconscious night:
> Trembling and poor, I still remain
> To meet unconscious night again.
>
> (George Crabbe, "My Birth-day", 5-8)

Here are some more examples of the figure WS-2 coupled with the verbs of shaky, uneven motion, of a violent, sudden motion, or motion checked or stopped: Throwing the base throng from his bending crest (Sh.VA, 66:5); Throwing his mantle rudely o'er his arm (Sh.RL 25:2); Throwing restraint upon us . . . (Sh.Oth IV,III:93); Struggling for passage, earth's foundation shakes; Shaking her wings, devouring all in haste; Shaking their scratch'd ears, bleeding as they go (Sh.VA 175:3, 10:3, 154:6); Shaken with sorrows in ungrateful Rome ("Titus Andronicus" IV,III:17); Shaking the bloody darts as *he his bells* ("Henry VI", Part 2, III,I:366); *What raging of the sea, shaking of earth!* ("Troilus and Cressida" I,III:97); *Shaking the bloody fingers of thy foes* ("Julius Caesar" III,I:198); *Stagger with dizzy aim* . . . (James Thomson, "Winter" 157); *Fluttering between the dun wave and the sky* (Byron, "The Island" IV,I:3); *Flutter her lovely pinions o'er his theme* (Byron, "The Prophecy of Dante" III:116); *Flutt'ring 'twixt Good and Ill, that shar'd thy Life* (James Thomson, "Winter" 373); (cf. the noun "flutters:" *Flutters in blood, and panting beats the ground*: Pope, "Hunting and Fishing" 4); *Quivers, (as in a fleece of snow-like air)* (Shelley, "Epipsychidion" 99); *Quivered like burning emerald* . . . *Quivered beneath my feet* (Shel.RI I,IV:6, VII,XXXIX:7); *Deep heavy gasps quivering through all his frame* (A.SR 850); *Struggling with whirlwinds of mad agony* (Shelley, "Queen Mab" VII:255); *Struggling, aghast and pale the Tyrant fled away* (Shel.RI VII,VI:9); *And hard loose rocks rushing tumultuously* (Shel.RI VII,XXXIX:3); *Tottering beneath us. Plead with the swift frost*; *Shivered to dust! To see thee, Beatrice* (Shel.C V,IV:101,132); *Tossing and wakeful* . . . (A.SR 37); *Pausing for means to mourn* . . . (Sh.RL 195:7); *Pausing in breathless silence* . . . (Shel.RI XII,XIII:2).

"Acts of beating and breaking": *Beating his kind embracements with her heels* (Sh.VA 52; 6); *Beated and chopp'd with tann'd antiquity* (Sh.Son 62:10); *Beaten away by brain-sick rude desire*; *Beating her bulk, that his hand shakes withal* (Sh.RL 25:7, 67:5); *Beating your officers, cursing yourselves* ("Coriolanus" III,III:78); *Broken his staff of office and dispersed* (Sh.RII II,III:27); *Breaking his oath and resolution, like* ("Coriolanus" V,VI:94); *Dead! The sweet bond broken!* . . . (Shel.C V,IV:137); *Broken and trembling to the yoke she bore* (Byron, "Childe Harold" III,LXXXI:7); *Who, but to-day, hammered of this design* (Sh.WT II,II:49); *Striking the electric chain* . . . (Byron, "Childe Harold" IV,XXIII:9).

"Motion directed around, upward, downward, or ahead": *Circles her body in on every side*; *Her breasts, like ivory globes circled with blue* (Sh.RL 249:3, 59:1); *Circling through these contaminated veins* (Shel.C III,I:96); *Circles above his eyery, with loud screams* (A.SR 565); *Falling on Diomed* . . . ("Troilus and Cressida" V,II:176); *Burying in Lucrece' wound his folly's show*; *Rolling his greedy eyeballs in his head* (Sh.RL 259:4, 53:4); *Mounted upon a hot and fiery steed* (Sh.RII, V,II:7); *Casting their savageness aside, have done* (Sh.WT II,III:188); *Lifting the thunder of their acclamation*; *Sinking upon their hearts* . . . *Of those dead leaves, shedding their stars, whene'er* (Shel.RI V,XIV:1, I,LVII:8, VI,XXVIII:6); *Drowning both tenderness and dread; at last*; *Which, as a dying pulse rises and falls* (Shel.C III,I:354, III,II:12); *Plunging all day in the blue waves, at night* (A.SR 287); *Rushing from forth a cloud* . . . (Sh.RL 54:2); *Hasting to th' court* . . . (Sh.WT II,III:197); *Crosses a deep ravine* . . . *Crosses the chasm* . . . (Shel.C III,I:179,245); *Crossing the stream in summer* . . . (A.SR 19).

"A floating, flowing, winding motion": *Fanning the hairs who wave like feather'd wings* (Sh.VA 51:6); *Streaming the ensign of the Christian cross* (Sh.RII IV,I:94); *Wafting his eyes to th'contrary, and falling* (Sh.WT I,II:372) (cf. *Waft on the Breeze . . .* : P.RL II:60); *Flowing, it fills the Channel vast and wide* (George Crabbe, "The Borough", 38); *Flowing o'er ocean as it stream'd in air* (Byron, "The Island" IV,V:8); *Floated, dilated as it came, the storm*; *Floated the shattered plumes . . . Floating at intervals the garments white* (Shel.RI I,VII:8, I,XI:6, VI,XLIV:7); *Loosening her star-bright robe . . . Loosened her, weeping then . . .* (Shel.RI I,XVIII:6, IV,XIX:3); *Winding among the lawny islands fair*; *Winding above the mountain's snowy term* (Shel.RI I,LI:1, VI,XVIII:3); *Sate one waving a sword . . .* (Shel.RI VI,XIX:7).

Verbs with the general meaning "to enclose", "restrict", "hold tight": *Cover the shame that follows sweet delight* (Sh.RL 51:7); *Prison my heart in thy steel bosom's ward* (Sh.Son 133:9); *Of Bolingbroke, covering your fearful land*; *Cover your heads, and mock not flesh and blood* (Sh.RII III,II:110,171); *Covering discretion with a coat of folly* ("Henry V" II,IV:38); *Even so. Cover their faces . . .* ("King Lear" V,IV:241); *Cover her face! Mine eyes dazzle; she died young* (Webster, "The Duchess of Malfi" IV,II:279); *Cover thy face from every living eye*; *Cover me! let me be no more! . . .* (Shel.C I,III:154, V,IV:129); *Closing in night and dreams . . .* (Shel.C V,III:3); *And pluck it o'er your brows, muffle your face* (Sh.WT IV,IV:657); *Stifled the captive's cry . . . Clasping its gray rents with a verdurous woof* (Shel.RI II,IV:4, VI,XXVII:8).

"Emotions and their physical display" is another typical semantic group of verbs forming the WS-2 figure. Some examples: *We did, my lord, weeping and commenting* (Sh.AYLI II,I:65); *Weeping again the king my father's wreck* ("The Tempest" I,II:394); *Weeping before for what she saw must come* ("The Comedy of Errors" I,I:71); *Weeping as fast as they stream forth thy blood* ("Julius Caesar" III,I:201); *Mewling and puking in the nurse's arms*; *Sighing like furnace, with a woeful ballad* (Sh.AYLI II,VII:144,148); *Kissing with golden face the meadows green* (Sh.Son 33:3); *Kissing with inside lip? . . .* (Sh.WT I,II:286); *Kissing his feet with murmurs . . .* (Byron, "Childe Harold" III,CI:6); *Blushing at that which is so purified* (Sh.RL 250:7); *Blushing in bright diversities of day* (P.RB 84); *Smiling upon her from her nursing breast*; *Smiling and slow, walk through a world of tears* (Shel.C IV,I:149, V,IV:113); *Over his loathed meal, laughing in agony, raves* (Shel.RI III,XXXVI:7); *Laughing the clouds away with playful scorn* (Byron, "Childe Harold" III,XCVIII:3); *As from the roots of the sea, raging and bubbling* (Shel.RI VII,XI:3); *Raging among the caverns . . . ; Of his own blood raging between us . . .* (Shel.C III,I:259, IV,I:114); *Rolling his greedy eyeballs in his head*; *He faintly flies, sweating with guilty fear* (Sh.RL 53:4, 106:5); *And stood erect, Trembling with rage . . . Deep heavy gasps quivering through all his frame* (A.SR 449,850).

Linked with the previous group "emotions and their physical display" are words denoting the processes of "eating, drinking, and swallowing": *Eater of youth, false slave to false delight* (Sh.RL 133:3); Feeding *on that which doth preserve the ill* (Sh.Son 147:3); Drinking *my griefs, whilst you mount up on high*; Eating *the bitter bread of banishment* (Sh.RII IV,I:189, III,I:21); Chewing *the food of sweet and bitter fancy* (Sh.AYLI IV,I:101); Swallow *them up. Now, by yond marble heaven* (Sh.Oth III,III:462).

"Suffering, pain, death, evil" is another sizeable group: Wounding *itself to death, rise up and fall* (Sh.RL 67:4); Wounding *supposèd peace: all these bold fears* ("Henry IV", Part 2, IV,V:194); Threatening *cloud-kissing Illion with annoy* (Sh.RL 196:5); Beating *his kind embracements with her heels* (Sh.VA 52:6); Prison *my heart in thy steel bosom'd ward* (Sh.Son 133:9); Frighting *her pale-faced villagers with war* (Sh.RII II,III:94); Killing *myself to die upon a kiss* (Sh.Oth V,II:360); Slaughters *a thousand waiting upon that*; Strangle *such thoughts as this with any thing* (Sh.WT I,II:93, IV,IV:47) (cf.: *What death?— *Strangling; *here are your executioners:* Webster, "The Duchess of Malfi" IV,II:221); Strangled; *and Giacomo, I think, will find* (Shel.C IV,I:47); Stifled *the captive's cry . . .* ; *(. . . like agonies)* Stifled *afar . . .* (Shel.RI II,IV:4, X,XII:7); *The red artillery's bolt* mangling *among them falls*; *Women, and babes, and men,* slaughtered *confusedly;* Languished *and died . . .* (Shel.RI VI,IV:9, VI,XLVI:9, X,XIII:7); Tortured *between just hate and vain remorse*; Torture *your dog, that he may tell when last (He lapped the blood his master shed . . .)* (Shel.C III,II:27, V,III:62); Poisoned, *perchance, by the disease and woe*; Poisons *no more the pleasure it bestows*; Poisoned *the springs of happiness and life* (Shelley, "Queen Mab" IV:128, VII:130, IX:88); *(. . . Paolo Santa Croce)* Murdered *his mother yester evening* (Shel.C V,III:19).

"Lightning, shining, darkening; kindling fire; getting cold" is one more recurring semantic group of verbs in the figure WS-2. Examples: Cooling *his hot face in the chastest tears*; *Thy eye* kindled *the fire that burneth here* (Sh.RL 98:3, 211:5); Darkening *thy power to lend base subjects light* (Sh.Son 100:4); Darkening *each other?—Should the offender live?* (Shel.C III,I:172); *His sorrow's eyes,* glazèd *with blinding tears* (Sh.RII II,II:16); Glitter *and boil beneath . . .* ; Blotting *its sphered stars with supernatural light*; *A lamp of vestal fire* burning *internally*; Kindled *intenser zeal . . .* ; Shining *beside a sail . . .* (Shel.RI I,III:4, I,LV:9, Dedication,XI:9, II,XXXII:2, III,XXX:5).

8.5.2. Nouns forming the figure WS-2, unless they are vocatives, belong to semantic categories not unlike those of verbs. They are usually words with a strong emotive connotation, positive or, more often, negative. For example, in Shakespeare's Sonnets, out of the eighteen disyllabic nouns coupled with the figure WS-2 the only repeated word is the noun beauty (beauty's), which occurs five times (almost 28% of the cases), while outside the figure WS-2 in the 602 lines analyzed (43 sonnets chosen at random), of 243 disyllabic non-oxytonic nouns the word beauty recurs 24 times, or in only about 10% of the cases. The word beauty, one of the key words of Shakepeare's Sonnets, is clearly emphasized by its position in WS-2. The same tendency is observed with the adjective beauteous.

Nouns with a strong negative connotation are particularly frequent in "The Cenci:" _Parricide_ with his alphabet . . . . _Parricide_ grows so rife . . . But not its cause: _suffering_ has died away; Which have no form, _sufferings_ which have no tongue; Could but despise _danger_ and gold . . . _Misery_ has killed its father . . . _Ravage_ on thee . . . (. . . let her food be) _Poison_, until she be encrusted round (cf. _Poison_, or fire . . . : Sh.Oth III,III:391); (Upon such evidence as justifies) _Torture_. -What evidence? This man's? -Even so; _Bloodhounds_, not men . . . ; _Infamy_, blood, _terror_, despair? . . . (Shel.C II,I:132, V,III:20, III,I:35,142, II,II:130, III,I:37,372, IV,I:129, V,II:77,166, V,III:45). The grammatical functions of the nouns in the WS-2 figures are usually those of a subject or, in cases of an enjambment, an object. Their coupling with the rhythmical figure emphasizes the rhematic function of the nouns.

Another typical semantic group of nouns in the figure WS-2 is "natural phenomena", particularly those associated with motion, sound, or light. For example: _Waterfalls_ leap . . . _Lightning_, and hail . . . (Shel.RI Dedication,II:6, I,III:6); Rightfullest arbiter!—If the _lightning_ (Of God has e'er descended to avenge) (Shel.C III,I:179-180); _Darkness_ arose . . . ; Till in the azure East _darkness_ again was piled (Shel.RI I,LV:7, III,XXXIII:9); Is conscious of a change. _Darkness_ and Hell (Shel.C IV,III:40).

Yet another group of repeated words can be generalized as "end of order". It is mainly comprised of the words _chaos_ and _ruin_, for example: _Ruin_ hath taught me thus to ruminate (Sh.Son 64:11); _Chaos_ is come again (Sh.Oth III,III:93); _Ruin_ to Thebes ("The Two Noble Kinsmen" I,II:92); _Chaos_ of ruins! who shall trace the void; _Ruins_ of years, though few, yet full of fate (Byron, "Childe Harold" IV,LXXX:7; IV,CXXXI:4); _Ruin_, already proud of the deeds done (Byron, "The Prophecy of Dante" II:73); _Ruin_ on ruin:— Thou art slow, my son (Shelley, "Hellas" 878); _Ruin_ upon the tyrants . . . (Shel.RI II,XXXIX:6);

Other often repeating words in the figure WS-2 are the verbs _pity_, _harden_, _mocking_, the nouns _pity_, _hardness_, and the adverbs _sudden_, _only_, and particularly _never_. For example, in Shakespeare's Sonnets the verb _pity_ (in the imperative mood) occurs three times, and all of them in the figure WS-2: _Pity_ the world . . . (Son. 1:13); _Pity_ me then . . . (Son. 111:8,13). The adjective _pitiful_ occurs only once, but also coupled with the figure WS-2: _Pitiful_ thieves . . . (Son. 125:8). Some more examples of recurring words are: _Never_ till now defiled . . . _Never_ the black and dripping precipices; _Never_ was that field lost, or that foe saved (A.SR 498,571,328); _Sudden_ he view'd . . . _Sudden_, these Honours shall be snatch'd away; _Sudden_, with starting Tears each Eye o'erflows (P.RL III:143,103, V:85). The former adverb is merely emphasized by the rhythmical figure WS-2, while the latter also builds a metaphoric image of an action abruptly beginning or ending.

8.6. The infrequent cases of the trisyllabic figure WSW-2 contain many vocative nouns; otherwise, semantically, the figures WSW-2 are not unlike the disyllabic WS-2. The recurring semantic components are motion, change, and speech. Recurring words, apart from proper names, are again the adverbs never, sudden, and only. Some examples are: *Uttering bare truths* . . . (Sh.Son 69:4); *Crossing so high* . . . (A.SR 163); *Spreading swift wings* . . . (Shel.RI VI,XXIX:5); *Never lack'd gold* . . . ; . . . *never loved Cassio*; *Never pray more* . . . (Sh.Oth II,I:151, V,II:62, III,III:371); . . . *never kept seat in one* (Sh.Son 105:14); . . . *Never saw I* (Sh.WT V,II:198); *Never so much* (Sh.AYLI I,III:51). Two causes seem to determine the grammatical and semantic properties of the WSW-2, probably even more strongly than with the other figures: (a) purely syntactic: words occupying the first two syllabic positions are often verb forms in the imperative, and vocative nouns; (b) arrangement of the sentence perspective: the disyllabic noun in WS is often syntactically a subject, while in terms of the sentence perspective (its "theme", or the "given", and the "rheme", or the "new" information) it is not the theme, but the rheme (on the rhematic subject and two rhematic "peaks" in an English sentence see, for example, Černjaxovskaja 1976:58-60, 69-169); examples: *Roses have thorns* . . . (Sh.Son 35:2); . . . *lions make leopards tame* (Sh.RII I,I:174); *Wretches so quacke* . . . (Sh.WT V,II:198); *Chloe stepp'd in* . . . (P.RL V:68); . . . *Sohrab lay dead* (A.SR 857).

8.7. We now will make a general resumé of the semantic functions of the various rhythmical figures. At the beginning of the chapter six questions were asked: (1) What meanings are emphasized and imitated by rhythm? (2) Are there specific semantic classes and groups of words italicized by rhythmical figures, or are the figures used randomly to emphasize words important for the poet in each individual context? (3) Are there any semantic characteristics of different rhythmical figures in terms of (a) their frequency of bearing a semantic load, (b) the intensity of the load, and (c) the image repertoire itself? (4) Is there any connection, within the same rhythmical figure, between its part-of-speech and syntactic structure, and (a) the frequency with which the figure bears semantic information, and (b) the kinds of semantic information it bears? (5) Is there any difference in the poets' attitude to the semantic potential of the figures in different genres, both Shakespeare's and other poets? (6) Is there any evolution in the attitude to the semantic potential of rhythm (a) within Shakespeare's literary career, and (b) within the history of the English literary tradition, for example, Shakespeare's epoch vs. the nineteenth-century verse? I drew provisional conclusions at the end of every section discussing individual figures; now we can generalize even further and provide the answers with more certainty, although still in many ways only provisionally. There is much more verse still to be examined, and many links are still missing, for example, pre-Shakespearean verse, or the verse of his older contemporaries (Sidney and Spenser; Kyd and Marlowe); the verse of his younger contemporaries (Jonson and Donne) and followers (Webster or Massinger; Herrick or Suckling); the verse of the end of Renaissance and post-Restoration poets (Milton and Dryden).

8.7.1. Rhythmical figures most certainly italicize words of definite semantic classes, and are thus tied to a specific image repertoire. It is hard to draw a line between mere emphasis and the mimetic (metaphoric) function of rhythm; but the most general semantic categories associated with all rhythmical figures analyzed are as follows. (1) Motion, particularly fast, forward, or downward; flowing, gliding, but more typically uneven, quivering; changed, restricted, or stopped; associated with force (delivering a blow; seizing and clutching). (2) Emotions and their physical display, as well as other kinds of facial movements (laughing, crying, kissing, turning red or pale; yawning, eating and swallowing; breathing). (3) Pain, destruction, and death, their physical causes and display (delivering a blow, wounding, breaking, bleeding, destroying; suffocation and strangulation; poisoning). (4) Speech and other sounds; cessation of sounds, lack of words, sounds stopped. (5) An unbalanced state of mind or thinking processes (being mad, drunk, frantic; doubting, or lacking knowledge). (6) Natural phenomena and their physical display (the activity of winds, waters; thunder and lightning; getting dark and, particularly, light; shining brightly). All these semantic categories also appear in the verse text outside the rhythmical figures; however, their frequency within the rhythmical figures is definitely higher.

To generalize further, one can say that rhythmical italics in most cases emphasize and represent iconically (metaphorically) a very general seme (an archiseme): a semantic feature referring to an uneven, discontinuous (beginning or, more often, ending) action (movement, state, or sound). Thus, even when the immediate constituents of a figure are non-verbal (like adjectives in the SW-1), the semantic and stylistic function of the figure, viewed in a broader situational context, is verbal, adding to the characteristics of a verbal style (R. Wells 1966; M. Lotman 1982:25-31). Being coupled again and again, in the course of the English literary tradition, with a limited "bundle" of semantic categories, rhythmical figures have acquired a semiotic character and a tendency to become a mimetic stylistic device, not unlike onomatopoeia. The same tendency is observed in the infrequent cases of the figure WS-1 in Russian verse. Examples like *Kon' upiraetsja, drožit* (The steed keeps backing, trembling), or *Boj barabannyj, kliki, skrežet* (Beat of the drums, shouts, grinding of teeth) (Puškin) indicate that the iconic potential of rhythmical figures, based on their physical properties of breaking the prevailing rhythmical momentum, is not limited to the English literary tradition alone.

8.7.2. There are some differences among the different rhythmical figures in terms of frequency with which they bear a supplementary semantic load, the amount of the additional information, and the types of semantic features added or emphasized. Some of the differences are related to the characteristics of genres and periods; others might be caused by the structural difference of the figures themselves (the rising accentual structure of the SW, the falling structure of the WS).

In terms of the increasing frequency of bearing supplementary information and the growing intensity of the semantic and connotative features emphasized or added, the figures can be conditionally arranged in the following order: W : SW-1 : WS-1 : WS-2 : WSW-2 : WSW-1. The number of neutral adjectives is higher in W than in SW-1; there are more verbs of broad and vague semantics in SW-1 than in WS-1 and particularly in WSW-1, while verbs with the feature "extra" are more numerous in WS-1 and particularly in WSW-1 than in SW-1; the incidence of the semantic feature "motion" increases in frequency and intensity from the least in verbs outside rhythmical figures, through the verbs in W and SW to the most in verbs forming the WS-1, WS-2, and WSW-1. The purely grammatical function of words in the rhythmical figures (notional verbs approaching link-verbs in the SW-1, verbs used to form imperatives and questions in the WS-1, nouns used as vocatives in the WS-1 and WS-2) decreases in frequency from SW-1 and WS-1, WS-2 through the WSW-1.

In spite of the general, and very strong, semantic similarity between different rhythmical figures, there are some individual differences in the types of semantic components regularly coupled with each figure. For example, the component "unbalanced state of mind" seems to be more typical of the SW-1 than of WS-1, though the reason may be purely grammatical: the word combinations to go (get, run, grow) mad (frantic, drunk) fit better into the structure of SW than WS. Conversely, the components "motion downward, falling" or a motion associated with weight and force seem to be more typical of the WS than SW. The explanation probably lies in the fact that both WS-1 and WS-2 disrupt the rhythmical momentum more strongly than the SW-1, where the usually syntactically subordinated elements on W tend to be also accentually subordinated by the following strongly stressed word; in cases where no subordination is observed (for example, subject + predicate) the semantic potential of the figure SW-1 strongly increases. The semantic component "falling", so frequent in the figure WS-1, probably has something to do with the accentual-syllabic structure of the figure itself, which usually begins a verse line or a phrase within the line (on the "phrase-initial" preferences of the figures see Hayes 1983:375): it is a stressed syllable followed by two unstressed ones; possibly this arrangement does produce a physical impression of a heavy weight falling down.

8.7.3. There is undoubtedly some connection between the part-of-speech and syntactic properties of the words forming rhythmical figures and the frequency and intensity of additional semantic information communicated by the figure. For example, the general frequency of additional semantic information and frequency of the semantic component "motion" of the type "extra" increases in the SW-1 from adverbs and adjectives *via* verbs through nouns. These are in the function of a subject coupled with a predicate, with its stress on the following ictic position.

8.7.4. In the course of the analyses we discovered connections between rhythm, grammar, semantics, and vocabulary. This connection results in rhythmical- grammatical-semantical-lexical patterns that have become conventional in the course of English literary history.

We have found recurring elements in all rhythmical figures. These are: (a) words of a particular part of speech in a particular morphological form, for example, adjectives in the figure SW-1, verbs in the figures WS-1 and WS-2, verbal forms of present participles in the WS-2; (b) particular syntactic patterns, for example, verb/predicate + adjective/attribute to the following noun, usually an object, in the WSW-1 and WSW-2 (*Pluck the keen teeth . . . Uttering bare truth . . .*); (c) words belonging to specific semantic classes, such as verbs of violent or uneven motion in the figures WS-1 and WS-2; and finally, (d) individual words or combinations of such words which have formed, as it were, in the course of English poetic tradition, "prefabricated blocks". The latter keep recurring, with variations, in the verse of the same or different poets.

Recurring rhythmical-grammatical-lexical patterns can in part be attributed to self-repetitions; for example:

> She is a woman, therefore may be wooed;
> She is a woman, therefore may be won
>
>   ("Titus Andronicus" II,I:82-83)
>
> She's beautiful and therefore to be wooed;
> She is a woman, therefore to be won.
>
>   ("Henry VI", Part 1, V,III:78-79)
>
> Was ever woman in this humour wooed?
> Was ever woman in this humour won?
>
>   ("Richard III" I,III:227-228)

Some repetitions occur at times within the same short text, as *Tired with all these . . .* in Sonnet 66; these are stylistically motivated.

Sometimes rhythmical-grammatical-lexical repetitions can be attributed to direct borrowings, allusions, reminiscences, or parody[4] (see, e.g., Collins 1904, Robertson 1924, Hieatt 1983). Compare, for example, *The tott'ring China shook without a Wind* (Pope, "The Rape of the Lock" IV:163) and *The shivering china dropped upon the ground* (John Gay, "The Toilette" 64); the deliberate connection between the two lines seems obvious.

Often, however, recurring rhythmical figures formed by particular parts of speech and syntactic patterns, coupled with similar situations and even common vocabulary and images, do not have a definite source and can rarely be attributed to a particular author. Indeed, one can hardly call it a borrowing when poet after poet after poet uses the present participle of the verbs shake, flutter, or tremble coupled with the figure WS-2, or the verbs run, rush, or fall with monosyllabic prepositions coupled with the figure WS-1. Apparently, combinations of certain grammatical and semantic classes of words coupled with a certain kind of rhythmical figure just exist in the English literary tradition belonging to nobody in particular but used by many.

The existence of rhythmical-grammatical-semantical "formulas" in Homeric verse and folklore literatures is acknowledged by many scholars; see, e.g., Meillet 1923; Parry 1928a,b, 1930, 1932, 1971; Lord 1960; Russo 1963, 1966; Nagler 1967; Žirmunskij 1962; Tronskij 1973; Kumaxov 1979; Schumann 1979-1982; and many others. Francis Magoun (1953) applied Parry-Lord's oral-formulaic ideas to Anglo-Saxon narrative poetry. Magoun's major concepts, (1) that Anglo-Saxon verse was totally formulaic and (2) that it was the product of an oral composition by generations of singers, were criticized in later years: for example, Arthur Brodeur (1959) and William Whallon (1961) questioned the completely formulaic structure of "Beowulf:" "*Beowulf* corresponds closely to the Homeric poems, but its diction is much less completely stereotyped" (Whallon 1961:319, cf. Bogatyrjëv 1971). Benson (1966) expressed his doubt that the formulaic structure of verse is typical only of oral poetry. He felt that a poet can be traditional without being oral; and some literary periods actually prefer tradition to "originality". "Literate poets," according to Benson, "could quite easily write in a formulaic style" (Benson 1966:336). The general idea that metrical-grammatical-semantic-lexical formulas played an important role in the composition of Anglo-Saxon poetry seems to be accepted nowadays (e.g., Creed 1959, Stevick 1962, Diamond 1963, Fry 1967, Watts 1969, Shippey 1979, Smirnickaja 1980).

It appears that a typologically similar phenomenon exists also in literary verse of modern times, particularly of certain epochs (cf. Benson 1966:335, footnote 6). Here is Parry's definition of "the formula:" it is "a group of words which is regularly employed under the same metrical conditions to express a given essential idea" (Parry 1971:272). And now let us recall the numerous examples cited above; all the countless cases of trembling coupled with a WS-2, or fall to (by, from . . .) coupled with a WS-1, or the grammatical pattern verb + adjective (+ noun, usually an object) expressing "the essential idea" of a violent or uneven motion and coupled with the figure WSW-1 (*Throw your vile guesses . . . Pluck the keen teeth . . . Shrink his thin essence . . . Clasped that bright shape . . . Wound his long arms . . .* and many others). Obviously, the recurring "patterns" in literary verse have a different proportion, different causes, and different functions than the "formulas" of ancient or folk poetry; but there is some unmistakable typological similarity. The recurring rhythmical-grammatical-lexical "patterns", so obvious in folklore and less noticeable in literary poetry, are part of the general multi-level parallelism which is an essential structural principle of verse (see Jakobson 1966, 1979d).

Here are some more examples of recurring rhythmical- grammatical patterns expressing closely related ideas and filled with identical or semantically related words. Most of the examples display only partial similarity. Identical rhythmical-grammatical patterns or their variants coupled with identical or closely related situations are arranged below in three "clusters". Each cluster expresses the same general idea and contains repeating words, their synonyms, or other related words belonging to the same or an adjacent semantic field. Examples within the "clusters" are arranged in such a way that similar or common lexical elements constitute "bridges" between the cited lines.

A. Bent with his load, and he at length was lame
(George Crabbe, "Peter Grimes" 129)
Bent its broad arch: her breath began to fail
(Byron, "The Island" IV,XIV:6)
Bent was his head, and hidden was his brow
(Byron, "Lara" II,XXIV:12)
Bent his thin head to seek the brazen rein
(Shelley, "The Revolt of Islam" VI,XLIII:4)
Bow thy white head before offended God
(Shelley, "The Cenci" I,III:157)
Bowing her head, and ready to expire
(Keats, "To Hope" 34)

B. Shakes the thin roof, and echoes round the walls
(George Crabbe, "The Poorhouse" 48)
Shake the red cloak and poise the ready brand
(Byron, "Childe Harold" I,LLXVIII:6)
Shook the weak hand that grasped it; of that crew
(Shelley, "Adonais" XXXIII:7)
(Cf.: Shaking a fist at him with one fierce arm:
Browning, "Fra Lippo Lippi" 154)
Stretch your blind hands and trifle with a match
(Browning, "Karshish" 176)
Clasp the fond arms and mix their kisses sweet
(Erasmus Darwin, "The Botanic Garden" 20)
Beats his weak arms against his tarry side
(George Crabbe, "The Borough" 56)

C. Borne on the wings of vain philosophy
(John Arbuthnot, "Know Yourself" 133)
Borne on whose Wings, each heavy Sot can pierce
(John Wilmot, "A Satire against Mankind" 84)
Spreads his black Wings, and slowly mounts to Day
(Pope, "The Rape of the Lock" IV:88)
Clapp'd his glad Wings, and sate to view the fight
(Pope, "The Rape of the Lock" V:54)
Claps her pale cheek, till clapping makes it red
(Shakespeare, "Venus and Adonis" 78:6)

<u>Climb with swift wings</u> after their children's souls
(Shelley, "The Cenci" I,III:85)
<u>Shaking her wings</u>, devouring all in haste
(Shakespeare, "Venus and Adonis" 10:3)
<u>Spreading swift wings</u> as sails to the dim air
(Shelley, "The Revolt of Islam" VI,XXIX:5)
<u>Spreading his azure sail</u> where breath of Heaven
(Shelley, "The Revolt of Islam" VIII,XXVI:8)
<u>Spread a green kirtle</u> to the minstrelsy
(Keats, "Lamia" 188)

The first four syllables of the English pentameter line are, as we know, more rhythmically diverse than the rest of the line, because the first three syllabic positions, beginning both a line and a phrase, allow the highest ratio of rhythmical variation (see Chapter 1). However, it is the first "hemistich" that usually contains the recurring rhythmical-grammatical-lexical patterns. This phenomenon, "unity in variety", seems to suggest that both the rhythmical figures themselves and the grammatical-lexical patterns that accompany them were "constructed" consciously some time ago, became in part automatic, and were deliberately used again and again to form a literary convention. Obviously there were periods, genres, and authors with greater or lesser numbers of these recurring patterns, for example, more in the Elizabethan dramas or in the eighteenth-century Classicists' verse, fewer in the nineteenth-century late Romantic and post-Romantic poetry; more in the verse of epigons than original poets (cf. Žirmunskij 1978). Still, rhythmical-grammatical-semantical-lexical patterns recurring fully or partially in the works of different authors seems to be a fact of the English literary tradition, an element of its "continuity" (cf. Miles 1951, 1955). Rhythmical-syntactical (and lexical) "figures" were also discovered in Russian verse (cf. Brik 1927, Xodasevič 1937, Jakobson 1979:466, Taranovsky 1963, Gasparov 1976, 1979, 1983). Such "figures", typologically comparable with the "formulas" of archaic and folk verse, are, naturally, more scarce in modern than in Old English poetry and are harder to find. But they do <u>exist</u>. Their origin and functions differ radically from the Old-Saxon "formulas;" and still there is some typological similarity.

The "patterns" of literary verse require further research. We still do not know, for example, when rhythmical figures began to be coupled with particular grammatical forms and especially with particular semantic classes of words,[5] we do not know if their proportion and functions are the same in iambic pentameter and tetrameter, and if any recurring patterns can be found in English poems written in other meters, e.g., trochaic or trisyllabic. The problem obviously needs more study.

8.7.5. There seem to be <u>genre and period characteristics in use of the semantic and stylistic potential of different rhythmical figures</u> found in iambic pentameter. These characteristics were discovered within Shakespeare's canon and in comparing Shakespeare's verse with that of later poets.

<u>Genre features</u> are observed in both Shakespeare's canon and the works of later poets. Some examples are as follows. Shakespeare's lyrical poem "The Rape of Lucrece" not only contains on its W more adjectives with alliteration than does his chronicle "Richard II;" the poem also has fewer adjectives with a neutral connotation than does the play. There is also a genre opposition in the way adjectives are treated by the disyllabic figure SW-1, both in Shakespeare's and in later verse. The highest number of neutral adjectives in the figure SW-1 was discovered in long narrative poems, the lowest in the lyrical verse, while dramatic verse occupies an intermediate position (Fig. 8.1). The number of verbs with the intensifying component "extra" both in the SW-1 and WS-1 is higher in lyrical and narrative verse than in dramas; this is true of both Shakespeare and Shelley. The opposition of genres through their utilization of rhythmical figures is not clear cut, but it is undoubtedly there.

<u>Period characteristics</u> are seen already in the correlation between the number of the figures SW-1 and WS-1: the incidence of the figure SW-1 increases in the verse of the nineteenth-century poets (before that, however, it decreased in the eighteenth-century verse), particularly in Arnold's "Sohrab and Rustum". There seems to be an evolution even in Shakespeare's canon: the correlation between the SW-1 and WS-1 in "The Winter's Tale" differs from his earlier works.

Shakespeare's attitude to the stylistic potential of rhythmical figures seems to have changed: the results of the analyses so far suggest that the poet made more use of the stylistic potential of verse rhythm in his <u>earlier</u> than later dramas. "Richard II", for example, is closer in its rhythmical style to Shakespeare's lyric verse than "The Winter's Tale". One can, of course, argue that it is natural for chronologically close works, as are "Lucrece", the Sonnets, and "Richard II", to resemble each other in style. It is also possible, however, that Shakespeare's own attitude to the semantic potential of verse rhythm evolved in time; dramatic verse is heard from the stage, and subtleties of rhythm probably escape the audience, a fact the poet came to realize. Isn't it at least one of the reasons why alliteration, or rhymed lines, become scarce in Shakespeare's later dramas? Isn't it also one of the probable reasons why Shakespeare makes less use of the stylistic and semantic potential of rhythmical figures in "The Winter's Tale" than in his earlier works?

The semantic load on rhythmical figures, particularly the SW-1, seems to have increased and become conventional in the English poetic tradition with the passage of time. The general trend is clearly seen already in Shakespeare's verse, and later poets, even not of the first rank, keep matching specific rhythmical patterns to particular grammatical structures, semantic categories of words, and even individual words and word combinations with greater and greater confidence and regularity. To trace the origin of the trend and the evolution of the strengthening link between rhythmical figures and semantic categories in the English poetic tradition of iambic verse is a fascinating problem for future study.

Notes to Chapter 8

[1] Componental analysis of meanings of words is a well- known procedure; see, for example, Hjemlslev 1961: Chapter 14, Greimas 1966:50-54, Melčuk 1974, Nida 1975.

[2] Semantic classifications of words in a poetic text can be done in several ways; one of them is singling out really elementary components of meaning, such as *Magn*, *AntiMagn*, *Mult*, *Oper*, and *ResultOper*, used by Melčuk 1974, and classifying words into more abstract classes (cf. Petöfi 1973). Another way is referring words to relatively more concrete conceptual-associative fields, such as "life", "death", "time", "youth", "old age", "evil", "goodness", and others (Levin 1975, Tarlinskaja and Coachman 1986). The second approach seemed more convenient for the type of the analysis undertaken here.

[3] The number of illustrating examples here and below may seem high; but my intention is to convince the readers of the recurring syntactic, semantic, and lexical patterns coupled with particular rhythmical figures. The repeating patterns tend to form, as it were, "prefabricated blocks" of building materials conventionalized in the English literary tradition.

[4] One interesting example of interliterature reminiscences is the fate of Shakespeare's *I know a bank where the wild thyme blows* ("A Midsummer Night's Dream", II,I:249): Goethe, *Kennst du das Land wo die Zitronen blühn* ("Die Leiden des Jungen Werthers", Mignonas Lied, 1): Byron, *Know ye the land where the cypress and myrtle* ("The Bride of Abydos", I,I:1); the Russian *Kto videl kraj, gde roskoju prirody* (Who saw the land where by the nature's splendour . . .) by Puškin or *Ty znaeš kraj gde vsë obil'em dyït* (You know the land where everything breathes of plenty) by A.K. Tolstoy. See also Žirmunskij 1978, 1981:112, Fridlender 1973, Altman 1973, Sajtanov 1977, Hieatt 1983.

[5] G.T. Wright (1985) suggests that Wyatt has been the first to use variations of lines for aesthetic and semantic purposes.

Chapter 9

Conclusion: Iambic Pentameter and Shakespeare's Idiosyncrasy

9.0 Preliminary remarks

In every chapter of this book I have, in one way or another, touched upon the following problems: (1) Meter of English iambic verse and the form it assumed in Shakespeare's works in the course of his career. (2) Metrical/rhythmical problems of genres and style; and the evolution of rhythmical styles of English poets during and after Shakespeare. (3) Verse form and meaning: rhythmical variations of meter reflected in the "stress profiles" of text fragments and in various "rhythmical figures", and their contributions to verse semantics. (4) Verse form and attribution: rhythmical characteristics seemingly indicative of collaboration, followed by a close analysis of four of Shakespeare's most questionable plays. In this concluding chapter I organize the results of the previous chapters under these four subjects.

9.1 English iambic meter and Shakespeare's verse

What is the relationship between English iambic verse as a whole system of versification and Shakespeare's individual metrical practice? What place does Shakespeare occupy within the English national variant of iambic meter, and what are his rhythmical peculiarities compared with those of his contemporaries? To answer these questions we shall have to bring together all the basic principles and minute details about English iambic meter, and compare them with the major principles and minor details that we have discovered about Shakespeare's verse.

9.1.0. I can summarize in the following way the basic accentual-syllabic features of phrase structure in the English language that influence the form of stress profiles.

1. A definite tendency to avoid back-to-back stressing. In the experimental, speech model of syllabic verse (Fig. 1.1), where the only conditions for "lines" were that they (1) begin syntagmatically and (2) end with a stress on position 10, the stress profile shows a rudimentary iambic tendency: an alternation of more strongly and more weakly stressed positions. Why? English phrases often begin "iambically" with an unstressed first syllable (i.e., an article, preposition, etc.), and position 2 is stressed because it is a notional (lexical) word. These are stressed; if polysyllabic, they are typically stressed on the first

syllable. Position 10 of the line is stressed (by condition), so 9 is by contrast unstressed, then 8, by contrast, slightly more strongly stressed, and so on. Thus the tendencies born at the beginnings and ends of "lines" mesh throughout the whole line. We conclude that an iambic tendency in a rudimentary form already exists in English prose; but this tendency becomes, of course, strongly amplified by the poets. The ontological iambic tendency of the English language in part explains the absolute predominance of iambic meters in the English poetic tradition.

2. English phrases tend to begin "iambically;" thus the "anacrusis" (syllabic position 1) of the speech model of iambic pentameter is the least stressed of all "non-ictic" positions. But in English poetry, all iambic pentameter lines have much greater stress on position 1 than on other non-ictuses (cf. Figs. 1.1, 2.1, 2.2, 2.3); thus all poets, even those who wrote the loosest verse closest to prose, deliberately modified the phrase stressing tendency. The extra-heavy stress on the anacrusis and the concentration of "rhythmical inversions of stress" at the beginning of the verse line are specific features of verse and not the result of prose tendencies influencing poetry.

3. The length of typical syntactic word groups ("phrases") in English is, on the average, definitely longer than 4-5 syllables, perhaps 6 or 7. Thus "lines" of a speech model of iambic pentameter (Fig. 2.1) show an asymmetrical bipartite structure: a reduced stress ("dip") on position 8 indicating a syntactic line segmentation 6+4 or 7+3. Poets who wrote more rigid verse had to deliberately shorten the initial phrases of their lines to 4 or 5 syllables, to generate maximum stress on 4 and minimum on 6, the symmetrical "hemistich" structure 4+6 or 5+5. The accentual and phrasal line structure of English iambic pentameter indicates that the bipartite line segmentation into "hemistichs" is a strong tendency in English verse.

9.1.1. The most general definition of the English variant of iambic pentameter can be reduced to a basic principle: the language material is to be organized in the form of a perceptible—to the people of English language and culture—alternation of weakly stressed or unstressed syllables in odd (W) syllabic positions with strongly-stressed syllables in even (S) syllabic positions of a verse line of ten syllabic positions. Loss of stress on any S and stressed syllables on any W in individual lines is well within the metrical norm, as long as the difference between $\bar{S}$ and $\bar{W}$ (mean stress values for strong and weak positions for the whole text) remains above a certain threshold. Phrasal stresses on W positions are not only considerably fewer than on S positions but also normally weaker than the adjacent stresses on S: back-to-back, "level" stressing is avoided and, though acceptable ("metrical"), it is not normative. The main condition of the stress weakening is a syntactic subordination of the words on W to either the preceding, or, more often, the following word with a strong ictic stress (. . . thĭne ŏwn brĭ́ght èyes; Wĭthĭn thĭne ŏwn bŭ́d bŭrĭĕst. . .). Accentual subordination of the words on W to adjacent words with an ictic stress is a part of a specific intonation pattern that accompanies "extrametrical" stresses or "inversions of stress" in the figures W, WS, WSW, or SW. Even on such a general, basic level of defining English iambic meter, syntax cannot be left out; it is part of the national characteristic of the English iambic meter.

The perceptible alternation of stressed and unstressed syllables on S and W in the English iambic pentameter requires that the mean difference between $\bar{S}$ and $\bar{W}$ be not below 50%. The iambic index of the loosest metrical form in our collection, Swinburne's verse, is 55.5%. True, the index of Donne's "Satyres" is even lower, only 48%, but "Satyres" are a unique form, transitory from syllabo-tonic to syllabic systems. If we take the indices of Pope's verse (79.2%) and of the "Satyres" (48%) to represent the extremes, then the range of variation between the most rigid and the loosest variants of the English iambic pentameter is a little over 30%. What is the position of Shakespeare's verse between the two poles? The highest iambic index of the dramas is displayed by "Henry VI",3: 68.3%, of the non-dramatic verse by "Lucrece:" 70.5%, while the lowest index characterizes "Timon of Athens:" 60.2%. "The Rape of Lucrece" is positioned a little more than one-fourth of the distance from the most rigid toward the loosest variant of iambic pentameter, "Henry VI",3, is a little over one-third of the way, while "Timon of Athens" is almost two-thirds of the way, and is in fact closer to Donne's "Satyres" than to Pope's verse. Thus the rhythmical diapason in Shakespeare's canon is considerable; it opposes his earlier plays (particularly chronicles) to the later dramas and his non-dramatic to dramatic verse. Loosening of Shakespeare's metrical norm in the course of his career is seen on various levels of his verse structure. However, even "Timon of Athens" does not display the maximum looseness typical of the Jacobean dramatic iambic pentameter: the iambic index of Webster's "The Duchess of Malfi", for example, is only 56.9%. The verse form of this drama is almost three-quarters of the way from the most rigid to the loosest form of English iambic pentameter; in fact the iambic index of "The Duchess of Malfi" is close to the conventional threshold, cf. with Swinburne's 55.5%. And it must be pointed out that only four later dramas by Shakespeare display indices approaching 60%: "Measure for Measure", "King Lear", "Timon of Athens", and "Henry VIII". Shakespeare was not only well within the norm for his epoch, but also on a slightly more conservative, "smoother" side.

9.1.2 Stress profiles as an element of meter

Analyses of all periods of English iambic verse tradition (cf. Tarlinskaja 1976) highlight the most general, most basic principles of the English iambic verse. The data indicate that not only the mean indices of stressing acceptable for Ws and Ss are constituents of English iambic meter; the most typical correlations of positional stressing within the line are also a substantial component of meter.

Though stressing on W and loss of stress on S are within the basic pentametrical norm, not all positions tolerate untypically stressed syllables with equal ease. The most stable ictus is the fifth S, the end of the line; but, unlike Italian or Russian verse, it is not constant; it is only predominantly stressed (i.e., >80%). The second S (position 4) is usually also strongly stressed and forms a "peak" between the two adjacent ictuses. The weakest ictuses are I, and either III (a "dip" in position 6) or IV (a "dip" in position 8). A particularly strong stress in position 4 and a "dip" in 6, optionally accompanied by a relative maximum of "extrametrical" stresses in position 5 and a syntactic seam after positions 4 or 5, are signs of a more rigid verse form and a "symmetrical", 4+6 or 5+5 bipartite line segmentation. A weakening of ictus II and an increased stress on ictus III, accompanied by a relative maximum of non-ictic stresses in position 7 and either shifting of the syntactic seam to the right or to the left, or effacing of a strong syntactic break in midline, are indications of a looser iambic form and of an asymmetrical bipartite line structure, or absence of any clear-cut tendency in line segmentation.

The weakly stressed (odd) syllabic positions usually decrease in stress from the anacrusis to the end of the line. Optional absolute maxima in stressing on non-ictuses in the middle of the line are always weaker than the stressing of the anacrusis; the first W and the first S of the English iambic pentameter line may be qualified as optionally stressed. The difference in stressing between W_1 and $\bar{W}_{3,5,7,9}$ is greater in a more rigid variant and tends to approach zero in a loose variant of English iambic pentameter. This is a deliberate "break" by the poet from a basic tendency of English phrase structure, forming a specific, conventional feature of iambic verse.

Shakespeare's dramatic verse went through an evolution from a more constrained form with a "dip" in 6, strong ictus II and a nine-fold difference between positions 1 and 9 ("Titus Andronicus") to a looser form with a "dip" on 8, weakened stress on ictus II (positions 4 and 6 are practically leveled, as in "Antony and Cleopatra" and "Cymbeline") and with the difference between stressing of the anacrusis and position 9 falling to less than two times ("The Winter's Tale"). Some typical examples of lines are: **Early Shakespeare**: *Sister, farewell, / I must to Coventry*; *Swear by the duty / that you owe to God* ("Richard II" I,II:56, I,III:180). **Late Shakespeare**: *Ănd făvŏur ŏf thĕ clĭmăte: / ăs bȳ strănge fŏrtŭne; Ŏur mŏst dĭslŏyăl lădȳ: / fŏr ās shĕ hăth* (Been publicly accused. . .) ("The Winter's Tale" II,III:179,203). Notice the syllabic duplications on W (position 7) which accompany the changed rhythmical-syntactic segmentation within the line of later Shakespeare. The changed principle of bipartite line segmentation is emphasized by the changed position of the split within the line when the latter is shared by two or more personages: the typical place of the split after position 4 in earlier dramas moves to 7 in "Henry VIII".

In addition to the accentual and syntactic peculiarities of late Shakespeare discussed in detail in this book, the last two examples above also contain disyllabic combinations in position 7. Disyllabic combinations filling non-ictic positions of dramatic iambic pentameter are very typical of later Elizabethan-Jacobean poetry (see section 2.8).

Shakespeare's poem "Venus and Adonis" (1592), bracketed by "The Two Gentlemen of Verona" and "Love's Labour's Lost" (Wentersdorf 1951:164), displays a stress profile tendency which differs from that of dramatic verse of the same time: ictus IV is somewhat weaker than III. This is a sign of a different bipartite line segmentation with a frequent syntactic seam after position 6; examples are:

O, what a sign it was,/wistly to view!	(58,1)
Didst thou not mark my face?/was it not white?	(108,1)
Lo, here the gentle lark,/weary of rest	(143,1)
Thy mark is feeble age;/but thy false dart	(157,5)
But when Adonis lived,/sun and sharp air	(181,5)

The rhythmical evolution of Shakespeare's non-dramatic verse ("Venus and Adonis;" "The Rape of Lucrece;" the Sonnets) proceeds in a reverse order from the dramatic verse of the same periods. The reason, it seems, is the following. In his non-dramatic verse Shakespeare must have followed the Italian verse form (Shakespeare's lyrical verse displays several features of Italian lyrics), and Italian verse makes extensive use of a longer first "hemistich" ("*A mayore*"). In his dramatic verse Shakespeare accepted a different model which strictly canonized a shorter first "hemistich" ("*A minore*") (cf. the two tendencies in "Gorboduc", section 3.1). A shorter first "hemistich", as in French verse, was widely used by earlier Elizabethan playwrights (cf. Table 2.3). Probably a shorter first "hemistich" made it easier for the actors of the early Elizabethan theatre to recite the dramatic pentameter verse line. Then in his later non-dramatic poetry Shakespeare followed the established momentum of his dramatic verse.

Why did the line model with a shorter first "hemistich", rather than with a longer one, become coupled with the strictest, the most canonized form of English pentameter? The answer to this question is not solely "the outer influence:" the French line form, rather than the Italian, providing the prevailing model. Another probable reason is the inner laws of English prosody. The pattern with a longer first "hemistich" happens to resemble the structure of the English prose phrase (syntagma) and diminishes the "verse-prose" opposition, so essential for a stricter metrical form. It is not accidental that the line variant with a longer first "hemistich" is typical both of the earliest English pentameter form, when the canon was still in the making and dominated by the prose syntagma structure, and of the much later, decanonized verse when the verse-prose opposition was already being effaced.

The evolution of line endings is another sign of verse form loosening: the proportion of unstressed monosyllables in position 10 increased ten times and the proportion of non-masculine endings grew three times from Shakespeare's earlier to later plays. An excessive use of unstressed monosyllables in the final ictic position—the result of strong enjambments—is more typical of Shakepeare's rhythmical style than of other Elizabethan-Jacobean poets, even Massinger. This rhythmical-syntactic feature reappears and is exaggerated two centuries later in the dramas of English Romanticism.

In his use of feminine line endings Shakespeare was ahead of his epoch at the beginning of his career but began to lag behind at the end: Shakespeare handled feminine endings with much more restraint than did Fletcher.

The evolution of the line structure in Shakespeare's canon progressed within the mainstream of Elizabethan-Jacobean dramatic verse (cf. Kyd's "The Spanish Tragedy", 1589, and Shirley's "Cardinal", 1641: Tarlinskaja 1976: Table 50; see Fig. 2.2). Shakespeare was the son of his time; but the evolution proceeded within different chronological segments in every poet's career: cf. the chronological contemporaries Marlowe's "Edward II" and Shakespeare's "Richard III", or Chapman's "Bussi d'Ambois" and Shakespeare's "Antony and Cleopatra" (Table 2.3).

9.1.3 Meter and rhythmical figures

The data on the proportion and grammatical (hence, intonational) characteristics of <u>rhythmical figures</u> are another element of English iambic meter. Analysis of rhythmical figures in Shakespeare's verse also help to locate the place of his verse style within his own epoch and within the whole English poetic tradition, and to trace a rhythmical evolution within Shakespeare's canon.

Let us sum up the information about the rhythmical figures (a) both normative and "metrical", (b) not normative but still "metrical" (acceptable), and (c) "unmetrical" (unacceptable by most poets).

The seven normative (traditionally acceptable) rhythmical figures are: S (missing stresses on an ictus), W ("extrametrical" stresses on a non-ictus), and their disyllabic and trisyllabic combinations: SW-1 and WS-1 (realized by two monosyllables); WS-2 (realized by a disyllabic non-oxytonic word), WSW-1 (three monosyllables) and WSW-2 (the first disyllabic group is realized by a disyllabic non-oxytonic word); examples are: (S) *and <u>I</u> have stood*; (W) *<u>Girl!</u> nimble with thy feet* . . . ; (SW-1) *The armies <u>are drawn</u> out* . . . ; (WS-1) *<u>Poised on</u> the top* . . . ; (WS-2) *And stood erect, <u>trembling</u> with rage* . . . ; (WSW-1) *<u>Miss'd, and went</u> quivering down* . . . ; (WSW-2) *<u>Sohrab came forth</u>* . . . . The non-normative (not acceptable by all poets of all epochs) figures are: SW-2, realized by an oxytonic disyllable (*shĕ rēpl͞ied ĕarnestly*. . .) and a variant of WSW-2, the disyllabic oxytonic word filling the last two positions (*L͞ĕss āppēar sŏ*. . .).

The following figures are also non-normative: SWS (*<u>Admit impediments.</u> <u>Love is</u> not love*) and WSWS; the latter is more acceptable if it is filled with accentually ambivalent monosyllables or if there is a syntactic seam in the middle of the figure (*<u>Uncle, even in</u> the glasses of thine eyes*).

The seven on the whole normative "rhythmical figures" have more normative and less normative grammatical realizations. W is usually realized by an adjective or another monosyllabic attribute; the normative subordination is to the following rather than to the preceding word (proclitic rather than enclitic): *Or laid great bases* . . . rather than *Ere beauty's dead fleece made*. . . . Within enclitic patterns, words of broad or vague semantics (capable of weakening or losing their sentence stress) are more acceptable than words of full lexical meaning (. . . *the best thing God invents* is more normative than *Those great rings serve more purposes*. . .).

Attributive grammatical structures are also typical of SW-1: . . . *with his brief hours and weeks*; an untypical syntactic pattern is "subject" (on W) followed by a predicate with an ictic stress (*And the hell reeks*. . .); the least normative pattern is phrase-terminal and has a strong syntactic break after SW (*If I doubt, prove*. . .). In both latter cases there is little or no accentual subordination of the element on W to the following word with an ictic stress. Absence of subordination causes back-to-back clashes of stress: these are definitely not normative.

Typical grammatical realizations of both WS-1 and WS-2 are verbs: imperatives are typical of the former, present participles of the latter. In cases of the infrequent line-internal nominal WS-1, enclitic accentual subordinations of the noun on W to the preceding word, usually its attribute, are on the whole not normative (even though metrical). The syntactic tie in such cases is stronger with the preceding rather than the following notional word (*Resembling strong youth \ in his middle age*). Enclitically-oriented nominal WS-1 were normative (acceptable and widely used) only during certain periods (e.g., the Jacobean epoch) and exceptional (and not normative) in others (e.g., early Elizabethan epoch, or Classicism).

WS-1, WS-2, WSW-1, and WSW-2 are normally line-initial or "hemistich"-initial, and at the same time they are usually phrase-initial. The least normative (but "metrical"!) non-phrase-initial syntactic elements on WS are disyllabic modified nouns (*Are base people. Believe them not*. . .), next come direct objects (*And peace proclaims olives of endless age*). The usual place of non-phrase-initial WS is the beginning of the line or of the second half- line: the implied by the tradition bipartite rhythmical line segmentation, as it were, neutralizes the absence of a syntactic break before WS(W), as in *And peace proclaims olives*. . . . This relatively frequent use of WS (and W) figures in line-initial positions accounts for the uniquely high stressing of position 1 in contrast with the other non-ictic positions.

Polysyllabic figures other than WS/WS are definitely avoided, and can be qualified as unmetrical; they appear as the rarest of exceptions and always play an important semantic or stylistic role as in *But shakes it not—Murder! Murder! Murder!*. "Unmetrical" segments used by poets for emphasis are typologically similar to "ungrammatical" utterances that are sometimes intentionally used by authors of verse and prose with a stylistic aim in mind (cf. Gindin 1981:234).

Shakespeare's "metrical idiolect" stays well within the norm of his epoch. Actually, in some respects his verse form is less loose than that of this contemporaries, and in many ways resembles the more rigid form of post-Restoration poets (cf. Shakespeare and Milton; see Chapter 6). Syllabically or syntactically "non-normative" figures are scarce in Shakespeare's verse; figures over four syllables long are practicaly non-existent (if the famous *Never, never, never, never, never* from "King Lear" is classified as a "headless" line with a zero anacrusis); we hardly ever find lines like <u>That's the greatest torture souls feel in hell</u> (Webster, "The Duchess of Malfi" IV,I:69) even in late Shakespeare. Webster's septasyllabic group WSWSWSW, which, although containing a syntactic seam (after <u>torture</u>), also comprises two disyllabic non-oxytonic words closely linked syntactically: a modifying adjective plus a modified noun on positions WSWS—a more striking "deviation" than Beaumont's and Fletcher's *Are base <u>people</u>. Believe them not: they lied* . . . Webster's line, by the way, is an excellent example of semantic functioning of a rhythmical figure: the "tortured" rhythm appropriately accompanies the contents of the line.

Another example of a more rigid pentameter form of even late Shakespeare, compared to his contemporaries, is the spare use of heavy feminine endings of phrases: Shakespeare seemed to avoid the syncopated rhythm of enclitic phrase structures even in "Henry VIII", working with Fletcher and, presumably, consciously or unconsciously imitating to some extent the rhythmical idiosyncrasy of his co-author. The predominantly proclitic character of Shakespeare's "extrametrical" stresses, the high proportion of more weakly stressed words of broad semantics in his enclitic phrases, and the prevailing syntactic structures in the latter (<u>a modifier + a modified noun</u>, and <u>a verb + an adverb</u>, as in *By adding óne thíng* . . . or . . . *that séals úp all in rest*) result in a smoother rhythm of his verse than in most of his contemporaries'. These facts show once again that <u>syntactic and semantic categories cannot be avoided in defining the English variant of iambic meter</u>.

The relative proportion of the various rhythmical figures evolved in the course of Shakespeare's career. The most significant change was the increased number of the figures SW-1; their proportion in Shakespeare's later works reminds us of the nineteenth-century poets. However, the elements on W in Shakespeare's dramas are usually words of broad or vague semantics liable to a stress weakening (*Othello shall <u>go</u> mad*), while the nineteenth-century poets chose words of full lexical meaning and used them in such syntactic functions that ensured their strong phrasal stress (*And the <u>sun</u> melts the snow*. . .). The semantic function of the figure SW-1 is more noticeable in the verse of Romantic and post-Romantic poets than in Shakespeare (see 9.3).

9.2 Problems of genre and style: rhythmical markers

Shakespeare's iambic pentameter displays not only period peculiarities but other, more subtle kinds of variation. Variations of verse form help the poet to set apart different genres and to create oppositions of various styles and substyles.

9.2.1. Variations of iambic pentameter form oppose Shakespeare's genres; first and foremost, his dramatic and non-dramatic verse. Non-dramatic verse is structurally more rigid than dramatic: (a) iambic indices are higher (cf. "The Rape of Lucrece" and "Richard II", Tables 2.2 and 2.6); (b) positions 4 and 10 are stressed more often (mean non-ictic stress, however, is slightly higher in non-dramatic verse, particularly in the Sonnets); (c) the rhythm of proclitic stresses on W is smoother: non-dramatic verse avoids syntactic breaks after the "extrametrical" stresses on W and favors syntactic and accentual subordination of stressed monosyllables on W to the following word; (d) polysyllabic rhythmical figures are more frequent in dramatic than non-dramatic verse.

Other features that oppose the genres are as follows: (a) a different stress profile tendency and bipartite segmentation in "Venus and Adonis" than in dramatic verse of the same period (see 9.1.2); (b) the proportion of verbs, particularly imperatives, in the figure WS-1 is the highest in the dramatic verse, the lowest in the narrative poem "Lucrece", while the lyrical verse (Sonnets) occupies an intermediate position; (c) the proportion of present participle forms in WS-2 is higher in non-dramatic than dramatic verse; (d) the semantic potential of rhythmical figures is more fully utilized in the non-dramatic than in dramatic verse, particularly of Shakespeare's final period. For example, in the rhythmical figures W and SW-1 there are fewer monosyllabic adjectives with a neutral connotation and more verbs with an "extra" component of meaning in the non-dramatic verse.

The rhythmical difference between the dramatic and non-dramatic genres is explained not only functionally but, presumably, also by the difference in perception: dramatic verse is heard from stage, and subtleties of stresses interacting with the metrical scheme are probably lost, or at least not fully grasped by the listening audience. On the other hand, the readers of poems and sonnets, who perceive the text visually and have time to peruse slowly or go back, notice more minute details of verse form which go unnoticed in dramatic verse (cf. also Hamm 1954).

Another hypothetical reason is the social difference between the broad public of the Elizabethan theatres and the more sophisticated, aristocratic addressees and readers of Shakespeare's lyrical poetry: the "vnpolisht lines", the "vntutord Lines" of Shakespeare's poems dedicated "To the Right Honourable Henry Wriothesley, Earle of Southampton, and Baron of Titchfield" are so much more polished than those of his dramas of the same period.

Probably also the time factor played a role: writing his dramas for a particular theatre season Shakespeare quite possibly had no time to pay attention to minute details, lost in an oral presentation anyhow. And in his later dramas Shakespeare seems to have grown more careless than in his earlier work (cf. "Richard II" or "Othello" on the one hand, and "The Winter's Tale" on the other; see Chapter 8).

There are rhythmical oppositions between genres both within dramatic and non-dramatic verse.

In Shakespeare's dramatic verse the genre of comedies is marked by several distinctive features. Most of them are signs of a looser verse form of this genre. For example, the difference in stressing between positions 8 and 6 ("rigidity index") tends to be lower in the comedies (e.g., "The Two Gentlemen of Verona"), and for the first time in his evolution equals zero also in a comedy ("The Merchant of Venice"). The genre of comedies displays the highest degree of rhythmical heterogeneity: the stress profiles of separate acts show considerable deviations, sometimes even developing opposing rhythmical tendencies as in "A Midsummer Night's Dream". Comedies have the highest proportion of non-masculine, particularly compound, line endings. Comedies tend to have more lines split between personages than chronicles and tragedies. In the course of time the place of the split in the comedies moves sooner to the right of the half-line boundary typical of a more rigid iambic pentameter than in other types of plays.

The looser verse form of the comedy may be in part explained by the poetic tradition: the verse of "Satyres" and comedies was evidently supposed to be rough and uncouth. Secondly, the personages of comedies frequently belong to the lower *emploi* (commoners; wits and their victims; simpletons, jesters, and clowns), while the exchange of utterances often takes place in the form of a fast give-and-take dialogue; and as we found out, the roles of lower characters and the fast-moving scenes with shorter repartees are characterized by a looser variant of iambic pentameter (Chapter 4). Thirdly, the texts of the comedies include long passages of prose and non-iambic verse which probably break the rhythmical inertia of the main, iambic pentameter text and make every new passage differ from the previous one.

On the other hand, the genre of historical plays (chronicles) demonstrates the most rigid variant of pentameter in Shakespeare's dramatic canon. The rigidity is seen in the structure of their stress profiles and line endings and in the number of split lines and the place of the split. One of the "external" reasons was very plausibly explained by Karl Wentersdorf (1951:186-187): . . . "the poetry of the historical works is more formal." The poet moves with more deliberation "in view of the necessity for closer adherence to the facts of the chronicles which served the dramatist as his sources. This meant less speed, less fluency, and therefore less freedom in writing. . ." The other reason, as it were, "internal", seems to be the peculiarity of the plot and dramatis personae of historical plays: the pathos and flourish of the dramatic situations, the prevalence of noble and royal characters typically speaking in the form of long monologues, orations, and soliloquies result in a more canonized, rigid form of verse (see Chapter 4).

The overall pathos of the play and the large share in its text of the roles of the main, noble personages result in more canonized stress profiles of other genres or their subtypes, e.g., "Romeo and Juliet", "Julius Caesar", or "Othello" (particularly the first two acts).

In Shakespeare's non-dramatic verse, both poems seem to be opposed along several parameters to the Sonnets; cf. their stress profiles, their iambic indices, and the stanzaic composition, for example, the final couplet in the rime royal stanzas of "Lucrece" and in the Sonnets (Chapters 2 and 7).

9.2.2. Rhythmical features differentiate styles within plays, reveal various compositional laws within both plays and poems, and help to trace structural isomorphism of different verse units.

The most striking stylistic differentiation with the help of verse form is the opposition of "plays within plays" to the main text of the dramas: the plays within plays in "Hamlet" and "Merry Wives of Windsor" are written in end-stopped rhyming lines, and their stress profiles are much stricter than those of the main texts. This opposition emphasizes the artificial, conventional character of "theatre within theatre" and at the same time produces a comical, mock-heroic effect.

The already mentioned opposition between monologues and dialogues, elevated scenes of pathos, and everyday scenes revolving around more trivial matters are coupled with specific rhythmical features. In Shakespeare's Period I, for example, lines with an unstressed final ictus caused by a polysyllable (*Stay, Roman brethren! Gracious conqueror*) are more typical of pathetic scenes containing monologues than of scenes of everyday life filled with fast exchanges of repartees. In later Shakespeare, scenes of meditation or pathos typically containing soliloquies and monologues are characterized by relatively few non-masculine line endings, while everyday-life situations with a faster action call forth shorter utterances with feminine (often compound feminine) endings of lines (see Chapter 5).

Rhythmical features mark compositionally relevant parts of separate stanzas and of the whole text of a poem. The first lines of poems, stanzas (e.g., a quatrain), and, to a lesser extent, the second couplets within a quatrain are characterized by "extrametrical" stressing on the anacrusis and/or by rhythmical figures WS(W)-1. For example, the number of line-initial figures WS-1 in each of the six lines of the 199 rime royal stanzas in "Venus and Adonis" is as follows: (1) 28,(2) 11,(3) 10,(4) 8,(5) 16,(6)11. The highest index marks the first opening lines of the stanzas; next comes the index of line five—another structural foothold, the beginning of the final couplet. Some examples of the first two lines are:

<u>Touch but</u> my lips with those fair lips of thine -
Though mine be not so fair, yet are they red -

(20: 1-2)

<u>Bid me</u> discourse, I will enchant thine ear,
Or, like a fairy, trip upon the green,

(25: 1-2)

<u>Say, that</u> the sense of feeling were bereft me,
And that I could not see, nor hear, nor touch,

(74: 1-2)

<u>Call it</u> not love, for Love to heaven is fled
Since sweating Lust on earth usurp'd his name;

(133: 1-2)

<u>More could</u> I tell, but more I dare not say;
The text is all, the orator too green.

(135: 1-2)

The figure WS-2, usually a present participle, often marks the even lines of Shakespeare's sonnets, for example:

O, how I faint when I of you do write,
<u>Knowing</u> a better spirit doth use your name,

(Son. 80: 1-2)

No, neither he, nor his compeers by night
<u>Giving</u> him aid, my verse astonished.

(Son. 86: 7-8)

The injuries that to myself I do,
<u>Doing</u> thee vantage, double-vantage me.

(Son. 88: 11-12)

That tongue that tells the story of thy days,
<u>Making</u> lascivious comments on thy sport,

(Son. 95: 5-6)

Spend'st thou thy fury on some worthless song,
<u>Darkening</u> thy power to lend base subjects light?

(Son. 100: 3-4)

Line-initial participles coupled with a WS-2 are a sign of longer syntactic periods; that is why they are less frequent in iambic tetrameter quatrains with their simpler syntax.

The <u>final</u> lines of poems and, to a lesser degree, ends of stanzas, are usually marked in two different ways. A less typical finale, characteristic of poems with a resumé, a moral, or a maxim, is an extra-heavy line bearing stresses on both S's and W's (e.g., the final lines of Shakespeare's Sonnets). A more typical finale, characteristic of both ends of poems <u>and</u> stanzas, is a lighter line, containing one or more missing ictic stresses. A typical position with a missing stress is the final S. Here are some typical examples of the two last lines of a poem:

And then my heart with pleasure fills,
And dances with the daffodils.
                    (Wordsworth, "I Wondered Lonely as a Cloud . . . ": 23-24)
So angels walk'd unknown on earth,
But when they flew were recogniz'd!
                    (Thomas Hood, "To an Absentee": 15-16)
My light in even the darkest hour,
My crowd in deepest solitude!
                    (Thomas Moore, "Tibulus to Sulpicia": 19-20)

    The rule of a general increase of rigidity (constraint) works in poems both horizontally and vertically. Horizontally: beginnings of lines (and "hemistichs") are rhythmically more variable than their ends. Vertically: the first line of a couplet, a stanza, and particularly of a poem has a greater number of "extrametrical" stresses on the anacrusis and/or line-initial disyllabic or trisyllabic rhythmical figures WS(W), while the final line has a lower number of "deviations".

    The obvious similarity of rules operating within verse units on various levels, such as "hemistich"-line-couplet-stanza-whole poem, are indications of isomorphism of verse units.

    Dramatic verse displays specific compositional rules of its own. For example, the first one or two acts are often rhythmically more constrained than the final two acts; consequently, the first and/or the fifth acts often deviate considerably from the mean stress profile of the whole play.

    A similar tendency of opposing the "beginning" to the "end" is observed in the whole of Shakepeare's canon: on the one hand, the plays of his first period have a more rigid iambic pentameter form than the drama of the final period; on the other hand, the earlier plays are characterized by a more heterogeneous rhythm by acts than the later ones.

    The opposition of beginnings and ends of plays is probably explained not only by the laws of plot development, but also by the typical dynamics of rhythm within a poem: at the beginning of a long text the poet is more constrained, while by the end he becomes freer, as it were, feels more at ease, and his rhythm becomes looser, like one's handwriting by the end of a letter.

    The opposition of a more constrained verse at the beginning of a poet's career and a looser verse at the end was noticed not only in Shakespeare's canon. It was observed in Marlowe's and Byron's cycles (see Chapter 2; cf. also the stress profiles of Byron's earlier poem "Childe Harold" and later poems, "Beppo" and "Don Juan"), and even in Pope's verse (Tarlinskaja 1976: Table 41). It was observed in the poetry of Russian authors, too, e.g., the early and late works of both Lomonosov and Puškin. The isomorphic loosening of the verse form both within one long text and within a poetic canon is probably explained by some psychological laws governing the dynamics of creative processes (see Snoll and Zamjatin 1974).

9.2.3. One of the pertinent stylistic features of verse is <u>rhythmical-grammatical-semantic-lexical patterns</u> that keep recurring in the texts of different poets. The recurring patterns, especially obvious within "rhythmical figures", are also formed outside the figures, and may embrace the whole line. Particular accentual and word boundary line variants are normally coupled with definite parts of speech in specific syntactic functions; for example, the rhythmical line variant (U⊥U/⊥/U⊥/ U⊥U/⊥) is often coupled with a grammatical pattern <u>modifier</u> + <u>modified noun</u> + <u>verb</u> + <u>modifier</u> + <u>modified</u> noun; the first noun is usually a subject, the second an object or an adverbial modifier (Tarlinskaja 1984). Some examples are:

And mighty/hearts/are held/in slender/Chains
        (Pope, "The Rape of the Lock" II:24)
While China's/Earth/receives/the smoking/Tyde
        (Pope, "The Rape of the Lock" III:110)
Of golden/leaves/inlaid/with silver/down
        (Wordsworth, "The Wild Duck's Nest": 11)
For thirteen/hours/he ran/a desperate/race
        (Wordsworth, "Hart-leap Well" Part II:49)
The orange/tints/that gild/the greenest/bough
        (Byron, "Childe Harold" I,XIX:6)
His early/youth/misspent/in maddest/whim
        (Byron, "Childe Harold" I,XXVII:8)
The Poet's/eye/can reach/those golden/halls.
        (Keats, "Epistle to my Brother George": 35)
And full-grown/lambs/loud bleat/from hilly/bourn
        (Keats, "To Autumn", III:8)

And even:

And every/tree/up stood/a rotting/trunk
        (Robert Frost, "The Census-Taker:" 22)
A sunny/morning,/or take/the rising/wind
        (Robert Frost, "A Servant to Servant:" 28)

The joining of particular rhythmical patterns and definite grammatical structures with words of certain semantic classes is particulary noticeable in "rhythmical figures". For example, the figure WSW-1 is typically coupled with the grammatical pattern <u>verb</u> + <u>modifier</u> (+ <u>modified noun</u>) filled with words conveying the idea of violent motion or change; e.g., *Shákes the thín róof* (Crabbe)—*Sháke the réd clóak* (Byron)—*Shóok the wéak hánd* (Shelley)—*Béats his wéak árms* (Crabbe)—*Clásp his fónd árms* (Darwin); or: *Cláps her pále chéek* (Shakespeare)—*Cllápp'd his glád wíngs* (Pope)—*Spréads his bláck Wíngs* (Pope)—*Clímb with swíft wíngs* (Shelley); cf. *Bórne on the wíngs* (Arbuthnot) (see section 8.7.4). As a result, a conventional, recurring rhythmical-grammatical-semantic-lexical pattern has emerged: WSW-1 → Verb +

Adjective (+ Noun) → situation of swift or violent motion → recurring individual words: clap (clasp, shake, beat, spread. . .) + (Adjective) + wings (hands, arms, sail. . .). Common themes and vocabulary coupled with specific rhythmical figures and grammtical patterns tend to produce, as it were, "prefabricated blocks" which keep recurring in the verse of the same or different poets, particularly of certain epochs, such as Classicism or early Romanticism. This phenomenon cannot be fully attributed to borrowings or reminiscences; the patterns born of convention just exist in the English literature belonging to nobody in particular but used (with modifications and variations) by many. Poetic "formulaes", evidently, exist not only in folklore verse traditions, but in later poetry too, though their proportion, causes, and stylistic functions in old and modern verse are undoubtedly dissimilar. This subject, naturally, needs more study and elucidation.

The problem discussed in 9.2.3 is transitory; it belongs both to the sphere of verse form and stylistics (9.2) and verse form and semantics (9.3).

9.3 Verse form and meaning

9.3.1 Variations of iambic pentameter and meaning

Shakespeare used specific rhythmical types of lines assembled to form the roles of particular characters, thereby opposing his dramatis personae by specific rhythmical variations of iambic pentameter that emerge from their role texts. The parts of typologically similar personages (*emploi*) are characterized by similar rhythmical tendencies and are opposed to the parts of other types of personages, e.g., heroes to villains, sophisticated to impulsive, monarchs to commoners; also female to male. The first member of the opposed pairs listed above is characterized by a relatively stricter variant of iambic pentameter, while the second member by a looser variant. Identifying the variant of pentameter verse spoken by different characters thus helps to clarify Shakespeare's own interpretation of his dramatis personae (Chapter 4).

Verse form is one of the means of showing a character evolution within a play. One example is the rhythmical evolution of Othello's part. The stress profiles of his text in Act I and in the last three acts show an opposition of a more rigid to a looser variant of iambic pentameter. At the beginning of the play Othello is portrayed as a noble character whose love for Desdemona has brought him inner peace and harmony of soul. By the end of the play, poisoned by jealousy, Othello's character passes from harmony to chaos and acquires many features of his antagonist, the villain Iago. The transformation from love, harmony, and goodness to hatred, chaos, and villainy is seen on various levels of Othello's text, e.g., in his syntax, choice of words, and figures of speech. This transformation is also reflected in the evolution of Othello's verse, which changes from a more symmetrical line structure and a more rigid iambic pentameter form to an asymmetrical line and a looser iambic pentameter variant. It becomes obvious that a more rigid verse form within Shakespeare's plays is invariably coupled with the notions of nobility, goodness, sophistication and wisdom, peace, and harmony of mind, while a looser verse form is associated with lower character traits, with villainy, folly, impulsiveness, inner discord, and madness.

Rhythmical characteristics of Shakespeare's personages have generalizing features: certain types of *emploi* are coupled with a particular variant of iambic pentameter; thus, Shakespeare's variations of iambic pentameter acquire semiotic functions.

9.3.2 Rhythmical figures and meaning

Rhythmical figures are usually coupled with particular parts of speech, syntactic patterns, and words of specific semantic classes (Chapters 7, 8). It is hard to draw a line between a mere foregrounding and the metaphorical (mimetic) functions of rhythm; but the most general semantic categories associated with all rhythmical figures are as follows. (1) Motion, paticularly extra fast or violent; often a motion downward; uneven, changed, forcefully restricted or stopped. (2) Emotions and their physical display, often mimic; other kinds of facial movements (yawning, eating, swallowing). (3) Pain, destruction, and death, particularly associated with their physical causes and displays (delivering a blow, torturing, wounding; suffocation and strangulation). (4) Speech and other sounds, as well as speech (or another sound) stopped.

Thus, rhythmical figures emphasize the following general semes and connotations: physical phenomena of motion or, less frequently, of sound; frequently their beginning, uneven or halting progress, and abrupt end; negative connotations or emotions often provided by an unsettling, destructuve motion (e.g., end of life). Even when the immediate constituents of the figure are not verbs, as in SW-1, the semantic and stylistic functions of the figure, viewed in a broader situational context, add to the peculiarities of a "verbal style".

Being coupled again and again with a limited "bundle" of particular semantic categories, rhythmical figures have acquired, in the course of the English literary tradition, a semiotic function and a tendency to become a mimetic stylistic device, not unlike onomatopoeia.

Different rhythmical figures have unequal semantic potentials. Arranged in the order of increasing frequency of bearing a supplementary semantic load and the growing intensity of the semantic and emotive feature emphasized, the rhythmical figures assume the following order: W : SW-1 : WS-1 : WS-2 : WSW-2 : WSW-1.

The semantic potential of rhythmical figures is materialized unequally in different genres (more in non-dramatic than in dramatic verse) and has increased in the course of the English literary history (cf. the less obvious semantic function of the figure SW-1 in Shakespeare's dramas and its heavy semantic load in Shelley's verse, sections 8.1 and 8.2).

To trace the origin and history of the semiotic function of English verse rhythm is a subject for further research.

9.4 Verse form and the poets' idiosyncrasy (additional clues for periodization and attribution)

9.4.1 General summary

Distinctive features of Shakespeare's iambic pentameter idiolect by periods were in part reviewed in 9.1. In studying (1) the stress profiles of Shakespeare's plays, each analyzed as a whole and by separate acts; (2) the number and place of line splits occurring between utterances of different characters; (3) the structure of line- and phrase-endings, and (4) the poets' use of rhythmical figures, one cannot help observing a relatively smooth process of evolution within Shakespeare's canon.

The rhythmical peculiarities of individual plays confirm the puissance of Wentersdorf's modifications to Chambers' chronology. For example, "Titus Andronicus", particularly Act I, has features of an earlier rhythmical style which indicates that this tragedy may have been Shakespeare's first work. "Henry VI", Part 1, probably did precede "Henry VI", parts 2 and 3. "Timon of Athens", judging by its verse form, seems to belong to the theatre season 1604-05 and to precede "King Lear" and, of course, "Macbeth", "Antony and Cleopatra", and "Coriolanus", rather than to theatre season 1607-08, two years after "King Lear". "Pericles" also seems to have preceded rather than followed "Coriolanus".

The evolution is by no means mechanical ("so many changed from play to play")—a poet is no machine; besides, he writes in different genres, modifies his style (as probably in "Troilus and Cressida" or "Othello"), and works on earlier plays later (as, possibly, on "Titus Andronicus"). Still, the rhythmical evolution is unmistakably there, and it is smooth and logical enough for such a long canon written over a quarter of a century. The very fact that there is an evolution seems to be one of the proofs of a single authorship of Shakespeare's canon. Though all Elizabethan-Jacobean play-wrights apparently passed through a similar evolutionary process, e.g., from a more canonized form with a "dip" in position 6 and a major syntactic seam after positions 4/5 to a looser form with a "dip" in position 8 and a seam after positions 6/7, and from fewer to more feminine line endings, each of the poets proceeded within his own time bracket and at his own speed; plays by different authors written the same year show marked differences, for example, Marlowe's "Edward II" and Shakespeare's "Richard III", or Chapman's "Bussi d'Ambois" and Shakespeare's "Antony and Cleopatra" (see Table 2.4).

Striking dissimilarities between "Edward II" and "Richard III" are one more proof that Marlowe was not the author of Shakespeare's canon ("Shakespeare, thy name is not Marlowe!").

9.4.2 Four questionable plays

The examination of Shakespeare's works from different angles, and the discovery in almost every chapter of more and more minute particulars about their iambic pentameter form, has resulted in a host of data scattered throughout the book. Now we assemble all the details found out about four questionable plays: "Titus Andronicus", "Timon of Athens", "Pericles", and "Henry VIII".

"Titus Andronicus"

The scenes arranged into two groups with a lower and a higher proportion of feminine endings display a considerable difference in their stress profiles: group one shows a "dip" in position 8 while group two in position 6 (Chapter 3). A "dip" in position 8 is a sign of either a canon in the making or of a canonized form becoming looser. With "Titus Andronicus" the first explanation seems to be more reasonable; the scenes of group one, characterized by a low proportion of feminine endings and a "dip" in position 8, are more archaic than other works of young Shakespeare and must be either the sign of his earliest efforts as a playwright or the remnant of a source text used by Shakespeare as a basis of his tragedy.

The earlier date of group one scenes is also confirmed (a) by the proportion of losses of final ictic stress caused by unstressed syllables of polysyllabic words and unstressed monosyllables (Chapter 5) and (b) by the number of enclitic phrases in both groups (Chapter 6). The proportion of enclitic phrases in the hypothetically earlier scenes is considerably below the indices for Shakespeare's other early works and must be an indication of a particularly early date of these scenes.

"Timon of Athens"

Indices of stress profiles or line endings do not seem to indicate that either acts III or V, suspected of having been written by a collaborator, belong to a different author than the rest of the play (Chapters 3 and 5). Stress profiles and line endings oppose acts I-II and III-V in a way contrary to the general tendency of the verse form to become looser by the end of a long poem or a play. In "Timon of Athens" an opposite tendency is at work: acts III-V are more constrained than I-II, but the text of "Timon" is so obviously corrupt that the irregularity in tendency has probably no deeper reason than mere fortuitousness.

Interesting rhythmical oppositions of scenes caused by stylistic differences were observed earlier (cf. 9.2.2), but they shed little light on the problem of authorship. Thus, rhythmical analysis of "Timon of Athens" has so far provided little additional insight into its attribution.

"Pericles"

The iambic pentameter text of the play falls rhythmically into two different parts: acts I-II and III-V. Acts I-II deviate from III-V and from other plays of Period IIIb in a number of ways: (1) in their stress profiles: (a) too strong stressing of position 4, emphasizing a more canonized $4+6$ or $5+5$ bipartite line segmentation and (b) absence of a relative maximum of "extrametrical" stresses in position 7, another sign that the "hemistich" model $6+4$ or $7+3$ typical of later Shakespeare does not prevail in acts I-II; (2) the number of split lines (too few) and the position of splits (too close to the middle of the line), typical of a more rigid variant of English iambic pentameter; and (3) the structure of line endings (too few cases of missing ictic stresses in position 10 caused by unstressed monosyllables; too many masculine line endings). The indices of acts III-V are much closer to the plays by Shakespeare of the same period. The structural peculiarities of acts I-II might be the sign of either their considerably earlier date, which is unlikely, or of their non-Shakespearean authorship.

"Henry VIII"

The scenes of the play, grouped into two clusters, "Shakespearean" and "Fletcherean", display considerably difference in their rhythmical structure along various parameters.

(1) Stress profiles and line segmentation.

(a) Fletcherean scenes have too strong stresses in positions 4 and 10: a strong stress in position 4 indicates a rhythmical-syntactic seam after the fourth or fifth syllable; a strong stress on 10 is a sign of syntactically end-stopped lines.

(b) Fletcherean scenes display at the same time a high peak of "extrametrical" stresses in position 7 and a deep "dip" in 8: these are indications of another rhythmical-syntactic seam, after positions 6/7; characteristics (a) and (b) point to a typically Fletcherean three-part line segmentation. In Shakespeare's canon a strong stress in position 4 is typically accompanied by a "dip" in position 6, not 8, and a "peak" of extrametrical stresses in position 5, not 7.

(c) In Shakespearean scenes of "Henry VIII" all ictic positions are more evenly stressed; this is a sign of the next stage of decanonization: the verse text begins to resemble its experimental prose model. There are fewer signs of any prevailing types of a rhythmical-syntactic line segmentation: Shakespeare's syntactic periods are longer than Fletcher's; they frequently overrun his lines and end in almost any position of the next line.

(d) On the whole, both ictic and non-ictic positions in the Fletcherean scenes are more strongly stressed than in the Shakespearean portion: Fletcher's verse is "heavier" than Shakespeare's.

(e) Fletcherean scenes display a more marked split between utterances after position 7, another sign of a second rhythmical-syntactic seam in the Fletcherean portion of the play.

(2) Line endings.

(a) There are too many non-masculine line endings in Fletcherean scenes; particularly numerous are compound feminine endings, both light and heavy (almost twice more than in the Shakespearean portion). There are more fully-stressed notional (lexical) words in Fletcher's heavy feminine endings, while Shakespeare's heavy feminine endings contain more words of broad or vague semantics liable to losses of strong phrasal accent.

(b) The proportion of unstressed monosyllables in position 10 is nine times higher in Shakespeare's than Fletcher's scenes, another sign of syntactic freedom and abundance of run-on lines in the Shakespearean portion of the play.

(3) Phrase endings.

There are considerably more enclitic phrases in the Fletcherean cluster of scenes; the difference is particularly striking with the syntactic patterns attribute + noun and verb + adverb. In Fletcher's scenes the proportion of enclitic structures sometimes outnumbers proclitic. The enclitic component in Fletcher's phrases is usually a strongly stressed word of full lexical meaning (as in *thy drý'd dŏg*), while in Shakepeare's enclitic phrases it is more often a word of broad semantics liable to at least a partial loss of phrasal accent, as in *I do not tálk múch*. These peculiarities cause a specific "syncopating" effect typical of Fletcher's verse style.

Idiosyncrasies of Fletcher's rhythmical style are more pronounced in dramas belonging to him alone, such as "Bonduca". In plays written in collaboration, such as "Henry VIII", Fletcher was apparently influenced by the style of his co-author. The influence, however, was reciprocal. There are signs that Shakespeare, too, consciously or subconsciously picked up some peculiarities of Fletcher's syncopated rhythm. These peculiarities are more marked at the beginning of a Shakespearean scene, and as the scene progresses Shakespeare lapses back into his own, more "procilitic" phrase rhythm (Chapter 6).

9.5 Final remarks

Thus, being the son of his epoch, Shakespeare displays a number of iambic pentameter characteristics typical of Elizabethan-Jacobean poets, e.g., the general evolution from a more constrained to a looser form which coincided with the evolution of the epoch. At the same time Shakespeare's verse has marked idiosyncratic features. Some of them seem to be ahead of the epoch, e.g., frequent use of unstressed monosyllables in position 10, reflecting Shakespeare's long syntactic periods and freer line syntax producing more enjambments than in the verse of his contemporaries. Other features of Shakepeare's rhythmical style mark it as more "conservative" than his contemporaries' and add more smoothness to his verse rhythm, e.g., his predominantly proclitic phrase structures. The study of minute particulars of Shakespeare's individual style enriches our understanding of the dynamics of English poetic tradition; it also helps to address the complicated problems of Shakespeare's chronology and authorship.

'Tis ten to one this play can never please
All that are here. Some come to take their ease,
And sleep an act or two; but those, we fear,
We've frighted with our trumpets; so, 'tis clear,
They'll say 'tis naught; others, to hear the city
Abused extremely, and to cry 'That's witty!'
Which we have not done neither . . .
 ("Henry VIII", The Epilogue: 1-7)

No Epilogue, I pray you—for your play needs no excuse.
 ("A Midsummer Night's Dream" V,I:356-357)

Bibliography

Aksënov, I.A. (1938). *Elizavetincy [The Elizabethans]*. Moskva: Xudožestvennaja Literatura.
Alexander, Peter. (1931). "Conjectural History, or Shakespeare's Henry VIII." *English Association. Essays and Studies*, 16: 85-120.
Alexander, Peter. (1939). *Shakespeare's Life and Art*. London: James Nisbert.
Allen, W. Sidney. (1973). *Accent and Rhythm. Prosodic Features of Latin and Greek: A Study in the Theory and Reconstruction*. Cambridge: University Press.
Altman, M.S. (1973). "Puškinskije reminiscencii u Bloka [Puškin's Reminiscences in Blok]." *Philologica*. Leningrad: Nauka: 350-359.
Anikst, A.A. (1963). *Tvorčestvo Šekspira [Shakespeare's Art]*. Moskva:Izdatel'stvo Xudožestvennoj Literatury.
Appleton, William Worthen. (1956). *Beaumont and Fletcher. A Critical Study*. London: George Allen and Unwin.
Armstrong, Edward Allworthy. (1963). *Shakespeare's Imagination; A Study of the Psychology of Associations and Inspiration*. (Rev. ed.) Lincoln: University of Nebraska Press.
Attridge, Derek. (1982). *The Rhythms of English Poetry*. London and New York: Longman.
Bailey, James. (1968). "The Basic Structural Characteristics of Russian Literary Meters." *Studies Presented to Professor Roman Jakobson by his Students*, ed. Charles E. Gribble. Cambridge, Mass.: Slavica Publishers: 17-38.
Bailey, James. (1973a). "The Evolution and Structure of the Russian Iambic Pentameter from 1880 to 1922." *International Journal of Slavic Linguistics and Poetics*, 16: 119-146.
Bailey, James. (1973b). Review of: W.K. Wimsatt, ed. and foreword. *Versification: Major Language Types*. New York: Modern Language Association and New York University Press, 1972, xxvii, 252. In: *Slavic and East European Journal*, 17, No. 4: 471-474.
Bailey, James. (1975). *Toward a Statistical Analysis of English Verse*. Lisse/ Netherlands: Peter de Ridder Press.
Bailey, Richard W. (1969). "Statistics and Style: A Historical Survey." *Statistics and Style*, ed. Lubomir Doležel and Richard W. Bailey. New York: American Elsevier Publishing Company: 217-236.
Bajevskij, V.S. (1972). *Stix Russkoj Sovetskoj Poezii [The Verse of the Russian Soviet Poetry]*. Ed. B.F. Egorov. Smolensk: Smolenskij pegagogičeskij institut.
Baker, George Pierce. (1965). *The Development of Shakespeare as a Dramatist*. New York: Ams Press.

Baker, William Edwin. (1967). *Syntax in English Poetry, 1870-1930*. Berkeley: University of California Press.
Baskervill, Ch.R., V.B. Heltzel, and A.H. Nethercot, eds. (1965). *Elizabethan and Stuart Plays*. New York-Chicago-San Francisco-Toronto-London: Holt, Rinehart and Winston.
Baxter, John. (1980). *Shakespeare's Poetic Styles. Verse into Drama*. London: Routledge & Kegan Paul.
Beaver, Joseph C. (1968). "A Grammar of Prosody." *College English*, 29: 310-321.
Beaver, Joseph C. (1969). "Contrastive Stress and Metrical Verse." *Language and Style*, 2: 257-271.
Beaver, Joseph C. (1971). "The Rules of Stress in English Verse." *Language*, 47, No. 3: 586-614.
Bennett, Paul E. (1954). "The Statistical Measurement of a Stylistic Trait in *Julius Caesar* and *As You Like It*." *Shakespeare Quarterly*, 8: 33-50, repr. in *Statistics and Style*, ed. Lubomir Doležel and Richard W. Bailey. New York: American Elsevier Publishing Co., 1969: 29-41.
Benson, Larry D. (1966). "The Literary Character of Anglo-Saxon Formulaic Poetry." *PMLA*, 81: 334-341.
Bentley, G.E. (1948). "Shakespeare and the Blackfriar's Theatre." *Shakespeare Survey*, 1, ed. Allardyce Nicoll. Cambridge: At The University Press: 38-50.
Berman, Arlene, and Michael Szamosi. (1972). "Observations on Sentence Stress." *Language*, 48, No. 2: 304-325.
Bethell, S.L. (1952). "Shakespeare's Imagery: The Diabolic Images in Othello." *Shakespeare Survey*, 5, ed. Allardyce Nicoll. Cambridge: At The University Press.
Bjorklund, Beth. (1978). *A Study in Comparative Prosody: English and German Iambic Pentameter*. Stuttgart: Akademischer Verlag Hans-Dieter Heinz.
Boas, Frederick S. (1925). *Shakspere and his Predecessors*. London: John Murray.
Boas, Frederick Samuel. (1953). *Christopher Marlowe. A Bibliographical and Critical Study*. Oxford: Clarendon Press.
Bobrov, S.P. (1965, 1966). "Sintagmy, Slovorazdely i Litavridy: Ponjatie o Ritme Soderžatel'no-effectivnom i o Estestvennoj Ritmazacii Reči [Syntagmas, Word Boundaries and Sound "Kettle-drums:" Differentiation Between Semantically- Effective Rhythm and Natural Speech Rhythm]." *Russkaja Literatura*, 1965, No. 4: 80-101 and 1966, No. 1: 79-97.
Bogatyrjëv, P.G. (1971). "Tradicija i Improvizacija v Narodnom Tvorčestve [Tradition and Improvisation in Folklore]." *Voprosy Teorii Narodnogo Iskusstva*, Moskva: Nauka: 393-400.
Bogatyrjëv, P.G. and R.O. Jakobson. (1971). "Folklor kak Osobaja Forma Tvorčestva [Folklore as a Specific Form of Creativity]." *Voprosy Teorii Narodnogo Iskusstva*. Moskva: Nauka: 369-383.
Bolinger, Dwight L. (1965a). "Intonation: Levels versus Configurations." *Forms of English. Accent, Morpheme, Order*. Cambridge, Mass.: Harvard University Press: 3-16.
Bolinger, Dwight L. (1965b). "A Theory of Pitch Accent in English." *Forms of English. Accent, Morpheme, Order*. Cambridge, Mass.: Harvard University Press: 17-55.
Bolinger, Dwight L. (1965c). "Stress and Information." *Forms of English. Accent, Morpheme, Order*. Cambridge, Mass.: Harvard University Press: 67-83.

Bolinger, Dwight L. (1965d). "Pitch Accent and Sentence Rhythm." *Forms of English. Accent, Morpheme, Order*. Cambridge, Mass.: Harvard University Press: 139-180.
Bolinger, Dwight L. (1972). "Accent is Predictable (If You're a Mind-Reader)." *Language*, 48, No. 3: 633-644.
Boyle, Robert. (1880-1886a). "Henry VIII. An Investigation into the Origin and Authorship of the Play." *New Shakspere Society. Transactions*, 1, No. 10: 443-488.
Boyle, Robert. (1880-1886b). "Beaumont, Fletcher, and Massinger." *New Shakspere Society. Transactions*. Ser. 1, No. 10 (no. 26): 579-628.
. Bradley, Andrew Cecil. (1902). *Oxford Lectures on Poetry*. London: Macmillan.
Bradley, Andrew Cecil. (1905). *Shakespearean Tragedy. Lectures on 'Hamlet', 'Othello', 'King Lear', 'Macbeth'*. 2nd ed. London: Macmillan.
Bresnan, Joan W. (1971). "Sentence Stress and Syntactic Transformations." *Language*, 47, No. 2: 257-281.
Bresnan, Joan W. (1972). "Stress and Syntax: A Reply." *Language*, 48, No. 2: 326-342.
Brik, O.M. (1927). "Ritm i Sintaksis [Rhythm and Syntax]." *Novyj Lef*. No. 3: 15-20, No. 4: 23-29, No. 5: 32-37, No. 6: 33-39.
Brodeur, Arthur Gilchrist. (1959). *The Art of Beowulf*. Berkeley and Los Angeles: University of California Press.
Brooke, Charles Frederick Tucker, ed. (1908). *The Shakespeare Apocrypha*. Oxford: Clarendon Press.
Brooke, Charles Frederick Tucker. (1912). "The Authorship of the Second and Third Parts of '*King Henry VI*'." New Haven: Yale University Press: 141-211. (*Transactions of the Connecticut Academy of Arts and Sciences*, vol. 17, July, 1912.)
Burton, Dolores M. (1968). *Shakespeare's Grammatical Style*. Austin and London: University of Texas Press.
Bynum, David E. (1978). *The Daemon in the Wood: A Study of Oral Narrative Patterns*. Cambridge, Mass.: Center for Study of Oral Literature. Harvard University.
Byrne, M. St. Clare. (1932). "Bibliographical Clues in Collaborate Plays." *The Library*, 4th Ser., 13: 21-48.
Cercignani, Fausto. (1981). *Shakespeare's Works and Elizabethan Pronunciation*. Oxford: Clarendon Press.
Černjaxovskaja, L.A. (1976). *Perevod i Smyslovaja Struktura [Translation and the Sense Structure]*. Moskva: Meždunarodnyje Otnošenija.
Chambers, Edmund Kerchever. (1930). *William Shakespeare. A Study of Facts and Problems*. Oxford: The Clarendon Press. v. 1, 2.
Chatman, Seymour. (1965). *A Theory of Meter*. London, The Hague, Paris: Mouton.
Chisholm, David. (1977). "Generative Prosody and English Verse." *Poetics*, 6: 111-154.
Chomsky, Noam, Morris Halle and Fred Lukoff. (1956). "On Accent and Juncture in English." *For Roman Jakobson: Essays on the Occasion of His Sixtieth Birthday*, ed. Morris Halle et al. The Hague: Mouton: 65-80.
Chomsky, Noam and Morris Halle. (1968). *The Sound Pattern of English*. New York: Harper and Row.
Churchill, R.C. (1958). *Shakespeare and His Betters. A History and a Criticism of the Authorship Question*. London: Max Reinhardt.
Collins, John Churton. (1904). *Studies in Shakespeare*. Westminster: Archibald Constable and Co., Ltd.
Cone, Mary. (1976). *Fletcher Without Beaumont: A Study of the Independent Plays of John Fletcher*. Institut für Englishche Sprache und Literatur. Universitat Salzburg.

Craig, Hardin. (1948). *An Interpretation of Shakespeare*. New York: Dryden Press.
Creed, R.P. (1957). "The Andswarode-System in Old English Poetry." *Speculum*, 32: 523-528.
Creed, R.P. (1959). "The Making of an Anglo-Saxon Poem." *Journal of English Literary History*, 26: 445-454.
Čudovskij, Valerij. (1914). "O Ritme Puškinsoj 'Rusalki' [On the Rhythm of Puškin's 'Rusalka']." *Appollon*, Nos. 1-2: 108-121.
Curme, George O. (1914, 1915). "The Development of Modern Groupstress in German and English." *Journal of English and Germanic Philology*, 13 (1914): 493-498, and 14 (1915): 163-168.
Curme, George O. (1931). *Syntax*. Boston, New York, etc.: D.C. Heath and Co.
Dahl, Liisa. (1969). *Nominal Style in The Shakespearean Soliloquy*. Turku: Turun Yliopisto.
De Groot, A.W. (1932). "Der Rhythmus." *Neophilologus*, 17: 81-100, 177-197, 241-265.
Diamond, Robert E. (1963). *The Diction of the Anglo-Saxon Metrical Psalms*. The Hague: Mouton.
Dobson, E.J. (1957). *English Pronunciation, 1500-1700*. Oxford: Clarendon Press.
Dobson, E.J. (1967). "Milton's Pronunciation." *Language and Style in Milton*. New York: F. Ungar: 154-192.
Doležel, Lubomir, and Richard W. Bailey, eds. (1969). *Statistics and Style*. New York: American Elsevier Publishing Co.
Draat, P. Fijnvan. (1912). "Rhythm in English Prose": "The Adjective"; "The Pronoun." *Anglia*, 36: 1-58, 492-538.
Edwards, Philip. (1952). "An Approach to the Problem of '*Pericles*'." *Shakespeare Survey*, 5: 25-49.
Edwards, Phillip. (1968). *Shakespeare and the Confines of Art*. London: Methuen.
Eitrem, H. (1903). "Stress in English Verb + Adverb Groups." *Englische Studien*, No. 32: 69-77.
Elizabethan Critical Essays. (1971). G. Gregory Smith, ed. London: Oxford University Press. 2 vols.
Ellis, Alexander John. (1968). *On Early English Pronunciation, with Especial Reference to Shakespeare and Chaucer*. New York: Greenwood Press. 5 v.
Elwert, W. Theodor. (1973). *Versificazione Italiana Dalle Origini ai Giorni Nostri*. Firenze: Le Monnier.
Farnham, W.E. (1916). "Colloquial Contractions in Beaumont, Fletcher, Massinger and Shakespeare as a Test of Authorship." *PMLA*, 31, No. 2: 326-358.
Feuillerat, Albert. (1953). *The Composition of Shakespeare's Plays. Authorship. Chronology*. New Haven: Yale University Press.
Filippov, V. (1925). "Problemy stixa "Gore ot uma". material dija sceničeskix xarakterixtik [Problems of the Verse of "Woe from Wit". Materials for the scene characteristics]." *Iskusstvo, Žurnal Gos. Akad. Xudož. Nauk*, Moskva 1925, No. 2: 146-175.
Fleay, F.G. (1874a). "On Metrical Tests as Applied to Dramatic Poetry." *New Shakspere Society. Transactions*. London, 1874: 1-84.
Fleay, F.G. (1874b). "On the Authorship of 'Timon of Athens'." *New Shakspere Society. Transactions*. London, 1874: 130-151.
Fleay, F.G. (1874c). "On the Play of 'Pericles'." *New Shakspere Society. Transactions*. London, 1874: 195-209.

Fleay, F.G. (1874d). "On Certain Plays of Shakspere of which Portions were Written at Different Periods of His Life." *New Shakspere Society. Transactions.* London, 1874: 285-317.

Fleay, F.G. (1874e). "On Two Plays of Shakspere's, the Versions of which as We Have Them are the Results of Alterations by Other Hands." *New Shakspere Society. Transactions.* London, 1874: 339-366.

Fleay, F.G. (1874f). "A Fresh Confirmation of Mr. Spedding's Division and Date of the Play of 'Henry VIII'." *New Shakspere Society. Transactions.* London, 1874, Appendix: 23*.

Fleay, F.G. (1874g). "Mr. Hickson's Division of 'The Two Noble Kinsmen', Confirmed by Metrical Tests." *New Shakspere Society. Transactions.* London, 1874, Appendix: 61*-64*.

Foakes, R.A., ed. (1957). *King Henry VIII.* The Arden Edition, London.

Fridlender, G.M. (1973). " 'Poltava' Puškina i 'Mazepa' Bajrona [Puškin's 'Poltava' and Byron's 'Mazeppa']." *Philologica.* Leningrad: Nauka: 337-340.

Frye, Northrop. (1957). "Introduction." *Sound and Poetry*, ed. Northrop Frye. New York and London: Columbia University Press.

Fussell, Paul. (1954). *Theory of Prosody in Eighteenth-Century England.* New London: Connecticut College, Monograph No. 5.

Fussell, Paul. (1979). *Poetic Meter and Poetic Form.* New York: Random House.

Gascoigne, George. (1971). "The Making of Verse (Certayne Notes of Instruction). 1575." *Elizabethan Critical Essays*, ed. G. Gregory Smith. Oxford University Press, v. I: 46-57.

Gasparov, M.L. (1973). "Russkij Jamb i Anglijskij Jamb [Russian Iamb and English Iamb]." *Philologica Issledovanija po Jazyku i Literature.* Leningrad: Nauka: 408-415.

Gasparov, M.L. (1974). *Sovremennyj Russkij Stix. Metrika i Ritmika [Modern Russian Verse. Metrics and Rhythmics].* Moskva: Nauka.

Gasparov, M.L. (1976). Metr i Smysl. K Semantike Russkogo Trëxstopnogo Xoreja [Meter and Meaning. On the Semantics of Russian Trochaic Trimeter]." *Izvestija Akademii Nauk SSSR, Serija Literatury i Jazyka*, 35, No. 4: 357-366.

Gasparov, M.L. (1979). "Semantičeskij Oreol Metra (K Semantike Russkogo Trëxstopnogo Jamba) [Semantic Halo of a Meter (On the Semantics of the Russian Iambic Trimeter)]." *Lingvistika i Poetika.* Moskva: Nauka: 284-308.

Gasparov, M.L. (1980). "Italjanskij Stix: Sillabika ili Sillabo-tonika? (Opyt Ispol'zovanija Verojatnostnyx Modelej v Stixovedenii) [Italian Verse: Syllabic or Syllabo-tonic? (An Experiment in Using Probability Models in Metrics)]." *Problemy Strukturnoj Lingvistiki 1978*, ed. P.V. Grigorjev. Moskva: Nauka: 199-218.

Gasparov, M.L. (1982). "Semantičeskij Oreol Trëxstopnogo Amfibraxija [The Semantic Halo of Amphibrachic Trimeter]." *Problemy Strukturnoj Lingvistiki 1980.* Moskva: Nauka: 174-192.

Gasparov, M.L. (1983). " 'Spi, Mladenec Moj Prekrasnyj': Semantičeskij Oreol Raznovidnosti Xoreičeskogo Razmera ['Spi, Mladenec Moj Prekrasnyj': The Semantic Halo of a Trochaic Variant]." *Problemy Strukturnoj Lingvistiki 1981.* Moskva: Nauka: 181-197.

Gasparov, M.L. (1984a). *Očerk Istorii Russkogo Stixa [A Sketch of the History of Russian Verse].* Moskva: Nauka.

Gasparov, M.L. (1984b). "Ješčë Raz k Sporam o Russkoj Sillabo-tonike [Once More

Concerning the Discussions on the Russian Syllabo-tonic Verse]." *Problemy Teorii Stixa*, ed. D.S. Lixačëv et al. Leningrad: Nauka: 174-178.
Gasparov, M.L. (1984c). "Ritmičeskij Slovar' i Ritmiko-sintaksičeskije Kliše [Rhythmical Vocabulary and Rhythmic-syntactic Clichés]." *Problemy Strukturnoj Lingvistiki 1982*, ed. V.P. Grigorjev. Moskva: Nauka: 169-185.
Giammati, A.B. (1972). "Italian." *Versification, Major Language Types*, ed. W.K. Wimsett. New York: Modern Language Association, New York University Press: 148-164.
Gibson, H.N. (1962). *The Shakespeare Claimants. A Critical Survey of the Four Principal Theories Concerning the Authorship of the Shakespearean Plays*. New York: Barnes and Noble.
Gimson, Alfred Charles. (1967). *Everyman's English Pronouncing Dictionary, Containing over 58,000 Words in International Phonetic Transcription*, by Daniel Jones. 13th ed., ed. A.C. Gimson. London: Dent; New York: Dutton.
Gimson, Alfred Charles. (1980). *An Introduction to the Pronunciation of English*. 3rd ed. London: Edward Arnold.
Gindin, S.I. (1981). "Ritmika, Intonacija i Smyslovaja Kompozicija v Poeme Vl. Lugovskogo 'Kak Čelovek Plyl s Odissejem' [Rhythm, Intonation and Semantic Composition of the Poem by Vl. Lugovskoj 'Kak Čelovek Plyl s Odissejem']." *Problemy Strukturnoj Lingvistiki 1978*, ed. V.P. Grigorjev. Moskva: Nauka: 230-265.
Greg, Walter Wilson. (1942). *The Editorial Problems in Shakespeare: A Survey of the Foundations of the Texts*. Oxford: Clarendon Press.
Greg, Walter Wilson. (1955). *The Shakespeare First Folio, Its Bibliographical and Textual History*. Oxford: Clarendon Press.
Greimas, Algirdas Julien. (1983). *Structural Semantics: An Attempt at a Method*. Lincoln: University of Nebraska Press.
Grigorjev, V.P. (1971). "Finali 'Soglasnyj + Sonant' v Poetičeskoj Reči [Finals 'Consonant + Sonant' in Poetic Speech]." *Fonetika, Fonologija, Grammatika*. Moskva: Nauka: 43-49.
Halle, M. and S.J. Keyser. (1971). *English Stress. Its Form, Its Growth, and Its Role in Verse*. New York, London: Harper and Row.
Hamm, V.M. (1954). "Meter and Meaning." *PMLA*, 69, No. 4, Part 1: 695-710.
Hart, Alfred. (1934). "Shakespeare and the Vocabulary of 'The Two Noble Kinsmen'." *Review of English Studies*, 10: 274-287.
Hart, Alfred. (1943a). "Vocabulary of Shakespeare's Plays." *Review of English Studies*, 19: 128-140.
Hart, Alfred. (1943b). "The Growth of Shakespeare's Vocabulary." *Review of English Studies*, 19: 242-254.
Hatcher, O.L. (1910). "Fletcher's Habit of Dramatic Collaboration." *Anglia*, 33. Neue Folge Band 21: 219-231.
Hayes, Bruce. (1983). "A Grid-Based Theory of English Meter." *Linguistic Inquiry*, 14(3): 357-397.
Hayes, Bruce. (1986). "The Prosodic Hierarchy in Meter" *Linguistic Inquiry* (special issue).(in press).
Heller, J.R. (1977). "Enjambment as a Metrical Force in Romantic Conversation." *Poetics*, 6: 15-26.
Hensman, Bertha. (1974). *The Shares of Fletcher, Field and Massinger in Twelve Plays*

of the Beaumont and Fletcher Canon. Salzburg: Institut für Englische Sprache und Literatur. Universität Salzburg, v. 1,2.

Hickson, Samuel. (1874a). "A Confirmation of Mr. Spedding's Paper on the Authorship of 'Henry VIII'." *New Shakspere Society. Transactions*, London, 1874, Appendix: 18*-20*.

Hickson, Samuel. (1874b). "The Shares of Shakspere and Fletcher in 'The Two Noble Kinsmen'." *New Shakspere Society. Transactions*, London, 1874, Appendix: 25*-61*.

Hieatt, A. Kent. (1983). "The Genesis of Shakespeare's *Sonnets*: Spenser's *Ruins of Rome*: by Bellay." *PMLA*, 98, No. 5: 800-814.

Hill, R.F. (1957). "The Composition of 'Titus Andronicus'." *Shakespeare Survey* 10: 60-70.

Hinman, Charlton. (1961). *Six Variant Readings in the First Folio of Shakespeare*. Lawrence: University of Kansas Libraries.

Hinman, Charlton. (1963). *The Printing and Proof-Reading of the First Folio of Shakespeare*. 2 vols. Oxford: Clarendon Press.

Hjelmslev, Louis. (1953). *Prolegomena to a Theory of Language*. Baltimore: Waverley Press.

Hoffman, C. (1955). *The Murder of the Man Who Was "Shakespeare"*. New York: J. Messner.

Hollander, John. (1966). "The Metrical Emblem." *Style in Language*, ed. Thomas A. Sebeok. Cambridge, Mass.: The Massachusetts Institute of Technology: 191-192.

Hollander, John. (1975a). " 'Sense Variously Drawn out': On English Enjambment." *Vision and Resonance: Two Senses of Poetic Form*. New York: Oxford University Press: 91-116.

Hollander, John. (1975b). "The Metrical Frame." *Vision and Resonance: Two Senses of Poetic Form*. New York: Oxford University Press: 135-164.

Honigmann, E.A.J. (1965). *The Stability of Shakespeare's Text*. Lincoln: University of Nebraska Press.

Hotson, Leslie. (1931). *Shakespeare versus Shallow*. Boston: Little, Brown, and Company.

Hotson, Leslie. (1949). *Shakespeare's Sonnets Dated and Other Essays*. New York: Oxford University Press.

Hoy, Cyrus. (1956-1962). "The Shares of Fletcher and his Collaborators in the Beaumont and Fletcher Canon." *Studies in Bibliography*, VII (1956): 129-146; IX (1957): 143-162; XI (1958): 85-106; XII (1959): 91-116; XIII (1960): 77-108; XIV (1961): 45-67; XV (1962): 71-90.

Ingram, John K. (1874). "On the 'Weak Endings' of Shakspere, with Some Account of the History of the Verse-Texts in General." *New Shakspere Society. Transactions*. London, 1874: 442-451.

Jackson, MacD.P. (1962). "Affirmative particles in 'Henry VIII'." *Notes and Queries*: 372-374.

Jackson, MacD.P. (1963). "Shakespeare and 'Edmund Ironside'." *Notes and Queries*: 331-332.

Jackson, MacD.P. (1975). *Studies in Attribution; Middleton and Shakespeare*. Salzburg: Institut für Anglistik und Amerikanistik, Universität Salzburg.

Jakobson, Roman. (1935). "Metrika." *Ottův Slovnic Náuchy Nové Doby*, Dodatky, IV, Praha: 213-218.

Jakobson, Roman. (1966). "Linguistics and Poetics." *Style in Language*, ed. Thomas A. Sebeok, Cambridge, Mass.: The M.I.T. Press: 350-377.
Jakobson, R.O. (1976). "Igra v Adu u Puškina i Xlebnikova [A Card Game in Hell in Puškin and Xlebnikov]." *Sravnitel'noe Izučenie Literatur*. Leningrad: Nauka: 35-37.
Jakobson, Roman. (1979a). "O Českom Stixe [On Czech Verse]." *Selected Writings*, V: *On Verse, Its Masters and Explorers*. The Hague, Paris, New York: Mouton: 3-130.
Jakobson, Roman. (1979b). "Ob Odnosložnyx Slovax v Russkom Stixe [On Monosyllables in Russian Verse]." *Selected Writings*, V: *On Verse, Its Masters and Explorers*. The Hague, Paris, New York: Mouton: 201-214.
Jakobson, Roman. (1979c). "Toward a Description of Macha's Verse." *Selected Writings*, V: *On Verse, Its Masters and Explorers*. The Hague, Paris, New York: Mouton: 433-485.
Jakobson, Roman. (1979d). "Retrospect." *Selected Writings*, V: *On Verse, Its Masters and Explorers*. The Hague, Paris, New York: Mouton: 569-601.
Jakobson, Roman, and Stephen Rudy. (1977). *Yeats' 'Sorry of Love' Through the Years*. Lisse: Peter de Ridder Press.
Jarxo, B.I. (1984). "Metodologija Točnogo Literaturovedenija (Nabrosok Plana) [Methodology of Scientific Literary Criticism (The Draft of a Plan)]" (publ. by M.L. Gasparov). *Kontekst 1983*. Moskva: Nauka: 195-236.
Jespersen, Otto. (1952). *Growth and Structure of the English Language*. 9th ed. Oxford: B. Blackwell.
Jespersen, Otto. (1966). "Notes on Metre." *The Structure of Verse. Modern Essays on Prosody*. Ed. Harvey Gross. Greenwich, Conn.: Fawcett Publications, Inc.: 111-130.
Jones, Daniel. (1927). *An English Pronouncing Dictionary*. London and Toronto: J.M. Dent & Sons, New York: E.P. Dutton & Co.
Jones, Daniel. (1964). *An Outline of English Phonetics*. 9th ed. Cambridge: W. Heffner.
Jones, Daniel. (1966). *The Pronunciation of English*. 4th ed. Cambridge: University Press.
Kadžaznuni, L. (1980). "K Voprosu ob Avtorstve Pjesy 'Dva Znatnyx Rodstvennika' [Towards the Authorship of the Play 'The Two Noble Kinsmen']." *Šekspirovskije Čtenija 1977*. Moskva: Nauka: 248-256.
Kennedy, A.G. (1920). "The Modern English Verb-Adverb Combinations." *Stanford University Publications, University Series, Language and Literature*, 1, No. 1, 1920.
Kenyon, John Samuel. (1950). *American Pronunciation*. 10th ed. Ann Arbor, Mich.: G. Wahr.
Kingdon, Roger. (1958a). *The Groundwork of English Intonation*. London, New York: Longmans, Green.
Kingdon, Roger. (1958b). *The Groundwork of English Stress*. London, New York: Longmans, Green.
Kiparsky, Paul. (1975). "Stress, Syntax, and Meter." *Language*, 51: 576-616.
Kiparsky, Paul. (1977). "The Rhythmic Structure of English Verse." *Linguistic Inquiry*, 8, No. 2 : 189-247.
Kökeritz, Helge. (1974). *Shakespeare's Pronunciation*. New Haven and London: Yale University Press, 4th printing.
Kolmogorov, A.H., and A.V. Proxorov. (1968). "K Osnovam Russkoj Metriki [Towards the Basis of the Russian Metrics]." *Sodružestvo Nauk i Tajny Tvorčestva*, ed. B.S. Mejlax. Moskva: Iskusstvo: 397-432.
König, Goswin. (1888). *Der Vers in Shakespeares Dramen*. Strassburg: K.J. Trübner.

Košutič, Radovan. (1919). *Gramatika Ruskog Jezika* [*Russian Grammar*]. 2. izd. Petrograd: Ruska Akademija Nauka, 3 v.
Kreider, Paul Vernon. (1941). *Repetitions in Shakespeare's Plays*. Princeton: Princeton University Press.
Kroeber, A.L. (1958). "Parts of Speech in Poetry." *PMLA*, 73: 309-314.
Kruisinga, Etsko. (1932). *A Handbook of Present-Day English*. 5th ed. Groningen: P. Noordhoff.
Kumaxov, M.A. (1979). "K Probleme Jazyka Epičeskoj Poezii [Towards the Problem of the Language of Epic Poetry]." *Voprosy Jazykoznanija*, 2: 48-60.
Langworthy, Charles A. (1931). "A Verse-Sentence Analysis of Shakespeare's Plays." *PMLA*, 46: 738-751.
Law, Robert Adger. (1959). "The Double Authorship of 'Henry VIII'." *Studies in Philology*, 56, No. 3: 471-488.
Lees, Robert B. (1968). *The Grammar of English Nominalizations*. 5th printing. The Hague: Mouton.
Lehiste, Ilse. (1970). *Suprasegmentals*. Cambridge, Mass.: The M.I.T. Press.
Lehman, Winfred P. (1956). *The Development of Germanic Verse Form*. Austin: University of Texas Press.
Legois, Emile and Louis Cazamian. (1971). *A History of English Literature*. London: J.M. Dent & Sons.
Levin, Ju.I. (1966). "O Nekotoryx Čertax Plana Soderžanija v Poetičeskix Tekstax [On Some Features of the Plane of Contents in Poetic Texts]." *Strukturnaja Tipologija Jazykov*. Moskva: Nauka: 199-215.
Levin, Ju.I. (1969). "O Nekotoryx Čertax Plana Soderžanija v Poetičeskix Tekstax. Materialy k Izučeniju Poetiki O. Mandel'tama [On Some Aspects of the Plane of Contents of Poetic Texts. Some Materials on O. Mandeltam's Poetics]." *International Journal of Slavic Linguistics and Poetics*, 12: 106-164.
Levin, Ju.I. (1975). "Leksiko-Semantičeskij Analiz Odnogo Stixotvorenija O. Mandeltama [Lexico-Semantic Analysis of a Poem by O. Mandeltam]." *Slovo v Russkoj Sovetskoj Poezii*. Moskva: Nauka: 225-233.
Levin, Ju.I. (1982). "Semantičeskij Oreol Metra s Semiotičeskoj Točki Zrenija [The Semantic Halo of a Meter from the Semiotic Point of View]." *Finitis Duodecim Lustris*, ed. S.G. Isakov. Tallin: Eesti Raamat: 151-154.
Lévy, Jiri. (1966). "The Meanings of Form and the Forms of Meaning." *Poetics, Poetyka, Poetika*, II. The Hague, Paris: Mouton; Warszawa: PWN—Polish Scientific Publishers: 45-59.
Lévy, Jiri. (1969). "Mathematical Aspects of the Theory of Verse." *Statistics and Style*, ed. Lubomir Doležal and Richard W. Bailey. New York: American Elsevier Publishing Co.: 95-112 (from *Mathematik und Dichtung*, 1967).
Liberman, M. and A. Prince. (1977). "On stress and linguistic rhythm." *Linguistic Inquiry* 8(2): 249-336.
Lord, Albert B. (1960). *The Singer of Tales*. Cambridge, Mass.: Harvard University Press.
Lotman, M., ed. (1982). *Učebnyj Material Po Analizu Poetičeskix Tekstov* [*Materials on Poetic Text Analysis*]. Compilation and comments by M. Ju. Lotman. Tallin: Tallinskij Pedagogičeskij Institut.
Macaulay, George C. (1883). *Francis Beaumont. A Critical Study*. London: K. Paul, Trench & Co.

Magoun, Francis P. (1953). "Oral-Formulaic Character of Anglo-Saxon Narrative Poetry." *Speculum*, 28, 3: 446-467.

Magnuson, Karl and Frank G. Ryder. (1970). "The Study of English Prosody: An Alternative Proposal." *College English*, 31: 789-820.

Martin, M.W. (1965). *Was Shakespeare Shakespeare?* New York: Cooper Square Publishers.

Maxwell, Baldwin. (1939). *Studies in Beaumont, Fletcher, and Massinger*. Chapel Hill: The University of North Carolina Press.

Maxwell, Baldwin. (1956). *Studies in the Shakespeare Apocrypha*. New York: King's Crown Press.

Maxwell, J.C. (1950). "Peele and Shakespeare: A Stylometric Test." *Journal of English and Germanic Philology*, 49: 557-561.

Maxwell, J.C., ed. (1968). *The New Shakespeare: 'Timon of Athens'*. Cambridge, paperback edition.

McMichael, George. (1962). *Shakespeare and His Rivals. A Casebook on the Authorship Controversy*. New York: The Odissey Press.

Meillet, Antoine. (1923). *Les Origines Indo-européennes des Mètres Grecs*. Paris: Les Presses Universitaires de France.

Melčuk, I.A. (1974). *Opyt Teorii Lingvističeskix Modelej 'Smysl—Teks'* [*Toward the Theory of Linguistic Models 'Sense—Text'*]. Moskva: Nauka.

Metz, G. Harold. (1979). "A Stylometric Comparison of Shakespeare's 'Titus Andronicus', 'Pericles', and 'Julius Caesar'." *The Shakespeare Newsletter* 28: 42.

Miles, Josephine. (1946). *Major Adjectives in English Poetry from Wyatt to Auden*. Berkeley and Los Angeles: University of California Press.

Miles, Josephine. (1957). *Eras and Modes in English Poetry*. Berkeley: University of California Press.

Miles, Josephine. (1965). *The Continuity of Poetic Language; the Primary Language of Poetry, 1540's-1940's*. New York: Octagon Books.

Miles, Josephine. (1967). *Style and Proportion: The Language of Prose and Poetry*. Boston: Little, Brown.

Milič, Louis T. (1967). *A Quantitative Approach to the Style of Jonathan Swift*. The Hague: Mouton.

Mincoff, Marco. (1952). "The Authorship of 'The Two Noble Kinsmen'." *English Studies*, 33: 97-115.

Mincoff, Marco. (1961). " 'Henry VIII' and Fletcher." *Shakespeare Quarterly*, 12: 239-260.

Mincoff, Marco. (1971). "The Source of 'Titus Andronicus'." *Notes and Queries*, April: 131-134.

Muir, Kenneth. (1960). *Shakespeare as Collaborator*. London: Methuen.

Muir, Kenneth. (1973). *Shakespeare the Professional, and Related Studies*. Ottawa, New York: Rowman and Littlefield.

Murray, Peter B. (1962). "The Authorship of 'The Revenger's Tragedy'." *Papers of the Bibliographical Society of America*, 56(162): 195-218.

Nagler, M.R. (1967). "Towards a Generative View of the Oral Formula." *Transactions and Proceedings of the American Philological Association*, 98: 269-311.

Neilson, W.A. and A.H. Thorndike. (1961). *The Facts About Shakespeare*. New York: Macmillan.

Newmeyer, Frederick J. (1983). *Grammatical Theory*. Chicago: The University of Chicago Press.
Nicolson, Marjorie. (1922). "The Authorship of 'Henry the Eighth'." *PMLA*, 37: 484-502.
Nida, E.A. (1975). *Componential Analysis of Meaning*. The Hague: Mouton.
Nikolaeva, T.M. (1982). *Semantika Akcentnogo Vydelenija [Semantics of the Accentual Emphasis]*. Moskva: Nauka.
Nowottny, W.M.T. (1959). "Acts IV and V of 'Timon of Athens'." *Shakespeare Quarterly*, 10, No. 4: 493-497.
Oliphant, Ernest Henry Clark. (1927). *The Plays of Beaumont and Fletcher; an Attempt to Determine their Respective Shares and the Shares of the Others*. New Haven: Yale University Press; London: H. Milford, Oxford University Press.
Oliver, H.J., ed. (1971). *The Merry Wives of Windsor*. Arden Edition. London: Methuen.
Oppel, Horst. (1966). "Shakespeare Oder Fletcher? Die Bankett-Szene in 'Henry VIII' als Kriterium der Verfasserschaft." Mainz: *Akademie der Wissenschaften und Literatur*: 479-508.
Oras, Ants. (1953). "Extra Monosyllables in 'Henry VIII' and the Problem of Authorship." *Journal of English and Germanic Philology*, 52: 198-213.
Oras, Ants. (1960). *Pause Pattern in Elizabethan and Jacobean Drama; an Experiment in Prosody*. Gainesville: University of Florida Press.
Oras, Ants. (1966). *Blank Verse and Chronology in Milton*. Gainesville: University of Florida Press.
Panov, M.V. (1967). *Russkaja Fonetika [Russian Phonetics]*. Moskva: Prosveščenije.
Parrott, Thomas Marc. (1919). "Shakespeare's Revision of 'Titus Andronicus'." *Modern Language Review*, 14: 16-37.
Parrott, Thomas Marc. (1923). *The Problem of 'Timon of Athens'*. London: Publications for the Shakespeare Association by H. Milford, Oxford University Press.
Parrott, Thomas Marc. (1934). *William Shakespeare, a Handbook*. New York, Chicago, etc.: C. Scribner's Sons. Rev. ed., New York: Scribner, 1955.
Parry, Milman. (1928a). *L'épithete Traditionelle dans Homère*. Paris: "Les Belles Lettres".
Parry, Milman. (1928b). *Les Formules et la Métrique d'Homère*. Paris: "Les Belles Lettres".
Parry, Milman. (1930). "Studies in the Epic Technique of Oral Verse Making. I. Homer and Homeric Style." *Harvard Studies in Classical Philology*, 41: 73-148.
Parry, Milman. (1932). "Studies in the Epic Technique of Oral Verse-Making. II. The Homeric Language as the Language of an Oral Poetry." *Harvard Studies in Classical Philology*, 43: 1-50.
Parry, Milman. (1971). *The Makings of Homeric Verse: The Collected Papers of Milman Parry*, ed. Adam Parry. Oxford: Clarendon Press.
Partridge, Astley Cooper. (1949). *The Problem of 'Henry VIII' Reopened; Some Linguistic Criteria for the Two Styles Apparent in the Play*. Cambridge, England: Bowes & Bowes.
Partridge, Astley Cooper. (1953). *Studies in the Syntax of Ben Jonson's Plays*. Cambridge, England: Bowes & Bowes.
Partridge, Astley Cooper. (1964). *Orthography in Shakespeare and Elizabethan Drama*. Lincoln: University of Nebraska Press.

Partridge, Astley Cooper. (1969). *Tudor to Augustan English; a Study of Syntax and Style from Caxton to Johnson.* London: Deutsch.

Partridge, Astley Cooper. (1976). *A Substantive Grammar of Shakespeare's Nondramatic Texts.* Charlottesville: Published for the Bibliographic Society of the University of Virginia by the University Press of Virginia.

Pekovskij, A.M. (1938). *Russkij Sintaksis v Naučnom Osveščenii [Russian Syntax Viewed Scientifically].* Moskva: Gosudarstvennoe Učebno-Pedagogičeskoje Izdatel'stvo.

Petöfi, J.S. (1973). "Text-Grammars, Text-Theory and the Theory of Literature." *Poetics,* 7: 36-76.

Plutarch. (1969). *Plutarch's Lives,* ed. Charles W. Eliot. The Harvard Classics, v. 12. New York: P.F. Collier & Son Corporation.

Pollard, Alfred W. (1967). *Shakespeare's Fight with the Pirates and the Problem of the Transmission of his Text.* 2nd ed., revised with an introduction. Cambridge: University Press, 1920, reprinted 1967.

Prior, Moody E. (1955). "Imagery as a Test of Authorship." *Shakespeare Quarterly,* 6: 381-386.

Proxorov, A.V. (1984). "O Slučajnoj Versifikacii (K Voprosu o Teoretičeskix i Rečevyx Modeljax Stixotvornoj Reči) [On Fortuitous Versification (On the Problem of Theoretical and Speech Models of Verse)]." *Problemy Teorii Stixa,* ed. Lixačëv et al., Leningrad: Nauka: 89-98.

Ramsey, Paul. (1979). *The Fickle Glass: A Study of Shakespeare's Sonnets.* New York: AMS Press.

Ransom, John Crowe. (1972). *Beating the Bushes. Selected Essays 1941-1970.* New York: New Directions Publishing Corporation.

Rauschenberger, Maria. (1981). *Shakespeare's Imagery: Versuch Einer Definition.* Amsterdam: Verlag B.R. Gruner.

Ribner, Irving. (1960). *Patterns in Shakespearean Tragedy.* London: Methuen.

Richards, I.A. (1954). *Practical Criticism, A Study of Literary Judgment.* London: Routledge and Kegan Paul Ltd.

Richards, I.A. (1979). "Rhythm and Meter." *The Structure of Verse. Modern Essays on Prosody,* ed. Harvey Gross. New York: The Ecco Press: 68-76.

Robertson, J.M. (1924). *An Introduction to the Study of the Shakespeare Canon.* London: George Routledge; New York: E.P. Dutton.

Russo, Joseph A. (1963). "A Closer Look at Homeric Formulas." *Transactions and Proceedings of the American Philological Association,* 94: 235-247.

Russo, Joseph A. (1966). "The Structural Formula in Homeric Verse." *Yale Classical Studies,* 20: 219-240.

Šajkevič, A.Ja. (1968). "Opyt Statističeskogo Vydelenija Funkcional'nyx Stilej [An Experiment in Differentiating Functional Styles Statistically]" *Voprosy Jazykoznanija,* 1: 64-76.

Šajkevič, A.Ja. (1976). "Distributivno-statističeskij Analiz v Semantike [A Distributive-Statistical Analysis in Semantics]." *Principy i Metody Semantičeskix Issledovanij,* ed. V.N. Jarceva et al. Moskva: Nauka: 353-378.

Sajtanov, V.A. (1977). "Puškin i Kol'ridž [Puškin and Coleridge]." *Izvestija ANSSSR, Serija Literatury i Jazyka,* 36, No. 2: 153-164.

Sampley, A.M. (1933). "'Verbal tests' for Peele's plays." *Studies in Philology,* 30: 473-496.

Sarrazin, G. (1897). "Wortechos bei Shakespeare." *Shakespeare Jahrbuch*, 33: 121-165.
Sarrazin, G. (1898). "Wortechos bei Shakespeare." *Shakespeare Jahrbuch*, 34: 119-169.
Schoenbaum, Samuel. (1966). *Internal Evidence and Elizabethan Dramatic Authorship*. Evanston: Northwestern University Press.
Scholl, E.H. (1944). "New Light on Seventeenth Century Pronunciation from the English School of Lutenist Song-Writers." *PMLA*, 59, No. 2: 398-445.
Schumann, Otto. (1979-1982). *Lateinisches Hexameter-Lexikon: Dichterisches Formelgut von Ennius bis zum Archipoeta*. München: Monumenta Germaniae Historica, 6 v.
Červinskij, S.V. (1961). *Ritm i Smysl. K Izučeniju Poetiki Puškina [Rhythm and Meaning. Towards Studying Puškin's Poetics]*. Moskva: Izdatel'stvo Akademii Nauk SSSR.
Shippey, J.A. (1972). *Old English Verse*. London: Hutchinson.
Sicherman, Carol M. (1982). "Meter and Meaning in Shakespeare." *Language and Style*, 15: 168-192.
Sipe, Dorothy L. (1968). *Shakespeare's Metrics*. New Haven: Yale University Press.
Slater, Eliot. (1975). "Shakespeare: Word Links Between Poems and Plays." *Notes and Queries*, 220: 157-163.
Slater, Eliot. (1978). "Word Links Between 'Timon of Athens' and 'King Lear'." *Notes and Queries*, 223: 147-149.
Smirnickaja, O.A. (1970). "Lingvističeskije Faktory Razvitija i Gibeli Alliteracionnogo Stixa v Anglii [Linguistic Factors of the Development and Decline of Alliterative Verse in England]." *Voprosy Anglijskoj Filologii*, Tula: Tul'skij Pedagoičeskij Institut: 71-90.
Smirnickaja, O.A. (1980). "Sinonimičeskije Sistemy v 'Beovul'fe' [Systems of Synonyms in 'Beowulf']." *Vestnik Moskovskogo Universiteta*, Serija 9, Filologija, No. 5: 44-57.
Smirnickij, A.I. (1957). *Sintaksis Anglijskogo Jazyka [English Syntax]*. Moskva: Izdatel'stvo Literatury na Inostrannyx Jazykax.
Smith, Barbara Herrnstein. (1968). *Poetic Closure. A Study of How Poems End*. Chicago, London: The University of Chicago Press.
Smith, G.S. (1981). "Stanza Rhythm in the Iambic Tetrameter of Three Modern Russian Poets." *International Journal of Slavic Linguistics and Poetics*, 24: 135-152.
Šnol', S.E. and A.A. Zamjatin. (1974). "Vozmožnyje Bioximičeskije i Biofizičeskije Osnovy Tvorčestva i Vosprijatie Ritmičeskix Xarakteristic Xudožestvennyx Proizvedenij [Probable Biochemical and Biophysical Bases of Creative Activity and the Perception of Rhythmical Characteristics of Poetic Works]." *Ritm, Prostranstvo i Vremja v Literatur i Iskusstve*, ed. B.F. Egorov. Leningrad: Nauka: 289-297.
Spalding, William. (1876). "A Letter on Shakspere's Authorship of 'The Two Noble Kinsmen'; and on the Characteristics of Shakspere's Style and the Secret of his Supremacy." New ed., with the life of the author, by John Hill Burton. London, Publications for the New Shakspere Society, by N. Trubner, 1876.
Spedding, James. (1874). "On the Several Shares of Shakspere and Fletcher in the Play of 'Henry VIII'." *New Shakspere Society. Transactions*. London, 1874, Appendix: 1*-18*.
Spevack, Marvin. (1974). *The Harvard Concordance to Shakespeare*. Cambridge, Mass: Belknap Press of Harvard University Press.
Sprott, S. Ernest. (1953). *Milton's Art of Prosody*. Oxford: Basil Blackwell.

Spurgeon, Caroline F.E. (1931). "Shakespeare's Iterative Imagery." *Studies in Shakespeare*, ed. Peter Alexander. London, New York, Toronto: Oxford University Press: 171-200.
Spurgeon, Caroline F.E. (1981). *Shakespeare's Imagery and What It Tells Us.* Cambridge: At the University Press. (10th Reprint of 1935 First Edition.)
Steblin-Kamenskij, M.I. (1978). *Istoričeskaja Poetika [Historical Poetics].* Leningrad: Nauka.
Steblin-Kamenskij, M.I. (1979). *Drevneskandinavskaja Literatura [Old Scandinavian Literature].* Moskva: Nauka.
Stein, Arnold. (1951). "Structures of Sound in Donne's Verse." *Kenyon Review*, 13: 20-36, 256-278.
Stein, Arnold. (1953). "Structures of Sound in Milton's Verse." *Kenyon Review*, 15: 266-277.
Stevick, R.D. (1962). "The Oral-Formulaic Analysis of Old English Verse." *Speculum*, 37: 382-389.
Suhamy, Henry. (1984). *Le Vers de Shakespeare.* Lille: Atelier National Reproduction des Thesis Universite Lille.
Sweet, Henry. (1958). *A New English Grammar; Logical and Historical.* Oxford: Clarendon Press.
Sykes, Henry Dugdale. (1919). *Sidelights on Shakespeare: Being Studies of 'The Two Noble Kinsmen'. 'Henry VIII'. 'Arden of Feversham'. 'A Yorkshire Tragedy'. 'The Troublesome Reign of King John'. 'King Leir'. 'Pericles Prince of Tyre'.* Stratford-upon-Avon: The Shakespeare Head Press.
Sykes, Henry Dugdale. (1924). *Sidelights on Elizabethan Drama: A Series of Studies Dealing with the Authorship of Sixteenth and Seventeenth Century Plays.* London: Oxford University Press.
Taranovsky, Kiril. (1953). *Ruski Dvodelni Ritmovi [Russian Binary Metres].* I-II. Beograd: Srpska Akademija Nauk.
Taranovsky, Kiril. (1963). "O Vzaimootnošnii Stixotvornogo Ritma i Tematiki [On the Correlation Between Verse Rhythm and the Themes]." *American Contributions to the Fifth International Congress of Slavists.* The Hague: Mouton: 287-322.
Taranovsky, Kiril. (1966a). "Osnovnye Zadači Statističeskogo Izučenija Slavianskogo Stixa [The Main Aims in Statistical Study of Slavic Verse]." *Poetics, Peotyka, Poetika*, II. The Hague, Paris: Mouton; Warszawa: PWN—Polish Scientific Publishers: 171-196.
Taranovsky, Kiril. (1966b). "Iz Istorii Russkogo Stixa XVIII v. (Odičeskaja Strofa AbAbCCdEEd v Poezii Lomonosova) [From the History of Russian Verse of the XVIII-th c. (The Ode Stanza AbAbCCdEEd in Lomonosov's Poetry)]." *XVIII Vek*, No. 7: 106-115.
Taranovsky, Kiril. (1980). "The Rhythmical Structure of Russian Binary Meters." *Russian Poetics in Translation*, v. 7: *Meter, Rhythm, Stanza, Rhyme*, ed. G.S. Smith. Colchester, Essex: Department of Language and Linguistics, University of Essex: 20-30. (First published in 1971.)
Taranovsky, K.F. and A.V. Proxorov. (1982). "K Xarakteristike Russkogo Četyrexstopnogo Jamba XVIII Veka: Lomonosov, Trediakovskij, Sumarokov [Towards Characteristics of the Russian Iambic Tetrameter of the Eighteenth Century: Lomonosov, Trediakovskij, Sumarokov]." *Russian Literature*, 12: 145-194.
Tarlinskaja, Marina. (1973). "The Syllabic Structure and Meter of English Verse from

Tarlinskaja, M.G. (1974a). "Meter and Rhythm of Pre-Chaucerian Rhymed Verse." *Linguistics*, 121: 65-88.

Tarlinskaja, M.G. (1974b). "K Voprosu o Sredneanglijskom Slovesnom Udarenii [Towards the Problem of Middle English Word Stress]." *Sbornik Naučnyx Trudov*, 81. Moskva: Moskovskij Gosudarstvennyj Pedagogičeskij Institut Inostrannyx Jazykov Imeni Morisa Toreza: 104-141.

Tarlinskaja, M.G. (1976). *English Verse. Theory and History*. The Hague, Paris: Mouton.

Tarlinskaja, M.G. (1980). "Izomorfnost' Stixotvornyx Tekstov i ix Sostavljuščiz [Isomorphism of Verse Texts and their Constituents]." *Sbornik Naučnyx Trudov* 158, Moskva: Moskovskij Gosudarstvennyj Pedagogičeskij Institut Inostrannyx Jazykov Imeni Morisa Toreza: 77-90.

Tarlinskaja, M.G. (1981). "Metriko-Grammatičeskaja Modeliruemost' Stixa [Metrical-Grammatical Verse Modeling]." *Actual'nye Problemy Stixovedenija i Voprosy Finno-ugorskogo Stixovedenija. Studia Metrica et Poetica*, 587: 120-133.

Tarlinskaja, M.G. (1983). "Evolution of Shakespeare's Metrical Style." *Poetics*, 12: 567-587.

Tarlinskaja, M.G. (1984). "Rhythm-Morphology-Syntax-Rhythm." *Style*, 18, No. 1: 1-26.

Tarlinskaja, M.G. (1986a). "Vertical Parameters of Meter [Stress Profiles of Russian and English Iambic Pentameter and Italian Hendecasyllabic Verse]." *Proceedings. Stanford Metrics Conference 1984*. New York: Academic Press.(in press).

Tarlinskaja, M.G. (1986b). "Aspects of Meter [Phonological and Grammatical Aspects; the General Rule and the Individual Norm]" *Proceedings. Stanford Metrics Conference 1984*. New York: Academic Press.(in press).

Tarlinskaja, M.G. and L.M. Teterina. (1974). "Verse-Prose-Metre." *Linguistics*, 129: 63-86.

Tarlinskaja, M.G. and L.K. Coachman. (1986). "Text-Theme-Text: Semantic Correlation Between Thematically Linked Poems (Seven Sonnets by Shakespeare)." *Language and Style* (in press).

Tarlinskaja, Marina and Naira Oganesova. (1986). "Meter and Meaning: The Semantic 'Halo' of Verse Form in English Romantic Lyrics (Iambic and Trochaic Tetrameter)." *American Journal of Semiotics* (in press).

Thompson, Elbert N.S. (1909). "Elizabethan Dramatic Collaboration." *Englische Studien*, 40: 30-46.

Thorndike, Ashley Horace. (1901). *The Influence of Beaumont and Fletcher on Shakespeare*. Worcester, Mass.: Press of O.B. Wood.

Tillyard, Eustace Mandeville Wentenhall. (1938). *Shakespeare's Last Plays*. London: Chatto and Windus.

Timberlake, Philip W. (1931). *The Feminine Endings in English Blank Verse*. Menasha, Wisc.: George Banta Publishing Company.

Tomaševskij, B.V. (1923). *Russkoje Stixosloženije [Russian Verse]*. Nachdruck der Ausgabe Petrograd 1923, Wilhelm Fink Ferlag, Munchen, 1971.

Tomaševskij, B.V. (1929). *O Stixe. Statji [On Verse. Articles]*. Leningrad: Priboj.

Tomaševskij, B.V. (1959). *Stix i Jazyk [Verse and Language]*. Moskva, Leningrad: Gosudarstvennoje Izdatel'stvo Xudožestvennoj Literatury.

Trager, Edith Crowell. (1956). "Superfix and Sememe: English Verbal Compounds." *General Linguistics*, 2: 13.

Trager, George Leonard and Henry Lee Smith, Jr. (1951). *An Outline of English Structure*. Norman, Ok.: Battenburg Press.

Tronskij, I.M. (1973). "K Voprosu o 'Formul'nom Stile' Gomerovskogo Eposa [On the Problem of the 'Formulaic Style' of Homeric Epos]." *Philologica. Issledovanija po Jazyku i Literature*. Leningrad: Nauka: 48-57.

Trubetzkoy, N.S. (1963). "K Voprosu o Stixe 'Pesen Zapadnyx Slavian' Puškina [On the Problem of the Verse of Puškin's 'Songs of the Western Slavs']." *Three Philological Studies*. Michigan Slavic Materials, No. 3, Ann Arbor: Department of Slavic Languages and Literature: 55-67. (First published in 1937.)

Tynjanov, Ju. (1924). *Problema Stuxotvornogo Jazyka* [*Problems of Poetic Language*]. Moskva: Academia.

Vanvik, Arne. (1961). *On Stress in Present-Day English*. Bergen: Norwegian Universities Press.

Vinogradov, V.V. (1959). *O Jazyke Xudožestvennoj Literatury* [*On the Language of Literature*]. Moskva: Goslitizdat.

Waith, Eugene M. (1952). *The Pattern of Tragicomedy in Beaumont and Fletcher*. New Haven: Yale University Press.

Waller, Frederick O. (1966). "The Use of Linguistic Criteria in Determining the Copy and Dates for Shakespeare's Plays." *Pacific Coast Studies in Shakespeare*, ed. Waldo F. McNeir and Thelma N. Greenfield. Eugene, Ore.: 1-19.

Warnken, Henry L. (1964). "Iago as a Projection of Othello." *Shakespeare Encomium*, ed. Anne Paolucci. The City College Papers, I. New York: The City College: 1-15.

Wasson, John. (1964). "In Defense of 'King Henry VIII'." *Research Studies* (Washington State University), 32: 261-276.

Watts, Ann Chaimers. (1969). *The Lyre and the Harp: A Comparative Reconsideration of Oral Tradition in Homer and Old English Epic Poetry*. New Haven: Yale University Press.

Wells, J.C. (1965). "The Phonological Status of Syllabic Consonants in English." *Phonetica*, 13. *Proceedings of the Fifth International Congress of Phonetic Sciences*. New York: S. Karger Basil: 110-113.

Wells, Rulon. (1966). "Nominal and Verbal Style." *Style in Language*, ed. Thomas A. Sebeok. Cambridge, Mass.: The M.I.T. Press, Massachusetts Institute of Technology: 213-220.

Wells, William. (1920). 'Timon of Athens.' *Notes and Queries*, 6: 266-269.

Wentersdorf, Karl. (1957). "Shakespearean Chronology and the Metrical Tests." *Shakespeare-Studien: Festschrift für Heinrich Mutschmann*, ed. Walther Fischer und Karl Wentersdorf. Marburg: N.G. Elwert: 161-193.

Wexler, W.J. (1964). "On the Grammetrics of the Classical Alexandrine." *Cahiers de Lexicologie*, 4: 61-72.

Whallon, William. (1961). "The Diction of 'Beowulf'." *PMLA*, 76: 309-319.

Williams, Carrington Bonsor. (1970). *Style and Vocabulary: Numerical Studies*. London: Griffin.

Williams, David Rhys. (1966). *Shakespeare, Thy Name is Marlowe*. New York: Philosophical Library.

Williams, Philip. (1956). "New Approaches to Textual Problems in Shakespeare." *Studies in Bibliography*, 8: 3-14.

Wilson, E.P. (1953). *Marlowe and the Early Shakespeare*. Oxford: Clarendon Press.
Wilson, John Harold. (1928). *The Influence of Beaumont and Fletcher on Restoration Drama*. Columbus: The Ohio State University Press.
Wimsatt, W.K., Jr. (1950). "Verbal Style: Logical and Counterlogical." *PMLA*, 65, No. 2: 5-20.
Wimsatt, W.K., Jr. (1970). "The Rule and the Norm: Halle and Keyser on Chaucer's Meter." *College English*, 31: 774-788.
Wright, George T. (1983). "The Play of Phrase and Line in Shakespeare's Iambic Pentameter." *Shakespeare Quarterly*, 34, No. 2: 147-158.
Wright, George T. (1985). "Wyatt's Decasyllabic Line." *Studies in Philology*, 82, No. 2: 129-156.
Xodasevič, V.F. (1937). *O Puškine [On Puškin]*. Berlin: Petropolis.
Xolševnikov, V.E. (1969). "Pereboi Ritma [Rhythmical Irregularities]." *Russkaja Sovetskaja Poezija i Stixovedenije*. Moskva: MOPI: 173-184.
Xolševnikov, V.E. (1984a). "Suščestvujet li Stopa v Russkoj Sillabo-tonike? [Is There a Foot in the Russian Syllabo-tonic Verse?]" *Problemy Teorii Stixa*, ed. Lixačëv et al. Leningrad: Nauka: 58-66.
Xolševnikov, V.E. (1984b). "K Sporam o Russkoj Sillabo-tonike [Concerning the Discussions of the Russian Syllabo-tonic Verse]." *Problemy Teorii Stixa*, ed. D.S. Lixačëv et al. Leningrad: Nauka: 168-173.
Yates, Frances Amelia. (1936). *A Study of 'Love's Labour's Lost'*. Cambridge, England: The University Press.
Youmans, Gilbert. (1983). "Generative Tests for Generative Meter." *Language*, 59, No. 1: 67-92.
Yule, George Udny. (1944). *The Statistical Study of Literary Vocabulary*. Cambridge, England: The University Press.
Zavarin, Valentina, and Mary Coote. (1979). "Theory of the Formulaic Text." *Working Papers and Pre-Publications of Centro Internazionale di Semiotica e di Linguistica*, Nos. 88-89: 1-48. Urbino: Universita di Urbino.
Žirmunskij, V.M. (1962). *Narodnyj Geroičeskij Epos. Sravnitel'no-Istoričeskie Očerki [Folklore Heroic Epos. Comparative-Historical Essays]*. Moskva, Leningrad: Nauka.
Žirmunskij, V.M. (1977). "O Nacional'nyx Formax Jambičeskogo Stixa [On the National Forms of Iambic Verse]." *Toerija Literatury, Poetica, Stilistika*. Leningrad: Nauka: 362-375.
Žirmunskij, V.M. (1978). *Bajron i Puškin [Byron and Puškin]*. Leningrad: Nauka. (First published in 1924.)
Žirmunskij, V.M. (1981). *Gëte v Russkoj Literature [Goethe in the Russian Literature]*. Leningrad: Nauka. (First published in 1937.)
Zholkovsky, A.K. (1980). " 'Prevosxoditel'nyj Pokoj': ob Odnom Invariantnom Motive Puškina ['Superior Rest': On One Invariant Motive in Puškin's Poetry]." In: A.K. Žolkovskij and Ju.K. Sčeglov, *Poetika Vyrazitel'nosti [Poetics of Expressiveness]*. Wiener Slawistischer Almanach, Sonderbandt, 2.
Zholkovsky, Alexander. (1984). *Themes and Texts*. Ithaca and London: Cornell University Press.

Sources analyzed and quoted in the text

Arnold, Matthew: *The Poetical Works of Matthew Arnold*, with an introduction by Sir A.T. Quiller-Couch. London: Oxford University Press, 1942.
Blake, William: *The Complete Poetry and Prose of William Blake*, ed. David V. Erdman. Berkeley: University of California Press, 1982.
Bloomfield, Robert: *Bloomfield's Works*. 3 vols. London: Longman, Hurst, Rees, Orme, and Brown, 1819-1826.
Browning, Robert: *The Complete Works of Robert Browning*, ed. Roma A. King, Jr., et al. 4 vols. Athens: Ohio University Press, 1969-1973.
Bryan, Daniel: *The Mountain Muse*. Harrisonburg: printed for the author by Davidson and Bourne, 1813.
Byron, George Gordon: *The Poems and Dramas of Lord Byron*. New York: Crowell, 1884.
Campbell, Thomas: *The Complete Poetical Works of Thomas Campbell*. Boston: Phillips, Sampson and Co., .
Carew, Thomas: *The Poems of Thomas Carew*, ed. Rhodes Dunlap. Oxford: Clarendon Press, 1957.
Chaucer, Geoffrey: *The Complete Works of Geoffrey Chaucer*, ed. Rev. Walter W. Skeat. Oxford: Clarendon Press, 1844.
Clough, Arthur Hugh: *The Poetical Works of Arthur Hugh Clough*. London: G. Routledge and Sons, 1906.
Coleridge, S.T.: *The Complete Poems of Samuel Taylor Coleridge*, ed. Morchard Bishop. London: Macdonald, 1954.
Collins Albatross Book of Longer Poems, ed. Edwin Morgan. London and Glasgow: Collins, 1964: James Thomson and John Wilmot.
Cornwall, Barry [pseud.]: Procter, Bryan Waller. *Dramatic Scenes. With other poems, now first printed.* By Barry Cornwall [pseud.]. New York, London: D. Appleton and Co., 1857.
Crabbe, George: *Poems*, ed. Adolphus William Ward. 3 vols. Cambridge: The University Press, 1905-1907.
Darley, George: *Selected Poems of George Darley*, ed. Anne Ridler. London: Merrion Press, 1979.
Donne, John: *The Complete Poetry of John Donne*, ed. John T. Shawcross. Anchor Books, Garden City, New York: Doubleday and Co., 1967.
Dryden, John: *Dramatic Works*, ed. Montagne Summers. 6 vols. London: Nonesuch Press, 1931-1932.
Elizabethan and Stuart Plays, ed. Charles Reed Baskervill, Virgil B. Heitzel, Arthur H. Nethercot. New York, Chicago, San Francisco, Toronto, London: Holt, Rinehart and Winston, 1965: Norton and Sackville, Kyd, Anon. 'Arden of Faversham', Ben Jonson, Beaumont and Fletcher ('The Maid's Tragedy'), Dekker, Massinger, Webster, Middleton and Rowley, Ford, Shirley.
Elliott, Ebenezer: *The Poetical Works of Ebenezer Elliott*, ed. by his son, Edwin Elliott. London: H.S. King and Co., 1876.
English Poetry of the Nineteenth Century, ed. G.R. Elliott and Norman Foerster. New York: Macmillan, 1958: R.S. Hawker.
Fielding, Henry: *The History of Tom Jones, A Foundling*, ed. Fredson Bowers. 2 vols. Middletown, Conn.: Wesleyan University Press, 1975.

Fletcher, "Bonduca": *The Dramatic Works in the Beaumont and Fletcher Canon*, ed. Fredson Bowers. 4 vols. London, New York, Melbourne: Cambridge University Press, 1979.

Frost, Robert: *The Poetry of Robert Frost*, ed. Edward Connery Lathem. New York: Holt, Rinehart and Winston, 1975.

Heber, Reginald: *Poems and Translations*. London: Longman, Hurst, Rees, Orme, and Brown, 1812.

Hemans, Mrs. Felicia Dorothea (Browne): *The Poetical Works of Felicia Hemans*. Complete in one volume. Philadelphia: J.B. Smith and Co., 1860.

Hood, Thomas. *Poetical Works*. 5 vols. Boston: Ticknor and Fields, 1866- 1871.

Jones, William: *Poems*. Selected by Jonathan Benthall. Cambridge: Sebastian Carter, 1961.

Keats, John: *The Complete Works of John Keats*, ed. H. Buxton Forman. 5 vols. Glasgow: Gowans and Gray, 1900-720 .

Landor, Walter Savage: *The Complete Works of Walter Savage Landor*, ed. T. Earle Welby. 16 vols. London: Chapman and Hall, 1927-1976.

Marlowe, Christopher: *Complete Plays*, ed. Irving Ribner. New York: Odyssey Press, 1963.

Marlowe, Christopher: *The Complete Works of Christopher Marlowe*, ed. Fredson Bowers. New York: Cambridge University Press, 1979.

Middle English Verse Romances, ed. Donald B. Sands. New York, Chicago, San Francisco, Toronto, London: Holt, Rinehart and Winston, 1966: "King Horn", "Sir Orfeo".

Milton, John: *The Complete Works of John Milton*, ed. Harris Francis Fletcher. Cambridge, Mass.: The Riverside Press, 1941.

Montgomery, James: *The Poetical Works of James Montgomery*. 4 vols. London: Longman, 1855.

Moore, Thomas: *The Poetical Works of Thomas Moore*. New York: Leavitt and Allen, 1856.

(The) Oxford Book of English Verse 1250-1918, ed. Arthur Quiller-Couch, Oxford: Clarendon Press, 1948: Samuel Rogers, Robert Stephen Hawker.

(The) Penguin Book of Ballads, ed. G. Grigson. Harmondsworth: Penguin Books, 1977: No. 7, "The Royal Fisherman", No. 23, "Tam Lin", No. 36, "Little Musgrave and Lady Barnard".

(The) Penguin Book of Eighteenth-Century English Verse, ed. Dennis Davison. Harmondsworth: Penguin Books, 1975: John Arbuthnot, John Armstrong, Robert Blair, John Byrom, William Cowper, Erasmus Darwin, John Gay, Samuel Johnson, William Somerville.

Pope, Alexander: *The Complete Poetical Works of Alexander Pope*, ed. Henry W. Boynton. Cambridge Edition. Boston: Houghton Mifflin Co., 1931.

Praed, Winthrop Mackworth: *Selected Poems*, ed. Kenneth Allott. London: Routledge and Paul, 1953.

Rogers, Samuel: *The Pleasures of Memory*. Boston: printed by David Carlisle, for West and Greenleaf, No. 56, Cornhill, 1801.

Shakespeare, William: *The Complete Works of William Shakespeare*. The Cambridge Text established by John Dover Wilson for the Cambridge University Press. Octopus Books, 1980.

Shakespeare, William: *The Arden Edition of the Works of William Shakespeare*, ed. Una Ellis-Fermor. 36 vols. London: Methuen, 1951-1982.

Shelley, Percy Bysshe: *The Complete Poetical Works of Percy Bysshe Shelley*, ed. Thomas Hutchinson. London: Oxford University Press, H. Milford, 1927.

Smith, Horace. *The Poetical Works, Comic and Miscellaneous, of Horace Smith. Now first collected.* 2 vols. London: Henry Colburn, 1851.

White, Henry Kirke: *The Poetical Works of Henry Kirke White*. Boston: Phillips, Sampson, 1854.

Wordsworth, William: *The Complete Poetical Works*. London: Macmillan, 1894.

Index

A mayore: *see* hemistich
"A Midsummer-Night's Dream", 72, 96, 106, 114, 115, 117, 120, 121, 131, 146, 192, 340
A minore: *see* hemistich
Accent, phrasal (*see also* stress), 6, 17, 33;
  combined with word stress, 35;
  sense differentiation by, 37;
  distribution in a phrase, 204, 214;
  emphatic, 33, 34, 205, 221, 222;
  proclitic/enclitic, 33, 35, 76-77, 128, 209ff., 254;
  evolution of tendencies, 217, 218;
  in attributive phrases, 219-223;
  in adverbial phrases, 223-225;
  subordinate, 32, 35, 214, 222, 235, 236, 246, 256, 257;
  weakening, loss of, 33-34, 35, 209, 214, 221, 222, 223, 239, 253, 254, 255, 256, 263;
  semantic reasons for weakening and loss of, 34, 204, 205, 221, 222, 225;
  ambivalent, 221, 239
Actual verse: *see* models of verse
Adjectives, 17, 35, 36, 211;
  in rhythmical figures, 235, 241, 242, 245-248, 253, 256, 262-264, 289, 292ff., 301-302, 323, 337, 339;
  stylistic connotations of, 288, 289-293, 339
Adverbial:
  modifiers, 211, 224, 236, 262, 303;
  phrases, 223-224
Adverbs, of broad semantics: 179, 224;
  stressing of, 204, 209, 211, 212, 224;

in rhythmical figures, 235, 241, 242, 245, 246, 248, 253
Aksënov, 14
Alexander, 54, 124, 126, 193
Allen, 227
Alliteration, 288-290, 292
"All's Well that Ends Well", 61-62, 115, 143
Altman, 24, 329n
Amphibrach, 16
Anacrusis, 14, 16, 40, 67, 72, 76, 77, 87, 92, 147, 254, 267, 272, 273, 274, 332, 334, 341;
  zero anacrusis, 338
Analysis:
  vertical, horizontal, 4, 7, 15, 31, 231;
  componental, 293-295, 329n.
Anapest, 16
Anikst, 54, 162
"Antony and Cleopatra", 22, 56, 61, 65, 114, 126, 142, 143, 147, 148, 150, 152, 156, 157, 170-171, 186, 190, 197, 334, 336, 347
Appleton, 19, 187, 217
Armstrong, 24
Arnold, 233, 241, 248, 251, 258, 259, 282, 291, 295ff., 299ff., 316
"As You Like It", 23, 106, 190, 233, 241, 259
Attribute, attributive phrase (*see also* adjectives *and* phrase): 17, 18, 22, 211, 221-223, 235, 236, 246, 253, 256, 258, 260, 262, 337, 344
Attribution: *see* authorship
Attridge, 27, 28, 32, 232, 235
Authorship, 18ff., 63, 93, 105, 106, 108, 114, 117, 143, 147, 157, 190, 192,

193, 195, 196, 197, 198, 207, 215, 221, 223, 226, 262, 347;
tests of:
  metrical, 20, 198;
  grammatical, 20-23, 198;
  lexical, 23-24;
  stylistic, 24;
  collaboration (co-authorship), 19-20, 65, 96, 117, 124, 125, 126, 127, 129-131, 190, 195, 196, 197, 198, 199, 200, 217, 221, 224, 226, 338, 347-350

Bailey, James, 38, 39, 222, 3, 4, 6, 13, 14, 15, 18, 32, 33, 34, 35, 37, 38, 39, 222, 232, 233, 235, 267
Bailey, Richard W., 3, 22
Bajevskij, 272
Baker, 22
Baskervill, Heltzel, and Nethercot, 114, 129
Baxter, 288
Beaumont and Fletcher, 44, 108, 113, 200, 208, 215, 221, 224, 236
Beaver, 33, 35, 205
Bennett, 23
Benson, 325
Berman and Szamosi, 204
Bipartite line segmentation: see break, hemistich, syntactic seam
Bjorklund, 6, 15, 16, 36, 37, 88, 116, 235, 236, 238, 252, 262, 278
Boas, 61, 80
Bobrov, 27
Bogatyrjëv, 325
Bolinger, 17, 31, 32, 33, 34, 36, 37, 204, 205, 221, 237
Boyle, 20, 23, 126, 178, 179, 187, 208, 212
Break (seam), rhythmical-syntactic: 30n., 127, 128, 130, 132, 169, 171, 175, 208, 235, 236, 237, 253, 255, 257-258, 260, 272, 334, 337, 339, 347, 349
Bresnan, 34, 204, 205
Bridges, 36
Brik, 266, 327

Brodeur, 325
Browning, 13, 40, 41, 43, 44, 54, 208, 218, 221, 222, 223, 224
Burton, 22-23
Byrne, 23
Byron, 31, 65, 79, 83-85, 105, 108, 113, 143, 144, 147, 188, 189-190, 208, 217, 218, 221, 222, 223, 224, 233, 254, 343

Caesura: *see* break, hemistich, syntactic seam
Canonized iambic pentameter: *see* iambic pentameter
Cercignani, 36, 88
Černjaxovskaja, 321
Chambers, 3, 20, 24, 47ff., 59, 61, 104, 115, 124, 126, 143, 177, 190, 191, 196, 347
Chapman, 44, 65, 66-67, 108, 114, 130, 208, 214, 218, 225, 228, 336, 347
Chatman, 32
Chaucer, 44, 60, 85
Chisholm, 238
Chomsky and Halle, 204
Chomsky, Halle, and Lukoff, 210
Chronology (*see also* periods, evolution): 18ff., 47ff., 54, 82, 83, 96, 181ff., 190-191, 192ff., 257, 259, 305, 312, 328, 338, 347;
  of Marlowe's plays, 80, 82
Churchill, 65, 66
Classicism, 5, 16-17, 39, 54, 189, 206, 217, 235, 260, 337, 345
Collins, 324
Composition (of plays, poems, stanzas): 103-104, 115, 116, 147, 266ff., 281, 282, 341, 342, 343;
  of "The Rape of Lucrece" stanza, 272, 275;
  of the Sonnets, 272-273, 282;
  last line of a poem, stanza, 274, 275, 276, 278, 342-343;
  first line of a poem, stanza, 278, 279;
  midlines of a poem, stanza, 279-280, 341
"Coriolanus", 104, 143, 190, 191, 197, 347

Craig, 126
Creed, 325
Čudovskij, 135, 157
Curme, 32, 204, 221
"Cymbeline", 23, 63, 92, 104, 128, 143, 148, 150, 152, 157, 171-172, 197, 334

Dactyl, 16
Dactylic endings, of lines: *see* line endings; of words: *see* word endings
Dahl, 23
Decanonized iambic pentameter, *see* iambic pentameter
Diamond, 325
Diapasons of stress variation, 105
Disintegrators (of Shakespeare), 23
Dissimilation:
 of adjacent verse units:
  of strong and weak ictuses, 105;
  of lines in a stanza, 267;
 of epochs, 218
Dobson, 36, 88, 284n.
Donne, 9, 13, 14, 18, 57, 65, 115, 237, 333, 340
van Draat, 17, 32, 37, 204, 206, 237
Dramatic verse: *see* genre variations

Edwards, 195
Eitrem, 204, 206
Elizabethan, 5, 21, 92, 121, 132, 178, 181, 192, 214, 335, 337
Elizabethan-Jacobean, 14, 20, 23, 39, 44, 54, 127, 146, 177, 181, 218, 237, 335, 336, 347, 350
Elizabethan Critical Essays, 227
Ellis, 88
Elvert, 7
Enclitic/proclitic: *see* accent, phrase, syntax
Endings of lines: *see* line endings
Enjambment: *see* line endings

Farnham, 21
Feminine endings, of lines: *see* line endings; of words: *see* word endings

Feuillerat, 3
Filipov, 157
Fleay, 20, 124, 126, 177
Fletcher, 16, 41, 44, 105, 106, 126, 127ff., 147, 188, 189, 190, 198, 199-201, 207, 208, 212, 214, 217, 218, 221, 222, 223, 224, 254, 260, 262, 336, 338, 349-350
Foakes, 126
Foot, 4, 16, 223;
 feet-emphasizing and feet-effacing word boundaries, 226-228, 232
Franz, 21
Fridlender, 329n
Fry, 325
Frye, 27
Fussell, 88

Gascoigne, 236
Gasparov, 6, 7, 8, 11, 16, 25, 26, 27, 28n., 29n, 103, 116, 135, 136, 206, 218, 234, 235, 237, 238, 264, 274, 275, 327
Genre variations:
 of general rhythm, 18, 57, 58, 59-60, 63-67, 72, 82, 85-87, 96, 105, 106, 115, 117, 118, 120, 136, 146, 335, 339-341;
 of rhythmical figures, 237, 239, 241, 246, 247, 255, 281, 288, 289, 292, 296, 303, 305, 312, 313, 323, 328, 339, 346
 of line endings, 190, 191, 192;
 of verse grammar, 250, 251-252, 255, 259, 260, 262
Giamati, 7
Gibson, 65, 66
Gimson, 89, 206
Gindin, 2, 338
Grammar and verse form: *see* meter and grammar, rhythmical figures, patterns, parts-of-speech, syntax, phrase, break
Greimas, 329n.
Grigorjev, 88

Half-line: *see* hemistich, break, syntactic seam

375

Halle and Keyser, 32, 88, 284n.
"Hamlet", 59, 60, 61, 72, 80, 92, 114, 115, 117, 120, 131-132, 143, 146, 152, 168, 431
Hamm, 27, 288, 339
Hart, 23, 53
Hatcher, 18
Hayes, 3, 6, 15, 16, 32, 37, 79, 88, 113, 116, 203, 204, 205, 207, 218, 228n., 236, 238, 260
Hemistich, half-line, bipartite line segmentation, A mayore, A minore: 12, 13, 14, 30n., 33, 39-40, 43, 47, 56-57, 58, 62, 63, 65, 72, 76, 78, 82, 83, 85-86, 96, 103, 105, 106, 116, 125, 127, 129, 130, 132, 146, 148ff., 160, 162, 165, 169, 172, 174, 227, 228n., 236, 246, 261, 278, 327, 332, 334, 335, 347, 349
Hendecasyllabic verse, Italian: 7-9, 12, 14, 85-86, 237
"Henry IV", 59, 104, 185, 190, 191
"Henry V", 72, 104, 106, 115, 143, 197
"Henry VI", 53, 57, 85, 96, 106, 114, 115, 117, 118, 191, 333, 347
"Henry VIII", 20, 61, 63, 67, 73-79, 105, 116, 121, 125ff., 143, 144, 146-147, 157, 187, 190, 191, 192, 196, 198-201, 207, 208, 215, 217, 221, 223, 224, 226, 261, 333, 334, 338, 348, 349-350
Heterogeneous rhythm: *see* homogeneous/heterogeneous rhythm
Hickson, 20, 126, 177
Hieatt, 324, 329n.
Hill, 23, 24, 121, 192, 193
Hinman, 53
Hjelmslev, 329n.
Hoffman, 66
Hollander, 25, 27, 28
Homogeneous/heterogeneous rhythm, 95, 104, 105, 106, 108ff., 113ff., 123, 128
Hotson, 53, 61
Householder, 36
Hoy, 21

Hyperdactylic endings, of lines: *see* line endings; of words: *see* word endings

Iambic hexameter and septameter (heptameter): 226-228
Iambic index, 8, 9, 12, 13, 15, 41, 67, 72, 85, 125, 333, 339
Iambic pentameter, 3, 4, 7, 13, 18, 58, 67, 79, 104, 105, 106, 113, 156, 206, 223, 226, 231, 234, 331, 332, 333;
rigid (canonized) and loose (decanonized): 7, 9, 12, 13, 39-44, 47, 54, 62, 63, 67, 93, 104, 108, 113, 116, 130, 146, 147, 148, 152, 162, 164, 168, 170, 173, 175, 187-188, 196, 228n., 235, 236, 237, 238, 241, 246, 261-262, 332, 333, 334, 335, 338, 340-341, 343, 345;
ambivalent lines, 180;
genre variations of: *see* genre variations;
syllabic variations of, 87-93, 334-335;
national variants of, 8, 9, 13, 14, 218, 237, 275, 278, 332
Iambic tendency, 12, 14, 15, 332
Iambic tetrameter, 25, 116, 266ff., 342; quatrain stanza, 116
Ictic/non-ictic, ictus/non-ictus: *see* syllabic positions
Imperative, 209, 258, 259, 262
Inertia (momentum): *see* rhythmical inertia
Ingram, 20, 177
Interjections, 208, 209, 241
Intonation, 32, 204, 205, 238, 253, 255, 263, 264, 333
Inversion of stresses: *see* stress
Isomorphism in verse, 116, 278, 341, 343

Jackson, 19, 20, 21, 23, 24, 53, 54, 104, 121, 177, 193, 195
Jacobean, 21, 179, 188, 189, 190, 207, 208, 214, 217, 218, 223, 226, 237, 260, 333, 337
Jakobson, 6, 24, 25, 26, 37, 228n., 230n. 238, 326, 327

Jakobson and Rudy, 266
Jarxo, 28, 135, 136
Jespersen, 237
Jones, 31, 32, 34, 84, 90, 204, 206
Jonson, 44, 108
"Julius Caesar", 23, 59, 60, 67, 106, 148, 150, 151, 152, 156, 165-168, 197, 341

Kenyon, 89, 204
"King John", 57, 146, 148, 152, 156, 157, 165, 191
"King Lear", 61-62, 64, 85, 114, 143, 151, 152, 170, 191, 200, 333, 347
Kiparsky, 3, 6, 16, 32, 113, 207, 218, 223, 235, 238, 260
Kökeritz, 36, 88, 91, 252
Kolmogorov and Proxorov, 7
König, 20, 88, 91, 177
Košutič, 88
Kreider, 24
Kroeber, 17, 22, 248
Kumaxov, 325
Kyd, 44, 214, 336

Langworthy, 22, 203
Law, 19, 20, 127, 177, 178, 198
Legois and Cazamian, 80
Lehiste, 33
Lehmann, 7
Levin, 24, 25, 301, 329n
Lévy, 5, 27
Liberman and Prince, 31
Line endings, 20, 25, 66, 121, 124, 125, 126, 151, 177ff., 196, 198, 335-336;
  classification of:
    accentual, 177-178;
    syllabic, 178-180;
  masculine, 25, 179, 186, 190, 191, 335, 349;
  non-masculine, 188, 190, 191, 196, 200, 336, 340, 349, 350;
  feminine, 20, 25, 66, 121, 122, 126, 180, 188, 199, 336, 341, 347, 348;
  compound, 179, 189, 190ff., 196, 200-201;
  light and heavy, 169, 178, 189, 199, 350;
  dactylic, 169, 179, 180;
  hyperdactylic, 179, 180;
  end-stopped, 127, 128, 131, 163, 178, 188, 197, 217, 341;
  enjambment (run-on-line), 20, 61, 162, 172, 177, 186-187, 190, 200, 217, 260, 263, 320, 336, 350;
  unstressed or weakly stressed, caused by monosyllables or polysyllables: 177, 178, 186-187, 188, 189, 190, 191, 194, 197, 200, 336, 350;
  reasons of evolution, 187-188
Line types (word boundary, rhythmical, grammatical): 2, 16, 18, 265-266 (*see also* patterns)
Line variants: *see* line types
Lord, 325
Lotman, 322
"Love's Labour's Lost", 57, 72, 96, 106, 115, 190, 191, 192, 335
Lyrical verse: *see* genre variations

"Macbeth", 56, 61-62, 96, 104, 143, 157, 170, 172, 186, 347
Magnuson and Ryder, 16, 238
Magoun, 325
Marked/unmarked syllables (phonologically), 5, 6
Marlowe, 31, 65-66, 79-83, 108, 113, 114, 130, 188, 207, 214, 217, 221, 336, 343, 347
Marlowe and Chapman, 108, 129, 130-131
Martin, 66
Masculine endings, of lines: *see* line endings; of words: *see* word endings
Massinger, 156-157, 178, 187, 188, 189, 190, 208, 215, 217, 218, 225, 336
Maximum range of dispersion (RD), 105ff.
Maxwell, Baldwin, 22, 126, 198
Maxwell, J.C., 22, 53, 121, 192, 193
McMichael, 65
Mean deviation of ictic stress (MD), 105, 116ff.

"Measure for Measure", 61, 96, 115,
   143, 146, 333
Meillet, 325
Melčuk, 329n.
Meter, metrical:
   general notions, 2, 4-5, 6, 206, 331ff.;
   perception of, 15, 28n., 332, 339;
   elements (components) of, 16, 226,
      228, 238, 332, 333, 336, 338;
   norm, period variations of, 18, 206,
      207, 218, 234, 237-238, 239, 252,
      280, 333, 336;
   scheme, 1, 2, 20;
   "metrical-unmetrical", 15, 113, 205,
      206, 236, 238, 252, 280, 281, 336,
      337;
   degrees of "metricality"
      (acceptability), 207, 236, 238,
      281, 332;
   national forms of, 2, 4, 5, 6, 7, 9, 14,
      15, 16, 37, 206, 218, 332, 334,
      335, 338;
   rules, laws of: 3, 16, 18, 43, 206, 218;
   meter and meaning, 25 (*see also*
      rhythm and meaning, verse form
      and meaning);
   meter and grammar: 16-17, 337, 338;
   metrical subordination, 235;
   metrically transitory forms, 333
Metrical positions: *see* syllabic positions
Metrical word, 103
Metricality: *see* meter
Metz, 23, 24
Micro-situation, micro-text: 294, 295,
   296, 301
Miles, 22, 327
Milton, 208, 217, 218, 220, 221, 223, 224,
   225, 254, 338
Mincoff, 19, 20, 21-22, 24, 125, 127, 128,
   157, 177, 178, 197, 198, 199, 217
Models of verse:
   language models, 8, 12, 28n;
   speech (prose) models, 9, 12, 13, 14-15,
      29n., 41ff., 54, 63, 65, 72, 76, 86,
      93n., 331;
   actual verse, 41, 43
Monosyllables:
   stressing of, 14, 17, 36-37, 61, 76-77;
   see also stressing;
   line-final, 177, 186-187, 189-190, 350;
   see also line endings;
   ambivalent (syllabically, accentually),
      180, 239;
   as phrase endings, 208ff.;
   in rhythmical figures: *see* rhythmical
      figures
Morphology: *see* parts of speech
"Much Ado About Nothing", 62, 72, 96,
   190
Muir, 24, 124

Nagler, 325
Narrative poems: *see* genre variations
Neilson and Thorndike, 19, 126
Newmeyer, 228n.
Nicolson, 126
Nikolaeva, 32, 205, 228n.
Non-ictic, non-ictus: *see* syllabic
   positions
Norton and Sackville, 44, 108, 114, 129-
   130, 335
Nouns:
   syllabic variants of, 35, 87-92, 194;
   stressing of, 204, 212, 221-223, 224;
   of broad semantics, 179, 212, 221-223;
   in rhythmical figures, 18, 235, 236, 241,
      242, 245, 246, 248, 235-255, 256,
      257, 260, 262-264, 299-301, 306,
      319, 321, 337, 344
Nowottny, 53, 104, 195

Object, 211, 213, 225, 236, 255, 256, 260,
   263, 303, 320, 337, 344
Oliphant, 19, 20, 156-157, 177, 178, 180,
   187, 200, 208
Onomatopoeia, 293, 322, 346
Opposition "verse-prose", 44, 83, 143,
   151, 162, 172, 187, 241, 242, 245,
   248, 249, 309, 335
Oras, 19, 20, 21, 24, 126, 127, 177, 178,
   179, 193, 199, 203, 206, 221, 222,
   223, 230n.
"Othello", 5, 53, 61-62, 114, 125, 143,
   146, 152, 156, 157, 168-170, 174,
   175-176, 191, 233, 241, 252, 257,
   259, 292, 313, 340, 341, 345, 347

Panov, 88
Parrott, 20, 23, 53, , 121, 177, 181, 192, 193
Parry, 325
Partridge, 21, 91, 128, 198, 208
Parts of speech (morphology; *see also* nouns, verbs, adjectives, and adverbs), 16, 17, 171-172;
 in heavy feminine endings, 199;
 in two-word phrases on WS or SW, 210-211, 212, 213, 221-223, 224-225;
 alliterating, 289;
 in rhythmical figures: *see* rhythmical figures
Patterns (clichés, formulas), 18, 21, 146, 171-172, 265-266, 281, 302, 306, 311-312, 315, 324ff., 344-345
"Pericles", 53, 61, 63, 105, 114, 115, 121, 124-125, 143, 190, 192, 196-198, 347, 348, 349
Periods, evolution of:
 in a poet's canon, 54ff., 72ff., 124, 136, 144, 146-147, 178, 181ff., 188, 189, 191, 215, 257, 259, 296ff., 304, 312, 327, 333, 334, 335, 336, 338, 340, 343, 347, 350;
 in a poetic tradition, 207, 218, 228, 232, 233, 234, 235, 237, 241, 257, 258, 259, 260, 281-282, 283, 295, 296, 303, 305, 311, 312, 327, 328, 335, 336, 346, 350
Personages (characters, dramatis personae, roles): 26, 62, 95, 104, 115, 135ff., 148;
 differentiation of, 152ff., 156, 157ff., 176;
 types of, emploi: 164, 166, 170, 171, 172, 173-174, 176, 340, 341, 345-346;
 evolution of a character, 174-176, 194, 345
Peškovskij, 228n.
Phrase, 16, 33, 34, 35, 73, 203, 228n., 331-332;
 microphrase, 17, 208ff.;
 principles of segmentation into, 210;

place of a word in, 76, 180, 256, 257;
phrasal accentuation (stressing): *see* accent, stress;
phrase rhythm, 32, 180, 203, 204, 331-332;
phrase and line, 177, 203, 331, , 335;
phrase endings, 199, 200, 203, 212, 226, 338;
proclitic/enclitic two-word phrases, 203, 204, 338, 348, 350, 351;
 stressing of, 207, 212, 213;
 patterns of, 213-214;221-223, 223-224, 225;
 correlation between, 214ff.;
 evolution of, 218;
 grammar of, 203, 209, 210ff., 213, 219ff., 225-226, 350;
Play within a play, 115, 131ff., 341
Plot development, 103, 104, 106, 115, 116, 192, 196, 343
Plutarch, 166, 167
Poetic universe, 293
Polysyllables, 16, 31, 62, 181, 194, 275-276;
 stress variants of, 35, 78;
 syllabic variants of, 87-91, 180-181;
 in rhythmical figures, 236, 248, 252-253, 262, 280, 315-321, 337, 338, 342, 343 (*see also* rhythmical figures);
 non-oxytones, 17, 77-79, 228n., 235, 238, 248, 278;
 oxytones, 35-36, 78-79, 235, 238, 248
Pope, 2, 13, 14, 18, 40, 41, 43, 54, 208, 217, 220, 221, 223, 233, 239, 241, 259, 303, 313, 333, 343
Post-Romanticism, 18, 39, 54, 206, 218, 338
Predicate: *see* subject and predicate
Prior, 24
Proclitic/enclitic: *see* accent, phrase, syntax
Prose models of verse: *see* models of verse
Prose tendencies in verse, 41, 43, 44, 63, 64ff., 76, 332, 334
Proxorov, 2

Quatrain, 266ff., 278, 279

Ransom, 26-27, 292
Rauschenberger, 24
Repetitions, rhythmical-grammatical-lexical: *see* patterns
Reworking of a play, 114, 115, 121, 124, 193, 215, 226, 348
Rheme, rhematic function: 33, 260, 263, 265, 278, 321
Rhymed verse, 266ff.
Rhythm:
  as a variant of meter, 2-3, 5, 28n., 95ff.;
  phrase (speech) rhythm, 32, 36, 37, 180;
  verse rhythm, 37, 38, 266;
  and syntax: *see* syntax
  and meaning (*see also* rhythmical figures), 25-28, 152, 156, 157ff., 232, 278, 287ff., 301, 302, 312, 322, 345;
    rhythmical italics, 232, 287, 302, 310, 322, 325, 346;
    iconic (mimetic, metaphoric) function of, 27, 287, 299, 301, 311, 321, 322, 346
Rhythmical figures, 17, 18, 26, 28, 218, 222, 223, 231, 232, 233, 239, 241, 281, 321ff., 336ff., 346;
  position in a line/phrase, 234, 235, 236, 238, 246, 256-257, 260, 261, 264, 337;
  monosyllabic, 233-234, 242, 253-255, 266ff., 288-292, 336, 337;
  disyllabic, 234-237, 248ff., 255, 262, 264, 292-293, 303ff., 310-312, 315-321, 336, 337;
  polysyllabic, 237-239, , 248, 252, 262, 264, 312-315, 321, 336, 337, 339;
  grammar of, 232, 236, 241ff., 281, 336, 337;
    morphology of, 235, 241, 242, 245-248, 251, 252, 253ff., 262, 264, 279-280, 281, 288, 292, 295, 299, 303, 315ff., 319-321, 337, 346;
    syntax of, 235, 236, 253ff., 257ff., 263, 264, 303, 320, 321, 337, 338, 346;

stylistic functions of, 232, 236, 237, 239, 288ff., 293, 338;
compositional functions of, 232, 237, 266ff., 278ff., 282, 341, 342;
semantic functions of, 232, 237, 239, 241, 253, 254, 256, 263-264, 278, 287ff., 293, 295, 299, 301, 302, 305-319, 321-323, 338, 339, 344, 346;
semiotic function of, 312, 322, 346
Rhythmical fluctuation, 95, 96ff., 118, 333
Rhythmical inertia (momentum), 32, 106, 115, 116, 191, 231, 235, 237, 246, 257, 292, 322, 335, 340
Rhythmical style, 2, 4, 5, 18, 31, 37, 44, 54, 63-67, 82, 87ff., 106, 116, 120, 124, 127, 132-133, 333, 336, 337, 338, 339-340, 341, 350
"Richard II", 22, 73-79, 106, 117, 125, 136, 142, 146, 156, 164, 191, 207, 217, 220, 225, 233, 239, 252, 253ff., 259, 263, 266ff., 275-276, 281, 282, 288ff., 312, 328, 339, 340
"Richard III", 57, 65, 67, 147, 152, 156, 157, 160, 174-175, 188, 191, 336, 347
Richards, 25, 27
Rigidity index, 53, 56, 61, 63ff., 123, 148-149, 150, 151, 162, 165, 169, 170-171, 175, 340
Robertson, 23, 324
Romanticism, 5, 17, 217, 218, 235, 336, 338, 345
"Romeo and Juliet", 57, 67, 72, 125, 136, 156, 160, 162-164, 341
Russo, 325

S – *see* syllabic positions *and* rhythmical figures
Šajkevic, 23, 95, 154
Sajtanov, 329n.
Sarrazin, 23
Schmidt, 36
Schoenbaum, 3, 19, 20, 23, 24, 126, 177
Scholl, 88, 91
Schumann, 325
Semantic component (seme), 293, 294, 295, 296, 297, 299ff., 305ff., 310,

314-319, 321, 322, 346
Semantic group (class), 294-295, 296, 298, 299, 322, 346
Šervinskij, 27
Shelley, 16, 17, 73, 77, 78, 108, 227, 229-230n., 233, 241, 246, 250, 251, 252, 256, 258, 259, 262, 263, 282, 291, 292, 295ff., 299ff., 346
Shippey, 325
Sipe, 88
Slater, 23, 53, 121, 124
Smirnickaja, 7, 325
Smirnickij, 210
Smith, Barbara Herrnstein, 116, 275
Smith, G.S., 103, 267, 274
Šnol' and Zamjatin, 343
"Sonnets", 85, 207, 217, 220, 221, 222, 223, 225, 233, 250, 252, 257, 259, 260, 261, 262, 266ff., 272-273, 274, 275ff., 278ff., 282, 288, 290ff., 299, 306, 328, 335, 339, 341, 342
Spalding, 20, 126, 177
Spedding, 20, 24, 125-126, 177
Spevack, 36, 91, 306
Split lines (between characters), 125, 136-148, 334, 340, 349;
  the place of split, 143ff.;
  stress profiles of, 147-148
Sprott, 88, 91
Spurgeon, 24
Stein, 27, 292
Stevick, 325
Stress (*see also* accent), 4;
  constant, predominant, optional (tendency): *see* syllabic positions;
  degrees of, 31, 32, 204-206, 209ff.;
  relative, 31, 32;
  phrasal, 32 (*see also* accent);
  word stress, 6, 32, 35-36;
    variations of, 36;
  inversion of, 15, 17, 33, 67, 79, 147, 205, 228-230n., 232, 272, 274, 332;
  extra-metrical (non-ictic), 9, 32, 37, 39, 43, 67-79, 83, 128, 147, 231, 239, 242, 245, 266ff, 274, 289, 338, 339, 341;

proclitic, enclitic (*see also* accent), 128, 209ff., 221, 253 ff.;
  evolution of, 217, 218;
  subordinate; weakening and loss of, 32, 35, 209ff., 214, 221-223, 234-236, 246, 257, 332, 339;
  emphatic, 32, 33, 221;
  back-to-back (adjacent), 15, 16, 17, 37, 209, 235, 237, 255, 332, 337
Stress maximum, 32
Stress profile, 4, 7, 8, 14, 28n, 31, 32, 39ff., 53, 231, 333-335, 339, 340, 347, 349;
  evolution of ictic stresses, 54-67, 96ff., 123ff.;
  evolution of non-ictic stresses, 67-79;
  variation by acts, 105ff.;
  of split lines, 147;
  of long and short utterances, 148;
  of role texts, 161ff.;
  and composition, 267ff., 276ff.
Stressing:
  principles of, 31, 32;
  influence by meter, 37-38;
  of monosyllables, 32, 36, 37, 38-39 (*see also* accent *and* monosyllables);
  in verse, revealing prose tendencies, 204;
  in a phrase, 204;
  semantic reasons of, 205;
  enclitic, 205
Style:
  author's, 2, 3, 23, 188, 189, 198, 199, 203, 206, 207, 212, 214, 217, 223, 226, 228, 239, 259, 263, 281;
  of scenes in a play, 194-195, 196;
  verbal, 322
Stylistic connotations, 290-293, 294, 297, 299, 302, 303, 304, 312, 319, 320, 323, 339, 346
Subject, predicate: 17, 35, 39, 210, 211, 213, 225, 235, 236, 256, 257, 258, 259, 260, 262, 265, 299-301, 321, 323, 337, 344
Suhamy, 3-4, 20, 230n.
Sykes, 23, 126
Syllabic positions: ictic (strong, S) and non-ictic (weak, W): 1, 4, 5-6, 8, 9, 12, 13, 14, 15, 16, 29-30n,

53ff., 96ff., 332ff., 336ff.
more strongly and more weakly
  stressed ictuses, 40, 57, 58;
non-ictuses, 67ff., 83, 147, 203ff.,
  233ff.;
constantly, predominantly, optionally
  stressed, 7, 8, 9, 12, 13, 334
Syllabic verse, 6, 7, 8, 12, 13, 14, 40, 334
Syllabo-tonic verse, 1, 6, 7, 13, 40, 334
Syntax, syntactic:
  as an element of meter, 16, 17, 333;
  syntactic links (ties), 40, 73, 75-77;
    hierarchy of, 210;
    strength of, 236, 260;
    proclitic/enclitic, 75, 76, 128, 210,
      253, 254, 255, 337;
  and line rhythm, 61, 157, 160, 162, 165,
    166, 169, 171, 175, 177, 178, 187,
    266, 332;
  seam (break), 47, 56, 58, 130, 169, 171,
    175, 208, 235, 236, 237, 238, 239,
    253, 255, 257-258, 260, 334, 347
    (*see also* break (seam)
    rhythmical-syntactic);
  and syllabic variants of words, 88;
  and phrasal accent, 34, 204;
  and genre, 250;
  functions of stressed words on W, 76-
    79, 208ff., 235, 236, 253-255,
    256, 260, 332, 337;
  syntactic patterns, *see* patterns;
  of rhythmical figures, *see* rhythmical
    figures

Taranovsky, 11, 16, 25, 27, 32, 103, 105,
  207, 218, 267, 275, 327
Taranovsky and Proxorov, 218
Tarlinskaja, 3, 4, 5, 6, 8, 11, 15, 16, 24,
  27, 35, 37, 39, 44, 47, 54, 61, 83,
  85, 86, 87, 88, 92, 103, 105, 113,
  122, 130, 188, 189, 203, 207, 218,
  230n., 233, 235, 248, 266, 275,
  285n., 288, 333, 336, 343, 344
Tarlinskaja and Coachman, 329n.
Tarlinskaja and Oganesova, 25
Tarlinskaja and Teterina, 3, 6, 8, 13, 16,
  29n., 39, 57, 63, 76, 115, 235,
  237, 238, 239, 267, 284n.
"The Comedy of Errors", 48, 72, 96,
  106, 114, 115, 146, 190, 191
"The Merchant of Venice", 58, 60, 72,
  96, 115, 190, 191, 340
"The Merry Wives of Windsor", 48, 60,
  72, 96, 115, 131-132, 341
"The Rape of Lucrece", 85-86, 233, 239,
  250, 252, 253ff., 262, 266ff.,
  275ff., 281, 288ff., 313, 328, 333,
  335, 339, 341
"The Taming of the Shrew", 53, 131,
  190, 191
"The Tempest", 143, 146, 188, 200
"The Two Gentlemen of Verona", 53,
  57, 58, 106, 152, 190, 191, 335
"The Two Noble Kinsmen", 20, 24, 125,
  127, 198
"The Winter's Tale", 88, 143, 200, 207,
  233, 241, 252, 257, 259, 282, 292,
  312, 328, 334, 340
Thompson, 19
Thorndike, 19, 20, 125, 126, 187, 217
Timberlake, 122, 177, 188, 192
"Timon of Athens", 48, 53, 61-62, 104,
  114, 115, 143, 151, 191, 192, 195-
  196, 333, 347, 348
"Titus Andronicus", 24, 48, 57, 72, 86,
  92, 96, 106, 114, 115, 117, 118,
  121-124, 181, 191, 192-195, 207,
  214, 217, 221, 334, 347, 348
Tomaševskij, 2, 15, 16, 28n., 33, 34, 65,
  218, 264
Tonic (accentual) verse, 6
Tradition, literary: 37, 232, 237, 260, 296,
  303, 306, 312, 322, 328, 340, 346,
  351 (*see also* periods, evolution
  of)
Trager and Smith, 31, 37, 39
Translation, 14, 105
Trochaic tetrameter, 25
Trochee, 5, 15-16, 25
"Troilus and Cressida", 58, 60-61, 62,
  72, 106, 143, 146, 191, 347
Tronskij, 325
Trubetzkoy, 7, 8, 15
"Twelfth Night", 60, 66, 72, 96, 125
Tynjanov, 301

Utterances of characters, 95, 135ff., 148ff., 152, 156, 340, 341 (*see also* personages)

Vanvik, 17, 248
Varma, 23
"Venus and Adonis", 57, 85-86, 124, 130, 233, 280, 335, 339, 341-342
Verbs, verbal:
  rhythmical forms of, 17, 35, 36, 38; phrases, 209, 211, 213, 214, 223-225;
  in rhythmical figures, 235, 236, 241, 242, 245, 246, 247, 248, 249, 252, 253, 255, 256, 258, 262, 279-280, 295-299, 303ff., 305-310, 315-319, 323, 337, 339, 346;
  verbal style, 346
Verse form and meaning, 25-28, 120, 152, 156, 157, 164, 345ff. (*see also* rhythm and meaning, meter and meaning *and* rhythmical figures: semantic function of)
Vinogradov, 25
Vocative, 34, 179, 205, 208, 209, 227, 237, 248, 253, 260, 263-264, 319, 321

W – *see* syllabic positions *and* rhythmical figures
Waller, 21
Warnken, 95, 135, 156, 170, 176
Watts, 325

Webster, 44, 92, 187, 188, 333, 338
Wells, J.C., 89
Wells, Rulon, 322
Wells, William, 53, 195
Wentersdorf, 20, 47ff., 53, 59-60, 115, 121, 136, 177, 190, 191, 192, 193, 335, 340, 347
Whallon, 325
Williams, 66
Wilson, 65, 80, 108
Words:
  syllabic variants of, 35, 88-92, 180-181;
  stress variants of, 36, 78-79;
  endings of (boundaries):
    masculine, feminine, dactylic, hyperdactylic: 17, 226-228;
    feet-emphasizing and feet-effacing, 226-228;
  of broad semantics, 204, 205, 212, 213, 221, 224, 337, 338, 350
Wright, 22, 85, 176n., 178, 203, 329n.

Xodasevič, 327
Xolševnikov, 6, 7, 8-9, 27, 206

Yates, 191
Yule, 23

Zholkovsky, 24
Žirmunskij, 6, 14, 24, 266, 325, 327, 329n.

John W. Crawford

EARLY SHAKESPEAREAN ACTRESSES

American University Studies: Series IV (English Language and Literature).
Vol. 8
ISBN 0-8204-0099-8   205 pages   hardback US $ 25.00*

*Recommended price - alterations reserved

One of the innovations of the Restoration in England was to introduce publicly the female actor on stage, with the reopening of the theatres. Charles II not only created two companies with his return to England, but promoted the concept of females as actors. It took courage for the first ones to enter this questionable vocation, considering the history the stage had achieved in Elizabethan and Stuart times, a history that demonstrated much criticism about the morality of dramatists and actors. Restoration actresses like George Anne Bellamy and Dora Jordan, as well as early eighteenth-century actresses like Catherine Clive and Peg Woffington proved that much individuality did indeed exist among the first; and even though the theatre had gained a much better reputation by the early nineteenth century, still actresses like Ellen Terry and Julia Marlowe were often the talk of the town because of their personal lives. Yet, these women proved that there is a place for the actress in modern drama.

Contents: 1. Brief background of the world of actors of the sixteenth century – 2. Individual sketches of various early actresses of Shakespearean roles – 3. Summary essay of certain actresses and their influence on Shakespearean drama.

PETER LANG PUBLISHING, INC.
62 West 45th Street
USA - New York, NY 10036

Peter Nicholas Baker, Jr.

MODERN POETIC PRACTICE
Structure and Genesis

American University Studies: Series III (Comparative Literature). Vol. 22
ISBN 0-8204-0343-1   222 pages   hardback US $ 35.45*

*Recommended price - alterations reserved

This book attempts to develop a generative criticism of poetic practice. The order of presentation follows a certain model for how the poem comes into being. Poetic practice as it is actualized in the work of the creative imagination stems from: *memory* as the place where the poem arises among the conflicts of the imagination; *absence* or the loss which weighs on the utterance and gives it urgency; *desire* as the force structuring the poem according to the subject's need; *knowing* or how the subject's experience of the world and other people finds expression; and *style* or how the poem exemplifies a compassionate understanding. Poets whose work is examined include Hardy, Mallarmé, Williams, Ungaretti, Apollinaire, Saint-John Perse, John Ashbery, and Frank O'Hara.

Contents: A generative criticism of poetic practice: models from memory, absence, desire, knowing, and style - Extended analyses of poetry by poets - English, American, French and Italian - University level.
This is a highly original, authoritative, and also engaging book.
(Albert Cook, Brown University)

PETER LANG PUBLISHING, INC.
62 West 45th Street
USA - New York, NY 10036

David L. Hoover

A NEW THEORY OF OLD ENGLISH METER

American University Studies: Series IV (English Language and Literature).
Vol. 14
ISBN 0-8204-0137-4   207 pages   hardback US $ 24.00*

*Recommended price - alterations reserved

A New Theory of Old English Meter sets out a simple new theory of Old English meter that is based on a bare minimum of initial assumptions and metrical principles, and supported by rigorous arguments and by evidence from a computer-assisted analysis of *Beowulf* and *The Battle of Maldon.* The new theory is revolutionary in concluding that alliteration rather than stress is the most important feature of the meter, and in rejecting the traditional assumptions of two lifts and four metrical positions per verse. It provides improved solutions for many of the perennial problems of Old English meter, makes possible an elegant logical explanation for the kinds of verses that occur and those which do not occur, and prepares the way for the most radical conclusion of the book: that Old English meter is not based on rhythm.

Contents: Old English meter, *Beowulf, The Battle of Maldon,* rhythm, metrical theory, stress, alliteration.

PETER LANG PUBLISHING, INC.
62 West 45th Street
USA - New York, NY 10036